ALLYN & BACON CLASSICS

THE EXPANDED FAMILY LIFE CYCLE

INDIVIDUAL, FAMILY, AND SOCIAL PERSPECTIVES

THIRD EDITION

Edited by

BETTY CARTER

Family Institute of Westchester

and

MONICA McGOLDRICK

The Multicultural Family Institute

With a new Foreword by

DONALD A. BLOCH

PEARSON

New York   San Francisco   Boston
London   Toronto   Sydney   Tokyo   Singapore   Madrid
Mexico City   Munich   Paris   Cape Town   Hong Kong   Montreal

To the future of my family, the grandchildren generation: Dylan, Grace, Patrick,
Danny, Michael, Jessica, Adrienne, Jacob, and Joseph, and to those as yet unborn.
B. C.

To John, Guy, and Hugh, all of our godchildren, and nieces and nephews: Stefan,
Ariane, Natalie, Claire, Maria, Gina, Patti, Christiana, Terry, Ryan, Irini, Angeliki, Gabe,
Irene, Stefan, Evan, and William. And to all who will come after them in our family.
M. M.

Copyright © 2005, 1999, 1989 by Allyn & Bacon
A Pearson Education Company
75 Arlington Street
Suite 300
Boston, MA 02116

Internet: www.ablongman.com

Series Editor, Social Work and Family Therapy: Patricia Quinlin
Series Editorial Assistant: Annemarie Kennedy
Marketing Manager: Kris Ellis-Levy
Production Editor: Greg Erb
Manufacturing Buyer: JoAnne Sweeney
Cover Administrator: Kristina Mose-Libon
Electronic Composition: Omegatype Typography, Inc.

Library of Congress Cataloging-in-Publication Data

The expanded family life cycle : individual, family, and social
    perspectives / edited by Betty Carter and Monica McGoldrick. — 3rd
    ed., classic ed.
        p. cm.
    Includes bibliographical references and index.
    ISBN 0-205-40981-4
    1. Life cycle, Human.   2. Family counseling—United States.
3. Family psychotherapy—United States.   I. Carter, Elizabeth A.
II. McGoldrick, Monica.

HQ536.C417   2004
306.85—dc22   2004053432

ISBN 0-205-40981-4

90000

9 780205 409815

Printed in the United States of America

10 9   11 10 09

Contributors

Constance R. Ahrons, Ph.D.
Professor of Sociology and Director of the Marriage
and Family Therapy Training Program, University
of Southern California, Los Angeles, CA
Private Practice, Santa Monica, CA

Rhea V. Almeida, L.C.S.W., Ph.D., D.V.S
Executive Director, Institute for Family Services,
Somerset, NJ
Faculty, Family Institute of New Jersey,
Metuchen, NJ

Carol M. Anderson, M.S.W., Ph.D.
Professor, University of Pittsburgh Medical School,
Pittsburgh, PA
Editor, *Family Process*

Waymon Benton, Ed.D.
Faculty, Counseling Psychology Department,
Columbia University Teachers' College,
New York, NY
Private Practice, Metuchen, NJ

Claudia S. Bepko, M.S.W.
Private Practice in family therapy,
Brunswick and Portland, ME
Faculty, Family Institute of Maine Foundation,
Portland, ME

Kathy Berliner, M.S.W.
Faculty, Family Institute of Westchester,
White Plains, NY

Lynn A. Blacker, L.C.S.W.
Clinical Coordinator, Family Intervention Services,
Morristown, NJ

Mary Ann Broken Nose, B.A.
Comprehensive Services of Aging (COPSA),
Institute for Alzheimer's Disease,
University Behavioral HealthCare, University
of Medicine and Dentistry of New Jersey,
Piscataway, NJ

Betty Carter, M.S.W.
Founder and Director Emerita, Family Institute of
Westchester, White Plains, NY

Patricia L. Colucci, M.S.W.
Faculty, Family Institute of Westchester,
White Plains, NY

Celia Jaes Falicov, Ph.D.
Department of Psychiatry, University of California in
San Diego, San Diego, CA
Private Practice, San Diego, CA

Richard H. Fulmer, Ph.D.
Private Practice, New York, NY
Faculty, National Institute for the Psychotherapies,
New York, NY

Miguel Hernandez
Roberto Clemente Center, New York, NY
Ackerman Institute for Family Therapy,
New York, NY

Paulette Moore Hines, Ph.D.
Director, Office of Prevention Services, University
Behavioral HealthCare, University of Medicine
and Dentistry of New Jersey, Piscataway, NJ
Faculty, Family Institute of New Jersey,
Metuchen, NJ

Jacqueline Hudak, M.Ed.
Director, Family Therapy Associates,
Monmouth County, NJ
Faculty, Family Institute of New Jersey,
Metuchen, NJ

Evan Imber-Black, Ph.D.
Faculty, Ackerman Institute for Family Therapy,
New York, NY

Demaris A. Jacob, Ph.D.
Faculty, Family Institute of Westchester,
White Plains, NY

Thomas W. Johnson, L.C.S.W., Ed.D.
Faculty, New Jersey Center for Family Studies,
Plainfield, NJ
Associate Faculty, Department of Psychiatry,
University of Medicine and Dentistry of New
Jersey, Piscataway, NJ
Private Practice, Metuchen, NJ

Jodie Kliman, Ph.D.
The Center for Multicultural Training in Psychology, Boston Medical Center, Boston, MA
The Family Institute of Cambridge, Watertown, MA
Private Practice, Brookline, MA

Jo-Ann Krestan, M.A., M.F.T.
Writer and Consultant, Surry, ME and Castle Valley, UT
Visiting Faculty, Family Institute of New Jersey, Metuchen, NJ

Stephen Lerner, Ph.D.
Private Practice, Topeka, KS

William C. Madsen, Ph.D.
Training Coordinator, Family Institute of Cambridge, Watertown, MA
Private Practice, Cambridge, MA

Monica McGoldrick, M.A., L.C.S.W., Ph.D. (hon.)
Director, The Multicultural Family Institute, Highland Park, NJ
Faculty, Fordham University School of Social Service, New York, NY
Faculty, Psychiatry Department, Robert Wood Johnson Medical School, New Brunswick, NJ
Private Practice, Metuchen, NJ

Mildred Potenza, C.S.W.
Geriatric Services, University Behavioral HealthCare, University of Medicine and Dentistry of New Jersey, Edison, NJ

Nydia Garcia Preto, L.C.S.W.
Faculty and Clinical Director, Family Institute of New Jersey, Metuchen, NJ
Private Practice, Metuchen, NJ

John S. Rolland, M.D.
Associate Clinical Professor of Psychiatry
Co-Director, Chicago Center for Family Health, University of Chicago, Chicago, IL

Elliott J. Rosen, Ed.D.
Director, Family Institute of Westchester, White Plains, NY

Natalie Schwartzberg, M.S.W.
Faculty, Family Institute of Westchester, White Plains, NY

Froma Walsh, M.S.W., Ph.D.
Co-Founder, Chicago Center for Family Health, University of Chicago, Chicago, IL
Professor, School of Social Service Administration, University of Chicago, Chicago, IL
Editor, *Journal of Marital and Family Therapy*

Marlene F. Watson, Ph.D.
Director, Graduate Programs in Couple and Family Therapy, Department of Mental Health Sciences, Allegheny University of the Health Sciences, Philadelphia, PA

Susan Weltman, M.S.W.
Private Practice, Highland Park, NJ
Faculty, Center for Family Studies, Springfield, NJ

CONTENTS

PART 3
CLINICAL APPLICATIONS

CHAPTER 26   COACHING AT VARIOUS STAGES OF THE LIFE CYCLE   436
Betty Carter and Monica McGoldrick

CHAPTER 27   ALCOHOL PROBLEMS AND THE FAMILY LIFE CYCLE   455
Jacqueline Hudak, Jo Ann Krestan, and Claudia Bepko

PREFACE

FOR WHOM WE ARE WRITING

The Expanded Family Life Cycle is a book for health care and social service professionals and students from medicine and nursing to social work and family therapy, to psychology, to sociology, and to all fields of counseling, school guidance counseling, vocational, college, addictions, and pastoral counseling. Although our original edition was written primarily for family therapists, the overwhelmingly positive response we have had from those in related professions who have used the book has led us to broaden our thinking about the applications of a life cycle perspective for all work with families.

The book also bridges the traditionally separate spheres of individual development and the family life cycle with cultural and social perspectives in a way that transforms the traditional categories and proposes a new, more comprehensive way to think about human development and the life cycle.

REDEFINING FAMILY

In this edition, we celebrate diversity as we welcome the multiculturalism of the twenty-first century. We refer not only to cultural diversity, but also to the diversity of family forms. There are many ways to go through life in a caring, productive manner, and no specific family structure is ideal. Indeed, it was dissatisfaction with the traditional nuclear family that produced the 50 percent divorce rate of the recent past. Most of the criticisms of life cycle theory have actually been justified criticism of the limited focus of theoretical and research attention to the developmental stages of only one family form: the White, Anglo, middle-class, nuclear family of a once-married heterosexual couple, their children, and their extended family. In this edition, we have expanded that definition of family in ways that attempt to include everyone in our society.

Although it is statistically accurate to outline the widely experienced stages of the family life cycle, focusing on marriage, the birth and development of children, and aging, no single list of stages is sufficient or inclusive. Throughout this edition, we recognize the vast numbers of families whose family life cycle varies in significant ways from this traditional stage outline. Individuals of different cultures and socioeconomic groups go through the stages at very different ages. A growing number of adults are choosing not to marry or, like gays and lesbians, are prevented from marrying or, like the poor, find it almost impossible to afford. Growing numbers of women are delaying childbearing (in 1995 one-third of first-time mothers were age 35 or older) or are choosing to remain childless. The prevalence of divorce and remarriage is requiring a large proportion of our society to manage additional life cycle stages and complete restructuring of their families (Chapters 22, 23, and 25). There has been a dramatic increase in the percentage of permanent single-parent households created by divorce or single-parent adoption (Chapters 19, 21, and 24). Finally, vast differences in family life cycle patterns are caused by oppressive social forces: racism, sexism, homophobia, classism, ageism, and cultural prejudices of all kinds (Chapters 4, 5, 6, 8, 10, 18, 19, 20, 21, and 24). This edition seeks to include all of these elements in our thinking while still providing clear and manageable clinical suggestions related to the family's place in its many contexts.

WIDENING OUR LENS

Our expanded view of family thus actively includes the reciprocal impact and the issues at multiple levels of the human system: the individual, the immediate family household(s), the extended family, the community, the cultural group, and the larger society. Although the family levels are usually the optimal levels for therapeutic intervention, we have widened our lens to deal more concretely in large and small ways with the fact that every family is a group of individuals and that the individuals and families are embedded in communities and the larger society whose impact is definitive and must be taken into account for interventions at the family level to succeed. Our choice of language symbolizes our recognition of the vast changes in family structure. We have replaced the limited term "nuclear family" with the more comprehensive term "immediate family," which includes nuclear, single-parent, unmarried, remarried, and gay and lesbian households. We consider "commitment" to be the family bond for many households in which no marriage exists or even no adult partnership. "Couples therapy" usually replaces the term "marital therapy." Further expanding our view of family relationships, we have added chapters on men, siblings, gays and lesbians, and single people.

THE INDIVIDUAL LEVEL

Although family therapists, even systems therapists, have always operated from some notion of the individual's role in the system, there has been a tendency in psychology, social work, medicine, and even family therapy to compartmentalize theorizing about family separately from theorizing about the individual. When evaluating individual behavior, the tendency has been, even for many family theorists, to shift to psychodynamic or psychoanalytic thinking. In our view, such splitting is not compatible with systems thinking. It leads to divergent and inconsistent definitions of the problem and its locus. Bowen's family systems theory, like Engel's biopsychosocial model in medicine, is a notable exception to this tendency to split individual and family thinking. Bowen's theory places individual behavior and feelings squarely in the context of the family system, elaborating on the intricacies of the impact and the interaction between an individual and the family system of three or more generations. Bowen's theory also holds each adult individual responsible for creating change in the system.

The mental health professions have also tended to perpetuate the splitting of theorizing about individuals and systems by accepting theories of individual development evolved in the field of human development, which has espoused primarily psychodynamically oriented schemas (especially Erikson's modifications of Freudian theory) that ignore the gender, race, sexual orientation, and class norms of society that have produced deeply skewed models of "normal" child and adult development which make those who don't conform to dominant norms seem deficient.

To address these problems, we have made a beginning effort in this edition to spell out a more comprehensive framework for individual development in the context of relationship and society (Chapter 2, "Self in Context"). We have also included a chapter based on Bowen's model of obtaining family systems change through individual coaching (Chapter 26). Other cases using this coaching method are discussed in various chapters throughout the book. Other chapters that expand on these more inclusive perspectives include Chapters 6 ("Women and the Family Life Cycle") and 7 ("Men in Transition: The 'New Man'"), Chapters 4, 8, 10, and 19 (on cultural issues), Chapters 5 and 10 (on class), and Chapter 20 (on gay and lesbian families).

THE SOCIAL PERSPECTIVE

In addition to focusing down from family to individual, we have expanded our focus up to the community and larger society levels. This focus, as we have indicated above, is an effort to help us to include in our clinical evaluations and treatment all of the major forces that make us who we are: race, class, sexual orientation, gender, ethnicity, spirituality, politics, work, time, community, values, beliefs, and dreams. In this edition, therefore, we have added chapters on class, violence, migration, and several cultural groups. As our awareness has grown of societal patterns of domination and privilege, we have greatly expanded our analysis of the impact of social norms on every family. We have also included throughout the book cases that reflect the social forces that impinge on individual and family functioning. It is our strong belief that this expanded family life cycle context is still the best framework for family therapy because it deals with the development over time of individuals in their family relationships and within their communities as they struggle at this millennium to define and implement life's meanings within a larger society that helps some more than others. To be lasting, change must encompass every level of our lives.

BETTY CARTER'S ACKNOWLEDGMENTS

Anything good that I've written in this book I learned from my family, friends, clients, trainees, mentors, and colleagues. I especially learned a lot during my twenty years of work with Peggy Papp, Olga Silverstein, and Marianne Walters in the Women's Project in Family Therapy.

I am grateful to all of my family and friends who have accepted my almost total isolation for the past year while Monica and I tried to finish the job of explicating the enormous amount and complexity of family change over the past decade. I often had the thought that if this is retirement, why did I leave paid work? But I confess that it pleased me, having long hours of uninterrupted time to think and write. And now that I have turned Family Institute of Westchester over to the capable hands of Elliott Rosen and the rest of the faculty, maybe there will be time to smell a rose or two.

I thank every author. We are critical, hands-on, in-your-face editors, full of requirements, requests, and suggestions. It couldn't have been easy for the authors, but they came through with wonderful, thoughtful material. And those of you who answered our cries for help very late in the process—you know who you are—we will never forget your rescue of several important chapters.

Special thanks to Monica and her staff at The Multicultural Family Institute, who so cheerfully handled all of the hard stuff that manuscripts require because they were in an office and I was at home, technologically impaired.

Monica and I wrote our first article together in the early 1970s. I have never worked with any-one, before or since, with whom I so completely shared every frame of reference: family background, philosophy of life, theoretical orientation and clinical ideas, interests, sense of humor, and response to people. I will never retire from working and playing with her, laughing with her, and loving her.

Even with all of the above help, this work wouldn't have gotten done without the total support of my dear husband, Sam. For all of this time, he has cheerfully done *all* of the shopping, cooking, and all other domestic chores so that I could be free to work. All that and emotional support too! As this book appears, we'll be close to celebrating our forty-sixth anniversary, happy in the belief that some part of our joint wisdom about marriage and family has surely found its way into these pages.

MONICA McGOLDRICK'S ACKNOWLEDGMENTS

Many people have provided me support over the many years that this third edition has been in process. It was twice as difficult to produce as the second edition, which, itself, was twice as difficult as the first edition. Our understanding of the complexities of families in their developmental and social context has greatly expanded, making it hard to write in as straightforward a way as we like. Each time we would write a sentence, we would say, "On the other hand, there is this other factor which influences that phenomenon." Space limitations have been especially constraining, and I am very grateful to the authors for their hard work on this endeavor and for their commitment to the material. I especially thank my guardian angel, Rene Campbell, who keeps my life working and whose smile and good nature keep me going on even my worst days. For their love I thank my son John, who moved from early latency to adolescence during the production of this book, and my husband, Sophocles, for his quiet support and for keeping the homefires burning, while I was preoccupied or off working to make this book come forth. Mary Ann Broken Nose was of enormous help on the research for this book, which was a mega-task, as the information explosion makes it ever less possible to keep up with what is written in the area. I thank also Mary Jean Battistella for all her help with the manuscript. I thank my sister Morna, who often sat by my side as we worked on our respective book projects and who is a major source of inspiration and solace to me. My aunt Mildred, who keeps developing at age 94 as I complete this book, is an amazing, witty, and sweet woman in the last phase of her life. I hope that as I grow, I will keep expanding emotionally as she has. And I thank my wonderful parents, my caretaker Margaret Bush, my Aunt Mamie, Elliot and Marie, Jack Mayer, Hughie McGoldrick, and all the other wonderful people who have gone before, who loved me and made me who I am. I hope I am worthy of their generosity in my life. And I thank my relatives, friends, colleagues, students, and clients who continuously inspire, support, and nurture me. Finally, I thank my sister, soulmate, friend, and collaborator, Betty Carter, for the friendship and intellectual stimulation she has provided me now for thirty years. This edition saw her into her retirement and grandparenthood, and I trust we will now find new ways to collaborate as we age and must cope with distance and losses that are painful and difficult. I greatly admire her for her life force, her humor, her intelligence, her sticking power, and the warmth of her friendship.

JOINT ACKNOWLEDGMENTS

We both give heartfelt thanks to our editor, Patricia Quinlin, for her unfailing patience and helpfulness throughout this entire process. We would also like to acknowledge the help of the reviewers who provided valuable feedback for this edition: Audrey Begun, University of Wisconsin-Milwaukee; Patricia A. Emerson, Azusa Pacific University; and Candyce S. Russel, Kansas State University.

FOREWORD

The perspective that the human family can be described in life cycle terms is a valuable, indeed, a fundamental orientation to human life. The concept girds and informs all of those fields concerned with human development, health, and education. The decision to issue this updated volume fully deserves our appreciation and respect. The editors, Betty Carter and Monica McGoldrick, have been major contributors to the clinical literature over their long, productive careers. They have also been a commanding presence in the field as teachers and theoreticians, particularly with regard to the influence of gender, race, and social class on both psycho-social dysfunction and treatment.

The individual and family life cycles are not simply isomorphic with each other; they are related, but not identical. The individual life cycle is familiar and clear. From the moment of conception humans follow a path with well defined stations and biological markers: prenatal development and birth, infancy, childhood, adolescence, young adulthood, maturity, senescence, death. The biological markers—and the dedicated sequence whereby they come on stage—are, for all practical purposes, constant.

In comparison with the individual, definitions of family are more variable and culturally sensitive. Family is the intimate emotional and relational context within which these individual developmental stages occur. The stages of family development— new family formation leading to parenting of new family members, to their rearing and acculturation, and so on—along with the associated family role and structural patterns, provide the conceptual trellis that we speak of as the family life cycle.

As the authors note, the family is a system moving, and changing, through time. Membership changes, and at any given point in time there may be multiple foci of the family emotional work and associated role development. A family does not march chronologically through these stages. At any given point in time they may be caring for a failing senior, struggling with integrating a daughter's new in-laws, and processing the recently announced sexual preference of a young adult, along with other life cycle events moving on and off stage. These overlaps may drive both conflicts and the creation of new roles that become family assets.

Differences between cultures and within cultures play a large part in how these stages are perceived and the meaning given to them. Gender, race, social class, and sexual orientation, among other socio-cultural dimensions, are critical determinants of the fates of individuals, and these are mediated by the particular family, its relationship structures, and history. To be a younger daughter in a culture and family where females are devalued is a vastly different experience from growing up as the eldest brother in the same family.

The case illustrations throughout this volume are excellent. The family life cycle is related to real life dilemmas as these are experienced in the consulting room as well as to solutions generated by inventive and sensitive clinicians. Carter and McGoldrick and their chapter authors are especially good in their sensitivity to these cultural concerns. The description of family life cycle issues, observed with socio-cultural sensitivity and related to understandable clinical problems and therapeutic interventions, creates the distinctive and valuable fabric of this book. Especially laudable is the real recognition of the limits of therapeutic intervention.

The family that joins us in the consulting room is in the midst of the work of living. Looking at that work through the lens of the family life cycle at any given point in time allows us to develop interventions that are liberating, non-blaming, growth-enhancing, and economic. A life cycle orientation tells us where to look.

A young couple, the Hayakawa/Goldensohns, who have been married less than a year, make an appointment for help with their escalating marital conflict. The differing ethnicities of their names jumps off the page. I anticipate being interested in how each person is resolving the separation from their family of origin associated with the formation of this new family, and I wonder what leftover family conflicts are being played out in their new family.

A woman calls for help with her mother, who is distraught at the news that her husband, newly retired, is suddenly told he is dying of a brain tumor. The mother is on the edge of a breakdown; her golden years with her husband are being snatched from her. I ask the daughter who is in the family. She has two brothers, and I invite all three adult siblings to convene with me to face this new stage in their family journey. The meeting helps them heal an incipient split in their generation and realize the strength they have to help their parents with their father's dying. No further intervention is necessary.

A great strength of this volume is its excellent exposition of the family genogram as a revealing map of family development over time. As clinicians, history is always with us. We search for old patterns that are recycled in significant new forms. It helps to have a good choreographic notation of this dance and the genogram provides one.

To think in terms of the family life cycle, especially from an historic multi-generational per-

spective is to be in touch with human life in deep, complex, endlessly revealing, and fascinating ways. It is as if we are looking first at a person, then a couple, then a family with children, then a network of families extending laterally in space and forward and back in time. This means using the novelist's eye and voice, the musician's creative ear, the film director's composition.

The family life cycle is a majestic concept. It is spacious and complex, and clinically fruitful. It allows for useful comparisons—family to family, culture to culture, by class, and by historical epoch. It embeds the essential stories about who we are, where we came from, and what elements shape our identity. The engines of our fears from the past and our hope for the future can be found in the matrix of our current families and with their representation of past families. The braiding together of these relational threads both creates and grows out of the family life cycle. This excellent volume is truly a "classic," serving as a solid introduction to the family life cycle orientation for the newcomer and deepening the understanding of the experienced reader.

Donald A. Bloch M.D.
March 31, 2004

CHAPTER 1

OVERVIEW: THE EXPANDED FAMILY LIFE CYCLE
INDIVIDUAL, FAMILY, AND SOCIAL PERSPECTIVES

BETTY CARTER
MONICA McGOLDRICK

THE FAMILY LIFE CYCLE

We are born into families. Our first relationships, our first group, our first experience of the world are with and through our families. We develop, grow, and hopefully die in the context of our families. Embedded within the larger sociopolitical culture, the individual life cycle takes shape as it moves and evolves within the matrix of the family life cycle. Our problems are framed by the formative course of our family's past, the present tasks it is trying to master, and the future to which it aspires. Thus, the family life cycle is the natural context within which to frame individual identity and development and to account for the effects of the social system.

Until recently, therapists have paid little attention to the family life cycle and its impact on human development. Even now, most psychological theories relate at most to the nuclear family, ignoring the multigenerational context of family connections that pattern our lives. But our dramatically changing family patterns, which in our times can assume many varied configurations over the life span, are forcing us to take a broader view of both development and normalcy. It is becoming increasingly difficult to determine what family life cycle patterns are "normal," causing great stress for family members, who have few consensually validated models to guide them through the passages they must negotiate.

Just as the texture of life has become more complicated, so too must our therapeutic models change to reflect this complexity, appreciating both the context around the individual as a shaping environment and the evolutionary influence of time on human development. From a family life cycle perspective, symptoms and dysfunction are examined within a systemic context and in relation to what the culture considers to be "normal" functioning over time. From this perspective, therapeutic interventions aim at helping to reestablish the family's developmental momentum so that it can proceed forward to foster the uniqueness of each member's development.

THE FAMILY AS A SYSTEM MOVING THROUGH TIME

Families comprise people who have a shared history and a shared future. They encompass the entire emotional system of at least three, and frequently now four or even five, generations held together by blood, legal, and/or historical ties. Relationships with parents, siblings, and other family members go through transitions as they move along the life cycle (see Table 1.1 on page 2). Boundaries shift, psychological distance among members changes, and roles within and between subsystems are constantly being redefined (Norris & Tindale, 1994;

TABLE 1.1   The Stages of the Family Life Cycle

FAMILY LIFE CYCLE STAGE	EMOTIONAL PROCESS OF TRANSITION: KEY PRINCIPLES	SECOND-ORDER CHANGES IN FAMILY STATUS REQUIRED TO PROCEED DEVELOPMENTALLY
Leaving home: single young adults	Accepting emotional and financial responsibility for self	a. Differentiation of self in relation to family of origin b. Development of intimate peer relationships c. Establishment of self in respect to work and financial independence
The joining of families through marriage: the new couple	Commitment to new system	a. Formation of marital system b. Realignment of relationships with extended families and friends to include spouse
Families with young children	Accepting new members into the system	a. Adjusting marital system to make space for children b. Joining in child rearing, financial and household tasks c. Realignment of relationships with extended family to include parenting and grandparenting roles
Families with adolescents	Increasing flexibility of family boundaries to permit children's independence and grandparents' frailties	a. Shifting of parent/child relationships to permit adolescent to move into and out of system b. Refocus on midlife marital and career issues c. Beginning shift toward caring for older generation
Launching children and moving on	Accepting a multitude of exits from and entries into the family system	a. Renegotiation of marital system as a dyad b. Development of adult-to-adult relationships between grown children and their parents c. Realignment of relationships to include in-laws and grandchildren d. Dealing with disabilities and death of parents (grandparents)
Families in later life	Accepting the shifting generational roles	a. Maintaining own and/or couple functioning and interests in face of physiological decline: exploration of new familial and social role options b. Support for more central role of middle generation c. Making room in the system for the wisdom and experience of the elderly, supporting the older generation without overfunctioning for them d. Dealing with loss of spouse, siblings, and other peers and preparation for death

Cicirelli, 1995). It is extremely difficult to think of the family as a whole because of the complexity involved. As a system moving through time, the family has different properties from those of all other systems. Unlike all other organizations, families incorporate new members only by birth, adoption, commitment, or marriage, and members can leave only by death, if then. No other system is sub-ject to these constraints. A business organization can fire members that managers view as dysfunctional, or members can resign if the organization's structure and values are not to their liking. In families, by contrast, the pressures of family membership with no exit available can, in the extreme, lead to psychosis. In nonfamily systems, the roles and functions of the system are carried out in a more or less stable way, by replacement of those who leave for any reason, or else the system dissolves and people move on into other organizations. Although families also have roles and functions, the main value in families is in the relationships, which are irreplaceable. If a parent leaves or dies, another person can be brought in to fill a parenting function, but this person can never replace the parent in his or her personal emotional aspects (Walsh & McGoldrick, 1991). Even in the divorce of a couple without children, the bonds very often linger, and it is difficult to hear of an ex-spouse's death without being shaken.

Despite the current dominant American pattern of nuclear families living on their own and often at great geographical distances from extended family members, they are still emotional subsystems, reacting to past, present, and anticipated future relationships within the larger three-generational family system. The options and decisions to be made are endless and can be confusing: whether or whom to marry; where to live; how many children to have, if any; how to conduct relationships within the immediate and extended family; and how to allocate family tasks. As Hess and Waring (1984) observed:

> As we moved from the family of obligatory ties to one of voluntary bonds, relationships outside the nuclear unit (as well as those inside it)...lost whatever normative certainty or consistency governed them at earlier times. For example, sibling relationships today are almost completely voluntary, subject to disruption through occupational and geographic mobility, as indeed might be said of marriage itself. (p. 303)

Cultural factors also play a major role in how families go through the life cycle. Not only do cultural groups vary greatly in their breakdown of family life cycle stages and definitions of the tasks at each stage, but it is clear that even several generations after immigration, the family life cycle patterns of groups differ markedly (Chapters 4 and 10; McGoldrick, Giordano, & Pearce, 1996). Furthermore, families' motion through the life cycle is profoundly influenced by the era in history at which they are living (Cohler, Hosteler, & Boxer, 1998; Elder, 1992; Neugarten, 1979). Family members' world views, including their attitudes toward life cycle transitions, are profoundly influenced by the time in history in which they have grown up. Those who lived through the Great Depression and World War II, those who came of age during the Vietnam War, those who experienced the Black migration to the North in the 1940s, the baby boomer generation that grew up in the 1950s—all these cohorts will have profoundly different orientations to life, influenced by the times in which they lived (Cohler et al., 1998; Elder, 1986).

The family of days gone by, when the extended family reigned supreme, should not be romanticized as a time when mutual respect and satisfaction existed between the generations. The traditional stable multigenerational extended family of yore was supported by sexism, classism, and racism. In this traditional patriarchal structure of families, respect for parents and obligations to care for elders were based on their control of the resources, reinforced by religious and secular sanctions against those who did not go along with the ideas of the dominant group. Now, with the increasing ability of younger family members to determine their own fate in marriage, work, and economic security, the power of elders to demand filial piety is reduced. As women are expecting to have lives of their own, whereas before their roles were limited primarily to the caretaking of others, our social institutions are not shifting enough to fit with these changing needs. Instead of evolving values of shared caretaking, our social institutions still operate mainly on the notions of the individualism of the pioneering frontier, and the most vulnerable— the poor, the young, the old, the infirm—suffer the consequences. What we need is not a return to a rigid, inequitable three-generational patriarchal family, but rather to recognize our connectedness in life—regardless of the particular family structure or culture—with those who went before us and those who follow after. At the same time, it is important to appreciate that many problems are caused when changes at the societal level lag behind those at the family level and therefore fail to validate and support the lives and choices of so many individuals.

In our time, people often act as though they can choose membership and responsibility in a family. However, there is very little choice about whom we are related to in the complex web of family ties. Children, for example, have no choice about being born into a system, nor do parents have a choice, once children are born, adopted, or fostered, as to the existence of the responsibilities of parenthood, even if they neglect these responsibilities. In fact, no family relationships except marriage are entered into by choice. Even in the case of marriage, the freedom to marry whomever one wishes is a rather recent option, and the decision to marry is probably much less freely made than people usually recognize at the time (see Chapter 14). Although partners can choose not to continue a marriage relationship, they remain co-parents of their children, and the fact of having been married continues to be acknowledged with the designation "ex-spouse." People cannot alter whom they are related to in the complex web of family ties over all the generations. Obviously, family members frequently act as if this were not so—they cut each other off because of conflicts or because they claim to have nothing in common—but when family members act as though family relationships were optional, they do so to the detriment of their own sense of identity and the richness of their emotional and social context.

The tremendous life-shaping impact of one generation on those following is hard to overestimate. For one thing, the three or four different generations must adjust to life cycle transitions simultaneously. While one generation is moving toward older age, the next is contending with the empty nest, the third with young adulthood, forming careers and intimate peer adult relationships and having children, and the fourth with being inducted into the system. Naturally, there is an intermingling of the generations, and events at one level have a powerful effect on relationships at each other level. The important impact of events in the grandparental generation is routinely overlooked by therapists who focus on the nuclear family. Painful experiences such as illness and death are particularly difficult for families to integrate and are thus most likely to have a long-range impact on relationships in the next generation.

Of course, in different cultures, the ages of these multigenerational transitions differ markedly. Certainly, the stages of the life cycle are rather arbitrary breakdowns. The notion of childhood has been described as the invention of eighteenth-century Western society and adolescence as the invention of the nineteenth century (Aries, 1962), related to the cultural, economic, and political contexts of those eras. The notion of young adulthood as an independent phase could easily be argued to be the invention of the twentieth century, and that of women as independent individuals could be said to be a construct of the late twentieth century. The lengthy phases of the empty nest and older age are also developments primarily of the twentieth century, brought about by the smaller number of children and the longer life span in our era. Given the current changes in the family, the twenty-first century may become known for developing the norms of serial marriage and unmarried motherhood as part of the life cycle. Developmental psychology has tended to take an ahistorical approach to the life cycle. But in virtually all other contemporary cultures and during virtually all other historical eras, the definition of life cycle stages has been different from our current definitions. To add to this complexity, cohorts born and living through different periods differ in fertility, mortality, acceptable gender roles, migration patterns, education, needs and resources, and attitudes toward family and aging.

Families characteristically lack time perspective when they are having problems. They tend generally to magnify the present moment, overwhelmed and immobilized by their immediate feelings; or they become fixed on a moment in the future that they dread or long for. They lose the awareness that life means continual motion from the past into the future with a continual transformation of familial relationships. As the sense of motion becomes lost or distorted, therapy involves restoring a sense of life as process and movement from and toward.

THE INDIVIDUAL IN THE FAMILY
AND IN HISTORY

The search for the meaning of our individual lives has led to many theories about the process of "normal" development, most of them proposing supposedly inherent, age-related, developmental stages for the individual (Levinson, 1978, 1996; Sheehy, 1977, 1995; Valliant, 1977; and others) and/or the traditional family (e.g., Duvall, 1977). From the beginning of our work, we have placed the individual in the context of family and have indicated the importance of the impact of cultural and structural variation on life cycle tasks for individuals and families. However, we do not espouse family life cycle stages as inherent, that is, identical for families of all kinds. But neither do we reject a flexible concept of predictable stages with appropriate emotional tasks for individuals and family groups, depending on their type of structure, specific cultural background, and current historical era. We disagree with those life course or life span theorists who, like many feminist theorists of development, in their effort to move on from the traditional family, essentially bypass the family level altogether and consider the individual in society as the essential unit for study.

We strongly believe that individual development takes place only in the context of significant emotional relationships and that the most significant relationships are family relationships, whether by blood, adoption, marriage, or commitment. Individuals and families must then also be seen in their cultural and historical context of past and present to be understood or changed. We see the family level as ideal for therapeutic intervention because it is the product of both individual and social forces, bridging and mediating between the two. However, since the family is no longer solely organized around a married heterosexual couple raising their children, but rather involves many different structures and cultures with different organizing principles, our job of identifying family stages and emotional tasks for various family groups is much more complex. But even within the diversity, there are some unifying principles that we have used to define stages and tasks, such as the primary importance of family relationships and the emotional disequilibrium caused by adding and losing family members during life's many transitions (Ahrons & Rodgers, 1987; Hadley, Jacob Milliones, Caplan, & Spitz, 1974). We embrace this complexity and the importance of all levels of the human system: individual, family, and social.

THE VERTICAL AND HORIZONTAL FLOW
OF STRESS IN THE LIFE CYCLE

To understand how individuals evolve, we must examine their lives within the context of both the family and the larger cultural contexts with their past and present properties, which change over time. Each system (individual, family, and cultural) can be represented schematically (see Figure 1.1 on page 6) along two time dimensions: one of which brings past and present issues to bear reciprocally on all other levels (the vertical axis) and one of which is developmental and unfolding (the horizontal axis). For the individual, the vertical axis includes the biological heritage and intricate programming of behaviors with one's given temperament, possible congenital disabilities, and genetic makeup. The horizontal axis relates to the individual's emotional, cognitive, interpersonal, and physical development over the life span within a specific historical context. Over time, the individual's inherent qualities can become either crystallized into rigid behaviors or elaborated into broader and more flexible repertoires. Certain individual stages may be more difficult to master, depending on one's innate characteristics and the influence of the environment.

At the family level (Carter, 1978), the vertical axis includes the family history, the patterns of relating and functioning that are transmitted down the generations, primarily through the mechanism of emotional triangling (Bowen, 1978). It includes all the family attitudes, taboos, expectations, labels, and loaded issues with which we grow up. These aspects of our lives are the hand we are dealt.

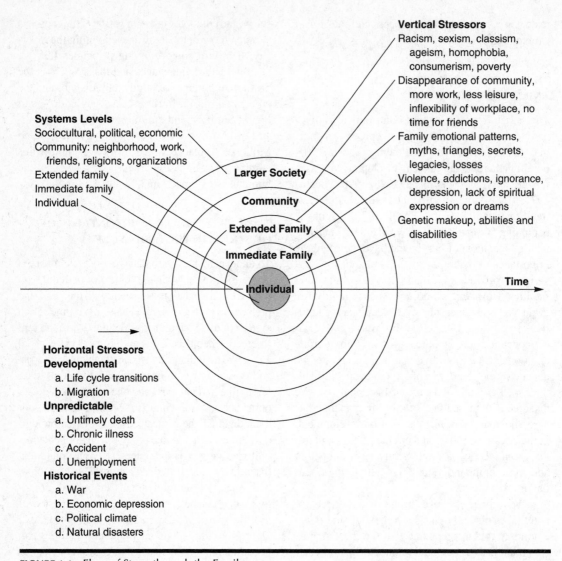

FIGURE 1.1   Flow of Stress through the Family

What we do with them is the question. The horizontal flow at a family level describes the family as it moves through time, coping with the changes and transitions of the family's life cycle. This includes both predictable developmental stresses and unpredictable events, the "slings and arrows of outrageous fortune," that may disrupt the life cycle process, such as untimely death, birth of a handicapped child, chronic illness, or job loss.

At a sociocultural level, the vertical axis includes cultural and societal history, stereotypes, patterns of power, social hierarchies, and beliefs, which have been passed down through the generations. A group's history, in particular the legacy of trauma in its history, will have an impact on families and individuals as they go through life (e.g., the Holocaust on Jews and Germans, slavery on African Americans and on slave-owning groups, homophobic crimes on homosexuals and hetero-sexuals). The horizontal axis relates to community connections or lack of them, current events, and social policy as they affect the family and the indi-vidual at a given time. It depicts the consequences in people's present lives of the society's inherited (vertical) norms of racism, sexism, classism, and homophobia, as well as ethnic and religious preju-dices, as these are manifested in social, political, and economic structures that limit the options of some and support the power of others.

ANXIETY AND SYMPTOM DEVELOPMENT

As families move along, stress is often greatest at transition points from one stage to another in the developmental process as families rebalance, rede-fine, and realign their relationships. Hadley and his colleagues (1974) found that symptom onset cor-related significantly with the normal family devel-opmental process of addition and loss of family members (e.g., birth, marriage, divorce, death). Walsh (1978) and McGoldrick (1977) both found that a significant life cycle event (death of a grand-parent), when closely related in time to another life cycle event (birth of a child), correlated with pat-terns of symptom development at a much later transition in the family life cycle (the launching of the next generation). Such research supports the clinical method of Murray Bowen, which tracks patterns through the family life cycle over several generations, focusing especially on nodal events and transition points to understand dysfunction at the present moment (Bowen, 1978). There is the strong implication that emotional issues and devel-opmental tasks that are not resolved at appropriate stages will be carried along and act as hindrances in future transitions and relationships (see Table 1.1). Given enough stress on the horizontal, devel-opmental axis, any individual family will appear extremely dysfunctional. Even a small horizontal stress on a family in which the vertical axis is full of intense stress will create great disruption in the system. The anxiety engendered on the vertical and horizontal axes where they converge and the interaction of the various systems and how they

work together to support or impede one another are the key determinants of how well the family will manage its transitions through life. It becomes im-perative, therefore, to assess not only the dimen-sions of the current life cycle stress, but also their connections to family themes and triangles coming down in the family over historical time. Although all normative change is to some degree stressful, when the horizontal (developmental) stress inter-sects with a vertical (transgenerational) stress, there tends to be a quantum leap in anxiety in the system (Carter, 1978). To give a global example, if one's parents were basically pleased to be parents and handled the job without too much anxiety, the birth of the first child will produce just the normal stresses of a system expanding its boundaries at the present time. On the other hand, if parenting was a problem in the family of origin of one or both spouses, and has not been dealt with, the transition to parenthood may produce heightened anxiety for the couple. Even without any outstanding family of origin issues, the inclusion of a child could po-tentially tax a system if there is a mismatch be-tween the child's temperament and the parent's. Or if a child is conceived in a time of great political upheaval that forces a family to leave its roots and culture and migrate to another country, the child's birth may carry with it unresolved issues.

In addition to the anxiety-provoking stress that is inherited from past generations and the stress that is experienced in moving through the family life cycle, there is, of course, the stress of living in a given place at a given time. Each cohort, or group born at a given time in history, that lives through various historical and sociocultural experiences at the same life cycle phase, is to an extent marked by its members' experiences. The World War II gener-ation and the baby boomers are examples of this ef-fect. However, we must also pay close attention to the enormous anxiety generated by the chronic un-remitting stresses of poverty and discrimination, especially as the economic and racial divide in our society widens (West, 1993). And at the end of the twentieth century, as the conservative crusade for so-called family values intensifies, it becomes nec-essary to evaluate the stress for families, especially women, that is caused by the relentless criticism of working mothers; the attacks on abortion rights; and the stigmatizing of divorce, gay and lesbian families, and unmarried mothers and their children.

THE CHANGING FAMILY LIFE CYCLE

Within the past few decades, the changes in family life cycle patterns have escalated dramatically, owing especially to the lower birth rate; the longer life expectancy; the changing role of women; very high divorce and remarriage rates; the rise of unmarried motherhood, unmarried couples, and single-parent adoptions; the increased visibility of gay and lesbian couples and families; and the increase in two-paycheck marriages to the point where they are the American norm. While it used to be that child-rearing occupied adults for their entire active life span, it now occupies less than half of the adult life span prior to old age. The meaning of family has changed drastically, but there is no agreed-upon definition. The changing role of women is central to these shifting family life cycle patterns. Seventy percent of working-age women are in the work-force. Even women who choose primary roles of mother and homemaker must now face an "empty nest" phase that equals in length the years devoted primarily to child care. Perhaps the modern feminist movement was inevitable, as women have come to need a personal identity. Having always had primary responsibility for home, family, and child care, women necessarily began to struggle under their burdens as they came to have more options for their own lives. Given their pivotal role in the family and their difficulty in maintaining concurrent functions outside the family, it is perhaps not surprising that women have been the most prone to symptom development at life cycle transitions. For men, the goals of career and family are parallel. For women, these goals conflict and present a severe dilemma. Surely, women's seeking help for family problems has much to do with their socialization, but it also reflects the special life cycle stresses on women, whose role has been to bear emotional responsibility for all family relationships at all stages of the life cycle (Chapter 6).

Men's roles in families are also beginning to change (see Chapter 7). They are participating more in child care (Levine, 1993) and housework (Barnett & Rivers, 1996), and many are realizing, in their minds if not always in action (Hochschild, 1989, 1997), that equality and partnership (Eisler, 1987) are a sensible ideal for couples. Michael Kimmel, a sociologist and spokesman for the National Organization for Men Against Sexism, holds out to men the ideal of "democratic manhood," which "requires both private and public commitments—changing ourselves, nurturing our relationships, cherishing our families, to be sure, but also reforming the public arena to enlarge the possibilities for other people to do the same" (1996, p. 334). Kimmel welcomes feminism, gay liberation, and multiculturalism as blueprints for the reconstruction of masculinity. He believes that men's lives will be healed only when there is full equality for everyone (Kimmel & Mosmiller, 1992; Kimmel, 1995).

Another major factor affecting all families at one time or another is the break in cultural and family continuity created by migration (Chapter 10; Sluzki, 1979). This break and its repercussions throughout family relationships affect family life cycle patterns for generations. An enormous number of Americans have immigrated within the past two generations.

Thus, overall, our paradigm for middle-class American families is currently more or less mythological, relating in part to existing patterns and in part to the ideal standards of the past against which most families compare themselves.

It is imperative that therapists at least recognize the extent of change and variations in the norm that are now widespread and that we help families to stop comparing their structure and life cycle course with that of the family of the 1950s. While relationship patterns and family themes may continue to sound familiar, the structure, ages, stages, and culture of the American family have changed radically.

It is time for us professionals to give up our attachments to the old ideals and to put a more positive conceptual frame around what is: two-paycheck marriages; permanent single-parent households; unmarried, remarried, and gay and lesbian couples and families; single-parent adoptions; and women of all ages alone. It is past time to stop thinking of transitional crises as permanent traumas and to drop from our vocabulary words and phrases that link us to the norms and prejudices of the past, such as broken or fatherless homes, children of divorce, out-of-wedlock children, and working mothers.

THE EXPANDED FAMILY LIFE CYCLE: INDIVIDUAL DEVELOPMENT

Part of the pull that family therapists feel to revert to psychoanalytic thinking whenever the individual is under consideration comes from the fact that our models of individual development have been built on Freud's and Erikson's ideas of psychosocial development. Compared to Freud's narrow focus on body zones, Erikson's (1963, 1968) eight stages of human development which have clearly been equated with male development; (Broverman et al., 1972) are an effort to highlight the interaction of the developing child with society. However, what Erikson's stages actually emphasize are not interdependence and the connectedness of the individual in relationships, but rather the development of individual characteristics (mostly traits of autonomy) in response to the demands of social interaction (Erikson, 1963). Thus, trust, autonomy, industry, and the formulation of an identity separate from his family are supposed to carry a child to young adulthood, at which point he is suddenly supposed to know how to "love," go through a middle age of "caring," and develop the "wisdom" of aging. This discontinuity—a childhood and adolescence focused on developing one's own autonomy supposedly in preparation for an adulthood of intimacy, caring, and wisdom—expresses exactly what we believe is wrong with male socialization as it is still practiced today in the belief that this is normal human development.

Although there has always been a "his" and "hers" version of development, until recently (Dinnerstein, 1976; Gilligan, 1982; McGoldrick, 1989;

Miller, 1976), only the former was ever described in the literature. Most male theoreticians, such as Freud, Kohlberg, Erikson, and Piaget, tended to ignore female development or subsume it under male development, which was taken as the standard for human functioning (Broverman et al., 1972; Notman, Klein, Jorden, & Zilbach, 1991; Tavris, 1992). Separation and autonomy have been considered the primary values for male development, the values of caring and attachment, interdependence, relationship, and attention to context being primary in female development. However, healthy development requires finding an optimal balance between connectedness and separateness, belonging and individuation, accommodation and autonomy. In general, developmental theories have failed to describe the progression of individuals in relationships toward a maturity of interdependence. Yet human identity is inextricably bound up with one's relationship to others, and the notion of complete autonomy is a fiction. Human beings cannot exist in isolation, and the most important aspects of human experience are relational.

Most developmental theorists, even those who have been feminist, have espoused psychodynamic assumptions about autonomy and separation, overfocusing on relationships with mothers as the primary factor in human development. They have assumed that masculine identity is achieved by separating from the mother and feminine identity through identification and attachment to her. Silverstein (1994) and Gilligan (quoted in Norman, 1997) effectively challenge this assumption that male development requires separating from one's mother. Gilligan (1982) critiques Piaget's conception of morality as being tied to the understanding of rights and rules and suggests that for females, moral development centers on the understanding of responsibility and relationships, whereas Piaget's description fits traditional male socialization's focus on autonomy (see Chapters 2 and 7). Eleanor Maccoby (1990) and Jean Baker Miller (1976) have tried to expand our understanding of the power dimensions in the social context of development. Their work suggests a broader conception of development for both males and females.

Developing a schema that would enhance all human development by including milestones of both autonomy and emotional connectedness for both males and females from earliest childhood has drawn us, not surprisingly, to the work of those whose perspectives go beyond white male development. These include Hale-Benson (1986), who explored the multiple intelligences and other developmental features she identified in African American children; Almeida, Woods, and Messineo (1998), who have been articulating a broad-based cultural conception of human development; Comer and Poussaint (1992), who have factored racism and its effects into their blueprint for development of healthy black children; Ian Canino and Jeanne Spurlock (1994), who outline many ways in which minority ethnic groups socialize their children; and Joan Borysenko (1996), whose descriptions of the stages of female development appear to have universal applicability for both males and females from all cultural groups. Borysenko's outline reflects the human need for responsible autonomy, which recent decades have granted in some measure to females, and emphasizes the importance of understanding interdependence, a concept that girls and children of color learn early but that is ignored in traditional male development.

CONTEMPORARY FAMILIES

It is high time we gave up on our traditional concept of family and expanded our very definition of the term. As Johnetta Cole (1996) has put it:

> No one family form—nuclear, extended, single-parent, matrilineal, patrilineal, fictive, residential, nonresidential—necessarily provides an environment better for humans to live or raise children in. Wife beating, child abuse, psychological terror, material deprivation and malnutrition take place in each of those family forms. And our responsibility, whether single parents or coparents or no parents at all, is to do all in our power to help create a healthy nonoppressive family environment for every living human being. (p. 75)

Families have many forms: multigenerational extended families of three or four generations, gay or lesbian couples and children, remarried families with shifting membership of children who belong to several households, single-parent families, families consisting of brothers and/or sisters or aunts and nieces, unmarried partners and their children and possibly a parent or an unmarried sibling of one. Yet, however much we accept the idea that family diversity exists, our society still tends to think of "family" as meaning a heterosexual, legally married couple and their children. This family form is taken all too frequently as the ideal against which all other family forms are judged and found wanting (McCarthy, 1994). All other family forms, which former President of the Republic of Ireland Mary Robinson has termed "unprotected families" (Burke, 1991), require our special consideration. Their history and family experience have been invalidated (McCarthy, 1994).

The backlash forces in our society use code terms such as "family values" to imply that traditional nuclear families are the only valid families. We must resist such insidious definitions and insist on a more inclusive definition of family and family values.

Contemporary families may consist of traditional nuclear families or many other kinds of immediate family households with or without children: single divorced parents, single unmarried parents, remarried families, unmarried partners, gay or lesbian partners, single adults, or widows or widowers, whose other family members may live in other households. Most of these families live in more than one household; divorced, remarried, and unmarried families may have ex-spouses and/or children who visit periodically. If parents live separately, we regard children as emotionally members of both households, regardless of the legal custody arrangements, what Ahrons (Chapter 23) calls the "binuclear family." This is in keeping with our belief that divorce restructures but does not end the family.

Dilworth-Anderson, Burton, and Johnson (1993) have contributed a thoughtful analysis of the impossibility of understanding families of color by using the rigid perspective of the nuclear family model: "Important organizing, relational bonding of significant others, as well as socialization practices or sociocultural premises are overlooked by researchers when the nuclear family structure is the unit of analysis" (p. 640). They discuss the important ways in which social support networks within the Black community serve as a buffer against a discriminating environment. They call for a broadening of ideas of what constitutes a family and its positive characteristics to allow for "culturally relevant descriptions, explanations, and interpretations of the family." They argue for the importance of a life-course perspective because it is based on interdisciplinary ways of thinking, being a framework that emerged from the cross-fertilization of the sociology of aging, demographic cohort analysis, and the study of personal biography in social psychology and history, and because it represents a dynamic approach to the study of family lives by focusing on the interlocking nature of individual trajectories within kinship networks in the context of temporal motion, culture, and social change. A life cycle framework thus "offers the conceptual flexibility to design conceptual frameworks and studies that address a variety of family forms in culturally diverse contexts" (p. 640).

Indeed, the separation of families into generational subsystems, referred to as the "nuclear" and the "extended" family, creates artificial separation of parts of a family. Extended family may live in many different geographic locations, but they are still family. Adding or subtracting members in the family is always stressful, and the stress of restructuring in the extended family because of divorce, death, or remarriage adds to the normative stress of the immediate family's task of dealing with whatever family patterns, myths, secrets, and triangles make up the emotional legacy from the family of origin.

OUR LIFE CYCLES UNFOLD IN THE CONTEXT OF THE COMMUNITY OF OUR CONNECTEDNESS

Community also represents multiple levels of the human system, from the small face-to-face neighborhood, group, or local community to the larger cultural group, to the nation, and then to our increasingly "global" society. All these levels have an enormous impact on the individuals and families under their sway.

There is an African saying, "If I don't care for you, I don't care for myself," which expresses the African sense that our identity is bound up in our interrelatedness to others (see Chapter 19). This is the essence of community defined as the level of interaction that bridges the gap between the private, personal family and the great impersonal public sphere. During the "me-first" 1980s, in a whirlwind of corporate speculation and reckless disregard for the commonweal, of massive deindustrialization and urban instability, American communities were blown apart. Women, who had for generations done the unpaid work of keeping their families connected to the community had themselves joined the workforce, many for economic survival, and nobody has yet replaced them. This loss is devastating for individuals and families alike and is a loss of the spiritual sense of belonging to something larger than one's own small, separate concerns. With our ever greater involvement in work, time for anything "unnecessary" has disappeared, so many people have no time for church or synagogue, friends or dinner parties, the PTA or the children's school, political action or advocacy. They seem lost in the scramble to survive in a tense, high-wired, violent time that rewards nothing but the individual acquisition of power and money (Carter, 1995).

Shaffer and Amundson (1993), in a chapter entitled "A Return to Community, but Not the Kind Your Grandparents Knew," define community as a dynamic whole that emerges when a group of people participate in common practices; depend on one another; make decisions together; identify themselves as part of something larger than the sum of their individual relationships; and commit themselves for the long term to their own, one another's, and the group's well being. Choice is the operative idea here, not nostalgia. It is important to remember that many traditional communities were and are repressive as well as secure, exclusionary as well as supportive of their members, and then only as long as members conform to community norms.

Webs of friendship and collective association, however, are woven deliberately and can be severed. Our social networks are no longer a given. We must, as economist Paul Wachtel (1989) says, find our own place in a social network that is no longer given to us to the degree that it was in the past. "We have no reserved seats. We must win our place" (p. 62). Wachtel suggests that our commitment to consumption is, in fact, an increasingly desperate attempt to replace our old sense of community and security with things. Amitai Etzioni (1997), one of our leading theorists on the subject of community, holds out a vision of community grounded in dialogue rather than fundamentalist censorship. Community in our lives can provide the best antidote to violence and anomie in our society and our best hope of an alternative to consumerism as a way of life.

THE LARGER SOCIETY

This is the largest context that has direct impact on our daily lives. In peacetime, this means the United States as a whole with its laws, norms, traditions, and way of life. In wartime, of course, and in pursuit of global markets, the context grows larger than one nation, and environmentally, the context for everyone is "spaceship earth." But for our purposes, we will consider here the culture of the United States at the close of the twentieth century and the dawn of the twenty-first. It is not a pretty sight. Mary Pipher (1994) says, "It became clearer and clearer to me that if families just let the culture happen to them, they end up fat, addicted, broke, with a house full of junk, and no time" (quoted in Simon, 1997, p. 29). Robert Bly (1996) says that contemporary society has left us with spiritual flatness with the talk show replacing the family, the internet instead of art, and the mall instead of community. Paradoxically, the American people, resented and envied throughout the world for our luxurious though vacuous way of life, are among the most religious, though not necessarily spiritual, people in the world (Mason, 1997). However extreme we may think or hope these comments are, there is the ring of truth in them.

Therapists could have a meaningful role here, encouraging clients to express their ideas about the meaning of family and asking whether they are living according to their own values and ideals. But we have been trained to avoid topics that smack of religion or even philosophy, and after millennia of holistic approaches to healing by the doctors of preindustrial cultures, we try to keep physical, emotional, and spiritual healing separate (Butler, 1990). But we pay a price for our arbitrary divisions, and so do our clients: depression, cynicism, anomie, despair and a culture of drugs, both recreational and medicinal.

How did we become one of the world's most class-stratified nations, with seemingly impenetrable walls between people of different status? The overclass lives in gated communities (where the emphasis is on security, not community), the underclass lives behind prison bars, on the street, or in cell-like corners of the ghetto; and everyone in between is confused about what is going on. The gap between rich and poor continues to widen. The U.S. Census Bureau reported in the fall of 1997 that in the previous year, median family incomes rose and Black and Latino poverty rates fell. However, closer examination revealed that incomes rose because more wives worked and men and women worked more hours. The gap between men's and women's pay increased again, and the poorest 20 percent of the population showed no increase in income (*New York Times,* Sept. 15, 1997). The extreme division between the haves and have-nots may be attributable to the change of rules in the larger society in the 1980s, such as changes in the tax code for individuals and corporations, excessive CEO salaries, the decline of unions, and the plunge into global competition (Yeskel, 1997). The antidote to social injustice, as Yeskel (1997) emphasizes, is political and social action.

We are all part of the problem. The political climate may exist in spite of us, but the properties of the system cannot be maintained unless the people in the system maintain them. If they begin to change their values and assumptions, they will begin to change the system as well (Wachtel, 1989). Galbraith (1996) reminds us that the poor don't vote and that great political victories can be won with a small percentage of eligible voters. He says that if concerned citizens brought the poor into the system, things would change as politicians sought to please the voters. When was the last time any of us asked a poor client whether he or she planned to vote? When was the last time we discussed social or political action with a middle-class client? We have to remind ourselves and our clients that if we limit our efforts to personal and family change within an unchanged larger society, we are helping to preserve the status quo.

In recent years, as economic pressures and uncertainties have grown and sources of support and inspiration have dwindled, a new trend has appeared among the well-to-do: to redefine success on a slower track and deliberately construct a simpler life (Saltzman, 1992). Although many of us resist "downshifting," even though "success" is killing us, it can be exactly the intervention that prevents a divorce and/or reacquaints family members with each other (Carter & Peters, 1997).

To keep family therapy relevant to today's families, we have to learn how and when to discuss all of the important issues that shape and determine our lives. We have to learn to reconnect family members with their dreams and their values. We have to learn to frankly discuss the inequalities in our society—the racism, classism, sexism, and homophobia that are built into the system—and help clients to join together within their families to create change for themselves and then to look outward and help bring change to the community and larger society. To be lasting, change must occur at every level of the system.

THE CHANGING STRUCTURE OF FAMILIES

Various studies by the U.S. Census Bureau (1996 and others) report that shifts in family structure leveled off in the 1990s as those changes became embedded in the culture:

- The percentage of single-person households rose from 17 percent to 25 percent, many of them elderly women (Bryson, 1996). The num-

ber of never-married men and women doubled or tripled in various age groups since 1970; for example, among people 35 to 39 years old, the rate more than doubled for women (from 5 percent to 13 percent) and tripled for men (from 7 percent to 19 percent).

- Single-parent families headed by women rose 12 percent (to 12.2 million) and those headed by men also rose 12 percent (to 3.2 million). The steepest rise is among white women (Roberts, 1994).

- The nuclear family (married couples with children under 18) shrank from 40 percent in 1970 to 25 percent of all households in 1996. About 50 percent of American children live in nuclear families.

- In nuclear families with children under age 6, 60 percent of mothers and 92 percent of fathers work.

- The majority of unwed mothers are poor and uneducated, but there are never-married mothers at every income level. Teenage pregnancy rates are dropping. Fewer than one third of single mothers are teenagers. The fathers of most children born to teenagers are over 20 years old (Coontz, 1997).

- Birth rates vary according to the mother's education, age, race, and ethnicity. The highest rates are among women in their twenties with the least education. Latino women had a higher birth rate than non-Latino black or white women in every educational category (National Center for Health Statistics, 1997).

- Of the 25 percent of children who live with one parent, 37 percent live with a divorced parent and 36 percent live with a never-married parent (Saluter, 1996).

- The number of unmarried couple households grew from half a million in 1970 to almost 4 million in 1994. About one third had children under age 15 at home.

- The median age of first marriage rose from 20.8 for women and 23.2 for men in 1970 to 24.5 for women and 26.7 for men in 1994.

- Three fourths of welfare recipients leave welfare within two years, but the instability of jobs and lack of child care often drive them back. Only 15 percent stay on welfare for five consecutive years. The majority of welfare recipients are white.

- The divorce rate, after doubling between 1960 and 1990, stabilized in the mid-1990s at about 46 percent (Bryson, 1996).
- Between 1970 and 1990, the rate at which people remarry after divorce dropped considerably. Currently about two thirds of divorced women and three fourths of divorced men remarry.
- After divorce, 64 percent of women and 16 percent of men report an improvement in psychological health. Divorced men have three to four times the mortality rate of their married peers.
- Within a year after divorce, 50 percent of fathers have virtually lost contact with their children. About two fifths of divorced men do not pay any child support (Bruce, Lloyd, & Leonard, 1995), and on the average men pay more for their car payments than they do for their child support payments.
- Remarried families are among our most common family structures; 20 percent of children live in stepfamilies.
- Second marriages break up more frequently than first marriages do. They also break up sooner—after an average of four rather than seven years (Norton & Miller, 1992).
- "Co-provider" marriages, in which the wife contributes 30–70 percent of the family income, are now the American norm and the major model for young couples (Smock and Dechter, 1994). Although women generally earn less than their husbands, 23 percent earn more than their husbands. Typically, wives manage the money but husbands control it.
- In two-parent families, men do about one third of the housework and less child care, even when both parents work at outside jobs (Barnett & Rivers, 1996).
- Americans age 65 and older make up about 13 percent of the nation's population but account for about 20 percent of all suicides, probably because of chronic illness and/or social isolation. Men account for 81 percent of elder suicides (Centers for Disease Control and Prevention, 1996).

It is difficult to get accurate numbers and information about gays and lesbians and their families because of the stigma attached to these identities. However, researchers in the gay and lesbian community provide extremely useful information (see Chapters 15 and 20). Family researchers (e.g., Gottman, 1994; Patterson, 1992) have confirmed findings of normal adjustment for children in gay and lesbian families. One study compared three groups of adult women: one group raised by single, divorced, heterosexual mothers; one group raised by remarried heterosexual mothers; and one group raised by mothers in lesbian couples. No significant differences were found. The largest problem of children in gay and lesbian families is the hostility or ridicule in the outside world (Coontz, 1997).

The changing American family structure should be put in the context of similar changes occurring worldwide and at every economic level: vastly increased divorce rates, the rise of single parent families, two-income households, an increase in work time, especially for women, and high rates of unwed childbearing. In Northern Europe, for example, one third of all births are to unwed mothers (Bruce et al., 1995). As researcher Frank Furstenberg has said, "The mainspring of the worldwide change probably has to do with the economic status of women and changes in the gender-based division of labor" (*New York Times,* May 30, 1995). Experts have expressed hope that the universality of family change will bring about new thinking on social policy.

MULTICULTURALISM

Racial and ethnic diversity are a fact in the United States. In the mid-1990s, with a population of 262 million, there were 73.6 percent European whites, 12 percent African Americans, 10 percent Latinos, and 3.3 percent people of Asian ancestry. In the

1990 census, there were 1.5 million interracial couples with 2 million children, a total that had doubled in the 1960s, tripled in the 1970s, and slowed somewhat in the 1980s. However, projections are that by the 2050s, Whites will hardly be a majority, while Latinos will rise to about 25 percent, the Black population will remain stable at 12 or 13 percent, and Asians will rise to about 8 percent. The overall U.S. population will have risen to 394 million by that date. Such changes will immediately present a host of new issues. For example, if, as projected, Whites will make up fewer than half of those under age 18 but three fourths of those over age 65, what will happen to the amounts of money allotted to public education and to Social Security or Medicare? How will the composition of Congress, now almost entirely white and male, change? We should be alert for more and more backlash against families of color as these projections become more widely known.

THE POLITICAL AND ECONOMIC SYSTEM

As John Kenneth Galbraith (1996) has said, the political dialectic in the United States used to be between capital and labor, between employer and employee, but now the struggle is between the rich (and those aspiring to be so) and the poor, unemployed and those suffering from racial, age, or gender discrimination. Our democracy has become, in large measure, a democracy of the fortunate.

The role of government is disputed. For the poor, the government can be central to their well-being and even survival. For the rich and comfortable, the government is a burden, except when it serves their interests as in military expenditure, Social Security, or the bailout of failed financial institutions. The United States has the widest gap between the rich and poor of any industrialized nation in the world. In 1989, the top 1 percent of American households owned nearly 40 percent of the nation's wealth. The top 20 percent owned more than 80 percent and this gap has continued to grow (Galbraith, 1996).

We believe that this state of affairs—rich versus poor—marks the end of the "American dream," which promised upward mobility in exchange for education and hard work. Now, the poor are not given access to adequate education, technical training, or any but dead-end jobs. We who have lost the will to make the dream possible pay an unacknowledged price in increased cynicism and despair and a loss of pride in the unstable and violent world we are leaving to our children and grandchildren, for which we blame the poor.

THE AMERICAN FAMILY OF THE FUTURE

According to Gillis (1996),

> *If history has a lesson for us, it is that no one family form has ever been able to satisfy the human need for love, comfort, and security.... We must keep our family cultures diverse, fluid, and unresolved, open to the input of everyone who has a stake in their future.... Our rituals, myths and images must therefore be open to perpetual revision, never allowed to come under the sway of any orthodoxy or to serve the interests of any one class, gender or generation. We must recognize that families are worlds of our own making and accept responsibility for our own creations. (p. 240)*

The most important determinants of the future will be our handling of the issues of the present: the support that we, as a society, give or don't give to family diversity in structure and culture and to the aspirations of the poor to give a better life to their children. Work is a big problem waiting to be solved: too much of it for some, not enough for others, and the need to provide good-quality child care for all the children on whom the future rests. Adequate education and health care are needed for them and their parents, and a commitment of a society with relatively fewer young people to pay the medical bills and Social Security of an increasing aging population. We need men to join actively in the search for family-friendly solutions. Serious human and ethical issues loom—the echoes of life and death—as reproductive technology heads toward genetic engineering and human cloning at one end of life and the push for physician-assisted suicide proceeds at the other end. For two centuries, our political discourse and changes have been about individual "rights." Perhaps in the twenty-first century, we will remember "interdependence."

Family therapists are in a unique position to help families leave behind their worn-out images and blueprints for the good life and embrace what is actually happening to make it work for them. First, of course, we must work at this in our own lives and with our colleagues.

CLINICAL IMPLICATIONS: THE MULTICONTEXTUAL FRAMEWORK

The multicontextual framework (Carter, 1993) shown in Table 1.2 is a model of couple and family assessment to assist clinicians in the work of including the relevant issues at all levels of the system in our clinical thinking and treatment. Our intent is to make an enormous amount of informa-

tion manageable and clinically relevant without diminishing its complexity. This guide is meant to be suggestive and is always subject to clinical judgment for a particular case.

The use of a genogram to identify and track patterns, resources, and problems over the generations cannot be overemphasized. The genogram, a three- or four-generation map of a family, is a major tool for organizing the complex information on family patterns through the life cycle (McGoldrick, 1995; McGoldrick, Gerson, & Schellenberger, 1998). Neither of us ever sits down with clients without their genogram in hand. Doing a genogram is not a one-session task, but a perpetual exploration. Cultural genograms (Congress, 1994; Hardy & Laszloffy, 1995; McGoldrick, Giordano, & Pearce, 1996) map a family's race, ethnicity, migration history, religious heritage, social class, and important

TABLE 1.2 Multicontextual Framework

THE INDIVIDUAL	IMMEDIATE HOUSEHOLD	EXTENDED FAMILY	COMMUNITY AND SOCIAL CONNECTIONS	LARGER SOCIETY
• Age • Gender roles and sexual orientation • Temperament • Developmental or physical disabilities • Culture, race, ethnicity • Class • Religious, philosophical, spiritual values • Finances • Autonomy skills • Affiliative skills • Power/privilege or powerlessness/abuse • Education and work • Physical or psychological symptoms • Addiction and behavioral disturbances • Allocation of time • Social participation • Personal dreams	• Type of family structure • Stage of family life cycle • Emotional climate • Boundaries, patterns, and triangles • Communication patterns • Negotiating skills • Decision-making process	• Relationship patterns • Emotional legacies, themes, secrets, family myths, taboos • Loss • Socioeconomic level and issues • Work patterns • Dysfunctions: addictions, violence, illness, disabilities • Social and community involvement • Ethnicity • Values and/or religion	• Face-to-face links between individual, family, and society • Friends and neighbors • Involvement with governmental institutions • Self-help, psychotherapy • Volunteer work • Church or temple • Involvement in children's school and activities • Political action • Recreation or cultural groups	• Social, political, economic issues • Bias based on race, ethnicity • Bias based on class • Bias based on gender • Bias based on sexual orientation • Bias based on religion • Bias based on age • Bias based on family status (e.g., single parent) • Bias based on disability • Power and privilege of some groups because of hierarchical rules and norms held by religions, social, business or governmental institutions • How does a family's place in hierarchy affect relationships and ability to change?

cultural issues. A family chronology (listing the events of family history in chronological order) and a sociogram, a map of the social network of a person or family, are other useful tools to use for family assessment (Hartman, 1995; McGoldrick et al., 1998). The Person-In-Environment classification system is a useful diagnostic system that emphasizes conceptualizing the person in context. This assessment tool for problems in social functioning is social work's answer to the DSM (Karls & Wandrei, 1994).

Overall, we urge clinicians to go beyond the clients' presenting problems to discuss their values and dreams. Encourage them to reflect about their real lives as they are actually leading them: Is my life meaningful? Do my relationships work? Am I teaching my children what they need to know? Do I like my work? Do I care about money too much or not enough? Is my life balanced? Do I have caring connections to my family and to others? Am I contributing to anyone in life? Do I belong?

The following information can be gathered in a structured assessment or as it emerges over several sessions. It is obviously important to develop a method of gathering all relevant information sooner rather than later.

ASSESSING INDIVIDUAL DEVELOPMENT

Any assessment requires consideration of the following issues for each individual:

- *Age.*
- *Gender roles and sexual orientation.* It is important not only to clarify the individual's sexual orientation and general attitude about gender roles, but also to see how these fit with those of others in the family and community.
- *Temperament.*
- *Developmental or physical abilities or disabilities.* These may include learning disorders, developmental lag, high intelligence, or musical talent, among other things.
- *Culture, race, and ethnicity: sociocultural background and values.* How does the client relate to his or her sociocultural situation, whether with pride or discomfort? How does he or she

handle negativity of the larger society, if applicable? How might those values influence the current situation?
- *Class.* Class is a combination of culture, education, wealth, and social status; it is also determined by the culture, education, wealth, employment and the social status of the marital partner. Class mobility is a major factor in family relationships, often creating unacknowledged tension, isolation, and loss for family members. Clarify the client's class status in relation to others in the family and community.
- *Religious, philosophical, and spiritual values.* What are client's beliefs about the meaning of life, death, life after death, God, concern for those less fortunate, and belief in something larger than him/herself?
- *Finances.* What are the yearly income, each client's level of control over income, child support payments, level of debt, number of people the client supports.
- *Autonomy skills.* For example, is the client free to make independent choices? Is the client assertive? Does the client believe that his or her ideas and wishes are heard?
- *Affiliative skills.* Does the client have friends and confidants? Does the client initiate social contacts or share doubts and dreams with anyone? How developed is his or her level of empathy? What are the extent and depth of the client's friendship and intimate network? Does the client have the ability to work collaboratively as well as independently?
- *Power/privilege or powerlessness/abuse.* Does the client have psychological power, physical power, and financial resources in relation to his or her life, family members, or community? Any indications of abuse should be assessed immediately.
- *Education and work.* What are the client's income and control of work, level of education, educational values, skills, and talents?
- *Physical or psychological symptoms.* Such symptoms include sleep disturbance and mood disorder.

- *Addictions and behavioral disturbances.* These include alcohol, drugs, food, gambling, or debt.
- *Allocation of time.* What amounts of time are spent at work, with family, on the self, in child care, on housework, on leisure, or in caretaking of others?
- *Social participation.* Explore the client's friendship network and membership in community organizations.
- *Personal dreams.* What are the client's wishes for life and degree of pursuit or fulfillment of them?

All these individual factors can influence family relationships at any phase of the life cycle and should be carefully assessed.

ASSESSING THE IMMEDIATE FAMILY HOUSEHOLD(S)

Assessment of this level includes exploration of the following:

- *Type of family structure.* For example, if the household consists of a single parent or single person, extra attention should be paid to the person's friendships and community connections. If the client has been divorced or remarried, attention should be paid to communication and relationships with the ex-spouse, especially if there are children.
- *Normative tasks at their stage of the family life cycle.*
- *Emotional climate within the family.* The emotional climate may be intimate, disorganized, unpredictable, emotional, tense, angry, cold, or distant.
- *Boundaries, patterns, and triangles.* These include marital, parent/child, and sibling relationships and relationships with other family members or caretakers.
- *Communication patterns.* These include decision making (authoritarian, egalitarian, casual, rigid) and negotiation skills and intimacy.

ASSESSING THE EXTENDED FAMILY

Any family assessment should include consideration of multigenerational issues that may be influ-

encing the immediate situation. These include the following:

- *Relationship patterns.* These may include cutoffs, conflicts, triangles, fusion, or enmeshment.
- *Emotional legacies, themes, secrets, family myths, taboos.* These include beliefs such as that money is everything, or that upward mobility is essential.
- *Loss.* These may include ghosts and unresolved, traumatic, untimely, or recent losses.
- *Socioeconomic issues.* These include class, ethnicity, migration history and cultural change, religious and spiritual values, income, beliefs, and prejudices.
- *Work patterns.* These include belief in working to live or living to work, hopelessness about finding meaningful work, and extreme ambition.
- *Dysfunctions.* These include addictions, violence, chronic illness, and disabilities.
- *Social and community involvement.*

Exploring the extended family is not like filling out a form. The therapist should track the antecedents of the presenting problems by asking dynamic relationship-oriented questions such as How did your parents react when you adopted a child of a different race? What attitudes have they expressed about African Americans? Is anyone else in the family interracially married or adopted? Did they know that you had fertility problems? Have you and your mother had the only conflictual mother-daughter relationship in the family? How did she get along with her mother? How did her sisters get along with their mother?

The relevance of the extended family is not limited to the past. This is a current and supremely significant emotional system, whether or not family members acknowledge that and even if they are not speaking to each other.

ASSESSING THE FAMILY'S COMMUNITY AND SOCIAL CONNECTIONS

Assessing families' connections to work, friends, and their broader community is essential to understanding their problems and to figuring out strategies for intervention. Very often, our interventions need to involve helping families to increase their contextual supports. This is especially important for populations that tend to be isolated, such as divorced men, the widowed elderly, and single parents. We must realize that families cannot be successful in a vacuum or without positive linkages to the wider social system. Areas to assess include the following:

- *Links between the individual, the family, and society.* Is it a buffer or a social stress?
- *Friends and neighbors.*
- *Community supports and connections.* These include religious groups and groups formed around interests, sports, work, education, politics, culture, and the arts.
- *Involvement with government institutions.* This includes involvement with welfare, the legal system, immigration, the military, and entitlement programs such as SSI benefits, Medicare, and Medicaid.
- *Self-help, psychotherapy.* This may include Alcoholics Anonymous, and other 12-step programs.
- *Volunteer work.* This includes work for church and temple groups, the Rotary Club, the American Legion, the League of Women Voters, and other such groups.

Families often belong to formal or informal groupings, which meet for mutual activity and support. Such groups connect individuals and families to the larger society and buffer them from its stress. They may enhance our spirituality by connecting us to interests and purposes larger than our own; mitigate the impact of social inequities; and provide information, meaning, enrichment, mutual support, and joint action to the lives of its members. The powerful healing quality of such networks is probably a main reason why Alcoholics Anonymous and the other community-based self-help groups that have sprung from this informal networking system have developed worldwide standing as the most powerful intervention to combat addictions.

Community-level interventions have been recognized as essential within the social work field

for more than 100 years. The Community Mental Health movement of the 1960s made great strides forward in attending to the community level of services to maintain family members' health and mental health. Unfortunately, the capitalistic, me-first, "not in my backyard" dismantling of communities and community services that has been going on since the 1970s has had far-reaching implications in terms of making the rich richer and the poor poorer. But we do not need to lose our own moral sense or our essential common sense awareness of what is obviously in the best interest of families through the life cycle just because the dominant groups are trying to blind us to the common welfare of our whole society. And in spite of our hyperindividualistic times, some creative therapists are still daring to maintain their social perspective and challenge the dominant ideology. For example, Ramon Rojano, the Colombian-born Director of the Department of Human Services in Hartford, Connecticut, has made his agency a forum for doing community family therapy, which he sees as the answer to poverty and the key to restoration of the American dream. With a network of at least twenty community agencies and programs, he spreads hope and aspirations among the poor, combining family therapy with connecting clients to jobs, education, health care, parent education, political action groups, leadership training, and anything that will help them to take charge of their lives (Markowitz, 1997).

As another example of what is possible, Earl Shorris, an author (1997a) and a university professor in New York City, was given space and sponsorship by Jaime Inclan at the Roberto Clemente Family Guidance Center in New York to offer a broad-based course in the humanities to poor young people. The only requirements for the course were low income and the ability to read a tabloid newspaper. Shorris (1997b) says that he offered participants hope. He dared to be undaunted by their poverty and to provide them the best ideas available—what is taught at colleges such as Harvard and Yale. Using a curriculum of the classics ranging from Plato and Aristotle through political and moral philosophy, literature, poetry, original documents of U.S. history and more, he taught them about the nature of political power, control over their own lives, and the ability to reflect and negotiate instead of only reacting instinctively. (This, of course, is the prime component of differentiation or emotional maturity as defined by Bowen, 1978.) Volunteer experts served as faculty, and the program offered field trips to museums, learning through Socratic dialogues, and a comprehensive exam at the end of the year-long course. Seventeen of the thirty-one youths who began the course completed it, and a year later, ten of these were attending four-year colleges on full scholarships (Shorris 1997b). This is a stunning example of how the poor can respond when they are given the advantages of the privileged.

Therapists can make a difference in large and small ways, even in our office practices. For example, Lascelles Black (1997), a Jamaican-born family therapist, does office therapy with the poor that spills over into the community, as he talks with his clients' lawyers, doctors, and welfare workers and attends clients' parties, weddings, and funerals. He describes himself as "a middle class advocate for people who have less access than I do." He talks to them about drugs and guns, asking whether they voted and whether they are taking their AIDS medication. Black's motto is: Take your opportunities when you find them; Never write anyone off; and Never underestimate family bonds of caring. Dusty Miller, a therapist in Northampton, Massachusetts, focuses her community efforts on therapists, working to mobilize them to take social and political action rather than submit to the restrictions of "mismanaged care" (Miller, 1996–97). She has organized volunteer therapists to provide free services to women survivors of violence who are not covered by any insurance, and part of this service is supporting the clients' demands for better health care. She mentors doctoral students who develop new, creative projects and encourages colleagues and students to speak out and write for lay audiences, not only professionals.

Even in middle-class office practice, we can speak to our clients about the benefits of their connection to groups within their communities, which is an important part of lifting the burden of expect-

ing all things from marriage and family relationships. Such activities are an important part of giving back and thus fostering values that go beyond clients' immediate self-interest.

ASSESSING THE IMPACT ON CLIENTS OF HIERARCHY AND POWER INEQUALITY IN THE LARGER SOCIAL STRUCTURES OF SOCIETY

We are realizing increasingly that our assessment of families and our interventions must attend to the unequal ways that families are situated in the larger context so that we don't become part of the problem by preserving the status quo. Areas to assess include the following:

Current or Longstanding Social, Political, and Economic Issues

How have these become family problems? It is helpful to make a list of issues that you think have an impact on your locale, to help keep these issues in the forefront of your mind, since there are so many forces that would obscure them (McGoldrick, 1998). Such a list at the end of the twentieth century might include random violence, affirmative action, de facto school and neighborhood segregation, gay and lesbian adoption or marriage, welfare reform, abortion rights, prejudice against legal and illegal immigrants, health care and insurance, tax cuts, downsizing, social services to the elderly and other groups, cost and availability of infertility treatments, and physician-assisted suicide.

It is extremely important that we not "psychologize" social problems by searching for the roots of every problem in the interior motivations and actions of the individual and/or the family. Many clinical problems can be directly connected with the social system. A lesbian couple came to therapy because of ongoing conflict between them. The major argument presented was that one of them was "neurotic and restless," always wanting to move to a different neighborhood, pressuring her partner ceaselessly. A thorough assessment revealed that the "neurotic" partner was a schoolteacher who feared, realistically, that she would be barred from teaching if her sexual orientation were reported to the school system. Therefore, she was extremely anxious about contacts with neighbors and very sensitive to indications that neighbors were puzzled about or suspicious of their relationship.

Bias against Race, Ethnicity, Class, Gender, Sexual Orientation, Religion, Age, Family Status, or Disability

How does a person, family, or group's place in these hierarchies affect family relationships and limit or enhance the ability to change? Much has been written about the impact of the norms and values of the larger society on the individuals and families within it. What is most important for the clinician to grasp is that race, class, gender, and sexual orientation are not simply "differences"; they are categories that are arranged hierarchically with power, validation, and maximum opportunity going to those at the top: whites, the affluent, men, and heterosexuals.

We must learn to be aware of and deal with these power differences as they operate (1) in the therapy system, in which they add to the already existing power differential between therapist and client; (2) within the family system, in which social stress easily becomes family conflict; and (3) between the family and society, in which they either limit or enhance the options available for change.

Clinically, the therapist must be prepared to discuss explicitly how racism, sexism, classism, and homophobia may be behind the problems clients are taking out on each other. The goal is to help the family members to join together against the problems in society instead of letting these problems divide them. Explicit discussion and strategies will also be needed to overcome the obstacles to change, which unaware therapists may blame on the client's "resistance."

A severely injured Irish American fireman and his Italian American wife came to therapy because of the wife's complaints about his drinking and depression. She also expressed great concern about family finances because his disability pay could not support them and their two young children. The therapist discovered that although the wife was a trained bookkeeper, the sexist norms of their ethnicities and class did not permit either of them to even consider one obvious solution: that the wife could get a full-time job while the husband stayed home with the children and planned or trained for whatever new work he would be able to do in the future. Not until the therapist explicitly addressed this and tracked the relevant attitudes about gender roles in their families of origin and in their friends and community network did the couple realize that they could choose a different set of beliefs about gender roles—and did so.

A middle-class African American woman and her husband entered therapy because of marital conflict, which her husband blamed on her depression. She agreed, saying that her depression was caused by her lack of progress at work, which she blamed on herself. Only after detailed questioning from the therapist did she come to believe that her supervisor's racism might be behind her poor evaluations. Encouraged by the therapist and her husband, she then discussed the issue with a higher-level manager and was transferred to a different supervisor, who subsequently promoted her. It is disconcerting to contemplate how many therapists might have suggested Prozac and explored her marriage and family of origin for the source of her depression and "poor work performance."

Power and Privilege Given to Some Groups over Others Because of the Hierarchical Rules and Norms Held by Religious, Social, Business, or Governmental Institutions

It is important to assess the level of awareness of those in privileged and powerful groups as to the nature of their position and its responsibilities. Because most people compare themselves with those "above" them, we don't let ourselves become aware that our privileges are at the expense of those below us in the hierarchy. But it is important to realize that sexism, classism, racism, homophobia, anti-Semitism, and other prejudices are problems of the privileged groups, not of the oppressed, who suffer from the problems. Therefore, we need to find ways, *whether the issues are part of the presenting problem or not,* to raise the issue of racism with whites, sexism with men, classism with the well-to-do, homophobia with heterosexuals, and anti-Semitism or other religious prejudice with Christians. These are the groups who must change to resolve the problem.

We can ask: What community groups do you belong to? Is there diversity of membership? Is that because of exclusionary policies or attitudes? What are you doing about that? Do you belong to a church or temple or other religious organization? If so, do you agree with their attitude toward people of other religions? If not, why not? Do your children have friends of other racial and religious backgrounds? How are you preparing them for the rapidly increasing multiculturalism in our society? I notice your brother John has never married. Do you think he is gay? If he were, what would make it hard for him to tell the family? How did you and your wife decide on the allocation of household chores? How did you and your wife decide who should cut back at work to do child care? Are you ashamed of your son-in-law because he and his parents have less education and money than your family? You have much more education and money and social status than average. Are you aware of the power that gives you? How do you use it? Do you exercise your power to make a difference in social and political issues that concern you? What would it take for you to make time to do for others?

Asking such questions is obviously not enough, since these inequities are structured into our society and our consciousness at such a profound level that those of us with privilege have extreme difficulty becoming aware of this fact. Frederick Douglass has taught us that power concedes nothing without demand. We rarely become aware of or give up our privilege without pressure. But these questions are the beginning of such challenge, because they assert that the status quo is not necessarily acceptable to us or to our clients if we are pushed to think about such issues seriously.

The following are additional questions to help raise issues in routine couples and family therapy assessment:

1. Ask routinely exactly how much income each spouse earns or has access to. Inquire what effect a large disparity in income has on a couple's overall decision-making process. Ask who manages the money, who has veto power, how financial decisions are arrived at, whose name is on their assets. Find out the family's level of debt, exact number of credit cards, and number of people they support or expect to support in later years.
2. Challenge the expectation of middle- and upper-class women that they will be supported financially for life by their husbands.
3. Question a wife who plans to stay home with her children as to whether she is "economically viable"—that is, has enough money or skills to risk being a nonearner in a society with a 46 percent divorce rate, in which women are often left with inadequate resources to care for themselves.
4. Challenge the notion that work prevents greater involvement in the family or that a wife must be the primary parent or she is not a "good mother."
5. Explore the wife's work or career plans and the husband's fathering.
6. Ask what each spouse's ethnicity is. If they are of different races or ethnic backgrounds, ask what issues arise for them, their children, and their families of origin because of the differences. Ask—or think about—what impact their and your racial or ethnic values have on the presenting problem and its evaluation in therapy. Talk and think about the impact of racism on the lives of people of color and in the therapy.
7. Be aware that gender, race, class, and sexual orientation connect people to a more powerful or less powerful place in the operating hierarchies. Be alert to the ways in which racism, sexism, elitism, or homophobia are played out as couple or family problems.

8. When working with gay and lesbian clients, be aware of society's intense homophobia. Explore the impact of social stigma on gay and lesbian relationships and evaluate the wisdom or consequences of coming out in different contexts: work, family, church, or temple.

9. Be aware of the different value systems held by the different socioeconomic classes in the United States. For example, they have different approaches to gender roles, education, religion, and work. Be aware of the influence of your own value system when discussing these value-laden issues with the couple.

10. Ask how much time each parent spends with their children and how much time the couple has alone together. Explore their satisfaction with their sexual relationship and their method of negotiating differences of all kinds.

11. Ask specifically how child care and housework chores are divided between the couple and among the children. Note and comment when appropriate on whether these tasks are allocated according to traditional gender roles. Ask whether both spouses find involvement with children and task allocation to be fair and satisfactory.

12. Ask how much time each parent spends at work, how secure and satisfactory their work is, whether they control their own time at work, and whether they need to work as many hours as they do to support the family adequately.

13. Inform couples struggling with marital or divorce issues what the facts and statistics are in the larger society regarding alimony allocation, child support collection, contact between fathers and children, the divorce rate for first and subsequent marriages, and other factors relevant to their situation.

14. Ask routinely about clients' friendships and their neighborhood and community connections and include such reconnections in the work of therapy.

15. Help clients to think about the meaning of spirituality in their lives and what values make their lives meaningful to them. Encourage clients to consider changes that help them live according to their own values.

16. Connect all of the above issues from the sociocultural system by relating them to the presenting problem, and give them emotional relevance by exploring the impact of these issues on the client's family of origin.

17. The more we deal with these issues in our own lives, the easier it will be to notice and deal with them in clients' lives.

A METHOD OF INCLUDING THE SOCIOCULTURAL CONTEXT IN FAMILY THERAPY

Rhea Almeida and her colleagues in central New Jersey have organized a format for intervention that combines society, community, family, and the individual. Called the Cultural Context Model, it was originally designed for treatment of domestic violence but now covers a wide range of problems. Phase I of treatment consists of socioeducation groups in which film clips and readings are used to educate the clients about the power abuses of racism, sexism, classism, and homophobia. Men, women, and children are divided into separate "culture groups," in which sponsors, who have previously completed the program, help the clients to discuss their personal issues. Men are held accountable to others and prevented from emotional compartmentalizing. Women are empowered and prevented from overly focusing on guilt. Children are encouraged to explore their perceptions of race and gender, and adolescents also explore sexual orientation. Family therapy takes place in the separate groups for men and women, in family groups, and in individual family sessions, the basic idea being to establish a new norm of social accountability and support. All family problems are examined in the social as well as family of origin context. At the conclusion of therapy, family members are encouraged to give back by becoming sponsors and/or by educating community groups (e.g., police, schools, business groups) about racism, sexism, and homophobia (Almeida, Messineor, & Woods, 1998).

CONCLUSION

Families have always had problems. Adam and Eve disobeyed the landlord's rules and were evicted from their lovely estate. Adam immediately blamed Eve for luring him into it, and Eve said that the snake made her do it, showing how easily couple conflict follows social upheavals such as migration, homelessness, or unemployment. Having received a life sentence of hard labor for their infraction, their family remained under considerable stress and became quite dysfunc-

tional. Eventually, one of their children killed the other. This put domestic violence on our first genogram and made an emotionally loaded issue out of the question of our responsibility toward others ("Am I my brother's keeper?"). Families have been struggling ever since to get it right. Of course, there is no one "right" way, but many strengths will always emerge from the effort. It is crucial that we validate and build on those strengths in every type of family that we encounter. This is the real meaning of family values.

REFERENCES

Ahrons, C. R., & Rodgers, R. H. (1987). *Divorced families.* New York: Norton.

Almeida, R., Font, R., Messineo, T., & Woods, R. (1998). The cultural context model. In M. McGoldrick (Ed.), *Revisioning family therapy: Race, culture and gender in clinical practice.* New York: The Guilford Press.

Almeida, R., Woods, R., & Messineo, T. (1998). Contextualizing child development theory: Race, gender, class and culture. *Cultural Diversity and Mental Health, 2*(3).

Aries, P. (1962). *Centuries of childhood: A social history of family life.* New York: Vintage.

Barnett, R. C., & Rivers, C. (1996). *She works/he works: How two-income families are happier, healthier, and better-off.* San Francisco: Harper.

Black, L. W., "When opportunity knocks," in *The Family Therapy Networker,* Nov./Dec. 1997.

Bly, R. (1997). *The sibling society.* New York: Vintage.

Borysenko, Joan. (1996). *A woman's book of life.* New York: Riverhead Books.

Bowen, M. (1978). *Family therapy in clinical practice.* New York: Aronson.

Broverman, I. K., Vogel, S. R., Broverman, D. M., Clarkson, F. E., & Rosenkrantz, P. S. (1972). Sex-role stereotypes: A current appraisal. *Journal of Social Issues, 28*(2): 59–78.

Bruce, J., Lloyd, C., and Leonard, A. (1995). "Families in Focus," issued by The Population Council, NY.

Bryson, K. Report from U.S. Bureau of the Census, Nov. 27, 1996.

Burke, H. (1991). Changing demography, changing needs, and unprotected families. In G. Kiely, & V. Richardson (Eds.), *Family policy: European perspectives.* Dublin: Family Studies Centre, University College Dublin.

Butler, K. (1990). "Spirituality reconsidered: Facing the limits of psychotherapy," in *The Family Therapy Networker,* Sept.–Oct.

Canino, I., & Spurlock, J. (1994). *Culturally diverse children and adolescents: Assessment, diagnosis and treatment.* New York: The Guilford Press.

Carter, B. (1993). *Clinical dilemmas in marriage: The search for equal partnership.* [Videotape produced by Steve Lerner which demonstrates the multicontextual framework.] New York: The Guilford Press.

Carter, B. (1995). "Focusing your wide-angle lens," in *The Family Therapy Networker,* Nov./Dec.

Carter, B., & Peters, J. (1997) *Love, honor and negotiate: Building partnerships that last a lifetime,* NY: Pocket Books.

Carter, E. A. (1978). Transgenerational scripts and nuclear family stress: Theory and clinical implications. In R. R. Sager (Ed.), *Georgetown Family Symposium: Vol. 3, 1975–76.* Washington, DC: Georgetown University.

Census Bureau Report (1996). *Population projections of the U.S. by age, sex, race and hispanic origin: 1996 to 2050.*

Centers for Disease Control and Prevention. January 1996.

Cicirelli, V. G. (1995). *Sibling relationships across the life span.* New York: Plenum Press.

Cohler, B., Hosteler, A. J., & Boxer, A. (1998). In D. McAdams & E. de St. Aubin (Eds.), *Generativity and adult development. Psychosocial perspective on caring and contributing to the next generation.* Washington, DC: American Psychological Association Press.

Cole, J. B. (1996). In Elza Dinwiddie-Boyd (Ed.), *In Our Own Words,* New York: Avon Books.

Comer, J., & Poussaint, A. (1992). *Raising Black Children.* New York: Penguin.

Coontz, S. (1997). *The way we really are: Coming to terms with America's changing families.* New York: Basic Books.

Coontz, S. (1992). *The way we never were: American families and the nostalgia trap.* New York: Basic Books.

Congress, E. (1994). The use of culturagrams to assess and empower culturally diverse families. *Families in Society: The Journal of Contemporary Human Services,* November.

Dilworth-Anderson, P., Burton, L., & Johnson, L. B. (1993). Reframing theories for understanding race, ethnicity and families. In P. G. Boss, W. J. Doherty, R. LaRossa, W. R. Schumm, & S. K. Steinmetz (Eds.), *Sourcebook of family theories and methods: A contextual approach.* New York: Plenum.

Dinnerstein, D. (1976). *The mermaid and the minotaur.* New York: Harper & Row.

Duvall, E. M. (1977). *Marriage and family development* (5th ed.). Philadelphia: Lippincott.

Eisler, R. (1987). *The chalice and the blade.* New York: Harper & Row.

Elder, G. (1986). Military times and turning points in men's lives. *Developmental Psychology, 22,* 233–245.

Elder, G. (1992). Life course. In E. Gorgatta & M. Borgatta (Eds.), *Encyclopedia of sociology, Vol. 3.* (pp. 1120–1130). New York: Macmillan.

Erikson, E. (1968). *Identity: youth and crisis.* New York: Norton.

Erikson, E. (1963). *Childhood and society* (2nd ed.). New York: W. W. Norton.

Etzioni, A. (1997). *The new golden rule: Community and morality in a democratic society.* New York: Basic Books.

Galbraith, J. K. (1996). *The good society: The humane agenda.* New York: Houghton Mifflin.

Gilligan, C. (1982). *In a Different Voice.* Cambridge, MA: Harvard University Press.

Gillis, J. (1996). *A world of their own making: Myth, ritual, and the quest for family values,* New York: Basic Books.

Gottman, J. (1994). *What predicts divorce?* NJ: L. Erlbaum Associates.

Hadley, T., Jacob, T., Milliones, J., Caplan, J., & Spitz, D. (1974). The relationship between family developmental crises and the appearance of symptoms in a family member. *Family Process 13,* 207–214.

Hale-Benson, J. E. (1986). *Black children: Their roots, culture and learning styles.* Baltimore: Johns Hopkins University Press.

Hardy, K. V. and Laszloffy, T. A. (1995). The cultural genograms: Key to training culturally competent family therapists. *Journal of Marital and Family Therapy, 21* (3), July.

Hartman, A. (1995). Diagramatic assessment of family relationships. *Families in Society, 76*(2): 111–122.

Hess, B. B., & Waring, J. M. (1984). Changing patterns of aging and family bonds in later life. *The Family Coordinator 27*(4), 303–314.

Hochschild, A. (1989). *The second shift: Working parents and the revolution at home.* New York: Viking.

Hochschild, A. (1997). *The time bind: When work becomes home and home becomes work.* New York: Holt.

Karls, J. A., & Wandrei, K. E. (Eds.). (1994). *Pie manual.* Washington, DC: N.A.S.W. Press.

Kimmel, M. S. (Ed.) (1995). *The politics of manhood,* Philadelphia: Temple University Press.

Kimmel, M. S. (1996). *Manhood in America: A cultural history,* New York: Free Press.

Kimmel, M. S., & Mosmiller, T. E. (1992). *Against the tide: Pro feminist men in the U.S. 1776–1990.* Boston: Beacon Press.

Levine, J., Murphy, D., & Wilson, S. (1993). *Getting men involved.* New York: Scholastic.

Levinson, D. (1978). *The seasons of a man's life.* New York: Knopf.

Levinson, D. J. (1996). *The seasons of a woman's life.* New York: Knopf.

Maccoby, E. E. (1990)."Gender and relationships: A developmental account." *American Psychologist,* April.

Markowitz, L. (1997). Ramon Rojano won't take no for an answer. *The Family Therapy Networker,* November-December, 1997.

Mason, M. (1997). *Seven Mountains: The inner climb to commitment and caring,* New York: Dutton.

McCarthy, I. C. (1994). "Abusing norms: Welfare families and a fifth province stance. In I. C. McCarthy (Ed.) *Poverty and social exclusion, a special issue of human systems, 5* (3–4), 229–239.

McGoldrick, M. (1977). *Some Data on Death and Cancer in Schizophrenic Families.* Presentation at Georgetown Presymposium, Washington, DC.

McGoldrick, M. (Ed.). (1998). *Revisioning family therapy: Race, culture and gender in clinical practice.* New York: The Guilford Press.

McGoldrick, M., Gerson, R., & Schellenberger (1998). Genograms: Assessment and intervention (2nd ed.). New York: Norton.

McGoldrick, M. (1995). *You can go home again: Reconnecting with your family.* New York: Norton.

McGoldrick, M., Giordano, J., & Pearce, J. (Eds.) (1996). *Ethnicity and family therapy* (2nd ed.). NY: The Guilford Press.

Miller, D. Therapists in the community. *AFTA Newsletter, 66,* Winter 1996–97.

Miller, J. B. (1976) *Toward a new psychology of women.* Boston: Beacon.

National Center for Health Statistics. April 1997.

Neugarten, B. (1979). Time, age and the life cycle. *American Journal of Psychiatry,* 136, 887–894.

Norman, M. (1997, Nov. 9). From Carol Gilligan's chair. *New York Times Magazine,* p. 50.

Norris, J. E., & Tindale, J. A. (1994). *Among generations: The cycle of adult relationships.* New York: W. H. Freeman & Company.

Norton, A. J., & Miller, L. F. (1992). *Marriage, divorce, and remarriage in the 1990s.* (U.S. Bureau of the Census, Current Population Reports. Series P-23, No. 180). Washington, DC: Government Printing Office.

Notman, M., Klein, R., Jordan, J., & Zilbach, J. (1991). Women's unique developmental issues across the life cycle. In A. Tasman & S. Goldfinger (Eds.), *Review of Psychiatry, 10.* Washington, DC: American Psychiatric Press.

Patterson, C. (1992). Children of lesbian and gay parents. *Child Development, 63,* 1025–1042.

Roberts, S. (1994). *Who we are: A portrait of America based on the latest U.S. census.* New York: Times Books.

Pipher, M. (1994). *Reviving Ophelia: Saving the selves of adolescent girls.* New York: Ballantine.

Saltzman, A. (1992). *Downshifting: Reinventing success on a slower track.* New York: Harper Perennial.

Saluter, A. (1996). *Marital status and living arrangements, March, 1995.* (Current Population Reports, P20–491). Washington DC: U.S. Department of the Census.

Shaffer, C., & Amundsen, K. (1993). *Creating community anywhere: Finding support and connection in a fragmented world.* New York: Tarcher/Perigee Books.

Sheehy, G. (1977). *Passages.* New York: Bantam.

Sheehy, G. (1995). *New passages.* New York: Ballantine Books.

Shorris, E. (1997a). *A journey through poverty to democracy.* New York: W. W. Norton.

Shorris, E. (1997b). "Of Plato and poverty." *The Family Therapy Networker,* November–December.

Silverstein, O. (1994). *The courage to raise good men.* New York: Viking.

Simon, R. (1997). The family unplugged (an interview with Mary Pipher). *Family Therapy Networker,* Jan.–Feb., 24–33.

Sluzki, C. (1979). Migration and family conflict. *Family Process 18*(4): 379–390.

Tavris, C. (1992). *The mismeasure of women.* New York: Simon & Schuster.

U.S. Census Bureau (1996). Annual Demographic Survey, March Supplement. Revised September 26. Contact (pop@census.gov).

Valliant, G. (1977). *Adaptation to life.* Boston: Little Brown.

Wachtel, P. (1989). *The poverty of affluence: A psychological portrait of the American way of life.* Philadelphia: New Society Publishers.

Walsh, F. (1978). Concurrent grandparent death and the birth of a schizophrenic offspring: An intriguing finding. *Family Process, 17,* 457–463.

Walsh, F., & McGoldrick, M. (1991). *Living beyond loss.* New York: Norton.

West, C. (1993). *Race matters.* Boston: Beacon Press.

Yeskel, F. (1997). Welfare or wealthfare? *The Women's Review of Books,* XIV (5).

CHAPTER 2

SELF IN CONTEXT
THE INDIVIDUAL LIFE CYCLE IN SYSTEMIC PERSPECTIVE

MONICA McGOLDRICK
BETTY CARTER

Like the concept of zero in mathematics, a concept of self is pivotal in organizing experience, useful as an idea as long as it is not mistaken for a thing. Yet, even though we regard the self as logically central to any way of experiencing the world, we are trained to look through it like a pane of glass, only noticing when it becomes blurred or cracked. The Western insistence on a separate self carries its own blindness, its own nonrecognition of necessary connection…The very self we set out to affirm can become a hostage to fortune.

—Mary Catherine Bateson (1994, p. 66)

REDEFINING THE DIMENSIONS OF HUMAN DEVELOPMENT

As Almeida, Woods, and Messineo (1998) have stated:

> *Human development evolves within the context of our social roles, which are* fundamentally *organized and bounded by our position within the class, gender, racial and cultural structure of our society.… Traditional theories of child development have overfocused on discrete tasks and stages in the evolution of a self, defined primarily by a child's level of achievement and autonomy.*

This paper challenges traditional Western formulations of human development, which have begun with the individual as a psychological being and defined development as growth in the human capacity for autonomous functioning. It attempts to broaden this conceptualization to include more expanded ways of viewing the self. In Eastern cultures, for example, the very conception of human development begins with the definition of a person as a social being and defines development as the evolution of the human capacity for empathy and connection. We build on the seminal work of Almeida, Woods, and Messineo (1998) and others on contextualizing theories of child development (Comer & Poussaint, 1992; Goleman, 1997; Hale-Benson, 1986; Mathias & French, 1996). We present a theory of individual development that integrates race, class, gender, and culture as central factors that structure development in fundamental ways. This theory defines maturity as self in context, that is, by our ability to live in respectful relation to others and to our complex and multifaceted world while being able to control our own impulses, and our ability to think and function for ourselves on the basis of our own values and beliefs, even if others around us do not share them. In this conceptualization, maturity requires the ability to empathize, trust, communicate, collaborate, and respect others who are different and to negotiate our interdependence with our environment and with our friends, partners, families, communities, and society in ways that do not entail the exploitation of others.

DEVELOPING A SELF IN CONTEXT

Gender, class, culture, and race form a basic structure within which individuals learn what behaviors, beliefs, values, and ways of expressing emotion and relating to others they will be expected to demonstrate throughout life. It is this context that carries every child from birth and childhood through adulthood to death and defines his or her legacy for the next generation. And each generation is different, as cultures evolve through time, influenced by the social, economic, and political history of their era, which makes their world view different from the views of those born in other times (Cohler, Hosteler, & Boxer, 1998; Elder, 1992; Neugarten, 1979). The gender, class, and cultural structure of any society profoundly influences the parameters of a child's evolving ability to empathize, share, negotiate, and communicate. It prescribes his or her way of thinking for self and of being emotionally connected to others.

Healthy development requires establishing a solid sense of our unique selves in the context of our connections to others. Connecting to others becomes a particular challenge when they are different from us. Raising a nonracist child, for example, becomes a serious challenge in our racist society (Mathias & French, 1996). Racial, religious, and other kinds of prejudice are learned emotionally in childhood and are thus very hard to eradicate later, even if one's intellectual beliefs change (Goleman, 1997). Indeed, the most challenging aspect of development involves our beliefs about, and interaction with, others who are different from ourselves: men from women; young from old; black from white; wealthy from poor; heterosexual from homosexual. Our level of maturity on this crucial dimension will depend on how these differences and connections were dealt with within our family of origin, within our communities, within our culture of origin, and within our society as a whole.

Because our society so quickly assigns roles and expectations based on gender, culture, class, and race, children's competences are obviously not simply milestones that they reach individually, but rather accomplishments that evolve within a complex web of racial, cultural, and familial contexts. A child's acquisition of cognitive, communicative, physical, emotional, and social skills is necessarily circumscribed by the particular social context in which he or she is raised. Thus our evaluation of these abilities can be meaningful only if these constraints are taken into account.

We believe that children are best able to develop their full potential, emotionally, intellectually, physically and spiritually, when they are exposed in positive ways to diversity and encouraged to embrace it. Children who are least restricted by rigid gender, cultural, or class role constraints seem likely to develop the most evolved sense of a connected self (Almeida et al., 1998).

THE MYTHS OF COMPLETE AUTONOMY AND SELF-DETERMINATION

Given the American focus on individualism and free enterprise, it is not surprising that autonomy and competitiveness have been considered desirable traits to be instilled in children of the white middle class, leading toward economic success in the marketplace (Dilworth-Anderson, Burton, & Johnson, 1993). But development must be defined by more than intellectual performance, analytical reasoning ability, and a focus on one's own achievements, as if they resulted from completely autonomous efforts. The people who have the most privilege in our society—especially those who are white and male and who have financial and social status—tend to be systematically kept unconscious of their dependence on others (Coontz, 1992, 1997). They remain unaware of the hidden ways in which our society supports their so-called "autonomous" functioning. Thus, many white men who benefited from the GI bill to attain their education now consider it a form of welfare to provide education to minorities of the current generation.

Men of any class or culture who are raised to deny their emotional interdependence face a terrible awakening during divorce, illness, job loss, or other adversities of life. Those who are privileged develop connections amidst a web of dissociations. It is their privilege that maintains their buffered position and allows them the illusion of complete self-determination. While self-direction and self-motivation are excellent characteristics, they can be realized only in individuals who are permitted to attain them and helped to do so by their families and by society.

DEVELOPING A MATURE INTERDEPENDENT SELF

We believe that maturity depends on seeing past myths of autonomy and self-determination. It requires that we appreciate our basic dependence on each other and on nature. Viewed from this perspective, in addition to an adequate degree of self-direction, maturity involves skills such as the following:

1. The ability to feel safe in the context of the familiar *and* the unfamiliar or different.
2. The ability to read emotion in others, to practice self-control, to empathize, and to engage in caring for others and in being cared for (Goleman, 1997).
3. The ability to accept one's self while simultaneously accepting differences in others, to maintain one's values and beliefs, and to relate generously to others, even if one is not receiving support from them or from anyone else for one's beliefs (defined by Bowen as "differentiation").
4. The ability to consider other people and future generations when evaluating sociopolitical issues such as the environment and human rights.

IT TAKES A VILLAGE

Children's sense of security evolves through their connection and identification with those who care for them—mothers, fathers, siblings, nannies, babysitters, grandparents, aunts, uncles, and all the others who participate in their caretaking. Traditional formulations of child development have ignored this rich context and offered us the paucity of a one-dimensional lens for viewing a child's development: the mother-child relationship. In most cultures throughout history, mothers have not been the primary caretakers of their children, usually being busy with other work. Grandparents and other elders as well as older siblings have, for the most part, been the primary caretakers of children. When we focus so myopically on the role of mothers, we not only project impossible expectations of them, but we are also blinded to the richness of environments in which children generally grow up.

Most child development theories, even feminist theories (Chodorow, 1974; Gilligan, 1982), explain male development's focus on autonomy and independence (self in isolation) as being a result of the male child's need to separate from the mother by rejecting feminine qualities. Like Eleanor Maccoby (1990), we strongly "doubt that the development of distinctive interactive styles has much to do with the fact that children are parented primarily by women … and it seems likely … that … (their) 'identification' with the same-sex parent is more a consequence than a cause of children's acquisition of sex-typed interaction styles" (p. 519). Maccoby thinks that processes within the nuclear family have been given too much credit—or too much blame—for sex-typing. She places most emphasis on "the peer group as the setting in which children first discover the compatibility of same-sex others, in which boys first discover the requirements of maintaining one's status in the male hierarchy, and in which the gender of one's partners becomes supremely important" (p. 519). We know that parents treat boys and girls differently from earliest infancy (Romer, 1981). In general, they discuss emotions—with the exception of anger—more with their daughters than with their sons. They use more emotional words when talking to their daughters (Lewis & Haviland, 1993). Fathers tend to treat young boys and girls in a somewhat more gendered way than mothers do (Siegal, 1987).

We believe that all of these socialization influences are present and important. Parents, acting under the influence of all available social evidence and beliefs, expect and reinforce different behaviors in their sons than in their daughters. The correctness of these behaviors is then validated in all the media as well as by teachers, pediatricians, relatives, babysitters, and the parents' own observations of children's play groups. Meanwhile, science argues about whether these are inborn differences or self-fulfilling prophecies. Only if we expand our lens to children's full environment can we properly measure the characteristics that may help them to attain their full potential and see clearly the influences that limit it.

Indeed, the traditional norms of male development have emphasized many of these characteristics (see Chapter 7) including keeping emotional distance; striving for hierarchical dominance in family relationships; toughness; competition; avoidance of dependence on others; aggression as a means of conflict resolution; avoidance of emotional closeness and affection with other males; suppression of feelings except anger; and avoidance of "feminine" behaviors such as nurturing, tenderness, and expressions of vulnerability. Such norms make it virtually impossible to achieve the sense of interdependence that is required for maturity.

GENDERED DEVELOPMENT: FROM ADAM'S RIB

Female development was formerly seen in the literature only from an androcentric perspective, that is, learning to become an adaptive helpmate to foster male development. Most early male theoreticians, such as Freud, Kohlberg, and Piaget, tended to ignore female development, which has been described in the literature only for the last two decades (Dinnerstein, 1976; Gilligan, 1982; Miller, 1976; Pipher, 1994). While separation and autonomy were considered the primary values for male development, values of caring and attachment, interdependence, relationship, and attention to context were viewed as primary in female development. Values that were thought to be feminine were devalued by male theoreticians (such as Erikson, Piaget, Levinson, and Valliant), while values associated with men were equated with adult maturity. Concern about relationships was seen as a weakness of women (and men) rather than a human strength.

In fact, women have always been involved in defining and redefining themselves throughout their lives in the context of their changing relationships. The life cycle framework, developed as a perspective on self-in-relation, seems a much more appropriate way to think of life cycle development for both men and women (Korin, McGoldrick, & Watson, 1996; Jordan, 1997). Erik Erikson's widely accepted eight stages of development, for example, ignore completely the evolution of our ability to communicate—the one characteristic that most distinguishes us from all other animals. Erikson's scheme makes no reference between age 2 and 20 to interpersonal issues. It suggests that human connectedness is part of the first stage (Trust versus Mistrust), during the first two years of life. But further reference to human relationships does not appear again until stage 6 (Intimacy versus Isolation). All the other stages leading to adulthood described by Erikson involve individual rather than relational issues: Autonomy versus Shame and Doubt, Initiative versus Guilt, Industry versus Inferiority, and Identity versus Role Confusion. Thus, doubt, shame, guilt, inferiority, and role confusion are all defined as having no part in a healthy identity. Identity is defined as having a sense of self *apart from* rather than *in relation to* one's family and says nothing about developing skill in relating to one's family. Furthermore, in Erikson's scheme, generativity is ignored during the time of greatest human creativity: bearing and raising children.

Given these distorted definitions of healthy development, it is not surprising that men so often grow up with an impaired capacity for intimacy and human connectedness. Our culture's distorted ideals for male development have made it hard for men to acknowledge their vulnerability, doubt, imperfection, role confusion, and desire for human connections (Kimmel, 1996). In our view, all stages of the life cycle have both individual and interpersonal aspects, and the failure to appreciate this has led to seriously skewed human development. The most important aspects of human experience are relational.

DEVELOPING A SELF IN A NONAFFIRMING ENVIRONMENT

The developmental literature, strongly influenced by the psychoanalytic tradition, has focused almost exclusively on mothers, giving extraordinary importance to the mother-child relationship in the earliest years of life, to the exclusion of other relationships in the family or to later developmental phases (Lewis, Feiring, & Kotsonis, 1984). Kagan (1984) has recently drawn our attention to the mythology involved in our assumptions about the overriding importance of infancy and early childhood in determining the rest of human life. The psychoanalytic model has also stressed the view of human development as a primarily painful process. The assumptions about development in the early years led to a psychological determinism that held mothering responsible for whatever happened. Much of the feminist literature has continued to focus on mothering while locating the mother-child dyad within a patriarchal system (Chodorow & Contratto, 1982; Dinnerstein, 1976). We urge quite a different perspective of human development, which views child development in the richness of its entire context of multigenerational family relationships as well as within its social and cultural context.

It is also curious that the developmental literature has ignored the powerful impact of children on adult development. Thus, the potential for change and growth in parents, as they respond to the unfolding of their children's lives is lost. As Daniels and Weingarten (1983) note, "Because men have not traditionally occupied themselves with caring for children, parenthood—the core experience of what Erikson calls generativity, is oddly missing from their sense of their own development" (p. 5).

It is difficult to determine what behavioral differences between males and females are based on biology, since socialization affects people so powerfully and so early. We do know that females are more likely to survive the birth experience, less likely to have birth defects, and less vulnerable to disease throughout life. The major difference in early childhood is that girls develop language skills earlier and boys tend to be more active, but since studies of infants show that parents talk and look more at girls and engage in more rough play with boys, it is not possible at this point to say whether the gender differences are biological or social. Eleanor Maccoby, one of the leading researchers on sex differences, found that over the past two decades, the sex differences on various dimensions have not changed too much. Moderate differences were found between boys and girls in performance on mathematical and spatial abilities, while sex differences in verbal abilities had faded. Other aspects of intellectual performance continue to show gender equality (Maccoby, 1990), but differences in social behavior follow from societal patterns that orient boys to competition and girls to relationships. Preschool girls, who increasingly try to influence others by polite suggestions, have increasingly less ability to influence boys, who are more and more unresponsive to polite suggestions. Boys and girls would respond to a vocal prohibition by another boy. Maccoby thinks that girls find it aversive to keep trying to interact with someone who is unresponsive and begin to avoid such partners.

Kagan and Moss (1962) traced achievement-oriented adults back to their relationships with their mothers (they did not look at their relationships with their fathers). They found that these males had very close, loving relationships with their mothers in infancy, while the females had less intense closeness with their mothers than the average. Hoffman (1972) has suggested that a daughter is more likely to become achievement oriented if she does not experience the training in dependence that has generally been prescribed as typical for girls.

The data on children who are raised with only one parent are not clear. Some girls who are raised without a father have more difficulty in establishing relationships with men, while boys may display extremely "masculine" behavior, possibly because their mothers' sensitivity to the lack of a father encourages the mothers to emphasize this behavior (Romer, 1981), but the pattern depends on many factors, including the presence of other male figures in the children's lives and the age at which they lose their fathers. On the other hand, children who are raised with their mothers in a single-parent household may well experience more collaborative, democratic relationships throughout childhood, which may be a particular strength in our competitive, hierarchical society (Hartman, 1987).

Infants and toddlers begin developing trust in their immediate environment, which ideally supports their safety and development. As soon as they reach the point of leaving the safety of their home environment, however, developing trust depends on how one's cultural group is positioned in the larger world. It takes greater maturity to be able to develop one's sense of self in an unfamiliar setting, in which one has little support, than it does in a context in which everyone in the outside world affirms your values. Members of the dominant groups of our society receive this affirmation daily, whereas many others do not grow up with this affirmation of their selfhood: a gay or lesbian child, a disabled child, a girl, a child of color, or a poor child. These children, stigmatized and often vilified, are not the ones depicted in books, TV programs, and movies as the "valued" child. Thus, a nonprivileged child who does manage to develop a strong self has accomplished a developmental feat beyond that of a child who has always been affirmed both at home and in the larger society's cultural messages (Kunjufu, 1995). Our theories of child development must take this into account.

Paradoxically, children of privilege may lack adaptive skills because they live in such an affirming, nonchallenging environment. Their lives shelter them to an extreme degree from minority experiences, that is, from ever feeling "other" or being the only one of their values or opinions in a group, experiences that promote growth as well as difficulty.

In our view, the richness of possibilities for learning and expressive styles should be celebrated, and all children should be encouraged to develop

their potential and to appreciate others for their different ways of knowing and doing. Thus, girls should be allowed and encouraged to develop their individual abilities without being viewed as selfish. They should be supported in developing leadership skills and in being comfortable with their accomplishments without fearing that their success hurts others, while boys should be encouraged to develop their relational and emotional selves, which are currently devalued in our theories and in the dominant society, which sees these styles as "unmanly." Psychological studies reveal that when fathers are involved in child-rearing in a major way, sons become more empathic than sons raised in the traditional ways (Miedzian, 1991). A twenty-six-year longitudinal study of empathy found that the single factor most linked to empathic concerns was the level of paternal involvement in child care (Koestner, Franz, & Weinberger, 1990). This suggests that the negative role modeling of a distant father on his children is significant and should be considered clinically.

Peggy McIntosh (1985, 1989), in her article "On Feeling Like a Fraud," has described the ways in which women who have been socialized in the single track logic of academia can end up feeling stupid because they may have intellectual approaches other than, or in addition to, making outlines that lay out subcategories in hierarchical order. Catherine Bateson (1994) likewise challenges the very ordering of education as a precursor to living life, suggesting instead that it makes more sense to thread education throughout our lives. Our ability to acknowledge our ignorance and maintain openness to learning is essential, yet not highly valued in our culture: "An open mind, the willingness to learn from mistakes, the willingness to admit ignorance—these are not widely valued or rewarded characteristics in our leaders. When political leaders hesitate or revise their views, we mistake it for weakness, not strength" (p. 74).

The implications of these ideas are evident. People of privilege can be at an enormous disadvantage because of the smugness and inflexibility of mainstream learning styles, which may leave them unable to acknowledge their ignorance and place themselves in the position of learner. Indeed, as Bateson points out, very few societies reward those who take the risks of new learning. Many adults take on the challenge of new learning which requires and promotes profound change only when they are desperate. As Bateson (1994) says, "This is why so much adult learning is packaged today as therapy and why it must often offer the compensation of membership in a new community or relationship" (p. 72). We are in serious need of modifying our cultural norms so that one does not need to feel humbled or threatened to open oneself to new learning throughout life and so that there are affirmation and support for all of the ways of learning and of expressing the self.

OUR MULTIPLE INTELLIGENCES

Traditional child development theories would have us think that intelligence is almost unidimensional, but a contextual perspective broadens this frame immeasurably. Ogbu's studies (1981) demonstrate that the intellectual tasks that Western theorists such as Piaget have used as definers of maturity are extraordinarily narrow indicators of intelligence and totally inadequate as a schema for understanding the rich possibilities of a child's intellectual development (Almeida et al., 1998).

Many other forms of intelligence have been described (Ellison, 1984; Gardner, 1983; Goleman, 1997; Hale-Benson, 1986):

- *Emotional intelligence:* the ability to control impulses, empathize with others, and conduct responsible social, interpersonal, and intimate relationships.
- *Spatial intelligence:* the ability to find one's way around.
- *Musical intelligence:* the ability to perceive rhythm and pitch.
- *Bodily-kinesthetic intelligence:* the gift of fine motor movement as seen in a surgeon, an athlete, or a dancer.
- *Interpersonal intelligence:* the ability to understand others.

- *Intrapersonal intelligence:* the ability to understand oneself.
- *Artistic intelligence:* the ability to connect words, color, materials, music, and space in interesting and unique ways.

Traditional child development schemas reward only the development of the analytic style of processing information. "Aspects of analytic style can be found in the requirements that the pupil learn to sit for increasingly long periods of time, to concentrate alone on impersonal learning stimuli, and to observe and value organized time allotment schedules" (Cohen, 1969, p. 830). How might different groups react to this? In China, for example, there is no concept of the musical virtuoso. Studying music is all about learning to play in harmony together. So the highest development involves the most accomplished ability to be in harmony with others. American Indians, as another example, raise their children to be keen observers of the world around them. Intelligence in this context involves being able to look and listen carefully to animals, birds, and trees in ways that are almost totally unknown to many American children (Broken Nose, 1997).

Many values within other African American communities are at odds with the dominant priorities for child development. Lerome Bennett has described their verbal emphasis thus:

> *Black culture gives rise to highly charismatic and stylistic uses of language. There is no counterpart in white culture to the oratory of a Dr. Martin Luther King, Jr., a Rev. Jesse Jackson, a Barbara Jordon ... or a Shirley Chisholm. The verbal rituals, particularly of Black male children, expressed in woofin', soundin', signifyin', chants, toasts, and playin' the dozens are examples of stylistic uses of language. These language skills of Black children are not assessed on the standard measures of verbal intelligence. (Hale-Benson, 1986, citing Lerome Bennett, p. xiii)*

Black children must master two cultures to succeed (Hale-Benson, 1986). Even though Black children are using complex thinking skills on the street, the problem of transferring these skills to the classroom has not been solved (Cole, 1971). Our current theories of intellectual development fail to make room for people of color to look any way but deficient and pathological.

Black children are exposed to a high degree of stimulation from expressive performers of music and the visual arts, which permeate the Black community. Their cultural style is organized in a circular fashion, in contrast to the linear organization of Western culture (Hale-Benson, 1986). They are proficient in nonverbal communication and use considerable body language and interaction in communication. By contrast, white children in the United States are born into a world where their style of communication is everywhere given priority: linear language, minimal body language, a preference for written over verbal expression, and a tendency to view the world in discrete segments rather than holistically.

Daniel Goleman (1997) has laid out clearly the extreme importance of understanding and supporting the development of emotional intelligence. The medical value of emotional connectedness is made clear by the fact that all studies show that isolation is as significant a risk to health and mortality as are smoking, high blood pressure, high cholesterol, obesity, and lack of exercise. Empathy, the earliest emotion, is the root of all caring about others: intimacy, ethics, altruism, and morality itself.

All of the skills that are essential for good academic performance are related to emotional competence: curiosity, confidence, intentionality, self-control, relatedness, cooperativeness, and communication skills. School success is not predicted by a child's fund of facts or a precocious ability to read, but rather by emotional and social measures: being self-assured and interested; knowing what kind of behavior is expected and being able to rein in the impulse to misbehave; being able to wait, follow directions, and ask the teacher for help; being able to express one's own needs in relationships with other children. Almost all children who do poorly in school lack one or more of these elements of emotional intelligence, regardless of other cognitive abilities or disabilities (Goleman, 1997).

Feminists have long lamented the accepted traditional attitude of ignoring the emotional development of males. But Goleman reports on a global slide in emotional competence so great that it seems to be the universal price of modern life for all children.

According to Goleman, emotional incompetence and disconnection lead to:

- prejudice and self involvement (lack of caring for others personally and socially),
- aggression and criminal behavior (lack of empathy and poor self-control),
- depression and poor academic performance (see above), and
- addictions (attempts to calm and soothe oneself).

Goleman suggests a remedy for our current rampant worldwide tendencies toward depression and crime: Help families and schools to realize that a child's development and education must include "the essential human competencies such as self-awareness, self-control, empathy, and the arts of listening, resolving conflicts, and cooperation." To change our world, we must focus on childhood and adolescence, the critical windows of opportunity for setting down the essential emotional habits that will govern our lives. Later remedial learning or unlearning in adulthood such as therapy is possible, but lengthy and hard (Goleman, 1997).

THE CONNECTED SELF

The connected self is grounded in recognition of the interdependence of people and assumes this as a critical dimension of healthy psychological development. Skills in human interdependence leading to maturity include the ability to do the following:

- Participate in cooperative activities of many kinds at home, at work, and at play.
- Express a full range of emotions and tolerate such emotions in others.
- Express one's differences of belief or opinion to others without attacking them or becoming defensive.

- Relate with openness, curiosity, tolerance, and respect to people who are different from oneself.
- Nurture, care for, and mentor others.
- Accept the help and mentoring of others.

Bowen's (1978) concept of differentiation describes a state of self-knowledge and self-definition that does not rely on others' acceptance for one's beliefs but encourages one to be connected to others without the need to defend oneself or attack the other. Ironically, although Bowen's is the only early family therapy theory that gives equal weight to autonomy and emotional connectedness as characteristics necessary for the differentiation of adult maturity, he is widely misunderstood in the field. Bowen's term "differentiation," which he equated with "maturity," is commonly misused and misquoted as though it meant autonomy only, separateness, or disconnectedness. And because Bowen emphasized the necessity of distinguishing between thinking and feeling, some feminists have criticized him for elevating "male" attributes of rationality over "female" relationality. Actually, Bowen was addressing the need to train one's mind to control emotional reactivity so that, unlike animals, we can control our behavior and think about how we want to respond, rather than be at the mercy of our fears, phobias, compulsions, instincts, and sexual and aggressive impulses. This is not at all a criticism of authentic and appropriate emotional expressiveness, which is part of the primary goal of Bowen therapy: to ground oneself emotionally and to learn to connect emotionally by developing a personal relationship with every member of one's family as the blueprint for all subsequent emotional connections.

Goleman (1997) discusses this same process of mind over emotional reactivity, attributing to Aristotle the original challenge to manage the emotional life with intelligence: "Anyone can become angry. That is easy. But to become angry with the right person, to the right degree, at the right time, for the right purpose—this is not easy" (Aristotle, *The Nichomachean Ethics*) (p. ix). The question is, Goleman says, "How can we bring intelligence to

our emotions and civility to our streets and caring to our communal life?" (p. xiv).

The blind spot in Bowen's (1978) theory as we see it is that it does not account for the fact that women and people of color have grown up with an oppressive socialization that actually proscribes the assertive, self-directed thinking and behavior that are necessary for differentiation. Lack of acknowledgment of this prohibition promotes disparities among groups within our society by not acknowledging that they are not starting on an even playing field. Girls in this society are expected to put the needs of others before their own. People of color are expected to defer to dominant beliefs and behaviors. Thus, a white male who tries to differentiate will generally be responded to with respect, while a woman or person of color may be sanctioned or even harmed or ostracized by the community. Thus our assessment of a person's development needs to address obstacles to their accomplishing the tasks leading to maturity.

COUNTERING UNEQUAL GENDER, CLASS, CULTURAL, AND RACIAL SOCIALIZATION

In our clinical work, we celebrate the diversity of our clients' backgrounds. To counter our society's privileging of certain skills for only certain children, we can challenge families on their distribution of chores, and their role expectations. But we need to do more.

Canino and Spurlock (1994) have defined some of the basic information on a family's social style and expectations that are crucial to assessment and intervention, not just with culturally diverse children, but with all children:

- Is the family isolated or active in their community?
- Does their culture expect frequent and intense social interactions in an extended network or does it respect privacy and a nuclear family orientation?
- Is the family living in a socially and culturally homogeneous community or in a heterogeneous setting?

- Is the community viewed as safe?
- Who are the models or teachers of socialization skills in the family?
- Do the skills taught at home converge with or differ from those required at school, in the park, or on the playing field?

As they rightly point out, the diagnostic challenge is to "make a clinical judgment as to whether a behavioral or emotional attribute is a culturally syntonic way of manifesting distress, a behavior adopted to survive a particular sociocultural milieu, or a universal symptom of psychiatric disorder. These judgments can be sound only if clinicians are knowledgeable about the culture of their patients" (Canino & Spurlock, 1994, p. 86).

Many guidelines and programs have been shown to be effective in developing children's emotional competence in schools and other programs (Goleman, 1997). We should do all that we can as mental health practitioners to support the establishment of such programs in the clinics and schools of our communities. The most crucial factor in teaching emotional competence is timing (Goleman, 1997), with infancy as the beginning point and childhood and adolescence the crucial windows of opportunity.

THE INDIVIDUAL LIFE CYCLE IN CONTEXT

Evaluating problems in terms of both the individual life cycle and the family life cycle is an important part of any assessment. Human development involves the accomplishment of certain physical, intellectual, social, spiritual, and emotional life cycle tasks. Each person's individual life cycle intersects with the family life cycle at every point, causing at times conflicts of needs. A toddler's developmental needs may conflict with a grandmother's life plans. When individual family members do not fit into normative expectations for development, there are repercussions on family development. A family's adaptation to its tasks will likewise influence how individuals negotiate their individual development. And the cultural, socioeconomic, racial, and gender context of the family will influence all of these developmental transitions.

A suggestive schema for exploring normative individual life cycle tasks is offered in Table 2.1. There are serious limitations to any attempt to condense the complications of life in a schematic framework. The phases of human development have been defined in many ways in different cultures and at different points in history. This outline is a rough and suggestive guideline, not a statement of the true and fixed stages of life. People vary greatly in their pathways through life. It is always important to consider the cohort to which family members belong, that is, the period in history when they grew up (Cohler, Hosteler, & Boxer, 1998; Elder, 1992; Neugarten, 1979); as it influences their world view and their beliefs about life cycle transitions and may be an important factor in intergenerational conflicts. Furthermore, accomplishing the individual tasks of a stage depends on resources available to individuals and families to help them to develop their abilities.

The first stage of life might be thought of as covering a baby's first two years of life. During this time, babies need to learn to communicate their needs and have some sense of trust, comfort, and relationship to their caretakers and the world around them. Their needs have to be satisfied consistently so that they can develop trust in others and a sense of security. They learn to coordinate their bodies and begin to explore the world. It is during this stage that empathy, the earliest emotion, begins to develop. From earliest infancy, babies are upset when they hear another infant cry (Goleman, 1997).

The second stage, the child's preschool years from age 2 to 6, is a time of great strides in language and motor skills and ability to relate to the world around. Children learn to take direction, cooperate, share, trust, explore, and be aware of themselves as different from others. As early as age 2½, children recognize that someone else's pain is different from their own and are able to comfort others. How discipline is handled at this phase influences the development of emotional competence, for example, "Look how sad you've made her" versus "That was naughty" (Goleman, 1997). It is at this phase that children begin to form peer

TABLE 2.1   The Individual Life Cycle in Context

1. Infancy (Approximately Birth to Age 2)—The Development of Empathy and Emotional Attunement to Others

"Our brains are wired in a way that allows emotional learning throughout the lifespan, as long as our caretakers are reasonably well attuned to our emotions and capable of mirroring them back to us in the first 18 months of life." (Borysenko, 1996, p. 19)

- Communicate frustration and happiness
- Develop beginning of empathy for others
- Talk
- Make needs known and get them met
- Develop coordination

- Sit, stand, walk, run, manipulate objects, feed self
- Recognize self as separate person
- Trust others, primarily caretakers
- Overcome fears of new situations

2. Early Childhood (Approximate Ages 2 to 6)—A Growing Understanding of Interdependence

"The bio-psycho-spiritual basis of the … life cycle is wired firmly into place by the end of early childhood, conferring the gifts of empathy, relationality, interdependent perception and intuition." (Borysenko, 1996, p. 35)

- Develop language and ability to relate and communicate
- Learn to regulate and control emotions and impulses
- Develop motor skills, eye-hand coordination, etc.
- Develop control of bodily functions—bowels, urine
- Start to become aware of self in terms of gender and abilities
- Start to become aware of "otherness" in terms of gender, race, and disability

- Start to become aware of self in relation to world around
- Learn cooperative play, ability to share
- Learn to obey rules
- Learn to delay gratification
- Increase ability to develop trusting relationships
- Start to develop peer relationships
- Develop ability to dramatize and engage in fantasy play to master own behavior and control anxieties

3. Middle Childhood (Approximate Ages 6 to 11 or 12)—Moral Development: Including "Heart Logic" along with "Mind Logic"

"Developing the capacity to use linear logic while retaining the inter-relational, interdependent perceptual capability developed in early childhood." (Borysenko, 1996, p. 38)

- Increase skill with language
- Begin development of morality
- Increase capacity for empathy
- Increase physical coordination and motor skills
- Develop ability to play team games
- Learn reading, writing, and math
- Develop knowledge about nature
- Increase understanding of self in terms of gender, race, culture, and abilities

- Increase understanding of self in relation to family, peers, and community
- Develop intuition
- Increase awareness of "otherness" in terms of gender, race, sexual orientation, culture, class, and disability
- Increase ability to conduct peer relationships
- Increase ability to conduct relationships with authorities
- Develop ability to be intimate and to express anger, fear and pain in nondestructive ways
- Develop tolerance for difference

4. Pubescence (Approximate Ages 11–13 for Girls; 12–14 for Boys)—Finding One's Own Voice: The Beginning Development of Authenticity

"The ability to see relationships with clarity, the uncanny tendency to recognize instances of relational injustice and cry foul, and the development of the morality of the heart." (Borysenko, 1996, p. 59)

- Cope with dramatic bodily changes of puberty
- Ability to assert oneself
- Increase development of emotional competence
- Develop awareness of own and others' sexuality
- Begin to learn control of one's sexual and aggressive impulses
- Recognize injustices
- Increase capacity for moral understanding
- Increase physical coordination and physical skills

- Increase ability to read, write, and think conceptually and mathematically
- Increase understanding of self in terms of gender, race, culture, sexual orientation, and abilities
- Increase understanding of self in relation to peers, family, and community
- Increase ability to handle social relationships and complex social situations
- Increase ability to work collaboratively and individually

(Continued)

TABLE 2.1   Continued

5. Adolescence (Approximate Ages: 13 or 14 to 21)—Looking for an Identity: Continuing to Voice Authentic Opinions and Feelings in the Context of Societal, Parental, and Peer Pressure to Conform to Age, Gender, and Racial Stereotypes; Learning to Balance Caring about Self and Caring about Others

"By this time, we can think our own thoughts, we have opinions that are separable from other people's, we can group concepts and calculate probabilities and we can stand back and reflect on ourselves." (Borysenko, 1996, p. 75)

- Continue to deal with rapid bodily changes and cultural ideals of body image
- Increase awareness and ability to deal with one's own and others' sexuality
- Increase emotional competence and self management
- Learn to handle of one's sexual and aggressive impulses
- Develop one's sexual identity
- Increase physical coordination and physical skills
- Increase ability to think conceptually and mathematically and learn about the world

- Increase discipline for physical and intellectual work, sleep, sex, and social relationships
- Increase understanding of self in relation to peers, family, and community
- Begin to develop a philosophy of life and a moral and spiritual identity
- Begin to develop ability to handle intimate physical and social relationships as well as increase ability to judge and handle complex social situations
- Increase ability to work collaboratively and individually

6. Early Adulthood (Approximate Ages: 21 to 35)—Development of the Ability to Engage in Intense Relationships Committed to Mutual Growth and in Satisfying Work: A Commitment to Parity for Care of the Family and the Importance of Career

"The development of a core self, a strong, yet pliable identity in which the previous development of relationality, intuition and the logic of the heart are combined in a conscious way, bestows life's most precious gift—the ability to relate to both self and others with true intimacy." (Borysenko, 1996, p. 76)

- Increase ability to care for self and one's own needs, financially, emotionally, and spiritually
- Increase awareness and ability to deal with one's own and others' sexuality
- Increase discipline for physical and intellectual work, sleep, sex, and social relationships
- Learn to focus on long-range life goals regarding work, intimate relationships, family, and community
- Develop ability to negotiate evolving relationships to one's parents, peers, children, and community, including work relationships

- Develop ability to nurture others physically and emotionally
- Develop ability to support one's children financially and emotionally
- Increase tolerance for delayed gratification to meet one's goals
- Evolve further one's ability to respect and advocate for those less fortunate than oneself
- Evolve ability to help oneself if socially disadvantaged

7. Middle Adulthood (Approximate Ages: 35 to 50 or 55)—Emergence into Authentic Power. Becoming More Aware of the Problems of Others

"Along with balancing many life tasks, there is a review of one's priorities, a striving towards balance and harmony with self and others while resisting pressure to pursue traditional gender patterns. There is greater community involvement and participation in social and political action." (Borysenko 1996, pp. 135, 181)

- Firm up and make solid all of the tasks of early adulthood
- Nurture and support one's children and partner, including caretaking of older family members
- Deepen and solidify friendships
- Reassess one's work satisfaction and financial adequacy and consider possibility of changing work or career to achieve greater life balance

- Involve oneself in improving community and society whether one is personally advantaged or disadvantaged
- Recognize one's accomplishments and accept one's limitations
- Accept the choices that made some dreams and goals attainable but precluded others
- Focus on mentoring the next generation
- Solidify one's philosophy of life and spirituality

8. Late Middle Age (Approximate Ages: 50 or 55 to early 70s)—Beginning of the Wisdom Years: Reclaiming the Wisdom of Interdependence

"An intensification of the altruism and service begun in the previous phase. Helping others, serving the community and mentoring: passing along our values and experience…There is a need to resist our culture's dismissal of older people, especially older women…The pendulum swings away from the active and productive principles back to the spiritual principles that value nature as well as technology, that honor cultural diversity, that foster caring for the less fortunate and that seek physical, emotional and spiritual harmony." (Borysenko, 1996, pp. 202, 219)

TABLE 2.1   Continued

- Handle some declining physical and intellectual abilities
- Deal with menopause, decreasing sexual energies, and one's changing sexuality
- Come to terms with one's failures and choices with accountability but without becoming bitter
- Plan and handle work transitions and retirement

- Define one's own grandparenting and other "senior" roles in work and community
- Take steps to pass the torch and attend to one's connections and responsibilities to the next generations
- Accept one's limitations and multiple caretaking responsibilities for those above and below
- Deal with death of parents and others of older generations

9. Aging (Approximate Ages: from 75 on)—Grief, Loss, Resiliency, Retrospection, and Growth

"This is a time to reflect on and review one's life with appreciation of its successes and compassion for its failings, and with an effort to extract new levels of meaning that had previously been unappreciated." (Borysenko, 1996, p. 243)

- Respond to loss and change by using these as opportunities to reevaluate life circumstances and create new fulfilling pathways
- Remain as physically, psychologically, intellectually, and spiritually active and as emotionally connected as possible
- Come to terms with death while focusing on what else one can still do for oneself and others

- Bring careful reflection, perspective, and balance to the task of life review
- Accept dependence on others and diminished control of one's life
- Affirm and work out one's financial, spiritual, and emotional legacy to the next generation
- Accept death of spouse and need to create a new life
- Accept one's own life and death

relationships. They also develop various cognitive skills with numbers, words, and objects and motor skills in relation to the world around.

During this phase, children learn where, how, and when to show aggression (Comer & Poussaint, 1992). They need to be taught control of their anger, aggression, distress, impulses, and excitement and to regulate their moods and delay gratification. This self-management, along with the continued development of empathy, is the basis of relationship skill (Goleman, 1997). By age 3, children become actively interested in defining how they are like or different from others, including skin color and hair texture (Comer & Poussaint, 1992; Mathias & French, 1996). They can start to share and be fair rather than to exclude others; they take their cues from the adults around them for how to treat others.

The third developmental phase might be said to cover the elementary school years of childhood, from about age 6 to 12. During this time, children typically make many developmental leaps in their cognitive, motor, and emotional skills. They expand their social world in terms of their ability to communicate and to handle relationships with an increasing range of adults and children beyond their families. Children begin to understand their identity in terms of gender, race, culture, and sexual orientation and to differentiate themselves from others. They improve in their ability to follow directions, tolerate frustration, work independently, and cooperate with others. If deprived of support for these developments, the child may develop either physical, emotional or social symptoms—fears, anxieties, phobias, stomachaches or headaches, aggressive or withdrawn behaviors.

Between ages 6 and 8, children develop a great passion to belong. They exclude others so that they can feel "in." Children of color must be taught at this age to handle racist acts in ways that are not self-destructive (Comer & Poussaint, 1992), while children of privilege must be taught not to commit racist acts and to be proactive in relationship to others who are experiencing oppression. At this phase, children learn competitiveness by comparing themselves to others and cooperation to the degree their parents, caretakers, or teachers teach them. Otherwise, competitiveness remains a problem. By age 7 or 8, dreams and make-believe (e.g., Santa Claus) are no longer considered real. At this stage, children should learn the truth about slavery, colonialism, war, and the like, which can be done through the stories we tell them about our holidays such as Thanksgiving and Fourth of July. Children start to read and watch television independently and should be monitored by parents, especially for exposure to racial and gender content, which can have a profound influence on them. Children at this phase are deeply affected by parental and school definitions of "normal." They learn to imitate racial, gender, and other discriminatory words and actions.

Sex segregation increases greatly, influenced by the fact that boys' behavior, unless checked, becomes characterized by competition, demands, and dominance. Girls have such difficulty having influence in play with boys that they avoid them (Maccoby, 1990). Boys tend to play more roughly in larger groups, and girls to form close friendships with one or two other girls. Goleman (1997) reports studies in which 50 percent of 3-year-olds, 20 percent of the 5-year-olds, and virtually no 7-year-olds, have friends of the opposite sex.

At this time, children become chums and segregate themselves by gender and often by race, discovering that skin color is a code denoting rank and even fate (Comer & Poussaint, 1992; Ogbu, 1981; Ogbu & Maureen, 1994). Girls become adept at reading verbal and nonverbal emotional signals and at expressing and communicating their feelings. Boys minimize the emotions connected to vulnerability, guilt, fear, and hurt (Goleman, 1997). Without specific intervention, these differences will persist into adulthood. Boys especially, in their efforts to establish their own sexual identity, may focus on their dislike of girls; they need adult validation of the other gender's interests and feelings to avoid establishing a gender role split. Friendship and conversation with friends becomes very important for the development of language and social skills.

At this phase also, children have a better memory, a longer attention span, and can understand more complex explanations and ask constant questions. Parents' responses are very important. It is important that they should not pretend to know everything, but teach the child how to look up information (Comer & Poussaint, 1992). It is also a time

when children produce creative works of art, dancing, and singing. Parental responses will encourage or discourage the development of creativity.

Boys especially may have difficulty talking about subjects like race, sex, anger, and conflict and need adult encouragement to foster skill in this (Comer & Poussaint, 1992). Children begin to develop respect for the rights and needs of self and others. They tattle on wrong-doers, and discussion about rule-breaking and commitments to rules and fairness is very important at this stage (Comer & Poussaint, 1992). How children learn life's "rules" will form the foundation of their morals. If they are continuously put down, they will lose faith in others; if they are not admonished for selfish or unfair acts, they will grow up with a false sense of privilege. Boys especially can be physically aggressive and need to be taught fairness and to have plenty of outlets for their physical energy. Games and hobbies can mitigate social conflicts. By age 9 to 12, children spend a lot of time discussing, arguing, and changing the rules of games. As the independence-dependence struggle intensifies, it is important to teach children to do chores and meet responsibilities for their own sake, not because they are told, and thus to encourage them to begin to establish their own standards. Doing chores teaches them that their contribution to the family is valuable. They may talk in a mature way, but they are still fearful and insecure. Family rituals and celebrations are important to children at this age, who start learning how to plan and organize events if their parents do this well. It is very important whether children get the message "I can" or "I can't" from their school experiences.

By age 9 to 12 parental support is essential for helping children cope with peer pressure. It is at this age that children become able to distinguish their own values and attitudes from those of the peer group (Matthias & French, 1996). This is the last stage for parents to affirm their support of their children's competence and abilities before teen struggles for independence begin. It is also the last chance for parents to strongly influence a child's choice of peers and to widen the child's social circle by encouraging diversity (Matthias & French,

1996). They may be preoccupied with prepuberty bodily changes and be extremely sensitive to unkind remarks from others. They are not always cooperative or obedient and may not want to be affiliated with others who are "different." It is a very important age for children to see parents actively handling and dealing with social problems in constructive ways. It is at this stage that children become able to differentiate between what is expected of them at home and outside of home. By age 9 to 12, children's identification with the causes, problems, aspirations, and privileges of groups they belong to provides direction, limitations, and motivation to think and act in certain ways. At the same time, the most advanced level of empathy emerges, and children are able to understand distress beyond an immediate situation and to feel for the plight of an entire group, such as the poor, oppressed, or outcast (Goleman, 1997).

Children may play adults off against each other to get what they want because they do not yet know how to confront adults to let them know they feel neglected or ignored (Comer & Poussaint, 1992). The quality of a child's relationships with adults is more important than the gender of the adults, for both male and female children. Children between ages 9 and 12 are aware of unfairness and hypocrisy of adults and officials. It is important for adults to help them understand adult failings and model doing something about it so that they don't feel powerless and cynical. Abused or neglected children may become aggressive, picking fights. Children who are shy need encouragement from adults to participate. Children are very sensitive to racial attitudes at this period and may hide behind race or other "differences" to excuse poor performance, so adults should be careful not to permit children's outrage to act as an excuse for nonperformance. Self-esteem is precarious at this age (9 to 12), and pride in race is crucial to self-esteem (Comer & Poussaint, 1992).

We might consider the fourth developmental stage to be pubescence, from about age 11 to 13 for girls and age 12 to 14 or 15 for boys. At this time, children are normally ambivalent, rebellious, bored, uninterested, or difficult. They are highly critical of others who don't look or act like them, and they identify with a preferred group of friends who agree on dress, music, and even language. They now view morality and rules as imposed by parents, not society, and experiment with new rules, valuing peers' values more than those of parents (Matthias & French, 1996). To prepare white children for a multicultural world, it is important to choose a middle school with diversity in mind. Young teens do not turn to parents with problems, even major ones. Parents have to persevere and not ask yes-no questions; they can speak of their own worries at that age rather than questioning. At this phase, children benefit from diversity training and group experiences that encourage the expression of thoughts and feelings and from volunteering for community service. Children at this age are idealistic and respond to calls for help.

For some reason, during certain phases in development, including preschool and adolescence, children seem to hold rigidly to sex-role stereotypes, even more so than their parents or teachers. It is important not to encourage this stereotyping but instead to encourage girls to develop their own opinions, values, aspirations, and interests. It is in keeping with social norms that during the adolescent years girls often confuse identity with intimacy by defining themselves through relationships with others. Advertising and adult attitudes toward girls, which define their development in terms of their ability to attract a male, are bound to be detrimental to girls' mental health, leaving them lacking in self-esteem; fearing to appear smart, tall, assertive, or competent; and worrying about losing their chances of finding an intimate relationship with a male. It is important to raise questions about such norms, since they put the girl into an impossible bind: You are healthy only if you define your identity not through your self but through your mate.

The fifth phase, adolescence, goes from about age 13 for girls and about age 14 or 15 for boys and continues until about age 21. Erikson (1968) described the development of adolescent girls as fundamentally different from that of boys, in that girls supposedly hold their identity in abeyance as they prepare to attract men by whose name they will be known and by whose status they will be defined. But after the challenges of the women's movement in the 1970s, Gilligan in her landmark study of preadolescent and early adolescent girls (Gilligan, 1982; Pipher 1994) attributed the girls' loss of voice and low self-esteem to their fear of appearing too smart, assertive, or competent to attract a male. This sexist requirement is now seen as cultural, not inherent in girls' development. During this phase, young people go through major bodily, emotional, sexual, and spiritual changes; evolve their sexual and gender identities; learn to relate to intimate partners; and develop the ability to function increasingly independently. They renegotiate their identity with their parents as they mature; refine their physical, social, and intellectual skills; develop their spiritual and moral identity; and begin to define who they want to become as adults. Families of color will have special tasks to help their children negotiate the burdens and pressures of dealing with a racist world without becoming bitter, hopeless, or cynical. Adolescents react to social hostility and are attracted to causes. Black adolescents may succumb to despair and give up hope of a productive future. Minority adolescents have identity problems if they are completely segregated from Whites or if they live in mostly White communities. Middle- and upper-class Black adolescents have identity problems because Black poverty is both romanticized and vilified. They need to be helped to be Black without being self-defeating or consumed by antagonism toward Whites and White-controlled America (Comer & Poussaint, 1992).

Sexual issues and information should be discussed with adolescents at home and at school, building on earlier sex education. Powerful attraction to members of the opposite sex does not mean that gender segregation disappears. Young people continue to spend a good portion of their social time with same-sex partners (Maccoby, 1990). However, the higher rates of depression in females may have their onset during adolescence, because of the difficulties of cross-sex interaction (Powlishta, 1987; Maccoby, 1990). Adolescents who are not succeeding tend to form gangs and involve themselves in fighting, aggression, and violence. Adolescents who date exclusively outside of their own race probably have identity problems or are trying to provoke their parents.

Adolescents are actively searching for an identity. Sexual, religious, and racial issues that seemed settled are reevaluated and subject to new understanding and revision. Similarities and differences, even within groups, cause the formation of in-groups and out-groups and for and against attitudes. The community climate regarding race and religion is important. Minority-majority ratios in school have great influence on the social atmosphere.

In adolescence, children begin to look beyond their own needs. They identify with community ideas and idealistic causes as a way to establish their own identity. This is an excellent age to involve them in community service programs, especially those catering to young children, or national organizations dedicated to helping their particular group socially and politically (Matthias & French, 1996). Their sense of empathy buttresses their moral conviction, which centers on wanting to alleviate misfortune and injustice (Goleman, 1997). To promote a sense of power and participation in society, 18-year-olds should be encouraged to vote.

Older teens finally understand morals and values not as impositions but as necessary for order and fairness. The media depict teens as selfish, aimless, and immoral, a picture that can become a self-fulfilling prophecy. In a disorderly and unfair society, they can stumble into drugs, alcohol, eating disorders, sexually transmitted diseases, and pregnancy. Parents must try to have their influence felt to counteract that of the peer group and the larger society—an uphill struggle (Matthias & French, 1996). Teens are aware of social hypocrisy. To remain credible to teens, parents must reveal their own uncertainties, beware of double messages delivered nonverbally, speak clearly from the heart, and keep the door open for discussions (Matthias & French, 1996).

Adolescents who display homosexual interests should be directed to see a counselor if, and only if, they are upset by this. This is a normal sexual identity for perhaps 10 percent of males and 5 percent of females, for complex biological and environmental factors that are not yet understood. Family acceptance is very important.

We might think of the sixth phase of development as covering the decades of young adulthood (from about age 21 to the mid-thirties). Of course, there are great differences in the pathways at this phase, depending on a person's race, gender, class, and sexual orientation. But in general, it is the phase of generativity in terms of partnering, work, and raising children. It is a time when adults are expected to function without the physical or financial support of their parents, a time when they begin not only to care for themselves but also to take on responsibilities for the care of others, establishing themselves in work, partnering, and parenting. There are major developmental problems in this phase for several groups, however, because of social factors.

By age 30, one out of every four Black males, if not already dead, is on probation, on parole, or in prison (Roberts, 1994). Many of those who are able and ready to work find themselves increasingly shut out of meaningful jobs because they lack the necessary education, technical skills, or training. This obviously impedes their potential for marriage (see Chapter 19). This lack of stable wage earning for young Black men creates a problem for young women in this phase, who find a severely diminished pool of marital prospects. Taken together, the massive obstacles of racism and poverty impede the forward development of young adults of color at this phase and may derail potentially productive people into the underclass, from which escape becomes harder as the life cycle continues.

Gay and lesbian young adults also have difficulties at this stage because of the stigma attached to their partnering and parenting, as well as the frequent necessity to keep their true lives secret at work. These struggles, created by the social system, with what should be normal developmental tasks have implications for smooth emotional development and well-being.

As for specific problems due to gender, there is evidence that women feel at a disadvantage in mixed-sex interaction. Men are less influenced by the opinions of others in a group than are women and have more influence on group process than women do. Women are more likely to withdraw or take unilateral action to get their way in a dispute, a pattern that appears to reflect their greater difficulty in influencing a male partner through direct negotiation (Maccoby, 1990). Women tend to enter into deeper levels of reciprocity with their children than men do (Maccoby & Jacklin, 1974) and to communicate with them better. In this phase of adulthood, extensive gender segregation continues in workplaces (Reskin, 1984) and in some social-class and ethnic groups, in which leisure time is still spent largely with others of the same sex even after marriage (Maccoby, 1990).

The seventh stage of the life cycle, which might be thought of as middle adulthood, lasts from about age 35 to 50 or 55. It is a time when, generally speaking, adults are still in good health, and their children are teenagers or being launched into adulthood. This is the last opportunity for active, hands-on parenting. In addition to the usual power struggles with teenagers pushing toward launching, it is a time to shift parental gears and start treating adolescents more like the young adults they will soon be, emphasizing the wish to trust rather than constricting or punishing them. This is the last chance to help children develop emotional competence (Goleman, 1997). It is a time for parents—unmarried, married, divorced, or remarried—to realize the grave dangers and temptations facing today's adolescents and to resolve their own differences with partners or other adult family members enough to be able to guide their adolescents as a team, united in concern and advice for them.

This is a time when people often do a philosophical reexamination of their lives, or even several reexaminations, and may need to reinvent themselves in their work and community to fit changing circumstances. There is often caretaking responsibility for older or ailing relatives, as well as for their children.

The eighth stage of the life cycle (from about age 50 or 55 to the early seventies) might be considered late middle age blending into early aging, a time when adults are beginning to retire, take up new interests, and still, in our times, feel in good health and have the energy for major undertakings. During this phase, they are freed from immediate child-rearing or financial responsibilities, though they are often helping the next generation, their grandchildren, and mentoring those who will follow them in the work world. Especially today, in our economically changing world, young adults more frequently need extra support from parents, and increasingly, families have to accommodate to changing family constellations. Women go through, or have already gone through, menopause, which often frees them up to concentrate their energies on new projects. They have been freed up from major caretaking and decided that it is their turn. It is a time when people are coming to terms with the fact that they couldn't do it all. They have to let go of certain dreams, recognizing their limitations so that they can concentrate on what they can do. Men often "mellow" at this phase as they become less focused on work and more involved in family relationships and domestic life.

People have to be concerned about husbanding their financial resources and preparing for future health care needs. It is a time to work out increasing supports and find ways to manage decreasing physical strength and endurance. It is also a time of facing the death of parents and losses of older friends and relatives.

The ninth and last stage of life, aging and death, covers roughly the ages from the middle seventies to 100+ as people come to terms with their own mortality and that of their peer group. It is a time for working out one's legacy, as well as any other personal business with one's descendants, to be prepared for death. An essential task is the completion of a life review in which one assesses the pluses and minuses of one's life and comes to a relatively positive acceptance.

The longer one lives, the more losses one sustains: family members, colleagues and lifelong friends, even some younger than oneself. The death of a spouse, one of life's heaviest blows, will occur during this phase for those who are still married. This produces many mixed emotions, from relief, if the death was preceded by a lengthy period of caretaking, to guilt—for surviving and feeling relieved—to devastation, if the marriage was a long one, especially if the partners were insufficiently independent in emotional or other functioning. The surviving spouse then has the task, one last time, of creating a new vision of life.

This is a time of life when spiritual resources are important to keep from being depressed and to tolerate one's growing dependence on others while continuing to maximize one's abilities.

THE "SLINGS AND ARROWS" AS INDIVIDUAL, FAMILY, AND COMMUNITY INTERSECT

The special and unpredictable individual life cycle problems of members of a family affect other family members at both an individual and family level. These issues, of course, also have extended family implications. Siblings, aunts, and uncles are also affected by the problems, having to decide how much each of them can or should do to help out. The problems also have community ramifications. A person's disabilities require various community resources throughout the school age and adult years. The availability and access to community resources to help a person with an alcohol problem or a stroke and to help the rest of the family with the disabilities created by these problems will have profound implications for the whole family's negotiation of their individual and family life cycles.

DEVELOPING AN AUTONOMOUS AND EMOTIONALLY CONNECTED SELF

We have quoted or paraphrased on our developmental chart (Table 2.1) the relevant milestones from Borysenko's (1996) book about the development of women as we think they might and should apply to the development of both females and males in a nonsexist, nonracist culture.

Many of us have struggled against the cultural bestowing of power on whites and denigrating of all others and the splitting of males and females into half people, one half focused on achievement and autonomy and the other on the emotional connectedness of relationship. Thanks to the women's movement, females have received compensatory help with this problem of imbalance in recent decades with many parents supporting their daughters' autonomy and the wider culture accepting it up to a point. That point is usually reached in adolescence, when dating begins, or when women marry and have children and are then expected to revert to an exclusive focus on relationship. But the

threats, epithets, and punishments visited on parents who question the culture's definition of masculinity and try to raise sons with an enhanced capacity to relate emotionally are swift and unforgiving (Kimmel, 1996; Silverstein, 1994). Perhaps if we therapists expected the same development in autonomy for females and in the skill of emotional connectedness for males, we could help parents find ways to defeat the destructive gender and racial stereotyping of our children. We owe it to our children not to permit the current deterioration of relationship and of community life to continue. What more important goal could we have for our turn to shape the future?

REFERENCES

Almeida, R., Woods, R., & Messineo, T. (1998). Contextualizing child development theory: Race, gender, class and culture. *Cultural Diversity and Mental Health.*

Bateson, M. C. (1994). *Peripheral visions.* New York: HarperCollins.

Borysenko, J. (1996). *A woman's book of life: The biology, psychology and spirituality of the feminine life cycle.* New York: Riverhead Books.

Bowen, M. (1978). *Family Therapy in clinical practice.* New York: Aronson.

Brody, L., & Hall, J. (1993). Gender and emotion. In Michael Lewis & Jeannette Haviland (Eds.), *Handbook of emotions.* New York: The Guilford Press.

Broken Nose, M. (1997). Personal communication.

Canino, I., & Spurlock, J. (1994). *Culturally diverse children and adolescents: Assessment, diagnosis and treatment.* New York: The Guilford Press.

Chodorow, N. (1974). Family structure and feminine personality. In M. Z. Rosaldo & L. Lamphere (Eds.), *Woman, culture and society.* Stanford, Calif.: Stanford University Press.

Chodorow, N., & Contratto, S. (1982). The fantasy of the perfect mother. In B. Throne (Ed.), *Rethinking the family: Some feminist questions.* New York: Longman.

Cohen, R. (1969). Conceptual styles, cultural conflict and nonverbal tests of intelligence. *American Anthropologist,* 71: 828–56.

Cohler, B., Hosteler, A. J., & Boxer, A. (1998). In D. McAdams & E. de St. Aubin (Eds.), *Generativity and adult development. Psychosocial perspective on caring and contributing to the next generation.* Washington, DC: American Psychological Association Press.

Cole, M. (1971). *The cultural context of thinking and learning.* New York: Basic Books.

Comer, James P., & Poussaint, Alvin F. (1992). *Raising black children.* New York: Penguin.

Coontz, S. (1992). *The way we never were.* New York: Basic Books.

Coontz, S. (1997). *The way we really are.* New York: Basic Books.

Daniels, P., & Weingarten, K. (1983). *Sooner or later: The timing of parenthood in adult lives.* New York: Norton.

Dilworth-Anderson, P., Burton, L., Johnson, L. B. (1993). Reframing theories of understanding race, ethnicity and families. In P. G. Boss, W. J. Doherty, R. LaRossa, W. R. Schumm, & S. K. Steinmetz (Eds.), *Sourcebook of family theories and methods: A contextual approach.* New York: Plenum.

Dinnerstein, D. (1976). *The mermaid and the minotaur.* New York: Harper & Row. 627–649.

Elder, G. (1992). Life course. In E. Borgatta & M. Borgatta (Eds.), *Encyclopedia of Sociology,* Vol. 3 (pp. 1120–1130). New York: Macmillan.

Ellison, J. (1984, June). The seven frames of mind. *Psychology Today,* 21–26.

Erikson, E. (1968). *Identity: youth and crisis.* New York: Norton.

Gardner, H. (1983). *Frames of mind: The theory of multiple intelligences.* New York: Basic Books.

Gilligan, C. (1982). *In a different voice.* Cambridge, MA: Harvard University Press.

Goleman, D. (1997). *Emotional intelligence.* New York: Bantam.

Green, R. J. (1998). Norms of traditional male development. In R. Almeida (Ed.), *Transforming gender and race.* New York: Harrington Park Press.

Hale-Benson, J. E. (1986). Black children: Their roots, culture and learning styles. Baltimore: Johns Hopkins University Press.

Hartman, A. (1987). Personal communication.

Hoffman, L. W. (1972). Early childhood experiences and women's achievement motives. *Journal of Social Issues 28*(2), 261–278.

Jordan, J. V. (Ed.). (1997). *Women's growth in diversity: More writings from the Stone Center.* New York: The Guilford Press.

Kagan, J. (1984). *The nature of the child.* New York: Basic Books.

Kagan, J., & Moss, H. (1962). *Birth to maturity.* New York: Wiley.

Koestner, R., Franz, C., & Weinberger, J. (1990). The family origins of empathic concern: A 26-year longitudinal study. *Journal of Personality and Social Psychology,* 709–717.

Korin, E., McGoldrick, M., & Watson, M. (1996). Individual and family life cycle. In Mark Mengel, & Warren L. Holleman (Eds.), *Principles of clinical practice, Vol. 1: Patient, doctor and society.* New York: Plenum.

Kimmel, M. (1996). *Manhood in America: A cultural history.* New York: Free Press.

Kunjufu, J. (1995). *Countering the conspiracy to destroy black boys, Vol. 4.* Chicago: African American Images.

Lewis, M., Feiring, C., & Kotsonis, M. (1984). The social network of the young child. In M. Lewis (Ed.), *Beyond the dyad: The genesis of behavior series* (Vol. 4). New York: Plenum.

Maccoby, Eleanor E. (1990). Gender and relationships: A developmental account, *American Psychologist, 45,* 513–520.

Maccoby, E. E., & Jacklin, C. H. (1974). *The psychology of sex differences.* Stanford, CA: Stanford University Press.

Matthias, B., & French, M. A. (1996). *Forty ways to raise a nonracist child.* New York: Harper.

McIntosh, P. (1985). On feeling like a fraud. *Work in Progress, No. 18.* Wellesley, MA: The Stone Center Working Papers Series.

McIntosh, P. (1989). On feeling like a fraud: Part 2. *Work in Progress, No. 37,* Wellesley, MA: The Stone Center Working Papers Series.

Miedzian, M. (1991). *Boys will be boys: Breaking the link between masculinity and violence.* New York: Doubleday.

Miller, J. B. (1976). *Toward a new psychology of women.* Boston: Beacon.

Neugarten, B. (1979). Time, age and the life cycle. *American Journal of Psychiatry,* 136, 887–894.

Ogbu, J. U. (1981). Origins of human competence: A cultural-ecological perspective. *Child Development, 52,* 413–429.

Ogbu, R., & Maureen T. (1994). *Crossing the color line: Race, parenting and culture.* New Brunswick, NJ: Rutgers University Press.

Pipher, M. (1994). *Reviving Ophelia: Saving the selves of adolescent girls.* New York: Ballantine.

Powlishta, K. K. (1987). *The social context of cross-sex interactions.* Paper presented at biennial meeting of the Society for Research in Child Development, Baltimore, MD.

Reskin, B. F. (Ed.) (1984). *Sex segregation in the workplace: Trends, explanations and remedies.* Washington, DC: National Academy Press.

Roberts, S. (1994). *Who we are: A portrait of America based on the latest U.S. Census.* New York: Times Books, Random House.

Romer, N. (1981). *The sex-role cycle: Socialization from infancy to old age.* New York: McGraw-Hill.

Siegal, M. (1987). Are sons and daughters treated more differently by fathers than by mothers? *Developmental Review, 7,* 183–209.

Silverstein, O. (1994). *The courage to raise good men.* New York: Viking.

CHAPTER 3

HISTORY, GENOGRAMS, AND THE FAMILY LIFE CYCLE
FREUD IN CONTEXT

MONICA McGOLDRICK

USING GENOGRAMS TO TRACK FAMILY HISTORY THROUGH THE FAMILY LIFE CYCLE

Genograms and family chronologies are useful tools for assessing families in life cycle perspective—the spiral of family evolution as generations move through time in their development from birth to death. It is like music, in which the meaning of individual notes depends on their rhythms in conjunction with each other and with the memories of past melodies and the anticipation of those yet to come. As graphic pictures of the family history and patterns showing the basic structure, family demographics, functioning, and relationships, genograms are a shorthand for depicting family patterns at a glance. They can elucidate the family life cycle framework, which in turn can aid in interpretation of the genogram. Both the patterns that typically occur at various phases of the life cycle and the issues to be predicted when life events are "off schedule" are relevant to understanding family developmental process.

Using Sigmund Freud as an example, this chapter will illustrate the use of genograms to track family process through the life cycle. Freud's genogram can help us to see him in context and put in perspective the history he did not want us to tell. Many people would prefer to downplay family history. Sigmund Freud, who has probably influenced our thinking about human behavior more than any other individual, focused almost exclusively on the importance of childhood fantasies about parents while ignoring the realities of parents' lives, the role of siblings, and the importance of the extended family and historical events on our psyches.

Though his thinking was radical for his times and encouraged a revolutionary attention to children's experience of their parents, there was much that his theories obscured from our view. Freud's theories seem to have been shaped and limited by his own personal family history, in which there was much that he wanted to ignore or forget (Gay, 1988, 1990; McGoldrick, 1995; Roazen, 1993; Krull, 1986). He did his best to be sure that it would be told the way he intended—with the stories he himself could not handle erased. Several times in his life, he destroyed personal and family records, embarrassed, as so many are, by the mental illness, criminal acts, and embarrassing or shameful behavior of various family members. He wrote about himself that he felt like the heir of "all the passions of our ancestors when they defended their temple." He wrote to his fiancée in 1884:

> One intention I have in fact almost finished carrying out, an intention which a number of as yet unborn and unfortunate people (my biographers) will resent.... I have destroyed all my notes of the past 14 years as well as letters, scientific excerpts and the manuscripts of my papers.... I couldn't have matured or died without worrying about who would get hold of those old papers.... As for the biographers, let them worry, we have no desire to make it too easy for them. Each one of them will be right in his opinion of "The Development of the

Hero," and I am already looking forward to seeing them go astray. (Letter to Martha Bernays, April 28, 1885, in Freud, 1960, pp. 140–141)

Indeed, many of his followers have contributed to the cover-up of Freud's history. Many of the Freud documents (now kept in the Library of Congress) have been restricted until the middle of the twenty-first century—some even until the twenty-second century!

Freud's views were, of course, limited by his time and culture. Patriarchal ideas about women profoundly influenced him. He, in turn, perpetuated and contributed to inappropriate expectations for women through the theory he propounded, which our society has for so long taken as psychological truth. There is an overfocus in Freudian theory on mothers to meet one's needs and at the same time a strong tendency to keep women's lives and experiences invisible. This reflected Freud's own family experience. As Lisa Appignanesi and John Forrester (1992) put it in their study of the women in Freud's life, "Throughout his life Freud oscillated between recognizing his mother as the alpha and omega of human existence and passing over her in silence" (p. 11). Freud glorified the mother-son relationship as the most perfect and unconditional love relationship of all. "The mother is only brought unlimited satisfaction by her relationship to a son: this is the most perfect, the most free from ambivalence of all human relationships" (cited in Appignanesi & Forrester, 1992, p. 15). He spent his childhood surrounded by an adoring mother and five adoring younger sisters, with his father in a much more remote position. He lived out at home his theory of oedipal conflict, in which the son competes to win the mother from the father; and he had the sense that he had won out against his father. In later life, he had profound conflicts with virtually all his male peers, dissolving each relationship with a cut-off after what he generally viewed as the other man's betrayal. He ended his days as he began them, surrounded by devoted women. Though glorifying the mother-son relationship in general, and though his own mother always treated him with reverence as her

"Goldene Sigi," he ignored her almost totally throughout his writings and in everyday life, apart from weekly duty visits to her. When she died at age 95, he did not even attend her funeral, sending instead as the "family representative" his dutiful daughter Anna, who had by that time become his loyal follower.

Unfortunately, it is not possible to destroy our history. It lives on inside us, probably the more powerful for our attempts to bury it. We and our families are likely to pay a high price in the present for trying to block out the past. Attempts to cover up family history tend to cause problems to fester, influencing people who are born long after the original painful experiences and relationships. Freud's biographers have had to struggle to uncover the intriguing private mysteries he left behind; just as we have to search for underlying patterns that make our own family histories so full of mystery. Often, we must choose indirect methods to piece the puzzle together.

Recent research suggests that there were many secrets in the Freud family that he dared not talk about. It is interesting that so many of Freud's biographers have gone along with his blind spot about exploring the family. They might be compared to the children in a family who silently participate in secrets by not asking questions and accepting the cover-up of their history that their parents have constructed. One would assume, for example, that biographers of Freud would be interested in his mother, who lived so long and had her wits about her long after her son became famous and slated for biographical interest. But in spite of Freud's own emphasis on mothers, almost no attention has ever been paid to her role in their family. We know nothing of her early life and relationships with her parents and siblings. Why not? Did Freud never ask her? And his followers, accepting his theories, did not pay attention to her either. Freud's son, one of the few people ever to discuss her at all, described her first in relation to her cultural group, the Galician Jews:

The Galician Jews were a peculiar race ... absolutely different from Jews who had lived in the west for

some generations. They … had little grace and no manners; and their women were certainly not what we should call "ladies." They were highly emotional and easily carried away by their feelings. But, although in many respects they would seem to be untamed barbarians to more civilized people, they alone of all minorities, stood up against the Nazis. It was men of Amalia's race who fought the German army on the ruins of Warsaw.… These people are not easy to live with, and grandmother, a true representative of her race, was no exception. She had great vitality and much impatience; she had a hunger for life and an indomitable spirit. Nobody envied Aunt Dolfi, whose destiny was to dedicate her life to the care of an old mother who was a tornado. (Freud, 1983, p. 11)

COURTSHIP AND MARRIAGE OF FREUD'S PARENTS: THE JOINING OF FAMILIES

Since the life cycle is circular and repetitive, one can start at any point to tell the story of a family. With the Freud family, we might begin a few years before the birth of Sigmund, at the time of his parents' courtship. The suggestions made here about the Freud family are, of course, speculative, since so much information is missing from the historical record. They are meant only to illustrate the use of a family life cycle framework in evaluating family patterns on genograms.

At the marriage or remarriage phase (see Chronology 3.1), the genogram shows the coming together of two separate families, indicating where each spouse is in his or her own family life cycle. To start a new family, both partners must come to terms with their families of origin. The genogram gives clues to the roles and connectedness of the spouses to their own families. When one spouse competes with the other's family or when parents do not approve of their child's choice, in-law triangles may begin at this phase. The genogram also shows the previous relationships that may affect or interfere with current marital bonding. Unfortunately, we know virtually nothing of the in-law relationships of this generation of the Freud family.

As can be seen on the genogram of the Freud family in 1855 (Figure 3.1 on page 50), the marriage of Jacob Freud and Amalia Nathansohn had a number of atypical aspects. Jacob, who was 40, was marrying for the third time. Amalia was just 20. In fact, she was even younger than Jacob's sons from his first marriage. Virtually nothing is known about his first wife, Sally Kanner, or the two children from that family who died; even less is known about Jacob's second wife, Rebecca. We do not know what happened to either wife, whether the couple divorced or the wives died. The missing information evokes curiosity and speculation about the meaning of his third wife to him. In addition, Jacob's first marriage took place when he was only 16, suggesting the possibility of an unexpected pregnancy (Anzieu, 1986). The second marriage is even more mysterious. Rebecca was never mentioned

CHRONOLOGY 3.1

The Freud Family at Time of Jacob and Amalia's Marriage

1832	Jacob Freud, age 16, marries Sally Kanner.	1852	(October–December) Rebecca dies (?).
1833	(April) Jacob and Sally's first child, Emanuel, is born.	1853	(December) Jacob hands over his business to son Emanuel.
1834	Jacob and Sally's second child, Philipp, is born.	1854	(or earlier) Emanuel marries Maria.
1852	Jacob's first wife, Sally Kanner is recorded as alive. Did they divorce? Did she die by end of year?	1854	(or slightly earlier) Amalia's father loses his fortune and is disgraced.
1852	Jacob's second marriage, to Rebecca. Two entries list Jacob's wife as Rebecca that year, aged 31 and 32 (Krull, 1986).	1855	(July 29) Jacob and Amalia are married. Jacob is listed as widower since 1852.
		1855	(August 13) Emanuel's first son (later Sigmund's nephew) John is born.

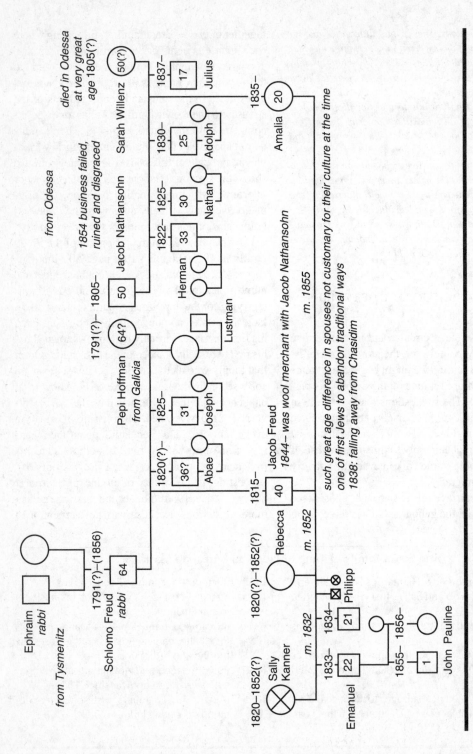

FIGURE 3.1 Freud/Nathansohn Families: 1855

50

by any family member, and we know of her existence only from public records. She appears to have married Jacob in 1852, Jacob's sons Emanuel and Philipp were grown and would obviously have known her. Surely Amalia would at least have known of her existence, as they all lived in the same town; yet if anyone ever did mention her to Freud, he never told anyone. One wonders why. Was there something about her of which the family was ashamed? In any case, Jacob and Amalia obviously began their new family in the shadow of Jacob's earlier marriages.

In examining a genogram, it is particularly important to note the ages of family members as they move through the life cycle. There is a normative timing for the transition to each of its phases. These norms are ever-changing and have varied across cultures and throughout history, but they can serve as a starting point for understanding more about life cycle transitions in a family. With any newly married couple, it is important to note the spouses' positions within the life cycles of their respective families. Jacob was already a grandfather, whereas Amalia, 20 years younger and a peer of his sons, was at the young adult phase. How did these two happen to marry? We know that such age differences were not the custom at this time and place (Krull, 1986). We know also that Jacob had no particular business prospects at that time (Swales, 1986), although it has been suggested that he may have misrepresented himself to her family. Otherwise, one wonders what led Amalia to agree to marry a man so much older, with grown sons and two previous marriages. It seems that her father had recently lost his fortune and been disgraced, which may explain the situation (Swales, 1986). In any case, Amalia was a vivacious young woman, one of the youngest in her family. Jacob, for his part, had experienced many ups and down. Having done fairly well in his thirties as a traveling salesman with his maternal grandfather, he seemingly came to a standstill in midlife. One would predict, upon seeing these differences in experience and expectation on a genogram, that this may be a problematic life cycle transition. Unresolved issues in earlier phases of the life cycle tend to lead to more difficult transitions and complexities in later life cycle stages. Thus, it is likely that with Jacob's previous marriages, his mysterious past, the discrepancies in their ages and expectations, as well as their financial precariousness, Jacob and Amalia entered their marriage with many complex issues unresolved.

It is also useful to examine the genogram for predictable triangles and patterns at different life cycle stages. There are at least two predictable triangles to search for in the genogram of a remarried family: that involving the two new spouses and the previous spouse (or the memory of the previous spouse) and that involving the two new spouses and the children of the previous marriage. We know nothing of Amalia's relationship with Jacob's previous wives. Nor do we know details of her relationship with Emanuel and Philipp. We do know that in Freud's fantasy, his mother and Philipp were lovers and that within three years of the marriage, Jacob helped to arrange for his sons to emigrate to England, which he may have done partly to have them at a safe distance from his wife.

THE TRANSITION TO PARENTHOOD AND FAMILIES WITH YOUNG CHILDREN

A genogram of the early parent years often reveals stressors that make this phase particularly difficult for the parents. By providing a quick map of the sibling constellation, the genogram may also reveal the particular circumstances surrounding the birth of a child and how those circumstances may contribute to the child's having a special position in that family. Finally, the genogram will show the typical mother-father-child triangles of this period.

Sigmund was born in 1856 in Freiburg, Moravia. As can be seen on the genogram of the Freud family for 1859 (Figure 3.2 on page 52), much was going on in the family around the time of his birth. His specialness for his father may have been intensified by the fact that Jacob's own father died less than three months before Sigmund was born and Sigmund was named for this grandfather, Schlomo, a rabbi. Sigmund was, perhaps, raised to follow in his footsteps by becoming a teacher and intellectual

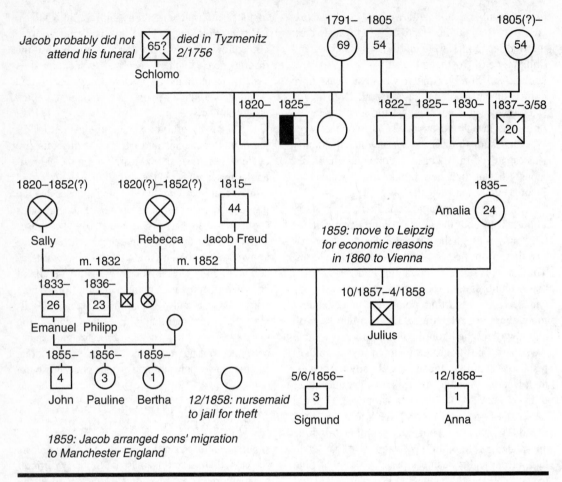

FIGURE 3.2 Freud Family: 1859

leader. Sigmund's family role was obviously also influenced by his innate brilliance. Another factor accounting for his special role was probably that he was born at the high point in the family's hopes. Shortly afterward, they had to migrate twice, and Jacob suffered from significant business failures from which he seems never entirely to have recovered. Sigmund's younger siblings, particularly Anna and Dolfi, may have borne the brunt of the negative effects of these changes on the family (see Chronology 3.2).

Equally important, Sigmund's brother Julius, born when Sigmund was 17 months old, lived for only seven months. The death of a sibling tends to

intensify parental feelings about the surviving children. The child nearest in age, especially a child of the same sex, often becomes a replacement for the lost child. Thus, Sigmund's closeness to his mother may have become even more important to her after the death of her second son. The loss of this infant would itself have been intensified by the fact that exactly one month before his death, Amalia's youngest brother, also named Julius, died at the age of 20 from pulmonary tuberculosis (Krull, 1986). Undoubtedly, she knew that her brother was dying when she named her son for him. The naming is especially interesting, since it goes against the Jewish custom of naming a baby in honor of someone who

CHRONOLOGY 3.2_____

The Freud Family, 1856–1859

1856	(Feb. 21) Schlomo Freud, Jacob's father dies. (Jacob is 40.)
1856	(May 6) Sigmund is born in Freiberg, Moravia (now Pribor, in Czech Republic).
1857	(October) Sigmund's brother Julius is born.
1858	(March) Julius Nathansohn, Amalia's 20-year-old brother, dies of tuberculosis.
1858	(April 15) Julius dies.
1858	Wilhelm Fliess is born. Sigmund identified Fliess with his brother Julius.
1858	(December) Sigmund's sister Anna is born.
1859	(January) Sigmund's nursemaid leaves—jailed for theft, reported by Sigmund's half-brother Philipp during Amalia's confinement with Anna.
1859	(August) Emanuel and Philipp emigrate with their families, including Sigmund's nephew, to whom he is very attached.
1859	(August) Freud family moves from Freiberg to Leipzig, apparently because of economic reversals.

---

has *already* died. One wonders whether the emotional imperative was somehow more powerful here than the cultural custom, which had been followed for Sigmund. In later life, Sigmund said that he had welcomed this brother with "ill wishes and real infantile jealousy, and his death left the germ of guilt in me" (cited in Krull, 1986).

The oldest sometimes resents the later-born, feeling threatened or displaced by the new arrival. From a very early age, Sigmund may have seen Anna as an intrusion, and she may have resented his special position and privileges in the family. She was conceived the month before the death of the second child, Julius. Sigmund's sibling rivalry might have been compounded by family ambivalence about the first child born after a lost son. These feelings of rivalry can linger into adulthood. Sigmund's relationship with his sister Anna seems never to have been very close, and they were alienated as adults.

Another complicating factor in terms of the sibling constellation can be seen on the genogram. For the first three years of his life, Sigmund was raised almost as a younger brother to his nephew John, who was a year or so older than he. Sigmund commented on the importance of this relationship:

> Until the end of my third year we had been inseparable; we had loved each other and fought each other and … this childish relationship has determined all my later feelings in intercourse with persons my own age. My nephew, John, has since then had many incarnations, which have revived first one and then another aspect of character and is ineradicably fixed in my conscious memory. At times he must have treated me very badly and I must have opposed my tyrant courageously. (Jones, 1953, p. 8)

This beginning phase of a new family, of which Sigmund was the first child, finally concluded with a splitting and emigration of the old family. We do not know the details of why the Freud family left Freiburg. When Sigmund was 3, his stepbrothers and their families went to England to find their fortunes, and Jacob moved his family first to Leipzig and then to Vienna, probably in part because of the economic reversals. Perhaps there were tensions between Amalia and her stepsons Emanuel and Philipp, who may have been reminders to her of Jacob's earlier loyalties. As mentioned, there is even a hint of a possible affair. Also, Jacob and Amalia shared a nursemaid with Emanuel and his wife, and the children played well together. The nursemaid was dismissed from the household for stealing while Amalia was confined for the birth of Anna; this was another loss for Sigmund. Thus, within a period of a few years, Sigmund experienced a multitude of losses: the death of his brother, the dismissal of the nursemaid, the emigration of his stepbrothers and their children, the birth of his sister, which took his mother away, and finally, the uprooting of his whole family. The Freuds were never to be as financially stable again (See Chronology 3.3).

CHRONOLOGY 3.3

Freud/Nathansohn Family, 1860s and 1870s

1860	Freud family settles in Vienna.
1860	(March) Sigmund's sister Rosa is born.
1861	(March) Sigmund's sister Marie (Mitzi) is born.
1862	(July) Sigmund's sister Dolfi is born.
1863	(May) Sigmund's sister Paula is born.
1865	(July 20) Uncle Josef Freud arrested for counterfeiting.
1865	(October) Maternal grandfather (Jacob Nathansohn) dies.
1866	(February) Uncle Josef Freud sent to prison for 10 years.
1866	(April) Sigmund's brother Alexander, named by Sigmund, is born.
1868	Sigmund enters gymnasium.
1873	Sigmund enters medical school.

Sigmund was the first of eight children (Figure 3.3). The genogram shows the family in the year Sigmund finished gymnasium and began medical school. It is the birth of the first child, more than the marriage itself, that most profoundly marks the transition to a new family. For the new spouse, the child tends to signify greater legitimization and power of the current family in relation to the partner's previous family. Sigmund definitely seemed to have a special place in his mother's heart. He had an intense relationship with her, and she always referred to him as her "golden Sigi." By all accounts, he was the center of the household. There is a well-known family story that when his sister Anna wanted to play the piano, their mother bought one but got rid of it immediately when Sigmund complained that the noise bothered him. His sisters got no further piano lessons. Sigmund's special position is further indicated by the fact that the family gave him the privilege of naming his younger brother, Alexander, born when Sigmund was 10. (In his own marriage, he himself named every one of his six children, all for his male heroes or one of their family female members!) The Freuds' cultural preference for sons further exalted Sigmund's position in his family.

FAMILIES WITH ADOLESCENTS

Once children reach adolescence, the task is to prepare the family for a qualitative change in the relationships between the generations, as the children are no longer so dependent on their parents. During this period, triangles are likely to develop involving adolescents, their peers, and their parents, or the adolescents, their parents, and their grandparents. We have little specific information on family events during Freud's adolescence, but the genogram suggests a family with many burdens of child-rearing, since there were seven children, all still in the home. We may also wonder whether the discrepancy in age between Jacob and Amalia would not be felt even more at this stage of the life cycle. Jacob, in his fifties, may have been feeling his age. Sigmund later described his father as rather grouchy and disappointed in his older sons, Emanuel and Philipp. In contrast, Amalia, in her thirties was still energetic, attractive, and youthful. We do not know whether these differences in age, energy level, and outlook led to tension or conflict between Jacob and Amalia, but given her devotion to Sigmund and the demands of a large household, it is likely that her energies were more focused on her children than on her spouse. Sigmund later reported that he felt as though he had to make up for his father's absence. We also know that Jacob's brother was jailed for counterfeiting, an experience that Sigmund later said turned his father's hair gray. It appears that Jacob was implicated in the scheme—or at least his sons were, which may have accounted for their earlier move to England (Krull, 1986; Swales, 1986).

It is during adolescence that children begin to have interests outside the family, both in school and with friends. Sigmund did very well in school

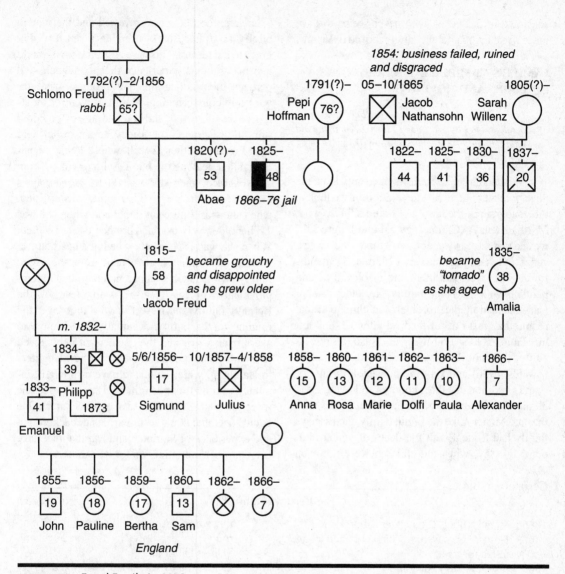

FIGURE 3.3 Freud Family in 1873

and was at the top of his gymnasium class for six of his eight years there. His success with his peers was less spectacular. By all accounts, he was a shy, intense, serious young man who focused more on his studies than on socializing. The genogram will sometimes indicate important peers in a child's life and whether family boundaries easily include outsiders. We know of Sigmund's having only one close friend at school, Eduard Silberstein, with whom he corresponded and formed a "secret society." At 16, he had a crush on a friend's sister, Gisela Fluss, but never expressed his feelings to her. Perhaps he was responding to a mandate from his family: to excel in school and to succeed in life and so justify his special position in his family and to make up for their other disappointments—in the older sons, and in the father, who never seems to have made a real living after the family moved to Vienna.

FAMILIES AT MIDLIFE: LAUNCHING CHILDREN AND MOVING ON

Little by little the young people are becoming independent and all of a sudden I have become the old man. (Freud, 1909, cited in Young-Bruehl, 1988, p. 61)

The genogram also allows us to anticipate the developments of the next generation. If we look at the genogram of the family of Freud's future wife, Martha Bernays (Chronology 3.4 and Figure 3.4), we see that the early years, particularly the adolescence and young adulthood of Martha, Sigmund's future wife, were turbulent and displayed certain parallels with the Freud family. Her older brother Isaac had had medical problems in childhood that required a great deal of medical attention and left him lame. As he was growing up, Isaac was reportedly a difficult child with destructive tendencies (Swales, 1986) and kept the household in an uproar. In addition, the three children following Isaac all died in early childhood. Finally came Eli, Martha, and Minna. Like the Freud family, the Bernays family had to deal with the death of young children. In 1867, when the children were not even teenagers, the father was arrested and then jailed briefly for fraud, surely bringing a sense of disgrace to the family. This is very similar to Sigmund and his sibling's experience that their uncle and perhaps their father and half brothers were involved in counterfeiting, Martha grew up in an atmosphere of secrets and forebodings of potential ruin and disgrace. There may be a parallel here with Freud's mother as well, whose father's business failed, leaving the family with a sense of ruin and disgrace when she was 18. In the Bernays's case, when Martha was 6 her father was arrested, when she was 7 he went to jail and when she was 11, her older, very troubled brother, Isaac, 17, died. When she was 18, her father died of a heart attack, leaving the family in great debt. Like the Freud family, with Jacob's apparent continued unemployment in his later years, it is not clear how the Bernays family survived. Eli, who took over the running of the family, eventually fled Vienna to avoid bankruptcy and the payment of debts owed to friends. The mother moved with her daughters to Hamburg, which seems to have infuriated Sigmund, who had met Martha in 1881 and became secretly engaged to her two months later. One could speculate that the similarities in background and experience of Sigmund and Martha may have been part of their attraction for one another.

CHRONOLOGY 3.4

The Bernays Family

1865	Minna, youngest daughter is born.
1867	Berman Bernays goes bankrupt and is arrested for fraud.
1868	Berman goes to prison.
1872	Isaac dies.
1879	Berman dies, leaving the family in great debt.
1882	Martha meets Sigmund and is secretly engaged two months later.
1882	Eli meets Anna.
1883	(June) Martha, Minna, and their mother move with their mother to Hamburg, a move arranged by Eli, probably because of

the embarrassment about their debts. Sigmund is very upset by the distance and blames Eli for it.

1883	Eli and Anna are married. Sigmund does not attend, nor does he even mention it in his letters to Martha.
1883	Ignaz Schonberg and Minna are engaged. Ignaz has TB.
1885	Ignaz breaks off the engagement.
1886	(June) Ignaz dies.
1886	(Sept) Sigmund and Martha marry.

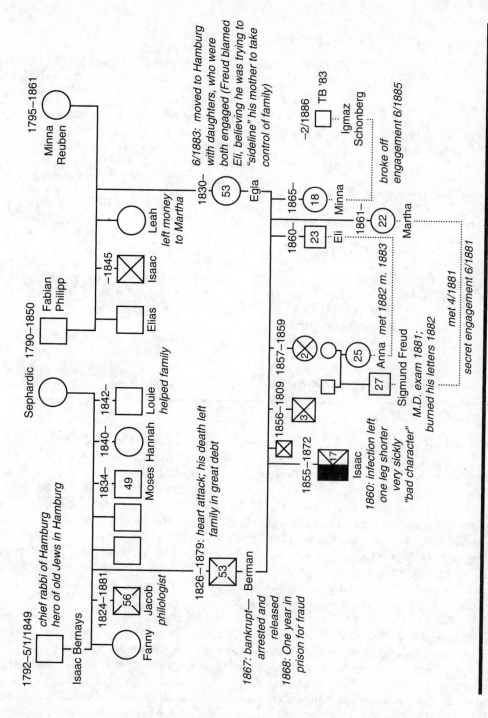

FIGURE 3.4 Bernays Family 1883: Family at Launching

The Freud Family in the 1880s

1873   Sigmund enters medical school.

1881   Sigmund completes medical school after 8 years.

1882   (April) Sigmund meets future wife, Martha Bernays.

1882   (April) Sigmund destroys his papers and letters just after meeting Martha.

1882   (June 17) Sigmund and Martha Bernays become engaged.

1883   Minna becomes engaged to Ignaz Schonberg, close friend of Sigmund.

1883   (June 14) Martha's mother moves with her daughters to Wandesbek.

1883   (September) Sigmund's friend Nathan Weiss commits suicide.

1883   (October) Eli Bernays and Sigmund's sister Anna are married. Sigmund does not attend or even mention the wedding in letters to Martha (at least not in published correspondence, although apparently only a small part has ever been published).

1884   (July 18) Sigmund becomes involved with cocaine and recommends it to others. He publishes cocaine paper. Evidence suggests that Freud went on using and recommending the use of cocaine until the mid-1890s (Isbister, 1985).

1884   Jacob Freud has business problems.

1885   (April) Sigmund destroys all of his papers.

1885   (June) Schonberg breaks his engagement to Minna.

1886   (February) Schonberg dies of tuberculosis, diagnosed in 1883.

1886   Sigmund writes paper on male hysteria.

1886   (September 14) Sigmund and Martha are married, enabled by a gift of money from Martha's aunt.

1887   (October) Sigmund and Martha's first child, Mathilda, is born (named for colleague Breuer's wife).

1887   Sigmund meets Wilhelm Fliess, who becomes his most important and intimate friend until their break in 1904 over an accusation of plagiarism.

The launching phases, when children leave home to be on their own, in the past usually blended into marriage, since children often did not leave home until they married. Now most go through a period of being a single adult. This phase is the cornerstone of the modern family life cycle and crucial for all the other phases that are to follow. The short-circuiting of this phase, or its prolongation, may affect all future life cycle transitions. The genogram often reveals the duration of the launching phase, as well as factors that may contribute to a delay of launching.

The information that we have on the Freud family during the launching phase is quite scanty. As has already been mentioned, Sigmund held a favored, almost exalted position in his family. Sometimes, this can lead to difficulties in launching, when a young adult is hesitant to leave such a favored position and the parents may be unwilling to let their special child go. In Sigmund's day, children usually did not leave home as single young adults but lived in their parents' household until they married and established a household of their own. This was true for Sigmund, who lived with his parents until he was 30, when he married Martha Bernays and they moved to their own apartment. As was customary, one other daughter, Dolfi, never married and remained at home to be the parental caretaker, as Anna did in the next generation.

One interesting fact from the perspective of the life cycle is how long it took Sigmund to complete his medical studies (Chronology 3.5). He took seven years to get his degree and did not practice for quite a few years after that. This was unusual for students in those days, particularly those who were not independently wealthy. Perhaps he was hesitant to finish and move on to the next phase: supporting himself. Or perhaps he felt that he was needed at home. In any case, he apparently did not seriously think about supporting himself until he wanted to marry Martha. When a delay in moving on to the next phase is indicated by the genogram, as in Freud's case with his prolonged time as a student and his lengthy engagement, one should explore what impediments to moving on in the life cycle there might be.

MARRIAGE: THE NEXT GENERATION

Having gone through several transitions of the Freud family life cycle, we come to the next phase: the marriage of Sigmund Freud and Martha Bernays. A genogram of the time of marriage will often provide valuable clues to the difficulties and issues involved in the joining together of two family traditions in a new family.

What is immediately apparent from the genogram (Figure 3.4 and Figure 3.5 on page 60) is the unusual double connection between the Freuds and Bernays in Sigmund's generation. Such unusual configurations often suggest complicated relationships between the two families and the possible existence of triangles. The oldest son in each family married the oldest daughter of the other family. As was mentioned earlier, Sigmund and his sister Anna never got along. Perhaps Sigmund felt the usual sibling rivalry of an oldest child with a younger sister. Or perhaps he associated Anna's birth with many losses: the brother Julius, who was born and died between them, the family's financial troubles and forced migration, the loss of the nursemaid, and the emigration of his uncles and cousins. Whatever the reasons, Sigmund seemed to resent the marriage of Anna to Eli Bernays and did not attend their wedding. In fact, he did not even mention the event in his letters to Martha, although he wrote to her almost daily and shortly after that discussed the possibility of attending the wedding of one of her cousins, certainly a much less important family event. Perhaps Sigmund resented Eli and Anna's being able to marry when his own marriage seemed so far off.

Indeed, it appears that Eli's control of a small legacy of Martha's from an aunt was at least part of the reason Sigmund and Martha could not marry sooner (Young-Bruehl, 1988). Sigmund's negative feelings toward his sister and brother-in-law seemed to intensify after the couple moved to New York and the less-educated Eli became very wealthy while the highly educated Sigmund had to struggle for the money to support his family.

We know that before their marriage, there were difficulties between Sigmund and Martha regarding their families. Both came from families with financial problems, and financial concerns stood in the way of their marrying for more than five years. Indeed, Sigmund blamed Eli for Martha's moving with her mother and sister to Hamburg the year after they were engaged, which made it extremely difficult for them to see each other for long periods of time. Freud felt threatened by Martha's relationship to her family of origin and was demanding and possessive about her loyalty to him. During their long courtship, he wrote to her:

> Are you already thinking of the day you are to leave, it is no more than a fortnight now, must not be more or else, yes, or else my egotism will rise up against Mama and Eli-Fritz and I will make such a din that everyone will hear and you understand, no matter how your filial feelings may rebel against it. From now on you are but a guest in your family like a jewel that I have pawned and that I am going to redeem as soon as I am rich. For has it not been laid down since time immemorial that the woman shall leave father and mother and follow the man she had chosen? (letter to Martha, 8/14/1882, in Freud, 1960, p. 23)

Sigmund was overtly jealous of Martha's relationship with Eli and even threatened to break off their engagement if she did not give up her loyalty to her brother. He later wrote to her:

> You have only an Either-Or. If you can't be fond enough of me to renounce for my sake your family, then you must lose me, wreck your life and not get much yourself out of your family. (cited in Appignanesi & Forrester, 1992, p. 31)

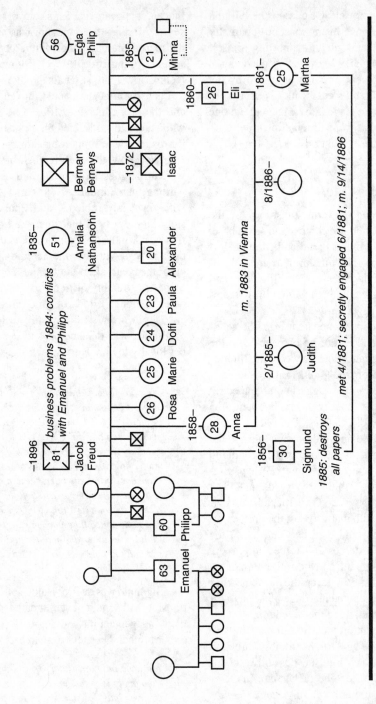

FIGURE 3.5 Freud's Family in 1886: Marriage Creates Freud/Bernays Family

Nevertheless, throughout their marriage, Martha did maintain contact with other members of her family and remained true to their faith, Orthodox Judaism, despite her husband's rejection of religion. After many years of marriage, she said that Sigmund's refusal to let her light the Sabbath lights on the first Friday night after her marriage was one of the most upsetting experiences of her life (Appignasesi & Forrester, 1992). As soon as Sigmund died, Martha, who was then 68 years old, began again to light the candles every Friday night.

PARENTHOOD: THE NEXT GENERATION

As can be seen on the Freud genogram for 1896 (Chronology 3.6 on page 62 and Figure 3.6 on page 63), Sigmund and Martha married and had six children within eight years. The early years of a family with young children are always an eventful time. While Martha handled virtually all parenting responsibilities, Sigmund struggled to enlarge his medical practice and began some of his most creative intellectual work. It can often be a difficult time for marriages, with so much of the spouses' energy focused on their children and work. When this phase is seen on the genogram, one should be alert to child-rearing pressures and normative strains in the marriage.

Like his own father's changes at midlife, it was during this part of his life cycle that Sigmund experienced a major life crisis. In his case, it led to his greatest intellectual discoveries and his major formulation, and then recanting, of the seduction theory (Masson, 1984). It was also during these years that Sigmund showed symptoms of depression and pseudo-cardiac problems. He complained of lethargy, migraines, and various other somatic and emotional concerns. He was clearly in a great deal of distress. It was during this period that he began his famous self-analysis and constructed the edifice of a new theory, which led to the publication of his most famous work, *The Interpretation of Dreams.*

A look at the genogram may elucidate why this was such a turbulent but productive time in Sigmund's life. In December 1895, Anna, their last child, was born. Martha, worn out by five pregnan-

cies in nine years, had been surprised and unhappy to learn that she was pregnant for the sixth time. It seems that after this last child, Sigmund and Martha decided not to have another. Sex between the couple apparently began to diminish considerably at this point (Anzieu, 1986; Roazen, 1993). Anna was conceived exactly at the time of one of Freud's most explosive professional consultations. He referred his patient Emma Eckstein to his friend Wilhelm Fliess, who believed in operating on people's noses to cure them of sexual problems, which he thought resulted from masturbation. Fliess made a mistake during the operation and left gauze in the wound, which almost killed the woman. Freud, who had an extremely intense relationship with his friend, experienced a profound sense of disillusionment and distress over this situation.

Often, the last child has a special position in the family. This was true of Anna, who was, by the way, not named for Freud's sister, but for the daughter of his friend and beloved teacher, Samuel Hammerschlag. This young woman, Anna Hammerschlag Lichtheim, was also a friend of the Freuds (Krull, 1986). Anna apparently felt that she was not the preferred child and spent an enormous amount of effort all her life trying to win her father's approval. She, rather than his wife, took care of him when he was ill. He became her analyst, beginning in 1918, when she was 23. She went in his stead to his own mother's funeral. She alone among his children, never married, devoted herself to her father, and chose to carry on his work.

The birth of the last child may be an important turning point in family life. It seems that Martha became very preoccupied with raising her six children, and Sigmund, who was not very much involved with the children, moved closer intellectually and emotionally to his sister-in-law, Minna, whom he had described in May 1894 in a letter to his friend Fliess as "otherwise my closest confidante" (Masson, 1985, p. 73).

Minna moved into the Freud household in early 1896. Fourteen years earlier, she had been engaged to Sigmund's best friend, Ignaz Schonberg, who had broken off the relationship shortly before his death from tuberculosis. According to

CHRONOLOGY 3.6_____

The Freud Family around 1896

1891   (February) Oliver, the third child is born (named for Freud's hero, Oliver Cromwell).

1892   Beginning of Freud's estrangement from Breuer.

1892   (April) Ernst, the fourth child is born (named for Freud's teacher, Ernst Brucke).

1892   Eli Bernays goes to America.

1893   Eli returns to take his family to the U.S. with him. Two daughters, Lucy and Hella, stay with Freud's family for a year. Sigmund gives Eli some money for the trip.

1894   Sigmund is having heart problems but does not tell his wife that he fears dying. He tries to give up smoking. He suffers depression, fatigue, and financial problems.

1895   (February) The Emma Eckstein episode begins. Freud has his friend Fliess operate on his patient, and Fliess makes a mistake, leaving gauze in the wound, which almost kills her.

1895   (March) Anna is conceived.

1895   Freud is still depressed, having cardiac symptoms. He treats himself with cocaine. He starts smoking after giving it up for over a year. He decides to begin self-analysis. Fliess performs a nasal operation on him.

1895   (December) Anna, the sixth and last child, is born (named for Freud's teacher Samuel Hammerschlag's daughter, a young widow and patient of Freud's) (Anzieu, 1986). Freud connects the expansion of his practice with Anna's birth.

1895   (December) Minna comes to live with the Freud family.

1896   Outbreak of extremely negative feelings about Breuer.

1896   (April) Sigmund writes of migraines, nasal secretions, fears of dying.

1896   (May) Sigmund writes clearest account of seduction theory, belief that women's anxieties are based on childhood sexual abuse. His presentation scandalizes his audience.

1896   Sigmund writes of the medical community's isolating him.

1896   Freud calls Emma's hemorrhages "hysterical."

1896   (October 23) Jacob Freud dies. (Sigmund is 40 at the time.) Jacob had been very ill for a month or so. Because Martha is away on her first trip in 10 years to visit her mother, only Minna is there to console Sigmund over the loss of his father.

1897   (January) Sigmund is passed over for university promotion.

1897   (February) Freud is informed that he will finally be proposed for the title of Professor. Martha's uncle Michael Bernays dies.

1897   (March) Sigmund's disgraced Uncle Joseph dies.

1897   (July) Freud takes a walking tour with Minna. He will take at least 17 vacations with her over the next years.

1897   (March) Mathilda has a very bad case of diphtheria.

1897   (May) Sigmund is again passed over for promotion and becomes anxious.

1897   (May) Sigmund has an incestuous dream about his daughter Mathilda.

1897   (September) Sigmund renounces his belief in "seduction theory." (He had thought that his father had an inappropriate relationship with his sister.) In despondence, he felt need for self-analysis. He outlined the oedipal theory.

1899   Freud writes *Interpretation of Dreams*.

1900   End of Sigmund's self-analysis.

1900   Trip with Fliess ends in falling out, which would turn out to be permanent.

1900   Trip with Minna in Italy. Did Minna become pregnant by Sigmund and have an abortion at a clinic? They traveled together extensively from September 12, 1900, through mid-February, 1901 (Swales, 1982). Jones said she was treated for TB, but there is no other mention of her having that illness.

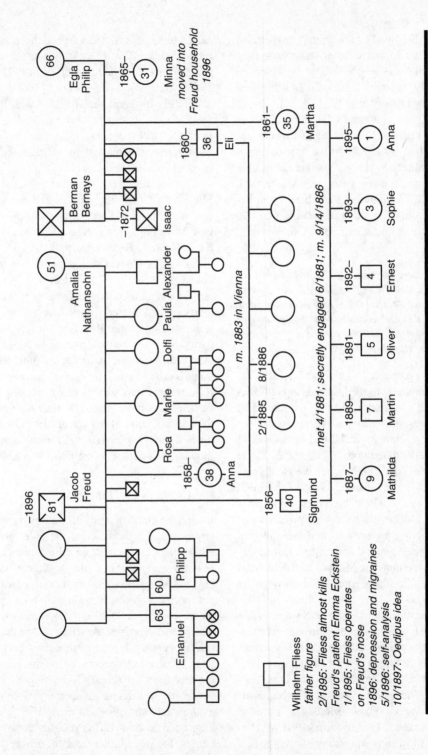

FIGURE 3.6 Freud's Family in 1896: Parenthood and the Next Generation in Freud's Immediate Household

Jones (1955), Sigmund's view in that early period was that he and Minna were alike because they were both wild, passionate people who wanted their own way, whereas Ignaz and Martha were good-natured and adaptable.

Also in 1896, Sigmund's father died, a loss that Sigmund said was the most significant and upsetting event in a man's life. At the time of his father's death, Martha was away visiting her mother for the first time in many years, and Minna, who had moved into the household less than a year before, was the only one there to console him. He wrote shortly after his father's death (November 2, 1895):

> By one of those obscure paths behind official consciousness, the death of the old man has affected me profoundly.... His life had been over a long time before he died, but his death seems to have aroused in me memories of all the early days. I now feel quite uprooted. (Masson, 1985)

The death of a parent marks a critical point in the life cycle. In addition to the loss, it is a painful reminder of one's mortality and that the mantle of tradition and responsibility has been passed to the next generation. Now Sigmund had his mother to support as well. In addition, his disgraced Uncle Josef and an uncle of Martha's had died that year.

Minna had never married. When other relatives appear as household members on a genogram, one should speculate about the possibility of triangles involving the spouses and the children. By all accounts, Sigmund and Minna had an extremely close relationship. Minna's bedroom in the Freud household could be entered only through the master bedroom (Eissler, 1978). Minna and Sigmund took many vacations together (Swales, 1987), apparently because they both enjoyed traveling, whereas Martha did not, at least not at Sigmund's pace (Freeman & Strean, 1981). Minna was much more interested than Martha in discussing Sigmund's ideas. Indeed, Martha said of psychoanalysis, "If I didn't realize how seriously my husband takes his treatments, I should think that psychoanalysis is a form of pornography" (Appignanesi & Forrester, 1992, p. 45). Recent research supports

Jung's report that Minna told him that she and Sigmund had an affair. There is evidence that she became pregnant and had an abortion in 1901 (Swales, 1986). We know nothing about Martha's attitude toward her husband's relationship with her sister. Interestingly, as can be seen on the Freud genogram for 1939 (Figure 3.7), Sigmund's oldest son, Martin, repeated this pattern and had an affair with his wife's sister (Freud, 1988).

It was around this time that Sigmund adopted Fliess as a father figure in his self-analysis. One can view Sigmund's self-analysis as the culmination of a number of events in the family and his own life cycle. He had just turned 40. He had had his last child. He was struggling to support a large family. His wife's sister had moved in for good. His father had died. Apparently, the passion of his marriage had cooled. In modern terms, Sigmund was suffering a "midlife crisis." Just as the midlife period for his father was marked by a new love relationship, occupational shift, and migration, Sigmund's crisis seemed to involve changing intimate relationships and career upheaval. He resolved it in certain ways more positively than his father with the consolidation of his career: the publication of his book, his appointment as a professor, and his growing recognition as the father of a new theory.

FAMILIES IN LATER LIFE

During the phase of aging, the family must come to terms with the mortality of the older generation, while relationships must be shifted as each generation moves up a level in the developmental hierarchy and all relationships must be reordered. There are special problems for women, who are more often the caretakers (Dolfi and Anna) and who tend to outlive their spouses (Amalia and Martha). When the last parent dies, the relationships between siblings become independent for the first time. Often, the genogram will reveal which child was delegated to become the caretaker of the aging parents, as well as the likely struggles and triangles in which siblings become involved in managing these responsibilities. Sibling conflicts and cut-offs at this point usually reflect triangles with parents that have come

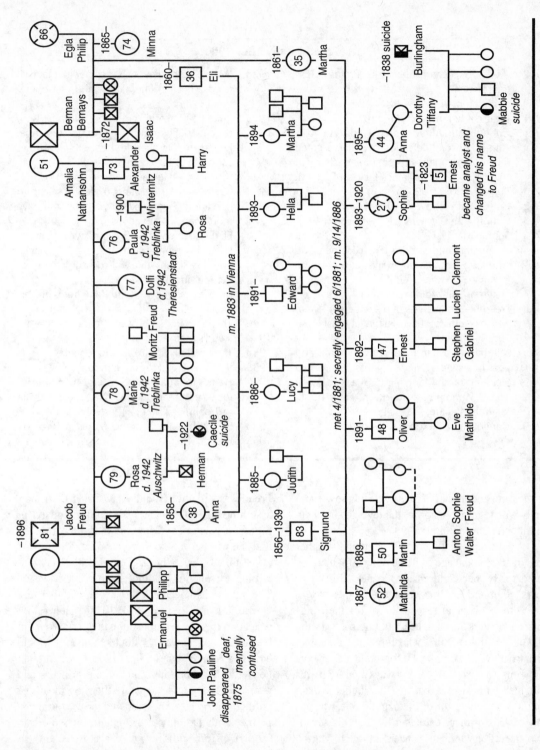

FIGURE 3.7 Freud Family in 1939

CHRONOLOGY 3.7

The Freud Family after 1900

1902	(March 5) Sigmund becomes Professor Extraordinary.
1909	Mathilda marries.
1911	Death of half-brother Philipp.
1911	Cut-off with Alfred Adler. Freud called it "the disgraceful defection of Adler, a gifted thinker but a malicious paranoiac" (letter of August 20, 1912 to James Jackson Putnam, quoted in Kerr, 1993, p. 416).
1912	Cut-off with follower William Stekel.
1913	Cut-off with Carl Jung.
1913	Sophie marries.
1914	First grandchild is born (Ernst Halberstadt, who later became an analyst and changed his name to Ernest Freud).
1914	Death of half-brother Emanuel
1918	Freud begins analysis of his daughter Anna, which seems to have lasted at least until 1922.
1919	Martha has a bad case of pneumonia and goes to a sanitorium.
1919	Sigmund and Martha go to a spa for a "cure." An important follower, Victor Tausk, commits suicide.
1920	Daughter Sophie contracts pneumonia and dies.
1923	(May) Sigmund goes to friend Felix Deutsch for diagnosis of the cancer and first operation.
1923	(June 19) Favorite grandson, Sophie's son, dies of TB. Sigmund weeps for the first time. He never gets over the loss, which follows so shortly on his own illness.
1923	(October 4) He has a second operation.
1923	(October 11) Sigmund undergoes a third operation. Over next 16 years he will have more than 33 operations.
1923	Eli dies in New York. Sigmund writes bitterly about his money and suggests that maybe now his sister Anna will do something for her four indigent sisters.
1924	Break with follower Otto Rank, rift with Ferenczi.
1926	Theodore Reik is prosecuted for "quackery."
1930	Freud's mother, Amalia, dies.
1938	The family is finally able to emigrate.
1939	Sigmund Freud dies in London.
1942	Freud's four unmarried sisters die in the Holocaust; Rosa in Auschwitz, Marie and Paula in Treblinka, Dolfi in Theresienstadt.
1943	Freud's brother, Alexander, dies in Toronto.
1955	Freud's sister, Anna, dies in New York.

down from much earlier life cycle phases, especially with regard to who was the favored sibling in childhood (Chronology 3.7).

As we saw in Figure 3.7, Sigmund's father died in 1896 at the age of 81, leaving Amalia to be cared for by her children for the next thirty-five years. Sigmund and his youngest brother, Alexander, took financial responsibility for their parents and sisters in later life, although it was the middle daughter, Dolfi, who remained at home, unmarried, with their mother. Sigmund also lived a long time, to the age of 83, and was cared for by his daughter Anna. Anna became her father's main follower and inheritor of his mantle. She was apparently his primary caretaker through his seventeen operations for jaw cancer, although Martha

Freud was still alive (she lived until 1951). Anna's assuming this role meant, as it had previously for Sigmund's sister Dolfi in relation to their mother, that she was never able to leave home. She was 44 at the time of her father's death. He had been unwilling to function without her for many years. Though she had been briefly in love with her first cousin, Edward Bernays, in 1913, she later said it was good that the relationship had not worked out because, since he was her double cousin, it would have been double incest. She had early dreamt that her father was the king and she the princess and people were trying to separate them by means of political intrigues. She resolved on becoming a partner with Dorothy Burlingham, an American mother of four children, who was the youngest of eight daughters of the glass millionaire Louis Comfort Tiffany. Though Dorothy was never officially divorced, she and Anna lived and vacationed together for the rest of their lives. Together, they ran a war nursery, a psychoanalytic training institute, and a world famous children's clinic. (Dorothy's husband committed suicide in 1938, having tried in vain to convince her to return to him.)

The genogram may be helpful in predicting or understanding the reactions of family members to key events at different stages of the life cycle. For example, Sigmund had a very strong reaction to the death of his 3-year-old grandson in 1923, shortly after he himself was diagnosed with cancer:

> He was indeed an enchanting little fellow, and I myself was aware of never having loved a human being, certainly never a child, so much.... I find this loss very hard to bear. I don't think I have ever experienced such grief, perhaps my own sickness contributes to the shock. I worked out of sheer necessity; fundamentally everything has lost its meaning for me. (June 11, 1923. In E. Freud, 1960)

A month later, he wrote that he was suffering from the first depression of his life (Jones, 1955, p. 92). And three years later, he wrote to his son-in-law that since this child's death he had not been able to enjoy life:

> I have spent some of the blackest days of my life in sorrowing about the child. At last I have taken hold of myself and can think of him quietly and talk of him without tears. But the comforts of reason have done nothing to help; the only consolation for me is that at my age I would not have seen much of him.

Sigmund's words suggest he was having to come to terms with his own mortality. This was particularly difficult not only because his grandson's death was so untimely, but also because his daughter, Sophie, this grandson's mother, had died three years earlier at the age of 27.

Contrast this grandson's death with Sigmund's reaction to the death of his own mother seven years later, in 1930:

> I will not disguise the fact that my reaction to this event has, because of special circumstances, been a curious one. Assuredly, there is no saying what effects such an experience may produce in deeper layers, but on the surface I can detect only two things: an increase in personal freedom, since it was always a terrifying thought that she might come to hear of my death; and secondly the satisfaction that at least she has achieved the deliverance for which she had earned a right after such a long life. No grief otherwise, such as my ten years younger brother is painfully experiencing. I was not at the funeral. Again Anna represented me as at Frankfort. Her value to me can hardly be heightened. This event has affected me in a curious manner.... No pain, no grief, which is probably to be explained by the circumstances, the great age, and the end of the pity we had felt at her helplessness. With that a feeling of liberation, of release, which I think I can understand. I was not allowed to die as long as she was alive, and now I may. Somehow the values of life have notably changed in the deeper layers. (quoted in Jones, 1955, p. 152)

In this case, Sigmund, at 74, more reconciled with his own eventual death, is relieved that the sequential order of the life cycle will be honored; first, the parents die and then the children. The untimely or traumatic loss of a family member is typically extremely difficult for families to mourn, and therapists are urged to be alert to dysfunctional patterns that develop in response to such losses (see also Chapter 11).

CONCLUSION

The genogram can be used to map the family at each phase of the family life cycle. Different configurations on the genogram suggest possible triangles and issues that can be explored for each phase. The genogram is only a schematic map of a family. Gathering the necessary information must be part of an extensive clinical interview, and the genogram is a summary graphic of the data collected. Much information, of course, must be omitted to make a genogram comprehensible. Despite these limitations, we believe that the genogram with an accompanying family chronology (McGoldrick, Gerson, & Shellenberger, 1998) is the best tool yet devised for tracking the family life cycle. Figure 3.7 presents an overview genogram of the Freud family, including his children and grandchildren, indicating that there are many more stories to tell as the family moves along and that this family, like all others, has many levels, many patterns and much fascinating richness.

REFERENCES

Anzieu, D. (1986). *Freud's self analysis.* Madison, CT: International Universities Press.

Appignanesi, L., & Forrester, J. (1992). *Freud's women.* New York: Basic Books.

Carotenuto, A. (1982). *A secret symmetry: Sabina Spielrein between Jung and Freud.* New York: Pantheon.

Eissler, K. R. (1978). *Sigmund Freud: His life in pictures and words.* New York: Helen & Kurt Wolff Books, Harcourt Brace Jovanovich.

Freeman, L., & Strean, H. S. (1981). *Freud and women.* New York: Frederick Ungar.

Freud, M. (1983). *Sigmund Freud: Man and father.* New York: Jason Aronson.

Freud, S. (1988). *My three mothers and other passions.* New York: New York University Press.

Freud, E. (Ed.) (1960). *The letters of Sigmund Freud.* New York: Basic Books.

Gay, P. (1988). *Freud: A life for our time.* New York: Norton.

Gay, P. (1990). *Reading Freud.* New Haven: Yale University Press.

Gerson, R., & McGoldrick, M. (1986). Constructing and interpreting genograms: The example of Sigmund Freud's family. *Innovations in Clinical Practice: A Source Book* (Vol. 5).

Glicklhorn, R. (1979). The Freiberg period of the Freud family. *Journal of the History of Medicine, 24,* 37–43.

Isbister, J. N. (1985). *Freud: An introduction to his life and work.* Cambridge, England: Polity Press.

Jones, E. (1953, 1954, 1955). *The life and work of Sigmund Freud* (3 vols.). New York: Basic Books.

Kerr, J. (1993). *A most dangerous method.* New York: Knopf.

Krull, M. (1986). *Freud and his father.* New York: Norton.

Mannoni, O. (1974). *Freud.* New York: Vintage.

Masson, J. (Ed.). (1985). *The complete letters of Sigmund Freud to Wilhelm Fliess: 1887–1904.* Cambridge, MA: Belnap Press.

Masson, J. (1984). *The assault on truth: Freud's suppression of the seduction theory.* New York: HarperCollins.

McGoldrick, M., Gerson, R., & Shellenberger, S. (1998). *Genograms in family assessment* (2nd ed.), New York: Norton.

Peters, U. H. (1985). *Anna Freud: A life dedicated to children.* New York: Shocken.

Roazen, P. (1993). *Meeting Freud's family.* Amherst, MA: University of Massachusetts Press.

Swales, P. (1982). Freud, Minna Bernays, and the conquest of Rome: New light on the origins of psychoanalysis. *The New American Review, 1*(2/3), 1–23.

Swales, P. (1986). *Freud, his origins and family history.* UMDNJ—Robert Wood Johnson Medical School. November 15.

Swales, P. (1987). *What Freud didn't say.* UMDNJ—Robert Wood Johnson Medical School. May 15.

Young-Bruel, E. (1988). *Anna Freud: A biography.* New York: Summit Books.

CHAPTER 4

CULTURE AND THE FAMILY LIFE CYCLE

PAULETTE MOORE HINES   *RHEA ALMEIDA*
NYDIA GARCIA PRETO   *SUSAN WELTMAN*
MONICA McGOLDRICK

Culture interacts with the family life cycle at every stage. Families differ in their definition of "family"; in their definition of the timing of life cycle phases and the tasks appropriate at each phase; and in their traditions, rituals, and ceremonies to mark life cycle transitions. When cultural stresses or transitions interact with life cycle transitions, the problems inherent in all change are compounded.

The consciousness of ethnic identity varies greatly within groups and from one group to another. Families vary in attitude toward their ethnicity, often as a result of pressures on them from the larger cultural context, at times regressively holding on to past traditions, at others denying any relevance of their ethnic heritage at all. In groups that have experienced discrimination, such as Jews and African Americans, family attitudes about allegiance to the group may become conflicted, with members turning against themselves or each other, reflecting the prejudices of the outside world. Some people have a choice about ethnic identification; others, because of their color or physical characteristics, do not. Ethnicity intersects with class, religion, politics, geography, the length of time a group has been in this country, the historical cohort, and the degree of discrimination the group has experienced (see Chapter 10). Generally speaking, Americans tend to move closer to the dominant American value system as they move up in class (see Chapter 5). People in different geographic locations evolve new cultural norms. Religion also motivates or reinforces certain cultural values. Families that remain within an ethnic neighborhood whose work, community and religion reinforce ethnic values are likely to maintain their ethnicity longer than those who live in heterogeneous settings without reinforcers of their cultural traditions. The degree of ethnic intermarriage in the family also plays a role in cultural patterns (McGoldrick & Preto, 1984). Nevertheless, there is burgeoning evidence that ethnic values and identifications are retained for many generations after immigration and play a significant role in family life throughout the life cycle (McGoldrick, Giordano, & Pearce, 1996). Second-, third-, and even fourth-generation Americans differ from the dominant culture in values, behavior, and life cycle patterns. While we are well aware of the problems of stereotyping and generalizing about groups in ways that may lead to prejudice and in no way mean to contribute to that tendency, we have taken the risk of characterizing intergenerational patterns over the life cycle for several groups to sensitize clinicians to the range of values that different people hold. Of course, each family must be dealt with as unique, and the characterizations used here are meant to broaden the therapist's framework, not to constrict it.

When we talk of families moving through the life cycle together, it is important to note how our clients themselves define "family." For example, the dominant American (Anglo) definition has focused on the intact nuclear family, often including other generations only to trace family genealogy to distinguish ancestors who were in this country before 1776 or, for southern Anglo families, noting family members who took part in the Civil War (McGill & Pearce, 1996). For Italians, by contrast, one might even say there is no such thing as the "nuclear family." For this group, family has tended to refer to the entire extended network of aunts, uncles, cousins, and grandparents, who are involved in family decision making; who share holidays and life cycle transition points together; and who tend to live in close proximity, if not in the same house (Giordano & McGoldrick, 1996). African American families tend to focus on a wide informal network of kin and community in their even broader definition of family, which goes beyond blood ties to close long-time friends, who are considered family members (Hines & Boyd-Franklin, 1996; Stack, 1974). The Chinese go even further, including all their ancestors and all their descendants in their definition of family. However, women traditionally moved into their husbands' family at the time of marriage, and their names disappear from the family tree in the next generation, leaving only the males as permanent members of the family (Kim, 1981). Thus, in a sense, Asian families consist of all one's male ancestors and descendants.

LIFE CYCLE STAGES

Groups differ in the importance given to different life cycle transitions. For example, the Irish have always placed great emphasis on the wake, viewing death as the most important life cycle transition, which frees human beings from the suffering of this world and takes them, it is hoped, to a happier afterlife. African Americans, perhaps as a result of similar life experiences with suffering, have also emphasized funerals. Both groups go to considerable expense and have traditionally delayed services until all family members can get there. Italian and Polish families have placed the greatest emphasis on weddings, often going to enormous expense and carry on the celebration and feasting for lengthy periods of time, reflecting the importance these groups place on continuation of the family into the next generation. Jewish families give special emphasis to the bar mitzvah and bat mitzvah, a transition to adulthood for boys and girls, respectively, reflecting the value placed on intellectual development, a transition that most other Western groups do not mark at all.

Families differ also in their intergenerational struggles. Anglo families (families of British extraction) are likely to feel that they have failed if their children do not move away from the family and become independent. Indeed, in Britain, many of those who can afford it send their children away to school by age 7. Even in this country, upper-middle-class Anglos often send their children away to boarding school by age 14. By contrast, Italian families may feel that they have failed if their children do move away. Jewish families will expect a relatively democratic atmosphere to exist in the family, children being free to challenge parents and to discuss their feelings openly (Rosen & Weltman, 1996). Greek families, by contrast, do not expect or desire open communication between generations and would not appreciate a therapist's getting everyone together to discuss and resolve their conflicts. Greek children are expected to respect parental authority, which is maintained by the distance parents keep from their children. Irish families are generally embarrassed to share feelings and conflicts across generations and cannot be expected to do so to any great extent.

Any life cycle transition can trigger ethnic identity conflicts, since it puts families more in touch with the roots of their family traditions. How the rituals of transition are celebrated can make an important difference in how well the family will adjust to the changes. All situational crises—divorce, illness, job loss, death, retirement—can compound ethnic identity conflicts, causing people to lose a sense of who they are. The more sensitive a therapist is to the need to preserve continuities, even in the process of change, the more he or she can help the family to maintain maximum control of its context and build upon it.

Groups differ not only in parent-child relationships in childhood, but also in the degree of intergenerational sharing and dependence expected between adult children and their aging parents. For example, whereas Italians or Greeks are likely to grow up with the expectation that they will eventually take care of their parents, Anglo parents' worst nightmare might be that they will eventually have to depend on their children for support. Minimal interdependence is expected or fostered, so adult children feel relatively guiltless when they have to put their parents in a nursing home. Conversely, adult children avoid asking their parents for support beyond paying for their education.

Groups differ in their definitions of responsibilities and obligations according to gender roles, in their expectations of motherhood and fatherhood, and in their treatment of sons and daughters. Marriage, child-rearing, leaving home, and caring for the elderly demand changes in relationships that are inherently stressful, especially when ascribed cultural rules for dealing with these stages are devalued or impossible to carry out in the new context. When conflict erupts, younger members may be most influenced by society's dominant values, while the older generations of a family usually attempt resolution by drawing on the strengths and legacies passed down from one generation to the next.

The portraits that we offer here are suggestive, not complete, and readers should consider the many other factors that may influence the particular values and behavior of each family they work with, including:

- the number of generations since the family came to the United States,
- their reasons for coming,
- socioeconomic factors that influence class status and class change,
- racial experiences in the United States and elsewhere,
- gender roles,
- migration history,
- religious influences, and
- the culture of the locale where the family lives.

AFRICAN AMERICAN FAMILIES

African traditions, the experience of slavery, assimilation into the U.S. mainstream, the psycho-logical scars of past and current discrimination, age, education, religion, and geographic origins make for great heterogeneity within African American culture. However, survival issues based on interdependence and oppression due to racism are commonalities that transcend individual and group differences. The legacy of slavery, racism, and oppression is a common bond for all African Americans, regardless of differences in educational or economic status (Hines & Boyd-Franklin, 1996; Mahmoud, 1998, Pinderhughes, 1998).

Despite conscious and consistent efforts by members of the dominant culture to erase all remnants of African culture from the memories and practices of African slaves and their descendants, the sense of oneness, exemplified in the practice of greeting one another as "sister" or "brother," is critical to understanding the dynamics of relationships among African Americans.

Family relationships, more than bank accounts, represent wealth and guarantee emotional and concrete support in the face of negative feedback from the larger society. The emotional significance of relationships is not determined solely by the immediacy of blood ties. In fact, "family" is an extended system of blood-related kin and people who are informally adopted into this system (Boyd-Franklin, 1989; Hines & Boyd-Franklin, 1996). Extended family systems tend to be large and constantly expanding as new individuals are incorporated through marriage and informal adoptions of children and fictive kin. Commonly, three or four generations live in proximity, sometimes residing in the same neighborhood.

Strong value is placed on loyalty and responsibility to others. This value is reinforced through the belief that everything one does in the public domain reflects on one's family and on other African Americans. Similarly, African Americans often believe that one does not succeed just for oneself, but for one's family and race as well. In essence, African Americans believe that "you are your brother's keeper." Personal accomplishments are considered the dual consequence of individual effort and the sacrifice of others. Success is to be acknowledged and celebrated but not overemphasized, as positive outcomes cannot be guaranteed despite one's efforts in a racist environment. Furthermore, even when success is achieved, it may be short lived. Intelligence and education without character and common sense have little value. Good character involves respect for those who helped one succeed and survive difficult circumstances. Family members are expected to stay connected and to reach out and assist others who are in need (McGoldrick, Garcia-Preto, Hines, & Lee, 1989).

The elderly are held in reverence. Older women, more than men, are called upon to impart wisdom as well as to provide functional support to younger family members. Older adults are testimony to the fact that one can not only survive, but even transcend difficult circumstances. They serve as models for self-sacrifice, personal strength, and integrity. By example, they show that although suffering is inevitable, one can grow from hardship and adversity. Children and adults are expected to show verbal and nonverbal respect to the elderly. Titles such as Mr., Mrs., Aunt, and Uncle are used to convey respect, deriving from the slavery and postslavery eras during which African American men and women, irrespective of their age, were treated and referred to as objects or children.

Children and adolescents may express their feelings and opinions but are not allowed to argue with adults after a final decision has been made. Although adults have the liberty to voice dissenting opinions to those who are older, younger adults are expected to acknowledge respectfully the older adult's opinion and perspective. To fail to do so shows disrespect for the life experience of the older person. Use of profanity in an intergenerational context is generally considered disrespectful and unacceptable.

Young adulthood for African Americans is a critical period during which poor decisions and impulsive behavior can have lifelong consequences (see Chapter 19). The usual stressors on intergenerational relationships during this phase of the life cycle can be both eased and complicated by the numerous adults who may be intensely concerned about a young adult's well-being. Young adults who have few employment possibilities and who find it difficult to achieve adult status while living at home may move in with relatives until they become economically self-sufficient. However, they remain subject to older family members' collective efforts to protect them from life's hardships.

Intergenerational issues may surface in families with young children and adolescents. The role flexibility (exchange of responsibilities) that is characteristic of African American families allows adults to help children thrive in an environment with many minefields (Hines, 1990). The proverb "It takes a village to raise a child" works well as long as roles are clearly defined, rules are consistent, and ultimate authority is clearly established. However, when distinctions between their functions and the process for decision making among various caretakers is not clearly delineated, confusion is likely to result. Intergenerational conflicts are most likely to arise when a child exhibits disrespectful behavior at home or school, poor academic functioning, and behavior that may put the youth at risk of compromising his or her personal freedom. More specifically, the primary concerns are that male adolescents will get into trouble with legal authorities and that female adolescents will act out sexually or, worse, become pregnant. Parents may resort to overfunctioning (i.e., become inflexible) and turn to relatives for help. Male adolescents in female-headed households are particularly inclined to rebel against the power and influence of their mothers and other females in positions of authority as they struggle to concretize their male identity (Hines, 1990).

Although African Americans have the capacity to be openly expressive of their feelings, such expression may be held in check in an effort to minimize intergenerational conflicts. Such conflicts threaten unity and diminish energy needed to deal with everyday life. Parent-child conflicts frequently occur, nevertheless, when individuals violate cultural norms by exhibiting hopelessness and a lack of self-respect. Tensions also are likely to arise when individuals are perceived to be wallowing in their sorrows, engaging in self-destructive behaviors, or pursuing individual interests without concern for significant others, particularly children and older adult family members.

Intergenerational conflicts may arise between family members over two, three, or even four generations based on differences as to whether children are being taught the traditional values that are considered critical to the survival of African American people. Youths who are oppositional in response to adults' push for their church involvement are seen as more vulnerable and defenseless in dealing with adverse circumstances. Conflicts may also surface between adults across generations as to how best to teach survival skills to youths without exposing them to hardships and depriving them of the fruits of the previous generation's labor. It is not uncommon for youths to have major differences with their parents and other adults in their extended families about their choices of clothing and/or hairstyles. While these issues are common sources of intergenerational conflict across ethnic groups, African American parents are likely to become upset not because of power and control issues but because such choices may limit their children's employment opportunities and further expose them to discrimination and problems with the police. African American youths may respond with equal intensity because they are not just rejecting adult authority, but struggling to express their racial identity and, often, anger at racist attitudes and practices. When the stakes are perceived to be so high, adult family members are reluctant to relax their positions; therapists must validate their goals before challenging them to shift maladaptive behavior.

Therapists are likely to encounter difficulty if they label any family member as a "villain" or "bad," regardless of how angry, disappointed, or rejecting family members may be because of that person's behavior. To attack one family member is to attack the entire family, which will arouse resistance. This does not mean that family members absolve one another of responsibility for problematic behaviors. However, families can become resentful or furious at the tendency of Whites to ignore the pernicious effects of racism and poverty. Families will gauge their therapist's attitude toward such

issues before they are willing to share personal information and subject themselves to the therapist's influence. African Americans are highly attuned to nonverbal as well as verbal communication, and therapists should be careful about what messages they convey at both levels. Giving family members permission to express their concerns facilitates trust so that the family can devote their attention to problem solving.

Because they are so invested in maintaining family unity, some family members may need encouragement to address topics that they anticipate might lead to intergenerational tension or cut-offs. One way to accomplish this is to offer examples that highlight how failure to discuss important issues can lead to damaged relationships that affect a family for generations. Family members are more likely to take the risk of bringing conflicts to the surface if they are clear that doing so is for the ultimate good of the family.

Family members often are inclined to make personal sacrifices "for the good of the family." Therapists should avoid suggesting that clients focus on their own needs before those of significant others (Hines, 1990). Behavioral changes can be encouraged by asking clients to consider the short- and long-term negative effects on significant others if they persist in their old behavior(s) while simultaneously emphasizing the individual's responsibility to self and the personal benefits of behavioral change.

When several people share caretaking responsibility for a child, the therapist should attempt to involve family members in clarifying who makes which decisions and how other family members can be supportive. Single mothers, especially those raising male adolescents, may benefit greatly when others within their social support systems are recruited to serve as mentors rather than as additional disciplinarians for their children.

When making referrals to self-help groups, therapists should be aware that the client may be uncomfortable if he or she is the sole African American participant. Clients should be offered the opportunity to discuss such concerns, and alternative options for seeking support should be made available if needed. For example, young adults, struggling under the weight of unrealistic family- or self-imposed expectations and/or challenged by the inherent stress of working in a bicultural setting can be encouraged to develop peer or professionally led support groups within their work and social environments.

LATINO FAMILIES

The web of relationships that extends across generations in Latino families provides a support network that is sustained by rules of mutual obligation. These rules are perpetuated by patterns of caretaking that fulfill expectations of emotional, physical, and economic support for those who need it from those who are capable of providing it. Rules of respect also play an important role in preserving this intergenerational network of close, personal relationships. For example, children learn to relate to others according to their age, sex, and social class. When the system works, that is, if sacrifices do not border on martyrdom, the support and emotional acceptance that are provided can be healthy and nurturing as well as reassuring and validating.

The sense of responsibility and mutual obligation can be so ingrained among Latinas and Latinos that individuals with few resources run the risk of self-sacrifice. Women, in particular, are expected to assume caretaking roles in the family and tend to experience more pressure than do men to devote their lives to the welfare of others. Becoming martyrs gives women special status, in that family members often see their sacrifice as exemplary. However, the price they pay for "carrying this cross" is often too high (Garcia-Preto, 1990). This behavior is reinforced by the cultural concepts of marianismo and hembrismo, a term derived from "hembra" and literally meaning "female" in Spanish, which contribute to the complexity of Latino gender roles.

Marianismo stems from the cult of the Virgin Mary, whereby women are considered morally superior to men and therefore capable of enduring the suffering inflicted by men (Stevens, 1973). Also implicit in the concept of marianismo are women's repression or sublimation of sexual drives and consideration of sex as an obligation. The cultural message is that if a woman has sex with a man before marriage, she will lose his respect, he will not marry her, and she will bring dishonor to herself and to her family. Traditionally, the line separating *doñas* (a respectful term for "Mrs.") from *putas* (whores) has been quite clear: no sex before marriage and afterward an accepting attitude without much demonstration of pleasure (Garcia-Preto, 1994).

Marianismo has been reinforced by the acclaim that the culture gives to mothers. Motherhood has been romanticized in Latino literature and their music, and the association made between mothers and the Virgin Mary is so strong that the mere mention of the word "mother" tends to evoke an almost religious response. Having children also raises the status of women in society and is a rite of passage into adulthood, eliciting respect from family members and friends. Mothers are glorified when they put their children's welfare above everything else and protect them. This sacrificial role is reinforced by the admiration of society. Feeling pressured and obligated to sacrifice themselves to be good mothers, women may assume positions of martyrdom in the family. Keeping the family together under all circumstances becomes their devotion, their cross to bear (Garcia-Preto, 1990).

Hembrismo, on the other hand, connotes strength, perseverance, flexibility, and the ability to survive. Within a historical context, hembrismo shares elements with the women's movement in the areas of social and political goals (Gomez, 1982). Also, in the same way that feminists have been perceived as men haters in this culture, Latinas who behave like hembras are sometimes viewed as trying to act like men or as challenging them. For instance, in the literature about Latinas, reference has been made to hembrismo as being a cultural reaction to machismo, or a frustrated attempt to imitate males. However, culturally, hembrismo can also translate into a woman's attempt to fulfill her multiple role expectations as a mother, wife, worker, daughter, and community member—in other words, the "superwoman" working a double shift, at home and on the job (Comas-Diaz, 1989). In therapy, we often see women presenting with symptoms related to pressure and conflict that they experience when they try to act like *marias* at home and *hembras* at work. At work, they assume responsibility and try to be flexible, strong, and assertive; at home they sacrifice themselves and suffer under the oppression of male dominance.

Men, for their part, are expected to assume financial responsibility for elderly parents, younger siblings, and nephews and nieces. This behavior, too, is admired and respected. Grandparents and other elderly relatives, although not expected to contribute financially to the family, often serve as caretakers for grandchildren, enabling parents to work or go to school. In return for this assistance, it is expected that the elderly will be cared for by their adult children. If such expectations are not met, intergenerational conflicts are likely to occur throughout the family system.

A common source of intergenerational conflict in Latino families who enter therapy is the struggle between parents and children who have grown apart while trying to adapt to American culture. Traditionally, Latino children tend to have closer relationships with their mothers than with their fathers. Perhaps because women are responsible for holding the family together, they tend to develop very strong relationships with their children and other family members. This central position in the family system yields them a degree of power that is reflected in the alliances mothers often build with children against authoritarian fathers, who are perceived as lacking understanding of emotional issues. Relationships between sons and mothers often are particularly close and mutually dependent, and it is not uncommon to see a son protecting his mother against an abusive husband. A family therapist working with this type of family may think that it is helpful to get the son to separate from the mother. The problem, however, is not the closeness between the mother and son, since strong loyalty ties between children and mothers are within the cultural norm among Latinos, but the lack of power that women in these positions experience. A more useful approach would

be to empower women to stop the abuse by linking them up with an antiviolence program and to address the alienation that is often created between fathers and children when men are uninvolved or abusive at home. Mothers and daughters also have close relationships, but these are more reciprocal in nature. Mothers teach their daughters how to be good women who deserve the respect of others, especially males, and who will make good wives and mothers. Daughters usually care for their elderly parents, often taking them into their homes when they are widowed, even though sons may provide financial support.

Relationships between Latinos and their fathers vary according to family structure. In families in which fathers assume an authoritarian position, there tend to be more distance and conflict. While attempting to be protective, fathers may become unreasonable, unapproachable, and highly critical of their daughters' behavior and friends. In contrast, they expect their sons to protect themselves, and they support sons' moves toward independence. On the other hand, in families in which fathers are more submissive and dependent on mothers to make decisions, they may develop special alliances with their daughters, who in turn assume a nurturing role toward them. With the increasing number of Latino families being headed by single women (for complex reasons including colonialist oppression of Latino cultures and the breakdown of patriarchal social structures), common scenarios are for fathers to be absent and distant or for daughters and sons to grow up having memories of their fathers' violent, abusive, and addictive behavior (Garcia-Preto, 1994).

When Latino families arrive in the United States, the children usually find it easier to learn English and adapt to the new culture than parents do. The parents may find English too difficult to learn and the new culture unwelcoming and dangerous. They may react by taking refuge in the traditional culture, expecting their children to do the same. When this occurs, children typically rebel against their parents' rigidity by rejecting parental customs, which are viewed as inferior to the American way of life.

Children may become emotionally distant from their parents, who often feel that they have lost control. Parents usually react by imposing stricter rules. Corporal punishment may be used. Commonly, parents will demand respect and obedience, cultural values that are traditionally seen as a solution to misbehavior. Parents may become very strict and highly protective of adolescents, especially if the family lives in a high-crime community. Daughters in particular may be overprotected because they are most vulnerable than males in a society with loose sexual mores. Such patterns of overprotection are most characteristic of families that are isolated or alienated from support systems in the community and when extended family members are not available (Garcia-Preto, 1996).

Children who are caught in the conflict of cultures and loyalties may develop a negative self-image, which can inhibit their chances for growth and accomplishment. Parents, then, may feel thwarted at every turn and consequently give up on their children. In therapy, it may be useful to see adolescents alone if they are unable to speak freely in front of their parents. Issues of respect and fear about their parents' reactions may inhibit adolescents from speaking about sex, drugs, incest, problems at school, or cultural conflicts at home and in the community. In such instances, obvious goals include helping adolescents to define and share with their parents personal issues that affect their relationship in an effort to find compromises. Discussing a family's migration history and acculturation process may help to clarify conflicts over cultural values. The therapist can also encourage parents to redefine privileges and responsibilities and to discuss their genuine concern for the child. By encouraging parents to express their love, concern, and fear to their children, therapists help parents and children to relate in a more positive manner (Garcia-Preto, 1996).

Disagreements that parents have with their own parents about child discipline can become another source of intergenerational conflict. This is especially true when grandparents live in the household with adolescents, who show disrespect toward them and reject Latino values. Parents often find themselves caught between two generations that pull them in opposite directions. Adolescents may feel that their grandparents are too old-fashioned and resent their attempts at discipline. Both adolescents and grandparents may complain to parents, who may try to mediate by explaining cultural differences but end up feeling powerless and confused about their own values.

Asking grandparents to attend therapy sessions to discuss adolescence and cultural values is sometimes helpful. The therapist might ask the family to identify the values that cause the most conflict at home. Ensuing discussions might lead to intergenerational compromise. For female adolescents, dating usually presents the greatest source of conflict. In traditional Latino culture, dating begins much later than it does in the United States. When dating is allowed, it is generally chaperoned by family or friends. Dating a number of boys is frowned upon, and girls gain bad reputations if they violate this rule of behavior. Once parents and grandparents recognize the difference between these rules and what is considered acceptable adolescent behavior in this culture, they are more willing to make compromises, especially when they realize the extent to which their children are affected by peer pressure. For instance, parents and grandparents may be more willing to accept their daughter's dating if, instead of going out alone with a boy, the dating is done with a group of friends. Meeting the girl's friends and their parents also helps them to feel less anxious about her going out.

As was stated earlier, intergenerational conflict is often caused by the inability of one generation to provide care for another. Adult children who are unable to care for their elderly parents, especially if the parents are ill, may experience stress and guilt. Conflicts with siblings and other family members may result. Practitioners need to encourage communication among family members to help them find ways to contribute to the care of elderly parents. Women who devote themselves to caring for elderly parents may express their stress and resentment through somatic complaints and or depression. Therapists can help these women to express their resentments openly as well as assist them in finding support from other family members or community resources.

Leaving the family system (e.g., through divorce or separation) is extremely risky for both men and women because it implies loss or control, support, and protection. For couples who are still adjusting to American culture, the loss of the family system can be devastating. For example, women usually depend on other women in the extended family to help with child-rearing and domestic tasks because men are not expected to share these responsibilities. Without the help of their mother, mothers-in-law, grandmothers, aunts, or sisters, Latinas may become overburdened and begin demanding assistance from their husbands. The husband may, in turn, resent these demands and become argumentative and distant, perhaps turning to alcohol, gambling, or extramarital affairs. The extended family can provide a measure of control for aggression and violence by intervening in arguments and providing advice to couples. Helping couples to make connections with relatives, friends, or community supports may be the therapist's most crucial task.

IRISH FAMILIES

Intergenerational relationships among the Irish often are not terribly intimate. Unlike groups that tend to view the extended family as a resource in times of trouble, the Irish often take the attitude that having a problem is bad enough, but if your family finds out, you have two problems: the problem and your embarrassment that your family knows. It is said of the Irish that they suffer alone. They do not like others to see them when they are in pain. It is not so much a fear of dependence, which it might be for Anglos, as a sense of embarrassment and shame at not being able to keep up appearances. Intergenerational secrets are common. The Irish would often rather tell almost anything to a stranger than to a family member. If they do share it with a family member, it is usually told to someone of the same sex and same generation as the teller. Intergenerational boundaries are strongly

maintained, even if this is very hurtful for everyone involved.

Within the family, intergenerational relationships throughout the life cycle were traditionally handled primarily by the mother. She cared for both the old and the young. Everyone is likely to view caretaking as her responsibility (McGoldrick, 1991). Her main supporters are her daughters, though she might also call on her sisters when she needs help. The therapist may have to teach both her and her husband how to involve him in handling problems.

The Irish sense of duty is a strong resource. Parents want to do the right thing for their children. It is not a lack of caring but a lack of attention to detail that most often interferes with appropriate nurturing of their children. This is the legacy of a history of oppression that forced parents to be overly vigilant about their children's behavior and left them often unable to attend adequately to their children's emotional needs because of their own deprivations. The Irish have tended to focus more on their children's conformity to rules than on other aspects of their child's development, such as emotional expression, self-assertiveness, or creativity. Traditionally, the Irish have believed that children should be seen and not heard. They should not bring outside notoriety to the family, especially for bad behavior. Less emphasis was placed on being a star student than on not standing out from the group for misbehavior. Irish parents traditionally tended to have little sense of child psychology. They hoped that keeping their children clean and out of trouble and teaching them right from wrong would get them through. When children develop psychological symptoms, Irish parents may be mystified. When children act out, parents tend to blame outside influences, although inwardly they blame themselves.

During the child-rearing phase, the greatest problem in Irish families occurs if a child gets in trouble with outside authorities, such as the school system. When parents have problems during this phase, for example, if the father is an alcoholic, Irish children can be remarkably inventive in developing strategies to obey family rules of denial while appearing to function well. However, they may later pay a high price emotionally for having learned at an early age to suppress their disallowed feelings.

During the adolescent phase and the launching years, drinking may become a major, often unidentified, problem that the parents do not know how to handle. They may ignore it, often with disastrous consequences. Parents do not want to be intrusive as long as the problem is not obvious and may not know how to talk through conflicts. They may hardly mention their concern at all until things reach an extreme.

Irish fathers have tended to play a peripheral role in intergenerational family relationships, whereas Irish mothers were always at the center (McGoldrick, 1996). Although Irish mothers have provided outstanding female role models of strong-minded, commanding, indomitable women, the stereotype of the "sainted Irish mother" is not totally positive (Diner, 1983; McGoldrick, 1996; McKenna, 1979; Rudd, 1984; Scheper-Hughes, 1979). She might be sanctimonious, preoccupied with black-and-white categories of right and wrong and with what the neighbors think, consciously withholding praise from her children for fear it would give them "a swelled head." Of course, this pattern makes sense in a culture with such a long history of foreign domination, in which the mother sought control through whatever means were available to her and felt the need to keep her family in line to minimize the risk of their being singled out for further oppression.

Sons and daughters rarely voice resentment toward their mothers. To do so is to risk guilt and to undermine their admiration for her stoic self-sacrifice. For generations, Irish women held a certain moral authority in their families, including control of the family money, even while being powerless in the larger context of the church and being unable to earn much money, except in low-paying jobs as caretakers or servants. Children tend to speak of "my mother's house," dismissing the role of the father (Diner, 1983). Irish mothers often fail to recognize their own strength or ability to intimidate their children, whether through teasing, ridicule, a disapproving glance, or a quick hand.

Perhaps because of their history of oppression, the Irish tend to communicate indirectly, often believing that putting feelings into words only makes things worse. They can also be uncomfortable with physical affection (Barrabe & von Mering, 1953; McGoldrick, 1996; Rudd, 1984) and tend to relate to their children through fixed labels: "Bold Kathleen," "Poor Paddy," and "That Joey." Children are loved, but not intimately known (Rudd, 1984).

What are we to make of these stereotypes of the Irish mother, who seems to be to blame for all sorts of problems—contempt for her husband, spoiling her sons and binding them in a love from which they will never be free while teaching her daughters to rely only on themselves, become overresponsible, and repeat these skewed patterns? We must take into account the very ancient tradition of Irish women, celebrated as formidable, tenacious, and powerful rulers from the time of ancient Irish legends (MacCurtain & O'Corrain, 1978). This tradition must be combined with awareness of the 900-year history of Irish oppression, which was focused especially on Irish men, who were systematically deprived of any sense of power and often turned to drink to blot out what was happening to them. Drink became institutionalized in the culture as an acceptable form of escape. Women were forced to run their families, and it is no wonder that they turned to their sons with the dreams their beaten-down husbands could not fulfill. They turned to their daughters to carry on with and after them.

As a result of the need of the Irish for ambiguous communication and ambivalence about self-assertion, parents may indirectly belittle a child for "putting himself ahead" while in the same breath chiding him for not being more aggressive and achievement oriented. Irish mothers tend to dote on their sons, overprotecting them and drawing them into powerful bonds, more intense than their marital tie. Sons might be pampered and protected much longer than daughters, and in traditional Irish families, they were called "boys" way into adulthood, probably largely because of the economic oppression that gave them no avenue to leave the parental home. A very high percentage of Irish men never married at all, and those who did were sometimes thought of as "married bachelors," more loyal to their mothers than to their wives (Connery, 1970). Conversely, Irish parents have tended to underprotect their daughters, treating them like sisters and often not allowing them much of a childhood by raising them to be overresponsible and self-sufficient, like the mothers themselves (Byrne & McCarthy, 1986). This failure to protect daughters teaches them to repress personal needs and contributes to an ongoing fatalism, emotional repression, and stoicism in the next generation of women. Irish women have little expectation of, or interest in, being taken care of by a man. Their hopes are articulated less often in romantic terms than in aspirations for self-sufficiency. They are often reluctant to give up their freedom and economic independence for marriage and family responsibilities. Generally, father-daughter relationships are distant, possibly because the father fears that closeness will be confused with trespass of sexual boundaries. Moreover, Irish families are not very good at differentiating among anger, sexuality, and intimacy. A father may maintain distance from his daughter or perhaps be sarcastic and teasing, not because such behavior reflects his true feelings but because he does not know how to approach her.

With a son, a father may share sports, work, and jokes, although the teasing and ridicule that are so common in Irish parent-child relationships may be very painful to sons as to daughters. Some Irish fathers remain silent, almost invisible, in the family. Another common pattern is the father who is jovial or silent except when drinking, at which time he becomes a fearsome, intimidating, larger-than-life antagonist, who returns to his gentler self when sober with no acknowledgment of this transformation. Children are kept off guard in such relationships. They may be drawn to the humor and fun, yet terrified of the unpredictable and violent moods.

Resentment over class differences may surface when Irish children marry. The Irish tend to measure others hierarchically as being "better than"

or "inferior to" themselves. Thus, parents may criticize children for "marrying up" and putting on airs (which usually means marrying an Anglo) or may criticize them for "marrying down." Both of these parental reactions are deeply rooted in tensions stemming from the Irish history of oppression by the British, which left them with a deep sense of inferiority. When Irish children reach their mid-twenties or older, they may begin to resent the family's patterns of denial and emotional suppression. Such resentments may be evident in their young adult relationships with others. The resentments that Irish children have buried since childhood often continue into adulthood without realization that resolution is possible.

Resentments and distancing may become more intense throughout the adults' life, especially if parents' subtle disapproval continues or if adult children assume caretaking responsibilities for their parents. Unlike other children who are freer to express their resentments, Irish children may be extremely sensitive to perceived slights, such as favors shown to siblings, or other imagined wrongs. They may never confront the parent or the sibling with their feelings, dutifully continuing their caretaking responsibilities while maintaining tense silence with regard to their emotional wounds.

As parents age, intimacy may not increase. Even unmarried children who continue to be emotionally and physically tied to their parents while outwardly denying this dependence may be shut down in terms of their emotional connectedness. The mother may maintain her matriarchal role while being unaware of the hold she has on her family because inwardly she feels that hold slipping. Placing a parent in a nursing home may be acceptable to both children and parents because the parents prefer to "suffer alone" and not become a burden to their children.

It is also extremely important to frame observations, especially regarding family members' intentions, as positively as possible while gently helping them to move beyond denial. A little assistance will go a long way with Irish family members in dealing with intergenerational problems. The Irish are generally cooperative, especially if therapy gives them a concrete sense of what they can do. It is often preferable to interview the generations, and even sometimes each parent, separately to help them avoid embarrassment in telling their story.

ASIAN INDIAN FAMILIES

In the past ten years, Asian Indian immigration to the United States has been opened to nonprofessional classes. Twenty years ago, families immigrating here were primarily of the professional class. Today, however, the influx of uneducated families settling into menial jobs has created many problems similar to those experienced by earlier groups of immigrants from other countries.

Despite the intersecting influences of caste, region, and religion, predictable intergenerational conflicts emerge among family members. Relationships within and across generations are influenced by beliefs in caste and karma. These beliefs are pervasive despite the diversity among Asian Indians in the "old country" and in the United States (Malyala, Kamaraju, & Ramana, 1984). However, the degree to which these beliefs affect adaptation to life in Western society is influenced by level of education and acculturation (Matsuoka, 1990; Segal, 1991). For example, an educated family living in this country for ten to twenty years will adapt to Western values around education and socialization for their children. However, they frequently revert back to Indian values as the marriage of a child approaches.

Hindu culture portrays women in paradoxical positions. Women are sacred in the afterlife, yet they are devalued in present life (Almeida, 1990; Bumiller, 1990; Wadley, 1977). Although men share power with women in the scriptures, in present life the male-centered family system exerts enormous social and economic power over women and children. With its concepts of "purity" and "pollution," the caste system shapes both intragenerational and intergenerational relationships. Prejudices related to lighter versus darker shades of skin color are deeply embedded within the culture, light skin symbolizing purity and dark skin symbolizing pollution. In fact, advertisements for brides place a high price on light-skinned women who have a green card. These ideals are carried into the acculturation process. Thus, Asian Indian immigrants move more readily toward white Americans than nonwhites and teach their children to passively learn to succeed in work. This response to obedience, which is a deeply held value, works against children and adults in many aspects of their lives. One example is the commonly held view that Asians embrace the work ethic. This pits these families against other minorities and immigrants in ways that isolate them further in the acculturation process. Asian Indian experiences of racism are generally not talked about, as though acknowledgment of racism might connect them with others who are similarly discriminated against. Although work and educational opportunities are available to all, women and lower-caste men have fewer choices regarding marriage partners and economic choices. Such contradictions are pervasive and are explained in terms of karma.

Karma focuses on past and future life space. Current life dilemmas are explained in terms of karma. For example, a wife who is mistreated by her in-laws might say, "I must deserve this for something bad I did in a past life. If I endure my current life, I know I will be taken care of by God in a future life." Making choices to alter current life struggles is possible within this belief system but often occurs in extreme forms. Such choices consist of sacrificial actions that alter one's current life and thus are meaningful. Fasting, praying, somatic complaints, head shaving, and suicide alter karma and move one toward a better life. In work with Asian Indian clients, therapists might suggest culturally appropriate constructions of less destructive solutions such as limited fasting, praying, meditating, or even haircutting.

Intergenerational patterns are embedded and negotiated within a collective consciousness. For example, a young woman leaving for college thinks about her decision as pleasing to her parents, grandparents, siblings, and, lastly, herself. Therefore, any exploration of her ambivalence toward this decision must include discussion of the implications of the decision for family and community relationships. Relationships are other-directed rather than self-centered. Spirituality and simplicity are applauded, and family-centered decisions take priority over individual preferences. Within the family of origin, older men assume decision-making authority over all members of the family. Fathers are responsible for the education, economics, and values of their male children and for the care of their elderly parents. Emotional connectedness between sons and fathers, as well as among other extended family members, is not expected. However, intimacy between the son and mother is emphasized. Fathers are responsible for their daughters' dowry and marriage; uncles or older male siblings take on this responsibility in the event of a father's death. Mothers expect their sons to control their wives with regard to money, work, and social activities. Older women gain status and power through the mother-in-law role; younger women are socialized by their mothers and sisters to idealize the role of mother-in-law. The cultural system (i.e., caste and karma with their values of tolerance and passivity), supported by the male family lineage (endorsing tolerance and passivity), embraces this process. In this system, women realize power by exerting control over women of lesser status. Caretaking of grandchildren and food preparation are used as covert means of gaining power in family relations. A mother-in-law, in charge of preparing food while the daughter-in-law works, might cook only according to her son's desires. Young children are generally overprotected by grandparents while being taught to respect their elders. Children are taught to avoid direct eye contact with their elders and to avoid disagreeing with them. Older sisters-in-law assume a degree of power over younger women entering the male-centered family system.

Education of male children is considered necessary for the economic needs of the entire family; education for female children increases their marketability as brides. Aging parents are cared for within the family by adult married male children and, in rare instances, by female children who have families of their own. The son provides economi-

cally and administratively for parents, but it is always his wife who does the actual caretaking in the home.

Child-rearing is a shared responsibility of the women in the male-oriented extended-family system. These women can be aunts or friends of the family from India who visit for extended periods during the family's initial years of child-rearing. When young mothers are forced to parent without this extended-kinship system, children are more at risk because family conflicts tend to be expressed in the mother-child dyad rather than in the marital dyad.

Power in Western marriages is directly connected to the economic resources of each partner. This notion of power and relationships is less applicable to Asian Indian families because a couple's economic resources are distributed across the extended male-oriented family system (Conklin, 1988). Unlike the white, American, middle-class nuclear family, in which marriage stands at the center of the family system, men and their mothers are at the center of the Asian Indian family system. The mother-son tie is prominent in both Hindu and Christian Asian Indian families (Almeida, 1996; de Souza, 1975). Sons provide their mothers and grandmothers with the ultimate pride and status afforded women in this life (Issmer, 1989). Young wives do not participate in this system of power, even when they contribute economically to the family unit (Chakrabortty, 1978).

Marriage is complicated by overarching problems of caste, dowry, expensive weddings, and arranged marriages, which are common among Indians in the United States as well as in India. When the family chooses to emphasize college education over marriage, or if the child asserts his or her personal rights over the parents' choice of mates or chooses career and money over marriage, major conflicts arise within the family system. Parents expect daughters to be married between 18 and 22 years of age and sons between the ages of 22 and 26. Many social gatherings by parents are spent planning and choosing possible mates for their children. Weddings are showcases for future brides and their grooms. When marriage does not occur, parents lack a clear role in their adult child's life. This can be a devastating loss for parents, because this transition is so important for them. Marriage rather than education is the primary marker of the transition to adulthood. The process of differentiation of self from family, which has various implications for Asian Indians as a result of their cultural norms, is particularly problematic at this stage. Despite their efforts to create choices for their sons and daughters, cultural expectations for arranged marriages take precedence.

An Asian Indian family entered therapy because of the 21-year-old daughter's difficulty completing her last semester of college. They expressed their helplessness in dealing with her launching. The mother said, "Shiva is very immature and irresponsible; it worries me that she does not know the meaning of money or getting a job, and yet she is about to graduate. I think of her as a selfish brat sometimes. She says she is not ready to think about marriage, and I believe it sometimes, but all of our friends and relatives think I am being neglectful in my responsibility to find her a nice man. If she waits until she is 30, then by the time she is 40, when she should be taking care of us, she and her husband will still have the responsibility of young children. I might be too old to be the kind of grandparent I have to be. Of course, I know that if Shiva gets married, then I will be pushing her to give me grandchildren, so I suppose I have to trust that my husband's and my choice to provide her with some independence will keep her loyal to our expectations as well."

An Asian Indian woman's status within the family is determined by the gender order of her children. First-born males are preferred. First-born females are vulnerable to conflict between the mother and her in-laws and are perceived as diminishing the father's status with the deities. However, a second-born male child helps to normalize the situation. For many families a second-born female child following a first-born female child is at risk for premature death through malnutrition and abuse, even in the United States, if the family does not have sufficient emotional, social, and economic support. Many female children in homes where there is a physically or developmentally delayed male child may present a range of psychological problems. The girls are often given an excess of adult responsibilities, not rewarded for their achievements, and isolated from their peers. Male children offer the family greater economic support and thereby lead to better marital opportunities for the female children in the family. A woman's relationship with her mother-in-law may become strained and the marriage may suffer if she is infertile and thus does not meet the family's role expectations. Sons who cannot support the elderly family members, widowed mothers, or unmarried sisters extort large dowries from their brides as solutions to this intergenerational legacy (Ramu, 1987).

These intergenerational patterns often conflict with Asian Indian acculturation (Sluzki, 1979). Although most Asian Indians accommodate to the work ethic and value of education, they maintain strong cultural ties to Asian Indian concepts of marriage, child-rearing, parenting, and the sharing and allocation of economic resources.

Western values of privacy and individualism conflict with Indian values of collectivity and family-centeredness. In the context of separation, less acculturated families view adolescent and young adult struggles around independence as disloyal cutting off from the family and culture. When Asian Indians speak of respect, they mean obedience to the family and culture. Similarly, it is difficult for them to comprehend that some aspects of the Western ideal of love includes separation and independence from the family of origin. For Asian Indians, the concept of love includes loyalty and control (Mukherjee, 1991).

Families are most likely to enter treatment through referral by outside organizations, such as schools and physicians, although in recent years, couples have entered therapy because of troubled marriages. Practitioners need to determine how the presenting problem fits with the belief system of the dominant culture by considering the following factors:

- Life-style in India before coming to the United States, to assess similarity to and difference from current life-style as well as status and story of immigration.

- Household composition, social organization, and domestic functioning and activities. (Concept of household may include relatives in India and in-laws here.)
- Religious affiliation.
- Details and status of arranged marriage as it relates to current intergenerational anxieties (marital satisfaction, as defined by dowry status, negotiation of "second-shift" responsibilities) when women work out of the home, money, child-rearing, emotional nurturing, and social activities.
- Relationship of couples to the in-law system, especially that of the husband.
- Young men's and women's, as well as children's, sense of physical beauty in a culture that values and often eroticizes white-skinned beauty and a caste system that embraces these values.

Clinical observations reveal that Asian Indians do not remain in therapy for long (six to nine months is typical). Therapists can help families with children to work through intergenerational conflicts by helping them to examine the underlying assumptions of individualism and self-determination as they relate to success and achievement and eliciting examples of individualism that demonstrate disregard for others (e.g., talking back, visiting friends whose parents are unknown to the family, not accounting for small amounts of money spent, talking on the telephone) in contrast with examples of individualism that are positive (e.g., good study habits, doing chores, spending allowances wisely, using good judgment with friends and recreation). Such work allows parents to promote their children's success while simultaneously addressing concerns regarding family disloyalty. Work with couples and in-law systems must empower women and help men to find constructive solutions that will support their nurturing of their partners while they maintain loyalties toward their families of origin.

Asian Indians address their problems within the hierarchy of "father knows best" and "mothers

and daughters should obey." The emotional difficulties of sons are ignored even when they are severe. Since emotions are neither identified nor acknowledged, families should be encouraged to speak about their problems within the context of their immigrant story and cultural heritage. Therapists must address family members' sense of loss over leaving home while struggling to be successful in their new country. Engaging the women in stories and myths about strong Asian Indian women can help them to achieve balance in their new culture (Almeida, 1996). Therapists should encourage families to discuss these experiences and identify their feelings so that families do not split their emotions from real life. Splitting has allowed men and women to uphold values of tolerance and passivity even when such values are not in their best interests. Therapists must inquire into the family's beliefs about tolerance (caste) and fate (karma). Asian Indians will not freely discuss these cultural beliefs unless they are specifically asked about them. Their responses might be couched in laughter, denial, or awkwardness. Gentle and respectful persistence will facilitate engagement of the family.

JEWISH FAMILIES

Judaism has the unusual distinction of being both a religion and an ethnic identity (Farber, Mindel, & Lazerwitz, 1988). Jews, who have a long tradition of intellectual debate and dialogue, carry on a never-ending discussion about who is a Jew and what it means to be a Jew. This debate has been engendered in part by the Jewish history of exclusion, discrimination, and wandering, culminating in the Holocaust and the founding of Israel. As waves of Jewish immigrants entered the United States, including early settlers from Germany who were relatively wealthy and assimilated, the poor and less assimilated (more observant) Eastern Europeans before and after World War I, Holocaust survivors, and, most recently, Russian and Israeli Jews, the question of essential Jewishness has continued to be debated. This is a legacy that has led to sensitivity over issues of discrimination and a sense of being "other." Although "Jewishness" may not be apparent to the outsider, most Jews are sensitive to interactions that might be perceived as anti-Semitic and may adopt a defensive posture that seems inexplicable to non-Jews.

Jews in the United States have been both fearful of and fascinated by assimilation into mainstream culture (Rosen & Weltman, 1996). Many families are overwhelmingly concerned that family members marry within the faith or, if members marry outside the faith, that they maintain their Jewish traditions. A primary concern for many parents who move to a new community is whether their children will have other Jewish children with whom to play and date. The issue is further complicated by the diversity of Jewish religious practice; acceptable Jewishness in one family may be considered too assimilated or too religious in another.

Families often enter treatment to deal with conflicting feelings with regard to intermarriage, which may be perceived as destroying the integrity of the family and the faith. Generally, the families' most immediate concerns revolve around who, if anyone, will be expected to convert, who will perform the wedding, and how the grandchildren will be raised. Intermarriage is often felt to be a failure on the part of the parents, who somehow should have prevented it from happening. Such feelings exist even in families that are culturally rather than religiously observant Jews and are not affiliated with a synagogue.

When intermarriage is an issue, it is important that the therapist attempt to gather concerned family members together. The parent or grandparent who is most upset may be the most difficult to engage. Because Jews traditionally have had a high regard for discourse and the transmission of cultural tradition and history, it can be helpful to review family history and to engage the family in searching for others within the extended family for whom intermarriage did not result in leaving the faith. Jewish families respond well to information and the sharing of stories; therefore, referral to a support group and/or interfaith classes run by Reform synagogues or other Jewish organizations can be effective.

Regardless of geographic distance, maintaining close family ties is important to Jewish families. It is useful for the therapist to identify family members who are critical to the treatment process but who are not immediately available. Soliciting their involvement as consultants (through inclusion in family sessions, a joint phone call, or a letter) can help to promote change.

Jewish families' focus on children, particularly their education and nurturing, can be a mixed blessing. Children are expected to be a source of pride and pleasure for parents and grandparents. However, children may find it difficult to be the focus of so much attention, with so many people having an expressed point of view. Young people may find it difficult to operate independently in their own interests. Separation and individuation are difficult to achieve if the family has rigid definitions of acceptable and successful behaviors. Young Jewish men and women often enter treatment because they are having difficulty dealing with issues of enmeshment. Parents may perceive themselves as being generous and supportive and feel hurt by their children's efforts to become more independent. Reframing and relabeling their adult children's need to separate as successful and productive behavior can be an effective treatment approach.

The changing mores of late twentieth-century American life have been stressful for Jewish families. Traditionally, Jewish women were expected to stay home, complying with the dictum to "be fruitful and multiply." Jewish law has rigidly defined rules for men's and women's behavior, women having a minor function in religious ritual in the synagogue. Reform and Conservative congregations have opened all aspects of religious observance to women, including being ordained as a rabbi; in contrast, Orthodox Jews continue to maintain strict adherence to the teachings of the Talmud, the traditional compendium of Jewish law that was written over a 500-year period during the first millennium. Although many Jewish laws concerning gender roles are barely observed in all but Orthodox families, these laws still have a subtle influence on role definition and expectations.

In Jewish families, women have traditionally held power at home while the husband faced the work world and the synagogue. Jewish mothers have been responsible for maintaining religious tradition and culture. However, because many Jewish women were employed outside the home during the Depression in the 1930s, many families remember grandmothers or other female relatives who worked, generally out of necessity. Their daughters were primarily homemakers, and their granddaughters now expect themselves to be "supermoms" (Hyman, 1991). The dilemma faced by all three generations (and now the fourth) has been how to reconcile social expectations with cultural expectations. Women who saw their mothers struggling to support the family during the Depression came to value their homemaker role. Their granddaughters have aspired to raise their family while participating in the professional world. Issues faced by American women in the 1980s and 1990s have been especially complicated for Jewish women because of the emphasis Jewish culture places on education, social consciousness, and tradition. In some situations, it may be the grandmother or great-grandmother who can serve as a role model for both working and maintaining a family.

Significant shifts in the role of the Jewish husband/father have also occurred. Jewish men have experienced discrimination and violence in the larger community. Traditionally, their home has been the place where they expected to achieve respect and authority. When both spouses work, the father may be called upon or may wish to be a more active parent than was his father. However, when he does take an active role, he risks the disapproval of his own parents, who may be uncomfortable in seeing him in an unconventional role. The extended family may also not be supportive of these changes.

Religious observance is another source of intergenerational conflict. The majority of Jews in the United States are affiliated with Reform congregations, which do not follow many of the laws (for example, keeping kosher, not driving or working on the Sabbath) that Orthodox and Conservative Jews follow. Intergenerational conflict may arise over the perceived religious laxity or conservatism of family members. Parents may be disappointed if their adult child chooses not to be affiliated with a synagogue or chooses not to have a bar mitzvah for their grandson or a bat mitzvah for their granddaughter when they turn 13.

Conversely, some young people have become more observant of the Jewish faith than their families, perhaps joining an Orthodox congregation and living in a style that is foreign to their families. Grandchildren's being unable to eat in their grandparents' non-kosher home can have a profound effect on intergenerational relationships. Conflicts in some families may occur if younger family members emigrate to Israel, thus separating parents from their children and grandchildren. Families may enter treatment to deal with feelings of loss and may need help in developing new ways to interact and to develop rituals that accept the differences in religious observance and practice.

The influx of immigrants from the former Soviet Union that began in the mid-1970s has significantly changed the face of the American Jewish community. Many of these families have come to the United States with little knowledge of Judaism, having been victims of anti-Semitism and State-declared atheism. Because of financial and living conditions it was not unusual for three generations of the family to live together and depend on each other; this pattern has frequently persisted in the United States and can lead to complex intergenerational patterns of relating (Feigen, 1996).

Jewish families tend to seek expert opinions and may ask a therapist many questions about professional degrees and competence. Although such inquiries may make practitioners feel uncomfortable and challenged, they may help clients to feel more comfortable in therapy. Directing Jewish families to appropriate reading materials about problems can be helpful because Jews tend to value being well-informed.

Jews have been avid consumers of psychotherapy, in part as a result of their comfort with discourse, their search for solutions, and the expectation that family life should follow predefined rules (Rosen & Weltman, 1996). However, extensive analysis does not always lead to resolution of problems. The therapist may find structural interventions and assigned tasks helpful in challenging verbal interactions that have not led to change.

Families may need to be reminded that the goal of therapy is not to tell a good story or to be "right" in the eyes of the therapist, but to resolve the conflict or assuage the pain that brought the family to therapy.

REFERENCES

Almeida, R. V. (1990). Asian Indian mothers. *Journal of Feminist Family Therapy, 2*(2): 33–39.

Almeida, R. V. (1996). Asian Indian families. In M. McGoldrick, J. Giordano, & J. K. Pearce (Eds.), *Ethnicity and family therapy* (2nd ed.). New York: The Guilford Press.

Barrabe, P., & von Mering, O. (1953). Ethnic variations in mental stress in families with psychotic children. *Social Problems, 1,* 48–53.

Boyd-Franklin, N. (1989). *Black families in therapy.* New York: The Guilford Press.

Bumiller, E. (1990). *May you be the mother of a hundred sons: A journey among the women of India.* New York: Random House.

Byrne, N., & McCarthy, I. (1986, September 15). Irish women. Family Therapy Training Program Conference, Robert Wood Johnson Medical School, Piscataway, NJ.

Chakrabortty, K. (1978). *The conflicting worlds of working mothers.* Calcutta, India: Progressive Publishers.

Comas-Diaz, L. (1989). Culturally relevant issues for Hispanics. In V. R. Koslow & E. Salett (Eds.), *Crossing cultures in mental health.* Washington, DC: Society for International Education, Training and Research.

Conklin, G. H. (1988). The influence of economic development and patterns of conjugal power and extended family residence in India. *Journal of Comparative Family Studies, 19,* 187–205.

Connery, D. S. (1970). *The Irish.* New York: Simon & Schuster.

de Souza, A. (1975). *Women in contemporary India.* New Delhi, India: Manohar.

Diner, H. R. (1983). *Erin's daughters in America.* Baltimore, MD: Johns Hopkins University Press.

Farber, B., Mindel, C. H., & Lazerwitz, B. (1988). The Jewish American family. In C. H. Mindel & R. W. Habenstein (Eds.), *Ethnic families in America: Patterns and variations.* New York: Elsevier.

Feigen, I. (1996). Soviet Jewish families. In M. McGoldrick, J. Giordano, & J. K. Pearce (Eds.), *Ethnicity and family therapy,* (2nd ed.), (pp. 631–637). New York: The Guilford Press.

Fogelman, E. (1996). Israeli families. In M. McGoldrick, J. Giordano, & J. K. Pearce (Eds.), *Ethnicity and family therapy* (2nd ed.). New York: The Guilford Press.

Garcia-Preto, N. (1990). Hispanic mothers. *Journal of Feminist Family Therapy, 2*(2), 15–21.

Garcia-Preto, N. (1994). On the Bridge. *Family Therapy Networker, 18*(4), 35–37.

Garcia-Preto, N. (1996). Puerto Rican families. In M. McGoldrick, J. Giordano, & J. K. Pearce (Eds.). *Ethnicity and family therapy* (2nd ed.), (pp. 183–199). New York: The Guilford Press.

Giordano, J. & McGoldrick, M. (1996). Italian families, in M. McGoldrick, J. Giordano, & J. K. Pearce (Eds.). *Ethnicity and family therapy* (2nd ed.), (pp. 567–582). New York: The Guilford Press.

Gomez, A. G. (1982). Puerto Rican Americans. In A. Gaw (Ed.), *Cross cultural psychiatry* (pp. 109–136). Boston: John Wright.

Habach, E. (1972). Ni machismo, ni hembriso. In *Coleccion: Protesta.* Caracas, Venezuela: Publicaciones EPLA.

Hines, P. (1990). The family life cycle of poor Black families. In B. Carter & M. McGoldrick (Eds.). *The Expanded Family Life Cycle: Individual, Family and Community Perspectives.* Boston: Allyn & Bacon.

Hines, P. (1990). African American mothers. *Journal of Feminist Family Therapy, 2*(2): 23–32.

Hines, P., & Boyd-Franklin, N. (1996). African American families. In M. McGoldrick, J. Giordano, & J. K. Pearce (Eds.), *Ethnicity and family therapy* (2nd ed.). New York: Guilford Press.

Hyman, P. (1991). Gender and the immigrant Jewish experience. In J. R. Baskin (Ed.), *Jewish women in historical perspective.* Detroit, MI: Wayne State University Press.

Issmer, S. D. (1989). The special function of out-of-home care in India. *Child Welfare, 68,* 228–232.

Kim, B.-L. C. (1981). *Women in the shadows: A handbook for service providers working with Asian wives of U.S. military personnel.* La Jolla, CA: National Committee Concerned with Asian Wives of U.S. Servicemen.

Mahmoud, V. (1998). The double bind dynamics of racism. In M. McGoldrick (Ed.), *Revisioning family therapy: Race, culture and gender in clinical practice.* New York: The Guilford Press.

Malyala, S., Kamaraju, S., & Ramana, K. V. (1984). Untouchability: need for a new approach. *Indian Journal of Social Work, 45,* 361–369.

Matsuoka, J. K. (1990). Differential acculturation among Vietnamese refugees. *Social Work, 35,* 341–345.

MacCurtain, M., & O'Corrain, D. (Eds.). (1978). *Women in Irish society: The historical dimension.* Dublin: Arlin House.

McGill, D. & Pearce, J. K. (1996). American families with English ancestors from the Colonial Era: Anglo Americans. In M. McGoldrick, J. Giordano, & J. K. Pearce (Eds.). *Ethnicity and family therapy* (2nd ed.). New York: The Guilford Press.

McGoldrick, M. (1991). Irish mothers. *Journal of Feminist Family Therapy, 2*(2).

McGoldrick, M. (1996). Irish families. In M. McGoldrick, J. Giordano, & J. K. Pearce (Eds.), *Ethnicity and family therapy* (2nd ed.). New York: The Guilford Press.

McGoldrick, M., & Garcia-Preto, N. (1984). Ethnic intermarriage: Implications for therapy. *Family Process, 23/4.*

McGoldrick, M., Garcia-Preto, N., Hines, P., & Lee, E. (1989). Ethnicity and women. In M. McGoldrick, C. Anderson, & F. Walsh (Eds.), *Women in families.* New York: W. W. Norton.

McGoldrick, M., Giordano, J., & Pearce, J. K. (1996). *Ethnicity and family therapy, 2nd edition.* New York: The Guilford Press.

McKenna, A. (1979). Attitudes of Irish mothers to child rearing. *Journal of Comparative Family Studies, 10,* 227–251.

Mukherjee, B. (1991). *Jasmine.* New York: Fawcett Crest.

Pinderhughes, E. (1998). Black geneology revisited: Restorying an African American family. In M. McGoldrick (Ed.), *Revisioning family therapy: Race, culture and gender in clinical practice.* New York: The Guilford Press.

Ramu, G. N. (1987). Indian husbands: Their role perceptions and performance in single- and dual-earner families. *Journal of Marriage and the Family, 49,* 903–915.

Rosen, E. J., & Weltman, S. (1996). Jewish families. In M. McGoldrick, J. Giordano, & J. K. Pearce (Eds.), *Ethnicity and family therapy* (2nd ed.). New York: The Guilford Press.

Rudd, J. M. (1984). Irish American families: The mother child dyad. Unpublished master's thesis, Smith College School of Social Work.

Scheper-Hughes, N. (1979). *Saints, scholars, and schizophrenics.* Berkeley, CA: University of California Press.

Schneider, S. W. (1985). *Jewish and female: A guide and sourcebook for today's Jewish woman.* New York: Simon & Schuster.

Segal, U. A. (1991). Cultural variables in Asian Indian families. *Families in Society, 72,* 233–241.

Sluzki, C. (1979). Migration and family conflict. *Family Process, 18,* 379–390.

Stack, C. (1974). *All our kin.* New York: Harper & Row.

Stevens, E. (1973). Machismo and marianismo. *Transaction Society, 10*(6), 57–63.

Wadley, S. (1977). Women and the Hindu tradition. *Journal of Women in Culture and Society, 3*(1), 113–128.

CHAPTER 5

SOCIAL CLASS AND THE FAMILY LIFE CYCLE

JODIE KLIMAN
WILLIAM MADSEN

In class-stratified society, social class shapes all families' lives, influencing the range, timing, and nature of their choices. Ideas about class and its impact on family life are often vague, contradictory, unexamined, and unspoken. Dominant U.S. discourse silences discussion of class, acknowledging only extremes of wealth or poverty. Contradictory myths that our society is classless *and* that anyone can be upwardly mobile obscure and strengthen the shaping power of class. Therapists must listen for both dominant and marginalized ideas about class's influence on the life cycle, exploring how families make meaning of their experiences and relate class to the paths they travel together.

This chapter adds a class perspective to an increasingly complex understanding of the family life cycle as embedded in multiple cultural contexts (Carter & McGoldrick, 1988). Mindful of the risks of stereotyping when incorporating class considerations of the family life cycle, we seek to avoid oversimplified generalizations as we attend to the central role of class in the shape and timing of movement through the family life cycle. Complex circumstances define the unique twists, turns, dead-ends, and open spaces of any one family's life. Some circumstances are clearly functions of class. Poor families do not expect grandparents to help with down payments; middle-class families

We thank David Trimble and Kathy Weingarten for invaluable conceptual and stylistic ideas and Laura Chasin, Jeffrey Kerr, and Michele Bograd for helpful conversation on class and families.

do not expect the parents of 18-year-olds to be their grandchildren's caregivers. Class intensifies or softens the impact of seemingly unrelated family crises, such as divorce, abuse, disability, or untimely death.

People living in relation to different class narratives and contexts make different meaning of being a 6-year-old or a 17-year-old, her parent or grandparent, or the child of a 70-year-old. Class-based assumptions inform negotiations of obligation and privilege between generations. The age at which people "should" become responsible for themselves, children, parents, or extended kin varies with economic and social circumstances. Class standing and intervals between generations change when the youngest of six children in a working-class family becomes the first to go to college, delay marriage, and have his first child at the age when his father had his last. They change when a breadwinner's early death brings poverty.

Class-influenced narratives permeate expectations of family life: when and if children leave home, whether youths have time or money to "find themselves," and even how long people live. These narratives—received or created, consistent or contradictory—build on generations of learning about class and the family life cycle. Because dominant U.S. discourse denies class, families and therapists may not see family experiences as being about class. Social class nevertheless shapes the timings, expectations, and cautionary tales of opportunity and risk that families carry through their lives (Fulmer, 1988; Stack & Burton, 1993). Class narratives contribute to family, network, and community stories about what is possible, acceptable, or conceivable (Kliman, 1998; Madsen, 1996).

UNDERSTANDING SOCIAL CLASS

Therapists' understanding of class evolves with the class and cultural narratives of our families and networks. They change as the shifting economy transforms family life cycle challenges for our family, community, and professional lives. Our clients' and colleagues' class experiences challenge and add to our understanding. As part of a society which mystifies class, we cannot know what social class is, but we can explore its workings and its intersection with the family life cycle.

Class is a difficult concept to define. It involves multiple relationships to economic and social phenomena, including race, ethnicity, religion, gender, sexuality, geography, and mental and physical ability. Prevailing definitions of class are inadequate. When dominant U.S. discourse does acknowledges class inequality, it decontextualizes it, explaining class standing with individual attributes, as if laziness, ignorance, dependence, and depravity cause poverty while initiative, talent, and competitiveness generate wealth. A contradictory explanation suggests a natural order of things: "We will always have the poor among us." Such explanations obscure the fact that one's economic and social circumstances exist in relation to those of others; privileged classes live well at others' expense. In 1989, the top 1 percent of the nation's households owned 48 percent and the top 20 percent owned 93 percent of U.S. wealth, or the sum of one's assets (bank accounts, insurance, inheritances, investments, real estate, etc.) minus one's debts. The bottom 20 percent, owing more than they owned, held −2.3 percent of the wealth (Sklar, 1995, p. 6). As the economy shifts its resources upward, this inequity grows. In 1960, the ratio of average CEO income to average worker income was 41:1 (Sklar, 1995, p. 10). By 1996, it had soared to 209:1, by far the highest ratio in the industrialized world (Reingold, 1997).

As the income gap widens, the wealthy successfully lobby for huge tax breaks in personal and corporate income, capital gains, and estate taxes. In 1959, personal income over $400,000 per year was taxed at 91 percent, creating a de facto income cap. By the 1990s, the top tax rate had declined to 31 percent (Barlett & Steele, 1994). Yet from 1993 to 1997 alone, states erased 3 million people from the welfare rolls without tracking whether they were employed above the poverty line (Jackson, 1997) or at all. Popular views of a morally neutral continuum (upper, upper-middle, middle, lower-middle, and lower socioeconomic status) overlook the relationship of one class's wealth and privilege to another class's poverty and oppression. The "upper" classes benefit from an exploitative class relationship with those "below." Class stratification is a predictable structural outcome of free-market, capitalist society, along with the patriarchy, racism, and colonialism on which our society is founded.

Class definitions are context sensitive. Money defines class, as do inconsistently invoked criteria of social status including ethnicity, religion, and education. A professor is seen as being in a higher class than a contractor who has equal income—unless the professor is a Latina single mother and the contractor is an Anglo-American man from "an old family." Women's and children's class standing plummets after divorce. A Black executive has less effective class standing than White subordinates when trying to hail a cab, join a country club, buy an elegant house, or ensure his children's class stability. In restaurants or hotels, Whites may ask him to serve them. Popular descriptions of people who speak with their mouths full or ornately decorate their homes and bodies as having "no class" reflect a troubling discourse in which the trappings of class privilege carry moral and aesthetic superiority.

Familiar categories of class do not hold up in complex, rapidly changing postindustrial society. Although no schema can adequately reflect current economic structures' intricate connections with other social structures, we provisionally describe the following classes, in order of descending access to power and resources: the business-owning class, the professional-managerial class, the working class, and the underclass, all of which stand in relation to each other.

The *business-owning class* (or capitalist class) owns the vast bulk of the nation's wealth and has more political power and influence than all other "interest groups" combined. The very top 1 to 2 percent (also called the ruling class) of this class are the wealthiest owners of big business. Almost exclusively Anglo American (British American) and almost exclusively Protestant, their "old money" and power go back many generations. The other members of the business-owning class own large and medium-size businesses that produce services (including professional services such as for-profit health care, major law firms, or entertainment) or goods. They are predominantly White Protestants. Even the richest people of color and non-Protestants in the Fortune 1000 have less prestige and influence than monied Anglo-American Protestants, whose class roots go deep. The business-owning class depends on the work of the classes below them for its income and personal maintenance.

Most Americans—from prosperous business owners to the working poor—define themselves and are defined as "middle-class," so the term has little descriptive value. We therefore divide this confounding identification into two distinct classes. We use Ehrenreich's (1989) *professional managerial class* to describe the more privileged portion of those popularly called the "middle class." The work of the professional-managerial class supports the economic and cultural status quo. This class includes small and family business owners, managers, salaried or self-employed professionals, highly educated technical workers, academics and the intelligentsia, elected officials, and mid- to high-level government bureaucrats. Even wealthy members of this class, unlike business owners, do not control the means of their production. Entertainers, athletes, and writers who make millions at the peak of their careers can become unmarketable with age, disability, or new trends. This class places great value on career (as opposed to job or income); in recent decades, paid work has been recognized as fulfilling for both genders. Concurrently, however, many professional-managerial workers find themselves less fulfilled and more overworked as they lose economic stability and autonomy and have more experiences in common with the working class.

The less privileged among the so-called "middle class" are better described as the *working class,* traditionally divided into white-, blue-, and, more recently, pink-collar workers. These divisions blur somewhat as service work and skilled technical work replace factory work, working-class women's job possibilities expand, white-collar jobs require college, and real wages fall. Education and economic stability provide the best distinction between the upper (white-collar) and lower (blue- and pink-collar) ranks of the working class. The latter are more vulnerable to un(der)employment. Many working-class families live in grinding poverty, with low wages and no benefits. The work ethic is highly valued for this class, but expectations for work satisfaction are low.

The underclass consists of permanently unemployed, or illegitimately employed people living outside the mainstream economy and often outside the work ethic. They include those living without hope in communities whose employment base and social grounding have disappeared (Wilson, 1996). Some operate in an underground economy of drugs, weapons, the sex trade, and violent crime, often imprisoned, occasionally achieving some wealth. They also include the disabled, disturbed, or traumatized living on (or off) public assistance (Inclán and Ferran, 1990).

Class weaves into personal, family, and community ties to local, national, and global economies. The extent to which work is alienating or self-determining, nonexistent, dead-end, or hopeful, shapes narratives of self, family, and community, delineating one's expectations of life (Wilson, 1996). Job and salary define one's place in the economy, as do inheritances, unearned income, credit lines, consumption, job security, and debt. So do accessibility and security of employment and how many paychecks one is from homelessness. Beliefs about education, intergenerational responsibilities, when (or if) to start work or retire, and who cares for the elderly ill are forged in earlier generations' class contexts but shift with economic realities. A family's place in the economy is also defined by access to economic and social resources, which are influenced by race, ethnicity, gender, sexual orientation, geographical region, and physical and mental well-being. If equally educated men of different races have different chances of getting mortgages, good jobs, or dying young, their families' life courses will diverge accordingly. Because men make more money than women and because gays and lesbians have less class privilege than heterosexuals, the children of sisters who are partnered with a middle-class man and a middle-class woman, respectively, are likely to have very different class experiences. The children of a middle-class, divorced mother who is disabled by chronic illness may end up supporting her as young adults, rather than being supported by her.

Class position regulates access to disposable income. Preferential interest rates ensure that monied people can borrow liberally, without debts precluding retirement or inheritance. Class affects whether kin, neighbors, or paid caretakers help with children, the elderly, or sick family members. Class determines which adolescents drop out, work through college, help support the family, or expect parents to finance college, rent, and vacations. Some parents can remove lead from their homes; others can only pray that toddlers won't suffer neurological damage from eating lead paint chips, intensifying family needs through the life cycle. In 1996, 25 percent of all U.S. families had no health insurance (Knox, 1996), further stressing and shortening the lives of millions of working and unwillingly unemployed families.

Class structure regulates access to information, connections, and influence. Mediocre students from "old money" gain entry to top colleges whose buildings are named for their ancestors. A professor gets a life-saving second medical opinion and dances, thirty years later, at her grandson's wedding. Her nanny, a single uninsured "illegal" alien, is turned away at the emergency room and dies of a treatable illness, leaving her 17-year-old

to care for siblings. A stockbroker has his assistant update his Web site and help his teenaged son browse the Web for summer travel in the time that it takes an unskilled, unemployed father and his 20-year-old son to apply in person for three advertised minimum-wage jobs.

Class involves a multilevel relationship between families and the economy. It intersects with community. Boyd-Franklin (1993) argued that definitions of class vary across racial communities. Poor Black communities, for example, may define poor working families as middle-class because of their employment and "values, aspirations, and expectations for their children" (pp. 363–364). Wilson (1996) argued that in depressed communities, people rarely can help each other to find jobs, school does not prepare students for the workforce, and people often lose the connection to legitimate work "as a regular, and regulating force in their lives [or] a central experience of adult life" (pp. 52–53).

Consider the family of a janitor and a hospital aide. Living in the wife's parents' two-family house on a gentrifying block, the couple are "poor neighbors" whose children may be ashamed to bring home middle-class friends. In a ghetto or rural hamlet with dying schools, theirs would be a rare two-income household, and their children would be thought unusual for taking school seriously. The future possibilities of families that are exposed to such different realities would diverge accordingly. In one community, this couple's son might become a teacher, father, and local activist who will help them in old age; in another, he might become a gang member, a drive-by shooting statistic, or a farm worker who is disabled on the job. The child of teachers at the edge of a ghetto whose arson, drugs, and violence make their home unsellable and the child of drug dealers a few blocks away are both (if not equally) at risk of undereducation, violence, or seduction by drugs or gangs. Class position and its meanings extend beyond the household to social networks and beyond.

In a racist and classist society, race and class fundamentally organize family life; each shapes our experience of the other (Kliman, 1994). Together, they fashion families' dilemmas and possibilities. Dominant U.S. discourse equates "White" with "middle-class" and "Black" with "poor." Recent attacks on affirmative action and welfare can be read as coded racism and sexism. (Jackson, 1997). Racism inequitably impoverishes people of color and ensures that almost all the very wealthy are White. While 12 percent of Whites live under the poverty line, 15 percent of Asians and Pacific Islanders, 31 percent of Latinos and Native Americans, and 33 percent of African Americans do so (Sklar, 1995, pp. 11–12; U.S. Bureau of the Census, 1994, pp. 475–476). As for children, 17 percent of Whites, 40 percent of Latinos, and 47 percent of Blacks live under the poverty line. Among the aged, three times more Blacks than Whites are poor (U.S. Bureau of the Census, 1994, p. 476). Job and educational discrimination make "middle-class" status far less secure across the generations for people of color. Racial discrimination in education and decreasing job opportunities for unskilled and semiskilled workers in postindustrial society leave over 15 percent of adult and 47 percent of adolescent Black men officially unemployed (Rubin, 1994). Still more are underemployed, no longer looking, or earning nearly one third less than Whites (Rubin, 1994).

Patriarchy and class structure combine powerfully to shape family life, with different implications for male and female family members. Although most women are employed (reflecting economic necessity as much as changing gender politics), the glass ceiling is intact. Across class, women, on whom the responsibilities for child care or elder care and health emergencies usually fall, earn less than men and account for most involuntarily part-time and temporary workers. However, the economic strain on female caretakers and their families varies with class. Family illness can mean long-term unemployment or exhausting double duty for working-class women, who cannot call on paid help or voluntarily at-home relatives. Educational expectations and opportunities are generally less for White women than for White men. In a racist twist to sexism, however, women of color, although the lowest-paid of all groups, are

better educated and more often employed than men of color, perhaps because they are less threatening to Whites (Boyd-Franklin, 1993; De La Cancela, 1991; see also Chapter 19). Because women get identified with their men's class status, women of all races who are single, divorced, widowed, or in lesbian couples have significantly lower income and status than those with male partners (Penelope, 1994). Yet single-mother households' greater poverty (U.S. Bureau of the Census, 1994, p. 470) and stress levels are blamed on mothers, not on capitalism, racism, patriarchy, or fathers who don't support children.

Class and gender intersect differently for families of different races. Unemployment, racism, poverty, and violence reduce African American men's participation in family life; Black males ages 15–19 are shot to death ten times more often than their White peers; Black men ages 20–24 are fatally shot at eleven times the rate of their White agemates (U.S. Bureau of the Census, 1994, p. 101). Although these racial disparities disappear with higher class standing (Wilson, 1996), in 1989, one fourth of all Black men in their twenties were incarcerated, on probation, or on parole, compared to one tenth of Latino men and one sixteenth of White men (Sklar, 1995, pp. 120–121). Although Black women are more employable than Black men, coupling offers economic advantage: 15 percent of Black children in two-parent homes live on under $15,000, compared to 68 percent of those living with mothers only (U.S. Bureau of the Census, 1994, p. 66). These figures reflect the synergy of classism, racism, and sexism.

CLASS INFLUENCES ON THE FAMILY LIFE CYCLE: CHALLENGES AND POSSIBILITIES

When many variables combine to shape family life, definitive statements about class-specific normative sequences and timings are properly suspect. Nevertheless, experiences that are widely shared within a social class contribute to class-influenced narratives about family life cycle challenges, resources, constraints, and opportunities. These narratives in turn shape how, whether, and when families prepare for and navigate developmental milestones and dilemmas. Wealthier, more educated people tend to enjoy healthier and longer lives, have fewer children, and have children later, when they are better prepared financially and economically, than do those with less privilege. Poverty hits the young hardest, with great impact on their family lives; 22 percent of all children (some of whom are themselves parents) live below the poverty line (Sklar, 1995, pp. 11–12). Note that the 1993 poverty line for a family of four, $14,654 (Sklar, 1995, p. 12), doesn't account for soaring housing, child care, and medical costs. Of all U.S. homes with householders age 15 to 24, 38 percent live in poverty, compared with 11 percent for householders age 35 to 44 (U.S. Bureau of the Census, 1994, p. 478). Obstacles to teen parents graduating from high school and getting higher education cement their families' poverty.

Class determines many of the options and resources that are available (and conceivable) for coping with developmental challenges and unpredictable crises throughout a family's life cycle. It affects how families experience those challenges and crises. Economic privilege buffers families physically and psychologically against the stressful effects of death, divorce, illness, disability, and trauma. Divorce deprives a realtor and her children of vacations and private college; it leaves their daycare provider's family without heat, pushing the oldest child out of school and into a dead-end job. One quarter of the severely disabled live below the poverty line (U.S. Bureau of the Census, 1994, p. 476). An elderly widow with a paid-off house and investments can afford home health care; her children and grandchildren need not organize themselves around her care. In contrast, a family sharing a grandmother's subsidized housing becomes homeless on her death, and the mother, who had already lost many work days because of the grandmother's illness, may be fired while apartment hunting. Homelessness makes regular school attendance impossible for the children, derailing their hopes for finishing school.

Class position influences the institutional responses to major family events. A capitalist-class "cut-up" who is expelled from prep school for fighting is easily enrolled elsewhere, his college career assured. The family of a young fighter in the barrio visits him in prison—or at graveside. Aging forces many working-class seniors into dependence on relatives, who may argue over caretaking. Old age inserts lawyers and financial advisors into the triangles of the privileged, whose conflicts often play out in financial realms. Class privilege protects families from institutional scrutiny (Imber-Black, 1990). The White family of a surgeon and a homemaker who is addicted to alcohol maintain household and class position with discreet help from paid caretakers, family, and friends. The Black children of a single mother who loses her sales clerk job to crack abuse take care of each other until the school reports their neglect and they are separated by foster care from mother, each other, friends, kin, and school.

Descriptions of the family experiences of different social classes are necessarily imprecise. Members of one family may follow different class trajectories. Family members may not hold "predictable" class values; some may identify more with where they have been, others with where they are going in relation to class. Some highly educated and privileged people live meagerly, either involuntarily or for philosophical reasons. Many families would disagree with how we name their class position. Race, ethnicity, gender, sexual orientation, religion, region, health, ability, and other factors combine with class in many confusing ways that go beyond the scope of this chapter.

Underclass Families

The underclass includes families (not all poor) that participate in an underground economy, as well as the chronically unemployed. Many poor people are employed; some of what follows applies to them. Deindustrialization and "exported" manufacturing have brought families whose working-class roots influence their life cycle patterns into the ranks of the underclass.

The compressed intervals between the generations (Fulmer, 1988) of underclass families with short school careers and life expectancies have great life cycle impact. Thirtyish grandparents, middle-aged great-grandparents, or older siblings and aunts often raise the small children of teen-aged girls. When there are no prospects for col-lege, marriage, or steady jobs, adulthood can come with one's first child (or one's first criminal act), even at 13 or 14. Teen mothers, secondary caretakers in their first children's early years, may become primary parents to subsequent children, perhaps setting up households with new partners and all their children. Childbearing often precedes marriage. Mothers, with or without partners, often raise grandchildren or informally foster relatives' and friends' children while their own children are still at home (Fulmer, 1988; Stack & Burton, 1993). The family life cycle implications of pa-rental responsibilities shifting between genera-tions and households, with half-siblings variously co-parented by grandmothers, fathers, stepparents, each other, and relatives or friends, are enormously complex. Clearly, the notion of the "empty nest" does not apply.

Burton (1996a) described three distinct family life cycle patterns in poor Black communities, which also apply to other races. In urban on-time normative childbearing with 20- to 23-year gener-ations (also typical of working-class families), par-ents have primary responsibility for children, and intergenerational assistance is mutual. In urban early nonnormative childbearing, with 14- to 15-year generations, grandmothers or great-grand-mothers hold primary responsibility for three or four generations. Young mothers, pressured by older boyfriends or eager for babies, may not ques-tion this arrangement, which their elders generally find more burdensome than the on-time pattern. In rural early normative childbearing, teen parent-hood is valued as it provides still-vigorous grand-mothers with children to raise and allows teens to care for the ailing grandparents or great-grandpar-ents who raised them. These patterns reflect the systematic obstruction of the underclass from edu-cation (including education about birth control), decent wages, and hope for change. Burton (1996b) found that most families of expectant teen parents

in an urban poverty zone were resigned to women dying by age 60 and men dying by age 21. A mother lamented, "I let go of my son last year. He's 14 now. You might say he's grown. In my neighborhood . . . boys get killed or locked up—it's a matter of time" (Burton, 1996b). One study showed that in the previous six months, 61 percent of 150 expectant teen parents had friends jailed, 20 percent had friends killed, and 10 percent had both (Burton, 1996b). Such cruel statistics make babies still more precious.

Compressed intervals create role ambiguity and confusion for family members who must take on responsibilities before they are ready (Burton, 1996b; see also Chapter 19). Teens and their chil-dren vie for the attention of grandmothers (whose more privileged age-mates may be just starting families). Pubescent girls and their mothers may date young men of the same age. Girls face high risk of sexual abuse by mothers' partners and other non-kin. Many are impregnated by adult men (U.S. Bureau of the Census, 1994, p. 76) who do not help with childrearing. Grandfathers, fathers, and sons compete for grossly underpaid jobs or for drug-dealing territory. Most schools for the under-class (and working poor) are overcrowded and ill-equipped to teach children whose lives are long on crisis and short on reason to hope. Up to 60 percent of students in poverty zones drop out by ninth grade (Burton, 1996b) for the street (drugs, gangs, or prostitution); to care for siblings, drug-sick par-ents, or grandparents; or to renew the cycle by hav-ing their own babies.

Poverty and oppression increase vulnerability and exposure to chronic stressors that are impli-cated in alcohol and drug abuse and other serious health problems (see Chapter 19). Poor mothers, without adequate nutrition, lodging, or prenatal care, are exposed to environmental hazards impli-cated in infants' low birth weight, birth defects, re-tardation, lead- or drug-related learning disabilities, addiction at birth, HIV, and fetal alcohol syndrome (FAS)—all with terrible implications for individual and family life, immediately and for generations to come. Children born with FAS and IV-drug-related conditions are often mentally impaired, highly impulsive, and prone to addiction and often end up in jail, dead, and/or starting new and equally troubled generations of children. Many, removed from their birth families in early childhood, bring major developmental challenges to adoptive or foster families and never function as independent adults (Dorris, 1989). Furthermore, the medical needs of children, the elderly, or the disabled, which are demanding enough for wealthier families, create even more stress when medical care, pharmacies, and even groceries are three bus rides away.

Working-Class Families

Deindustrialization has radically altered working-class family life. As unskilled and semiskilled work disappears, high school diplomas (once unnecessary for working-class jobs) are becoming normative. Youthful responsibility and learning to manage in an unfair and unforgiving work world are emphasized. Teens often work to pay for expenses through high school, and older children often carry responsibilities for housework and siblings. Adult status is conferred upon full-time employment and/or marriage. As hard work no longer ensures decent income, more youths pursue and finance higher education (often in state, community, or technical schools). Those who delay parenthood for higher education elongate the intervals between generations. College can trigger family tensions when family and community class (and cultural) narratives include both valuing and suspicious messages about upward mobility ("Go to school to make a better life than we had—but don't think you're better than us, or abandon us").

Affordable housing and plentiful work encouraged post–World War II youths to leave home. Soaring housing costs and plummeting wages now keep them home, helping with finances and chores until—and often after—marriage and children in the early- to mid-twenties. (Marriage, if not children, often comes later for African American women than for other women.) Working-class parents often share parental authority and responsibility with grandparents and other relatives in the same building or neighborhood. Grown children's divorce,

job loss, or widowhood can bring one or two generations back home after years of living away. Such arrangements are consistent with the cultural norms of many immigrant and first-generation Americans, but families in dominant U.S. culture may regret needing such arrangements. Whatever a particular family's cultural narratives, the recent downward mobility of this entire class conflicts both with prior generations' view of "success" (steady work, good wages, benefits, and a family home) and with television's glamorous images.

Grandchildren expectably arrive in the forties in working-class families. Parents, although primary caretakers, are usually both employed and rely on relatives for child care. Working-class women historically did paid work, but being at home was the post–World War II ideal, and the generations may differ over gender role expectations. Middle-aged grandmothers (who may be employed) often juggle child care and keeping house for husbands and grown children who live at home while working or going to school. They are also often involved in full- or part-time care for elderly relatives and in-laws. As real wages decline and health and housing costs soar, retirement often comes later than age 65, with full- or part-time work augmenting Social Security, Medicare, and pensions. Retirement is a shaky proposition for those who came of age when factory jobs assured a lifelong career only to lose jobs and retirement security to downsizing and the export of industry to developing nations. It is even shakier for the currently middle-aged, for whom retirement may bring the poverty that Social Security and Medicare were designed to prevent. The risk is still greater for families that are grappling with occupational health hazards or inadequate (or nonexistent) insurance. Moreover, although younger relatives are generally responsible for the elderly, employed daughters (in-law) are now less available for their daily care.

Professional-Managerial-Class Families

Couples that are on dual-career fast-tracks may delay marriage and children until the mid-thirties or later (Fulmer, 1988), perhaps forming second, remarried families even later, when their own parents are past retirement age. Professional and managerial-class families tend to view childhood as a time for protection and indulgence (by family, school, friends, and, often, paid helpers) and adolescence and young adulthood as times of experimentation and individuation, relatively free of family or work obligation. This view, which is historically recent (and only for the privileged classes), informs dominant cultural ideas about "normal development."

Families with adolescents expect an extended familial subsidizing of education and training before grown children start careers, marry, acquire mortgages, and have children. Children usually go away to college (the more privileged go to prep school) and live separately, often with parental subsidies, while working or in graduate training. However, young adults, squeezed between higher housing costs and lower real wages, are increasingly moving back home after school. Unlike their working-class peers, they tend to put their earnings toward consumer goods and entertainment rather than into the family coffers. Families may perceive this living arrangement as a family failure because home ownership was a given for the previous generation. Both generations may find it difficult to negotiate the transition from parents supporting youths to young adults supporting themselves.

Grandparents, having enjoyed good health care and relatively safe work, are typically healthier than in lower classes. They may engage in work, leisure, and volunteer activities long past "retirement" age, remaining independent until old-old age. Grandparents whose cultural values favor familial interdependence may occasionally or regularly perform child care. Some take care of aged or disabled relatives (whose life expectancies exceed those of the less privileged), although financially ruinous long-term institutional or paid home care is becoming increasingly common as sick people live longer and more women are in the labor force. Many families, particularly dual-career or single-parent ones, depend on working-class "help" to care for children, elders, and the chronically ill or disabled while parents are at work or play.

Business-Owning-Class Families

The details of the family life cycle of the business-owning class (as well as of organized crime's upper ranks, who have high incomes but operate within an underground economy) are less documented than for other classes; class privilege assures privacy. Most families in this class are born into it, but some begin in the working or professional-managerial class and are catapulted up by the success of relatively small businesses. These families may identify themselves as "upper-middle-class," and their developmental patterns resemble those of the upper professional-managerial class, despite operating in an economically secure and rarified realm. Other families, of more "aristocratic" descent, have dissipated their resources and influence over generations. Comparing themselves to wealthier kin and neighbors, they may worry about depleting principal for graduate school, never noting that higher education requires most families to go deeply into debt.

Business-owning-class families rely heavily on paid help for managing family tasks. Parents, children, and paid caretakers face particular challenges in navigating their changing relationships across the family life cycle, when live-in servants and/or boarding schools provide most child care. (The families of live-in servants also face challenges, albeit very different ones.) When interaction between parents and younger children is largely mediated by paid helpers, it may be difficult to deal directly with each other at later stages. Close relatives may find themselves separately managing death, illness, divorce, or even birth without avenues for initiating intimate contact to ease the transition emotionally. The buffering effects of financial security, paid help, and professional advice, ease other aspects of such transitions. These families can support wide-ranging exploration of life choices for youths, without financial worry. However, financial support may be coupled with demands for maintaining the family legacy and daunting consequences (including disinheritance) for not meeting such class specifications as attending the "right" schools or "marrying well." Options and expectations may differ for the genders (if less so in recent years), men being responsible for growing the family fortune and women for doing highly visible good works and being decorative.

The almost exclusively Anglo American Protestant families at the top 1 to 2 percent of the social and economic pyramid, being even more socially insulated than the rest of the business-owning class, are both more and less constrained by class narratives about the family life cycle. These narratives may reflect a long-established legacy as much as current circumstances. Business and social obligations, travel, multiple households, and the use of boarding school from a very early age make parents and relatives far less available to children than is the case for other classes or even most of the business-owning class. This arrangement poses class-specific challenges for negotiating parent-adult child and sibling relationships. When parents have not, directly and without mediation, supplied nurturance, discipline, or economic support, their adult progeny may be less moved to do the hard work of renegotiating an adult relationship with them. They may be more likely to do so with siblings and cousins, with whom they share financial resources and the obligations of family investments, foundations, and the like. Youths, often lavishly financed by trust funds rather than directly by elders (or their own work), can leave home as children or adults (for boarding school, college, travel, or independent, employee-run households) without concern for income, money management, or domestic skills. One's name, rather than hard work or ability, guarantees entry into the best schools and support for any venture. When family coffers are undrainable, adulthood need not be defined by self-sufficiency, "responsibility," or involved parenthood and may involve decades of "holding pattern." Divorce, bereavement, disability, and extreme old age are mediated by employees and financial arrangements; family members may be emotionally, but never fiscally, bereft.

THREE FAMILIES

The following three families entered therapy with different class experiences, generating different family life cycle challenges. We invite you to consider how current and lingering class stories shape their developmental challenges, resources, and expectations. Consider how these families and their therapists respond to each other's understandings, for instance, of intergenerational expectations through the family life cycle. Imagine how your own narratives might connect with theirs.

Jim and Abigail Sinclair, a CPA and a professor, came to private therapy through their son's suburban school when Eddie's grades plummeted (See Figure 5.1). They were distressed over his drug use, truancy, learning problems, and worsening college prospects. Their daughter, Jean (age 24), a law student, was insisting that they get tough with Eddie (age 17). She had been distant from her parents since they had reluctantly acknowledged Jean's partner, Linda, but threatened to stop paying tuition if Jean came out to relatives. Jean's partner and friends urged to her stand up to her family and work her way through school. She resisted this argument, hoping to lose neither family nor financial help. Meanwhile, Jim and Abby were pouring saved or borrowed money intended for tuition, retirement, and Jim's mother's medical bills into therapy, tutors, and wrecked cars. Eddie alternated between angrily rejecting their anxious lectures about college and admitting that he feared that college would be too hard. He had fallen in with regular drug users who attended high school sporadically. He avoided his mother's family, who expected him to follow their Ivy League tradition. Abby avoided mentioning Eddie to them for fear of upsetting her ailing father and of being judged. Eddie felt less pressure from his father's family but dismissed them as "clueless." Jim and Abby argued over Abby's "overprotectiveness" and "financial bail-outs" and Jim's "undue harshness" toward Eddie.

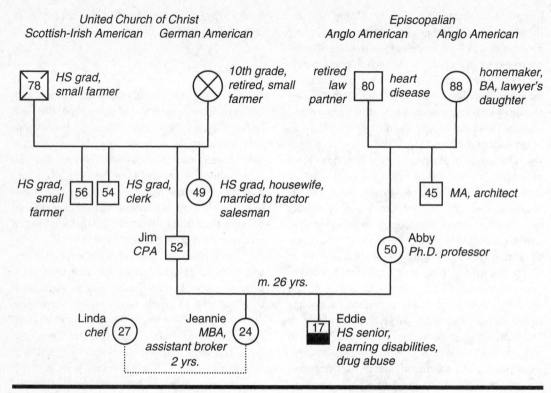

FIGURE 5.1 The Sinclair Family. The half-shaded square represents substance abuse.

Curious about such different responses, their therapist asked about their respective families' class backgrounds. Jim's parents were Anglo- and German-American hardscrabble farmers. Abby came from a long line of High Church Episcopalians, highly successful law partners. No one else in Jim's rural working-class family had gone to college, while the Ivy League was *de rigueur* for Abby's kin. Eddie's failing grades evoked reactions that were colored by markedly different ideas about education. Both parents worried how Eddie could become independent and successful. The therapist, wondering what "independent" and "successful" meant to spouses and families of such different class backgrounds, asked about relatives' responses to the current situation. They reported that Jim's family worried about the drug use but not about college plans. Jim agonized that Eddie would destroy the comfortable life he had struggled to provide for him while worrying that his hu-

miliation at the thought of Eddie's leaving school reflected shame over his "salt of the earth," uneducated family. Abby's family, privileged for generations, viewed Eddie's behavior as needing to be "fixed" immediately, perhaps by having the right boarding school shape him up for college. Abby, however, feared losing him—as she was already losing her daughter—if she and Jim took a hard line with Eddie. She recalled whisperings about a great-uncle, expelled from Yale, whom her father never mentioned. The Sinclairs had not considered class-based expectations as being relevant to their difficulties with each other. Connecting their class differences and different responses to Eddie's school and drug problems helped them to personalize their conflict less and consider a wider range of possibilities.

Richard and Mabel Edwards, their children, and their youngest son's girlfriend came to a clinic in their depressed industrial city in bitter conflict over the impending birth of the young couple's baby. (See Figure 5.2 on page 100 for the Edwards family.) Richard (age 45), an African American deliveryman, had been a factory worker until being laid off four years before. Mabel (age 43), also African American, was a home health care aide. Saundra (age 23), a temporary secretary with an Associate's Degree, lived with her husband, a youth worker. Richie (age 20), on scholarship in an electrician program, worked to pay expenses, including rent to his parents. Greg (age 17), a high school junior with learning and attentional disabilities, had been missing school and getting drunk often.

Greg and his girlfriend, Arlette Patterson (also age 17 and African American), wanted to leave school and work to support their child, who was due in three months. They weren't sure that they wanted to get married just yet. Arlette's mother and grandmother wanted the young couple to marry but couldn't afford to offer them space in their crowded apartment or help with expenses. Greg's parents and grandparents, by contrast, were vehemently opposed to teen parenthood or marriage, which they believed would ruin Greg's already precarious future. Mabel, in particular, insisted that Arlette and her family were "trouble" and that Greg should break off his relationship with her. Greg's family argued that he and Arlette were too young for responsible parenthood and that, with their parents all working and Greg's grandparents (who lived upstairs) too disabled to help, no one could provide regular child care. What's more, they worried, the baby would be uninsured, since the family no longer had health coverage and teen parents rarely find jobs with benefits. Greg's family urged the young couple to place the baby for adoption (preferably informally with Mabel's cousin, who had no children and was "getting on in years"), finish high school, and improve Greg's chances for economic security before starting a family. Greg and Arlette insisted rather vaguely that they would manage somehow, even without help, but that their parents should help with child care as their grandmothers had helped their parents with them a generation earlier.

The therapist interrupted the mutual recriminations to ask whether the city's economic decline might have any influence on Greg's and his parents' differing hopes and expectations for parenthood and career. In fact, Richard and Mabel had grown up in a company town that had assured unskilled and semiskilled workers steady employment, good benefits, and upward mobility from their own parents' sharecropping background. Until Richard was laid off and Mabel's job stopped offering benefits, the couple had provided their children with a sense of economic security and even upward mobility. Greg, the youngest, grew up in harder times than his siblings had. His vision of his future was constricted by his family's and his community's recent downward mobility, with its falling real wages and high unemployment, especially for young Black men; violence, drug abuse, White and middle-class flight, and failing schools. In these historical circumstances and with learning disabilities that required more skilled attention than his overburdened school could offer, Greg saw little reason to stay in school or delay parenthood.

The therapist also wondered aloud whether the Edwardses and the Pattersons had lived through different formative economic experiences. He learned that Arlette's mother and grandmother had alternated between unskilled labor and welfare for most of Arlette's life and that her mother was convinced that the Edwardses looked down on them as a result. His detailed questions about coming of age in different historical and economic contexts allowed the Edwardses and Arlette to explore the different meanings that each member of two families gave to teen parenthood, marriage, and education. His questions also opened up discussion of unspoken, powerful class-based tensions between the two families. This therapeutic conversation depolarized relationships within the Edwards family and between the Edwardses and the Pattersons. Arlette's family was invited to attend future meetings. All the adults therefore could cooperate in facilitating the young couple's difficult decision making (both individual and shared) about their own, their baby's, and their families' future. This collaboration, in turn, enabled the

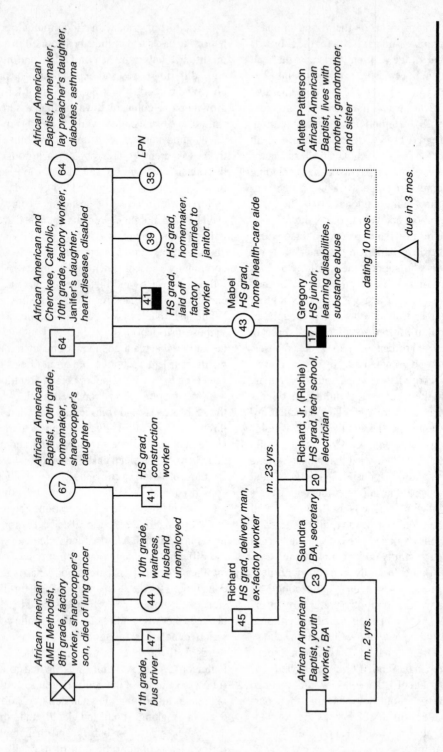

FIGURE 5.2 The Edwards Family. The half-shaded squares represent substance abuse.

young couple to think more carefully about the long-term implications and consequences of their decision.

Luanne Johnson (age 56), her daughter Mary (age 37), her granddaughter Caroline (age 20), and their four-generation household began mandated home-based therapy when an emergency room doctor, worried about Caroline's baby Ashley's failure to thrive, filed neglect charges. (See Figure 5.3 for the Johnson family.) Also at home were

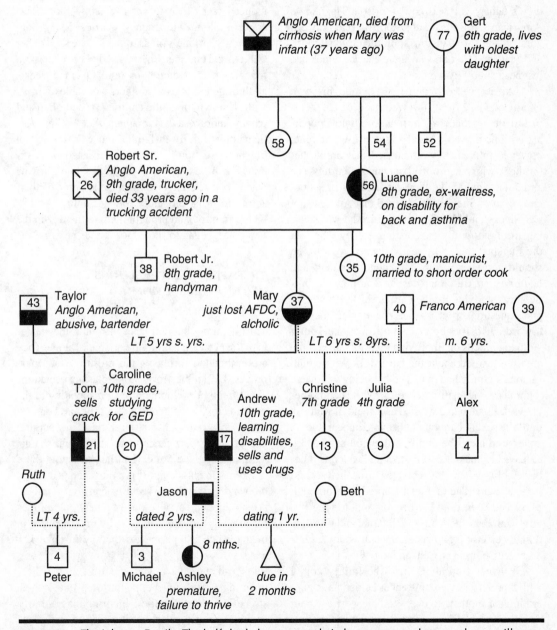

FIGURE 5.3 The Johnson Family. The half-shaded squares and circles represent substance abuse or illness.

Mary's son Andrew (age 17), whose girlfriend Beth (age 16), was pregnant; Mary's daughters Christine (age 13), and Julia (age 9); and Caroline's 3-year-old son Michael. Mary's son Tom (age 21) lived with his girlfriend and their 4-year-old son Peter. Caroline had recently stopped seeing her children's father, who was now in prison. This Anglo American family had subsisted for years on Luanne's disability pension, sporadic child support, and Mary and Caroline's welfare checks, which had just been cut off by welfare reform.

Experience with home visits (and his own childhood visits from "the Welfare") led the therapist to predict that the Johnsons would not cooperate until he proved himself trustworthy. Christine, however, immediately announced that unlike her brothers, who had dropped out and sold drugs, she and Julia would (like their father) stay in school and get jobs. She angrily charged that Andrew, not Caroline, should be in trouble, since he was stealing from the family and scaring Ashley. She told the therapist that if he really wanted to help, he should get Mary a job. This announcement and learning that Caroline (despite learning disabilities) was studying for the G.E.D. shifted the therapist's questions from assessing parental negligence toward curiosity about what allowed the young women to focus on improving their lot. He and the children learned about the hard work with which Luanne's family had managed her being widowed, without death benefits, at age 23. While her mother babysat, Luanne had worked as a cocktail waitress until the sexual harassment became unbearable. A generation later, the family had encouraged Mary to leave her abusive first partner and welcomed her back home when she separated from her second partner, Sam. The therapist learned that although Mary had been drinking heavily and arguing bitterly with her older children, Luanne and Caroline reliably cared for two generations of younger children, with help from Sam and his wife.

Conversation about how the family coped with their difficult circumstances helped three generations of mothers to express their worries about Andrew's escalating drug problems and angry outbursts and their effects on the younger children.

They had welcomed the births of Peter and Michael, untroubled by teen parenthood, which was normative in their experience. They all agreed, however, that neither they nor Andrew was ready for his parenthood. They attributed Ashley's health problems more to being around Andrew's drug-induced rages than to her premature birth. This concern, along with money worries, Mary's depression, Caroline's plans to work once she got her G.E.D., and cramped quarters added up to no room for a new baby in their household. Over the weeks, all three generations of mothers were able to insist, with Sam (whom all the children visited often and whom Andrew saw as a father), that Andrew participate peacefully in family and work or school life or leave home. They also insisted that Andrew's baby either live with Beth's family or be placed elsewhere. As they became surer of their ability to insist on safety for the family, Ashley, whose fragility had brought them to therapy in the first place, began to show more robustness.

THERAPEUTIC IMPLICATIONS OF THE INTERSECTION OF CLASS AND THE FAMILY LIFE CYCLE

The dilemmas that families confront as they negotiate life cycle transitions are not theirs alone. They are embedded in class- and culture-based narratives. Difficulties in meeting class expectations about family development or in responding to the contradictory ones generated in multiple contexts (as when a family has several class and cultural backgrounds) can generate mystification, shame, guilt, anxiety, and family conflict. Situating these dilemmas in class context provides perspective on the ways in which class stories constrict families' possibilities. It can also open up new possibilities for moving forward, individually and together, in their lives. Class permeates therapy in three key ways.

First, class narratives constitute all families' meanings, life cycle expectations, challenges, strengths, and difficulties. Ignoring class stratification promotes selective attention to individual family failures and selective inattention to constraining social factors, further burdening families that are struggling with life transitions. Unless poverty, great wealth, or a rapid class shift make class salient, most families do not consider class on entering therapy. When they perceive class-related difficulties as stemming from other sources (e.g., trauma, incompetence, or pathology), bringing class into therapeutic discourse can alleviate shame, guilt, and stigmatization.

Naming and externalizing class realities can discredit dominant social myths of classlessness and counter their shaming, blaming, and limiting effects on families. For instance, a family's shame over needing food stamps or bouncing checks after a layoff can be ameliorated by learning that welfare to corporations (i.e., in the form of subsidies and tax breaks) alone exceed *all* social spending, including that on health and education (Sennott, 1996). Many "welfare reformers" benefited from the G.I. Bill's free college tuition and stipends (for nearly half the college students in 1947); low-interest, no-down-payment home loans; and free medical care for veterans and their families (Brady, 1996). The G.I. Bill facilitated upward mobility for an entire generation of poor and working-class veterans. Its demise left their progeny wondering why they cannot afford equivalent homes or tuition. Knowing about such radical social change can counter self-blame and mutual recriminations for families in reduced circumstances whose goals and expectations, formed in easier times, are out of reach.

Second, class narratives shape professional understandings of families and the family life cycle. Many of our field's "truths" about the family life cycle embody class biases. Although therapists need navigational tools to orient us to a family's progress along their developmental path, we must use those tools to fit our understandings to families rather than fitting families to our understandings. We must hold our own narratives alongside, and not superordinate to, families' narratives. We must try to avoid reproducing class privilege by imposing class narratives and overlooking what families know about their own lives (White, 1995). For instance, therapists who assume homogeneity both

of class and of the intervals between generations might miss the class implications of a 27-year-old's anxiety about not being a mother when her mother had four children by that age. Similarly, they might pathologize as "parentifying" a family's pragmatic expectations that older children in large families and/or with single working, very young, or disabled parents take domestic responsibility (and thereby feel qualified to become young parents themselves).

Third, most family therapy involves cross-class relationships. Therapy tends to represent professional-managerial-class belief systems (Ehrenreich, 1989), which are consistent with many therapists' own experiences. Even when we do not see ourselves as privileged or as supporting the status quo, our less privileged clients may see us that way. Many difficulties in treatment with less privileged clients involve cross-class negotiation whose history transcends the individuals involved. But not all therapists have professional-managerial-class backgrounds, and both families and therapists usually have complex and confusing class histories. Therapists, in exploring their own struggles and their experiences of shame, confusion, domination, silence, entitlement, guilt, or loss over how class has shaped their family life cycle, can clarify the resources and blind spots they bring to the therapeutic encounter. A therapist from a working-class family may react strongly to some clients' assumption that everyone's family pays for higher education or even down payments on first homes. A therapist who shares a father's expectation of young adults showing responsibility may not realize that such life skills as sticking to a budget or studying hard in college, which were essential in the therapist's and father's own youth, are irrelevant to the father's 20-something son, who was raised in the household of a self-made millionaire.

A therapist who was raised in the professional-middle class and a couple (one of whom grew up in the business-owning class and the other in the white-collar working class) all identify themselves as "middle class." They may jointly construct the couple's bitter conflict about college and retirement investments versus splurging on expensive clothes, vacations, and Christmas presents as reflecting unresolved conflicts in their families of origin. However, if they explore how class history informs the spouses' divergent priorities, they might uncover class diversity. Perhaps one's grandfather's Depression-era death forced a generation to give up college, while the other's great-grandfather's steerage-class immigration allowed his children to go to college and celebrate upward mobility with heartfelt generosity.

We hope that this chapter clarifies the centrality of class in creating the meanings, expectations, and courses of the family life cycle. We hope that it helps therapists of all class backgrounds to limit

harmful assumptions by being open about class differences, willing to ask and answer questions about class in therapy, and respectfully curious about families' understandings of how class operates on their course through the family life cycle. We hope that it helps to limit the reproduction of class privilege in therapy. We invite the reader to continue to explore the neglected intersection of family life cycle and class in your own work. Breaking silence about class and its impact on the family life cycle can counter the mystifying effects of the dominant discourses that obscure and perpetuate class privilege and do harm to the families we treat and the families of which we are part.

REFERENCES

Barlett, D., & Steele, J. (1994). *America: Who really pays the taxes?* New York: Touchstone.

Boyd-Franklin, N. (1993). Class, race, and poverty. In F. Walsh (Ed.), *Normal family processes* (2nd ed.) (pp. 361–376). New York: The Guilford Press.

Brady, J. (1996, August 4). In appreciation, the GI Bill. *Parade,* 4–5.

Burton, L. (1996a). Age norms, the timing of family role transitions, and intergenerational caregiving among aging African American women. *The Gerontologist, 36*(2), 199–208.

Burton, L. (1996b, June). *Multigenerational families, adolescence, and high-risk neighborhoods: How ethnographic studies can inform clinical research.* Paper presented at the annual meeting of the American Family Therapy Academy, San Francisco.

Carter, B., & McGoldrick, M. (Eds.). (1988). *The changing family life cycle: A framework for family therapy* (2nd ed.). New York: Gardner Press.

De la Cancela, V. (1991). Working affirmatively with Puerto Rican men. *Journal of Feminist Family Therapy, 2*(3/4), 195–212.

Dorris, M. (1989). *The broken cord: A family's ongoing struggle with fetal alcohol syndrome.* New York: Harper & Row.

Ehrenreich, B. (1989). *Fear of falling: The inner life of the middle class.* New York: HarperCollins.

Fulmer, R. (1988). Lower-income and professional families: A comparison of structure and life cycle process. In B. Carter & M. McGoldrick (Eds.), *The*

changing family life cycle: A framework for family therapy (2nd ed.) (pp. 545–578). New York: Gardner Press.

Imber-Black, E. (1990). Multiple embedded systems. In M. Mirkin (Ed.), *The social and political contexts of family therapy.* Boston: Allyn & Bacon.

Inclán, J., & Ferran, E. (1990). Poverty, politics, and family therapy: A role for systems theory. In M. Mirkin (Ed.), *The social and political contexts of family therapy.* Boston: Allyn & Bacon.

Jackson, D. (1997, July 23). The media's skewed image. *The Boston Globe,* p. A17.

Kliman, J. (1998). Social class as a relationship: Implications for family therapy. In M. McGoldrick (Ed.), *Re-visioning family therapy: Race, culture and gender in clinical practice* (pp. 50–61). New York: The Guilford Press.

Kliman, J. (1994). The interweaving of gender, class, and race in family therapy. In M. Mirkin (Ed.), *Women in context: A feminist reconstruction of psychotherapy* (pp. 25–47). New York: The Guilford Press.

Madsen, W. (1996). A narrative approach to family-based services. In E. Walton (Ed.), *Empowering families: Papers from the 9th annual conference on family-based services.* River Sale, IL: National Association for Family-Based Services.

Penelope, J. (Ed.). (1994). *Out of the class closet: Lesbians speak.* Freedom, CA: Crossing Press.

Reingold, J. (1997, April 29). Executive pay. *Business Week,* 58–102.

Rubin, L. (1994). *Families on the fault line: America's working class speaks about the family, the economy, race, and ethnicity.* New York: HarperPerennial.

Sennott, C. (1996, July 7). The $150 billion 'welfare' recipients: US Corporations. *The Boston Globe,* p. A1.

Sklar, H. (1995). *Chaos or community: Seeking solutions, not scapegoats for bad economics.* Boston: South End Press.

Stack, C., & Burton, L. (1993). Kinscripts. *Journal of Comparative Family Studies, 24*(2), 157–170.

U.S. Bureau of the Census. (1994). *Statistical abstract of the United States.* Washington, DC: U.S. Government Printing Office.

White, M. (1995). *Re-Authoring lives: Interviews and essays.* Adelaide, South Australia: Dulwich Centre Publications.

Wilson, W. J. (1996). *When work disappears: The world of the new urban poor.* New York: Knopf.

CHAPTER 6

WOMEN THROUGH THE FAMILY LIFE CYCLE

MONICA McGOLDRICK

*Composing a life involves a continual reimaging of the future and reinter-
pretation of the past to give meaning to the present.... Many of the most
basic concepts we use to construct a sense of self or the design of a life
have changed their meanings: Work, Home, Love, Commitment....Our
lives...take on new directions. Each of us is involved in inventing a new
kind of story.*

—Catherine Bateson, *Composing a Life* (1989, p. 2)

WOMEN'S CHANGING LIFE CYCLE ROLES

Women's lives have always required amazing improvisation, but never more than today. They were
never about following a single thread of the evolution of the hero into the undaunted, courageous
and goal-oriented achiever, as seemed to be the life
plan for Western men. As Catherine Bateson (1989)
puts it: "Life...[is] an improvisatory art...We combine familiar and unfamiliar components in response to new situations...[My writing] started
from a disgruntled reflection on my own life as a
sort of desperate improvisation in which I was constantly trying to make something coherent from
conflicting elements to fit rapidly changing settings" (p. 3). Women's lives always involved a
weaving together of many strands, attending to
multiple tasks, sounds, and images at once. They
created the "nest" that was home for everyone else;
they provided the food, the nurturance, and the
care for all from the youngest to the oldest; they
created the family rituals, bought the presents,
made birthdays and Thanksgivings happen. They
nursed the sick, washed and mourned the dead, and
attended to the needs of other mourners.

But women were systematically kept out of
the public spheres of life—government, business,
the world of power and money—all of which had
to change, for women to have a life cycle of their
own (Walters, Carter, Papp, & Silverstein, 1988).
As Carolyn Heilbrun has discussed in her now-
classic analysis of women's biography, *Writing a
Woman's Life* (1988), women's selfhood, her right
to her own story, depends on her ability to act in the
public domain. Heilbrun sees power as "the ability
to take one's place in whatever discourse is essential to action and the right to have one's part
matter" (p. 18). Women's life cycles have been
changing because women have been asserting the
right to have their part matter in the public domain,
which determines their possibilities also in the intimate, personal domain—from infant care to
physical, psychological, spiritual, and financial security in old age, a phase of life that has always
been for women only but that has until now been
controlled by men, not by women themselves.

Mirra Bank, in her touching book *Anonymous
Was a Woman* (1979), about American women's
roles in the last century, quotes Mary Boykin Ches-
nut as writing in her diary in 1862,

Why (do I) feel like a beggar, utterly humiliated and degraded when I am forced to say I need money? I cannot tell, but I do; and the worst of it is, this thing grows worse as one grows older.... What a proud woman suffers under all this, who can tell? (p. 92)

The conundrum of responsibility without power has long characterized women's lives. Women had responsibilities for clothing their children, but fashion and advertising have always been a man's world; women were the cooks at home, but they were not the chefs of record; they were the artistic creators of the home, but they were not the artists of record. Another of Bank's (1979) "anonymous women" described her 25-year endeavor in making a quilt in her stolen evening hours:

My whole life is in that quilt. All my joys and all my sorrows are stitched into those little pieces. When I was proud of the boys and when I was downright provoked and angry with them...and...John (my husband) too. Sometimes I loved him and sometimes I sat there hating him as I pieced the patches together. So they are all in that quilt, my hopes and fears...my loves and hates. I tremble sometimes when I remember what that quilt knows about me. (p. 94)

For centuries, women remained voiceless in the public sphere, having to stitch their lives together here and there as they could. This was a tragedy, but it has also given them an adaptive strength, making them able to weave lives out of many disparate strands. Even in the private sphere, in their homes, the pervasive private abuse, persecution, and humiliation of women has been an unacknowledged societal shame for many centuries. Battering of women, date rape, marital rape, dehumanizing treatment of women as sex objects, psychological abuse, financial control, sexual harassment, and exploitation of women in the workplace are problems of incredible proportions that have only recently begun to become visible. President Clinton, for example, spoke publicly of the problem in 1995:

If children aren't safe in their homes, if college women aren't safe in their dorms, if mothers can't raise their children in safety, then the American

Dream will never be real for them. Domestic violence is now the number one health risk for women between the ages of 15 and 44 in our country. It is a bigger threat than cancer or car accidents. (quoted in Barnett, Miller-Perrin, & Perrin, 1997, p. 15)

The systematic exclusion of women from participation in the societal institutions is indeed being challenged (Goldberger, Tarule, Clinchy, & Belenky, 1996). The exclusion of women from public spheres of education, lawmaking, business, the arts, money, and power is gradually changing. But the issues remain, and for women of color, they are dramatically more complex and difficult than they are for White women (Almeida, 1993, 1998). Audre Lorde (1984) described a key difference between Black and White women boldly:

Black women and our children know the fabric of our lives is stitched with violence and with hatred, that there is no rest. We do not deal with it only on the picket lines, or in dark midnight alleys, or in the places where we dare to verbalize our resistance. For us, increasingly, violence weaves through the daily tissues of our living—in the supermarket, in the classroom, in the elevator, in the clinic and the schoolyard, from the plumber, the baker, the saleswoman, the bus driver, the bank teller, the waitress who does not serve us.

Some problems we share as women, some we do not. You fear your children will grow up to join the patriarchy and testify against you; we fear our children will be dragged from a car and shot down in the street, and you will turn your backs upon the reasons they are dying. (p. 9)

African American and other marginalized women perceive their womanhood differently than White women and may distance themselves from feminists and the feminist movement, seeing it as White, privileged, and underestimating the integral role of cultural traditions and racism in their lives (Hall & Greene, 1994). Paula Gunn Allen (1992) summarizes the context of American Indian women's lives:

Within this geopolitical charnel house, American Indian women struggle on every front for the survival of our children, our people, our self-respect, our value systems, and our way of life. The past five hundred years testify to our skill at waging this struggle. For all the varied weapons of extinction pointed at our heads, we endure. We survive war and conquest; we survive colonization, acculturation, assimilation; we survive beating, rape, starvation, mutilation, sterilization, abandonment, neglect, death of our children, our loved ones, destruction of our land, our homes, our past, and our future. We survive and we do more than just survive. We bond, we care, we fight, we teach, we nurse, we bear, we feed, we earn, we laugh, we love, we hang in there, no matter what. Of course many of us just give up. Many are alcoholics, many are addicts. Many abandon their children, the old ones. Many commit suicide. Many become violent, go insane, Many go "white" and are never seen or heard from again. But enough hold on to their traditions and their ways so that even after almost five hundred years, we endure. And we even write songs and poems, make paintings and drawings that say: "We walk in beauty. Let us continue." (p. 43)

We must be careful to acknowledge differences in women's life cycle experiences, depending on where they are in the larger sociopolitical structure, even as we assert their common experiences, to keep their lives from remaining invisible (Chapter 2; Almeida, Woods, & Messineo, 1998). And we must pay attention to their adaptive strengths even as we assert the traumatic inequities they have experienced. Women have always played a central role in families, but the idea that they have a life cycle apart from their roles as wife and mother is a relatively recent one and is still not fully accepted. Until very recently, "human development" referred to male development. Women's development was defined by the men in their lives, their role being defined by their position in someone else's life cycle: daughter, mother, sister, grandmother. The expectation for women has been that they would take care of the needs of others, first men, then children, then the elderly. Rarely has it been accepted that they have a right to a life for themselves. Nevertheless, women lead far more complex, varied, and unpredictable lives than men do (Shapiro, 1996), reinventing themselves many times to meet different exigencies (Bateson, 1994).

While men's work life tends to follow a linear course, women's usually consists of starts, stops, meanders, interruptions, revisions, and detours as they accommodate to the others in their lives (Shapiro, 1996).

Women's roles have been changing dramatically in recent years. They are delaying marriage. Instead of being passed from their fathers to their husbands, they are claiming an increasing span of time to define their own lives. A much higher proportion of women than ever before is experiencing a period of independent living and work before marriage (Coontz, 1997). Whereas only 28 percent of women age 20 to 24 were single in 1960, now more than two thirds of women that age are unmarried (Coontz, 1997). The typical first-time bride in 1993 was 24, almost four years older than her counterpart of 1970. Since 1980, childbearing has fallen below replacement levels, as women are increasingly electing to postpone childbearing. Women are refusing to stay in stifling or abusive marriages. Divorce is at 46 percent, and women with the most education and income are more likely to divorce and less likely to remarry, in contrast to men, the most wealthy and well educated of whom are the most likely to stay married or to remarry quickly. But women are also more likely to move down to poverty after divorce, while men's income actually rises after divorce (Peterson, 1996). Currently, 75 percent of the poor are women or children, most of whom live in one-parent households. The number of single-parent households (86 percent headed by women) has more than doubled. For the increasing number of teenaged unmarried mothers, their mothers, aunts, and sisters share responsibility for the children. In addition, for the first time, a fair number of women in their thirties and forties are choosing to have and raise children without partners, a new phenomenon altogether (Anderson, 1994; see also Chapter 21). Lesbians, who are increasingly having children together, are broadening and reworking the concept of family to include their own special relationships with friends, extended family, and ex-lovers (Slater, 1995). And many more older women are living longer, having adventurous lives, and reinventing themselves well into their seventies, eighties, and nineties (Heilbrun, 1997). Finally, the majority of people who live alone are women (11 million versus 6.8 million men), who tend to be widowed and/or divorced elderly. Between 1970 and 1993, there was a large increase in the percentage of women over age 75 who live alone, from 37 percent to 52 percent.

WOMEN AND EDUCATION

Many more women are concentrating on education. Since 1979, more women than men have been enrolled in college, and among people age 25 to 29, women match men in the percentage that have completed at least four years of college (25 percent). Women now make up 55 percent of college students and 65 percent of students over age 35, so they will soon become a majority of Americans with higher education (Collins, 1997).

But for education to work for women, it, like all other institutions of our society, needs to change. Within the hallowed halls of academia, women are likely to feel like frauds. Peggy McIntosh (1985, 1989), in her articles "On Feeling Like a Fraud," has described the ways in which women who have been socialized in the "single track logic" of academia can end up feeling stupid because they find themselves unable to make an outline that lays out categories and subcategories in hierarchical order. McIntosh (1989) asserts that the very requirement of acting as if all ideas fit in logical and hierarchical sequence is absurd.

> Language is an invention.... Life doesn't come in sentences, paragraphs or arguments. For me, the outline now joined the argumentative paper as a problematical form, requiring pretenses, such as subordinating all ideas to one "main" or governing idea.... For me the outline is, and always has been, a fraudulent form. My genre,...is the list.... On a list everything matters; you need not rank, subordinate, and exclude; you can add or subtract, elaborate or delete.... With an outline, one must (pretend to) justify the sequence, and to know and deal appropriately the relative significance of each item or idea. One cannot be generous in an out-

> line...The list allows me to keep everything, to expand, to add at any time. (p. 2)

We must challenge the categories of description to gain better perspective on the values of our society and particularly to gain an appreciation for the complex threads of a woman's life cycle. McIntosh calls for developing a "double vision" regarding a woman's sense of being a "fraud." On the one hand, we need to help women to overcome their feelings of inadequacy and of not deserving a place to stand or speak out. On the other hand, we need to validate and appreciate women's acknowledgment that they do not know everything and their resistance to making pronouncements from on high as if they held "the" truth, as men have done so often. McIntosh's intuition about lists and outlines seems particularly apt for understanding women's need to reinvent themselves continually to meet ever changing circumstances throughout the life cycle. It helps if we keep a broad perspective on women's expanding lives in the public domain of work, school, governance, business, power, and money. And we must pay more attention to the community networks that women have always been responsible for maintaining and that are crucial to their safety and ability to have a life. We must also attend to the possibilities of equal partnership, connection, and flexibility in couple relationships, friendships and intergenerational bonds through the life cycle. In addition, we must bear in mind that women of color experience double jeopardy and lesbians of color experience triple jeopardy in adjusting to a world in which the institutions have been defined by others. Lorraine Hansberry (1969), author of *Raisin in the Sun,* provides an example that still has relevance:

> She had begun her college career awkwardly and it had stayed that way. The point of things eluded her—things like classes and note-taking and lecture and lab. She found most of them unspeakably dull and irrelevant to virtually anything she had ever had on her mind or ever expected to. Worst of all was something called "Physical Geography," which required, among other things, that she spend some four hours a week knocking on rocks with a little metal hammer. (p. 37)

How many women, especially lesbian women and women of color, have been thrown into experiences in which, as for Hansberry, societal assumptions had absolutely no connection to their life experience in which, to survive, they had to draw from inner resources and make improvisatory connections and transformations to bridge to what was relevant in their souls. Hansberry, for one, proved more than up to the task. Before she turned 30, in her play *Raisin in the Sun,* she had articulated the intergenerational relationships of African American men and women through the life cycle and became the youngest person, the only African American, and only the fifth woman ever to win the New York Drama Critics award for best play.

Therapists have important work to do with women at every phase of the life cycle in encouraging their ideas, intuitions, and adaptive resourcefulness, helping them to realize that they are not "frauds" and validating their "ways of knowing" (Belenky, Clinchy, Goldberger, & Tarule, 1986; Goldberger, Tarule, Clinchy, & Belenky, 1996).

WOMEN AND WORK

The majority of women, even mothers of small children, are now in the paid workforce. But the continuing differential roles of men and women in the larger context is illustrated by the fact that a large portion of women are still in sex-segregated, low-paying jobs. Women who work full time have lost ground in the battle for equal pay in the past decade. They have gone from making 77 percent of what men make down to 74 percent—and older women make only 65 percent of what working men make (Lewin, 1997b). One quarter of all employed women are crowded into just 22 of 500 occupations distinguished by the Bureau of the Census.

The issue of achieving equal pay for equal work is the top concern of American women, one third of whom earn more than half of their family's income (Lewin, 1997a). Indeed two fifths of working women are the sole heads of their households. Among African American women, the issue of undercompensation is even greater than it is for others, while for Latina and Asian women, balancing

work and family appears to be the number one issue (Lewin, 1997a). Nevertheless, the impact of women working is overall a positive one for them and for their children (Barnett & Rivers, 1996). Daughters appear to benefit most of all from having a working mother. They have been shown to be more self-confident, to get better grades, and to be more likely to pursue careers themselves than children of nonemployed mothers (Hoffman, 1989). For African American families, a mother's working has been shown to improve not only her self-esteem (Hoffman, 1989), but also her daughters' likelihood of staying in school (Wolfer & Moen, 1996). Furthermore, a fascinating and little-publicized finding has suggested that the high achievement of mothers is even more predictive of high achievement of both their sons and their daughters than is the high achievement of fathers (Losoff, 1974; Padan, 1965).

But the main point is that very few families can afford to have children these days unless both husband and wife have paying jobs. Still, while for men the relationship of family and work is seen as mutually supportive and complementary, for women, work and family have involved conflicting demands. The family is seen as supporting and nurturing the male worker for his performance on the job, whereas women are seen as depriving their families by working. There is no sense of the family's being a refuge for women as it has been for men (Almeida, 1993). In fact, the high level of psychological demands in their jobs at home and often in the workplace, with little actual control or power over their situation, can put women in particularly stressful situations much of the time (Baruch, Barnett, & Rivers, 1983; Barnett & Rivers, 1996).

Women have been in a double bind in this regard. Although the dominant belief has been that women belong in the home, participation in the labor force has been shown to be the most important determinant of a woman's psychological well-being. Women who work outside the home show fewer symptoms of psychological and physiological distress, and the evidence is that maternal employment is not harmful for children (Barnett & Rivers, 1996). Indeed, in traditional cultures, mothers typically always worked, and children were raised primarily by grandparents and older siblings. Yet there are many social pressures against women feeling good about working. But it is not the number of activities that is burdensome to a woman's well-being. Rather, it is the lack of support and the inability to choose one's roles and organize one's resources to meet the demands.

Couple relationships are changing dramatically in dual-worker families. Barnett and Rivers (1996) and Stacey (1996) found that employed wives are not as anxious as 1950s homemakers were, nor are their children suffering from their working. They found the major source of stress for working women to be sexual harassment, followed by efforts to "mommy track" mothers out of their jobs. They found fathers to be much more involved with all aspects of their children's care than the previous generation of fathers was and to experience distress when they do not have enough time with their children. Men's participation in household chores has risen dramatically, even in working-class families, though it still lags far behind the participation of women (Barnett & Rivers, 1996; Hochschild, 1989). The real problem, though, is our nation's refusal to support good-quality child care for all children, as other advanced nations of the world have done, which is essential in a country that requires dual-worker families.

In any case, economic independence for women, which has profound implications for traditional family structures, appears to be crucial for women's protection from the high risk of abuse, divorce, and poverty and powerlessness in old age. To accomplish this independence, massive power changes are required in our culture. Wives' economic dependence, which is the greatest factor in their returning to abusing husbands (Aguirre, 1985), creates a seriously problematic power imbalance that threatens marriage altogether. As Rachel Hare-Mustin (1991) has put it, the problem in women's relationships with men is power: "Unless therapists are aware of the effects of unequal power on women, they will be unlikely to move beyond the status quo to challenge the sources of stress in male-female relationships" (p. 39).

In spite of household and other strains, the more roles a woman occupies, the healthier she is likely to be. Employed married parents have the best health profile, whereas people with none of these roles have the worst profile. Employed women are healthier than nonemployed women, and lack of employment is a risk factor for women's health (Arnetz, Wasserman, Petrini, & Brenner, 1987). Multiple roles may provide cognitive cushioning in the face of stress. There is a significant relationship between underemployment and decreased physical and mental health. Jobs with no flexibility, poor pay, poor benefits, no security, irregular schedules, and low control may jeopardize health, whereas having high-quality roles, even if they are numerous, may help to maintain or enhance health. Women with more high-powered, high-status careers obviously have more advantages. Job-related social support has particularly beneficial effects on women's health.

While work seems to be a stress on men, indications are that paid work actually improves the health of women. Women who are homemakers end up with a lower sense of self-esteem and personal competence, even regarding their child care and social skills, than do mothers in the paid workforce. Women who take any time off from full commitment to the paid workforce lose a great deal of ground in their power in their relationships, their work flexibility, and their financial options (Barnett & Rivers, 1996).

As more women have entered the workplace, they have become more aware of the external constraints on them in the labor force. As a result, they often become more aware of pay discrimination, job discrimination, and sexual harassment than they were in the past, and this awareness can be intensely stressful, even when it leads to change. Again, the main clinical implication is that we need to be active educators in our therapy, helping women to realize that they are not alone, encouraging them to network to diminish their sense of isolation, and empowering them to join forces to change the way society operates. A woman who must bring a charge of sexual harassment against her boss by herself will have great difficulty. A class action suit is enormously easier to handle, and women are more likely to win when they operate together. Linking women to other women is one of the most important tools we have as clinicians.

WOMEN IN FAMILIES

Being part of a family and the breaking up of a family have profoundly different implications for men and women. Indicators are that married women have more symptoms than married men or unmarried women. They experience more depression and more marital dissatisfaction. Women in traditional marital relationships have poorer physical health, lower self-esteem, less autonomy, and poorer marital adjustment than women in more equal relationships (Avis, 1985). Indeed, being part of a family has been a serious danger for many women but rarely for men. For example, women are 10 times more likely than men to be abused by an intimate partner and 6 times more likely to be abused by an intimate partner than by a stranger. At least 29 percent of the violent crimes against women are committed by husbands or boyfriends. The number of women murdered by their intimates in the United States during the years of the Vietnam War (51,000) approximated the number of soldiers killed in the war (58,000), yet we have heard virtually nothing about these tragic losses, and there are no memorials to these women.

Yet, as problematic as traditional patterns have been for many women, changing the status quo has been extremely difficult. Even as women are rebelling against the burden of bearing full responsibility for making family relationships, holidays, and celebrations happen, they still feel guilty when they do not do what they have grown up expecting to do. When no one else moves in to fill the gap, they often feel blamed that family solidarity is breaking down and believe that it is their fault. Men's emotional and physical distance is still largely ignored in writings about the changing family. In earlier times, when community cohesion was greater, women often had at least a network of extended family and neighbors to help out. But now, increasingly, extended families are not easily accessible, and those essential networks that ease the burdens of child-rearing by providing supplementary caretakers are not available. The importance of these invisible networks has rarely been acknowledged by society, which has espoused values that have uprooted families regularly and intentionally for jobs, military duty, or corporate needs. Thus, when women have found themselves without such supports, they have often been unable to articulate what is wrong, since the need for such community and family support has not been socially validated. In the absence of such acknowledgment, women often blame themselves or are blamed by society when they cannot hold things together. The argument typically moves between the use of the word "mother" and the word "parent" in such a way that mothers are blamed for abandoning their children, while fathers' traditional absence from the interior of the child's life is continuously obscured. Commentators (e.g. Whitehead, 1993) talk about the selfishness of "parents," who are spending less time with their children, but it is clear that the attack is directed against mothers, because they fail to refer to the fact that fathers have been absent from families for a long time already.

Such backlash responses to the changes in women's roles in our times typically harks back nostalgically to that idiosyncratic period in U.S. history: the 1950s for white middle-class families, when women, at higher rates than at any time in history, were isolated in nuclear families as homemakers with their children. As Stephanie Coontz (1997) has pointed out, the "traditional" marriages of that generation created the most drug-oriented, rebellious children of the 1960s as well as the fastest-growing divorce rate in the world, so we should think twice about our reverence for that phase of the "good old days," not to mention the suppression of women entailed in that family arrangement. Susan Faludi (1991) has detailed brilliantly the conservative backlash response to the changing roles of women, which has blamed women for destroying families by their selfishness in considering their own needs first.

By far the majority of household labor is still done by women. The household remains primarily women's responsibility, with other family members still thinking that their role in participating in chores is to "help her." Arlie Hochschild (1989) actually calculated a few years ago that over a year, women averaged an extra month of 24-hour work days, and over 12 years, they averaged an extra year of 24-hour work days. Recent indications are that the skew in housekeeping and child care is diminishing but that mothers of preschoolers still work 17 hours more a week than their mates, and once their children enter school, mothers still work an extra 5.6 hours a week more than their husbands (Barnett & Rivers, 1996). A large research study (Blumstein & Schwartz, 1983, 1991) found that money buys power in marriage. It buys the privilege to make decisions—concerning whether to stay or leave, what the family will purchase, where they will live, and how the children will be educated. In other words, money talks.

WOMEN IN THE MIDDLE:
WOMEN AND CARETAKING

Unfortunately, the well-being of both children and the elderly, who are mostly women, may be gained at the expense of the quality of life of the middle generation of women who are most burdened, squeezed by overwhelming demands of caretaking for both other generations. Sometimes referred to as "the sandwich generation," they are often caught in a dependency squeeze between their parents and their children and are also often squeezed to accept work their lives had not prepared them for, since they did not expect to have to seek employment after midlife. The realities of their financial future as older women is increasingly hitting women at midlife. They are realizing how severely the inequalities of their position in the power structure limit their other options for the rest of their lives (Dowling, 1996).

Women are exposed to higher rates of change and instability in their lives than men and are also more vulnerable to life cycle stresses, because of their greater emotional involvement in the lives of those around them. They are more responsive to a wider network of people for whom they feel responsible (Antonucci, 1994). Their role overload leaves them further burdened when unpredictable stresses such as illness, divorce, or unemployment occur. This means that they are doubly stressed, exposed to more network stresses and more emotionally responsive to them. Women are much more emotionally affected than men by deaths and by other events in their networks (Kessler & Me-Leod, 1984). Men respond less to events at the edge of their caring networks. They respond less to the distress of neighbors and friends than women do. They actually hear less about stress in their networks. The help-seeking literature indicates that people who need emotional support more often seek out women as confidants. Therefore, women have more demands for nurturance made on them. Daughters are more involved with and visit parents more than sons do. Grandmothers are twice as likely to have warm relationships with grandchildren as grandfathers are. Indeed, grandfathers tend to be active with their grandchildren only if their wives are (Lott, 1994).

Traditionally, women have been held responsible for all family caretaking: for their husbands, their children, their parents, their husband's parents, and any other sick or dependent family members. Even now, almost one fifth of women aged 55 to 59 are providing in-home care to an elderly relative. Over half of women with one surviving parent can expect to become the parent's caretaker. Usually one daughter or a daughter-in-law has the primary responsibility for care of elderly women. Clearly, caring for the very old (who are mostly women) is primarily a woman's issue. But increasingly, younger women are in the labor force and thus unavailable for caretaking without extreme difficulty. Presently more than half of all women age 45 to 64 are in the labor force, and most of these are working full time. Increasingly, with more and more four-generation families, the caregivers themselves are elderly and struggling with declining functioning. Twelve percent of caregivers are themselves over age 75.

WOMEN'S EXCLUSION FROM POWER UNDER THE LAW AND SOCIETAL EXPECTATIONS

The overwhelming majority of lawmakers in our society are males. Their record on legislation in support of family caretaking is a travesty. This is a critical issue for divorced women, mothers of small children, women of color, the elderly, who are mostly women, and other groups that do not have the power to make the laws and thus get doubly burdened: with the responsibility and without the power or resources to take care of their families. The laws regulating social services do not support the women. Contrary to the claim that government services sap the strength of family supports, the failure to provide public services to families will most likely exacerbate marital and intergenerational conflicts, turning family members against each other (Hess, 1985).

Friedan (1985), Hochschild (1989), and others have urged us to move farther and faster to tackle the hard political tasks of restructuring home and work so that women who are married and have children can also earn money or have their own voice in the decision-making mainstream of society. The guilts of less-than-perfect motherhood and less-than-perfect professional career performance are real, because it's not possible to "have it all," when jobs are still structured for men whose wives take care of the details of life and homes are still structured for women whose only responsibility is running their families (Friedan, 1985). As Goldner (1985) has stated:

> By ignoring the complex relationship between the structure of family relations and the world of work, family therapists tacitly endorse the nineteenth-century fiction that the family is a domestic retreat from the market place economy.... The dichotomization of these social domains is a mystification and a distortion that masks a fundamental organizing principle of contemporary family life. The division of labor (both affective and instrumental) and the distribution of power in families are structured not only according to generational hierarchies but also around gendered spheres of influence that de-

rive their legitimacy precisely because of the creation of a public-private dichotomy. To rely on a theory that neither confronts, nor even acknowledges, this reality is to operate in the realm of illusion." (pp. 43–44)

The pressures on women to lower their sights for educational or career opportunities may be intense. They are presented with more obstacles in the work world and negative pressure from media, community, and family. Often, they have also internalized beliefs about their own limitations and the role of a woman as secondary to men. As Sassen (1980) pointed out about Horner's (1972) classic study of women's "fear of success," their success anxiety was present only when success was at the expense of another's failure, showing their sophisticated sensitivity to the interpersonal context of success.

Clinically, it may be useful to help clients to outline all the unrecognized work that their mothers and grandmothers did to raise their families and keep a household going. This emphasizes their courage, abilities, hard work, and strength as role models for positive identification, since women are typically hidden from history. Harriet Lerner's books *The Dance of Anger* (1985), *The Dance of Intimacy* (1989), and *The Dance of Deception* (1993) and Betty Carter's *Love, Honor and Negotiate* (1996), as well as my own *You Can Go Home Again* (1995), provide illustrations to use in coaching women on transforming their family relationships and redefining their own lives.

WOMEN AND MARRIAGE

The rate of marriage has increased since 1960, but marriage now plays a less comprehensive role in defining a woman's social and personal life than in earlier times. Nevertheless, as Jessie Bernard (1982) long ago described it, "his" marriage is still very different from, and a great deal less problematic than, "her" marriage. Although many men remain ambivalent about getting married, fearing ensnarement, it is women who become more symptomatic and prone to stress in the married state on virtually every indicator (Gove, 1972; Goleman, 1986; Heyn, 1997). It is striking that women tend to be so positive about marrying and men so ambivalent about it, since marriage appears to be so much more advantageous for men than for women. Often, the woman has given up more to be married than the man has (her occupation, friends, residence, family, name). She adjusts to his life (Goodrich, Rampage, Ellman, & Halstead, 1988; Heyn, 1997). Although men are willing to spend time with women during courtship in ways that enhance the women's sense of intimacy, after marriage, men tend to spend less and less time talking to their wives. Husbands often consider that doing chores around the house should be an adequate demonstration of caring and that sex should provide an adequate demonstration of intimacy; they may feel mystified about what women want when they seek more emotional contact. Women are often frustrated by the limited degree of relating that their husbands offer. Women are more willing than men to admit to problems and to acknowledge their part in them. While men's and women's priorities in marriage differ (for example, regarding the place of sex and of financial security), men generally rate their marital communication, relationships with parents, and sexual relationships as good, while women rate all of these as problematic (Goleman, 1986). Furthermore, it seems that the double standard continues to operate, with women considering their husband's fidelity more important than men do and men more likely to expect fidelity from their wives than from themselves. Developmentally, women have been expected from the point of early adulthood to accept being uprooted every time their husbands moved for a better job, to accept their husbands' lack of communication and unavailability, and to handle all relationships themselves. It is ironic that women, who are seen as dependent and less competent than men, have had to function without emotional support in their marriages—to be, indeed, almost totally emotionally self-sufficient (Bernard, 1982), while men were assumed to need the emotional support of another human being who sacrificed all her own needs for his. Women have typically had

to bolster their husbands' sense of self-esteem but have been seen as "nags" when they sought emotional support for themselves. In clinical practice, men's marital complaints typically center on their wives' nagging and emotional demands, while wives' complaints center on their husbands' lack of emotional responsiveness and their own sense of abandonment (Gottman, 1985; Weiss, 1985).

In any case, the general lack of political and social equality between marital partners makes the mythology of marital equality a dangerous mystification for most women. The transition to marriage is an important time for helping young women (and men) look beyond the inequitable, often dysfunctional couple roles that were prominent in previous generations. Patterns that get set at this point in the life cycle may have great importance later on. Many young women resist challenging the romantic myths about marriage until later stages, when problems surface in seriousness. Yet it is a lot easier to change patterns in the early years of marriage than later, when they have become entrenched and when women's lack of power in the social domain increases.

BECOMING MOTHERS

Although our society has been changing rapidly, normative expectations for men and women in families have lagged behind emerging realities of family life (Carter, 1996; McGoldrick, Anderson, & Walsh, 1989; Garcia Coll, Surrey, & Weingarten, 1998). Mothers are particularly vulnerable to blame and guilt because of societal expectations that they bear primary responsibility for the care and well-being of homes, their husbands, their children, and their aging parents. The traditional family not only encouraged, but even required, dysfunctional patterns such as the overresponsibility of mothers for their children and the complementary underresponsibility or disengagement of fathers (Avis, 1985). Daughters and daughters-in-law carry those responsibilities for their own and their husbands' extended families. Now that most women are combining work and family responsibilities, they are increasingly overburdened.

Even for today's dual-career couples, the transition to parenthood tends to mark a reversion to a more traditional division of roles, with women doing the lion's share of household maintenance and child care planning (Carter, 1996; Hochschild, 1989). Still, having a child per se does not appear to cause women psychological distress, but leaving the labor force does (Barnett & Rivers, 1996; Wetherington & Kessler, 1989). Yet parenthood is a powerful generator of development, giving us new opportunities to redefine and express who we are and who we can be (Daniels and Weingarten, 1983; Lerner, 1998). As mothers have always known, and fathers are learning now,

> Children battle you into being more than you thought you were, into giving more than you thought you had it in you to give. Those middle of the nights, you learn something about yourself. (Mother's comment cited in Daniels & Weingarten, 1983, p. 1)

But our culture still leaves women with the primary responsibility for child-rearing and blames them when it goes wrong (Caplan, 1996; Caplan & Hall-McCorquondale, 1985). Seventy-three percent of mothers with children in the home work, and 60 percent of working mothers have no guaranteed maternity leave (a basic right in most industrialized countries). However, since 1980, the amount of public money that we spend on daycare has decreased 25 percent. Thus, it is clear that mothers are by no means receiving social support for the tasks that are expected of them in parenting.

Remarried families offer a number of particularly trying situations for women. Most difficult of all family positions is undoubtedly the role of stepmother. Given our culture's high expectations of motherhood, the woman who is brought in to replace a "lost" mother enters a situation fraught with high expectations that even a saint could not meet. One of the major clinical interventions is to remove from the stepmother the burden of guilt for not being able to accomplish the impossible—taking over the parenting for children who are not her own. Our general guidelines involve putting the biological parent in charge of the children, however difficult that may be when the father works full-

time and feels that he has no experience with "mothering." The problem for the stepmother is especially poignant, since she is usually the one who is most sensitive to the needs of others, and it will be extremely difficult for her to take a back seat while her husband struggles awkwardly with an uncomfortable situation. The fact is that she has no alternative. The major problem for women in remarried families is their tendency to take responsibility for family relationships, to believe that what goes wrong is their fault and that if they just try hard enough, things will work out, since the situation carries with it built-in structural ambiguities, loyalty conflicts, guilt, and membership problems (see McGoldrick, 1996 for a videotape illustration of the problems of remarried families).

Eleanor Maccoby, who has been writing for many years about gender differences in sex-role development, has repeatedly pointed out that while innate gender differences do not appear to be major, the social context constricts girls from earliest childhood, and gender segregation is pervasive. Maccoby (1990) cites boys' orientation toward competition and dominance, to which girls seem to be averse, and the fact that girls appear to have little ability to influence boys when they are together as factors contributing to this. It seems natural that girls are averse to interacting with someone who is unresponsive and that they begin to avoid such partners. But what is it in the social context that reinforces boys for being unresponsive to girls? And what can we do to change these patterns? Obviously, there is much that we need to do as adults to ensure that girls' opinions are validated and given space in social interactions, but we must change our socialization of boys to increase their sensitivity and responsiveness to others (Almeida et al., 1998; see also Chapter 2). This is something that must be worked on from earliest childhood if girls are to achieve equity in relationships.

Among the questions therapists can ask to challenge the status quo regarding a mother's over-responsibility might be the following:

- Do both parents equally attend children's school plays and sports events?

- How are your children changing your perspective on the meaning of your life?
- Does the father get to spend time alone with each child? (It is almost impossible to develop intimacy if he does not.) Is the time spent fairly equally divided among the daughters and sons?
- How are domestic responsibilities divided?
- How is money handled and by whom? Who makes decisions about spending?
- What are each parent's hopes and expectations for each child in adulthood?
- How do you as parents try to counter societal preferential treatment of boys and show your daughters they are valuable?

ADOLESCENCE

Adolescence is a time when traditional deferential behaviors for girls come particularly to the fore. School sports, for example, are unfortunately still too often organized to highlight boys' competitive prowess, with girls cheerleading on the sidelines. Clinically, in working with adolescents and their families, it is important to ask questions about the roles each is asked to play in the family. What are the chores and responsibilities of boys and of girls? Are girls spending too much time and money on their clothes and appearance in response to media messages that they should concentrate on being sex objects? Are sons encouraged to develop social skills, or are parents focused primarily on their achievement and sports performance? Are daughters encouraged to have high academic aspirations? Are both sexes given equal responsibility and encouragement in dealing with education, athletics, aspirations for the future, extended family relationships, buying gifts, writing, calling, or caring for relatives? Do both sexes buy and clean their own clothes? Are daughters encouraged to learn about money, science, and other traditionally "masculine" subjects? Clinicians can help by asking questions about these patterns.

We also need to help families find more positive ways of defining for their daughters the changes of the menstrual and reproductive cycle so that they do not see themselves as "unclean" or "impure." For so long, if sex was even discussed in the family, mothers have taught their daughters that menstruation was "the curse" and that sexuality was dangerous and would reflect negatively on them. Sons, by contrast, were taught to view their bodily changes, especially their sexuality, as positive, powerful, and fulfilling aspects of their identity.

Adolescence is a key time in a young woman's life. It is the time when, traditionally, she was specifically inducted into the role of sex object and when, instead, she needs to be encouraged to form her own identity and life plans (Gilligan, 1982; Gilligan, Lyons, & Hanmer, 1990; Mirkin, 1994; Pipher, 1994). Although acceptance of conventional gender values is at an all-time high during adolescence, it is also during this phase that crucial life-shaping decisions are made. It is extremely important for therapists to support and encourage parents to be proactive with their daughters, to counter discriminatory messages that girls receive within the culture, and to encourage them not to short-circuit their dreams or submit to objectification in their relationships or work.

This phase may mark a time for conversion to a feminist position for fathers of daughters, as they want to support their daughters' having the same rights and privileges that men do. This awareness is important to capitalize on therapeutically. Mothers may be feeling a strain as their children pull away, particularly as they realize the limitations of their own options if they have devoted themselves primarily to child-rearing. On the other hand, mothers may feel a special sense of fulfillment in their daughters' going beyond the constrictions that limited their own lives.

LAUNCHING CHILDREN AND MOVING ON

For women, this may be a time of special opportunity to reinvent themselves, but also a time of special stress, since women often feel very much behind in the skills to deal with the outside world. Just when their children no longer need them and they are beginning to be defined by the male world as too old to be desirable, they must venture outward. The initial steps are usually the hardest. Once they have begun to move in this arena, many women experience a new confidence and pleasure in their independence—no longer having to put everyone else's needs first. Because of the social and management skills they have generally developed in the previous life cycle phases, women have remarkable resources for building a social network. Their lifelong skills in adapting to new situations also serve them in good stead. But the world of work still does not recognize their efforts in a way that is commensurate with their contribution, and women have generally been excluded from the financial world—and experience frequent discrimination in banks and legal and business institutions. In addition, women have typically not been socialized to expect or demand the recognition they deserve.

Of course, the divergence of interests for men and women, as well as the shift in focus of energies that is required at this phase, often creates marital tensions, perhaps leading to divorce. Hayes, Anderson and Blau (1993) challenge the idea that divorced women over age 40 are lonely, frightened, and unhappy. On the contrary, for the majority of midlife and older women who divorce, it is a catalyst for self-discovery, change, and growth (Anderson, 1994; Apter, 1995). These women tend to develop new confidence and self-esteem, despite the staggering drop in their income after divorce. However, 90 percent of them had no long-term financial goals or any idea how to confront the financial realities of their lives. The financial empowerment of women is an issue that deserves much more clinical attention. For women, whose options are much more limited than men's, the likelihood of remarriage after a divorce at this phase is quite slim. In part, this is due to the skew in availability of partners, and in part, it appears to be due to older women's having less need to be married and thus, perhaps, being less willing to "settle," particularly for a traditional marriage, which would mean a return to extensive caretaking and sacrifice of their own needs and interests.

Obviously, women who have developed an identity primarily through intimacy and adaptation to men will be particularly vulnerable in divorce during the launching phase, when they may feel that their very self is disintegrating. Women's risks at midlife due to their embeddedness in relationships, their orientation toward interdependence, their subordination of achievement to care, and their conflicts over competitive success are a problem of our society more than a problem in women's development.

This life cycle phase has often been referred to as the "empty nest" and depicted as a time of depression for women. Menopause, which usually occurs in a woman's late forties or early fifties, has generally been viewed negatively as a time of physical and psychological distress, especially for those whose whole lives have been devoted to home and family. However, the recent literature on this phase suggests that such a phenomenon is much more apparent than real (McQuaide, 1998). Typically, women are grateful and energized by recapturing free time and exploring new options for themselves. They are not nearly as sorry to see the child-rearing era end as has been assumed. For many women, it is a turning point that frees them sexually from worries about pregnancy and marks a new stabilization in their energies for pursuit of work and social activities (see Chapter 17).

OLDER FAMILIES

The final phase of life might be considered "for women only," since women tend to live longer and, unlike men, are rarely paired with younger partners, making the statistics for this life cycle phase extremely imbalanced. Since women are the primary caretakers of other women, these problems will affect at least two generations of women, who will be increasingly stressed as time goes along.

Women who need care and those who give it are statistically the poorest and have the least legislative power in our society. As was mentioned earlier, legislators have given little consideration to services that support family caregivers. The immediate cause of nursing home admission is more likely to be the depletion of family resources than a deterioration in the health of the older relative. While the increase in remarried families might mean that a wider kinship network is available for caregiving, the increasing divorce rate will probably mean that fewer family members will be willing or available to provide care for elderly parents. Since both those who give care to the elderly and most of those who receive it are women, the subject tends to escape our view. As therapists, we can counter this imbalance by redefining the dilemmas of both the elderly and their caretakers as serious, significant issues.

WOMEN AND THEIR FRIENDSHIP NETWORKS

Friendship is an extremely important resource for women throughout the life cycle. From earliest childhood, girls concentrate more energy on working out friendships than boys do. Girls assess activities in terms of their impact on relationships, whereas boys usually subordinate relationships to the games they are playing. Throughout life, women tend to have more close friends than men do, but the relationships that women have are often not validated by the larger society (Antonucci, 1994). Schydlowsky (1983) shows that the importance of women's close female friendships diminishes from adolescence to early adulthood, as they focus on finding a mate and establishing a marriage, and then increases throughout the rest of the life cycle. Close female friendships were reported to be more important than close male friendships throughout the life cycle, second only to good health in importance for life satisfaction.

We urge family members to respect and nurture friendship systems and challenge in therapy societal values that would allow a husband to block his wife's friendships or invalidate their importance. In traditional heterosexual couples, women were expected to make friends with their husbands' friends' wives to facilitate their husbands' social or business contacts, rather than to form their own friendships based on common needs and interests. In such traditional arrangements, women were expected to replace friends whenever they moved for their husbands' jobs. Such arrangements do not respect friendship as a basic support

throughout the life cycle and show a distorted prioritizing of career networking over friendship.

The expanded networks of many lesbian communities can provide a corrective model, emphasizing the importance of friendship and neighborhood networks, even including ex-partners in a permanent extended community network. Lesbians' careful nurturing of their networks is an excellent adaptation to a society that has been unsupportive and invalidating of their life cycle rituals and transitions, leaving them one of the most invisible of minorities. Their adaptive response is a transformative one, from which we could all benefit.

WOMEN AND LOSS

The usual coping strategies of women for dealing with loss leave them isolated and overburdened (Videcka-Sherman, 1982). For example, in a study of parents' reactions to sudden infant death syndrome, fathers reported anger, fear, and a loss of control, along with a desire to keep their grieving private, whereas mothers responded more with sorrow and depression (DeFrain, Taylor, & Ernst, 1982). Fathers are more likely to withdraw, to take refuge in their work, and to be uncomfortable with their wives' expressions of grief, not knowing how to respond and fearful of losing control of their own feelings. Mothers may perceive their husbands' emotional unavailability as abandonment when they need comfort most, thereby experiencing a double loss. When husbands are expressive and actively involved in a child's illness and death and in the family bereavement process, the quality of the marriage improves markedly.

Most commonly, when there is a loss, it is women who present themselves—or are sent by their husbands—for treatment of depression or other symptoms of distress concerning loss. Interventions need to be aimed at decreasing the sex-role split so that all family members can experience their own grief and be supportive to one another in adapting to loss. It is important to facilitate fuller involvement for men in the social and emotional tasks of the loss process, which will enrich their experience of family life as it lessens the disproportionate burden for women. A greater flexibility of allowable roles for both men and women will permit the full range of human experiences in bereavement as in other areas of family life.

The full participation of male and female family members in mourning rituals should be encouraged. One woman, at the death of her 100-year-old grandmother, expressed her desire to be a pallbearer at the funeral. One cousin replied that only males could do that; another added that they already had picked six pallbearers (who all happened to be male grandchildren). She persisted, suggesting that they simply have more than six. In the end, all twelve grandchildren, including five women, shared that important experience.

THAT THE BUMBLE BEE SHOULD FLY: AFFIRMING WOMEN THROUGH THE LIFE CYCLE

In *Reinventing Womanhood,* Carolyn Heilbrun (1979) said:

> If I imagine myself whole, active, a self, will I not cease in some profound way to be a woman? The answer must be: imagine, and the old idea of womanhood be damned.... When I was a girl, my father told me the story of the bumble bee. According to the science of aeronautics, so the story went, it was impossible for a creature of the size and weight and construction of a bumble bee to fly. But the bumble bee, not having been told this, flies anyway.

Carolyn Heibrun's advice seems essential to clinical work that would free women from the oppressive structures that would tell them they cannot fly. Therapy requires recontextualizing women's history, countering societal pressures for voicelessness and invisibility, and affirming women's own life stories (Carter, Papp, Silverstein & Walters, 1988). Traditional therapies have probably done more harm than good, failing as they did to acknowledge women's oppression and invalidation in the larger context and psychologizing social problems that made women think they were re-sponsible for creating problems in which they were, in fact, trapped by the social structure. Thus, is it most important, in working with women of every age, to be a force for liberation, validating the ways in which women are different and encouraging them to follow their dreams. The following poetic narrative by Pat Parker (1985) illustrates the power of this multigenerational perspective—one that puts us within the context of "herstory," not denying the problems that remain but validating the power of the women who have come before and the connectedness they have to the present generation and whose who will come after:

> It is from this past that I come, surrounded by sisters in blood and in spirit It is this past that I bequeath, a history of work and struggle
> Each generation improves the world for the next.
> My grandparents willed me strength, My parents will me pride. I will you rage.
> I give you a world incomplete, a world where women still are property and chattel
> where color still shuts doors, where sexual choice still threatens, but I give you a legacy of doers of people who take risks to chisel the crack wider.
> Take the strength that you may wage a long battle.
> Take the pride that you can never stand small.
> Take the rage that you can never settle for less

CONCLUSION

In 1976, Jean Baker Miller's brilliant essay *Toward a New Psychology of Women* outlined a new pathway for women's relationships that would involve reorganizing all men's relationships as well. In the two decades since that book appeared, we have been going through nothing less than a revolution in the pathways of the life cycle of women. We hope that our clinical interventions become a liberating force, fostering the creative and adaptive changes in human development that allow more latitude for both men and women in their ways of relating to their mates and peers, in their intergenerational connectedness, and in their relationships to work and community. We do not believe that the relational and emotionally expressive aspect of development is intrinsic to women (see Chapter 2).

We see the romanticization of "feminine" values as inaccurate and unhelpful to families (Hare-Mustin, 1983). It is also not enough for women to adopt the "male" values of the dominant culture and to devalue what have been traditionally "female" values.

We aim toward a theory of family and individual development where both instrumental and relational aspects of each individual will be fostered. The "feminine" perspective has been so devalued that it needs to be highlighted, as Harriet Lerner, the Stone Center, bell hooks, Audre Lorde, Paula Gunn Allen, Carol Gilligan, Betty Friedan, Mary Field Belenky, Mary Pipher, and so many others have recently been doing. It is hoped that both men and women will be able to develop their potential without regard for the constraints of gender stereotyping that have been so constricting of human experience until now. It is clear that traditional marriage and family patterns are no longer working for women, if they ever did, and the statistics reveal women's dissatisfaction. In our view, these patterns will change only when we have worked out a new equilibrium that is not based on the patriarchal family hierarchy. And we will understand and appreciate women's potential and dilemmas only when we consider all women together: gay and straight, young and old, black and white and all the hues in between.

REFERENCES

Aguirre, B. E. (1985). Why do they return? Abused wives in shelters. *Social Work. 30*(3), 350–354.

Almeida, R. (1993). Unexamined assumptions and service delivery systems: Feminist theory and racial exclusions. *Journal of Feminist Family Therapy, 5* (1), 3–23.

Almeida, R. (1998). The dislocation of women's experience in family therapy. *Journal of Feminist Family Therapy, 10*(1).

Almeida, R., Woods, R., & Messineo, T. (1998). Child development: The intersection of race, gender, class and culture. In R. Almeida (Ed.), *Transforming gender and race.* New York: Harrington Park Press.

Anderson, C. (1994). *Flying solo.* New York: W. W. Norton.

Antonucci, T. C. (1994). A life span view of women's social relationships. In B. F. Turner & L. E. Troll (Eds.), *Women growing older.* Thousand Oaks, CA: Sage.

Apter, T. (1995) *Secret paths: Women in the new midlife.* New York: W. W. Norton.

Arnetz, B. B., Wasserman, J., Petrini, B., & Brenner, S. (1987). Immune function in unemployed women. *Psychosomatic medicine. 49*(1), 3–12.

Avis, J. (1985). The politics of functional family therapy: A feminist critique. *Journal of Marital and Family Therapy, 11*(2), 127–138.

Bank, M. (1979). *Anonymous was a woman.* New York: St. Martin's Press.

Barnett, O. W., Miller-Perrin, C. L., & Perrin, R. D. (1997). *Family violence across the lifespan.* Thousand Oaks, CA: Sage.

Barnett, R. C., & Rivers, C. (1996). *She works/he works: How two-income families are happier, healthier, and better-off.* San Francisco: Harper.

Baruch, G., Barnett, R., & Rivers, C. (1983). *Lifeprints: New patterns of love and work for today's women.* New York: New American Library.

Bateson, M. C. (1989). *Composing a life.* New York: The Atlantic Monthly Press.

Bateson, M. C. (1994). *Peripheral Visions.* New York: Harper Collins.

Belenky, M. F., Clinchy, B. M., Goldberger, N. R., & Tarule, J. M. (1986). *Women's ways of knowing.* New York: Basic Books.

Bernard, J. (1982). *The future of marriage.* New Haven, CT: Yale University Press.

Blumstein, P., & Schwartz, P. (1983). *American couples: Money, work, sex.* New York: William Morrow.

Blumstein, P., & Schwartz, P. (1991). Money and ideology: Their impact on power and the division of household labor. In Blumberg, Rae Lesser (Ed.), *Gender, family and economy: The triple overlap.* New York: Sage.

Caplan, P. J. (1996, October). Take the blame off mother. *Psychology Today.*

Caplan, P. J., & Hall-McCorquondale, I. (1985). Mother-blaming in major clinical journals. *American Journal of Orthopsychiatry, 55*(3), 345–353.

Carter, B. (1996). *Love, honor and negotiate.* New York: Pocketbooks.

Collins, L. V. (1997). *Facts for women's history month.* Washington DC: U.S. Census Bureau.

Coontz, S. (1997). *The way we really are.* New York: Basic Books.

Daniels, P., & Weingarten, K. (1983). *Sooner or later: The timing of parenthood in adult lives.* New York: Norton.

Defrain, J., Taylor, J., & Ernst, L. (1982). *Coping with sudden infant death.* Lexington, MA: D. C. Heath.

Dowling, C. (1996). *Red hot mamas: Coming into our own at fifty.* New York: Bantam.

Faludi, S. (1991). *Backlash: The undeclared war against American women.* New York: Crown Publishers.

Friedan, B. (1985, November 3). How to get the women's movement moving again. *New York Times Magazine.*

Garcia Coll, C., Surrey, J. I., & Weingarten, K., (Eds.). (1998). *Mothering against the odds.* New York: The Guilford Press.

Gilligan, C. (1982). *In a different voice.* Cambridge, MA: Harvard University Press.

Gilligan, C., Lyons, N. P., & Hamner, T. J. (1990). *Making connections: The relational worlds of adolescent girls at the Emma Willard School.* Cambridge, MA: Harvard University Press.

Goldberger, N., Tarule, J., Clinchy, B., & Belenky, M. (1996). *Knowledge difference and power.* New York: Basic Books.

Goldner, V. (1985). Feminism and family therapy. *Family Process.* 24(1), 31–48.

Goleman, D. (1986, April 1). Two views of marriage explored: His and hers. *New York Times,* 19.

Goodrich, T. J., Rampage, C., Ellman, B., & Halstead, K. (1988). *Feminist family therapy: A casebook.* New York: Norton.

Gove, W. R. (1972). The relationship between sex roles, marital status and mental illness. *Social Forces,* 51, 34–44.

Gunn Allen, P. (1992). Angry women are building: Issues and struggles facing American Indian women today. In M. L. Anderson & P. H. Collins (Eds.), *Race, class, and gender.* Belmont, CA: Wadsworth.

Hall, R. L., & Greene, B. (1994). Cultural competence in feminist family therapy: An ethical mandate. *Journal of Feminist Family Therapy,* 6(3), 5–28.

Hansberry, L. (1969). *To be young, gifted and black.* New York: Signet.

Hare-Mustin, R. T. (1983). Psychology: A feminist perspective on family therapy. In E. Haber (Ed.), The Women's Annual: 1982–83 (pp. 177–204). Boston: G. K. Hall.

Hare-Mustin, R. T. (1991). Sex, lies and headaches: The problem of power. *Journal of Feminist Family Therapy, 3.*

Heilbrun, C. G. (1979). *Reinventing womanhood.* New York: Norton.

Heilbrun, C. (1988). *Writing a woman's life.* New York: Norton.

Heilbrun, C. (1997). *The last gift of time: Life beyond sixty.* New York: The Dial Press.

Hess, B. B. (1985). Aging policies and old women: The hidden agenda. In A. S. Rossi (Ed.), *Gender and the life course.* New York: Aldine.

Heyn, D. (1997). *Marriage shock: The transformation of women into wives.* New York: Villard.

Hochschild, A. (1989). *The second shift: Working parents and the revolution at home.* New York: Viking.

Hoffman, L. (1989). Effects of maternal employment in the two parent family. *American Psychologist.*

Horner, M. S. (1972). Toward an understanding of achievement-related conflicts in women. *Journal of Social Issues, 28,* 157–175.

Kessler, R. C., & McRae, J. A. (1984). A note on the relationships of sex and marital status with psychological distress. In J. Greenley (Ed.), *Community and mental health* (Vol. 3). Greenwich, CT: JAI.

Lerner, H. (1985). *The dance of anger.* New York: Harper & Row.

Lerner, H. (1989). *The dance of intimacy.* New York: Harper & Row.

Lerner, H. (1993). *The dance of deception.* New York: Harper & Row.

Lewin, T. (1997a, September 5). Equal pay for equal work is no. 1 goal of women. *New York Times,* p. A20.

Lerner, H. (1998). *Mother dance.* New York: Harper & Row.

Lewin, T. (1997b, September 15). Women losing ground to men in widening income difference. *New York Times.*

Lorde, A. (1984). *Sister outsider.* Freedom, CA: The Crossing Press.

Losoff, M. M. (1974). Fathers and autonomy in women. In R. B. Kundsin (Ed.), *Women and success: The anatomy of achievement.* New York: William Morrow.

Lott, B. (1994). *Women's lives* (2nd ed.). Pacific Grove, CA: Brooks/Cole.

Maccoby, E. E. (1990). Gender and relationships: A developmental account. *American Psychologist, 45*(4): 513–520.

McGoldrick, M. (1995). *You can go home again: Reconnecting with your family.* New York: W. W. Norton.

McGoldrick, M. (1996). *The legacy of unresolved loss: A family systems approach.* New York: Newbridge Communications.

McGoldrick, M., Anderson, C., & Walsh, F. (Eds.). (1989). *Women in families and family therapy.* New York: Norton.

McIntosh, P. (1985). *On feeling like a fraud.* Work in Progress, No. 18. Wellesley, MA: The Stone Center Working Papers Series.

McIntosh, P. (1989). *On feeling like a fraud,* (Part 2). Work in Progress, No. 37, Wellesley, MA: The Stone Center Working Papers Series.

McQuaide, S. (1998, January). Women at midlife. *Social Work, 43*(1), 21–31.

Miller, J. B. (1976). *Toward a new psychology of women.* Boston: Beacon.

Mirkin, M. (1994). Female adolescence revisited: Understanding girls in their sociocultural contexts. In M. Mirkin (Ed.), *Women in Context.* New York: The Guilford Press.

Padan, D. (1965). *Intergenerational mobility of women: A two-step process of status mobility in a context of a value conflict.* Tel Aviv, Israel: Publication of Tel Aviv University.

Parker, P. (1985). *Jonestown & other madness.* Ithaca, NY: Firebrand Books.

Peterson, R. R. (1996). A re-evaluation of the economic consequences of divorce. *American Sociological Review, 61*(3), 528–536.

Pipher, M. (1994). *Reviving Ophelia.* New York: Ballantine Books.

Sassen, G. (1980). Success anxiety in women: A constructivist interpretation of its sources and its significance. *Harvard Educational Review, 50,* 13–25.

Schydlowsky, B. M. (1983). Friendships among women in midlife. Unpublished doctoral dissertation, University of Michigan. Microfilm.

Shapiro, P. G. (1996). *My turn: Women's search for self after the children leave.* Princeton, NJ: Peterson's.

Slater, S. (1995). *The lesbian family life cycle.* New York: The Free Press.

Stacey, J. (1996). *In the name of the family: Rethinking family values.* Boston: Beacon.

Videka-Sherman, L. (1982). Coping with the death of a child: A study over time. *American Journal of Orthopsychiatry, 52,* 688–698.

Weingarten, K. (1994). *The mother's voice.* New York: Harcourt, Brace & Co.

Weiss, R. S. (1985). Men and the family. *Family Process, 24*(1): 49–58.

Wetherington, E., & Kessler, R. (1989, December). Employment, parental responsibility and psychological distress. *Journal of Family Issues.*

Whitehead, B. D. (1993, May/June). The new family values. *Utne Reader,* 61–66.

Wolfer, L. T., & Moen, P. (1996). Staying in school: Maternal employment and the timing of Black and White daughters' school exit. *Journal of Family Issues, 17*(4), 540–560.

CHAPTER 7

MEN IN TRANSITION
THE "NEW MAN"

ELLIOTT J. ROSEN

THE NEW MAN AND THE LEGACY OF MASCULINITY

In a provocative memoir, Jane Lazzare relates her experience as a white mother raising two black sons. She emphasizes that understanding and talking about race must include an awareness of Whiteness, because "understanding racism does not occur automatically or quickly... [that] racism involves power, an intricate pattern of privilege we enjoy" (Lazzare, 1996, p. xvi). What is true of race is similarly true of gender. While it is often noted that much of history is about men, written by men, and focused on men's accomplishments, men themselves have seldom been consciously aware of gender as a dimension of their lives (Kivel, 1992). This lack of awareness of maleness, much like the blindness to Whiteness, perpetuates power inequities that will never be addressed unless consciously examined. Explorations of maleness, fueled by the liberation movements and growing awareness of gender, class, race, sexual orientation, and ethnicity may even raise the question of whether we stand at the threshold of an era of the "new man" (Kimmel, 1996). When a million men can march on Washington to claim—or reclaim—their maleness, and when scores of sports stadiums throughout the country can fill to the voices of men vowing to keep their promises, we most surely take notice.

If you have practiced family therapy long enough, you are sure to have compiled a "fan mail" file. I have an enlightening letter in my fan mail file dated February 8, 1983:

Dear Dr. Rosen:

Thank you for meeting with my wife and me this past evening. By now I assume she has called to tell you that we cannot continue marriage counseling with you. You seem like a warm and sympathetic fellow and _____ spoke highly of you. However, I do not believe you can be helpful to us.

I do not know exactly what you meant when you spoke of my wife as being (and I think this is a direct quote) "one-down and powerless" in her marriage, but anyone who can say this about a woman, who plays more tennis in one week than I get to play in a year, has no idea what the real world is all about.

Thank you for your time. Enclosed is a check for our meeting.

Sincerely,

This was the early 1980s, and in the flush and pride of new-found therapeutic feminism, my first reaction was the familiar sigh and the expletive *"men."* Yet I could not get the experience out of my mind. It had been a *good* session! I had done a solid job of clarifying the issues in this first consultation: Theirs was an arrangement that mirrored how men and women counterproductively align themselves in traditional marriage. Unless she understood that her depression and rage were related to her dependence on him and he understood that his sense of powerlessness and frustration were the result of his believing his power and privilege to be a burden, as his having no option other than to work harder and harder to satisfy the inexhaustible needs of his family, they would continue to struggle. In this, a new era in social history, it would be necessary for both to critically address traditional gender roles; while feminism had begun to face the issues for women, challenging the norms of masculinity would be an even greater task. Such norms as avoiding femininity; suppressing emotional vulnerability; elevating the primacy of work; glorifying self-reliance, aggression, and toughness; striving for dominance; sexual objectification; and homophobia are among those enumerated by Robert-Jay Green (1998). To change them would be virtually to invent a "new man."

IS THERE A "NEW MAN"?

Garrison Keillor, in *The Book of Guys,* writes that "years ago, manhood was an opportunity for achievement, and now it is a problem to be overcome" (Keillor, 1993, p. 11). When was this "years ago" that Keillor writes about and how do the lives of American men differ from those of previous generations? Sociologist Michael Kimmel, in his superb cultural history *Manhood in America,* traces the American notion of "maleness" from its earliest roots in the oedipal revolt of the Sons of Liberty against Father England and suggests that maleness has meant different things at different periods of American history. He argues that American men have always had some anxiety about gender, at times to the point of pathology (Kimmel, 1996).

The notion of the "self-made man," for example (a term that was first coined in the nineteenth century), has been a category within which many American men have sought to define themselves for generations, and that, of course, obscures their connections to those who have nurtured and raised them. This notion, forged in tandem with the peculiarly American sociopolitical belief in manifest destiny and the frontier, allowed for enormous creativity and exploration while simultaneously burdening men with a sense of rootlessness and difficulty in determining a firm sense of identity. It may also contribute to their valuing their own experience over their accountability to others they live with. The additional phenomenon of many boys coming of age in families without fathers has added to the difficulty of forging identity (Pittman, 1993). The strong cultural strain for American men of going forth to seek one's fate and destiny is well documented in fact and fiction. As long as there is a wilderness, an uncharted frontier, there remains an opportunity to prove one's ability to create oneself as a man. The premise of Kimmel's work is that the cultural history of American men is the drive to define themselves—by either excessive efforts at self-control, reactive exclusion, or escape. These three themes, which he traces over two centuries, are now evident as contemporary men attempt to come to grips with their identity: the appeal of the Christian men's movements; the rising tide of neo-Nazi, nativist, and xenophobic movements; and the glorification of native American wilderness quests and sweat lodges are just a few of many latter-day efforts to grapple with masculine identity.

Homophobia is usually presumed to refer only to the fear of the homosexual, but more universally, it is an ingrained fear of other men. As Kimmel (1996, p. 120) has pointed out, men fear not "women, but of being ashamed or humiliated in front of other men, or being dominated by stronger men." When I asked male friends and colleagues, "What is your most negative or unpleasant childhood social memory?" almost every one reported an incident in which he was humiliated or bullied by a bigger or older boy or in which he felt dominated or weak in a social situation.

The dilemma of male identity and the meaning of masculinity has been even more pronounced for Black men and homosexuals. With a legacy of slavery and oppression, African American men have been faced with the agonizing task of reclaiming a manhood that was stolen from them as part of their initiation into America. Literary and journalistic images of freed Black slaves through the turn of this century had focused on the familiar idea of the self-made man who would reclaim his manhood (Kimmel, 1996). This theme continued to be articulated by the Black liberation movement of the 1960s, which focused on concepts such as pride and manhood; Eldridge Cleaver's manifesto of Black manhood, *Soul on Ice,* ignited the imagination of young Black men. Today's Black Muslim movement has much appeal in the Black community because it is unambiguous in its identification of who men need to be. A traditional belief in men as strong, protective warriors and family providers (and women as in need of protection) is the cornerstone of the Black male revival movement, which is most publicly represented by the Nation of Islam. It has, perhaps not incidentally, provided a strong rationale for some African American women to support what appears to many White feminists as a sexist credo. There are some women's voices in the African American community who publicly grapple with male-female issues, but they are not well known. One example is Pearl Cleage, whose call for a new understanding of "brotherhood," in which awareness of and compassion for women and children are a cornerstone, is poignant and powerful (Cleage, 1990). But in a community in which the anomie and alienation of men have created much pain and arrested development, Black women are far more willing to exercise patience with their men and to defend them against White criticism. I was recently chastised by the wife of an African American man I was treating when I mildly challenged what I characterized as her husband's irresponsibility regarding finances. "I don't expect perfection from him," she scolded me, "and I think it's pretty patronizing of you to."

For gay men, the difficulty of conforming to traditional male roles is an important aspect of their having been prevented from achieving a sense of themselves as "acceptable" men. Ironically, there have been times when society has been more welcoming to the gay life, particularly in the larger cities (Kaiser, 1997). However, brief periods of open acceptance have nearly always met with extreme reactivity and anxiety—with the dangers of feminization and homosexuality being linked as scourges on the purity of family and society. Historically, a direct accusation of homosexuality, or even the suggestion of femininelike behavior, has proven a death knell to the success of public figures. The social institutionalization of homophobia has been well documented (Cohler, Hostetler, & Boxer, 1998; Eisler, 1995). From the public attacks on political personalities such as Adlai Stevenson, Michael Dukakis, and others as "effeminate" to the more localized travails of untold numbers of teachers, coaches, and clergy, to be

identified as "less than masculine" has been a frightening prospect. The Stonewall riots of 1969 marked the beginnings of a shift in self-confidence and self-regard for gay men. Moreover, it would seem that gay men have been more successful than heterosexuals in breaking out of the stereotypical models of manhood. Because of the forced or chosen nonconformity on the part of gay men "and especially gay men who create and sustain couple relationships…[they] have been socialized differently than other men and therefore have distinctive relational styles, abilities, and values that differ from those of heterosexual men" (Green, Bettinger, & Zacks, 1996, p. 209).

The theme that dominates the life cycle of heterosexual men is a profound sense of challenge, a sense of being constantly tested, whether at home or in the world of work. How a man perceives himself as meeting that challenge is likely to underlie his fundamental sense of self. Although Hamlet's famous soliloquy is usually characterized as the ultimate existential challenge, it can be viewed even more pointedly as a peculiarly masculine dilemma: "*To be*," we recall is "to take arms against a sea of troubles and, by opposing, end them." "*Or not to be*," on the other hand, is "to suffer the slings and arrows of outrageous fortune." This reflects a uniquely male conundrum: If I let down my guard or allow myself to be vulnerable I will be hurt, defenseless against the vicissitudes of life and relationships; if I mobilize my defenses, I will be safe. This tension between perceived strength and weakness lies at the core of male being (Brod, 1988). It is also at the core of what one clinician refers to as "male relational dread" (Bergman, 1996). Among the many beliefs that attend to this dread is that relationships will ultimately end in disaster, that they will cause damage, or that they may result in violence. Often, when men do become self-aware as men in relationships they tend to focus on their internal experience rather than on the impact of their social privilege. As one group of clinicians working with men points out, their "men's groups emphasize personal accountability to others rather than to self. In our experience, one of the most common problems men have is overfocusing on

'self' and the 'resolution' of their feelings."
(Almeida, Wood, Messineo, & Font, 1998).

The definition of masculinity is, of course, a
social construct. While we are born biologically
male or female, the notions of feminine and masculine are cultural and socially determined. When
it comes to defining "maleness" or "masculinity,"
we often find that these terms are defined by what
a man is *not*—not a woman, not a boy, not a homosexual (Green, 1998). What we do know about
being a man is that masculinity is something that
needs to be proved, constantly and regularly, to
one's self and to others—to men, to women, to
parents, to co-workers. This may be among the
heaviest burdens borne by men. A man's psychological life is a constant struggle with what he believes are the demands of his masculinity, and for
children, there is a paucity of alternative models
for manhood. Paul Kivel (1992) offers a personal
reminiscence:

> When I was a teenager I lived in a world inhabited
> entirely by men. All my friends were the other guys
> on the block or at school. I spent almost every
> minute with them. Every book I read, every televi-
> sion show or movie I watched was by and about
> men. Everything I learned in history…was about
> men. At home I tried to be like my father—I dis-
> counted my mother and ignored my sister. Girls
> were distant, shining sex objects that I dreamed
> about but who did not fit into my daily experience.
> (pp. 31–32)

A number of metaphors for masculinity are
incorporated at an early age for boys, and chief
among them is sports. I can recall the hours I spent
as a young adolescent shooting hoops alone on the
playground, accompanied by a leitmotif of myself
as sports announcer, describing my prowess and
competition against various NBA opponents—
against whom I always triumphed. Even for many
young boys who lack physical athletic prowess,
the identification with sports teams and sports heroes forms a powerful framework for thinking
about the world. I recently treated a man who suffered crippling polio in childhood and who became
a virtual encyclopedia of sports information, which,

he explained, allowed him to relate companionably
to the other boys in his neighborhood—to be
"one of the guys."

MEN AND POWER

Few subjects have demanded more attention in the
family therapy literature in recent years than that
of the power imbalance between men and women.
The subtlety and hidden nature of this power
imbalance are often at the core of resistance to
change in couples therapy. While examples of how
this power is manifested in terms of physical intimidation or financial leverage are common, the
more subtle evidence often perplexes therapists.
For example, it can be demonstrated in a description of the decision-making process for infertile
couples. Even in situations in which the man is infertile, it is the woman who must make decisions
and take action (Lorber & Bandlamudi, 1993).
Without his cooperation, of course, she can neither
use his sperm nor opt for donor insemination; but
since she bears more painfully the social onus of
childlessness—and thus is often more desperate to
conceive—her bargaining power is compromised.
"Even though the man seems to be in a disadvantaged position, since he is the one with the physiological problem, the combination of social
pressures and men's marital power reduces the
woman's ability to bargain for what she wants in
the situation" (Lorber & Bandlamudi, 1993, p. 33).
Nevertheless, it is in such situations that men often
accuse women of owning all the power. "It's *you*,"
he may argue, "who wants a child…and I'm willing to cooperate. Why are you being so difficult
about it?"

Any discussion of power in marriage must address not only tradition-bound male privilege, but
also the many significant advantages that come with
financial control and physical strength. Not surprisingly, the notion of the man as the head of household
remains firmly entrenched, despite dramatic demographic changes in women's employment outside
the home. Even though only about 15 percent of
American households are supported solely by a
male breadwinner (down from 42 percent in 1960),

a large percentage of men continue to espouse a belief that men should maintain the sole provider role (Wilkie, 1991, 1993). Of course, since many men believe that their identity as men depends on their maintaining decision-making prerogatives, it is difficult for them to imagine a marital system in which such decision-making is more equitable. This blindness, culturally instilled and reinforced at every turn, permits men to experience the demand that they change as a demand that they relinquish power while continuing to bear the overresponsibility of manhood. Even in marriages that begin with a more equal or shared notion of gender role, the arrival of children often signals a "backsliding into traditional marriage" (Carter, 1996, p. 13). Many factors contribute to this regression, but certainly a primary factor is the husband's belief that he is now burdened with far too much "real-world" responsibility (i.e., earning money—and lots of it) to compromise that pursuit with more mundane—and less productive—household chores. This thinking has been reinforced by modern-day male polemicists such as Warren Farrell who argue that marriage is an unfair deal for men in that women have many options and men are stuck with only one choice: to work full-time (Farrell, 1986). This neatly deflects the focus from a consideration of men's privilege and power to self-pity for being "burdened" to provide for others. It also ignores the potential for mutual decision making about career choices, life-style, child-rearing practices, and a host of other matters that are seldom addressed if they interfere with this privilege.

The issue of men's power as manifested in domestic violence and abuse is discussed more fully in this volume (see Chapter 28). What must be noted here, of course, is the fact that violence and physical abuse are fundamentally problems that must be addressed by men. The early feminist critiques of family therapy's treatment of domestic violence rightfully highlighted the further victimization of women in a therapy devoted to uncovering how "the system" contributed to an atmosphere in which violence could occur (Goodrich, Rampage, Ellman, & Halsted, 1988; Walters, Carter, Papp, & Silverstein, 1988) Needless to say, child-

rearing patterns and social acceptance of violence continue to reinforce the image of men as "real men" when they are physically tough and willing to show it. In a recent TV series, a 30-something attorney was explaining to his female colleague the zeal he was bringing to the defense of a young man accused of slugging another fellow in defense of his girlfriend, whom the latter was insulting. Despite his many life successes, the lawyer claimed, he was plagued by the memory of being bullied on the playground by a bigger boy. It was only when finally, as an adult, he hit a man who was intimidating him in a bar that he was able to reclaim his wounded manhood. His female colleague argued feebly with this notion, but it was clear to the viewer that she understood—as did the jury that acquitted the young man. No mention was made of the degree to which such violence "in defense" of women is a subtle demonstration of the "ownership" of women. As one clinician has pointed out, a man's need to control the "dangerous sexuality of women" has often resulted in homicide or suicide (Pittman, 1993). The preponderance of violent themes in television, movies, and video games designed for young children continue to reinforce the acceptability of the notion that "boys will be boys." Certainly the glorification of military culture, reinforced by a sports vocabulary replete with murder, mayhem, and military metaphor, will continue to encourage more aggressive, violent behavior in young men (see Chapter 13).

The contemporary Black and Christian men's movements have, to their credit, been willing to take clear ownership of violence as a male problem. A frequent message in many of their rallies and meetings has been that violence against women and children must cease and that men must atone for their history of physical abuse and change their ways. However, there is an inherent paradox in this message. The men's movement, in general, has strongly espoused a return to traditional gender roles and traditional family values. Such roles and such values have historically fostered violence, abuse, and physical control of weaker members of the system. A return to this traditional family model will inevitably perpetuate a rigid system in which power and gender hierarchy prevail—and violence and abuse are likely to occur. Some 80 percent or more of lethal violence in America is perpetrated by men, and one study that examined gender, intimacy, and lethal violence revealed that there has been little change over time in the pattern of men killing their wives and unmarried partners (Browne & Williams, 1993; see also Chapter 28).

MEN, FRIENDSHIP, AND THE MEN'S MOVEMENTS

It has become a commonplace observation that men have difficulty creating and sustaining same-sex friendships or communicating their emotional problems or vulnerability. One of my clients, Barbara, described a conversation with her husband upon leaving his company's holiday party: She commented on how sad it was that Bob (one of her husband's partners) and Susan (his wife) had finally been forced to place their adult, retarded son in an institution. "Bob has a retarded son?" he replied. Barbara sighed and rolled her eyes. "You've worked with him for ten years and you never knew they were caring for a profoundly retarded son at home?" she said. "It never came up," replied her husband.

It has been frequently noted that men's friendship patterns differ dramatically from those of women (Miller, 1983; Walker, 1994). Indeed, there does seem a longing on the part of men for a more sustaining, nurturing connection with other men, although this need for same-sex companionship is often thwarted by powerful cultural strains of homophobia (Swain, 1989). Each generation has created its own rendition, from the hypermasculine Jacksonian version of the 1830s and the blatantly homophobic Red-baiting of 1950s McCarthyism (Kimmel, 1996) to the pages of our present-day newspapers. The presidential politics of this past decade have continued that theme. Recall that George Bush had gone to great lengths to fashion himself a president in the "tough guy" likeness of his predecessor, Ronald Reagan. President Bush's military victories in Panama and the Gulf War cre-

ated his image as a manly leader. Ironically, he was defeated by Bill Clinton, who campaigned as a "new man," willing to express emotion and acknowledge weakness—and even to admit that he and his family had been in family therapy. Yet within months of his election, Clinton's popularity was eroded by the controversial debate over gays in the military and the accusation that his wife was too powerful—the implication, of course, being that he was not man enough to control her.

The desire for male camaraderie is a frequent theme in any discussion about male socialization. "Men court men," says one observer of the male condition (Tiger, 1969, p. 14). The popularity of buddy movies reflects this, as does the emphasis on team sports, fraternities, clubs, and other group activities for men. Jokes, sarcasm, and humor serve a similar purpose, reaffirming values of friendship, generosity, and heterosexuality (Walker, 1994). Camaraderie, play, and "hanging out" notwithstanding, it is difficult for men to form deep friendship bonds in adulthood. A common theme in therapy with men is that of loneliness. It is probably fair to say that most men seek women nearly exclusively as confidantes and look to men as playmates rather than as sources of emotional support (Pittman, 1993). I make it a practice to question men in treatment carefully about their friendship patterns. Their wives are often quick to observe that their husbands have no close friends and are fairly alone, with no one to talk to. A man is likely to reply that, of course, he has friends—and mention the names of a few other men. His wife will immediately counter by pointing out that he seldom talks with these guys and may not see or speak to them for months on end.

It would appear than an obstacle to male friendship is the loss of power that closeness with another might create. If one leaves oneself vulnerable, exposes one's frailties, and shares one's uncertainties about managing life, it is difficult to remain in control, in the "one-up" position. Since much of a man's life is fraught with the necessity of proving himself, there is no doubt that his performance is a necessary mask for deeper feelings of low self-esteem and insecurity. This may be one aspect of why men turn to women for their more intimate friendships and why these friendships often result in extramarital affairs. For in a world in which gender and power are so closely related, it is infinitely safer for a man to risk closeness with a woman than with a competitive male.

> John and Carrie came to couples therapy to try to save their marriage after it was revealed that John had had an extramarital affair with Carrie's close friend, Tanya. Carrie was devastated by the dual betrayal, and John was ashamed and contrite. In a lengthy discussion of friendship, John described how easy it was to talk to Tanya about his doubts and uncertainties and how agonizing a similar conversation would be with his wife. "If I ever told you some of the things I've told her," John told Carrie, "you'd pack your bags and run out the door. You wouldn't want to stay with a pitiful wimp like me. You admire your father and his strength so I know what you want in a man!" Carrie was bewildered. "What's marriage for if it's not a place where you can share your doubts and insecurity? I didn't marry my father. I married you."

Men, of course, often confuse intimacy with sexuality, partly because they are not particularly comfortable with nor know much about the former (Pittman, 1993). Telling another the details of one's life is a common experience for women. At an early age, girls are encouraged to share their thoughts and feelings with others, and boys are discouraged from such intimacies (Tannen, 1990). Women have also learned that real closeness with men is likely to demand sexual as well as emotional intimacy, and they play by these gender rules. Not to do so would most often spell the end to a relationship that they wish to maintain. In recent years, as men and women have interacted in more equal relationships in school and the workplace, it has become more common for platonic friendships to be maintained between sexes and to be tolerated more easily by both of the friends' significant other.

In many ways the growth of the men's movements—from Robert Bly and Sam Keen's mythopoetic drum banging through the Nation of Islam's Million Man March and the Promise Keepers—reflects a longing on the part of men for connection with other men. Many of these movements recapitulate earlier phenomena in our cultural history. For example, at the end of the nineteenth century, some 20 percent of American men were members of organizations or fraternal orders that supported a masculine ideal of camaraderie and grew in reaction to a perceived feminization of society (Kimmel, 1996). One recent exception to the typical pattern of men's movements has been the National Organization of Men Against Sexism. This group supports a program that condemns racism and sexism but, needless to say, has not gained the kind of public notice or interest among men that the more traditional conservative movements have.

Particularly interesting are the similarities between the Promise Keepers and the "muscular Christianity" movements of the 1930s and 1940s and Billy Sunday's Christian mission earlier in the century. In these organizations, much of the same language used by today's Christian movements was present. Jesus was portrayed as hypermasculine, and women were depicted paradoxically as potentially dangerous while in need of protection. As Billy Sunday loudly proclaimed, Jesus was "the greatest scrapper who ever lived," and another evangelist counseled that Jesus should be the model for "magnificent manliness" (Kimmel, 1996). This mission to hold back the demon of feminization and "revirilize" boyhood reverberates in today's men's movements when leaders assert that American men face a moral and spiritual crisis in their lives and need to "reclaim" leadership in the family from women.

However, as was mentioned, there is an inherent danger in a movement that espouses a return to a gender-based family hierarchy, in which men are encouraged to "reclaim leadership." Louis Farrakhan's Nation of Islam has espoused much the same philosophy, albeit in a racially separate model of manhood. In response to the phenomenon in the African American community of men who have been marginalized, underemployed, humiliated, and oppressed, the appeal of the movement is understandable. The unease with which White America has greeted Farrakhan is certainly a reflection of historical fear of Black male potency and rage, as well as a legitimate uneasiness with a rhetoric fraught with threats, anti-Semitism, and distortion of generally accepted historical realities. There is no question, however, that much of what latter-day movements have responded to is the two-centuries-old quest on the part of American men for a viable identity, a sense of belonging, friendship, and a need to be nurtured. Once again, the self-made man is searching for the anchor of self-definition.

MEN AND THEIR RELATIONSHIPS THROUGHOUT THE FAMILY LIFE CYCLE

Among the many significant shifts in family configuration are the continued shrinkage of the traditional nuclear family to only one quarter of all households, and the dramatic increase in single-parent families. Further, the fact that within a year of divorce, some 50 percent of fathers cease contact with their children and 40 percent fail to pay child support is a disturbing phenomenon and certainly tells us much about men's conceptions of themselves as fathers (Furstenberg, et al., 1983).

As we examine the stages of the family life cycle and men's roles, rewards, and expectations at each stage, we need to keep in mind that there continues to be a deplorable lack of preparation for men to take their place in collaborative relationships in the family. Gender-biased child-rearing practices remain in many ways as entrenched today as they have ever been. The encouragement that girls receive to be emotionally expressive and that boys receive to be tough and resilient remains part of the fabric of our child-rearing and our popular culture (Maccoby, 1990; Gilligan, 1982). As Deborah Tannen has pointed out, "even if they grow up in the same neighborhood, on the same block, or in the same house, girls and boys grow up in different worlds of words" (1990, p. 43). Whereas the language of young girls reflects intimacy and sharing, the language of boys is competitive and boastful, thus creating male-female relationships that are nearly cross-cultural. This is not to say that advances have not been made to-

ward creating a more level field of play for boys and girls, men and women. Title IX guidelines have created enormous opportunities for girls and women in competitive sports. Domestic violence and sexual harassment laws and other wide-ranging legislation have made both the home and the workplace a safer and more congenial place for women and have clarified expectations for men. But much remains to be done to ensure gender equality in both spheres.

Becoming an Adult: The Task of Differentiation

In a world of protracted adolescence, the tasks attendant on growing up have become ever more complex and confounding. The gap between haves and have-nots grows wider and is most glaringly visible through the lens of race. There appear to be two distinct developmental patterns for boys becoming men: for "White middle-class" adolescents, the task of achieving manhood is focused primarily on envisioning a future that includes a career, financial success, family, and social privilege.* For others, the tasks of becoming an adult may be as narrow as avoiding death or arrest (one of three African American males is dead or in prison by age 21) (Roberts, 1994) or avoiding scorn and violence (gay boys experience at an early age a distinct sense of being different and of being treated differently) (Savin-Williams, 1996).

Developmental theorists have long contended that the chief task for adolescent boys is to effect *separation* from their families—especially their mothers—to achieve a full male identity. Far too often, this means an emotional disengagement that leaves many young men stranded in early adulthood, devoid of the emotional anchor that their parents, especially their mothers, have heretofore

---

*The term "White middle-class" has become almost useless as a description of socioeconomic status. I use it here to describe a social stratum that is *not* poor, *not* Black or Latino, and *not* gay. For example, it *also* includes those who *are* rich, *are* Asian, and have a reasonable chance of achieving and maintaining social privilege.

provided. *Differentiation,* a more comprehensive and complex concept, better describes the developmental process of becoming autonomous while remaining linked to sources of emotional succor. This essential need for healthy attachment has been undervalued and even disparaged and obscures men's hidden dependence by devaluing and making invisible those who serve their needs. The disdain in which society often holds men who remain emotionally connected to their mothers takes on near-burlesqued dimensions, as in the film *Only the Lonely,* in which John Candy plays a schlemiel-like young man whose attempts to have a love life are constantly thwarted by his controlling mother, Maureen O'Sullivan, or in Philip Roth's classic novel *Portnoy's Complaint,* in which a man's obsessive masturbatory fantasies center on his mother as the source of his psychic pain.

> George, a 22-year-old medical student, first appeared in treatment with severe anxiety about beginning his clinical rotation. His father, an emotionally distant physician, dismissed his fears, although his mother was sympathetic, reassuring him that she would help him if he wanted to take some time off to reconsider his decision to be a doctor, something that they had covertly discussed since college.

> George: I know my mother's being too easy on me and Dad's right. It's time I grew up and became a man.
> Therapist: Does being a man mean being a doctor?
> G: No, I think being a man means being tough enough to face the stuff I don't want to do...and not hiding behind Mom's protection.
> Th: The stuff you don't want to do?
> G: Yeh, like being a doc. It's ridiculous to believe that I'll ever make a living as a musician, and Mom's support for that fantasy is preventing me from doing what I have to do.
> Th: Dad wouldn't accept a decision to leave med school and pursue music?
> G: Not Dad! Me! How do you just throw away what you're supposed to do? I think because Mom feels she never did what she wanted, I should...But it's different.

Mothers often prematurely disengage from their sons in puberty, and even earlier, to serve what they have been told is the adolescent's need for autonomy (Silverstein, 1994). George's mother remains involved and concerned about her son, but he perceives her as standing in the way of his growing up. But George is torn: To please his father he needs to embrace a premature and uncertain career path; in doing so, he risks being emotionally alone and abandoned, treated as if he had no emotional needs for vital *inter*dependence, which he desperately desires with his mother but has been taught to resist and disparage. This is especially common for young men like George whose fathers are physically absent or emotionally unavailable—the case in a large percentage of American families. Among the consequences of premature disengagement are the tendency on the part of young men to either shut down emotionally or desperately seek a female companion to act in mother's stead and heal the pain of "abandonment" (Pittman, 1993). Other typical patterns for young men include an intensified desire for connection to an unavailable father (witness the extraordinary popularity of movies that reflect the yearning for an idealized father-son relationship, such as the 1989 film *Field of Dreams*) and hostility toward the mother, who is perceived as preventing a relationship with Dad. Society's normalization of anger and hypercriticism toward mothers (and thus toward women in general) and a failure to develop the relationship skills needed in marriage and later parenting will serve as dire impediments to marital success. At this sensitive moment in their development, young men, feeling little success or encouragement to connect emotionally, turn toward the powerfully reinforced male goals of achievement, money, and power. This may also be an underlying factor in the pervasive problems with alcohol and drugs among adolescent boys and young adults.

What is often referred to as "father hunger" is deeply felt by many young men (Silverstein, 1994; Pittman, 1993), but the clinical challenge at this stage of the family life cycle, as with George, is not merely to reconnect a man with his father, but rather to help to clarify the important distinction between separation and differentiation. The work with this young man primarily centered on how he could achieve three important tasks: (1) safely pursue experimentation with another possible career option, (2) aggressively pursue a relationship with his father despite the latter's disappointment, and (3) feel the support offered from his mother not as an obstacle to his growth but as support for his taking a risk. This latter task is often particularly difficult for a man, whose mother's support is so glibly characterized as intrusive and a potential impediment to his autonomy. Robert Bly expresses bluntly that a man must make "a clean break from the mother" (1990, p. 19). The goal of therapy, however, is to help him to establish an adult relationship with his father *and* mother—to differentiate without emotionally disengaging.

Becoming a Couple: The Task of Connecting

It is nearly impossible to compare the process of two young people forming a committed relationship today with that process as recently as a generation or two ago. Given the dramatic changes in courtship, marriage, and family life, a typical marriage as characterized by popular culture until the early 1970s can no longer be taken for granted (Carter, 1996; see also Chapter 14). Traditional gender roles that, until recently, guided and defined the character of marriage have lost universal acceptance, leaving young adults frantically searching for guidance as to how to do it. For young men, in particular, a vague awareness that *something* has changed ("this is not my parents' marriage") seldom translates into much more than an intellectual acknowledgement that the prerogatives of being a male are no longer taken for granted. An integrated awareness of how to manage emotional intimacy outside the bedroom or participate in domestic chores as more than an affable helper is much more difficult to achieve.

James and Veronica, a "30-something" African American couple, were on the brink of splitting after less than two years of marriage. They reported irreconcilable arguments in which Veronica raged at James for his refusal to "put her first" in his life. James countered that he was not going to "give my whole life away," just because he was married.

Veronica, a successful corporate executive, expressed her consternation that if James wasn't willing to do something to advance professionally and contribute an equal financial share, he could at least devote more attention and affection to her. James's failure to advance from a junior position at work while others at his level were doing so left him frustrated and feeling unsuccessful. He found solace in time spent with old high school buddies three or four nights a week and often did not come home until early morning, precipitating blow-ups that left both of them feeling hopeless about their survival as a couple.

Hank and Gabriella, a "30-something" "White middle-class" couple, were on the brink of splitting after less than two years of marriage. They reported irreconcilable arguments in which Gabriella raged at Hank for his refusal to "put her first" in his life. Hank countered that he was not going to "lose my entire career" just because he was married. Gabriella, a middle management administrator, expressed her strong desire to begin a family but feared that Hank's preoccupation with his work would later render her a single parent. Hank's fast rise in his law firm demanded increasingly more hours to compete with his other junior partners— male and female. He found solace in tennis and golf with his friends on weekends (when he wasn't working) and often arrived home with only time enough to shower and dress before going out, precipitating blow-ups that left both of them feeling hopeless about their survival as a couple.

Although both couples' conflicts reflect a common problem faced by young adults creating a marriage, they also mirror a significant distinction between young "White middle-class" adults and African American couples. Defining the parameters of emotional intimacy is a frequent field of combat for young couples. The notion that for a man, "the most terrifying thing he can imagine is making a commitment to an equal, honest, intimate relationship with a woman" (Pittman, 1993, p. 241) has been so consistently reinforced as to create a self-fulfilling prophecy in which men are led to believe that their masculinity cannot survive closeness with the opposite sex. The perception must be directly addressed for therapy to be successful; this entails directly challenging the traditional norms of masculinity and its social supports and encouraging a man to develop his own definition.

The other significant challenge at this stage of the family life cycle is effecting an appropriate disengagement from one's family of origin. Since differentiation entails achieving autonomy while maintaining connectedness, the need to remain part of one's own family, while creating a new one—with different values, different goals, and different expectations—can be a daunting prospect. Young men, of course, are taught to invite their female partners to manage social encounters, thus ceding contacts with the man's family of origin to the woman. The result is that many men find themselves ill equipped to stay connected on their own. They thus unwittingly create an enmity between themselves and their families of origin, particularly their mothers, who may perceive the wives as preventing contact. Young women often are baffled: "Why is it *my* responsibility to call your mother?" For young gay couples, the issues of differentiation are greatly complicated by the fact that often, one or both of the partners has yet to "come out" to his family of origin (see Chapter 20). The sense of stigmatization, already felt in society at large, is reinforced by the subterfuge that is created to avoid confrontation with parents and extended family. Clinical work with these couples entails balancing sensitivity to social and internalized homophobia while helping them to develop the skills to risk self-disclosure.

Becoming Parents: The Task of Guiding and Nurturing

The shift in generational responsibility from being taken care of to taking care of often creates a crisis for couples. At this crucial crossroads of the family life cycle, many young adults falter. Ill-equipped to skillfully assume the guidance and responsibility of children ("I feel like a child myself!") and seeking some sense of grounding in how to parent, both men and women often initially embrace a return to tried-and-true traditional parenting roles. Even if they have been successful in negotiating a work-

able marital system, the arrival of children may shake its foundation.

Maria and Fred were referred by their pediatrician after reporting difficulties with disciplining their two young children, ages 6 and 3. Married thirteen years, they described their life as "perfect" until the arrival of children. First-generation college graduates, they were the envy of their immigrant families. Both had been working as credit managers, earning good money, vacationing regularly, and living a life neither had imagined growing up. When their first child was born, Maria left work and had only recently returned, although her husband continued working the second job he had taken to augment the loss of her salary. Child care, finances, and Fred's long work hours and unavailability to share domestic responsibilities seemed even more overwhelming than their concern with disciplining their kids.

While it is important to respond to parents with practical guidance on discipline, if the couple has an unequal relationship, concrete suggestions are unlikely to work. In a distant world in which one salary was adequate to support a family and few couples had any models other than Ozzie and Harriet, Fred and Maria would probably have not been referred for help. Maria's mother and other relatives (and perhaps Fred's) would have been close by to support and guide her in raising her children, and Fred might have been a friendly but distant dad, adored by his children but clueless about their needs. Underlying discontent on both their parts might have made their relationship tense and distant, but neither would have imagined an arrangement different from what they had. Today, however, Maria refuses to tolerate Fred's distance, and he feels unappreciated for how hard he works. When he is angriest at her, his worst denunciation has become "You're a ball-busting feminist!" The once-loving couple now live parallel lives, barely meeting except to argue and express their helplessness at how difficult the children are and how overwhelmed they feel.

Addressing the gendered power imbalance in the marriage as an underlying source of the problem is often the most important issue at this stage of the family life cycle but a hard point for men to grasp. They are usually in touch with their personal anxiety but not their social power. This is commonly reflected in their choices about how to be a parent. "Fathering"—the active and intimate involvement in the lives of one's children—is too frequently diluted for and by men to the comfortable notion of "quality time." The fact that no qualitative parenting can be accomplished without hands-on responsibility for both the pleasures and pains of children's lives is a frequent source of conflict between husbands and wives. Having never spent an entire day planning and caring for his two children, Fred can malign Maria's contention that she now has *two* full time jobs. "My father barely ever spent time with me," claims Fred. "I play with my kids all the time. I also tell them I love them and hug them and kiss them—something my old man never did. So don't tell me I'm not a good father." Since the model for high-quality fathering is so abysmally lacking in our society, their boasts about the quality of their own involvement is hard to assail. Further, since the parental behaviors of empathy, compassion, and emotional engagement are so often characterized as maternal, many men see them as trivial and, at best, a luxury (Taffel & Masters, 1989).

Contemporary fathers, however, seem to be caught in an either-or dilemma regarding their roles as parents. Either they relinquish the role to their wives because they believe themselves incapable or too responsible for the real-world tasks to do it themselves, or they assume the most superficial ("quality time") dimensions of the role, since even that is far more than what their fathers did. The clinical task is to help couples to envision parenthood as a shared, equal task, in which providing nurturing, discipline, empathy—and even throwing a baseball—are the province of *both* parents, regardless of gender. An added benefit, of course, is that the road to a better marital relationship often goes through a shared, collegial parenthood in which both are active and mutually respected partners.

As an increasing number of gay couples look to adopt children—or together raise one or the other's biological children—we encounter a new perspective on men as parents. Given that "gay" often has an antifamily connotation and "father" implies heterosexuality, the gay father often struggles with a divided identity (Bigner, 1996). While some states have begun to grant adoptive privileges to gay men, the road to overall social acceptance will remain bumpy. In a clinical context, it is interesting to note that gay men are likely to bring very different gender role assumptions to the parenting process. Is there a concern that the child will be deprived of a mother's "unique" nurturance? Is there a belief that the family's makeup must be kept secret from a hostile outside environment? Do internalized homophobic feelings create self-doubt in one's role as a parent? What are the parents' beliefs about the "contagion" of homosexuality? Have arrangements been made in the case of divorce or death of one parent? These are only a few of many issues that need to be addressed in working with gay parents.

The Family with Adolescents: The Task of Renegotiation

A man whose family has begun the raising of adolescents is also likely to face a midcourse examination of his own life. As adolescents flex the muscles of their burgeoning adulthood, assess the boundaries of newfound sexual awakenings, explore the limits of imagining an identity, and consider where they have been and where they are going, their fathers are often surprised at the degree to which they themselves are affected. This stage of the family life cycle is likely to coincide with a man's midlife crisis, in which he, too, reflects on the course of his life. If men have been acculturated to judge their worth by how high they have risen and how much money they have accumulated, then their mid-forties may indeed create a crisis. (Note the popular bumper sticker "Whoever dies with the most toys, wins.")

Men and women at this stage of the life cycle find themselves sandwiched between their children and their parents, creating a tension that often results in a woman's assuming more responsibility and a man's disengaging from the demands of heightening emotional expectations.

Susan and Byron, a couple in their late forties with three adolescents, presented a multitude of problems in their first session. Susan had just completed a round of adjuvant chemotherapy for breast cancer, Byron's mother had been placed in a nursing home as her Alzheimer's disease worsened, Byron was smoking marijuana regularly, and their three children, while apparently well-adjusted, were behaving like adolescents and challenging their parents at every turn. Susan angrily reported that her husband was retreating further and further from contact with her, seemed nearly always high, left her to attend to his mother's needs, and barely spoke to the kids. Byron accused Susan of being occupied only with herself and unconcerned with how out of control he was feeling in the face of her illness, his mother's deterioration, and the children's lack of respect. In the midst of their fights, he frequently threatened to leave. Susan's basic response to him was: "Grow up. I don't need four teenagers."

This case illustrates a number of crises that are nearly normative in the family at the life cycle stage of adolescence. It is frequently a stage at which the family is first likely to confront the specter of physical illness; the family will probably be dealing with one or more ill or infirm grandparents; children will begin testing the limits of their independence; and a man will find himself examining his life and wondering whether his work and his marriage have met his expectations. He is less likely to consider the question of whether he has met the expectations of others. In Byron's case, of course, his preoccupation with his own needs allows him to rationalize his inattention to the crisis of his wife's life-threatening illness.

Many men at this stage seize the opportunity to affect a midcourse correction and focus on deepening family ties, carving out recreational opportunities, reconnecting with extended family, renegotiating their marriages, and intensifying efforts to spend more time with their children. However, this confluence of predictable life cycle crises may also result in men suddenly confronting their mortality, contemplating leaving, retreating from contact from their wives and children, turning to alcohol, to drugs or to an extramarital affair. Ronald Taffel (1990) suggests that what presents in a ther-

apist's office as a vague family dysfunction—often with an acting-out adolescent—may mask a father's unacknowledged depression, which has been normalized in the family, naively accepted simply as a reflection of how men are. His formulation suggests that the family may operate—as does Byron's—in the throes of a double bind: They must take responsibility for a condition (Dad's depression) that supposedly does not exist.

Byron was having difficulty finding a way to positively frame his life when he and Susan appeared for therapy. Unfortunately, his emotional floundering added to his inability to focus on his wife's health crisis in any helpful way. In fact his emotional dependence on Susan was further affected by her illness, and it emerged early on that her caring for his mother—a task she resented and demanded that he also share—was necessary to reassure him that she would not abandon him. In particular, Byron's father's death a few years earlier had given him a sense of his own mortality; in addition, he reported feeling that his distance from his children had the potential to become a rewrite of his history with his father. Despite Susan's reassurances that his children did, indeed, want more contact with him, Byron's failed relationship with his own father and unresolved issues with his mother left him feeling inadequate in his dealing with them. Some direct suggestions with men at this stage of the family life cycle can be effective in helping them to form deeper emotional ties with their children. If their parents are still living, this is an appropriate time to employ a coaching method for helping them heal the wounds in their families of origin. In the case of this couple, however, it was also necessary to impress on both Byron and Susan that his emotional needs—consistently attended to by Susan throughout their marriage—could not be allowed to eclipse the larger issue of his failure to respond helpfully to her illness.

In an often chaotic world, issues of letting go of one's children often become paramount. Coping with the distancing behavior of adolescents can be a painful experience for fathers, who are unprepared to manage what they experience as personal rejection. In addition, for fathers who have fashioned themselves as the protectors of their families, the risk taking in which adolescents engage can be disconcerting and result in their overprotecting and stifling children who are best left free to experiment within reason. This can be a uniquely troubling issue for African American and gay fathers who are aware that the potential physical danger to their children—particularly their sons—is not imagined, but quite real. With an astronomical mortality rate for African American adolescent boys and the cruel stigmatization and violence for homosexual adolescents, it is difficult to find the line that separates overconcern from good sense.

Extramarital affairs, not uncommon for men at this stage, are motivated by a variety of factors: fear of mortality and a desire to recapture a sense of youth, confusing their needs for emotional connectedness with sex, a feeling of missed opportunities mirrored in their observation of their adolescent children, an inability to address their dissatisfaction with the marriage, making it easier to escape than negotiate, and loneliness created by the awareness that they no longer occupy the center stage of their wives' and childrens' lives. Further, since men are raised in a culture in which pornography is often their introduction to sexuality, there is a natural tendency to objectify women. There is certainly no one way to deal clinically with a man's affair, but it should be emphasized that the necessity of his facing his own responsibility and the ways in which the affair reflects some sense of failure in his life is a vital element in treatment. Whatever else the affair represents, most men need to face the hard fact that, like their adolescent sons, it is mostly about trying to feel like a man.

Launching Children: The Task of Moving On

It is hardly unusual in a group of people in their fifties, and even sixties, to find that nearly everyone has at least one living parent, and many still have both. There was a time when this stage of the family life cycle barely existed, when the task of most families was exclusively raising children, well into old age. The need to create a new life after children have left home is a relatively new phenomenon, given our extended life span and other changes in family life (see Chapter 18). Men once again face the need to reevaluate their lives, a process that commonly begins in the previous period.

> Harold, a 56-year-old plumber, was referred for therapy by his cardiologist, who also prescribed Prozac to his patient. Harold had been taking the medication for about six weeks when he called me, and although he reported some mood enhancement, he still felt "pretty bummed." Two of his three children had left home, and the third was completing high school and would soon be off to college. Harold had been an active, involved father, often scheduling work around his children's activities. As his daughter prepared to leave home, he reported feeling increasingly annoyed by his wife's demands, doubtful about following through with their plans to retire to Florida, and asking "What's it all about anyway?"

Harold's lament about the meaning of his life is a common concern, as is the need to face a marriage that may have been conveniently marginalized during the raising of children. This existential crisis, coupled with the demands from a spouse that the marriage take a new direction with the exit of children, is the highlight of this stage of the family life cycle. The "empty nest syndrome," long considered exclusive to women, is increasingly described by men. Even when children return to the nest, their presence seems tenuous, and this period is characterized by frequent entrances and exits—not only of children, but of the previous generation as well. A man may be faced with an overwhelming task of retooling a multitude of relationships simultaneously: with his parents, his wife, his children, and the new generation, his grandchildren.

The realignment of relationships with the previous generations demands the settling of unresolved issues and the acceptance of some responsibility for the welfare of parents, while the realignment of relationships with one's children may demand a flexibility that has heretofore been untested. Both offer an excellent opportunity for the therapist to utilize Bowenian-style family of origin coaching to achieve those ends. It is important for a man to realize that caretaking of elderly parents may require more than merely sending money and leaving the rest to his wife or other female family members. There is a direct relationship between involvement with parents and the ability to mentor the next generation. Even so, most men will need specific coaching on how to conduct their own relationship with their young adult children, especially if they have previously left this to their wives or are divorced.

The paradox of this period for men is that it ought to be liberating. Finally, there is time, and often the financial wherewithal, to do all those things that have been postponed, and indeed, for many men, this can be freeing and stimulating. Yet for others, the quest for that elusive meaning of masculinity leaves them unable to relinquish the status that both defines them and weighs upon them. Additionally, their having failed to master the skills of sustaining interpersonal relationships may make this a painful period of life. Marriages can be sorely tested at this point, and indeed, while unheard of only a generation or two ago, divorce after twenty-five years of marriage is becoming increasingly common. At this particular stage, women are likely to feel far more vulnerable in a marital breakup, and men seldom leave without already having become involved in another relationship—frequently with a much younger woman. As in the previous stage, one must investigate the meaning of the affair, probe the degree of satisfaction with his life and achievement to date, and connect these to the attitudes about men that predominate in the larger social system. Separation and divorce may serve as a substitute for undone personal emotional work or a search for the fountain of youth. They may also, if they have been long postponed, provide a catalyst for this needed work.

Families in Older Age: The Task of Reassessment

Aging, of course, is not a disease, but neither is it the universal opportunity for continued vigor increasingly portrayed by the media or in popular films. Indeed, in his dotage, the self-made man feels compelled to continue remaking himself and proving his entitlement to manhood. While men often mellow somewhat in their later years, the need to continue

striving to win and to maintain control remain paramount. Recent reports of drug companies investing exorbitant sums on the research and development of medications to assure male potency, even in the face of aging and prostate failure, is one indication of this drive. The reality for most men, however, is facing their diminishing physiological and psychological health, remaining optimistic in the face of shrinking opportunities for making their mark, relinquishing a place to the next generation, and facing the increasing number of losses in their lives as well as their own prospective demise.

> When Anders and Lorraine Parsons came to their first session, Lorraine said, "We're here because I can no longer tolerate my husband's irritability and aimless puttering. I feel like since he retired, my job is to be his playmate, and if I am even momentarily unavailable, he turns on me angrily." Anders, a 72-year-old architect, had retired two years previously, reluctantly turning his firm over to his son and niece. He claimed to have many projects planned, but he seemed unable to get much started. He sought out old acquaintances for golf, but many had moved to warmer climes, others were ill, and some had died. His retirement had not turned out as he'd hoped, he was embittered at feeling pushed out of his business, and he discovered that Lorraine—whom he had counted on to manage the household and his social life and who he assumed would be available for him—was occupied with her friends, volunteer work, and grandchildren.

Anders is at risk, of course, given the disproportionate number of elderly men who, depressed and bewildered by confrontation with their final years, take their own lives. Recent reports suggest that nearly a quarter of all suicides are committed by people over 65 and that some 80 percent of these suicides are men. When one sees a couple in their later years struggling with issues similar to those of the Parsonses, one is struck by how fragile the traditional marriage becomes over time. Certainly, such marriages were more viable when the age of mortality was in the forties and fifties, rather than the seventies. The harsh awareness for men at this stage of the family life cycle is that they have cultivated few interests outside their work and few independent friendships, and so they encounter a barrenness in their lives. Increasingly, younger men, more aware of the prospect of a protracted and even vigorous old age, have taken steps to ensure more opportunities for themselves in the future. However, for most men, especially for those who have already reached this point in their lives, the problem of creating an active, fulfilling retirement remains. In addition, for men who have failed to achieve the goals of success as defined by society, retirement can be a grim reminder of failure. Even if they are judged as having been successful, for men like Anders, feeling compelled to leave work—the only world in which they felt unambivalently valued—can be devastating.

One important clinical task with men at this stage of life is to help them "reauthor" their lives as fully as possible. This may entail embracing a definition of oneself in marked contrast to what has been deemed important thus far. Anders is typical of many men at this stage of life who, rather than a sense of integrity in who they have become, experience despair at lost opportunities and lives perceived as devoid of meaning. His depression, a common symptom among males in later life, reflects a profound existential condition that his internist is likely to suggest be treated with medication. However, the condition can be better understood as the final chapter in many men's lives, when they realize that the accumulation of wealth and control at home and in the world of work are not enough. The sense of loneliness and emptiness when one has only oneself can be overwhelming. This is, in fact, a spiritual crisis, that is faced by many men but unacknowledged as such. Exploring with Anders his religious roots and connecting him with a community—perhaps in a church setting where he may be encouraged to become more involved in activities and volunteer charity work—could be quite helpful. The revelation that one can

be valued for one's presence is an astounding one for many men and may inspire them to take more public positions about the role of men.

Among the problems for men at this stage of the life cycle is the difficulty with accepting the partner's autonomy. Like Anders Parsons, many men expect that when they become available, women will schedule their lives to satisfy their husbands' whims. I have found that men frequently express astonishment that their wives have conducted lives in their "absence" (of many decades) that cannot be easily abandoned to accommodate their presence. This is hurtful for men and misunderstood as indifference by their wives to their newfound need for emotional engagement. In therapy with couples newly facing retirement, I have found it helpful to work with them on very concrete plans for time together and time apart. Both naively believe that the other should be able to comfortably manage the new regimen. For men, this means that women should simply accommodate to their needs; for women, it is often portrayed as disbelief that "he cannot do something as simple as figure out what he's going to do today without me." For a man who has spent his entire adult life living out a belief in his own supremacy (which he and everyone else have called "autonomy"), retirement can be threatening.

Finally, an important goal at this stage of life is maintaining relationships with one's children and grandchildren. A large percentage of men over age 65 have grandchildren, and many have great-grandchildren. In addition, for men who have assumed that their wives would take responsibility for maintaining ties to the next generations, there is a need to develop the skills to manage these relationships independently. This process may even provide a man with the enlightenment to communicate to his adult sons and grandsons a new vision of what it means to be a man

REFERENCES

Almeida, R., Wood, R., Messineo, T., & Front, R. (1998). The cultural context model. In M. McGoldrick (Ed.), *Revisioning family therapy: Race, gender and culture in clinical practice.* New York: The Guilford Press.

Bergman, S. J. (1996). Male relational dread. *Psychiatric Annals, 26*(1), 24–28.

Bigner, J. J. (1996). Working with gay fathers: Developmental, postdivorce parenting, and therapeutic issues. In J. Laird & R. J. Green (Eds.), *Lesbians and gays in couples and families* (pp. 370–403). San Francisco: Jossey-Bass.

Bly, R. (1990). *Iron John.* Reading, MA: Addison-Wesley.

Brod, H. (Ed.). (1988). *A mensch among men: Explorations in Jewish masculinity.* Freedom, CA: The Crossing Press.

Browne, A., & Williams, K. R. (1993). Gender, intimacy, and lethal violence: Trends from 1976 through 1987. *Gender and Society, 7*(1), 78–98.

Carter, B. (1996). *Love, honor and negotiate.* New York: Pocket Books.

Cleage, P. (1990). *Mad at Miles: A Blackwoman's guide to truth.* Southfield, MI: The Cleage Group.

Cohler, B. J., Hostetler, A. J., & Boxer, A. (1998). Generativity, social context, and lived experience narratives of gay men in middle adulthood. In D. McAdams & E. de St. Aubin (Eds.), *Generativity and adult development: Psychological perspectives on caring and contributing to the next generation.* Washington, DC: The American Psychological Association Press.

Eisler, R. (1995). Masculine gender role stress. In R. F. Levant & W. S. Pollack (Eds.), *A new psychology of men.* New York: Basic Books.

Farrell, W. (1986). *Why men are the way they are.* New York: Berkley.

Gilligan, C. (1982). *In a different voice: Psychological theory and women's development.* Cambridge: Harvard University Press.

Goodrich, T. J., Rampage, C., Ellman, B., & Halstead, K. (1988). *Feminist family therapy.* New York: W. W. Norton.

Green, R. J. (1998). Traditional norms of the male role. *Journal of Feminist Family Therapy.*

Green, R. J., Bettinger, M., & Zacks, E. (1996). Are lesbian couples fused and gay male couples disengaged? In J. Laird & R. J. Green (Eds.), *Lesbians and Gays in Couples and Families.* (pp. 185–230). San Francisco: Jossey-Bass.

Kaiser, C. (1997). *The gay metropolis: 1940–1996.* Boston: Houghton Mifflin.

Keillor, G. (1993). *The book of guys.* New York: Viking.

Kimmel, M. (1996). *Manhood in America: A cultural history.* New York: The Free Press.

Kivel, P. (1992). *Men's work: How to stop the violence that tears our lives apart.* New York: Ballantine.

Lazarre, J. (1996). *Beyond the whiteness of whiteness.* Durham, NC: Duke University Press.

Lorber, J., and Bandlamudi, L. (1993). The dynamics of marital bargaining in male infertility. *Gender and Society, 7*(1), 32–49.

Maccoby, E. (1990). Gender and relationships: A developmental account. *The American Psychologist, 45* (4), 513–520.

Miller, M. (1983). *Men and friendship.* Boston: Houghton Mifflin.

Pittman, F. (1993). *Man enough: Fathers, sons, and the search for masculinity.* New York: Perigee.

Roberts, S. (1994). *Who we are: A portrait of America based on the latest U.S. Census.* New York: Time Books, Random House.

Savin-Williams, R. C. (1996). Self-labeling and disclosure among gay, lesbian and bi-sexual youths. In J. Laird & R. J. Green (Eds.), *Lesbians and gays in couples and families.* (pp. 153–182). San Francisco: Jossey-Bass.

Silverstein, O. (1994). *The courage to raise good men.* New York: Viking.

Swain, S. (1989). Covert intimacy: Closeness in men's friendships. In B. Risman & P. Schwartz (Eds.), *Gender and intimate relationships* (pp. 71–86). Belmont, CA: Wadsworth.

Taffel, R., & Masters, R. (1989). An evolutionary approach to revolutionary change: The impact of gender arrangements on family therapy. In M. McGoldrick, C. M. Anderson & F. Walsh (Eds.), *Women in families: A framework for family therapy* (pp. 117–134). New York: W. W. Norton.

Taffel, R. (1990, September/October). The politics of mood. *The Family Therapy Networker,* 49–54.

Tannen, D. (1990). *You just don't understand: Women and men in conversation.* New York: Ballantine.

Tiger, L. (1969). *Men in groups.* New York: Random House.

Walker, K. (1994). Men's friendships: 'I'm not friends the way she's friends.' *Masculinities: Interdisciplinary Studies on Gender, 2*(2), 38–55.

Walters, M., Carter, B., Papp, P., & Silverstein, O. (1988). *The invisible web: Gender patterns in family relationships.* New York: The Guilford Press.

Wilkie, J. R. (1991). The decline in men's labor force participation and earnings and the changing structure of family economic support. *Journal of Marriage and the Family, 53*(1), 11–22.

Wilkie, J. R. (1993). Changes in U.S. men's attitudes toward the family provider role, 1972–1989. *Gender and Society, 7*(2), 261–279.

CHAPTER 8

THE LATINO FAMILY LIFE CYCLE

CELIA JAES FALICOV

FAMILY ORGANIZATION, MIGRATION, AND THE FAMILY LIFE CYCLE

Public or prescriptive Latino life cycle views are consonant with extended, three-generational families or large nuclear families. Extended families usually exert more directive control, giving children a sense of security and connectedness, but may curtail their self-expression and autonomy (Falicov & Brudner-White, 1983). But the values of democracy, egalitarianism, and individualism that typify smaller nuclear families are making greater inroads among Latinos.

Family size is also an important modifier of family development. Small families experience stress during launching but eventually accept the need for separation. Large families emphasize togetherness, tend to induce older children to take on parenting roles, and rely on sibling solidarity. Family size also affects developmental transactions between spouses. In large Latino families, husband and wife may never have to adapt to living "alone" as a couple after their children are grown up, because they typically remain involved in the lives of their many children and grandchildren. Pressures to achieve certain milestones "on time" are felt more intensely when one lives close to family. A wedding, a birth, a relative's illness, or a death has reverberations upon an extended network that maintains close practical and emotional ties (Falicov & Karrer, 1980).

When a family moves to another country, the cultural meanings attached to life cycle events may differ between the family and the dominant culture models. For example, the model of child-rearing is likely to be incongruent with the dominant culture's model, yet the original views may continue to be reinforced by similar attitudes held by other immigrants living in the ethnic neighborhood or by repeated return trips to the country of origin. Normal developmental stresses may be intensified thus by cultural dilemmas.

Latinos span a large number of nationalities and races from White to Black and several educational and economic classes. Although racism attached to skin color may be an issue in some of the countries of origin, migration compounds the sense of disempowerment by adding the stress of being a cultural and language minority (see Shorris, 1992). Bicultural exposure can gradually become an enriching resource by increasing alternative ways to cope with developmental change. Yet problems may also develop through attempts to force, merge, ignore, or reconcile contradictory cultural views about the life cycle.

Latinos are notorious for the preservation of life cycle markers and appropriate rituals. These can take the form of birthday celebrations, religious rituals, holiday dates, or Sunday picnic traditions. Every milestone is an occasion for a large family gathering or a festive party. The endurance of traditional rituals has important consequences for mental health and acquires particularly poignant therapeutic value for immigrants. (Falicov, 1998).

THE FAMILY WITH YOUNG CHILDREN: RELATEDNESS OR AUTONOMY?

Entrance into Parenthood

The baptism, or *bautismo,* initiates the infant into membership in the Roman Catholic Church and, even for Latinos who have joined other Christian religions in their country, the baptism crowns the acceptance of the new family. It also serves as an extended family reunion even when the marriage was accepted reluctantly by the elders. The infant is sponsored by godparents or *padrinos,* who are selected from the social network of relatives, friends, and prestigious acquaintances of the family for their capacity to supplement economic and other parental functions in case of need.

Entrance into parenthood may not be experienced as a major crisis for Latinos. One reason may be that, given the lower emphasis on romantic privacy for the couple, the perception of loss of time and activities together alone is not as keenly felt as it is by many Anglo American couples. Further, young Latino parents, even if they are single mothers, may have a dense network of grandparents and relatives who help with caretaking and offer plentiful coaching and advice. Traditional expectations may also organize this transition by moving the Latina wife towards her mother and other supportive women. This allows the husband to be concerned primarily with economic pursuits, and sometimes the young mother herself must return to work. Socialization of young children is provided by parents, grandparents, and relatives of all ages who convey the vitality of family connectedness and solidarity as well as other central values of Latino culture.

Social Relatedness or Individual Autonomy

From early on, Latino mothers stress to their children a cluster of cultural meaning systems summarized as "proper demeanor," such as social relatedness, valuing and teaching respect and obedience, responsiveness to adults and other children, dignity, conformity, and good social manners. In contrast, white Anglo American mothers emphasize self maximization, that is, self-esteem, autonomy, and self-confidence (González-Ramos, Zayas, & Cohen 1993; Harwood, Miller, & Irizarry, 1995; Okagaki & Sternberg, 1993: Ortiz-Colón, 1985). These Latino belief systems define lifelong conceptions of being in the world that privilege social relationships over self-development.

The Latino father may or may not be involved in caretaking during the early upbringing of the children. While fathers communicate very closely with babies and young children and have even been shown to do more holding of babies than mothers do (Guttman, 1996), this affectionate indulgence may slowly wane as the child gets older and the fathers' role becomes more circumscribed to enforcing discipline. Active shaming, which includes teasing and mocking, humiliation, scary threats, ridicule, and punishment, including mild corporal punishment, appears to be accepted in many cases as the prerogative of parents who must raise children to respect authority and understand their place in society.

External, Not Internal Transitions

The baby or young child enjoys a close relationship with mother and a special position in the family either until a new child is born or until he or she enters nursery school or kindergarten. An external marker, such as the arrival of a new child or entry into school, defines the child's passage to a new stage much more powerfully than processes of internal readiness for individual achievement that motivate parents to expect or demand more from their children in anticipation of the next stage.

Perhaps because of the low emphasis on the achievement of autonomous self-care, variations in weaning and toilet training depend on individual readiness and personal family history rather than on prescribed social norms. As long as childhood milestones are achieved within a "reasonable" length of time, no pride or shame is attached to them. Because Anglo therapists have internalized developmental expectations toward greater autonomy, they tend to judge negatively what appears to them as Latino parents' indulgent attitudes toward their young children. However, Latino parents place demands on children for a different type of behavior: the ability to get along with and be pleasant and caring toward others.

The storied recreation of family bonds and shared understandings of the fragmentation forced by migration pave the way for a smoother transition to school either preventively or for children who are already experiencing difficulty with school entry. This is a time when the child helps to open the family boundaries to closer contact with the unfamiliar host society's cultural constructions and treatment of minorities.

THE FAMILY WITH SCHOOL-AGE CHILDREN: BRAVE IN A NEW WORLD

Institutional Contact

For the family of Mexican descent and central Americans, such as Guatemalans or Salvadorans, the school may be the first direct sustained and structured contact with the institutions of the host country. Puerto Ricans and Cubans, given their greater exposure to U.S. institutions, may have more experience with how the school system functions. This transition from home to school may be difficult for many parents who lack formal education, but for immigrants, this transition may occur when the family is still weakened by the uprooting caused by their migration.

Latino children may differ from their Anglo peers in their social and the emotional readiness to move into the more autonomous stage of entering school. Like most other immigrant children, they are handicapped by limitations in language and communication skills. These limitations create learning barriers that are often associated with behavior problems (Aronowitz, 1984). School entrance may also be the child's first encounter with prejudice and racial discrimination, difficult issues for young children to articulate.

Separations and Reunions

Some cultural differences in child-rearing may account for Latino children appearing infantilized or overprotected to American teachers or counselors, but the family's reorganization due to migration may greatly intensify these behaviors. Many families leave some of their children in Guatemala, Mexico, or Puerto Rico for practical or financial reasons or because of feelings of loyalty toward their family of origin. When a child comes to the United States precisely around the time of school entry, the mother may quickly begin a campaign of overcompensation for the lost years of affection. The mother herself may have difficulties in separating from the child, even for a few hours a day, so soon after the reunion. The father may adopt a "tough-it-out" attitude that may reflect his internal denial of fears and losses precipitated by his own migration trajectory. Some Latino children may have been raised by several loving (and sometimes competing) mothers before migration and school entry and abruptly enter a much harsher reality when the emotional reunion with his or her parents coincides with entering school. One can see how bravery is required in this new world.

Boundary Negotiations

Preteenagers often assume responsibilities for errands, babysitting, cooking, or other forms of household help to the mother in poor families. In working-class, middle-class and upper-class Latino families, the presence of live-in domestic help drastically reduces children's chores relative to their Anglo American counterparts. Greater individual responsibility for handling an allowance, or small jobs outside the family, such as a newspaper route, are not customary or consonant, regardless of social class. This reflects a different boundary negotiation between the family and the extrafamilial environment than for Anglo Americans and a relative lack of preparation for the work world in the preadolescent years.

Rather than being too controlling or authoritarian, immigrant parents are probably attempting to define a firm boundary between home and the extrafamilial world, especially the peer group. Perceiving many dangers in the urban neighborhood, they may restrict their children's activities to indoors. Parents may promote siblings and cousins as the main playmates, even if they are far apart in age, to protect children from the many urban dangers and temptations.

Because underachievement, school failure, and early dropout are statistically very high among

Latinos, completing elementary school (as well as graduation from high school) is a matter of great pride and joy for Mexican American families, often accompanied by a happy celebration. Members of the extended family may attend this graduation (*graduación*) at the school. As a ritual celebration, it can be used to facilitate and mark family change during the transition to adolescence.

ADOLESCENCE: BETWEEN TWO WORLDS

Latino adolescents are immersed in the multiple struggles of being part of an ethnically and socially discriminated minority. They often face the impact of marginalized status on their self-esteem, the helplessness engendered by institutionalized racism, and internalization of low expectations. Their experience of growing up in the United States has been described as *entremundos* (between two worlds) (Zavala-Martinez, 1994), that is, an uneasy coexistence between two cultures, two languages, two sets of values, two philosophies of life. Developing a bilingual, bicultural competence within a framework of knowing and respecting a Latino identity could be thought of as additional developmental tasks of adolescence.

Parent-Adolescent Interaction: The Clash of Cultures

The new culture is no longer outside, as one could pretend it was when the children were small. It now sits in full force in the family's inner sanctum, like an overbearing guest, demanding intense attention. The coexistence of different views of family connectedness and individual separation and the different conceptions of age and gender hierarchies cannot be ignored any longer.

The axiom "be good to your parents" is probably universal. However, different cultural meanings about transgressions of this norm result in different consequences. For Latinos, if adolescents answer back verbally or deviate from obligations to their parents or other societal rules, parents do not necessarily feel guilty. They may be embar-

rassed about their bad luck in having a bad son or daughter. For Anglo Americans, when children deviate from society's norms, this represents an indictment of the parents' ability to raise good, healthy citizens. The Latino adolescent is often the guilty one, shamed by his or her parents for breaking rules. The American middle-class adolescent can more often blame his or her parents for the unreasonableness of their child-rearing, as being either too strict or too permissive. While Anglo American parents accept that young people need the autonomy to define themselves and thus may rebel against authority, Latino parents expect respect and obedience throughout life.

Children of immigrants living in the United States may begin to expect and demand "an adolescence" with its ensuing freedoms in the worst possible circumstances for the parents, whose ability to supervise and guide is weakened because of their ignorance of the language and ways of doing things. Add that sociohistorical frame to the social dynamics of tension and danger in the ghetto to arrive at a complex context that illuminates the mutually reinforcing cycle of repressive "old-fashioned" parents, and acting out "liberated" youth that we so often see in mental health clinics. The family is indeed between realities, divided within by two cultures and languages.

Latino adolescents have many responsibilities toward parents and younger siblings. Although this is a natural occurrence in large families, structural changes precipitated by migration complicate this situation. Parents who might otherwise work out a gradual separation find it nearly impossible to do so because of their dependence on their older child to mediate with the language and institutions. The younger children in the family may also cling to the older sibling who appears to be much less old-fashioned and more understanding than the parents. Having internalized the two languages and the two cultures, older children may find themselves in the confusing but influential position of "parent to their parents" and "parent to their siblings." This position can pave the way for competent independence, or it may result in an instrumental and emotional entrapment.

In situations of rapid culture change, when a veritable experiential chasm between one generation and the next exists, the peer group often assumes a crucial and controversial socializing role. The attraction of gangs is powerful for Latino adolescents, particularly those born in this country. Many factors related to urban poverty are involved, but gangs also provide a solution to identity confusion via a source of new cultural identification, values, and human support (Horowitz, 1983; Vigil, 1988).

Sexual Practices

Sexuality is a fundamental issue for adolescents. If there is any talk about sexuality between most Latino parents and children, it is almost always indirect, via allusions and certainly via restrictions, even in the mother-daughter relationships in which there could be more intimate conversation. The strength of Roman Catholicism and the practice of confession influence the equation of sexuality with sin and in theory support restrictions of sex to traditional reproductive ideology, which most Latinos are aware to be quite different from actual practice.

Strong social controls are also exerted on sexual orientations other than heterosexuality. I know of two middle-class Mexican families who sent their gay adolescent sons to live in the United States to escape intense stigmatization. Homosexuality and lesbianism are also repressed, hidden, and shunned among first-generation immigrants, but second and third generations appear somewhat more open about their sexual orientation. An interesting illustration of the social construction aspects of homosexuality is the fact that among Mexicans, the label of homosexual is applied exclusively to one of the two partners of a homosexual encounter. The homosexual is only the passive partner who is penetrated and is thought to be more effeminate. The aggressive one who penetrates is often bisexual and heterosexually married. He is thought to be manly and therefore not homosexual (Bronfman et al., 1995). This construction has many dangers for women whose husbands may not take precautions in practicing safe sex with men because they don't think of themselves as being involved in a homosexual encounter.

Teenage Pregnancy

A between-stage phenomenon that causes boundary ambiguity between youth and adulthood is teenage pregnancy, an event that is on the rise among Latinas. Mexicans are somewhat less likely to be sexually active before marriage. Yet once pregnant they are the most likely to give birth (Becerra & de Anda, 1984; Martínez, 1981). As for other groups, early out-of-wedlock childbearing is related to poverty and its low educational possibilities, unemployment, and bleak surroundings.

Pregnant Mexican and Cuban adolescents are more likely than Puerto Ricans and adolescents from other very poor groups to use this stage as a step to marriage and independent living. This is because they are more likely to be in long-term relationships with partners who accept the pregnancy and endeavor to support the family. The cultural value of a man's honor, and his pride in the virility of the conception may be motivating forces to legitimize fatherhood.

The strength of the adolescent's girl immigrant family usually prevails. The parents may initially be furious about the pregnancy, but they eventually look forward to the birth and may even afford special status to the young mother (de Anda, Becerra, & Fielder, 1988; Felice, Shragg, James, & Hollingsworth, 1987; Kay, 1980).

Rituals

A ritual that accompanies a girl's entrance into the romantic, premarital field is the *quinceañera*, a formal party given for a girl by her parents and relatives on her fifteenth birthday. Curiously, this is an event that all generations agree has to take place, and it is an important marker of maturation. It involves a religious ceremony, a dinner, and a dance for 100 to 200 people. The persistence of this ritual into second and third generations may be an example of the alternation theory or hybridization theory of acculturation whereby very traditional customs coexist with more "modern" views about premarital sex. As an initiation rite, the *quinceañera* is similar to the American tradition of the debutante ball or "sweet sixteen" party, but its celebration is common among all Latino social class levels. The absence of a comparable initiation rite for boys can sometimes be corrected for therapeutic purposes by inventing a passage rite or a maturation celebration that would allow for negotiation of privilege and responsibilities, for example.

Dating

A second arena for legitimization of the adolescent's maturation is dating. Casual dating without marriage as a goal has become common for both sexes after age 15 or 16. Unhappiness and intense depression, including suicidal thoughts, are not uncommon among Latino adolescents, particularly girls who are very strictly raised and closely supervised (Zimmerman, 1991). Six out of nine girls in a study of Puerto Rican adolescents in New York City (Canino & Canino, 1982) showed psychiatric symptoms that seem to have been due in part to conflicting cultural expectations in the area of dating, sexuality, and difficulties in establishing a sense of identity.

Psychoeducational Conversations

Conversation centered on generational and gender differences in culture change is a useful technique to normalize, diffuse, and facilitate conflict resolution between parents and adolescents. Conversations in the presence of the parents about racial, language, peer group acceptance, and other tensions facing Latino adolescents usually increases the emotional resonance with the parents' experience and provides other views of the problem and avenues for change.

In therapy, Latino families may be amenable to suggestions that their teenagers need to find a sympathetic ear in their parents, so that they can confide or honestly speak up, or even to the suggestion that adolescents need the freedom to experiment and learn from their own experiences. Nonetheless, it is very important to stress to the whole family that a modified equivalent of respect for parental authority remains in place. This stance helps to assuage parents' fears that the therapist may be siding with what they regard as the perils of American permissiveness.

Immigrant parents, and sometimes first-generation parents, extend their calls for help to their country of origin when they find themselves unable to deal with an unruly adolescent. They simply send the adolescent to live with relatives in Mexico or Puerto Rico. Often, this is a desirable move, certainly preferable to a life of drugs, crime, or jail. The teenager may later be reintegrated into the nuclear family in the United States. A mother I know in San Diego saved money to take her two gang-involved sons back to her hometown and saved them from a life of crime, using the excuse of a family vacation. But sometimes, the adolescent does not reform in the extended setting or is never integrated back into the original nuclear family.

YOUNG ADULTHOOD: STAYING HOME AND COURTSHIP

Staying Home and Gaining Autonomy

Latinos in late adolescence and early adulthood do not construct the leaving home transition as a solo act whereby an individual proves oneself capable of autonomy, decision making, or the ability to survive and support oneself emotionally and financially. Rather, Latinos tend to leave home in the context of forming a new and connected family of their own. Steady dating is the sanctioned manner to become more autonomous and private, and courtship may be the functional equivalent of Anglo American launching into adulthood by distancing from parents.

Gender expectations help to shape this separation process. Moving out of the home through dating occurs gradually. Sons may stay out of the home for increasingly long periods of time, coming home only at night to sleep. Parents may occasionally complain about not seeing the son often enough, but his peripheral role is acceptable, while more participation and visibility is expected of young women. Eventually, the young adult son moves out smoothly through work, marriage, or educational opportunities, most often in his early twenties. The most acceptable way for an adult daughter to leave home is through marriage. But within the last decade, an increasing number of young Latinas are leaving home to further their education. This may be a stressful event for the whole family. A college-educated Latina who decides to get her own apartment may be criticized, or at least frowned upon, by her parents.

Siblings are again very important in young adulthood. The roles of older and younger siblings may get even more sharply differentiated than during adolescence. The older siblings may pioneer the road to emancipation. But in other instances, as an older child leaves, parental dependency shifts to the next in line, who may be unprepared to assume the roles vacated by the older one. Other children may then be "recruited" or "elected" for these roles with various degrees of success.

When young adults marry and leave home, their relationship with their parents no doubt changes, but their availability to each other continues at a more intense level than Anglo Americans experience. The incorporation of the son-in-law or daughter-in-law may become problematic if the parents continue to cling to their married children or if the married adult is very involved with the parents, as may happen for immigrant parents.

Courtship: Sanctioned Distancing from Parents

Courtship is a very significant stage of the life cycle of Latino families. This may be partly because marriage is a weighty decision, a commitment for a lifetime. Parents often check out potential candidates for steady dating whenever a daughter appears to be seeing a young man with some frequency. Good manners, financial prospects, and educational level all enter into consideration in this covert assessment process. Once an opinion has

been formed, parents exert considerable pressure for or against the selection of a particular mate. In spite of greater openness toward premarital sex, double standards still make a woman's reputation dependent on her chastity. A young man's sexual dalliances, on the other hand, are accepted and often encouraged.

Steady courtship is usually legitimized by a *compromiso,* or an engagement party, which involves a public announcement, elaborate festivities, and a formal exchange of rings. After the *compromiso,* the two extended families will begin including each other in their family get-togethers.

If courtship never takes place or doesn't lead to marriage, the unmarried Latino man or woman tends not to move out of the parental household. If both parents die, it is more acceptable for the unmarried adult to live with a married sibling than to live on his or her own. The presence of a maternal or paternal aunt in our clients' households is a pattern observed so frequently that I label it *la tia* ("the aunt"). In some cases, the aunt serves useful affective and instrumental functions while subsystem boundaries are maintained. In other cases, depending on the age and role interactions within the family, the aunt may form a cross-generational coalition with a parent or with a child, or she may attempt to act as intermediary between the two, sometimes facilitating growth but other times blocking it (Falicov & Karrer, 1980).

MARRIAGE: SEPARATING OR RETURNING TO THE FOLD?

The late teens and early twenties are common and socially acceptable ages for marriage for both men and women, but there is greater tolerance for later marriage for men. A Latino wedding, or *casamiento,* is a colorful and joyous collective celebration. From working-class to upper-class settings, a *casamiento* is an elaborate church and dinner affair with formal attire and hundreds of guests. Many adult relatives or family friends become financially and instrumentally responsible for various aspects of the wedding, another indication of the collective meanings given to financial resources and the strength of social commitments. Thus, there are godparents of *cojines* (they put the pillows to lean at the altar), godparents of *flores* (they buy the flower arrangements), and godparents of *pasteles* (they provide the cakes and sweets). Financial debts related to this celebration may take the father of the bride years to pay.

Greater self-individuation and maturation may be slowly fulfilled in the dyadic, less hierarchical context of forming a marriage with common goals and negotiation of values, priorities, and everyday routines. The tendency to maintain harmony and communicate indirectly about differences and conflicts, which is learned in the family of origin, can make the early stage of marriage seem harmonious. But it can also be a tumultuous time in that the young man or woman may first begin to express more individualistic desires, desires that for young Latinos may reflect an expanding bicultural self. This is quite different from the Anglo American cultural belief that you have to develop yourself (i.e., differentiate as a person) before you can form a good marriage. (For a discussion of overlap of developmental stages see Falicov, 1984.)

While Latino subjective time appears to be slower than the American chronological milestones of infancy (weaning), childhood (school entrance readiness), and adolescence (leaving home), Latinos marry and have children chronologically earlier than their Anglo counterparts, regardless of social class. This means that they become parents and grandparents at a relatively early age, but by maintaining age hierarchies, they may remain "children" to their parents throughout life (Clark & Mendelson, 1975). This is manifested by the young couple's financial limitations and family economic interdependence, which slow down the process of truly setting up a separate household. The newly constituted family may live with or near the husband's family and receive temporary economic support; this may result in tensions between wife and mother-in-law. Occasionally, couples live with the wife's family, but this dependence may be perceived as a lack of masculinity on the husband's part. Young wives may talk on the phone to their mothers every day. Many young husbands may

visit their parents, particularly their mothers, once or twice a week. This interaction may become even more frequent after marriage than it was during their steady courtship, when the young couple was usually left alone to explore their relationship. Thus, paradoxically, marriage may signify a return to, rather than a separation from, the fold.

Marital therapy for Latinos often involves complex intergenerational issues. Conflicts of loyalty between obligations to one's aging parents and to one's own family of procreation may create considerable stress and may surface in any family member. Many Latinos are likely to resist the idea of publicly leveling hierarchies or using a direct assertive communication style with their parents.

Divorce may be more traumatic for Latinos than for Anglo Americans. The criticism and judgmental disappointment about the decision to divorce are most intense among first-generation immigrant Mexican parents. Since marriage is thought to be for life, a divorce on the basis of marital incompatibility may be alien to cultural and religious beliefs. There are also feelings of shame about the social stigma and what others in the extended networks will say about a divorce (Wagner, 1988). Unlike divorce, single parenthood is common at lower socioeconomic levels owing to teenage pregnancy and spousal abandonment.

MIDDLE AGE: A FULL NEST

Cultural meaning systems have prepared the Latino couple for parenting while deemphasizing meanings related to marital happiness. Satisfaction in marriage is seen as the result of good fortune and wise choices, rather than of working toward marital improvement or enrichment. Searching for compensation in other family bonds and simple resignation are common solutions. Educated middle-class or acculturated Latinos may see cause for alarm in the proverbial communication problems defined by Anglo Americans, but in general, marital therapy is reserved for severe difficulties.

Gender definitions are in flux. Although a patriarchal view of gender definitions continues to be the stereotypical view of Latinos, more complex dynamics from patriarchal to egalitarian and mixed styles are being documented, particularly for young couples (Kutsche, 1983; Vega, 1990; Ybarra, 1982). In middle age, a compromise is usually reached by finding an acceptable, somewhat less connected manner of parenting the married children, focusing on caretaking of grandchildren and perhaps increasing contact with relatives, in-laws, and other significant kin. A frequent pattern is a type of emotional separation, with both spouses continuing to live together, carrying on their family duties but hardly renewing their marital bond.

The sense of vitality in the involvement with the younger generations and continued usefulness make for a different configuration to the issues of middle life than the empty nest and the existential and marital reevaluations that are typically described for middle-class, Anglo Americans. Grandparents assume an important role in child-rearing. Indeed, their influence is felt and usually accepted by the young parents, who do not seem to experience the peripherality and fear of intrusion that their middle-class Anglo American counterparts express. When these avenues for continued connectedness with family are not available, reorganization of the mature marital relationship toward a more intimate and compassionate unit contributes to greater well-being. Considerable accommodation must take place to cope with the overlapping stresses of launching and marriage of children, new relationships with the in-laws, and illnesses or death of one's own parents all happening virtually under the same roof.

THE ELDERLY: LOSSES BUT A SHARED LIFE

Many parents of first-generation adult immigrants remain behind in their countries of origin. When these parents become too old to work, ill, widowed, or isolated, they are encouraged to move to the United States to be near their offspring, living either in the same house or close by. The older person arrives in an unknown setting, without knowledge of the language or any skills for independent living. She or he may or may not find a useful role. The older woman may be easily integrated into customary housekeeping and babysitting activities. The functions of the older man may be limited to babysitting and running small errands. He may sit for long hours on the porch or watch Spanish-language programs on television all day, deprived of his country's lifelong associations. In a given week, elderly Puerto Rican women, in particular, think about their relatives and friends very often (Mahard, 1989). The elderly may have traded the losses of uprooting for a shared life with their children, but the balance is often questionable, and even those who have been in this country for many years may long for their roots.

Hard Reality Issues First

The Latino elderly make up the fastest-growing subgroup among Latinos. Economic hardships, language difficulties, social isolation, and very limited adaptation to the unknown environment outside the home are the bane of older Latinos. Some derivative of these hard reality issues is what most often brings the elderly Latino into contact with mental health services.

Multiple Jeopardy

The Latino elderly experience multiple jeopardy (Dowd & Bengtson, 1978), that is, a vulnerable position in facing life stresses because of being old, being a social and class minority, not knowing the language and institutions, and not having transportation or support networks (Bastida, 1984). Most do not receive pensions, Social Security, or Medicare (Gallegos, 1991). It is difficult to imagine a more excruciating uprooting than the one that occurs in old age. Despite the prevalence of extended family caregivers (Greene & Monahan, 1984; Merkides, Boldt, & Ray, 1986) it is probably a disservice to the Latino elderly to assume, as the stereotype of close family ties invites us to do, that the family can meet all their needs (Gallegos, 1991).

Networking

Exploring and developing alternative natural social support networks is the most constructive solution to combat the problems of the elderly. A network that involves reciprocity and mutual assistance appears to work much better than simple charity or help for the elderly (Miranda, 1991).

Elderly Latinos who have been in this country for many years retain important positive roles when they live with their adult children. Their presence helps to reduce anxiety at times of stress for the younger nuclear family, such as illness of children, overtime work for the husband, or the wife's dilemmas of employment and child care. Wisdom, and even sorcery, are attributed only to the old. Their usefulness and wisdom, coupled with the younger generation's respect for authority, allow older people to continue to exert considerable influence on their married or single children through control, criticism, and reminders. The ability to become a "tough old bird"—energetic, involved, and self-confident—and perceive old age as arriving chronologically later than it does for Anglo Americans seems to be preserved among the Mexican American elderly. This finding may be accounted for by the fact that Latino culture values collectivism, conservation, cooperation, and continuity and therefore does not require the dramatic shifts in life orientation that are required for Anglo Americans in later life. In Latino culture, being old doesn't strand people on an experiential island; it allows them to remain in the mainstream of life.

Retirement

Retirement from their usual occupation may not represent as significant a turning point for older Latino men or for their families. Productive work in one's occupation is not as central a life task as it is for those raised in the Protestant ethic. In their Latin American countries of origin, few people retire in a prescribed manner. Older men continue to work while they can. They gradually reduce their output and begin to move closer to the family orbit. There, the man joins a houseful of people, rather than a wife who has learned to live alone during the past twenty years. In fact, retirement does not demand very significant shifts for the wife or adjust-

ment for the couple, since they may be able to maintain separate gender spheres of social contact and leisure. However, some of the original supportive structures found in siblings and same-sex leisure groups may have been painfully lost by the migration.

Nursing Homes

Because self-sufficiency isn't expected from an old or sick person, Latinos expect that the young will take care of the old until the end and not place parents in nursing homes. The entire family tends to respect cultural values that emphasize the importance of filial love, or at least obligation, more than efficiency and practicality.

Americans believe that those who worked hard, saved, planned ahead, or raised a good family deserve more comfortable aging than does the old derelict or the alcoholic, who never provided adequately for his family and may even have abused them. Among Latinos, children are obligated to care for and respect their parents whether the older person rightfully deserves it or not. A relational ethic of intrinsic duty and obligation toward one's own parents moves Latinos to obey this mandate regardless of whether the relationships have been reciprocal, balanced, or fair. Being old and being one's parents are more than sufficient reasons to merit care.

DYING AND GRIEVING

The immigrant's old memories and feelings of uprooting may return in facing death or bereavement in a foreign land. The fantasy of returning to be buried in the homeland may be keenly experienced as a much-wanted final recovery of belonging. The presence of supportive compatriots that share language, history, and values can provide invaluable support in dying or grieving for a loved one's death.

Latinos do not ignore death as a constant fact of life. In many Latin American countries, the Day of the Dead is a *fiesta* that is publicly held once a year in which folklore, religious litanies, sugar candy skulls, and tissue paper skeletons poke fun at death. Jokes and sayings about astute maneuverings that confuse and defeat death are common, an attempt to banter with a difficult but inevitable companion.

An important part of the Day of the Dead in Mexico is the ritualization of grief over a period of four years of annual repetition of mourning and offerings after a death. The family erects a home portable altar with a photograph of the dead person, some favorite objects surrounded by zimpazuchis— deep yellow and purple flowers (the only flowers that can be used on that day)—and the dead person's favorite foods. After a day's vigil at their open home, the family transports to the cemetery the altar with its hanging objects and a sample of the dead person's foods on plates covered with beautifully embroidered cloths. Family and friends sit around the grave chanting and swaying, with very tall lit candles all around. Close family members, particularly women and children, will sleep next to the grave until the following morning to "keep company with our poor dead ones" ("*a nuestros pobrecitos muertos*"). This ritual offers emotional release, and some household variant could be used as a natural therapeutic resource if the ritual has ever been meaningful to the particular family, although it would be hard to fathom an American cemetery as a place to spend the night with one's dead ones.

Gasping for breath, heart palpitations, or chest pains (*piquetes*) in the deeply bereaved are accepted as natural expressions of grief, because in most Latino cultures, emotional states are not conceived as separate from bodily reactions. Hallucinations of the deceased in the form of visitations of spirits and ghosts up to several years from the death do occur, especially among Puerto Ricans who practice *santería* and Cubans who engage in *macombe,* an Afro-Caribbean religion.

The physical and emotional support of the extended family and the community provide nurturance for the bereaved. Emotions may be vented within a closely knit group. Equally acceptable are stoic resignation and acceptance. Religion may resurface with impending loss, as guidance or consolation for the ill, elderly, or bereaved person. The Catholic belief in the immortality of the soul may ameliorate some of the most frightening aspects of death.

The custom of the oldest son's being responsible for the funeral arrangements may be maintained in this country, financial responsibilities being shared among siblings and other relatives. Those who immigrated as young adults have not been exposed to the cultural mechanisms and conduct expected at times of illness and death. They may have to learn those anew and alone and frequently feel confused.

During developmental transitions, immigrant families turn more intensely to the comfort and continuity of past traditions, such as the rituals of praying or trying folk remedies. Therapists can use the impetus toward one's own primary ethnicity as a resource to help discover the practices that enhance a family's sense of continuity and belonging and the ancestral rituals that push the life cycle forward while reaffirming past ties.

REFERENCES

Aronowitz, M. (1984). The social and emotional adjustment of immigrant children: A review of literature. *International Migration Review, 18,* 237–257.

Bastida, E. (1984). Reconstructing the world at sixty: Older Cubans in the U.S.A. *Gerontologist, 24,* 465–470.

Becerra, R. M., & de Anda, D. (1984). Pregnancy and motherhood among Mexican American adolescents. *Health and Social Work, 9*(2), 106–123.

Bronfman, M., Amuchástegui, A., Martina, R. M., Minello, N., Rivas, M., & Rodríguez, G., (1995). *SIDA en Mexico: migración, adolescencia y género.* Mexico: Informacíon Profesional Especializada.

Canino, G., & Canino, A. I. (1982). Culturally syntonic family therapy for migrant Puerto Ricans. *Hospital and Community Psychiatry, 33*(4), 299–303.

Clark, M. & Mendelson, M. (1975). Mexican-American aged in San Francisco. In W. C. Sze (Ed.), *Human life cycle.* New York: Jason Aronson.

de Anda, D., Becerra, R. M., & Fielder, E. (1988). Sexuality, pregnancy, and motherhood among Mexican-American adolescents. *Journal of Adolescent Research, 3*(3–4), 403–411.

Dowd, J. J., & Bengtson, V. L. (1978), Aging in minority populations: An examination of the double jeopardy hypothesis. *Journal of Gerontology, 33,* 427–436.

Falicov, C. J. (1984). Focus on stages: A response to Proudfit's developmental analysis of V. Wolff's *To the Lighthouse. Family Process, 23*(3), 329–334.

Falicov, C. J. (1998). *Latino families in therapy.* New York: The Guilford Press.

Falicov, C. J., & Brudner-White, L. (1983). The shifting triangle: The issue of cultural and contextual relativity. In C. J. Falicov (Ed.), *Cultural perspectives in family therapy.* Rockville, MD: Aspen Corporation.

Falicov, C. J., & Karrer, B. (1980). Cultural variations in the family life cycle: The Mexican-American family. In B. Carter & M. McGoldrick (Eds.), *The family life cycle: A framework for family therapy.* (pp. 383–425). New York: Gardner Press.

Felice, M. E., Shragg, G. P., James, M., & Hollingsworth, D. R. (1987). Psychosocial aspects of Mexican-American, White, and Black teenage pregnancy. *Journal of Adolescent Health Care, 8,* 330–335.

Gallegos, J. S. (1991). Culturally relevant services for Hispanic elderly. In M. Sotomayor (Ed.), *Empowering Hispanic families: A critical issue for the '90s.* Milwaukee, WI: Family Service America.

González-Ramos, G., Zayas, L. H., & Cohen, E. (1993). Cultural beliefs in Puerto Rican childrearing. Unpublished raw data, available from authors.

Greene, V. L., & Monahan, D. J. (1984). Comparative utilization of community-based long-term care services by Hispanic and Anglo elderly in a case mangement system. *Journal of Gerontology, 39,* 730–735.

Gutmann, M. C. (1996). *The Meanings of macho: Being a man in Mexico City.* Berkeley: University of California Press.

Harwood, R. L., Miller, J. G., & Irizarry, N. L. (1995). *Culture and attachment: Perceptions of the child in context.* New York: The Guilford Press.

Horowitz, R. (1983). *Honor and the American dream: Culture and identity in a Chicano community.* New Brunswick, NJ: Rutgers University Press.

Kay, M. A. (1980). Mexican American and Chicana childbirth. In M. Melville (Ed.), *Twice a minority* (pp. 52–65). St. Louis, MO: C. V. Mosby.

Kutsche, P. (1983). Household and family in Hispanic northern New Mexico. *Journal of Comparative Family Studies, 14,* 151–165.

Mahard, R. (1989). Elderly Puerto Rican women in the continental United States. In C. García Coll & L. Mattei (Eds.), *The psychosocial development of Puerto Rican women* (pp. 88–101). New York: Praeger.

Martinez, A. L. (1981). The impact of adolescent pregnancy on Hispanic adolescents and their families. In T. Ooms (Ed.), *Teenage pregnancy in a family context* (pp. 326–343). Philadelphia: Temple University Press.

Merkides, K. S., Boldt, J. S., & Ray, L. A. (1986). Sources of helping an intergenerational solidarity: A three-generations study of Mexican Americans. *Journal of Gerontology, 41,* 506–511.

Miranda, M. R. (1991). Mental health services and the Hispanic elderly. In M. Sotomayor (Ed.), *Empowering Hispanic families: A critical issue for the '90s.* Milwaukee, WI: Family Service America.

Okagaki, L., & Sternberg, R. J. (1993). Parental beliefs and children's school performance. *Child Development, 64,* 36–56.

Ortiz-Colón, R. (1985). Acculturation, ethnicity and education: A comparison of Anglo teachers' and Puerto Rican mothers' values regarding behaviors and skills. Unpublished doctoral dissertation, Harvard University, Cambridge, MA.

Shorris, E. (1992). *Latinos: A biography of the people.* New York: Norton.

Vega, W. (1990). Hispanic families in the 1980s: A decade of research. *Journal of Marriage and the Family, 52,* 1015–1024.

Vigil, J. D. (1988). *Barrio gangs: Street life and identity in Southern California.* Austin: University of Texas Press.

Wagner, R. M. (1988). Changes in extended family relationships for Mexican Americans and Anglo single mothers. In C. A. Everett (Ed.), *Minority and Ethnic Issues in the Divorce Process* (pp. 69–87). New York: Hawthorn Press.

Ybarra, L. (1982). Marital decision making and the role of machismo in the Chicano family. *De Colores, 6,* 32–47.

Zavala-Martinez, I. (1994). Quién soy? Who am I? Identity issues for Puerto Rican adolescents. In E. P. Salett & D. R. Koslow (Eds.), *Race, ethnicity, and self: Identity in multicultural perspective* (pp. 89–116). Washington, D.C.: National MultiCultural Institute.

Zimmerman, J. (1991). Crossing the desert alone: An etiological model of female adolescent suicidality. In C. Gilligan, A. Rogers, & D. Thomas (Eds.), *Women, girls & psychotherapy: Reframing resistance* (pp. 223–240). Binghamton, NY: Harrington Park Press.

CHAPTER 9

SIBLINGS THROUGH THE LIFE CYCLE

MONICA McGOLDRICK
MARLENE WATSON
WAYMON BENTON

My dearest friend and bitterest rival, my mirror and opposite, my confidante and betrayer, my student and teacher, my reference point and counterpoint, my support and dependent, my daughter and mother, my subordinate, my superior and scariest still, my equal. My sister is someone who lives out another part of myself, freeing me or limiting me to my role, which is by definition "not her."

—Elizabeth Fishel (1979, p. 16)

THE IMPORTANCE OF SIBLING RELATIONSHIPS THROUGH THE LIFE CYCLE

Sibling relationships are the longest that most of us have in life. Indeed, from a life cycle perspective, the sibling bond may be second only to the parent-child bond in importance. In later life, once parents are gone, the sibling bond can become our primary attachment (Gold, 1989; Norris & Tindale, 1994). Yet sibling relationships have been largely neglected in the family therapy literature and in the mental health field in general. Apart from Adler's (1959, 1979) early formulations, followed up by Walter Toman's *Family Constellation* (1976), there was for many years hardly any attention to siblings in the psychological literature. Luckily, a number of excellent works in the past few years can begin to counter this neglect, such as Bank and Kahn's *The Sibling Bond* (1982), Kahn and Lewis's "Siblings in Therapy" (1982), Barbara Mathias's *Between Sisters* (1992), Marianne Sandmaier's *Original Kin*

(1994), Susan Scarf Merrell's *The Accidental Bond* (1995), Frank Sulloway's *Born to Rebel* (1996), and Victor Cicirelli's *Sibling Relationships across the Life Span* (1995). In our view, the neglect of siblings reflects cultural attitudes that overvalue the individual and nuclear family experience to the neglect of lifelong connections that we all have to our extended family members throughout the life cycle. We can, through our therapeutic efforts, validate, empower, and strengthen family ties or, by ignoring them, perpetuate the invalidation, anomie, and disconnection promoted by the dominant society's value structure, which privileges autonomy, competition and materialistic values.

We hope that this chapter will encourage therapists to ask more questions about sibling relationships for people of every age, affirm the importance of sibling connections through the life cycle in all clinical assessments, and validate sibling relationships through therapeutic interventions that support and strengthen these bonds. We encourage therapists to hold specific sibling sessions when appropriate.

Perhaps our therapeutic approach would be facilitated if we worked on the basic assumption of including siblings unless there is a reason not to. That is, in doing an assessment, we could start with the question "Why *not* have a sibling session to understand or help clients in this situation?" rather than starting with the negative and including siblings only if there is a specific sibling conflict.

In some families, relationships with siblings remain each other's most important relationships. In others, sibling rivalry and conflict causes families to break apart. Siblings can become the models for future relationships with friends, lovers, and other contemporaries. In our modern world, spouses may come and go, parents die, and children grow up and leave, but if we are lucky, siblings are always there. Our parents usually die a generation before we do, and our children live on for a generation after us. It is rare that our spouses are closely acquainted with our first twenty or thirty years or for friendships to last from earliest childhood until the end of our lives. However, our siblings share more of our lives genetically and contextually than anyone else, particularly sisters, since sisters tend to be emotionally more connected and to live longer than brothers. In fact, we can divorce a spouse much more finally than a sibling (McGoldrick, 1989b).

In today's world of frequent divorce and remarriage, there may be a combination of siblings, stepsiblings, and half-siblings who live in different households and come together only on special occasions. There are also more only children, whose closest siblinglike relationships will be with their friends. There are more two-child families as well, in which the relationship between the children tends to be more intense for the lack of other siblings, especially if their parents divorce. Thus, sibling relationships may become more salient for the current generation because of all the factors that are diminishing the family and community network. Clearly, the more time siblings spend with one another and the fewer siblings there are, the more intense their relationships are likely to be. Furthermore, siblings who have little contact with outsiders grow to rely on each other, especially when parents are absent, unavailable, or inadequate.

Though there has been extremely little research on longitudinal aspects of sibling relationships, siblings generally seem to have a commitment to maintaining their relationships throughout life, and it is rare for them to break off their relationship or lose touch completely with each other (Cicirelli, 1985). Among the few findings that we have are data showing that siblings of the handicapped, especially sisters, are particularly vulnerable to emotional problems and to increased emotional demands from their families. Involving siblings in planning and treatment obviously benefits the whole family. Yet very few programs for the disabled include work with siblings (whether children or adults) as a focus of their intervention.

But the evidence is that sibling relationships matter a great deal. According to one important longitudinal study of successful, well-educated men (the Harvard classes of 1938–1944), the single best predictor of emotional health at age 65 was having had a close relationship with one's sibling in college. This was more predictive than childhood closeness to parents, emotional problems in childhood or parental divorce, and more predictive even than having had a successful marriage or career (Valliant, 1977).

AGE SPACING

Sibling experiences vary greatly. An important factor is the amount of time brothers and sisters spend together when they are young. Two children who are close in age, particularly if they are of the same gender, generally spend a lot of time together, must share their parents' attention, and are usually raised under similar conditions. Siblings who are born far apart spend less time with each other and have fewer shared experiences; they grow up at very different points in their family's evolution and are in many ways like only children.

Sulloway (1996) maintains that children who are closest in age have the greatest competition and rivalry for their parents care; therefore, the second sibling has the greatest need to differentiate from the oldest to find a niche for him or herself.

The ultimate shared sibling experience is that of identical twins. They have a special relationship that is exclusive of the rest of the family. Twins have been known to develop their own language and maintain an uncanny, almost telepathic sense of each other. Even fraternal twins often have remarkable similarities because of their shared life experiences.

The major challenge for twins is to develop individual identities. Since they do not have their own unique sibling position, there is a tendency to lump twins together. This becomes a problem especially when, as adolescents, they are trying to develop their separate identities. Sometimes twins have to go to extremes to distinguish themselves from each other.

GENDER DIFFERENCES

Sister pairs tend to have the closest relationships. Sisters generally have been treated differently from brothers in families, given the pivotal caretaking role that sisters typically have in a family. Both brothers and sisters report feeling more positive about sisters (Troll & Smith, 1976) and indicate that a sister was the sibling to whom they felt closest (Cicirelli, 1982). According to a survey by Cicirelli (1983), the more sisters a man has, the happier he is and the less worried about family, job, or money matters. Sisters seem to provide a basic feeling of emotional security. The more sisters a woman has, the more she is concerned with keeping up social relationships and helping others (Cicirelli, 1985). Siblings can provide role models for successful aging, widowhood, bereavement, and retirement. They act as caretakers and exert pressures on each other to maintain values.

With rare exceptions, fewer expectations for intellectual and worldly achievement are placed on, or allowed to, sisters than brothers. It is interesting that in Hennig and Jardin's classic study (1977) of highly successful women in business, not a single woman in the sample had had a brother. Research indicates that while the prefer-

ence for sons is diminishing (Entwistle & Doering, 1981), there is still a greater likelihood that a family with only female children will continue to try for a boy. We have come a long way from the infanticide that other cultures have resorted to when they had daughters instead of sons, but the remnants of those attitudes still exist. Families are more likely to divorce if they only have daughters, and divorced fathers are more likely to lose contact with children if they are daughters.

Unlike oldest sons, who typically have a clear feeling of entitlement, oldest daughters often have feelings of ambivalence and guilt about the responsibilities of their role. Whatever they do, they feel that it is not quite enough, and they can never let up in their efforts to caretake and make the family work right. They are the ones who maintain the networks; who make Thanksgiving, Christmas, and Passover happen; who care for the sick; and who carry on the primary mourning when family members die. They are central in family process, more often taking responsibility for maintaining family relationships than their brothers. Sisters not only do more caretaking, but they tend to share more intimacy and have more intense relationships than brothers, although they typically get less glory than brothers do. From childhood on, most sibling caretaking is delegated to older sisters, with brothers freed for play or other tasks (Cicirelli, 1985). Brother-to-brother relationships appear characterized by more rivalry, competitiveness, ambivalence, and jealousy (Adams, 1968; Cicirelli, 1985), while sister relationships are characterized by more support and caretaking.

Sister relationships, like those of women friends, are more often devalued than peer relationships involving men. A woman who wants to avoid a move for her husband's job to be near her sister is considered strange indeed. She will probably be labeled "enmeshed" or "undifferentiated." Yet it is the sister who was there at the beginning, before the husband, and who will most likely be there at the end, after he is dead and gone. A strong sense of sisterhood seems to strengthen a woman's sense of self (Cicirelli, 1982, 1985; Noberini, Brady, & Mosatche, in press).

With the best of intentions, parents may convey very different messages to their sons than to their daughters. In certain cultures, such as Italian and Latino, daughters are more likely to be raised to take care of others, including their brothers. Some cultural groups, such as Irish and African American families, may, for various historical reasons, overprotect sons and underprotect daughters (McGoldrick, 1989a; McGoldrick, Giordano, & Pearce, 1996). Other cultural groups have less specific expectations. Anglos, for example, are more likely to believe in brothers and sisters having equal chores. But, in general, it is important to notice how gender roles influence sibling patterns in understanding a family (McGoldrick, 1989b).

BIRTH-ORDER EFFECTS IN SIBLING RELATIONSHIPS

Although birth order can profoundly influence later experiences with spouses, friends, and colleagues, many other factors also influence sibling roles, such as temperament, disability, class, culture, looks, intelligence, talent, gender, and the timing of each birth in relation to other family experiences—deaths, moves, illnesses, changes in financial status, and so on.

Parents may have a particular agenda for a specific child, such as expecting him or her to be the responsible one or the baby, regardless of that child's position in the family. Children who resemble a certain family member may be expected to be like that person or to take on that person's role. Children's temperaments may also be at odds with their sibling positions. This may explain why some children struggle so valiantly against family expectations—the oldest who refuses to take on the responsibility of the caretaker or family standard bearer or the youngest who strives to be a leader. In some families, it will be the child who is most comfortable with the responsibility—not necessarily the oldest child—who becomes the leader. Parents' own sibling experiences will affect their children as well. But certain typical patterns often occur that reflect each child's birth order.

In general, oldest children are likely to be the overresponsible and conscientious ones in the family. They make good leaders, since they have experienced authority over and responsibility for younger siblings. Often serious in disposition, they may believe that they have a mission in life. In identifying with their parents and being especially favored by them, oldest children tend to be conservative even while leading others into new worlds; and while they may be self-critical, they do not necessarily handle criticism from others well.

The oldest daughter often has the same sense of responsibility, conscientiousness, and ability to care for and lead others as her male counterpart. However, daughters generally do not receive the same privileges, nor are there generally the same expectations for them to excel. Thus, they may be saddled with the responsibilities of the oldest child without the privileges or enhanced self-esteem.

The middle child in a family is in between, having neither the position of the first as the standard bearer nor the last as the baby. Middle children thus run the risk of getting lost in the family, especially if all the siblings are of the same sex. On the other hand, middle children may develop into the best negotiators, more even-tempered and mellow than their more driven older siblings and less self-indulgent than the youngest. They may even relish their invisibility.

Frank Sulloway (1996) argues on the basis of a large sample of historical figures that later-born children, both middle and youngest children, are very much more likely to be rebels than are oldest or only children because of the Darwinian imperative for survival. The niche of following in the parental footsteps has already been taken by the oldest, and they need to find a different niche to survive. They therefore tend to be less parent identified, less conscientious, and more sociable. Traditionally, in many European cultures, younger children, sons in particular, had to be disposed of, since the oldest took over the family from the father; younger sons became warriors or priests or fulfilled other less conventional roles in society.

A middle sister is under less pressure to take responsibility, but she needs to try harder to make her mark in general because she has no special role. She remembers running to catch up with the older sister from childhood and running frantically from the younger one, who seemed to be gaining on her every minute (Fishel, 1979).

The youngest child often has a sense of specialness that allows self-indulgence without the overburdening sense of responsibility of oldest children. This pattern may be more intense the more siblings there are in a family. The younger of two children probably has more a sense of pairing and twinship—unless there is a considerable age differential—than the youngest of ten. Freed from convention and determined to do things his or her own way, the youngest child can sometimes make remarkable creative leaps leading to inventions and innovations.

Youngest children can also be spoiled and self-absorbed, and their sense of entitlement may lead at times to frustration and disappointment. In addition, the youngest often has a period as an only child after the older siblings have left home. This can be an opportunity to enjoy the sole attention of parents but can also lead to feelings of abandonment by the siblings.

A younger sister tends to be protected, showered with affection, and handed a blueprint for life. She may either be spoiled (especially if there are older brothers) and have special privileges or, if she is from a large family, frustrated by always having to wait her turn. Her parents may have run out of energy with her. She may feel resentful about being bossed around and never taken quite seriously. If she is the only girl, the youngest may be more like the princess, yet the servant to elders, becoming, perhaps, the confidante of her brothers in adult life and the one to replace the parents in holding the family together.

Like middle children, only children show characteristics of both oldest and youngest children. In fact, they may show the extremes of both at the same time. They may have the seriousness and sense of responsibility of the oldest and the conviction of specialness and entitlement of the youngest. Not having siblings, only children tend to be more oriented toward adults, seeking their

love and approval and in return expecting their undivided attention. The major challenge for only children is to learn how to get along with others their own age. Only children often maintain very close attachments to their parents throughout their lives but find it more difficult to relate to friends and spouses.

LIFE CYCLE ISSUES IN FAMILIES WITH DISABLED SIBLINGS

We need to plan therapeutically for the lifelong implications that a handicapped child has for all family members, especially for the adjustment and caretaking responsibilities of the siblings. Siblings respond not only to the disabled child but also to parents' distress and/or preoccupation with the needs of the disabled child. Parents may also shift their hopes and dreams onto their other child, which can create burden and sibling strains (Cicirelli, 1995). Older children tend to make a better adjustment to disability than do younger ones because older children are better able to put the situation in perspective. Relative birth order is also important. A younger sibling may have difficulties associated with needing to assume a crossover leadership role (Boyce & Barnett, 1993). Normal siblings become especially stressed when parents expect them to treat a disabled sibling as normal or when parents expect them to be preoccupied with the needs of the disabled sibling. During adolescence, siblings may feel particular embarrassment about a disabled sibling. On the other hand, if they have developed greater maturity through sibling caretaking experiences, they may feel out of step with peers (Cicirelli, 1995).

Oldest sisters are at greatest risk because of increased parental demands on them. Brothers of disabled siblings tend to spend more time away from the family (Cicirelli, 1995), and this is something that we can help families change. These very parental expectations need to be questioned as we help parents to include brothers in caretaking and prevent sisters from becoming overburdened. Otherwise, in later life, brothers may become completely disengaged from the disabled sibling, while sisters must bear total responsibility for them.

Small families tend to experience more pressure when there is a handicapped child because there are fewer siblings to share the responsibility. The pressure seems increased when the handicapped sibling is a brother, probably because of parents', especially fathers', reactions of personal hurt to pride in having a disabled son. Sisters seem more ready to accept the role of caretaker for a brother and to have more sibling rivalry or competition with a handicapped sister. In a study of siblings of retarded children, older sisters were more affected than older brothers, undoubtedly because they got the lion's share of the caretaking responsibility for the retarded child. They experi-enced the greatest demands and were the most influenced by the retarded child in their career and family decisions. Sisters tended to be closer to the impaired child than brothers are and to have more responsibilities. They had less time for peer involvement and were more informed about the handicapped siblings than brothers were. Older sisters were found to enter the helping professions more often than other siblings (Cicirelli, 1995).

The following is an illustration of the life cycle implications of the imbalance in caretaking responsibilities between an older sister and younger brothers in providing care for a disabled brother (Figure 9.1). It provides a classic portrayal of the findings in the literature.

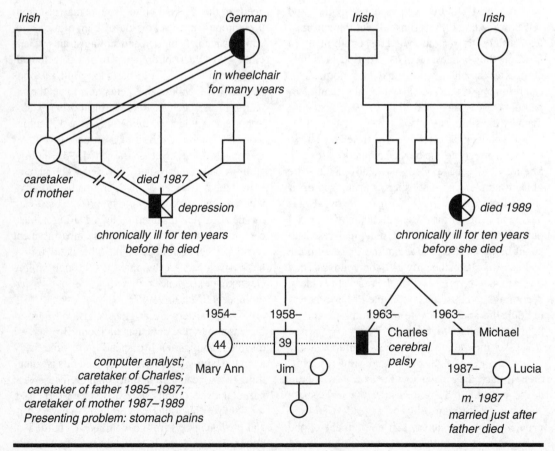

FIGURE 9.1   Donnelly Genogram

The Donnellys are a family of German-Irish and Roman Catholic background. Both parents died in the late 1980s of chronic illnesses, leaving behind an oldest daughter, Mary Ann, a younger brother, and youngest fraternal twin brothers, one of whom, Charles, had been handicapped since birth with cerebral palsy. The sister had been reared for such a caretaker's role since her preteens; she had taken care of her handicapped brother from the time she was 9 and of her chronically ill father for two years before his death. She had also cared for her chronically ill mother until her death two years later. Although she had attended college and had a successful career as a computer analyst, she was never free to take even an overnight vacation from her brother.

When her other brothers distanced themselves from her and Charles in the wake of the mother's death, she began to have unexplained stomach pains, and her family physician referred the family for therapy. The family therapist initially addressed the family's problems as unresolved mourning and attempted to involve the reluctant brothers in taking some responsibility for the disabled brother in an attempt to reconnect the family by helping them to mourn the death of their mother and challenge the directives of the mother's will, which identified Mary Ann as sole caretaker. Many attempts were made to assemble all family members together.

Charles's twin brother Michael was easier to involve in therapy than the older brother, Jim. Michael had almost cut off from the family when he married his Italian wife, Lucia, of whom the family disapproved. The marriage had occurred shortly after the father had died, and the mother had felt doubly bereft by the loss of her husband and her son, who, she said, chose to leave the family in their time of need. Michael almost seemed to have been waiting for the chance to sort out issues he had with the family. Within two months, he sought help for his own marital problems and continued working hard on his connections to his brother and sister.

The older brother, Jim, was much harder to involve in the therapy. He made one excuse after another for not attending sessions and then said that his wife's feelings were hurt because Mary Ann had not attended his daughter's christening. He wanted to accept unquestioningly that it was the sister's responsibility to care for Charles. Mary Ann also seemed to accept this role. She presented

as guilt ridden and depressed, having pledged undying loyalty to her mother's wishes that she care for her younger handicapped brother, despite the fact that her personal and social life had been sacrificed by this commitment.

To understand this better, we inquired about the sibling relationships of both parents and discovered that the father, also named Jim, also an oldest son, had been virtually cut off from his sole sister, who had cared for their widowed mother, who was wheelchair-bound with multiple sclerosis for many years. We were able to explore with the other siblings the father's longstanding depression, which they believed resulted from his own unhappy cutoff from his parents. We discovered that the sibling overfunctioning and underfunctioning in the current generation and the imminent cut-offs reflected similar imbalances in both parents' families that had led to sibling cut-offs at midlife. Mary Ann and Charles initially wanted to ignore Jim and his family, but we have been challenging them to try to overcome the family legacy of sibling cut-off. We have also challenged with Mary Ann and the others her "duty" and the long-held family and cultural beliefs about sisters' obligations in caretaking. She has recently been successful in asserting herself with Charles's doctors regarding their assumptions about Charles's need for continual monitoring. Recently, she took her first vacation in many years while Charles went to stay with Michael and his wife.

SIBLING POSITIONS AND PARENTING

If you have struggled in your own sibling position, as a parent you may overidentify with a child of the same sex and sibling position as yourself. One father who was an oldest of five felt that he had been burdened with too much responsibility while his younger brothers and sister "got away with murder." When his own children came along, he spoiled the oldest and tried to make the younger ones toe the line. A mother may find it difficult to sympathize with a youngest daughter if she always felt envious of her younger sister. Parents may also identify with one particular child because of a resemblance to another family member. Whether these identifications are conscious or unconscious, they are normal. It is a myth that parents can feel the same toward all their children. Problems develop when a parent's need for the child to play a certain role interferes with the child's abilities or with two siblings' relationship to each other or to outsiders. A parent's identification with a child may be so strong that he or she perpetuates old family patterns in the next generation. On the other hand, if their own experience has been different, parents may misread their own children. Two sisters may get along quite well though their mother expects them to fight as she and her sister did. And a parent who was an only child may assume that normal sibling fights are an indication of trouble.

SIBLINGS AND ADOLESCENT RELATIONSHIPS

By the time adolescence begins, siblings provide important models and alter egos. By adolescence, one sibling may begin to live out a life path for the other, so that they become alternate selves. But sisters in particular also often share secrets, clothes, and sensitivities about their parents' problems.

Gay and lesbian adolescents often have a particularly difficult time at this phase of their budding sexuality, both in dealing with peers and in dealing with parents and institutions. Having a supportive sibling network can be an extremely important cushion against the difficulties of school and neighborhood rejection, or it can contribute to the sense of isolation and rejection of children at this time.

Obviously, not all siblings are close. Childhood rivalries and hurts carry over into adolescence and adulthood. At family get-togethers, everyone tries, at least at first, to be friendly and cordial, but beneath the surface, old conflicts may simmer.

SIBLING RELATIONSHIPS IN YOUNG ADULTHOOD

Feelings of closeness to siblings have been found to be strong just before they leave their parental home (Bowerman & Dobash, 1974; Troll, 1994).

This is followed by a distancing during the early and middle years of adulthood, but in old age, people rate affectional closeness with siblings higher and conflict lower than do middle-aged siblings (Brady & Noberini, 1987). As they reach young adulthood, sisters often grow farther apart, each focusing on her own friends, work, and relationships, developing her own family. They may get together during holidays at the parental home, but often the focus is primarily on the relationship of each to the parents or spouses rather than on their relationships with each other. Support may be least at this phase, and competition may be strongest: Who went to the better school? Whose husband or children are more successful? Whose life is happier? The images that each develops of the other are often colored less by their personal interchanges than by the rivalries carried over from childhood or the parental images, which get transmitted to each other as they each hear from parents about the other's life. The oldest sister, once the responsible caretaker, may still resent her "bratty and irresponsible little brother," now six feet two, who teased her mercilessly throughout childhood. She soon finds herself falling into an old pattern of giving him advice. And he, though now a successful business executive, is immediately on the defensive because the old family script triggers his memories of being bossed around and of feeling impotent. A younger sister who felt dominated or abused by her older brother may feel uncomfortable even sitting at the same table with him. All the unpleasant memories flood back. Two brothers who spent their childhoods competing in sports, in school, and for parental attention may find themselves subtly competing in the holiday dinner table conversation. Even if there are no major flare-ups, family members may leave the dinner feeling bored or vaguely dissatisfied, glad that such occasions occur only a few times a year.

Whether deliberately or inadvertently, parents can perpetuate such old sibling patterns. A mother may compare one child with another, perhaps chiding one for not calling as often as another does. A father might talk repeatedly about how proud he is of his son, not realizing that he is ignoring his daughter. A parent may elicit the support of one sibling in an effort to "shape up" another. Clinically, we can do much to challenge such values on behalf of all siblings.

It is at this phase also that sisters may move into different social classes as they marry and move, according to the culture's expectations, to adapt to their husband's socioeconomic context. They themselves are often not able to define this context. It has traditionally been defined by the husband's education, work, and financial status. Although some cultures, such as African American and Irish, emphasize friendship between siblings more than other groups, such as Scandinavian or Jewish culture (Woehrer, 1982), the sister bond is generally continued through a mutual sense of shared understanding and responsibility for the family, more than through common interests, especially when class differences between the sisters have developed.

SIBLING POSITIONS AND MARITAL RELATIONSHIPS

Sibling relationships can often pave the way for couple relationships—for sharing, interdependence, and mutuality—just as they can predispose partners to jealousy, power struggles, and rivalry. Since siblings are generally our earliest peer relationships, we are likely to be most comfortable in other relationships that reproduce the familiar sibling patterns of birth order and gender. Generally speaking, marriage seems easiest for partners who fit their original sibling pattern, for example, if an oldest marries a youngest, rather than two oldests marrying each other. If a wife has grown up as the oldest of many siblings and the caretaker, she might be attracted to a dominant oldest who offers to take over management of responsibilities. But as time goes along, she may come to resent his assertion of authority, because, by experience, she is more comfortable making decisions for herself.

All things being equal (and they seldom are in life!), the ideal marriage based on sibling position would be a complementary one in which, for example, the husband was the older brother of a younger sister and the wife was the younger sister of an older brother. However, the complementarity of caretaker and someone who needs caretaking or leader and follower does not guarantee intimacy or a happy marriage.

In addition to complementary birth order, it seems to help in marriage if one has had siblings of the opposite sex. The most difficult pairing might be that of the youngest sister of many sisters who marries the youngest brother of many brothers, since neither would have much experience of the opposite sex in a close way, and they might both play the spoiled child waiting for a caretaker.

There are, of course, many other possible sibling pairings in marriage. The marriage of two only children might be particularly difficult, since neither has the experience of intimate sharing that one does with a brother or sister. Middle children may be the most flexible, since they have experiences with a number of different roles.

Coupling and marriage tend to increase the distance between siblings. Sisters may be pressured by their spouses to decrease their intimacy with each other, and that pressure may create sibling distance that lasts until later life. Maya Angelou (1981) has described the efforts siblings must make to remain connected in spite of spousal pressure:

> I don't believe that the accident of birth makes people sisters and brothers. It makes them siblings. Gives them mutuality of parentage. Sisterhood and brotherhood are conditions people have to work at. It's a serious matter. You compromise, you give, you take, you stand firm, and you're relentless.... And it is an investment. Sisterhood means if you happen to be in Burma and I happen to be in San Diego and I'm married to someone who's very jealous and you're married to somebody who's very possessive, if you call me in the middle of the night, I have to come. (p.62)

Sister-in-law and brother-in-law relationships can have some of the positives of sibling relationships without the tensions, but things seldom work out this way. Sisters-in-law share a future but not a biological or childhood history. As Bernikow (1980) put it:

At the border of family and friends stands my sister-in-law Marlene. We do not share a mother, do not worry about the pull of likeness and the need for separation. Much of the conflict and tension between sisters is missing for us. Still, as sister-in-law, it is possible that she might be my sister in spirit. The things that arise between us are things that arise between other women, touched by our family affiliation. (p. 105)

The interesting aspect of in-law patterns is the extent to which the structure of the family tends to determine in-law relationships in a family, even though family members are more sure than ever that it is just personality characteristics that they are reacting against in rejecting an in-law.

Sisters-in-law who marry into families that have only brothers probably have the greatest likelihood of developing positive connections to the new family. The wife of a youngest brother of older sisters is probably in the most difficult position, since this brother may have been treated like a prince. He may be resented though protected by his sisters, whom he probably tried to avoid for their "bossiness." When he finds a wife, his choice is likely to reflect in part his need for some protection against other powerful females, and his wife may then become the villain, supposedly keeping him from having a closer relationship with his sisters.

SIBLING RELATIONSHIPS IN MIDLIFE

Often, it is not until midlife that siblings reconnect with each other, through the shared experiences of caring for a failing or dying parent, a divorce in the family, or perhaps a personal health problem, which inspires them to clarify their priorities and to redefine which relationships in life really matter to them. Sometimes, at this point, relationships that have been maintained at a superficial level may break under the strain of caretaking or under the pain of the distance that has grown between them. On the other hand, siblings may now be brought closer to each other. Their relationships may solidify through the realization that their parents will not always be there and that they themselves must begin to put the effort into maintaining their own relationship.

In our culture, sisters are generally the caretakers of parents and other unattached older relatives or the managers who have responsibility to arrange for the caretaking. In other cultures, such as in Japan, this role goes to the wife of the oldest son. But in our culture, if sisters do not do the primary caretaking, they often feel guilty about it because the cultural pressure is so strong that they should, and they are often held responsible for it by others.

Sibling relationships can be a most important connection in adult life, especially in the later years. However, if negative feelings persist, the care of an aging parent may bring on particular difficulty. At such a time, siblings may have been apart for years. They may have to work together in new and unfamiliar ways. The child who has remained closest to the parents, usually a daughter, often gets most of these caretaking responsibilities, which may cause long-buried jealousies and resentments to surface.

While the final caretaking of parents may increase a child's commitment and closeness to them (Bass & Bowman, 1990), it may either draw siblings together or arouse conflicts over who did more and who did less. It is at the death of the last parent that sibling relationships become voluntary for the first time in life. While parents are alive, siblings may have contact with and hear news about each other primarily as a function of their relationships with their parents. If there are unresolved problematic issues in a family, they are likely to surface at this time in conflicts over the final caretaking, the funeral, or the will. Once the parents die, siblings must decide for the first time whether to maintain contact with each other.

Because it is women who tend to be so central in maintaining the emotional relationships in a family, sisters may focus their disappointments on each other or on their sisters-in-law more than on their brothers, who are often treated with kid gloves and not expected to give much in the way of emotional or physical support when caretaking is required. Brothers may provide financial support, but the usual excuse for their lack of involvement is that they don't have the time—they are busy with their work—as if sisters were not equally busy with their own work.

SIBLING RELATIONSHIPS AFTER THE DEATH OF PARENTS

Once both parents have died, sibling relationships become truly independent for the first time. From here on, whether they see each other will be their own choice. This is the time when estrangement can become complete, particularly if old rivalries continue. The focus may be on concrete disagreements: Who should have helped in the care of their ailing parent? Who took all the responsibility? Who was more loved? Strong feelings can be fueled by old unresolved issues. In general, the better relationships siblings have, the less likely it is that later traumatic family events will lead to a parting of the ways.

At the end of the life cycle, sisters are especially likely to be a major support for each other or even to live together. Older women are especially likely to rely on their sisters, as well as their daughters and even their nieces, for support (Anderson, 1984; Lopata, 1979; Townsend, 1957). Anderson (1984) found that sisters were the ones to whom older widows most often turned, more often than to children, even though they were not more available geographically. She speculated that the reasons might include sisters' shared history of experiences and life transitions. She concludes that siblings, especially sisters, take on added significance as confidants and emotional resources for women after they have been widowed.

Because siblings share a unique history, reminiscing about earlier times together is an activity in which they engage at many points in the life cycle. Such reminiscing tends to become even more important late in life. It helps all siblings to validate and clarify events and relationships that took place in earlier years and to place them in mature perspective, and it can become an important source of pride and comfort (Cicirelli, 1985). This seems especially meaningful for sisters who tend anyway to define themselves more in terms of context and to place a high value on the quality of human relationships. Cicirelli (1982) found that having a relationship with a sister stimulates elderly women to remain socially engaged with others as well. Although the relationships of sisters, like all female relationships, tend to be invisible in the value structure of the culture at large, sisters tend to sustain one another in time of need throughout life. In old age, they become indispensable. As Margaret Mead (1972) described it:

> Sisters draw closer together and often, in old age, they become each other's chosen and most happy companions. In addition to their shared memories of childhood and their relationships to each other's children, they share memories of the same house, the same homemaking style, and the same small prejudices about housekeeping.

Mead's comment is interesting in its focus on the details of life. Especially as we grow older, it is the details—of our memories, or of our housekeeping, or of our relationships with each other's children—that may hold us together.

We are coming to appreciate more the importance of adult sibling relationships as researchers have observed that family support for caregivers correlates with the presence of siblings (Bedford, 1989). As we age, some sibling relationships lose the competitive quality of childhood and become more like friendships (McGhee, 1985; Norris & Tindale, 1994). As personal resources may become overtaxed by the demands of frail or demented aging parents, sibling bonds may either become overtaxed or provide the extra energy for caretaking. Sibling relationships may also become closer with aging, as activities and preoccupations of earlier life cycle phases diminish. The loss of a spouse who may have interfered with sibling closeness leaves siblings with more time and need for the comfort and sharing of the sibling bond. Cicirelli (1989) found that attachment is more likely to characterize sibling ties when sisters are involved. It does appear that sibling rivalries diminish in later life. Generational solidarity increases and sibling bonds appear to have greater salience for siblings as they age (Norris & Tindale, 1994).

OTHER FACTORS THAT INTERSECT WITH SIBLING PATTERNS: CULTURE, CLASS, AND RACE

In addition to early parental loss, temperament, the child's physical attributes, family traumas, and major life changes related to politics, economics, and emotional factors affecting families, class, culture and race also powerfully influence sibling patterns. Cultures and classes differ in the expected roles and relationships of siblings (Leder, 1993; McGoldrick et al., 1996; Nuckolls, 1993; Sandmeier, 1994; Sulloway, 1996; Watson, in press; Zukow, 1989).

A family's ethnic identity may determine whether siblings are close, distant, or created equal (Leder, 1991) and the meaning of the siblinghood. Some ethnic groups, such as Asians, may show a greater preference for male children; some, such as African Americans, value the family unit over individual members; others, such as Anglos give priority to autonomy and self-reliance.

Even the concept of sibling rivalry is culture-bound, being largely a Western phenomenon that stems from a focus on individual achievement, competition, and status. In contrast, a huge segment of the world's population dissuades children from assuming the stance of sibling-as-rival by instilling in them a sense of "we-ness" rather than "I" (Sandmeier, 1994). In cultures that train their children to view each other as necessary, siblings are more likely to have lifelong, enduring ties.

In some oppressed cultures, the closely knit sibling bond is also influenced by historical needs for survival. Family members rely on mutual support and aid to fulfill basic material and emotional needs. In African American families, the tradition of tightly woven sibships that was passed down from African culture is combined with the family's need to function as a unit to deal with the forces of racism (Watson, 1998). Thus, strong sibling bonds may be more necessary for African Americans than for people in cultures that are not affected by oppression and in which siblings can live independently of each other. In cultures in which sibling caretaking is a major form of caretaking, as it is for African Americans, strong emotional attachment, positive or negative, may have a profound effect on siblinghood throughout the life cycle (Watson, 1998). Although large sibships such as those that may be found in Irish Catholic families may also produce older sibling caretakers, this role will probably end with childhood. Among African Americans, however, sibling caretakers tend to continue their role into adulthood. Childhood sibling caretaking helps to prepare them for their lifelong role as each other's keeper (Watson, 1998). Hence, the expectations of African American siblings have implications for individual and family development throughout the life cycle.

Some cultures use the term "brother" or "sister" to convey the depth of a cherished relationship. The Vietnamese, for example, address lovers and spouses as "big brother" or "little sister," and African Americans may greet one another with the term "Brother" or "Sister" to convey their sense of kinship (Sandmaier, 1994). Such terms of endearment express the particular culture's valuing of sibling relationships.

The family's emotional map is governed by its cultural roots. Families of Northern European and Anglo backgrounds may discourage strong displays of feeling or affection and will probably view themselves, their siblings and their parents as a related collection of individuals. German brothers and sisters would also be likely to refrain from showing strong or open affection toward one another because of the cultural prescription to maintain a stiff upper lip (Sandmaier, 1994).

In Italian culture, in which the family supercedes the individual, sibling relationships tend to be close, especially between same-sex pairs. In a study conducted by Colleen Leahy Johnson (1982), 63 percent of middle-aged Italian women saw a sibling daily, in contrast to 12 percent of their Anglo counterparts. Among college-educated older Americans, African American siblings were three times as likely as whites to focus on themes of loyalty, solidarity, and enduring affection. Hence, the cultural message that African Americans receive to stay together and help each other does not disappear as family members move up the class ladder or move toward old age.

In Greek and Jewish cultures, conflicting messages about family loyalty and individual success and competition may add to sibling tensions. Siblings may be fierce rivals at the same time that family cohesion is expected (Sandmaier, 1994). Irish siblings also seem to have ambivalent feelings toward one another. Irish culture's emphasis on dichotomies and labels may spark sibling rivalry while simultaneously inducing guilt in the sibling for having bad thoughts. Thus, buried resentments that enable siblings to appear connected while the parents are alive may lead to sibling cutoffs in the wake of parental death.

Culturally influenced family rules and scripts set the stage for sibling relationships (Sandmaier, 1994; Watson, 1998). As more Americans face longer lives without partners or children, sibling relationships must be revisited. Our brothers and sisters are potentially emotional and physical resources at all points of the life cycle, but individual needs for attachment and belonging are apt to be more critical at later junctures of the life cycle.

In cultures that prize individuality over family unity, siblings' life cycle patterns may remain distinct and separate as brothers and sisters keep their families of procreation apart. In cultures that demand family cohesion or enmeshment, siblings' life cycle patterns may become fused, making it difficult for families of procreation to establish their own traditions and ways of relating.

Understanding the cultural context of sibling relationships provides a larger framework for addressing individual issues of self-esteem and identity, unresolved issues of childhood and sibling relationships through the life cycle. A sister from a culture that prefers sons may stop blaming her brother and have greater compassion for her parents once she realizes the cultural script in which they all played a part.

Class differences are likely to have a major impact on adult siblings from oppressed cultures or poor families. Unacknowledged or overt resentments may characterize adult sibling relationships for siblings who end up in different socioeconomic groups. Lower-class African American siblings may hold their resentment of middle-class or professional brothers and sisters in check because of cultural expectations of familyhood and their need for physical support. Middle-class brothers and sisters may resent lower-class siblings for relying on them but not feel free to express such resentment because of the sense of family obligation.

In Jewish families, sibling resentment or cutoffs may result from intense feelings around the success or lack of success of one's brother or sister. Parental reactions to successful and nonsuccessful children may exacerbate sibling fissures related to class differences. The need to prove oneself intellectually superior and successful for Jewish siblings may be related to their cultural history and experience of the Holocaust. Class differences between Jewish siblings might adversely affect their relationship, especially if one perceives the other as having had an unfair advantage.

Class differences in Anglo families may result in sibling antagonism, but the cultural pattern of individuality and autonomy may obscure such resentments or conflicts. Since these siblings tend not to mingle except for formal family occasions, sibling tensions would go virtually unnoticed and probably would not be dealt with by the siblings themselves. Lower-class family members at family events may be treated like poor relations, or they may be closed out of family events because of cut-offs. Although lower-class family members could be treated negatively by middle-class African Americans, it would not go unnoticed, and the mother would probably intervene on behalf of the lower-class sibling.

Regardless of the ethnic or cultural group, class tensions are likely to surface when aging or ill parents require care from children.

Class may influence the way rebellion may intersect with sibling position. Just as oldest sisters may be more rebellious than oldest brothers because the gender inequities impinge on an oldest sister's "right" to be the leader, oldest siblings in minority families may become more rebellious than oldest siblings from the dominant groups because of the interaction of social privilege and status with sibling status. While one might think that since family members of oppressed groups might all be more resistant to the status quo than members of the upper classes, sibling position would exaggerate these class effects (for example, making a younger sibling of a poor family even more rebellious), Sulloway (1996) found that, as with the interaction of gender and birth order, the oldest child in a poor family may use a strategy of rebellion against the status quo as the best way to achieve eminence. The more radical reformers have tended to come from racial minorities and lower classes, and to be later-borns. In Sulloway's research, abolitionism attracted the highest proportion of later-borns of any reform movement he surveyed. Still, because Sulloway's study's were focused primarily on Europeans, who became involved in scientific revolutions, we need further research on culture, class, gender, and sibling patterns from other countries where lives include other spheres of activity and interest. Sulloway suggests that the early parental loss in the upper classes diminishes sibling differences based on birth order, as nannies and other caretakers come in to replace the lost parent, and siblings become more supportive of each other as they share their loss. In middle- and lower-class families, the opposite may happen. The oldest child is drawn into the burden of parenting younger siblings and becomes even more conservative, leading the younger siblings to become even more rebellious than otherwise. Large sibships reinforce the firstborn's duties as surrogate parent.

CONCLUSIONS

Throughout the family life cycle, relationships are constantly changing. Our relationships with our parents are the first and, perhaps, foremost in reminding us of our family lineage—where we come from. Without knowledge of our uncles, aunts, grandparents, and great-grandparents, how can we know who we are? Just as important in shaping our personality development are our relationships with

our siblings (Adler, 1959, 1979; Benton, 1992; Sulloway, 1996; Sutton-Smith & Rosenberg, 1970). Unlike our relationships with our parents, our friends, and our spouses (like it or not), our sibling relationships are lifelong. However, the gender differences are pronounced in sibling relationships. Sibships of sisters tend to differ from sibships of brothers. Whereas brother relationships are often more competitive and superficial, sisters tend to be more connected and deeply involved in each other's lives and the lives of other family members throughout the family life cycle. Although less honored or glorified, sisters are often the designated caretaker of disabled family members. They are confidantes and healers of the family. Their lifelong friendships become even more significant and stronger after parents die and as they themselves enter old age. Given the importance of these bonds, which are always present in the family therapy context, therapists should become more aware of their influence, initiate more clinical research, and integrate these observations in their interventions. Including siblings in therapy at any point of the life cycle can validate the importance of their relationships, help them to resolve their conflicts, whether recent or deep seated from unresolved childhood conflicts, and strengthen them for their future. Sibling sessions can unlock a client's stuckness, provide richness to an understanding of a client's history, and provide relief for dealing with current stresses. A single sibling session may become a pivotal experience in an adult's therapy. One isolated research scientist who sought therapy because of his wife's frustration with his emotional distance held a session with his siblings who came from all over the country for the meeting. All brothers over age 40, they discussed their different responses to their mother's mental illness in their childhood and learned that each had become isolated in his own way. Each brother thought his problems were unique and individual, but they discovered as they reviewed their life experiences how profoundly connected they had always been and would always be. This session shifted the client's basic relationship with his wife. He now saw himself as a man among brothers, going through life together, and felt strengthened in his ability to be open with his wife. As was described earlier, sibling sessions can help underfunctioning siblings to share caretaking burdens, modify gender imbalances, resolve longstanding conflicts, and increase collaboration.

RULES OF THUMB FOR SIBLING RELATIONSHIPS THROUGH THE LIFE CYCLE

1. Take a proactive stance about including siblings in families, whatever the presenting problem. Say to yourself, "Why not have a sibling session?" rather than thinking of including a sibling only when the client presents a sibling problem directly.

2. When one sibling is bearing the weight of sibling caretaking for a parent or a disabled sibling, work to improve the balance of sibling relationships so that the siblings can be more collaborative.

3. Assess and carefully challenge inequities in family roles and emotional and caretaking functioning of brothers and sisters. In general, sisters tend to be seriously overburdened and brothers to seriously underfunction in terms of meeting the emotional needs of the broader family.

4. Validate the importance of sibling relationships and encourage resolution of sibling conflicts whenever possible.

REFERENCES

Adams, B. N. (1968). *Kinship in an urban setting.* Chicago: Markham.

Adler, A. (1959). *The practice and theory of individual psychology.* Paterson, NJ: Littlefield, Adams.

Adler, A. (1979). *Superiority and social interest.* New York: W. W. Norton.

Anderson, T. (1984). Widowhood as a life transition: Its impact on kinship ties. *Journal of Marriage and the Family, 46*(1), 105–114.

Angelou, M. (1981). *The heart of a woman.* New York: Random House.

Bank, S. P., & Kahn, M. D. (1982). *The sibling bond.* New York: Basic Books.

Bass, D. M., & Bowman, K. (1990). Transition from caregiving to bereavement. The relationship of care-related strain and adjustment to death. *The Gerontologist, 30,* 135–142.

Bedford, V. H. (1989). Understanding the value of siblings in old age. *American Behavioral Scientist, 33,* 33–44.

Bernikow, L. (1980). *Among women.* New York: Harper & Row.

Bowerman, C. E., & Dobash, R. M. (1974). Structural variations in inter-sibling affect. *Journal of Marriage and the Family, 36,* 48–54.

Boyce, G. C., & Barnett, W. S. (1993). Siblings of persons with mental retardation: A historical perspective and recent findings. In Z. Stoneman & P. W. Berman (Eds.), *The effects of mental retardation, disability, and illness on sibling relationships: Research issues and challenges.* Baltimore: Paul H. Brookes.

Brady, E. M., & Noberini, M. R. (1987). Sibling support in the context of a model of sibling solidarity. Paper presented at the annual meeting of the American Psychological Association, New York, August.

Cicirelli, V. G. (1982). Sibling influence throughout the life span. In M. E. Lamb & B. Sutton-Smith (Eds.), *Sibling relationships: Their nature and significance across the lifespan.* Hillsdale, NJ: Lawrence Erlbaum Associates.

Cicirelli, V. G. (1983). Adult children's attachment and helping behavior to elderly parents: A path model. *Journal of Marriage and the Family, 45,* 815–825.

Cicirelli, V. G. (1985). Sibling relationships throughout the life cycle. In L. L'Abate (Ed.), *The handbook of family psychology and therapy.* Homewood, IL: The Dorsey Press.

Cicirelli, V. G. (1989). Feelings of attachment to siblings and well-being in later life. *Psychology and Aging, 4,* 211–216.

Cicirelli, V. G. (1995). *Sibling relationships across the life span.* New York: Plenum Press.

Entwistle, D. R., & Doering, S. G. (1981). *The first birth.* Baltimore: Johns Hopkins Press.

Fishel, E. (1979). *Sisters: Love and rivalry inside the family and beyond.* New York: William Morrow.

Gold, D. T. (1987). Siblings in old age. Something special. *Canadian Journal on Aging, 6,* 199–215.

Gold, D. T. (1989). Sibling relationships in old age: A typology. *International Journal of Aging and Human Development, 28,* 37–51.

Hennig, M., & Jardim, A. (1977). *The managerial woman.* Garden City: Anchor/Doubleday.

Johnson, C. L. (1982). Sibling solidarity: Its origin and functioning in Italian-American families. *Journal of Marriage and the Family, 44,* 155–67.

Kahn, M. D., & Lewis, K. G. (Eds.). *Siblings in therapy. Life span and clinical issues.* New York: Norton.

Lamb, M. E., & Sutton-Smith, B. (1982). *Sibling relationships: Their nature and significance across the lifespan.* Hillsdale, NJ: Erbaum.

Leder, J. M. (1991). *Brothers and sisters: How they stage our lives.* New York: Ballantine.

Lopata, H. Z. (1979). *Women as widows: Support systems.* New York: Elsevier.

Mathias, B. (1992). *Between sisters: Secret rivals, intimate friends.* New York: Delacorte Press.

McGhee, J. L. (1985). The effects of siblings on the life satisfaction of the rural elderly. *Journal of Marriage and the Family, 41,* 703–714.

McGoldrick, M. (1989a) Irish women. In M. McGoldrick, C. Anderson, & F. Walsh (Eds.), *Women in families.* Norton: New York.

McGoldrick, M. (1989b). Sisters. In M. McGoldrick, C. Anderson, & F. Walsh (Eds.), *Women in families.* Norton: New York.

McGoldrick, M. (1995). *You can go home again: Reconnecting with your family.* New York: Norton.

McGoldrick, M., Giordano, J., & Pearce, J. K. (Eds.). (1996). *Ethnicity and family therapy* (2nd ed.). New York: The Guilford Press.

Mead, M. (1972). *Blackberry winter.* New York: Washington Square Press.

Merrell, S. S. (1995). *The accidental bond: The power of sibling relationships.* New York: Times Books.

Noberini, M. R., Brady, E. M., & Mosatche, H. S. (in press). Personality and adult sibling relationships: A preliminary study.

Norris, J. E., & Tindale, J. A. (1994). *Among generations: The cycle of adult relationships.* New York: W. H. Freeman.

Nuckolls, C. W. (1993). *Siblings in South Asia: Brothers and sisters in cultural context.* New York: The Guilford Press.

Sandmaier, M. (1994). *Original kin: The search for connection among adult sisters and brothers.* New York: Plume.

Shanas, E., & Streib, G. F. (1965). *Social structure and the family.* Englewood Cliffs, NJ: Prentice-Hall.

Sulloway, F. J. (1996). *Born to rebel: Sibling relationships, family dynamics and creative lives.* New York: Pantheon.

Sutton-Smith, B., & Rosenberg, B. G. (1970). *The sibling.* New York: Holt, Rinehart & Winston.

Toman, W. (1976). *Family constellation* (3rd ed.). New York: Springer.

Townsend, P. (1957). *The family life of older people.* London: Routledge and Kegan Paul.

Troll, L. E. (1994). Family connectedness of old women: Attachments in later life. In B. F. Turner & L. E. Troll (Eds.). *Women growing older.* Thousand Oaks, CA: Sage.

Troll, L. E., & Smith, J. (1976). Attachment through the life span: Some questions about dyadic bonds among adults. *Human Development, 19,* 156–170.

Vadasy, P. F., Fewell, R. R., Meyer, D. J., & Schell, G. (1984). Siblings of handicapped children: A developmental perspective on family interactions. *Family Relations, 33*(1): 155–167.

Valliant, G. (1977). *Adaptation to life.* Boston: Little Brown.

Watson, M. (1998). African American siblings. In M. McGoldrick (Ed.), *Revisioning family therapy.* New York: The Guilford Press.

Woehrer, C. (1982). The influence of ethnic families on intergenerational relationships and later life transitions. *Annal of American Academy,* 65–78.

Zukow, P. G. (Ed.). (1989). *Sibling interaction across cultures.* New York: Springer-Verlag.

CHAPTER 10

MIGRATION AND THE LIFE CYCLE

MIGUEL HERNANDEZ
MONICA McGOLDRICK

The United States is a nation built largely by successive waves of immigrants. The current average is 1 million immigrants per year, 700,000 of whom are legal and the rest are undocumented. Despite the history and tradition of the United States as an immigrant nation, immigration has become a subject of increasingly bitter debate, often supported by myths about immigrants and their role in the current socioeconomic and political situation in the United States. Therefore, the following relevant demographics are useful to frame some facts about the issue:

The number of Americans who were born elsewhere has risen recently to about 23 million people or about 8.7 percent of the population, nowhere near the 15 percent foreign born in the early 1900s (Holmes, 1995). Indeed, the number of legal immigrants admitted to the United States in 1907 was 1.2 million; the number admitted in 1994 was only 804,416 (Labowitz, 1996).

Immigration patterns vary dramatically by region. For example, while nearly 25 percent of California's population is foreign born, the numbers are much lower in New York, only 15 percent of the population being foreign born (Holmes, 1995). These two states have the first and second highest percentage of foreign-born population in the United States (Ocasio, 1995).

Although the fearmongers would suggest that we must deter immigrants because they come only to take advantage of the U.S. economy and taxpayers, research reveals that immigrants pay more in taxes than they receive in public services, generate more jobs than they take, and are less likely to be on public assistance than U.S.-born residents are (Fix & Passel, 1994).

In fact, it has been reported that undocumented immigrants use social services far less than the typical working-class household (Vernez & McCarthy, 1995). This is not surprising, given that federal law already renders undocumented immigrants ineligible for most social and health services. Moreover, recent immigrants tend to be healthier than the typical U.S. citizen (Hinojosa & Schey, 1995).

Legal and undocumented immigrant families pay an estimated $70 billion a year in taxes while receiving $43 billion a year in services. Therefore, the U.S. economy benefits by $27 billion a year from the contribution of immigrants (Immigrants' Rights Sub-team of Combating Racism Task Force, 1996). In addition, the U.S. economy benefits from immigrant-owned businesses and from the national wealth generated by immigrants' consumer spending (Hinojosa & Schey, 1995).

Large parts of California's economy—in particular, agriculture and the garment industry—would simply not be viable without undocumented workers. The fact that undocumented immigrants are paid, on the average, 15 to 20 percent less than legal workers for comparable work means that there are significant price subsidies for the consumers of the goods and services that immigrants provide (Hinojosa & Schey, 1995).

Some of the largest consumers of immigrant low-cost services are older white property owners with high levels of disposable income to spend on gardeners, nannies, and house cleaners (Hinojosa & Schey, 1995).

The current immigration debate is not just about the U.S. economy but also about the future ethnic makeup of the United States. Whereas the immigrants in the nineteenth and early twentieth century were from "White" European countries, the most recent immigrant groups have come primarily from Asia, Africa, and Latin America. They are racially different (or, as more often defined, "people of color"), are not assimilating according to the lineal progression assumed by the "melting pot" ideology (Katz, 1993), and, through intermarriages, are creating the "new American face."

People immigrate for many reasons: for work, study, political and economic survival, or increased life options. Families may migrate to escape oppression, famine, or life without a future. Although migration has become the norm for many people worldwide, it is still a stressful and long-lasting transition and one that is not generally recognized by our society as a whole (Sluzki, 1992). Until recently, it almost always meant a permanent loss of one's homeland because of the expense and difficulty of traveling back to the country of origin. Indeed, immigration creates such long-ranging and profound family changes that it creates an entire new life stage for all families that go through it.

In the nineteenth century, the Irish celebrated the emigration of community members with a life cycle ritual that came to be known as the American Wake, indicating the seriousness of this transition for family and community, especially since poverty and distance generally made the separation permanent. Like the wake for the dead, the American Wake involved public participation, allowing the family and the community to grieve over the loss. Attendance reaffirmed family and group ties. Such celebrations allowed the community to rejoice ritualistically in a migrant's rebirth to a new state, since emigration, like death, freed one forever from the stark hopelessness of poverty (Metress, 1990). Public involvement acknowledged the altered relationships that emigration, like death, brought about. These were of concern not only to the individual, but also to the group as a whole.

While such rituals for the departure or the welcoming of the migrants facilitate the experience of uprooting, the profundity of the loss and transformation that immigrants experience cannot be overestimated. The readjustment to a new culture requires a prolonged developmental process of adjustment and affects families for generations. Its effects will differ, depending on the life cycle phase family members are in at the time of transition, the causes for migration, the family's experiences that lead to migration, and their experiences in their new context.

To understand a family's experience of migration, we need to learn about the circumstances that led them to migrate: Did the immigrant come alone as a young adult seeking adventure, or are the immigrants young children with their nuclear family in search of better life? Was the immigrant part of a mass exodus due to political or economic oppression? Sometimes, immigrants leave to escape a difficult social situation such as an oppressive political system. Women may leave rigidly patriarchal societies; homosexuals may leave sexist or homophobic societies; people of color may escape racist societies; and socially marginal individuals may wish to escape oppressive classist societies. Finally, although some families view the act of migration as something final, burning bridges with their country of origin, others experience migration as a temporary relocation, maintaining home bases in two or more countries.

In addition to the individual, idiosyncratic circumstances that led the family to migrate, we must be aware of the complex challenges that all immigrants face after migration. Although the style and type of migration will affect the immigrant's ability to accept a new social contract with the host society, all who migrate must deal with the conflict of cultural norms between the country of origin and the United States. This clash has a direct relationship to identity issues. A person's evolving cultural identity will depend on many factors: his or her facility with the new language; adaptation to the economic and political situation; flexibility in making new connections with work, friends, and community institutions such as church, schools, government bureaucracies, and the health care system; and the level and nature of the connection maintained with the country of origin. Some immigrants may attempt to wall off the past, forcing their children to speak only English and never talking about the country they left behind. Or they may wall off the new culture, living and working in an ethnic enclave, never learning English or negotiating the U.S. system. Others assume a pattern of biculturality, passing to the children their stories and traditions while embracing the ways of the new culture.

If families attribute positive motives to their migration, they may evade or repress feelings of loss or longing for their homeland (Sluzki, 1979). If families attribute negative motivations to their migrations, as when they have been forced by sociopolitical circumstances to flee their country, they may remain in a state of permanent collective remembrance, mourning, and involvement with the dreaded circumstances which their compatriots were unable to escape (Sluzki, 1979). When families have buried the past—under pressure to accommodate to the new environment and out of the pain of remembering what they have left behind—it may be important to help them break through the cultural cut-off and regain continuity with the culture of origin. This enriches their sense of continuous identity and broadens their potential for dealing with the present. In this regard, it is essential to keep a perspective on the entire course of the life cycle. For example, those who migrate in young adulthood may tend to disregard their culture in order to be accepted within their new context. However, as the young adult enters midlife, adulthood may become more important to them and inspire them to reconnect with their ethnic traditions. The migration experience affects and can alter a family's developmental progression and reconstruct its structure and dynamics by forcibly separating close relatives, postponing marriages and creating other family disruptions (Inclan & Hernandez, 1992).

These observations and the clinical approaches that will be presented in this chapter have evolved from our work with immigrants and from our personal experiences, MH as an immigrant and MM as a fourth generation American married to an immigrant.

THE MIGRATION EXPERIENCE

Migration forces a connection between two disparate social realities: that of the culture of origin and that of the new context. It requires the reconstruction of social networks and movement from one socioeconomic and cultural system to another (Rogler, Gurak, & Cooney, 1987; Mirkin, 1998; Sluzki, 1998). These experiences are mediated by gender, race, social class, and age (Rogler, 1994) and influence how a family copes with the natural stresses that are present at every family life cycle. Understanding of these experiences facilitates better appreciation for the complex dynamics initiated by migration.

CHANGES IN SOCIAL NETWORKS

While immigrants grieve specific losses of community, friends, and personal networks, their experiences of loss are often vague and pervasive because what they miss is not only the particular lost friends but also what Tichio (1971) refers to as the "average expectable environment." But their mourning is often minimized or bypassed because of the need to cope with the new environment. Immigrants must find ways to develop new networks to replace the links they have lost, a lengthy and difficult process. In the meantime, many interpersonal functions that the old network accomplished may remain unfulfilled, and the resulting social isolation can heighten the stress of other changes. Couple relationships often become overloaded, as each spouse may need or expect the other to fulfill functions that were previously met by a whole network of supports—parents, friends, siblings (Sluzki, 1998). In their old environment, the couple was cushioned by many social supports. In the new one, unmet needs tend to be interpreted as incompetence, betrayal, or abandonment by the partner. As each partner turns to the other, a vicious cycle of strain may develop, since the small context of one relationship cannot possibly meet all the partner's needs.

Children and adolescents may lose a major source of security: the peer group with whom they shared developmental landmarks and established reciprocal trust. They are often forced to start relationships in new environments that are dangerous and threatening. All this occurs while parents, bound up in their own adaptive struggles or difficulties understanding their new context, are understandably less available as sources of support. Elderly family members, whose natural networks have already shrunk by attrition, have even fewer social opportunities for reconstructing the peer component of their network. They become increasingly dependent on other family members, who, overloaded as they are, may react negatively to their increasing dependency. In summary, all family members are more in need and at the same time less available to each other (Sluzki, 1992).

CHANGES IN SOCIOECONOMIC STATUS

Migration tends to push immigrants into a new hierarchy of power, privilege, and prestige. Even if their gross earning potential improves, they often experience initial downward mobility in relation to their status in their culture of origin (Rogler, 1994). Both employment and family income have a direct impact on family structure, functioning, and development. Unemployment of a former breadwinner may challenge the family's hierarchy and create tension in the marriage or parental system. In addition, experiences of exploitation at the workplace or discrimination in the job search may provoke aggressive or hostile attitudes inside or outside the family (Mirkin, 1998). Difficulty or inability to fulfill the American Dream of upward mobility or even to feel included in the society creates a sense of failure, frustration, and isolation.

Finally, it is essential to realize that current anti-immigrant feelings and the consequent changes in global immigration laws and policies have resulted in a decrease of entitlements and supportive services for immigrants. Although these changes affect all immigrant families, they affect most critically families with members who are unable to produce revenue and families with disabled or elderly members or young children—leaving the most vulnerable families unsupported in caring for their vulnerable members.

The clinical consequences of these dynamics are many. Racism, ethnic prejudice, xenophobia, oppression, humiliation, invalidation, stereotyping, and negative overt and covert messages about differences undercut immigrants' self-esteem and ethnic identity (Arredondo, 1986). Anger, frustration, and fear associated with these humiliations and inequities instill even greater feelings of hopelessness and isolation.

CHANGES IN CULTURE

Acculturation is a nonlinear process that includes multiple possibilities of learning, negotiation, and accommodation to the beliefs and values of the new culture. It is a process of learning (Inclan, 1985). The type and pace of the changes made depend on multiple factors such as socioeconomic status, availability of support networks, and inner psychological resources. Acculturation takes place over many generations and has both unconscious and conscious dimensions (Ho, 1987). Acculturation conflicts arise when the values, belief systems, and worldviews of the homeland and the United States are in open opposition. Unless these conflicts can be resolved by accommodation and negotiation within the family, they result in stress that interferes with the performance of everyday tasks. Family members may become disoriented if they fail to fulfill the cultural roles they have grown up to expect. Acculturation conflicts may develop around changes in gender roles, intergenerational conflicts, differences in the pace of acculturation of various family members, social isolation, or changes in the permeability of family boundaries in the United States (Inclan & Heron, 1989). Families' external boundaries often become rigid to preserve the cultural roles and patterns of their culture of origin. This rigidity elicits intergenerational conflicts when parents react to the rapid acculturation of children, who are usually much more exposed to the new language through school and especially through their peers. Gender conflicts often arise from acculturation. Women tend to acculturate faster than men (Hernandez, 1996). Husbands become upset by their wives' ready acceptance of their new gender roles and by the consequent challenge to their patriarchal authority (Espin, 1987). Conflict is often manifested in power struggles, domestic violence, and other forms of marital oppression of women. Out of guilt and confusion, immigrant women may try to resume old roles, isolate themselves from friends, and work extra hard to please their husbands, masking their discontent in psychiatric symptoms and other relational conflicts (Hernandez, 1996). Traditional male roles are also challenged in the new cultural context. Many immigrant men feel socially powerless. Their new ethnic minority status, ethnic prejudice, racism, social invisibility, and new gender politics invalidate and challenge their traditional primary domain, the public sphere. Unfortunately, they often manifest their conflicts in domestic violence, substance abuse, illegal activities, or psychiatric symptoms (Hernandez, 1996).

LIFE CYCLE PHASE AT TIME OF MIGRATION

Young Adults

People who migrate in the young adult phase may have the greatest potential for adapting to the new culture in terms of career and relationship possibilities. While all young adults must master the complex tasks of defining their identity in relationship to their family of origin, developing intimate peer relationships, and establishing themselves in work, community, and social contexts, immigrants coping with this life transition are immersed in a parallel process of differentiating themselves from their families while separating from their country of origin. They have the complex task of forming a sense of coherent identity while having to establish themselves in a new sociocultural context. They are perhaps the must vulnerable to cut-off from their heritage, leaving themselves open to emotional isolation at later phases of the life cycle, when the need for cultural support and identification tends to increase (Gelfand & Kutzik, 1979).

The following case, seen by Miguel Hernandez, illustrates some of the complex dynamics experienced by young adults who are recent immigrants:

Ernesto is a 22-year-old Puerto Rican man who migrated to the United States to continue his education. Though his stated motivation was to become a film maker, underlying developmental and family issues affected his decision to leave his country. Feeling that it was time to become more independent from his parents, he thought that leaving Puerto Rico would finally prove to his parents that he was an adult. An only child, he described his parents, who were both college professors, as overinvolved in his college life, disapproving of his career choice, his average academic performance, and the women he dated. Against his parents' wishes, he applied for a scholarship and made plans to relocate to New York City. His parents predicted that he would fail, arguing that he was immature and unprepared for such an experience. In spite of their lack of support, Ernesto was able to move to New York, with the help of extended family and friends.

Excited and hopeful about his adventure, Ernesto looked forward to having his own apartment, a part-time job, an academic career, and freedom from his intrusive parents. However, three months after migration, he was already doubting himself and his decision to migrate. He found language a serious barrier, could not find meaningful peer relationships, and missed his family and friends. He called his friends in Puerto Rico often but could tell them only that everything was fine, ashamed of what he was experiencing as his failure in his new situation. He was cut off from his parents, resenting and blaming them for his misfortune. He was also stressed by financial problems but felt that asking for help would mean admitting failure. Feeling trapped, overwhelmed by anger, sadness, and fear, he became bitter and hostile. These feelings were acted out in his relationships with his professors and classmates. Being White, blond, and blue-eyed did not help Ernesto. On the contrary, the dissonance between his physical appearance and the stereotypes in his new contexts about Puerto Ricans made him feel more isolated and inadequate. Race and class separated him from certain groups. Culture, ethnicity, language, and migration history separated him from others. He began to experience racism, prejudice, and ethnic identity conflicts, which made him more angry and confused. Four months after arriving in New York and after failing his first college semester, Ernesto came for therapy. He was depressed, confused and ambivalent about returning to Puerto Rico.

My first move in helping Ernesto was to contextualize his present situation within his migration experience. Using this framework, I began by addressing his reasons for migrating. Instead of focusing on his conflict with his parents, I explored with him the limited options he had in Puerto Rico to become a film maker. Discussing the lack of academic film programs in Puerto Rico helped him to recognize and validate his adult decision to emigrate. The next step was to discuss his family conflict. First we addressed his anger toward his parents and his struggles to be more independent, contextualizing them as being within normal processes of separation and individuation. A multigenerational genogram revealed important family themes connected to his present situation.

Ernesto's paternal grandfather was a self-educated orphan who experienced many difficulties in becoming a successful writer. He married an upper-middle-class women, a feminist leader, who was a successful writer herself. They both valued education and culture. Because of his painful past, his grandfather also placed high value on family closeness. Their only son, Ernesto's father, Luis, had also migrated to the United States to complete his graduate education. While Luis was away, his father died quite suddenly, and feeling unable to cope with the loss and responsible for his mother, Luis moved back to Puerto Rico. Thus, since there were no academic programs in journalism in Puerto Rico, he had to give up his dream of becoming a news reporter. Although he became a successful history professor, he regretted that his dream was thwarted. Ernesto's mother Ana had also attempted to migrate for her education, but she too returned, in her case because she missed her family and had trouble adapting to the new country. Listening to these stories, I highlighted the positive aspects of Ernesto's family traditions rather than focusing on unresolved family conflicts and myths. We discussed how his family's values and traditions about education, literature, work, familism, and self-determination were important forces in his life. These values had influenced his career and personal choices, his

commitment to success, his courage to leave home, and his attempt to pursue his goals. Discussing the importance of these values and traditions in his family of origin also gave a different meaning to his parents' overinvolvement in his academic life. Although Ernesto was able to develop empathy for his parents and to connect his situation with their earlier lives, he wanted to be "well" before allowing them to become involved in his life again, by which he meant academically stable and better able to handle the challenges of his new environment. Our sessions focused on the transitions induced by his migration. We explored the emotional impact of losing social status and its meaning within his family history. By recognizing his new ethnic minority status, he was better able to deal with his experiences of racism, prejudice, and marginality. Validating his anger and confusion seemed most important. I also encouraged him to redirect his anger and frustration toward social action by participating in activities such as student political groups, which also helped to decrease his sense of isolation.

Another important aspect to Ernesto's treatment related to his sense of identity and acculturation. While he was trying to define his identity as a young adult, he was also continuously confronted with a cultural environment that challenged the values, beliefs, and behaviors that he associated with this developmental process. Discussing the language barrier marked a significant turning point in Ernesto's treatment. He could not understand why he was having so much difficulty when English had been a part of his previous education. I suggested that the uprooting experience of the immigrant, which called for a normal process of mourning his homeland, might not have left him enough cognitive and psychological space to apply what he knew in this unfamiliar setting. Through reminder of his mourning process, I was able to facilitate his recognition of how much he missed his parents. I encouraged him to share with them some of the new things he was doing and some of the details of his life as a recent immigrant. Indeed, their discussions about migration began a healing process between them.

The New Couple

New immigrant couples are confronted with the challenges of their migration-related transformations as they negotiate differences in world view, beliefs, religion, class, and cultural background. Often, the level of adaptation varies between the partners and causes serious conflicts. The lack of social supports forces partners to become more dependent on each other, a situation that fosters isolation and overwhelms each of the partners. Racial and ethnic prejudice can seriously compound a couple's conflict. Partners may not have the necessary skills to protect their self-perceptions and deal with such depersonalizing experiences. Loss of social status, financial difficulties, and social, political, and economic marginality become longstanding strains on a couple's relationship, greatly compounding its complexity and leaving them in great confusion. Many couples describe this process as one of constant internal and external crisis, which at times creates feelings of overwhelming chaos that can destroy self-esteem, mastery and relationship harmony.

Edgar (age 28) and Elsa (age 21), sought marital therapy at our agency (MH) after four years of marriage. Elsa, the oldest of two siblings, migrated from Mexico after her mother married a man of whom she disapproved. Her father, who was living in California with his second wife and children, got her a permanent visa and facilitated her coming to live with his sister in New York City. Although Elsa would have preferred to live with her father, she agreed to stay with her aunt, who had promised her a secure job in a leather factory. She also planned to get her high school diploma and become a secretary while in the United States, but adjusting to her new life was not easy. Her aunt's apartment was small and overcrowded. Elsa had no privacy and felt uncomfortable sharing a bedroom with a male cousin two years younger than she. She could not attend night school because she had to take care of her cousins while her aunt worked and to contribute to household expenses, which left her feeling exploited.

Edgar had migrated illegally from El Salvador two years before Elsa. The youngest of three siblings, he came to New York to attain a better life. His older brother has been killed in the war, and his middle brother had migrated to Mexico and not been heard from since. Edgar's parents were poor and in ill health and he hoped to bring them to the United States once he was established here.

Edgar met Elsa at work. At the time, he was living in a small rented room. He was socially isolated and held two jobs that helped him to support his parents. The couple became good friends shortly after they met. They shared their ambivalent feelings about migration, their difficulties with acculturation, and their loneliness. These similarities and their empathy toward each other led to courtship. They began to plan their future together, saved any money they could, and began to make the necessary arrangements to obtain legal residence status for Edgar. Almost immediately after the wedding, Edgar lost his job, and because of his undocumented status, his job search became a long and painful process. Finally, he got work as a handyman in his building, though this job was unreliable and did not pay enough to cover their bills. Elsa took a second job, working up to twelve hours a day. Though Edgar felt guilty for not being a better provider for his wife and parents, Elsa did not mind the long hours. At her evening job, Elsa met new friends, with whom she began to socialize in her spare time on weekends. Through these friends, Elsa learned about a program that offered recent immigrants job training and helped them to earn their high school equivalency diploma. She wanted to attend the program and began to pressure Edgar to get a steadier job. She resented that the little money he made went to his parents and to the legal expenses for his visa. In private moments, she wondered whether Edgar was taking advantage of her, as her aunt had done. Edgar felt lonely and abandoned by his wife, jealous of her friends and her time away. Tension grew between the spouses, though they felt some relief when Edgar found a better-paying job in a restaurant kitchen, which allowed Elsa to quit her evening job and attend school. She was an excellent student; within a year, she received her high school diploma and began a computer training program. Through this, she found a better part-time job, which allowed her to leave the factory. Meanwhile, Edgar, who hated his job, his abusive boss, and the long hours, became depressed and began to drink heavily. Tension between the couple mounted, and they grew apart. Edgar felt that Elsa had become too Americanized and snobbish. Though he had initially fallen in love with her determination, he now resented her interest in becoming a professional and her neglect of the marriage. Until now, they had managed to ignore their cultural and class differences, but these now became a common source of arguments. Elsa felt confused, depressed, angry, and disappointed in Edgar's lack of ambition for his future. The threat of separation brought them to therapy.

During my (MH) first session, the couple reported that they both wanted to save their marriage. Despite their severe conflicts, it became clear as we talked that they had become soulmates in the difficult process of adapting to their new context. Clearly, Edgar's undocumented status and their different life histories put them in different places in their migration transition process. Within this framework, I invited them to explore the ways in which their migration experiences had brought them together and had contributed to their current individual and marital struggles, including gender, class, and migration transitions.

As they discussed their migration history, Edgar was surprised to learn that one of Elsa's reason for migration was the fact that her stepfather had demanded sexual favors in return for his support of her impoverished mother and siblings. When Elsa told her mother of his sexual advances, the mother did not believe her, saying that Elsa wanted to prevent the mother's remarriage out of loyalty to her father. Scared, Elsa had contacted her father and asked to live with him. She felt rejected when he sent her to his sister. In her mind, her father's actions confirmed her mother's complaints that he did not care for her and that he had married Elsa's mother only because of her higher social status. He had originally worked for the maternal grandfather and began to have an affair with Elsa's mother, who became pregnant. The couple were forced into marriage, the mother lost her right to any financial support from her wealthy family, and they were sent to a different state in Mexico, where they lived until he abandoned the family and moved to California. Elsa was raised with dissonant class values. Becoming "someone" and reclaiming her mother's social status was an important hidden theme in her life. She had wished to protect her mother from loneliness and social criticism.

Edgar's story revealed a family tragedy common among Central American families. His family tragically deteriorated after his oldest brother died in the war, shortly after the father had required a leg amputation because of chronic diabetes. His mother, unable to recuperate from the loss of her favorite son, became depressed and dysfunctional. Concerned about the parents' rapid deterioration, the middle brother migrated to Mexico as a seasonal farmer, but, not hearing from him, the family suspected that he had died. Edgar was 12 at the time. He left school and became his family's primary provider. Emotionally isolated from friends and community, the parents became increasingly dependent on their youngest son. From this time on, Edgar devoted his life to his parents, becoming a good provider and unconditional caretaker. He did not have many friends and went through adolescence performing the responsibilities of an adult. At age 18, he lost his job because of the deteriorating economic situation of the country and felt forced to migrate. He was devastated about leaving his parents behind but believed that he had no choice. Once in New York, he remained very focused on helping his parents and worked extremely hard, writing to his parents constantly but keeping to himself all the hardships inherent in being an illegal immigrant. To survive emotionally, he learned to conceal his needs and emotions from others. Both his survival and his family's survival became important factors for understanding his migration process and his adaptive responses to his new environment.

Edgar and Elsa were surprised by how little they knew about each other's past. Learning about each other's family background and premigration experiences provided a context for better understanding their relationship. They gained compassion for each other as they became aware of the past traumas and emotions that had been repressed so that they could deal with their migration transitions. The need to cope and survive made sense out of their silence about their past. Therapy helped them to appreciate their complementarity and positive connections. Elsa's self-determination was a stimulus for Edgar to move forward in life. Edgar's unconditional caretaking and emotional support helped her to achieve her goals. Within this framework, I introduced the theme of acculturation. I guided them to explore how the lack of supportive networks and changes in their socioeconomic status brought on by migration contributed to their marital conflicts.

We explored the limitations that Edgar's legal status placed on them. It meant that he had no job security or everyday basic services such as a bank account, a lease, telephone service, gas and electricity, legal facilities to send money to his parents, or access to social or educational services, such as Elsa attended. Edgar was experiencing an emotional situation common to those who experience undocumented migration: social marginality, a sense of being illegal and invalid, and the need to conceal his ethnic identity to prevent deportation. These feelings create a constant and overwhelming sense of tension, which inevitably affects a person's overall psychosocial functioning. In Edgar's case, his job performance, ability to establish social relationships, and response to crises were all negatively affected. Validating his feelings and contextualizing them in relation to his migration helped to relieve his sense of guilt and inadequacy. We also addressed race and its impact on how he was perceived within U.S. society. This discussion helped him and Elsa to see the contrast in their experiences of prejudice. Given Edgar's dark skin and strong Indian features, he was more visible as racially different and consequently a target for social rejection and prejudice. We were also able to contextualize Elsa's better opportunities to navigate socially, given her white skin and Anglo features, which helped her to "pass" and be less visually threatening within a predominantly White society. In addition, she had had access to a good education while growing up, along with English and values that were closer to mainstream American standards. She also had legal access to jobs, education, and all the institutions of U.S. society. These opportunities facilitated the establishment of new supportive relationships and a sense of belonging that Edgar could not share. Through her social network, Elsa was able to buffer some of the stressors of migration and acculturation. In addition, her self-determination and goal-oriented behavior facilitated her integration into U.S. society. We discussed the impact of the couple's differing pace of acculturation on the power structure of their relationship. Elsa's focus on her career and her success in school and in her new job challenged Edgar's traditional gender role definitions and expectations of Elsa as a wife. He felt that Elsa had become opinionated, disrespectful, and disengaged from the home and feared what his parents would say if they knew his wife went to parties by herself and had lunch with male friends. He thought that Elsa was pursuing a career

because he was a bad provider, which made him feel less of a man. Confronting him with the underlying power issues of his gender belief and discussing gender politics helped him to explore his oppressive attitudes and behaviors toward women. This discussion also clarified for Elsa some of the confusion she experienced about the contradictory messages she received from her family of origin and culture about gender roles. Overtly, her culture and family espoused traditional gender roles as the way to achieve happiness in marital life. However, these messages were contradicted by her family and personal history. In her family, men took advantage of women. Her mother's life was controlled by her grandfather, father, and stepfather, and Elsa had decided at a young age that she did not want to end up like her mother. Instead, she wanted a career, a supportive husband, and the freedom to make her own decisions. Thus, she experienced Edgar's lack of solidarity as controlling and abusive, which exacerbated her mistrust of men and her unresolved family issues. Deconstructing their beliefs, gender politics, and myths provided a broader context to understand their feelings of inadequacy. At this point, therapy with Edgar and Elsa became a process of weaving all these complex events and processes together. Their goal became one of "restorying" their history as an immigrant couple in cultural transition.

Families with Children

Families that migrate with children are perhaps strengthened by having each other, but acculturation processes can threaten the family's structural composition by reversing hierarchies and family roles. If the family migrates with small children, there is a likelihood that the parents will acculturate more slowly than their children, creating a problematic power reversal in the family (Lappin & Scott, 1982). Immigrant children are frequently caught in a conflict between their parents' cultural values and peer pressure to assimilate, which may provoke disconnection from their ethnic roots (Landau, 1982). The family's inability to make overt their mourning and pain and the normal avoidance to make explicit the cultural conflict inadvertently fosters the assimilation of youngsters.

In addition, as children of immigrants move outside the family, to school and community, they often move away not only from the parents themselves but also from the parents' culture toward the new culture. This may separate children from parents dramatically more than is normative at this stage. Through school, children are more exposed to the new language and to formal education about the history and dominant values of the new country. They tend to have more flexible strategies for coping with the massive changes required by migration and may become their parents' culture brokers, helping them to negotiate their new world.

If the children must take on the task of interpreting the new culture for the parents, parental leadership may be so threatened that children are left without effective authority to support them and without a positive identification with their ethnic background to ease their struggle with life in this new culture (McGoldrick & Giordano, 1996). In addition, the need to fit into their new context tends to foster the acceptance of the new and rejection of the old, and to promote children's shame about their cultural heritage. Parents, on the other hand, tend to feel that by rejecting their culture of origin, their children are rejecting them. They experience a lack of control over their children's rapid movement towards assimilation, which leaves them feeling helpless. The family must struggle with multiple transitions and generational conflicts at once. In addition, the distance from the grandparents' generation may be particularly distressing as grandparents become ill or dependent or die. The parents may experience severe stress in not being able to fulfill their obligations to their parents in the country of origin. It is not uncommon for adolescents to develop symptoms in reaction to their parents' unexpressed distress. Because of the social isolation immigrant families tend to experience, they often feel lost without the support and guidance from grandparents and extended family. Yet when grandparents are in contact with the family, they may actually increase the stress for parents, who may feel caught up in the middle of serious intergenerational and cross-cultural conflicts. Grandparents may be more rigid in their attitudes toward the new culture. They tend to become the defenders of traditional values and preservers of the family's ethnic identity. They may criticize parents for being too lenient with children or may even interfere with their discipline.

Families that migrate when their children are adolescents may have more difficulty because they will have less time together as a unit in the new culture before the children move out on their own. During adolescence, teenagers become more involved with their peer culture, more rebellious about parental authority, and more demanding of their freedom. Ethnic identity conflicts become a source of family differences as teenagers begin to construct and reshape their own identities and question the values and role expectations of both cultures. If these teenagers have migrated to cosmopolitan cities, the acculturation process acquires an added multicultural dimension. They are acculturating not just to American culture, but to a multicultural context. Whereas the exposure to cultural diversity may facilitate the acquisition of more flexible sociocultural roles and world views, it can also add to the confusion and contradictions of teenagers' ongoing acculturation process. During this time, parents and teenagers usually experience serious intergenerational conflicts, which reflect the larger contradictions in cultural systems that clash in migration. A common issue is the pressure that teenagers put on their parents to belong, which may include having material goods that show assimilation or social status. Adolescents may demand expensive items or money for entertainment—the material indicators of belonging within their new context. Parents may feel pressured to provide for teenagers, which may overload an already burned-out system. In addition, teenagers will confront their parents with their contradictions about their acculturation process, accusing the parents of operating from the old culture's values and of not adjusting to their new context as expected. The following case seen by MH shows some of these dynamics.

Daniel (age 40) and Rita (age 35), a couple born in Chile, requested family therapy because they were having constant arguments with their oldest son Mauro (age 14). They complained about Mauro's poor school performance, disapproved of his friends, and were angry that he refused to work in their flower shop so that he could spend more time with his friends. Father and son were not talking to each other, and Rita said that she was tired of being in the middle but feared the potential for violence between father and son. Daniel accused his son of being irresponsible, was disgusted about the way he dressed and his overall physical appearance, and resented Mauro's preference for speaking English and his "Americanization," saying that he was a bad role model for his younger brother Emilio (age 7).

Mauro accused his parents of being old fashioned. He described his mother as overbearing and his father as distant. He hated his parents' "obsession" with the flower business and accused his parents of resisting learning about American culture and being anchored in old Chilean values. He resented his father's attitude toward him and his mother, describing him as an authoritarian father and husband who used his family for labor and for satisfying his own greed. The problem began shortly after Mauro started junior high school. Until then, he had attended a local Catholic school very near the flower shop, where 80 percent of the students were Latino immigrant children. The parents had taken him to school and picked him up every day, taking him to the flower shop, where he could help out and get help with his homework. Every night, the family drove home together, where they ate and spent the evening together. They socialized with other Chilean families, who shared their concern about protecting their children from the dangers of the larger culture.

But for junior high school, Mauro had to take a bus out of the neighborhood and go to public school, where most of the children were neither immigrants nor Latino. He liked the freedom of his new school, not having to wear a uniform, and not having to go to Mass. His parents reacted to his change in clothing and refusal to speak Spanish at home. As we explored the family's migration history, I learned that at the time of Rita's pregnancy with Mauro back in Chile, the county's economy hit a disastrous low, and Daniel, in desperation, developed a plan to come to the United States illegally on a merchant marine ship. He had no con-

ception of the emotional cost of this plan, and by the time he arrived in the United States, he was almost dead from the trauma of traveling hidden in a small storage room without ventilation. His dreams for his wife and child were what saved him. When he recovered, he began to work and save obsessively to bring his family to the United States. By the time the family was reunited two years later, Daniel had begun his flower business and had bought a small house, but the toll on him was tremendous. He suffered from insomnia and flashbacks of his traumatic migration. It took a while for him to work things out with Rita, who experienced him as distant and preoccupied with money until she learned that it was only his obsessive dreams of providing a better future for Mauro that had saved him from insanity in his years of deprivation and isolation.

Helping the family involved unveiling the consequences of trauma in their lives. I (MH) tried to normalize their conflicts by stressing that each family member had been taken in by the globalized propaganda of the American Dream. Daniel, who in Chile had been politically minded and liberal, connected easily with this reframing. Rita and Mauro were curious about my invitation to reconstruct their family history from the point at which Daniel decided to migrate. The first move was to ask Daniel and Rita about the sociopolitical and economic context of Chile at the time of their marriage. Stories about the political turmoil and eventual military occupancy and their participation in students' movements against the oppressive regime of Pinochet redirected them toward painful and unspoken life themes. Mauro was fascinated as he listened to his parents' stories of their political commitment. In spite of their opposition to the government, they were forced to surrender their ideals to survive in a changing economy, controlled by the new dictatorship regime. Eventually, they had to work for the government, a painful decision. They had resented the U.S. involvement in Chile, and both had strong anti-American feelings. As the couple spoke about their early relationship and their strong desire for a baby, Mauro began to reexperience closeness to his parents. The American history the parents had learned in school supported the fantasy of New York City as a fast city with multiple possibilities, the most welcoming place in America, where all their dreams could come true.

Daniel never heard about the prejudice, racism, and xenophobia of the United States, the high cost of living, or the difficulties of being an undocumented immigrant.

When Daniel had spoken of his immigration before, he had told it as a heroic tale. This time, I helped him to describe the trauma of it, and his wife and sons listened carefully, hearing the emotional force of the experience for the first time. Rita was surprised to learn details of the journey she had not known, including the exorbitant cost. Mauro was able to see his father as a human being, not the distant, obsessed businessman who was always in control. He heard for the first time about his father's pain at not being in Chile when Mauro was born and about his impulsive decision to leave everything behind in hopes of a better future. Daniel was able to share his overwhelming feelings of guilt toward Rita and Mauro for abandoning them. Emphasizing his courage and good intentions helped them to see his accommodations in a different light.

Mauro was given the opportunity to confront his parents with his feelings of responsibility for his father's misfortune. Deconstructing the meaning of Americanization facilitated the processing of Daniel's and Rita's ambivalence about being immigrants in the United States. For both of them, Americanization meant renouncing their traditions and history and losing their ethnic identity. "Without it," Daniel told Mauro, "You won't have a frame of reference to understand and explain yourself." Rita added, "Renouncing who you are is not going to erase who you are, our history is your history." Implicitly, both parents feared that without a strong sense of ethnic identity, Mauro would end up excluded and marginal, trapped in the politics of the disadvantaged. But they did not have an alternative model for him. Their own strategy was to protect themselves from assimilation by renouncing anything defined as American, which perpetuated their own marginality and exclusion. For Mauro, Americanization meant modernism, belonging, and moving forward in life. I introduced a different model of coping with acculturation by having positive connections to both cultural systems, recognizing the contradictions between them. This discussion helped to depolarize the family's ideas about their cultural differences. By the end of therapy, we integrated the new information they had learned about each other and their history so that they could see how their normal family development was affected by their migration and acculturation process.

Coaching the younger generation to show respect for the values of the older generation is usually the first step in negotiating conflicts due to acculturation. Families that migrate at this phase may also have problems down the road, particularly at the launching phase, when children may feel guilty about leaving parents who do not feel at home in the culture.

When families migrate in the launching phase, it is often less because they seek a better way of life and more because circumstances in their country of origin make remaining there impossible. Migration in this phase causes particular difficulties because it is much harder for the middle generation to break into new work and friendship networks at this age. The launching phase may be made more complex when children date or marry spouses in the United States from other backgrounds. This is naturally perceived as a threat by parents, since it means a loss of the cultural heritage in the next generation. One cannot underestimate the stress it creates for parents, who themselves have had to give up their country of origin, to fear the loss of their traditions when their children intermarry.

Families in Later Life

Migration in later life is especially difficult because families are leaving so much of themselves and their lives behind. Older immigrants tend to have a much slower pace of acculturation and a harder time learning and negotiating new situations. The general stresses of retirement, widowhood, and grandparenthood; fears of dependency; and difficulties accepting and coping with physical and mental decline, which always require family support, adjustment, reorientation, and readjustment, now demand even more effort because of the additional stresses of migration. Immigrants' inner and external resources are often depleted from having to cope with the massive changes of cultural transition. In addition, the family's way of dealing with these issues will depend on the cultural values they attach to old age. For example, in traditional Latino culture, aging is associated with wisdom, respect, and power. It is taken for granted that adult children should now return all the care and support parents earlier provided them. Elder family members may thus either become providers of positive support and guidance as experts on life, or the family may develop serious intergenerational structural conflicts. Elders in immigrant families may thus serve younger family members as a bridge to the original cultural patterns, but at times, they may intensify intergenerational conflicts with their children and grandchildren because of their difficulty adapting to the new cultural values.

There is evidence that even those who migrate at a young age have a strong need to reclaim their ethnic roots at this phase, particularly because they are losing other supports around them (Gelfand & Kutzik, 1979). For those who have not mastered English, life can be extremely isolating in late life. The need to depend on others may be particularly frustrating when one is in a nursing home where one cannot communicate easily. The following case illustrates some of the complex challenges that elderly recent immigrants face.

Maria (age 46) decided to bring her parents to live with her after a hurricane in their native Puerto Rico destroyed their house and community. Her father, Juan (age 72), a retired construction worker, was active in his community and enjoyed working as a volunteer for a vocational school. Sara (age 69) was involved in her church and in charity work for poor children. They had an active social life through a local senior center and made yearly visits to Maria, their only child, her second-generation Italian husband Antonio, and their son Tony (age 15), to whom Juan and Sara were very attached. Juan had also a special relationship with Antonio, who, with his broken Spanish, enjoyed playing dominoes and helping to fix things around the house with his father-in-law.

Things changed drastically for Juan and Sara after the hurricane. Many of their friends were forced to relocate with their children or extended family in other communities, while they, initially having nowhere to go and having lost all their possessions, went to a shelter until they decided to relocate at least temporarily with Maria and Antonio. They were emotionally devastated. Sara was depressed and scared about all their losses. Juan was angry at the government for not providing better financial support, felt guilty that he had not had an insurance policy, and worried about their financial status. Both of them feared becoming a burden to their daughter and living in a place where they had no friends and did not speak the language. They also feared dying far from their country. Maria, Antonio, and Tony, on the other hand, were initially very happy to have them. They had tried to persuade Sara and Juan to come earlier and were now glad to have them around. They rearranged the house to give them comfort and privacy and Tony was moved to the basement.

But problems emerged almost immediately. Sara and Juan were used to the freedom of walking around and busying themselves with their own projects, but here they were isolated and felt trapped in the house in a White, upper-middle class suburb where they knew no one. They missed their small community. Public transportation was inaccessible, and the only local church activities were bingo and celebrations to which they could not relate. Tony, who had loved spending time with his grandparents, now began to resent what he perceived as intrusiveness and constant nagging about his behavior. Maria felt uneasy that her mother took over the housekeeping but said nothing for fear of offending her parents. Sara and Juan disapproved of Maria's social independence and the lack of time Maria, Antonio, and Tony spent together as a family. Tension mounted, and Juan and Sara began to explore how to return to Puerto Rico, but their plans were interrupted when Sara fell on the ice and broke her hip. This increased tension even further, as Juan felt more dependent on Maria, even to talk to his wife's doctors. He felt that Maria was intentionally speaking English to exclude him when she was with her family. Sara felt even more depressed and miserable and stayed in her room to avoid further conflicts. This was the situation that precipitated their seeking therapy.

Therapy with this family was facilitated by working with its subsystems. I (MH) began with Maria and Antonio, helping Maria to work through her guilt for being unable to fulfill what she understood as her obligation as a daughter: to care for her parents in their old age. We addressed her unresolved feelings about having left her parents alone in Puerto Rico twenty-three years earlier. She also felt responsible for making her parents unhappy by pressing them to come to New York, not respecting their desire to stay in Puerto Rico. She felt unsure whether her parents' criticism of her parenting skills was justified. We then discussed her own issues of acculturation and distress about her process of cultural transition. Two major interventions facilitated the processing of Maria's guilt and feelings of distress. First, I helped Maria to reconnect her own migration history and transitions and those the family was currently experiencing, which helped her to use her own experience as a point of reference for understanding some of her parents' difficulties in their adaptive process. Second, Antonio and Maria were encouraged to explore ways to make room in their family for the wisdom and experience Sara and Juan brought to their family. This was made easier because of Antonio's own positive experience coping with his aging parents. An only son with two sisters, Antonio had had to facilitate a similar process for his mother when she went to live with his sister after their father died. At the time, his younger sister, who had suggested that their mother move in with her family, began to experience conflicts with her husband and children due to Antonio's mother's intrusiveness in their family life. Antonio, who had always been his mother's confidant, was aware of how his mother disapproved of his sister's Americanized life-style. From his sister and his brother-in-law, he heard how his mother tried to impose her more traditional values about parenting on them. The resolution of their conflict was facilitated by Antonio's direct involvement in taking his mother out to mother-son activities and by having her with him, Maria, and Tony for weekends and other social activities.

Drawing on Antonio's positive experience, we began to explore how they could address issues about family boundaries and support Sara and Juan in their difficult process of adapting to a difficult situation without underfunctioning or overfunctioning for them. It became clearer that they needed to better redefine and negotiate boundaries, family roles, and tasks to develop more open communica-

tion. Soon they were ready to invite Sara and Juan for a session, but they refused because they thought that discussing family business with a stranger was wrong. They finally agreed to come in for one consultation to please Maria. They were easily engaged and ready to talk about their migration-related conflicts. Juan missed his previous life in Puerto Rico and saw no possibilities for him in New York, but said that he liked being closer to Maria, Tony, and Antonio. Sara agreed with Juan but was even firmer than he in her resolve to return to Puerto Rico. She felt she was aging faster since she relocated to New York. She felt useless and bored, since she had no activities to engage in. However, they both agreed to stay until Sara was fully recovered and they could arrange housing in Puerto Rico. During the session, I used a metaphor commonly used by immigrants, which describes the process of migration as a rebirth experience. I attempted to establish some similarities between migration-induced transitions and the process of redefining life during later life. The couple engaged in this discussion and agreed to explore other ways to improve their coping with the multileveled processes they were experiencing: adjustment to later life, adjustment to a new environment and culture, and adjustment to a new family system. They agreed to meet for two more sessions, during which we discussed strategies to facilitate their integration into the community. For example, it was not difficult to engage them in learning how to travel to the city, where we found bilingual supportive services, which they enjoyed. Sara even agreed to take an English course, and Juan agreed to participate in a volunteer program working with foster care children. After these sessions, the whole family met together. Sara and Juan negotiated how to support Maria and Antonio's parental roles without being intrusive or critical. Boundary issues, collaborative roles, and communication rules were discussed and agreed upon. Maria and Antonio agreed to support Juan and Sara in learning how be more independent, that is, learning how to travel. For his part, Tony agreed to be more sensitive to and respectful of his grandparents' values and was helped to appreciate the value of their wisdom. After ten sessions, the family was doing better and agreed to continue the work by themselves. A follow-up session revealed that Juan and Sara had decided to stay longer but had moved into their own apartment and were actively involved in a senior citizen center in New York City for recent immigrants.

CONCLUDING REMARKS

Contextualizing family problems within the evolutionary process of the migration experience can be a powerful tool in therapy. Normalizing families' experiences can help to heal their emotional and relational conflicts. We have both repeatedly experienced the impact of migration and cultural transition on our lives as we move through the life cycle—Miguel as an immigrant himself and Monica as a fourth-generation American married to a man who immigrated from Greece at age 19. Understanding the larger forces that affect the life of immigrants helps us to manage the obstacles we face in trying to adapt and integrate ourselves into a new living context. We believe that is important for therapists working with recent immigrants to educate themselves about the complex phenomena of international migration. Anthropological curiosity, knowledge of politics, and sensitivity to culture, race, and ethnicity facilitate the work. Learning how to locate problems within the larger sociocultural, economic, and political context is indispensable for working with immigrant families. Feeling comfortable in sharing experiences and challenging views and belief systems provides the therapist with important intervention tools. Exchanging points of view with the family can result in a very empowering experience for both the therapist and the family. Encouraging social action will reduce marginality and will facilitate social and political participation, which strengthens integration within the new sociocultural context.

REFERENCES

Arredondo, P. (1986, May). Immigration as a historical moment leading to an identity crisis. *Journal of Counseling and Human Service Professions,* 78–82.

Espin, O. (1987). Psychological impact of migration on Latinas: Implication for psychotherapeutic practice. *Psychology of Women Quarterly, 2,* 489–503.

Fix, M., & Passel, J. S. (1994). *Immigration and immigrants: Setting the record straight.* Washington, DC: The Urban Institute.

Gelfand, D. E., & Kutzik, A. J. (Eds.). (1979). *Ethnicity and aging.* New York: Springer.

Hernandez, M. (1996). Central American families. In M. McGoldrick, J. Giordano, & J. K. Pearce (Eds.), *Ethnicity and family therapy* (pp. 214–224). New York: The Guilford Press.

Hinojosa, R., & Schey, P. (1995). The faulty logic of the anti-immigration rhetoric. *NACLA Report on the Americas, 29*(3), 18–23.

Ho, M. K. (1987). *Family therapy with ethnic minorities* (pp. 123–177). Beverly Hills, CA: Sage.

Holmes, S. (1995, August 30). A surge in immigration surprises experts and intensifies a debate. *New York Times,* p. A1.

Immigrants' Rights Sub-team of Combating Racism Task Force. (1996). Immigrant bashing: Get the facts. NOW-New Jersey State Conference, October 26, 1996.

Inclan, J. (1985). Variations in value orientation in mental health work with Puerto Ricans. *Psychotherapy, 22,* 324–334.

Inclan J., & Hernandez, M. (1992). Cross-cultural perspectives and codependence: The case of poor Hispanics. *American Journal of Orthopsychiatry, 62*(2), 245–255.

Inclan, J., & Heron, G. (1989). Ecologically-oriented therapy with Puerto Rican adolescents and their families. In J. T. Gibbs & L. N. Hung (Eds.), *Psychological treatment of minority children and adolescents* (pp. 251–277). San Francisco: Jossey-Bass.

Katz, M. B. (1993). *The underclass debate.* Princeton, NJ:Princeton University Press.

Labowitz, P. (1996, March 25). Immigration—Just the facts. *New York Times,* Op-Ed page.

Landau, J. (1982). Therapy with families in cultural transition. In M. McGoldrick, J. K. Pearce, & J. Giordano (Eds.), *Ethnicity and family therapy* (pp. 352–372). New York: The Guilford Press.

Lappin, J., & Scott, S. (1982). Intervention with a Vietnamese refugee family. In M. McGoldrick, J. K. Pearce, & J. Giordano (Eds.), *Ethnicity and family therapy* (pp. 483–491). New York: The Guilford Press.

McGoldrick, M., & Giordano, J. (1996). Overview: Ethnicity and family therapy. In M. McGoldrick,

J. K. Pearce, & J. Giordano (Eds.), *Ethnicity and family therapy* (pp. 1–27). New York: The Guilford Press.

Metress E. (1990). The American wake of Ireland: Symbolic death ritual. *Omega, 21*(2), 147–153.

Mirkin, M. P. (1998). The impact of multiple contexts on recent immigrant families. In M. M. McGoldrick (Ed.). *Revisioning family therapy: Race, culture and gender in clinical practice.* New York: The Guilford Press.

Ocasio, L. (1995). The year of the immigrant as scapegoat. *NACLA Report on the Americas, 29*(3), 14–17.

Rogler, L. H. (1994). International migrations: A framework for directing research. *American Psychologist, 49*(8), 701–707.

Rogler, R. S., Gurack, D. T., & Cooney, R. S. (1987). The migration experience and mental health: Formulations relevant to Hispanics and other immigrants. In M. Gavira & J. D. Arana (Eds.), *Health and behavior: Research agenda for Hispanics* (pp. 72–84). Chicago: University of Illinois.

Sluzki, C. E. (1979). Migration and family conflict. *Family Process, 18,* 379–390.

Sluzki, C. E. (1992). Disruption and reconstruction of networks following migration relocation. *Family Systems Medicine, 10*(4), 359–365.

Sluzki, C. E. (1998). Migration and the disruption of the social network. In M. M. McGoldrick (Ed.). *Revisioning family therapy: Race, culture, and gender in clinical practice.* New York: The Guilford Press.

Tichio, G. (1971). Cultural aspects of transference and counter-transference. *Bulletin of The Menninger Clinic, 35,* 313–334.

Vernez, G., & McCarthy, K. (1995). *The fiscal cost of immigration: Analytical and policy issues.* Paper prepared for the Irvine Foundation by the Center for Research on Immigration Policy, The Rand Corporation, February.

CHAPTER 11

DEATH AND THE FAMILY LIFE CYCLE

MONICA McGOLDRICK
FROMA WALSH

There is no love without loss. And there is no moving beyond loss without some experience of mourning. To be unable to mourn is to be unable to enter into the great human life cycle of death and rebirth—to be unable, that is, to live again.

—Lifton, 1975, p. vii

Death and loss are transactional processes involving those who die and their survivors in a shared life cycle that acknowledges both the finality of death and the continuity of life. Coming to terms with this process is the most difficult task a family must confront in life. Throughout history and in every culture, mourning rituals have facilitated not only the integration of death but also the transformation of survivors. Each culture, in its own ways, offers assistance to the community of survivors in moving forward with life.

By and large, the mental health field has failed to appreciate the impact of loss on the family as an interactional system. In dealing with any death, the fewer the family resources, such as extended family, friends, and financial supports, the more the system will be stressed. Insufficient attention has been given to the immediate and long-term effects for siblings, parents, children, and extended family. Legacies of loss find expression in continuing patterns of interaction and mutual influence among the survivors and across the generations. The pain of death touches all survivors' relationships with others, some of whom may never have even known the person who died.

FAMILY ADAPTATION TO LOSS

Death poses shared adaptational challenges, requiring both immediate and long-term family reorganization and changes in a family's definitions of its identity and purpose (Herz, 1989; Jordan, Kraus, & Ware, 1993; Rosen, 1998; Shapiro, 1994; Walsh, 1983; Walsh & McGoldrick, 1991). The ability to accept loss is at the heart of all strengths in healthy family functioning. The families that show the most maladaptive patterns in dealing with inevitable losses cling together in fantasy and denial to blur reality and to insist on timelessness and the perpetuation of never-broken bonds (Lewis, Beavers, Gossett, & Phillips, 1976).

Adaptation does not mean resolution in the sense of some complete coming to terms with the loss once and for all. Rather, it involves finding ways to put the loss in perspective and to move on with life. Adaptation has no fixed timetable or sequence, and significant or traumatic losses may never be fully resolved. The multiple meanings of any death are transformed throughout the life cycle as they are experienced and integrated with other life experiences, especially other losses (McGoldrick & Walsh, 1991).

It would be a mistake to impose expectations of fixed stages, sequences, or schedules on such a complex process as grief, given the diversity of family and individual coping styles, but we believe that there are crucial family adaptational tasks that, if not dealt with, leave family members vulnerable to dysfunction. Two major family tasks tend to promote immediate and long-term adaptation for family members and to strengthen the family as a functional unit.

Shared Acknowledgment of the Reality of Death and Shared Experience of Loss

All family members, in their own ways, must confront the reality of a death in the family. Bowen (1988) drew our attention to the importance of contact with the reality of death, in particular the inclusion of children.

Acknowledgment of the loss is facilitated by clear information and open communication about the facts and circumstances of the death (Wright & Nagy, 1992). Inability to accept the reality of death can lead a family member to avoid contact with the rest of the family or to become angry with others who are moving forward in the grief process. Long-standing sibling conflicts and cut-offs can often be traced back to the bedside of a dying parent or to the graveside.

Funeral rituals (Imber-Black, 1991; McGoldrick, 1991a) and visits to the grave (Paul & Paul, 1974; Williamson, 1978) serve a vital function in providing direct confrontation with the reality of death and the opportunity to pay last respects, to share grief, and to receive comfort in the supportive network of the community of survivors. A climate of trust, empathic response, and tolerance for diverse reactions is crucial. The mourning process also involves sharing attempts to put the loss into some meaningful perspective that fits coherently into the rest of a family's life experience and belief system. This requires dealing with the ongoing negative implications of the loss, including the loss of dreams for the future.

Reorganization of the Family System and Reinvestment in Other Relationships and Life Pursuits

The death of a family member disrupts the family equilibrium and established patterns of interaction. The process of recovery involves a realignment of relationships and redistribution of role functions needed to compensate for the loss and carry on with family life. Promoting cohesion and flexibility in the family system is crucial to restabilization. The upheaval and disorganization experienced in the immediate aftermath of a loss may lead families to make precipitous moves into new homes or marriages. The further dislocation may make matters worse. Some families may try to hold on rigidly to old patterns that are no longer functional to minimize the sense of loss and disruption in family life.

In Western societies before the present century, people died at home, and children were not protected from death but shared in its sights and smells. As is still prevalent in poor communities throughout the world, families had to cope with the precariousness of life, with death striking young and old alike. With high rates of mortality for infants, children, and women in childbirth, along with the much shorter lifespan (averaging 47 years in 1900 in the United States), it was rare to grow up without experiencing a death in the immediate family. Parental death often disrupted nuclear families and shifted them into other forms, producing complex networks of full, half, and step relationships and vast extended kinship systems (Scott & Wishy, 1982).

Thus, the nostalgic American image of the intact traditional "normal" family is a myth (Walsh, 1993); our denial of death contributes to the maintenance of that myth. In our time, we have come to hide death, making the process of adapting to loss all the more difficult (Paul and Grosser, 1965). In contrast to traditional cultures, our society lacks cultural supports to assist families in integrating the fact of death with ongoing life (Aries, 1974; 1982; Becker, 1973; Mitford, 1978; McGoldrick et al., 1991; Parkes, Laungani, & Young, 1997). Geographical distances separate family members at times of death and dying. Medical practice and technology have complicated the process by removing death from everyday reality while at the same time confronting families with unprecedented decisions about whether to prolong or terminate life. Most recently, families have begun to organize in efforts to reclaim the dying process.

The process of mourning is quite variable, often lasting much longer than people themselves expect (Wortman & Silver, 1989). Each new season, holiday, or anniversary is likely to reevoke the loss. Overidealization of the deceased, a sense of disloyalty, or the catastrophic fear of another loss may block the formation of other attachments and commitments (Rando, 1993). Family members may refuse to accept a new member who is seen as replacing the deceased when the loss has not been integrated.

The meaning and consequences of loss vary depending on many factors, including the particular phase of the life cycle at which it occurs. Whatever our therapeutic approach, a family life cycle perspective can enable us to facilitate adaptation to strengthen the whole family for future life passages.

TIMING OF LOSS IN THE FAMILY LIFE CYCLE

The timing of a loss in the three-generational family life cycle may place a family at higher risk for dysfunction (Walsh & McGoldrick, 1988). Factors that influence the impact of a loss include (1) the timing of the loss, (2) the concurrence of multiple losses or loss with other major life cycle changes, (3) a history of traumatic loss and unresolved mourning, (4) the nature of the death, and (5) the function of the person in the family.

Untimely Losses

Deaths that are untimely in terms of chronological or social expectations, such as early widowhood,

early parent loss, or death of a child, tend to be especially difficult for families. Prolonged mourning, often lasting many years, is common. Many families struggle to find some justification for the loss. Survivor guilt for spouses, siblings, and parents can block their life pursuits or satisfaction. The death of a child, which reverses the natural order of life, is probably the most painful loss of all.

In whatever different forms and circumstances, mourning must be experienced, although individual responses to bereavement vary widely (Wortman & Silver, 1989). Epidemiologic studies have found that the death of a family member increases vulnerability to premature illness and death for surviving family members (Osterweis, Solomon, & Green, 1984), especially a widowed spouse and parents who have recently lost a child (Huygen, van den Hoogen, van Eijk, & Smits, 1989). Furthermore, family developmental crises have been linked to the appearance of symptoms in a family member (Hadley, Jacob, Miliones, Caplan, & Spitz, 1974). In view of the profound connections among members of a family, it is not surprising that adjustment to death is more difficult than any other life change (Holmes & Rahe, 1967).

Concurrence of Multiple Losses or Loss with Other Major Life Cycle Changes

The temporal coincidence of loss with other major stress events, including multiple losses and other developmental milestones, may overload a family, posing incompatible demands. We pay particular attention to the concurrence of death with the birth of a child, since the tasks of mourning may interfere with parenting. In addition, a child who is born at the time of a significant loss may also assume a special replacement function that can be the impetus for high achievement or dysfunction. Similarly, a marriage in the wake of loss is likely to confound the two relationships, interfering with bereavement and with investment in the new relationship in its own right. When stressful events pile up, the support of one's partner and/or extended family is a crucial buffer that facilitates resilience.

Past Traumatic Loss and Unresolved Mourning

In family assessment, a genogram and a timeline are particularly useful in tracking sequences and concurrences of nodal events over time in the multigenerational family field (McGoldrick, 1991b; McGoldrick, Gerson, & Sohellenberger, 1998). In cases of marital breakdown, we are especially careful to inquire about losses that occurred at the start of the relationship, as well as losses coinciding with problem onset. When a child in a family is symptomatic, we pay particular attention to unresolved losses that coincided with his or her birth. Studies by Walsh (1978) and Mueller and McGoldrick Orfanidis (1976) have suggested that the death of a grandparent near the time of birth of a child may contribute to later emotional problems, particularly at later separation points such as leaving home.

We also pay attention to transgenerational anniversary patterns (Engel, 1975; Walsh & McGoldrick, 1991). Family patterns are often replicated in the next generation when a child reaches the same age or stage as the parent at the time of death or traumatic loss. It is crucial to assess a risk of suicide or self-destructive behavior when a child reaches the age at which a parent experienced an untimely or traumatic death. The more seriously dysfunctional a family, the more likely it is that such linkages go unrecognized by family members and become encoded in covert family scripts that may be enacted with dire consequences (Byng-Hall, 1991). In one chilling case, a 15-year-old boy stabbed an older man in the street in an apparently dissociative episode, which the family ignored. After a repeated offense, he was psychiatrically hospitalized. A family assessment revealed that the father, at the age of 15, had witnessed the stabbing death of his own father in the street. Study of such transgenerational anniversary patterns is needed to more fully understand the transmission processes

of such experiences. Clinical interventions should be aimed at making such covert patterns overt and helping family members to differentiate present relationships from the past so that history need not repeat itself.

LOSS AT DIFFERENT FAMILY LIFE CYCLE STAGES

The Young Adult Phase

It is remarkable that so little attention has been given to the impact of loss in young adulthood. At launching, the family must renegotiate intergenerational relationships, from the dependency and hierarchical authority of childhood and adolescence to a more equal balance as adults to adults. In families in which relationships have been especially close or intensely conflictual, young adults may cut off entirely to gain physical or emotional distance. Such cut-offs generally produce only a pseudo-autonomy, which disintegrates upon contact with the family. However, because of our society's assumption that young adults should become independent of their families, the significance of loss may not be recognized, and mourning may become more complicated.

The death of a young adult child is a tragedy for the entire family and may produce highly distressing and long-lasting grief (Gorer, 1965; Rando, 1986b). The family may experience a sense of cruel injustice in the ending of a life they have nurtured before it has reached its prime. The pain and guilt of parents and siblings may block them from continuing their own pursuits. Where the young adult had been distant or in conflict with the family or dies by suicide or drug-involved accident, mourning is likely to be complicated by the unresolved state of the relationship. Combat-related death in war, even when it is regarded as heroic or as a sacrifice in the patriotic defense of national or ideological values, is nevertheless heartbreaking for parents, whose grief may surface only over time. Siblings may be expected to carry the torch, and yet be blocked from realization of their own potential by prior sibling rivalry, survivor guilt, and conflicting family injunctions to attempt to replace but not replace the lost child (Arnold & Gemma, 1994; Cain & Cain, 1964; Cain, Fast, & Erickson, 1964; McGoldrick, 1995; Worden, 1996).

> Brian, age 29, sought therapy for a repeated cycle of setting rather grandiose career goals that he pursued at a fevered pitch, only to undermine himself each time he was on the brink of success. He felt extreme discomfort whenever he returned to his home, which his parents had made into a "shrine" to his older brother, who had been killed in Vietnam at the age of twenty-one. Pictures, medals, and plaques covered the walls. Although Brian was only 17 when his brother died, he felt a strong expectation from his parents to fulfill their dreams for their firstborn son. This expectation was coupled with a counterinjunction that it would be disloyal to surpass his brother. Brian gradually came to the realization that, try as he might, he could not measure up to his parents' idealized expectations. Therapy focused on shifting his triangulated position, helping him and his parents to unknot his bind.

Given the tendency in our society to deny the importance of family ties at this phase, the impact of loss of a parent for young adults may be seriously underestimated by them, their families, their friends, and even therapists. The terminal illness of a parent may be particularly difficult for young adult children who have moved away and are invested in launching a career and new relationship commitments (Walsh & McGoldrick, 1991). Torn between their own life pursuits and their filial caretaking responsibilities, young adults may be threatened by closeness and parental dependence when not yet secure on their own. Facing a parent's dying may stir fears of a loss of self. If the impact of the parental loss is not acknowledged, the young adult may distance still further from the family and may seek emotional replacement in a romantic involvement.

Another source of distancing is the fear that newly initiated adult life pursuits will have to be abandoned or put on hold while the young person cares for the dying parent or for the surviving parent and other family members. This expectation tends to weigh most heavily on the oldest or the child who has taken on the most parental roles. The oldest son may be expected to become the head of the family, whereas daughters are typically expected to assume major caretaking functions for the surviving parent, younger siblings, and aged grandparents. It is not uncommon for an adult child to move back home to assist in the immediate adjustment of a widowed parent. When caregiving responsibility becomes prolonged, forward movement in the life cycle may be blocked for the young adult.

The loss of grandparents at this phase may be upsetting, particularly if they played central caregiving roles, as is common for grandmothers in African American and other ethnic families and in single-parent families. More complicated emotional ramifications are likely to flow down the system if the parent and grandparent had a troubled relationship that remained unresolved at the time of death.

Young Couples: The Joining of Families through Marriage

Widowhood in early marriage is now relatively uncommon, and its untimeliness makes bereavement for the surviving spouse more difficult (Parkes & Weiss, 1983). Early widowhood tends to be a shocking and isolating experience without emotional preparation or essential social supports. Not surprisingly, sudden death is more traumatic at this phase (Kastenbaum, 1998; Parkes 1972) than in later life, when lingering deaths tend to produce greater strain (Gerber, Rusalem, Hannon, Battin, & Arkin, 1975). Not only do young widow(er)s have to cope with the loss itself, but siblings and peers often shun them in an attempt to avoid confronting their own mortality or possibility of widowhood. There is also a tendency for the family to minimize the significance of the experience by expecting the widowed spouse to move on quickly to a new relationship. Relationships between the surviving spouse and in-laws, which are commonly strained at this phase of the life cycle, often break off in the wake of the loss. If the surviving spouse rushes into a new relationship to avoid the pain of loss, unattended mourning will most likely be carried along, to surface later. Men tend to move on more rapidly, expecting a new partner to be sympathetic toward their continued mourning (Glick, Parkes, & Weiss, 1975). Not surprisingly, women are less likely than men to move precipitously into a new relationship, especially when in-laws imply guilt and disloyalty.

Infertility, Miscarriage, and Perinatal Losses

Infertility, often a hidden loss, represents the loss of one's dreams for the future. The incidence of infertility has been rising, associated in many cases with sexually transmitted diseases or, increasingly, with postponement of childbearing. The impact of loss may be gradual over time, becoming more painful as each monthly cycle passes and as menopause approaches, especially when medical interventions repeatedly fail to result in conception. When one feels out of phase with siblings and friends who are excited over their own pregnancies or involvement with newborns, distress is heightened, and couples may avoid contact and discussion of their own situation. Women and their partners who have pursued careers before starting a family are especially vulnerable to self-blame. It is crucial for clinicians to assuage feelings that they have not progressed "normally" in the family life cycle without children and to help them find meaningful ways to express their generativity.

Other significant hidden losses include stillbirths, miscarriages, and abortions. These losses are often unknown to others or unacknowledged and regarded as nonevents, making the loss more painful (Lewis, 1976). Women commonly feel the attachment and loss more deeply than their spouses do, especially when the child has grown in their bodies during pregnancy. Moral or religious controversy about abortion may complicate that decision. In cases of miscarriage or stillbirth, women are also more likely to be faulted or blame themselves. Disappointment and sorrow may include the loss of a desired child and the fear of future pregnancy complications. Well-intentioned

relatives and friends may encourage the couple to put the event behind them quickly and immediately try to conceive another child. It is important to help both partners acknowledge the meaning of such losses. In cases of perinatal loss, grief is facilitated by encouraging a couple to name and have contact with the newborn, hold a simple memorial service, and bury the child in a marked grave.

The trauma may challenge the equilibrium of a new couple, requiring friends and family support to absorb the stress. Where there is social stigma or a lack of resources, the couple may turn in on themselves, risking either fusion in a "two against the world" stance or mutual blame for the inability to fill each other's sense of loss and emptiness. Since the loss of a child places a couple's relationship at risk for breakdown, brief couples therapy or a focused couples group can be especially helpful to facilitate the mourning process and mutual support.

The death of a parent at this phase, when young couples are focused on establishing their own lives, may not be mourned as directly as at other life phases. When intergenerational relationships have become closer with the marriage, parental loss may be less difficult than it would be during the independent young adult phase. On the other hand, the death of one parent may leave a child (especially an only child or the only one living in the area) anxious about attending to the needs of the surviving parent as much as grieving for the one who is lost, or it may intensify expectations and needs from the marriage. Indeed, parental illness or death may propel an individual into marriage, embedding residuals of unresolved mourning in the couple relationship (see Chapter 14).

An issue that deserves much more clinical attention is the change in adult sibling relationships brought on by the death of a parent. Sisters are more likely to be stressed by our cultural expectation that daughters will be primary parental caretakers (see Chapter 9). Brothers tend to shoulder more of the financial responsibilities but less of the day-to-day caregiving. Old sibling rivalries may erupt into conflict over who was more favored at the end, more burdened by caregiving, or more neglectful. Competitive struggles may ensue over succession issues where a family business is involved.

The sense of responsibility to one's parents may produce conflicts between loyalty to the family of origin and the marriage. Increased attention, physical or financial caretaking of the dying or surviving parent, or absorption in the grief process may stress the couple relationship, especially if the spouse feels neglected over an extended period of time. Disappointment and distancing can have fallout for the intimate and sexual relationship (Paul & Paul, 1982). In cross-cultural marriages, a spouse who expects the marriage to come first may not understand that a partner—from a Latino culture, for example—is expected to place intergenerational obligations over spousal investment (Falicov, 1998). Encouraging mutual understanding and support will facilitate mourning and strengthen relational resilience (Walsh, 1998a).

Families with Young Children

The loss of a mate at this life phase is complicated by financial and caretaking obligations for children, which can interfere with the tasks of mourning. Children may try to cover their own grief to distract the bereaved parent from grieving out of anxiety about their only surviving parent (Fulmer, 1983). Families need extra support from other adult family members and friends to provide caretaking and concrete services, to permit the surviving parent to grieve. Generally, widowers receive such support more than widows do. However, men are less likely to have intimate friendships to facilitate emotional griefwork and more likely to confuse romance with needs for comfort and dependency in seeking support.

The death of a child is the most tragic of all untimely losses, reversing generational expectations. Grief tends to persist for years and may even intensify with the passage of time (Rando, 1986a). The effect can be devastating for the parents' health and marriage. A number of studies have documented the high distress of bereaved parents on such indicators as depression, anxiety, somatic symptoms, self-esteem, and sense of control in life. The marital relationship is particularly vulnerable after a child's death, with heightened risk of deterioration and divorce (Rando, 1986a; Videka-Sherman & Lieberman, 1985). Yet couples that are helped to pull together and comfort each other can emerge with deepened marital bonds (Walsh, 1998a).

It is often said, "when your parent dies, you have lost your past. When your child dies, you have lost your future." The untimeliness and injustice in the death of a child can lead family members to the most profound questioning of the meaning of life, involving as it does the loss of parents' hopes and dreams. Of all losses, it is hardest not to idealize a child who has died.

Particularly difficult may be the death of the firstborn, an only child, the only child of one sex, a gifted child, a difficult child for whom family members have had ambivalent or negative relationships, or a child who dies in an accident for which the parents blame themselves. Because small children are so utterly dependent on parents for their safety and survival, parental guilt tends to be especially strong in accidental or ambiguous deaths, such as sudden infant death syndrome (DeFrain, Taylor, & Ernst, 1982). Blame is particularly likely to fall on mothers, who are expected to carry the primary responsibility for a child's well-being, even when paternal abuse or neglect are implicated. Indeed, grieving may involve deep attachment to that dead baby rather than detachment (Vaisanen, 1996). Unattended parental difficulties with the loss of a child may be presented through symptomatic behavior of a sibling, as in the following case:

> The Lamb family was referred for therapy for a school refusal problem, when their 4-year-old son Danny refused to go to nursery school despite his good adjustment there the previous year. In taking a family history, the therapist learned that an older brother, Michael, had died suddenly at the age of 4, three years earlier, after developing a high fever. The parents attributed the death to a virus he had picked up at nursery school. Mr. Lamb (and his own mother) secretly blamed Mrs. Lamb for letting Michael go to nursery school when the flu was

going around. The parents kept Michael's room the way it had been, and the mother continued to celebrate his birthdays with Danny, each year making a birthday cake with candles for the age he would have been if still alive.

Bereavement is eased when both parents can participate in taking care of a sick child before death (Mulhern, Laurer, & Hoffman, 1983) and when they have a similar philosophy of life (Spinetta, Swarner, & Sheposh, 1981) or strong religious beliefs (Martinson, Moldow, & Henry, 1980). Self-help groups are extremely valuable for bereaved parents, providing a supportive network to facilitate dealing with the pain of the experience (Videka-Sherman & Lieberman, 1985).

In the death of a child, the needs of siblings and other family members are too often neglected. Some children experience prolonged grieving, including anniversary reactions for years afterward (Cain et al., 1964). Normal sibling rivalry may contribute to intense survival guilt that can block developmental strivings well into adulthood. A sibling's death is likely to be accompanied by the sense of losing one's parents as well, because they are preoccupied with caretaking or grieving or may even withdraw from their children out of their fear of ever being vulnerable to loss again. When illness is protracted, siblings must also cope with diminished attention to their own needs. In many cases, parents become overly protective and vigilant of surviving children and later have difficulty with the transitions of separation and launching.

A sibling may also be inducted into a replacement role for the family. Such a response is not necessarily pathogenic. Investing energy in surviving children has been found to facilitate positive adjustment over time for parents (Vidaka-Sherman, 1982). However, the long-term consequences for the replacement child need to be considered (Cain & Cain, 1964; Legg & Sherick, 1976). Our own clinical experience suggests that it becomes dysfunctional if the child's own needs and unique qualities can not be affirmed. In such cases, attempts at separation and individuation are likely to disrupt the family equilibrium and precipitate delayed grief responses in other members.

Children who lose a parent may suffer profound short- and long-term consequences (Furman, 1974; Osterweis et al., 1984), including illness, depression, and other emotional disturbances in subsequent adult life. They may later experience difficulty in forming intimate attachments and and carry catastrophic fears of separation and abandonment. Later difficulty in parenting is also common, especially if the same-sex parent was lost in childhood. A parent may function normally until a child reaches the same age at which the parent had been bereaved. At that point, the relationship may become blocked, the parent may distance, and/or the child may become symptomatic.

Children's reactions to death will depend on their stage of cognitive development, on the way adults deal with them around the death, and on the degree of caretaking they have lost. It is important for adults to recognize the limitations of a child's ability to understand what is happening and not to be alarmed by seemingly unemotional or "inappropriate" responses. For instance, a small child may approach strangers saying, "My mother died" as a way of seeking support and understanding through observing the reactions of others (Osterweis et al., 1984). It is crucial for adults not to exclude children from the shared experience of loss, hoping thus to spare them pain (Bowen, 1988). Role functions of the lost parent and of the bereaved spouse need to be carried out by other members. If, in addition to the loss of a parent, the child must cope with a vacuum in caretaking while the surviving parent is depressed or preoccupied, there may be serious lasting consequences. A child's handling of loss of a parent depends largely on the emotional state of the surviving parent and the availability of other caretakers (Rutter, 1966; Van Eerdewegh, Bieri, Parilla, & Clayton, 1982).

The loss of a grandparent at this phase is likely to be a child's first experience in learning how to deal with death. Children will probably be most helped if they are included in their parents' experience of mourning and will be reassured by seeing that the parents can cope with the loss. If the grandparent has suffered a prolonged illness with major caregiving demands, the parent will be stressed by pulls in two directions: toward the heavy responsibilities of caring for young children and toward filial obligations for the dying and surviving parent.

Families with Adolescents

Death at this phase in the life cycle may be particularly traumatic because the primary developmental task of adolescent separation conflicts with the experience of loss, which requires the family to move closer in support of its members. The most common adolescent deaths are from accidents (often complicated by risky or self-destructive behavior, such as drug and alcohol abuse and careless driving), suicide, and homicide. With life-threatening illnesses such as cancer, treatment becomes interwoven with adolescent rebelliousness, compounding the difficulty for parents. Children may resist medications or required treatments, taking severe risks with their health. Parents, more conscious of the long-term consequences, may struggle with the present-focused adolescent. Helping agencies are often caught in between.

When the death is associated with impulsive, risk-taking behavior, parents and siblings may carry intense anger, frustration, and sadness about the senseless loss. Reckless driving, especially under the influence of alcohol or drugs, accounts for a high percentage of teen deaths. Lethal firearms have contributed to an alarming increase in homicides and accidental shootings of youths by youths. Inner-city violence takes a tragic toll of young lives, particularly in poor, minority neighborhoods. The experience of daily threat is much like living in a war zone (Garbarino, 1992). As Burton's research has shown, poor minority adolescents in such dangerous and blighted communities often have a foreshortened expectation of their life cycle and a sense of hopelessness about their future. The high risk of early violent death, especially for young males, fuels doubts about even reaching adulthood and contributes to a focus on immediate gratification, early sex and parenthood, and self-destructive drug abuse (Burton, 1995).

Any number of problems in living, fueled by the strong peer and media pressure at this time,

may contribute to an adolescent's self-destructive behavior, such as eating disorders or actual decision to commit suicide (Pipher, 1994). When a suicide attempt occurs, the whole family should be convened, helped to understand and reconstruct meanings surrounding the experience, and helped to repair whatever family fragmentation has resulted from earlier adversities (Gutstein, 1991). It is crucial to explore possible connections to other traumatic losses in the family system (Coleman & Stanton, 1978; Dunne, McIntosh, & Dunne-Maxim, 1988; McGoldrick, 1991b; 1995; Walsh & McGoldrick, 1991), especially other suicides, as in the following case:

> David, a 13-year-old boy, was hospitalized after an attempted suicide. The boy and his family were at a loss to explain the episode and made no mention of the fact that an older brother had died shortly before David's birth. This fact was revealed only in doing the family genogram. David had grown up attempting to take the place of this brother he had never known to relieve his parents' sadness. The father, who could not recall the date or events surrounding the death, wished to remember his first son "as if he were still alive." David cultivated his appearance to resemble photos of his brother, finally acknowledging that he had attempted suicide "to join [his] 13-year-old brother in heaven." The timing corresponded to his surviving the age of his brother's death and to his concern about his growth spurt at puberty, which was changing him from the way he was "supposed" to look. Family therapy focused on enabling David and his parents to relinquish his surrogate position and let him move forward in his own development.

Adolescents frequently retreat from family and friends after a sibling's death. They may talk to no one about the experience, never even clarifying the nature of the death. The differences in coping styles of different family members may compound problems following loss. It is an important clinical issue to discuss with adolescents the meaning of death and help them to articulate their thoughts and feelings (Watkins, 1993). Typically, in our culture, adolescents may rebuff their mothers' attempts to share feelings, as their fathers withdraw or bury themselves in work. Such reactions will, of course, vary with cultural background and each family's prior experience with loss. Unfortunately, when family members have widely differing response styles, grieving becomes even more difficult.

Because our dominant culture encourages adolescents to push away from parental closeness, influence, and control, the death of a parent is likely to be complicated by conflicted feelings, or the significance of the loss may go unrecognized. If other family members idealize the deceased parent, an adolescent's experience of disqualification may lead to an increased sense of alienation and of not being understood.

Adolescents who earlier wished to be rid of parental control may develop considerable guilt. The death of a parent at this phase is also complicated by peer models of acting-out behavior to escape pain. Boys who lose a parent often turn to stealing, drugs, or fighting, or they withdraw socially, whereas girls are more likely to band together, become sexually active, or become pregnant in seeking closeness to comfort themselves and replace their loss (Osterweis et al., 1984). Adolescent acting-out behavior, in turn, stresses the family and may involve school or juvenile authorities. Such larger systems tend to focus narrowly on the child's problem behavior, which may only exacerbate the problem. It is crucial to assess the context of behavior problems routinely and, when there are recent or impending losses, to assist the family, not only the symptomatic child, in resolution. Weingarten (1996), following the work of Gilligan, Lyons, and Hanmer (1990), challenges traditional psychoanalytic assumptions that healthy adolescent development requires disconnection from parents and that adolescents will be damaged if parents "burden them" with their own concerns. Instead, drawing on her positive experience in sharing her battle with a life-threatening illness with her own teenage children, she argues that maturity, relational connectedness, and empathy are fostered if adolescents are encouraged to keep connected to their parents and come to understand their life struggles.

Since adolescents may not approach parents, it's crucial for parents to encourage them to voice their concerns.

A mother called after her husband found their 13-year-old daughter's letter to her camp counselor saying that she wanted to die. The mother, who had been battling breast cancer for several years, had recently learned that the cancer had spread and was no longer treatable. The parents, trying to be cheerful, kept their children busy with activities and avoided discussion of the mother's terminal condition. The daughter, not wanting to burden her mother, showed no sign of distress and got straight A's at school. It was crucial to help her share the unspeakable so that they could talk openly about the challenges ahead.

Teenagers, as well as younger children, worry not only about losing a parent, but also about how well the surviving parent will care for them and what will happen to them. In identification with their parent, they may also fear that they will get the same disease. The daughter in this family, with a heightened concern about her developing body at puberty, worried that she too would get breast cancer and die.

The death of a grandparent often turns out to be an underlying precipitant for adolescent problem behavior. Adolescents are often the barometer of family feelings, the ones who express the unexpressible and who draw needed attention to family problems. If the parents cannot deal with their own emotional loss issues, an adolescent will often pick up parental feelings and, not knowing a better way to help the parents, will draw fire by misbehavior.

Adolescents are often less ambivalent and more openly expressive of sadness about the loss of a grandparent. Naturally, a parent can feel conflicted when having to cope simultaneously with the grandparent's death and the adolescent's separation. This experience may be intensified if the parent's own adolescence was troublesome. Mourning is likely to be complicated by longstanding intergenerational triangles, in which problems between parent and grandparent a generation earlier have led to a coalition between grandparent and grandchild, with the parent (viewed as the common enemy) in the outside position. Without repair, such triangles can be repeated in the next generation.

Launching Children and Moving On

The family at launching experiences a major transitional upheaval as children leave and the two-generational household unit reorganizes as a marital dyad. At launching, the couple must renegotiate their relationship, which no longer centers on child-rearing. Concurrently at midlife, as men typically begin to confront their own mortality, concerns about widowhood become prominent for most women. In fact, women, who are commonly younger than their husbands, are four times more likely to outlive them, and are likely to be widowed at an earlier age and to remain widows with many years of life ahead. With this anticipation, women in traditional marriages, who have been financially dependent and emotionally centered on their husbands, may be even more concerned about the health of their husbands than about their own well-being (Neugarten, 1970). We encourage women to put their own lives in perspective—to consider how they will manage on their own and to build a supportive social network for the years they are likely to spend alone. Men, who are less likely to anticipate widowhood, may lack preparedness and experience greater shock at the loss of their wives. The suicide rate for men who are widowed at midlife is exceptionally high (Butler & Lewis, 1983).

Widowhood at midlife is much more difficult than in later life because it does not fit with social expectations and is not commonly experienced by peers. At launching, couples often reinvest energy in the marriage and make plans for their future together, with the anticipation of sharing activities that have been postponed while child-rearing consumed attention and financial resources. With the death of a partner, these dreams of a shared future are lost. Friends and other couples who are unready to confront their own mortality and survivorship may distance themselves from the survivor. The widow(er) may also be reluctant to burden recently launched children, who are not yet es-

tablished, or aging parents, who have diminished resources and increased needs for caretaking.

Couples at launching are typically confronting losses on both sides. As their children are leaving home, their aging parents may be declining in health or dying. Most adults in their middle years are prepared to assume increased caretaking responsibilities for aging parents and to accept their deaths as a natural, inevitable occurrence in the life cycle (Lewis, 1976; Neugarten, 1970). Nevertheless, adjustment to loss is frequently complicated by concerns about caretaker burden, neglect, or abandonment; caregiving children may feel that their efforts were unappreciated by the dying parent or by less involved siblings, who themselves may feel guilty that they didn't do more.

Caretaking and mourning processes are likely to be more complicated for the entire family when intergenerational tensions or cut-offs have been longstanding. Clinically, we move, whenever possible, to bridge cut-offs and promote intergenerational connectedness, to strengthen the family in coping with its loss. A conjoint family life review (see Chapter 18) can be valuable in structuring the sharing of memories to gain a more balanced, evolutionary perspective on family relationships. Members may have mellowed about issues that were painful at an earlier stage in the life cycle, viewing them differently, with new opportunity for resolution or at least more empathic understanding of differences and disappointments.

With the death of aging parents, adult children typically confront their own mortality and think more about the time that remains ahead of them. The death of the last surviving member of the older generation makes them especially aware that *they* are now the oldest generation and the next to die. Because the existence of grandchildren commonly eases the acceptance of mortality, there may be pressure on the recently launched generation to marry and start a family.

Families in Later Life

With increasing life expectancy, four- and five-generation families are becoming more common,

and postretirement couples with declining resources are increasingly called upon to care for
their very elderly parents. The central life cycle
task of old age—accepting one's own mortality—
becomes quite real as siblings, spouses, and peers
die around one. Surviving the death of an adult
child can be especially painful. Multiple concurrent losses, though common at this time, are nevertheless painful. In reaction, some older people
withdraw from closeness and dependency on other
elders or avoid funerals so as not to experience yet
another painful loss. Intergenerational family conflicts may erupt over issues of caretaking, dependency, loss of functioning and control as health
declines and death approaches (Chapter 18).

It is all but inevitable that one partner in a marriage will die before the other. As was noted above,
women are more likely to outlive their husbands,
by seven years on the average. Most men over 65
are married, whereas most women are widowed
(Butler & Lewis, 1983). This gender imbalance is
one of the most poignant problems of the elderly.
Older men, who tend to select younger partners,
have many more marital options; the odds are
against women remarrying, since there are fewer
men in their age group and relationships with
younger men are less socially acceptable. If the
prior marriage was deeply valued or, conversely,
too burdensome, older widow(er)s may simply
prefer not to remarry. Because so many widows
find themselves unprepared for the financial burdens of widowhood and may lack adequate retirement benefits of their own, one of the most
important areas for preventive intervention is to
help women become knowledgable and empowered regarding their economic security.

Widowers are at especially high risk of death
and suicide in the first year of bereavement because of the initial sense of loss, disorientation,
and loneliness and because of the loss of a wife's
caretaking functions. Husbands' vulnerability to
loss may also be greater because men are socialized to minimize their awareness of dependency on
their spouses. Furthermore, because men are less
likely to be widowed, they are less prepared for the
adjustment. Deaths of widowers during the first six

months of bereavement have been found to be 40
percent above the expected rate for married men of
the same age.

The psychosocial tasks for widowhood, as for
other losses, are twofold: to grieve for the loss of
the spouse and to reinvest in future functioning.
Lopata (1996) has described common phases and
tasks, which include loosening bonds to the spouse
and acknowledging the fact of the death, transforming shared daily experiences into memories.
Open expression of grief and loss is important at
this time. Typically within a year, attention turns
to the demands of daily functioning, self-support,
household management, and adjustment to being
physically and emotionally alone. Next, women
typically shift to new activities and interest in others. Loss in widowhood is often compounded by
other dislocations, particularly when the family
home and social community are given up or when
financial loss or illness reduce independent functioning. Though widows and widowers are the one
class of mourners given a specific title defining
their status, that identity is also a constant reminder of the loss and may impede the process of
reentry.

DEATH IN DIVORCED AND
REMARRIED FAMILIES

With current high rates of divorce, remarriage, and
redivorce expected to continue, family members
are likely to experience a variety of losses. Clinical
inquiry must extend beyond the immediate household to the broader network of family relationships
and not overlook deaths in prior marriages and
stepfamilies. The death of a former spouse may
bring a surprisingly strong grief reaction, even if
the marriage ended years earlier, as in the following case:

> Sarah learned of the death of her former husband,
> Paul, from a neighbor. Her grief, the intensity of
> which surprised her, was made more painful by her
> exclusion from the community of mourners, due
> to everyone's efforts to protect Paul's widow and
> their children from the potential upset of her pres-
> ence in the midst of their sorrow. Although Sarah

had been very close to Paul's parents and friends for many years, she had never met his second wife and children and was not invited to sit shiva at the family home. She attended the memorial service alone; as other mourners avoided contact with her, she felt like a ghost in the shadows. It was extremely important to her that her current husband and an old friend accompanied her to the gravesite the next day and were comforting to her in her grief.

Children's losses of kin or step-relations who have been important to them at some phase in their development should also be attended to. Where a stepparent has formed a strong attachment to stepchildren and assumed financial and other responsibilities, the death of his or her spouse, the biological parent, leaves him or her with no legal rights to continue a relationship with the children. In other cases, when loyalty conflicts are strong at the death of a parent, children may vehemently contest a will that favors a stepparent over the biological parent. Finally, couples may need to consider with which spouse they should be buried. For children from the divorced family, old wishes may be rekindled to reunite their parents for all time in their graves.

VARIED LIFE COURSE: CHALLENGES OF HIDDEN AND STIGMATIZED LOSSES

Many lives and relationships do not fit neatly into the categories and succession of stages described in the preceding section, and significant losses may be unrecognized. Loss issues concerning infertility and miscarriage are not confined to early, childless marriage and become more painful with the ticking of the biological clock. Single individuals or couples who have chosen not to have children may be assumed erroneously to be suffering or compensating for loss, as implied by our language, which labels them "*un*married" and "child*less*." Societal attitudes toward homosexuality complicate all losses in gay and lesbian relationships. Lacking the legal standing of marriage, a partner may be denied death benefits when a relationship is ended by death. The death of a partner

may be grieved for in isolation when the relationship has been a secret or has been disapproved of by the family or the community. When the relationship has been kept secret, the very loss must be hidden.

Cancer and AIDS have become the epidemics of our times, each generating tremendous stigma and fear of contagion (Rolland, 1994; Sontag, 1988). The AIDS epidemic has led many people who are HIV-positive to cover up their health status and other people to distance themselves from those who are known to have AIDS, impairing family and social support as well as the delivery of critical health care. Distinctions are too often made between "innocent victims," on one hand, such as children born with AIDS or individuals who have contracted the disease through blood transfusions, and, on the other hand, those who are condemned for having "brought it on themselves" through homosexuality or drug use. Clinicians can help to reduce social stigma and unfounded fears of contagion so that suffering and death by AIDS are not made all the more painful and isolating.

The epidemic of AIDS is especially devastating in the gay community—and increasingly for men, women, and children in poor inner-city neighborhoods—because of the multiple losses and anticipated losses experienced in relationship networks (Klein & Fletcher, 1986). As recent treatment advances have brought new hope to many, they must adjust from a prognosis of certain death to reengage in life with an uncertain long-term course (see Chapter 29). Tragically, the high cost and difficulty of complicated drug regimens limit their availability to those who are poor and lack adequate medical care.

Gender Differences and Constraints

Although our society has been changing rapidly, normative expectations for men and women in families have lagged behind emerging realities of family life (McGoldrick, Anderson, & Walsh, 1989). Traditional gender-based socialization has constrained and separated men and women in the mourning process, men being assigned to instrumental tasks, such as financial and funeral arrangements, and women being expected to be social and emotional caretakers. Mothers are particularly vulnerable to blame and guilt at the death of a family member because of societal expectations that they bear primary caretaking responsibility for the well-being of their husbands, children, and aging parents. Given our cultural indoctrination that "real" men don't cry, men have been constrained from "losing control" and showing vulnerability and sorrow. Helping family members to gain awareness of the cultural context of such constraints is an important part of helping families come to view their own and each other's reactions. Moreover, when men distance themselves from their wives' grief, the couple relationship is at risk of breakdown. It is important to address distancing and imbalance, encouraging families to question constraining responses in themselves and in their culture.

Respecting Cultural Differences

Helping family members to deal with a loss often means showing respect for their particular cultural heritage and encouraging them to be proactive in determining how they will commemorate a death. It is generally better to encourage families toward openness about death, but it is also crucial to respect their pain and their timing in facing the emotional aftermath of a loss. It is especially important to ask several questions about a particular cultural group's traditions:

1. What are the prescribed rituals for handling dying, the dead body, and the disposal of the body and rituals to commemorate the loss?
2. What are the group's beliefs about what happens after death?
3. What does the group believe about appropriate emotional expression and integration of a loss experience?
4. What are the gender rules for handling the death?
5. Are certain deaths particularly stigmatized (e.g., suicide) or traumatic for the group?

Religion and spirituality also need to be explored, as they offer meaning about a death and can provide solace and comfort through faith, congregational support, and transcending beliefs in a larger purpose and connectedness to all of life (Walsh, 1998b).

CONCLUSION

We are seeing a heightened recognition of the importance of facing death and loss. The worldwide AIDS epidemic has forced greater attention to death and dying. Also, the approach of middle age for the large baby boom generation has prompted a shift in public consciousness from preoccupation with youth to the realities of aging and mortality, along with increasing comfort in open expression of grief. Families are reclaiming the dying process through such directives as living wills and more active creation and participation in meaningful memorial rites. At the same time, controversy over end of life decisions is becoming the major issue facing families and society in our times.

Amidst social and economic upheavals of recent decades, families are dealing with multiple losses, transitions, and uncertainties. Family stability and security have been disrupted through such dislocations as divorce, migration, and job loss. Although this chapter has focused on loss through death, the family challenges and processes described for recovery and healing have broader application to other losses. Clinicians can play a vital role in helping families to transform and transcend their losses with courage in a rapidly changing world.

In sharing their experience of loss, family members gain one of the most important healing resources: each other. Without mutual support in times of death and loss, the pain is ultimately that much worse, not only for the one who mourns alone, but also for those who grieve silently on the sidelines or not at all. When we foster family resilience in the face of loss, individual members and their relationships emerge strengthened and more resourceful in meeting future life challenges (Walsh, 1998a).

The uniqueness of each life course in its context needs to be appreciated in every assessment of the multigenerational family life cycle and in our understanding of the meaning of loss. Our own personal, cultural, and spiritual beliefs and experiences surrounding loss need to be examined as they constrain or facilitate our efforts to help grieving families. By coming to accept death as part of life and loss as a transforming experience, we—and our field—will discover new possibilities for growth.

REFERENCES

Aries, P. (1974). *Western attitudes toward death: From the middle ages to the present.* Baltimore: Johns Hopkins University Press.

Aries, P. (1982). *The hour of our death.* New York: Vintage.

Arnold, J. H., & Gemma, P. B. (1994). *A child dies: A portrait of family grief* (2nd ed.) Philadelphia: The Charles Press.

Becker, E. (1973). *The denial of death.* New York: The Free Press.

Bowen, M. (1988). Family reaction to death. In F. Walsh, & M. McGoldrick, (Eds.), *Living beyond loss* (pp. 79–92). New York: W. W. Norton.

Bowlby, J. (1961). Process of mourning. *International Journal of Psychoanalysis, 42,* 317–340.

Burton, L. (1995). Intergenerational patterns of providing care in African American families with teenage childbearers: Emergent patterns in an ethnographic study. In V. L. Bengston, K. Warner Schaie, & L. Burton (Eds.), *Adult intergenerational relations.* New York: Springer.

Butler, R. & Lewis, M. 1983. *Aging and mental health.* St. Louis: C. V. Lewis.

Byng-Hall, J. (1995) *Rewriting family scripts.* New York: The Guilford Press.

Byng-Hall, J. (1991) Family scripts and loss. In F. Walsh & M. McGoldrick (Eds.), *Living beyond loss* (pp. 130–143). New York: Norton.

Cain, A., & Cain, B. (1964). On replacing a child. *Journal of the American Academy of Child Psychiatry, 3,* 443–456.

Cain, A., & Fast, I. (1972). The legacy of suicide: Observations on the pathogenic impact of suicide upon marital partners. In A. Cain (Ed.), *Survivors of suicide.* Springfield, IL: Charles C. Thomas.

Cain, A., Fast, I., and Erickson, M. (1964). Children's disturbed reactions to the death of a sibling. *American Journal of Orthopsychiatry, 34*(4): 741–752.

Coleman, S. B., & Stanton, D. M. (1978). The role of death in the addict family. *Journal of Marriage and Family Counseling, 4,* 79–91.

Crenshaw, D. A. (1996). *Bereavement: Counseling the grieving throughout the life cycle.* New York: Crossroads.

DeFrain, J., Taylor, J., & Ernst, L. (1982). *Coping with sudden infant death.* Lexington, MA: D.C. Heath.

Dunne, E., McIntosh, J., & Dunne-Maxim, K. (1988). *Suicide and its aftermath.* New York: Norton.

Engel, G. (1975). The death of a twin: Mourning and anniversary reactions. Fragments of 10 years of self-analysis. *International Journal of Psychoanalysis, 56,* 23–40.

Falicov, C. (1998). The cultural meanings of family triangles. In M. McGoldrick (Ed.), *Revisioning family therapy: Race, culture and gender in clinical practice.* New York: The Guilford Press.

Fulmer, R. (1983). A structural approach to unresolved mourning in single parent family systems. *Journal of Marital and Family Therapy, 9*(3), 259–270.

Furman, E. (1974). *A child's parent dies: Studies in childhood bereavement.* New Haven: Yale University Press.

Garbarino (1992). *Children in danger: Coping with the consequences of community violence.* San Francisco: Jossey-Bass.

Gerber, I., Rusalem, R., Hannon, N., Battin, D., & Arkin, A. (1975). Anticipatory grief and aged widows and widowers. *Journal of Gerontology, 30,* 225–229.

Gilligan, C., Lyons, N., & Hanmer, T. (1990). *Making connections.* Cambridge, MA: Harvard University Press.

Glick, I. O., Parkes, C. M., & Weiss, R. (1975). *The first year of bereavement.* New York: Basic Books.

Gorer, G. (1965). *Death, grief and mourning.* New York: Doubleday.

Gutstein, S. (1991). Adolescent suicide: The loss of rec-onciliation. In F. Walsh & M. McGoldrick (Eds.) *Living beyond loss.* New York: Norton.

Hadley, T., Jacob, T., Miliones, J., Caplan, J., & Spitz, D. (1974). The relationship between family develop-mental crises and the appearance of symptoms in a family member. *Family Process 13,* 207–214.

Herz, F. (1989). The impact of death and serious illness on the family life cycle. In B. Carter & M. McGold-rick (Eds.), *The changing family life cycle: A frame-work for family therapy* (2nd ed.). Boston: Allyn & Bacon.

Holmes, T., & Rahe, R. H. (1967). The social adjustment rating scale. *Journal of Psychosomatic Research, 11,* 213–218.

Huygen, F. J. A., van den Hoogen, H. J. M., van Eijk, J. T. M., & Smits, A. J. A. (1989). Death and dying: A longitudinal study of their medical impact on the family. *Family systems medicine, 7,* 374–384.

Imber-Black, E. (1991). Rituals and the healing process. In F. Walsh & M. McGoldrick (Eds.), *Living beyond loss* (pp. 207–223). New York: Norton.

Jordan, J. R., Kraus, D. R., & Ware, E. S. (1993). Obser-vations on loss and family development. *Family Pro-cess, 32,* 425–440.

Kastenbaum, R. J. (1998). *Death, society and human ex-perience* (6th ed.) Boston: Allyn & Bacon.

Klein, S., & Fletcher, W. (1986). Gay grief: An exami-nation of the uniqueness brought to light by the AIDS crisis. *Journal of Psychosocial Oncology, 4,* 15–25.

Legg, C., and Sherick, I. (1976). The replacement child: A developmental tragedy: Some preliminary com-ments. *Child Psychiatry and Human Development, 7,* 113–126.

Lewis, E. (1976). The management of stillbirth: Coping with an unreality. *Lancet, 2,* 619–620.

Lewis, J., Beavers, W. R., Gossett, J., & Phillips, V. (1976). *No single thread: Psychological health in family systems.* New York: Brunner/Mazel.

Lifton, R. J. (1975). Preface. In A. Mitscherlich & M. Mitscherlich (Eds.), *The inability to mourn.* New York: Grove.

Lopata, H. (1996). *Current widowhood: Myths and real-ities.* Thousand Oaks, CA: Sage.

Martinson, I., Moldow, D., & Henry, W. (1980). *Home care for the child with cancer* (Final report of Grant No. CA 19490). Washington, DC: National Cancer Institute.

McGoldrick, M. (1991a). Echoes from the past: Helping families mourn their losses. In F. Walsh & M. McGoldrick (Eds.), *Living beyond loss.* 50–78. New York: Norton.

McGoldrick, M. (1991b) The legacy of loss. In F. Walsh & M. McGoldrick (Eds.), *Living beyond loss.* (pp. 104–129). New York: Norton.

McGoldrick, M. (1995). *You can go home again.* New York: W. W. Norton.

McGoldrick, M., Almeida, R., Hines, P. M., Garcia-Preto, N., Rosen, E. & Lee, E. (1991). Mourning in different cultures. In F. Walsh & M. McGoldrick (Eds.), *Living beyond loss.* (pp. 172–206). New York: Norton.

McGoldrick, M., Anderson, C., & Walsh, F. (Eds.) (1989). *Women in families.* New York: Norton.

McGoldrick, M., Gerson, R, & Schellenberger, S. (1998). *Genograms: Family assessment and inter-vention.* New York: W. W. Norton,

McGoldrick, M., & Walsh, F. (1983). A systemic view of family history and loss. In M. Aronson & D. Wol-berg (Eds.), *Group and family therapy 1983.* New York: Brunner/Mazel.

McGoldrick, M., & Walsh, F. (1991). A time to mourn: Death and the life cycle. In F. Walsh & M. McGold-rick (Eds.), *Living beyond loss.* (pp. 30–49). New York: Norton.

Mitford, J. (1978). *The American way of death.* New York: Touchstone Books.

Mueller, P. S., & McGoldrick Orfanidis, M. (1976). A method of co-therapy for schizophrenic families. *Family Process, 15,* 179–192.

Neugarten, B. (1970) Dynamics of transition of middle age to old age: Adaptation and the life cycle. *Jour-nal of Geriatric Psychiatry, 4,* 71–87.

Osterweis, M., Solomon, F., & Green, M. (Eds.). (1984). *Bereavement: Reactions, consequences, and care.* Washington, DC: National Academy Press.

Parkes, C. M. (1972). Bereavement: Studies of grief in adult life. New York: International Universities Press.

Parkes, C. M., Laungani, P., & Young, B. (1997). *Death and bereavement across cultures.* New York: Routledge.

Parkes, C. M., & Weiss, R. S. (1983) *Recovery from be-reavement.* New York: Basic Books.

Paul, N., & Grosser, G. (1965). Operational mourning and its role in conjoint family therapy. *Community Mental Health Journal, 1,* 339–345.

Paul, N., & Paul, B. (1974). *A marital puzzle.* New York: Norton.

Paul, N., & Paul, B. (1982). Death and changes in sexual behavior. In F. Walsh (Ed.), *Normal family processes.* New York: The Guilford Press.

Pipher, M. (1994). *Reviving Ophelia.* New York: Ballantine.

Rando, T. (1986a). *The parental loss of a child.* Champaign, IL: Research Press.

Rando. T. A. (1986b). Death of the adult child. In T. A. Rando (Ed.), *The parental loss of a child.* Champaign, IL: Research Press.

Rando, T. A. (1993). *Treatment of complicated mourning.* Champaign, IL: Research Press.

Rolland, J. S. (1994). *Families, illness, and disability.* New York: Basic.

Rosen, E. (1998). *Families facing death* (rev. ed.). San Francisco: Jossey-Bass.

Rutter, M. (1966). *Children of sick parents.* London: Oxford University Press.

Scott, D., & Wishy, B. (Eds.). (1982). *America's families: A documentary history.* New York: Harper & Row.

Shapiro, E. (1994). *Grief as a family process.* New York: The Guilford Press.

Sontag, S. (1988). *AIDS and its metaphors.* New York: Farrar, Straus, & Giroux.

Vaisanen, L. (1996). Family grief and recovery process when a baby dies. *Acta Universitatis Ouluensis Medica, D. Medica,* 398.

Van Eerdewegh, M., Bieri, M., Parilla, R., & Clayton, P. (1982). The bereaved child. *British Journal of Psychiatry, 140,* 23–29.

Videka-Sherman, L. (1982). Coping with the death of a child: A study over time. *American Journal of Orthopsychiatry, 52,* 688–698.

Videka-Sherman, L., & Lieberman, M. (1985). Effects of self-help groups and psychotherapy after a child dies: The limits of recovery. *American Journal of Orthopsychiatry, 55,* 70–82.

Walsh, F. (1978). Concurrent grandparent death and birth of schizophrenic offspring: An intriguing finding. *Family Process, 17,* 457–463.

Walsh, F. (1983). The timing of symptoms and critical events in the family life cycle. In H. Liddle (Ed.), *Clinical implications of the family life cycle.* Rockville, MD: Aspen.

Walsh, F. (1993). Conceptualization of normal family processes. In F. Walsh (Ed.), *Normal family processes.* New York: The Guilford Press.

Walsh, F. (1998a). *Strengthening family resilience.* New York: The Guilford Press.

Walsh, F. (Ed.). (In press). *Spirituality in families and family therapy.* New York: The Guilford Press.

Walsh, F., & McGoldrick, M. (1988). Loss and the family life cycle. In C. Falicov (Ed.), *Family transitions: Continuity and change.* New York: The Guilford Press.

Walsh, F., & McGoldrick, M. (Eds.). (1991) *Living beyond loss: Death in the family.* New York: Norton.

Watkins, J. (1993). *Death and beyond: Answers to teens' questions about death, reincarnation, ghosts and the afterlife.* Wheaton, IL: Tyndale House Publishers.

Weingarten, K. (1996). *The mother's voice: Strengthening intimacy in families.* New York: The Guilford Press.

Williamson, D. S.(1978). New life at the graveyard: A method of therapy for individuation from a dead former parent. *Journal of Marriage and Family Counseling, 4,* 93–101.

Worden, J. W. (1996). *Children and grief.* New York: The Guilford Press.

Wortman, C., & Silver, R. (1989). The myths of coping with loss. *Journal of consulting and clinical psychology, 57,* 349–357.

Wright, L., & Nagy, J. (1992). Death: The most troubling family secret. In E. Imber-Black (Ed.), *Secrets in families and family therapy.* New York: Norton.

CHAPTER 12

CREATING MEANINGFUL RITUALS FOR NEW LIFE CYCLE TRANSITIONS

EVAN IMBER-BLACK

Every culture makes rituals. Anchoring us with the past and where each of us comes from, while simultaneously moving us into the future, rituals capture and express the duality of continuity and change, constancy and transformation, required for families and cultures.

The capacity of rituals to both make and mark transitions make them especially salient for life cycle changes. Life cycle events and transitions such as birth, marriage, and death are most frequently marked with familiar rituals. Many religious and ethnic groups also have rituals to mark young adult development (e.g., bar mitzvah, confirmation), or such development may be marked by secular rituals such as graduation. These rituals, while often seen as discrete events, such as *the* wedding, and *the* christening or baby-naming, are in actuality processes that occur over time, involving advance preparation and reflection afterward. Choices about who participates in the planning and execution of a life cycle ritual reflect family relationship patterns. Negotiations that occur during the preparation for life cycle rituals may be opportunities to change such patterns. Thus, such rituals may be seen as the visible and condensed drama of the life cycle transitions that they mark.

Relying on symbols, metaphors, and actions, which may have multiple meanings, life cycle rituals function to reduce anxiety about change. According to Schwartzman (1982), rituals make change manageable, as members experience change as part of their system rather than as a threat to it. Similarly, Wolin and Bennett (1984) suggest that rituals contribute to a family's identity, its sense of itself over time, facilitating the elaboration of roles, boundaries, and rules. Imber-Black and Roberts (1992) have delineated how rituals define family and group membership; heal losses; maintain and/ or change individual, family, and cultural identity; express core beliefs; and facilitate the celebration of life. Rituals enable us to hold and express contradictions. Thus, a wedding marks the loss of particular roles in the families of origin while at the same time marking the beginnings of the new couple and in-law relationships. Since the ritual event is time- and space-bounded, a safe and manageable context for the expression of strong emotions is created. Rituals marking life cycle transitions function at many levels, enabling individual change (e.g., from adolescent to young adult, from single adult to married adult), relationship change (e.g., from parent-child to two adults, from dating couple to married couple), family system change (e.g., expansion through the addition of members or contraction through members leaving), and family-community change (e.g., graduation marks not only a child's leaving school, but also a change in the family's relationship to larger systems; a retirement party marks not only a person's ending work, but also a change in the family's relationship to the outside world). Rituals may connect a family with previous generations, providing a sense of history and rootedness, while simultaneously implying future relationships. The performance of and participation in such rituals link a family to the wider community through the repetition of familiar rites.

The critical importance of rituals in our lives is evident in the responses of oppressed people when rituals are forbidden to them. African Americans held in slavery were not permitted to marry. They created their own secret wedding ceremony, "jumping the broom," to mark a committed relationship. Jewish women in Nazi concentration camps turned conversations with each other into remembering rituals and wrote out recipes for rich and delicious food in the midst of forced starvation. In so doing, they proclaimed connections to their villages, their faith, and their families (DeSilva, 1996).

Rituals can alter the stories that we tell about ourselves and that other people tell about us. They can powerfully connect us to a community of support. The family therapist Kathy Weingarten and her daughter Miranda Eve Weingarten Worthen created a moving ritual to decrease the loneliness Miranda felt as an adolescent with a rare, serious, and little-known genetic disorder, Beckwith-Wiedemann Syndrome (BWS). Having struggled since birth with severe pain, joint dislocations, and other complications of her illness, Miranda also faced tremendous isolation, since no one she knew had ever heard of her illness, nor could people outside of her family even begin to imagine what living with this illness meant.

At Kathy's urging, Miranda and Kathy designed an invitation to a special ceremony, one that would allow Miranda to tell her story to a trusted group of friends. Miranda created two rituals. In the first, she lit a candle and gave an unlit candle to each person gathered. "I began to tell the story of my living with BWS. I asked people to light their candle from mine when they understood the magnitude of my experience. As people lit their candles from mine...I felt that each lit candle took some of the burden off me" (Weingarten & Weingarten Worthen, 1997, p. 52).

In the second ritual, Miranda listed thirty different feelings connected to her illness on cards. She placed her negative feelings in one box and her positive feelings in another. Both boxes were beautiful, to honor the validity of all of her feelings. The people who gathered then helped Miranda to brainstorm more positive feelings. Following these rituals, the people who gathered to witness Miranda's story remained in her life as a special team, available in crises and knowledgeable about Miranda's unique story (Weingarten & Weingarten Worthen, 1997).

CREATING RITUALS AS A DEVELOPMENTAL TASK FOR COUPLES

Among the many developmental tasks facing any new couple is the creating of rituals. Coming from different families of origin, members of a couple often encounter differences in preferred and familiar rituals of everyday life, such as meals or greeting each other at the end of a busy day, family traditions such as birthdays or anniversaries, and holiday celebrations. Struggles over how to perform rituals are a lens through which couples can learn about each other's family of origin. Such struggles are particularly challenging for couples who come from different religions, ethnic groups, or social classes. While a couple may be able to create an interfaith wedding, they may find that rituals to mark the birth of children, how to celebrate religious holidays, or imagining what an interfaith funeral would look like become the crucible for working out loyalties to extended family and current differentiated beliefs and identities. Members of a couple who come from different social class backgrounds will have very different experiences with rituals.

Gay and lesbian couples may face unique challenges where rituals are concerned. Our culture has still not affirmed legal marriage for gay and lesbian couples, requiring such couples to think through what kind of ritual to create to mark a committed relationship. Many gay and lesbian couples find that they have acceptance and support from the extended family of one partner but not the other, leading them to adopt the rituals of only one partner while the other partner's legacy gets lost. Therapy with gay and lesbian couples should include conversations about meaningful rituals starting from the premise that each is bringing an encyclopedia of rituals from which to choose ways to make new meaning together.

Jerry Corbell and Stan Best had lived together for fifteen years. Since Jerry's family had rejected him, all of Stan and Jerry's holidays were celebrated only with Stan's family. Jerry felt so much pain over his family's cut-off that he abandoned all familiar rituals from his own childhood, leaving him with the double loss of family relationships and family rituals. The rituals with Stan's family, while warm and caring, were at the same time a sharp reminder of his losses. In our therapy, I suggested that Jerry's parents' rejection did not mean that Jerry needed to lose meaningful rituals that belonged to him. Rather, he needed to reclaim and alter those rituals to fit his life now. Jerry began by unpacking key symbolic objects that he had hidden away—his grandmother's candlesticks from Eastern Europe, Christmas ornaments that his aunt had given him every year as a child, a card file of recipes of his favorite dishes from his family of origin. Over time, Jerry and Stan integrated these special symbols into their ritual life together.

Many couples seeking therapy today come with multiple differences in religion, ethnicity, race, and social class. Often, the couple has not identified these differences as a source of difficulty, yet their struggles and conflicts over rituals will mirror these. Nonconfrontational conversation about each one's ritual life is often an excellent entry point, enabling couples to see the power of their own heritage in the present. Any therapy with bicultural couples needs to spend time on helping the couple to examine each one's history with rituals and negotiate meaningful rituals for their lives together.

CONTEMPORARY LIFE CYCLE TRANSITIONS

While all individuals and families experience some normative life cycle transitions and participate in rituals that facilitate these transitions, many individuals and families are faced with life cycle transitions that are new or novel and that, by virtue of their seemingly different or unusual nature, may not be marked by rituals or may have rituals that simply don't fit the circumstances and need to be

adapted. For instance, when Sherry and Bruce Callahan had their first baby, they planned a christening that was exactly like all such rituals, with the addition of one aspect. Their baby had been conceived through assisted insemination with donor sperm. They decided well before their baby's birth that they did not want their use of new birth technologies to be a secret that part of their family knew and others did not know. They also wanted to be able to speak about this easily with their child when the time came and not allow it to be a taboo subject. In our therapy, we talked of ways to adapt the christening ritual to include the fact of donor insemination. They decided that after the christening, Bruce would speak to all assembled, publicly thanking their anonymous donor for helping them to have the precious gift of their baby. Bruce told me later, "I was so scared to say those words, but when I did, any shame I had previously felt just lifted and flew out of the church" (Imber-Black & Roberts, 1992).

Idiosyncratic life cycle transitions may include bicultural marriage; gay or lesbian marriage; families formed by adoption, especially when there is overt or covert nonsupport from family members; families formed by new birth technologies; the birth of a handicapped child; the birth or adoption of a child by an unmarried mother or father; pregnancy loss; forced separation through hospitalization, imprisonment, or terror; reunion after such forced separations; migration; living together relationships; the end of nonmarried relationships; foster placement and the reunion after foster placement; sudden, unexpected or violent death, including suicide; the leaving home of a mentally or physically handicapped young adult, especially when this leaving has not been anticipated; and chronic, incapacitating illness. This list, which is intended to be suggestive rather than exhaustive, is shaped by broad social processes that may change over time and may differ with various cultural and socioeconomic groups. For example, pregnancy outside of a legal marriage may or may not be an idiosyncratic life cycle event with all of the aspects described below attendant on it, depending on the norms of the family, the family's reference group and the response of the wider community. While the list above may seem an unusual combination, all items in the list have several elements in common:

1. Familiar, repetitive, and widely accepted rituals do not exist to facilitate required changes and to link individual, family, and community.

2. All require complex reworking of relationships, similar to normative life cycle transitions, but lack the available maps that attend to more expected transitions.

3. Contextual support from family of origin, the community, and the wider culture is often lacking. Individual and family events and processes are not confirmed by family of origin, larger systems, and the community.

4. A balance of being both like others (e.g., a family with a severely handicapped member shares many features with other families) and being unlike others (e.g., a family with a severely handicapped member has certain aspects of their functioning that are different from those of other families) is often difficult to achieve, resulting in a skewed sense of either denying the differences or maximizing them to the exclusion of a sense of connectedness with others.

5. A sense of stigma is often experienced because of prejudice from the wider community. This, in turn, may lead to the emergence of secrets and conspiracies of silence that constrain relationship possibilities.

6. Involvement with larger systems is often problematic. Families with handicapped members, hospitalized members, imprisoned members, or fostered members are required to deal with larger systems in ways that alter family boundaries and relationships, often over many years. Families experiencing forced migration or migration for economic necessity are often involved with intimidating larger systems. Families whose organization and membership are not affirmed by the wider culture, such as gay couples and their children, are often stigmatized by larger systems. Because family identity and sense of competency include reflections from larger systems with whom they interact, families

with any of the idiosyncratic life cycle events and transitions listed above may be at greater risk of incorporating negative images.

7. The family may abandon or interrupt familiar rituals that contribute to its sense of itself, especially if these elicit painful memories. For instance, after the loss of a member through sudden death, hospitalization, or imprisonment, members may avoid family rituals. Families that are unable to accept members' gay relationships or nonmarried heterosexual relationships may restrict participation in rituals. Paradoxically, such ritual abandonment or interruption prevents healing and relationship development.

El Salvador and the Bronx

When the Torres family arrived in the Bronx from El Salvador, Mrs. Torres and her son Manuel, age 13, and her daughter Maria, age 11, were coping with the recent death of their husband and father in the Salvadoran civil war and recovering from their own terrifying wartime experiences. They remained very close for the first two years but abandoned many familiar rituals from their culture. Since most of their rituals were communal or religious and depended on people from their own country, they struggled with little success to find ways to develop meaningful rituals. Simply meeting the demands of daily life in the Bronx took precedence.

The children quickly learned English in school. Mrs. Torres became worried that they would forget Spanish and forget that they were Salvadoran. She spoke to them in Spanish at home, but they insisted on responding in English. In a fairly typical pattern among parents and adolescents who have migrated, they were soon struggling, as Mrs. Torres wanted to talk about "home," while her children insisted that home was in the Bronx.

When I met the Torres family in family therapy, I suggested that they bring symbols to our next session—symbols of El Salvador and the Bronx. Mrs. Torres was very surprised to see that Manuel and Maria brought symbols of El Salvador that showed how connected they still were to their original home. The teens brought toys and photographs that their mother didn't know they had kept. They talked with their mother about their memories, letting her know that they were involved with their homeland in deeply emotional ways. Their symbols from the Bronx included a music tape and a poster from a concert. Mrs. Torres listened respectfully to them describe what this music meant to them, replacing their usual arguments about North American music. Mrs. Torres brought food for both of her symbols, including her wonderful Salvadoran cooking and a small pizza to symbolize the Bronx and the arguments they had been having when her children wanted pizza instead of her ethnic dishes. The family and I sat and ate both foods together.

Following this ritual that enabled the holding and expressing of past and present, their prior life and their current life, their losses and their surviving, the Torres family agreed to hold a weekly story-telling session at home to include Mrs. Torres' stories of El Salvador and Manuel and Maria's stories of the Bronx. Over time, the children also shared memories of El Salvador, and Mrs. Torres began to tell stories of her daily life in the Bronx. This ritual enabled the family to express their deep sense of loss and sadness connected to their forced migration while providing healing as the ritual anchored them in a new life that could include elements of both El Salvador and the Bronx (Imber-Black & Roberts, 1992).

THE EMERGENCE OF SYMPTOMS

Family life cycle theorists (Carter & McGoldrick, 1980; Haley, 1973; Terkelson, 1980) have described the connection between normative life cycle derailment and the emergence of symptoms in individuals and families. Carter and McGoldrick (1980) alerted the clinician to assess for both horizontal and vertical stressors in family development. Terkelson (1980) added the category "paranormative" to include such transitions as marital separation, illness, and severe extrinsic and unexpected events with which a family must cope and under the stress of which a family may become symptomatic. Families who are experiencing idiosyncratic life cycle events and processes may be at particular risk for the development of symptoms in members. The convergence of lack of social support, intergenerational cut-offs and isolation, stigma,

secrecy, sense of shame in one or more members, and frequently stressful relationships with larger systems with whom the family must interact may be mirrored by a paucity of rituals to mark developmental change. Rigid and repetitive symptoms and interactions of family members in response to symptoms metaphorically express the family's stuck position. The clinician who searches for normative life cycle issues to hypothesize about the emergence of symptoms may find that idiosyncratic and often hidden life cycle processes are salient.

The House-Cooling Party

Candice Meyers first contacted me for therapy because she was depressed. Her family physician had prescribed antidepressant medication, but she wanted to try therapy first. In our first meeting, she told me through her tears that her husband, Brent, had left her for another woman six months earlier. Married for six years, they had been talking about starting a family. Brent had been secretly planning to leave for over a year.

After their separation, Candace became isolated from family and friends. She stopped participating in any family rituals, giving the excuse that she was exhausted and had frequent headaches. It was clear to me that Candace was suffering from many unacknowledged and unritualized losses—of her marriage, her hoped-for first child, and all of her relationships with family and friends. Her many symptoms—sleeplessness, headaches, weight loss, hopelessness—were directly related to her unanticipated divorce.

Candace felt very ashamed that she had been left by her husband. She stopped inviting anyone to her home, since hosting people alone seemed to emphasize her abandonment. This was in marked contrast to her earlier married life when her home had been the center for all of the holidays and other rituals with her extended family and friends. She called her house her "loneliness and her memories." I suggested that she might want to begin her healing by replacing some of the familiar and jointly owned items in her home with some new things that represented her individual tastes. As Candace began to put together a house that suited her, the acute depressive symptoms abated.

But for a long while, Candace was still unable to invite anyone to her home. "I feel like a strange sort of prisoner in my own home. But I'm not locked in—other people are locked out," Candace told me.

I was intrigued with her metaphor of the lock. I wondered with Candace what effect a new lock on her door might have. Candace agreed to buy a new lock and to simply sit with it each day and ask herself, "What would it take to put this new lock on my door—a lock that I could open to my family and friends?"

During that week, Candace went through many emotions—sadness, anger, a sense of betrayal. By the end of the week, she felt ready to reclaim her life. She decided to make a special ritual, a "house-cooling party." She told me, "People usually have house-warming parties when they move to a new home, I'd like to mark my divorce with some humor and have a "house-cooling party." She designed an invitation that read: "Please come to my house-cooling party. Please do bring gifts appropriate for the lovely home of a single woman—I need to replace the 'his and her' stuff!" Just before the party, Candace had the new lock put on her front door, symbolizing that she was now in charge of her life (Imber-Black & Roberts, 1992).

THERAPEUTIC RITUALS

Many clinicians have described the efficacy of therapeutic rituals in facilitating systemic change. (Imber-Black,1986a, 1986b; Imber Coppersmith, 1983, 1985; O'Connor, 1984; O'Connor & Horwitz, 1984; Palazzolli, Boscolo, Cecchin & Prata, 1977; Papp, 1984; Seltzer & Seltzer, 1983; van der Hart, 1983). Differing from simple tasks whose intent is to target the behavioral level and that the therapist expects to be performed as prescribed, rituals are intended to effect the behavioral, cognitive, and affective levels, and the family or individual is expected to improvise to tailor the ritual to particular and personal circumstances. Rather than relying only on concrete instructions, rituals utilize symbols and symbolic actions that may have multiple meanings.

Therapeutic rituals draw on elements attendant to normative life cycle rituals to highlight similarities to others, while including unusual elements that are capable of affirming differences rather than hiding them. Thus, Candace's house-cooling party began with the new lock as a powerful symbol of her autonomy after divorce. Many rituals include documents. Candace's invitation became a document to announce her divorce, and the party allowed her to ask others for support. Friends and family gathered to witness and celebrate her life cycle transition, just as they would with any other life cycle ritual.

Although there are several categories of rituals that may be useful in therapy, three categories are particularly beneficial for idiosyncratic life cycle events and processes. These include transition rituals, healing rituals, and identity redefinition rituals.

Transition rituals have been described extensively by van der Hart (1983), primarily in reference to normative life cycle transitions. Such rituals mark and facilitate transitions of specific members and of membership in the family, altering boundaries and making new relationship options available. The transitions in idiosyncratic life cycle events and processes often have no rituals. Indeed, the family may not have anticipated the transition and all of the relationship changes attendant on it.

The Giving of Gifts

A physician referred a family to me for therapy for what was identified as depression in the mother. The family consisted of two parents, Mr. and Mrs. Berry, and two young adult children, Karen, age 22, and Andrew, age 20. Karen was diagnosed as severely mentally retarded shortly after her birth. Karen's pediatrician advised Mrs. Berry to quit her job and remain at home to care for Karen. Extended family supported this advice and visited often while Karen and Andrew were small. The parents were told that Karen would never function on her own and would always remain "like a child." Eventually, Karen went to a special school, but the parents were never counseled in ways to prepare for Karen's adolescence or adulthood. Karen developed language and self-care skills. The family functioned well during Karen and Andrew's childhood. However, as both children became teenagers, severe difficulties arose. No one in the nuclear or extended family knew how to cope with Karen as an emerging young woman.

Fearful that Karen might be exploited sexually, the family became increasingly protective of her. Andrew was required to spend most of his free time taking Karen to any outside events that were scheduled by her special school, and he grew increasingly resentful and withdrawn. His own plans to go away to college seemed impossible to him. Karen became rebellious and difficult for the family to be with, and the parents felt that they had failed her and needed to try harder. At the same time, Karen's school began to push the family to put Karen in a group home. This option had not existed at the time of Karen's birth and had never been anticipated by the family. For a period of two years, the parents and the school struggled over Karen's future. The parents were unable to articulate their fears to the school personnel, who saw them as overinvolved with Karen. Consequently, adequate explanations of what the group home could offer Karen and her family were not forthcoming. During this time, everyone in the family deteriorated emotionally and functionally, culminating in the referral for family therapy by the mother's physician.

Through the course of a therapy in which I helped the family to anticipate the life cycle change of Karen's eventually leaving home, and that richly credited the family for their contributions to Karen, the family became able to ask for and receive adequate information from the group home about Karen's future there. As the leaving home was normalized, the parents were able to articulate expectations about visiting and holiday time together that would mark the relationship of most young adults and their families. Andrew became freer to live his own life and made plans for going away to college in four months, after Karen was to go to the group home. The family was preparing itself for many changes. However, as Karen began to visit the group home, first for dinners and then for brief overnights stays, conflicts began to break out between Karen and her parents. Mr. and Mrs. Berry became alarmed that Karen was not as ready to move out as they had thought. In a session alone with the therapist, they cried and said that they feared for Karen's future.

Since the family had made so many changes in the direction of Karen's leaving home and were on the verge of completing the actual leaving when the arguments emerged, the therapist decided that a ritual to mark Karen's leaving home was needed. The Berrys had stated frequently that they "didn't think we had given Karen enough in order to equip her for life in the outside community." This sense of not having given her enough was intensified by the school's criticism of the family. Their phrase "given her enough" was used to construct a leaving home ritual that would confirm Karen's young adulthood, would promote the family's confidence in her and themselves, and would highlight ongoing connectedness among the members.

I asked the parents and Andrew each to select a gift for Karen for her to take to her new home. I suggested that they choose a gift that would remind Karen of them and would also ease her way in her new setting. Karen, in turn, was asked to select a gift for each member that would remain with them when she left. The family members were told not to buy these gifts, but rather to choose something of their own or to make something. They were asked to bring these gifts to the next session and not to tell anyone else in the family about their gift before the session.

When the family arrived, they appeared very excited and happy in a way that had not been seen before during therapy. They had not shared their gifts before the session but had decided during the two weeks to wrap them and put them in a large bag, which Karen carried into the meeting. Mrs. Berry began by saying that during that week, they had decided on a definite date for Karen to move out, which they had not been able to do previously. Karen had gone for several visits to the group home. She also said that there had been a lot of secretive laughter during the two weeks, as people prepared their gifts, and no fighting!

I suggested a format for the exchange of gifts that was simple and largely nonverbal, which involved each member giving their gift, with a brief explanation if needed, and the recipient simply saying "thank you," other discussion being reserved for after the gift exchange. This was done to highlight the family as a group together and to facilitate equal participation, since Karen often fell silent when verbal discussions became rapid.

Mr. Berry began the ceremony. He reached into the bag and gave Karen an unusual-shaped package, which turned out to be his favorite frying pan.

Traditionally, Mr. Berry made Sunday breakfast. Because Karen was learning some simple cooking skills in school, she always wanted to use this frying pan, but her father had been afraid that she would ruin it and so had not let her use it. Karen beamed and said, "Thank you."

Mrs. Berry's package was small, and she shyly handed it to Karen. It contained an almost full bottle of perfume and a pair of earrings. Mrs. Berry related briefly that she had often scolded Karen for using her perfume and had never allowed her to wear earrings. She looked at Karen and said, "I think you're grown up enough for these—they belonged to my mother and she gave them to me and now I'm giving them to you." With tears in her eyes, Karen said, "Thank you."

The mood changed profoundly when it was Andrew's turn. He remarked that he couldn't bring his whole gift to the session, but that Karen would understand. She opened his package to find a partially used box of birdseed. Leaving for school meant that Andrew would have to leave his parakeet. He had been allowed various pets at home, and had been responsible for them, while Karen had not. He explained that he had called Karen's group home, and they would allow her to bring the bird. He said that he would teach her to care for it before she moved out. Karen said, "Thank you," and Mrs. Berry expressed relief that the parakeet was leaving home too.

Karen then gave her gifts. To her mother, Karen gave her favorite stuffed animal, which she had had since early childhood and with which she still slept. She said to her mother, "I can't sleep with this in my new home—please keep it." To her father, she gave a photograph of her that had been taken during one of her visits at the group home. The photograph showed her sitting with several young men and women, and she said to her father, "These are my new friends." To Andrew, she gave her clock radio. This was a prized possession that had been a Christmas present. She gave it to Andrew and said, "Don't be late for school!"

Two weeks after this session, Karen moved into the group home, and a month later, Andrew left for college. The family ended therapy. At their one year follow-up, the family reported that both children had adjusted well to their new settings and were visiting home for holidays. Mrs.

Berry had also returned to school to train for paid employment.

DISCUSSION OF THE RITUAL

This leaving-home ritual seemed to function in a number of ways. Through the course of the family therapy, the family had been preparing for Karen's leaving home but seemed to get stuck just on the verge of her actual leaving. Like many normative life cycle rituals, the therapeutic ritual worked to confirm a process that was already in motion and was not simply a discrete event. The ritual symbolically affirmed and made simultaneous the contradictions of separation and ongoing connectedness that are involved when any child leaves home. The family members, in their giving of gifts, were able both to give permission for separation and affirm their ongoing but changing relationships.

The ritual was designed to introduce symmetry into a system that had been primarily marked by complementary relationships. Thus, all members participated in the giving and receiving of gifts and in the planning and thoughtfulness that went into gift selection, altering the previous pattern in the family whereby the parents and Andrew were seen to be the "givers," the "providers," the "protectors," and Karen was seen to be the recipient of care, advice, and protection.

The ritual was also designed to confirm individual boundaries as each member was individually responsible for his or her own planning and selection of gifts. Individuation was promoted through the instruction of secret planning by each member. Dyadic relationships between Karen and every member were also confirmed, in a family that had previously operated with triads involving Karen as their primary mode of relationship. Finally, each member's contribution to the ritual was highlighted as important to the entire process, thus symbolically celebrating the whole family unit. Thus, various aspects of the ritual functioned to introduce differences in pattern to the family system.

By asking the family to bring their gifts to the therapy session, I was able to serve as witness to the process. Witnesses are frequently a part of normative life cycle rituals. Here, the therapist also may be seen to symbolically represent an outside helping system in a celebratory stance with a family which had been used to criticism and disparagement from outside systems.

HEALING RITUALS

Every culture has rituals to mark profound losses, deal with the grief of survivors, and facilitate ongoing life after such loss. There are many creative contemporary examples of cultural healing rituals. The Vietnam War Memorial in Washington, D.C., is visited by families and friends who lost men and women in the war and make pilgrimages to the memorial, during which they search for their loved one's name, perhaps leave items that have special meaning, and often make rubbings to carry back home. Public grieving for a war that held so much secrecy and shame is facilitated by this repeated ritual.

The AIDS quilt, consisting of several thousand hand-sewn patches, each memorializing a person who has died of AIDS, is displayed with a powerful ceremony in which all of the names of the dead are read aloud as the quilt is unfolded in planned, repetitive motions of connection and uplift. A quilt is often a community endeavor. The AIDS quilt connects a community of mourners with a symbol of warmth and care.

The Clothesline Project is a women's ritual devoted to recovery from abuse. A growing collection of hand-painted T-shirts is hung on a clothesline. This community ritual includes the ringing of gongs and bells and blowing of horns to symbolize how often a woman is assaulted, raped, and murdered. The marvelous contradiction of regaining power in the face of servitude is clearly contained in these hand-painted depictions of violence hung ironically on a clothesline for all to see.

Healing may also be necessary for losses sustained through the breakup of relationships, for the reconciliation of relationships after painful revelations such as affairs, for unresolved grief when normative healing rituals have not occurred or have not succeeded, for losses of bodily parts and functions due to illness, and for the often attendant loss of roles, life expectations, and dreams (see Imber Coppersmith, 1985, for case examples of healing rituals). Therapeutic healing rituals are particularly useful when normative healing rituals do not exist or are not sufficient for the magnitude of the loss.

Setting Fire to the Past

Alice Jeffers, age 35, requested therapy, saying that she was depressed and unable to live her life normally. Alice was single and lived alone. She was a trained and practicing veterinarian. In the first session, she described to me an eight-year-long relationship with a man. The relationship, which had included periods of living together, had been very stormy and had finally ended two years previously at his insistence. Alice's family had not approved of the relationship. They were relieved when it ended but seemed unable to extend any support to Alice for the pain she felt. Friends told her that she was well rid of him. Over the two years, Alice grew increasingly isolated, and by the time she came to therapy, she did not go out with any friends, spent all her free time thinking about her former lover, dreamed about him nightly, had gained a lot of weight, and felt that her work was being affected. Her family and friends' inability to confirm her pain and loss seemed to contribute to her own need to do nothing else but think about him and feel sad. She said she felt that if she had been married and divorced, people would have been more supportive of her, as they had been of her sister in such circumstances.

I began with simple confirmation of Alice's loss and grief and highlighted that, indeed, there are no agreed-upon processes for the end of a nonmarried relationship. I asked Alice to perform a task that would allow her both to grieve and to begin to get on with other aspects of her life. For one hour a day, Alice was told to do nothing but review memories of the relationship, since this was something that obviously still needed to be completed. I suggested that she write these memories out on separate index cards and bring them to the next session. Outside of the hour a day, I urged Alice to do other things.

Alice returned with a stack of index cards, which she had creatively color-coded, using purple for "mellow" memories, green for "jealous" memories, and blue for "sad" memories. With laughter, she stated, "And, of course, my angry ones are RED!" As the therapy session focused on the cards and their meanings, Alice stated that she had felt much better during the three weeks, that she began to find that an hour a day was too much time, and that she had stopped dreaming about her former love. I asked her whether there were cards she felt ready to let go of, and she said that there were. She was asked to take all the cards home and sort them out, differentiating between those she still wanted to hang on to and those she felt ready to let go of.

Alice arrived two weeks later, dressed more brightly than before and eager to talk. She had started to go out with friends a bit and had looked into an aerobics class. After reporting this, she took out two stacks of cards. She said she had decided she wanted to keep the purple "mellow" memories, as these were a part of her that she wanted to maintain. She felt the good parts of the relationship had changed her in positive ways, and she said she wanted to carry this into any new relationship she might have. This was the first mention of a sense of future. She also wanted to keep most of the red "anger" memories, as these helped her to remember how shabbily she had been treated many times and thus kept her from romanticizing the past. However she was very ready to let go of the green "jealousy" memories, which often made her feel bad about herself, and the blue "sad" memories, as she felt that she had been sad long enough. At that point, I left the room and returned with a ceramic bowl and a book of matches, which I silently offered to Alice, who smiled and said, "Oh, we should burn them!" It is important to note that she saw the burning as a joint endeavor by herself and me. I handed the cards back to Alice, who put them in a pile in the bowl and lit them. She used several matches to get a good fire going and then sat silently for several moments watching the flames. At one point, she said, "It's so final, but it's good." A few minutes later, she joked, "We should toast marshmallows—that would be the final irony," referring to the fact that her boyfriend had often criticized her body and her weight and yet brought her treats. Toward the end, she said, "This is good—my final memory is of warmth."

In sessions after to the burning ritual, Alice dealt with many family of origin issues that had previously been unavailable because of her stuck position vis-a-vis her boyfriend. She was able to renegotiate several family relationships, began going out more with friends, and joined a scuba class. When therapy ended, she was beginning flying lessons, an apt metaphor for her new beginnings.

IDENTITY REDEFINITION RITUALS

Identity redefinition rituals function to remove labels and stigma from individuals, couples and families and often realign relationships between the family and larger systems. This is especially necessary when the larger systems have held negative points of view toward a family. A reworking of an earlier idiosyncratic life cycle transition that went awry may be accomplished. New relationship options, previously unavailable because of the constraints of labels, become available (see Imber-Coppersmith, 1983). A balance of being both similar to others and different from others becomes achievable.

A Mutual Adoption Celebration

I met Bob Simmons, a 37-year-old single gay man, about a year and a half after he had adopted his 9-year-old son, Alan. "We're definitely a new sort of family," Bob told me in our first therapy session. "I don't have to tell you that as a gay man, I had to look all over the country to find an agency that would let me adopt a child. It took me four years, but I finally succeeded," Bob reflected proudly.

Bob had found an agency across the country that let him make a home for Alan, a biracial child with many special educational and emotional needs. Alan had been in six foster homes after his crack-addicted mother abandoned him when he was 2 years old. He had been severely abused, both in his biological family and in at least three of his foster homes. Now, living with Bob, Alan showed many of the signs of an abused and neglected child. Alan had learned to survive by drawing into himself, allowing little contact with others. Bob came to family therapy to help his son, to build their relationship, and to learn parenting strategies.

As I met with Bob and his young son, Alan refused to talk to me. No doubt, having met many professionals whose jobs had been to move him from one place to another, Alan was not about to take any risks with me. As Bob described his frustrations learning to parent, Alan sank lower and lower in his chair. My many attempts to reach him were met with shrugs and a cap pulled farther and farther over his eyes. "Tell me something," I said to Alan, "he adopted you, right?" "Right," Alan whispered in return. "Have you adopted him?" I asked. Alan's cap flew off, and his eyes grew as big as saucers. He rose up in his seat. "Oh, how could I do that?" his voice boomed. "I don't know," I replied. "How do *you* think you could do that?" "I would have to go to court and get some papers," Alan replied. "I think you've hit on something important here," Bob said.

For the rest of the session, we talked about how Bob adopted Alan. As a gay man, he was made to feel stigmatized everywhere he turned to realize his dream of being a father. When he finally adopted Alan, he didn't make a celebration. There was no ritual to mark and help make this critical transition. Most of Bob's friends couldn't understand his decision to be a single father. His sister yelled at him over the phone that he had no right to be a parent. When Bob and Alan began to live together as father and son, Bob was unprepared for how difficult parenting a boy who had been so abused would be. He often told Alan how lucky he was to be in a nice home. Without meaning to, Bob made Alan feel that he was in a very unbalanced situation. When I asked Alan whether he had adopted Bob, I struck an important chord of mutuality, one that excited Alan with its possibilities.

I met alone with Alan and told him that he wouldn't need to go to court to adopt Bob. He would just need to write out his own document on his computer at home. We agreed to keep this private between us as he worked on a "certificate to adopt my dad."

The therapy contained many other elements, including helping Bob to set appropriate limits for Alan, reconnecting Bob to his own mother, who wanted to be a loving grandmother for Alan, and aiding Bob in finding other single dads, both gay and straight. When our therapy concluded, Bob and Alan invited Bob's mother and some new and supportive friends over for a special ritual, a mutual adoption ceremony, in which Alan and Bob openly adopted one another.

DESIGNING AND IMPLEMENTING RITUALS FOR IDIOSYNCRATIC LIFE CYCLE TRANSITIONS

Designing and implementing rituals such as those discussed in this chapter, is a learnable skill. Several guidelines will enhance this process.

1. Just as normative rituals are processes, rather than discrete events, so therapeutic rituals are part of a larger therapeutic process. Their efficacy relies on planning, careful assessment, especially regarding life cycle phases and idiosyncratic life cycle events, and respect and rapport between family and therapist. The rituals intended here are not games or tricks, but rather rise out of a relational context that appreciates the ritualizing tendency of human beings and the need for meaning in human relationships.

2. The family and therapist search for the appropriate symbols and symbolic acts of the individual, family, ethnic group, and cultural group, which represents the possibility of relationship development. Such symbols and metaphorical action should connect the family with the familiar, while also being capable of leading to the unfamiliar.

3. The family and therapist design the ritual with a focus on special time and special space. Thus, rituals may occur at a particular time or over time. Time may be used to draw particular distinctions or to highlight simultaneity. A sense of connection to past, present, and future is made. The ritual may occur in the therapy session, at home, or at some other agreed-upon place, such as by a body of water, in a woods, or in a cemetery. If the ritual requires a witness, then the therapy session is often the preferred time and space, or the therapist may accompany the family to an agreed-upon place.

4. The therapist attends to alternations in order to incorporate contradictions. Thus, holding on may be alternated with letting go in a single ritual, or a ritual of termination or separation may be followed by a ritual of renewal or celebration.

5. The therapist looks for ways to involve the family in codesigning the ritual to facilitate imagination that may lead to problem solving and enhanced functioning. A sense of humor and playfulness are used when appropriate.

6. Therapeutic rituals for idiosyncratic life cycle events borrow heavily from normative rituals, yet utilize symbols and symbolic actions that are relevant to the particular life cycle transition.

7. The therapist remains open to the family's development of the ritual, including their choice to not perform the ritual. Therapeutic rituals, like normative rituals, should not be hollow events, practiced simply because someone said to do it. Rather, they are opportunities for the confirmation of existing relationships and for the beginnings of relationship change. Family readiness must be carefully gauged and respected. In successful therapeutic rituals, the ritual and its outcome ultimately belong to the family.

CONCLUSION

Idiosyncratic life cycle events and transitions pose particular difficulties for individuals and families. Lacking available maps that fit their situation and without wider contextual support and confirmation, complex feedback processes may be set in motion, resulting in symptoms and a high level of distress and isolation. Since rituals have the capacity to hold and express differences rather than homogenize them, they are particularly powerful resources for any life cycle transition that differs from the conventional. Therapy needs to include conversations about meaningful rituals. Creatively and sensitively crafted rituals, which both borrow richly from normative life cycle rituals and are simultaneously brand new, facilitate necessary transitions and the expansion of relationship possibilities.

REFERENCES

Carter, E. A., & McGoldrick, M. (1980). The family life cycle and family therapy. In E. A. Carter & M. McGoldrick (Eds.), *The family life cycle: A framework for family therapy.* New York: Gardner Press.

DeSilva, C. (Ed.). (1996). *In memory's kitchen: A legacy from the women of Terezin.* New York: Jason Aronson.

Haley, J. (1973). *Uncommon therapy: The psychiatric techniques of Milton H. Erickson.* New York: Norton.

Imber-Black, E. (1986a). Odysseys of a learner. In D. Efron (Ed.), *Journeys: Expansion of the strategic-systemic therapies.* New York: Brunner/Mazel.

Imber-Black, E. (1986b). Towards a resource model in systemic family therapy. In M. Karpel (Ed.), *Family resources,* (pp. 148–174). New York: The Guilford Press.

Imber-Black, E., & Roberts, J. (1992). *Rituals for our times: Celebrating, healing and changing our lives and our relationships.* New York: HarperCollins.

Imber Coppersmith, E. (1983). From hyperactive to normal but naughty: A multisystem partnership in delabeling. *International Journal of Family Psychiatry, 3*(2), 131–144.

Imber Coppersmith, E. (1985). We've got a secret: A non-marital marital therapy. In A. Gurman (Ed.), *Casebook of marital therapy,* (pp. 369–386). New York: The Guilford Press.

O'Connor, J. (1984). The resurrection of a magical reality: Treatment of functional migraine in a child. *Family Process, 23*(4), 501–509.

O'Connor, J., & Horwitz, A. N. (1984). The bogeyman cometh: A strategic approach for difficult adolescents. *Family Process, 23*(2), 237–249.

Palazzoli, M., Boscolo, L., Cecehin, G., & Prata, G. (1977). Family rituals: A powerful tool in family therapy. *Family Process, 16*(4), 445–454.

Papp, P. (1984). The links between clinical and artistic creativity. *The Family Therapy Networker, 8*(5), 20–29.

Schwartzman, J. (1982). Symptoms and rituals: Paradoxical modes and social organization. *Ethos, 10*(1), 3–23.

Seltzer, W., & Seltzer, M. (1983). Magic, material and myth. *Family Process, 22*(1), 3–14.

Terkleson, K. G. (1980). Toward a theory of the family life cycle. In E. A. Carter & M. McGoldrick (Eds.), *The Family life cycle: A framework for family therapy.* New York: Gardner Press.

van der Hart, O. (1983). *Rituals in psychotherapy: Transition and continuity.* New York: Irvington Publishers.

Van Gennep, A. (1960). *The rites of passage.* Chicago: University of Chicago Press.

Walzlawick, P. (1978). *The language of change: Elements of therapeutic communication.* New York: Basic Books.

Weingarten, K., & Weingarten Worthen, M. E. (1997). A narrative approach to understanding the illness experiences of a mother and daughter. *Families, Systems and Health, 15*(1), 41–54.

Wolin, S. J., & Bennett, S. A. (1984). Family rituals. *Family Process, 23*(3), 401–420.

CHAPTER 13

BECOMING AN ADULT
LEAVING HOME AND
STAYING CONNECTED

RICHARD FULMER

In the 1970s, family therapy writers began to use a developmental view of family life to describe the changing goals of the family system through time. In that era, authors emphasized separation between children and their parents as one of the primary developmental tasks of young adulthood. Stierlin (1977) and Haley (1980) especially focused on parental resistance to separation as a source of delayed development in this phase. Since that time, we have become aware of the overemphasis in the developmental literature placed on autonomy and separation, particularly for male development, which had previously been seen as the norm for both sexes. Studies of female development have broadened our understanding of the needs of both men and women for connection and the ability to function independently, a basic aspect of Murray Bowen's (1978) definition of maturity. Carol Gilligan (1982, 1991), for example, through her study of female development, drew our attention to the need to develop "a healthy resistance to disconnectedness" (1991, p. 241) while acquiring a "voice of one's own." Coontz (1992), writing on a societal level, emphasized the way women's support of men in modern families was determinedly unrecognized to preserve the myth of rugged individualism.

Miller (1976), Benjamin (1988), Bergman (1991), and others have highlighted the importance of relatedness in men's psychological development as well. Olga Silverstein and Beth Rashbaum (1994) developed the idea that cultural norms have permitted mothers to maintain relationships with their daughters but have mistakenly pushed them to sever their bonds with their sons. This too-early

or too-extreme separation is meant to help promote their sons' independence and male identity.

Clinically, this is the family life cycle phase when our clients may seem to be least "in relationships." In the middle class, children of both sexes have left their family of origin and may not yet be married and raising their own families. But the impact of their family of origin relationships is still primary, even though frequently unacknowledged.

YOUNG ADULTHOOD: DEVELOPMENTAL TASKS

Work Tasks

Young adults of all social classes depend on their families for tangible and emotional support as they develop themselves as workers. Support is necessary for such an extended period that the young adult's goal in this era can be called "preparing for productivity." The family's task, achieved by setting examples of how to approach work and providing material and emotional support, can be seen as "enabling preparation."

Relationship Tasks

In the realm of relationships, the young adults' task is more complex than "breaking ties." It is to develop the ability to become as deeply attached to a few select others as one has been attached to family members. I would like to call this family task "exporting relatedness." The quality of the intimate relationships that young adults make will be influenced by the marital relationships they have observed and the way they themselves have been treated. Their ties with their parents endure, in part in the form of the ongoing permission and support they receive from parents to transfer their affection to a few appropriate strangers.

To correct the usual split between concern for autonomy in male development and emotional connectedness in female development, I would like to emphasize the importance of relatedness in male development and to articulate the need for a period of self-focus and separateness during young adulthood in female development (see Chapter 2).

YOUNG ADULTHOOD IN THE 1990s

As real wages decrease and skill requirements for entry level jobs increase, it is taking longer for young adults to become self-supporting. Economists report that "a young man under 25 years of age employed full time in 1994 earned 31 percent less per week than what his same-aged counterpart earned in 1973" (Sum, Togg, & Taggert, 1996, pp. 83–84). They describe this period of working but being unable to support a family as "economic adolescence" and note that it has greatly lengthened in the last two decades. One striking piece of evidence is that "the 1990 census revealed that 21 percent of 25-year olds were living with one or both parents, up from 15 percent in 1970" (Mogelonsky, 1996, p. 29). Some stay at home after graduating from high school. More return home after having been away. In 1980–1994, 46 percent of young men returned home for at least four months after their first departure. In the same period, only 36 percent of young women did so. At least one writer speculates that a possible reason for this sex difference is that women have a greater incentive to leave. Young men returning home may not lose much of their autonomy. Young women tend to be drawn into more householding chores (Haddock, 1996) and don't want to explain why a boyfriend is still there in the morning.

Parents may be surprised by the return of their adult children. They may feel that they have done something wrong when their temporarily empty nest is refilled. They may be relieved to find that it is a common, often planned practice, not the result of some failure. At any rate, this return to the home in young adulthood is often a convenient, temporary, and orderly way to prepare for adulthood, not always an indulgence of insecurity or irresponsibility.

LATE ADOLESCENCE OR EARLY YOUNG ADULTHOOD: AGE 18–21

Learning to Work

Young men have always been expected to work at cash-producing jobs to support first themselves and then their families. Since the 1960s, women have also increasingly used this period to prepare to enter the workforce. Women of all social classes find meaning in work and want to increase their future independence from men. They also know that real wages have declined so much since the 1960s that it is very difficult for all but the most affluent families to survive on the husband's income alone.

So for both sexes one of the primary tasks of early young adulthood is learning how to work. This requires the young adult to form an interest in work for which others will pay. This sounds a little obvious, but it is by no means automatic. Many adolescent interests must be considerably transformed to become a job or a career. Often, this can only be accomplished by trial and error and may involve a great deal of disappointment, refocusing, and trying again. If a salable interest can be developed, young adults have the capacity to work with great concentration and intensity. If they cannot find an interest, they risk having to do work that only remunerates but does not express any meaning about themselves. This process may involve many false starts that may be sobering experiences for the young adult and nerve-wracking for their families.

Self-Involvement

Young adulthood is a period when both men and women may retreat from long-term relationship·

commitments. The middle classes observe a sort of moratorium on family obligations. This permits a period of relative solitude, a time when young adults may become more self-involved. They work to develop themselves, in terms of both skills and personal maturity. Their activity does not return much cash or service to anyone else.

Idealism

Not having much life experience, many young adults try to guide themselves with values. They feel that problems can be solved by living in accordance with ideals and renouncing personal interest. They are also often grandiose, feeling that they can fairly easily avoid the mistakes they perceive their elders to have made. This arrogance may not be fully mature, but it may be a necessary maturational stage on the way to the development of true personal authority, something that we do not even hope for until middle adulthood.

Young adults' consciously held values may often differ at least superficially from those of their parents. They may be quite righteous in their beliefs. If they are still accepting their parents' financial support, they may have to tolerate the moral dilemma of holding a benefactor in contempt.

Mentors

While this is a time of more or less polite contempt toward parents and their allies, the moral simplicity of young adults permits them to idealize the one or two teachers they may admire. This personal relationship to a mentor is extremely important. It can serve as a bridge between immersion in family and greater self-definition. It can be a way to submit to learning at an intense rate without a loss of pride. This worshipful relationship holds dangers, however, if the mentor uses the relationship to his or her own advantage. Young adults are especially vulnerable to leaders of cults and gangs. Such groups offer an idealistic focus, moral simplicity, and a socially reinforced identity that ease the fears of meaninglessness, disorganization, and loneliness that beset young adults.

This ability to idealize (even if it somewhat overestimates the mentor) is also a developmental achievement. In *The Sibling Society* (1997), Robert Bly argues that the loss of an age hierarchy in American society has made such idealization nearly impossible. His is not the usual rant against disrespectful youth, however. He also cites the unwillingness of older people to claim authority and speak with wisdom. He tells of a bumper sticker displayed by some grandparents: "We are spending our children's inheritance." He feels that older people are not spending, but squandering their ability to guide the young and resolve society's conflicts. If everyone's goal is to play like children, says he, we are a society of siblings, with no one looking up and no one to look up to. Such a leveling of age differences is particularly devastating for young adults who need the opportunity to idealize.

Perfect Love

Another manifestation of the idealism of this era is the search for a perfect love. Many young adults are looking for a love partner whom they can value and be valued by so intensely that all ambivalence, uncertainty, self-doubts, sadness, and fears of the future are swept away forever. They hope to be created anew, this time by the love of an ideal alternative to imperfect parents. This is not a desire for true relatedness, but a wish for fusion, a desire to be fulfilled without effort and without the responsibility to be a separate individual oneself.

This search for perfect love is often an important transaction between the young adult and his or her family of origin. Young adults are often eager to find someone outside their family to affirm the experimental part of their identities. It is a heady experience to be discovered and loved by someone who is brand new and whose love is not routine or based on role obligations. It is very gratifying to feel so needed by the other. Often, the perfect lover will be different in some important way from parents. This may be an attempt to display to parents the young adult's independence. The perfect love may also represent an attempt to solve certain problems that the young adult experienced in family of origin.

The loved one may be someone who needs the young adult's help. The hope of being able to save someone is a seductive lure for both young women and young men. It promises an increase in status (from being taken care of to taking care), an affirmation of a grandiose self-image, a chance to surpass parents at parenting, and an enactment of personal idealism. The helped partner must necessarily have some problems (drug abuse, low social status, financial or academic difficulties, or emotional disturbance) for the lover to help them with. That their child becomes so intensely involved with an underfunctioning partner is usually agony for parents.

Efforts to break up the relationship may be surreptitiously accepted by the daughters or sons if they are already looking for a way out, or parental disapproval may hold the couple together, sometimes at considerable risk to the participants. Perfect love is, of course, never perfect, and it never lasts. When the transition from adolescent-in-family to adult-between-families has progressed somewhat, the need for such love diminishes, and its imperfections can be evaluated realistically. The wounded lovers may approach their next relationship with more grounded idealism.

Alcohol and Drugs

Early young adulthood is the period when consciousness-altering drugs—such as coffee, marijuana, alcohol, hallucinogens, cocaine, pills, and heroin—are most enthusiastically used. There must be multiple reasons for this—the exercise of freedom from parental supervision, a social lubricant for the many anxiety-filled social contacts of the period, or an aid to ecstatic, sometimes sexual celebration at parties. Other possible reasons for such excess may be a desire to transcend the self, resolve inner conflicts, and find at least a temporary sense of certainty during such an uncertain time of life. While most will emerge from this phase eventually, young people whose family members are or have been addicted

to some substance are at serious risk of getting caught here.

From Self-Involvement to Beginning to Think Like a Householder

Early young adulthood, like late adolescence, is characterized by grandiosity, idealism, idealization, intense work, and using relationships to define the self. These are gradually replaced by a more realistic view of what can be accomplished, a more complex, situation-based morality, disillusionment, a focusing of work interests, and a wish for a home.

This last desire raises the importance of relationships in the personal economy of both men and women. In the television series *Taxi,* Louie complained about how his girlfriend, Zena, had "ruined" (his) life. "Before," he said, "I used to be perfectly happy just sitting and watching the Mets game! Now I'm not happy unless I'm sitting watching the game *with Zena!*" For many, this wish for an attachment to a particular other person becomes a primary concern. What I think is going on here is a wish to reproduce a good version of the family of origin, beginning with an ideal couple. The particular candidate for spouse is meant to fill in the deficits and resolve many of the conflicts experienced in that family. Now a gratifying relationship (but not necessarily marriage) becomes the most important objective. As that occurs, the singleness of purpose of earlier young adulthood is lost. A more complex balancing of the needs of self and other begins, necessitating compromise of ambitions, values, even ideals. This is the beginning of a shift from the self-involved identity to the identity of the householder. Romantic partners are now measured not only by whether they are fun to be with, but also by how well they will fit in the young adult's program for an ideal family. Interest shifts from the difficult task of definition of the self to the even more complex project of definition of a family and self-in-a-family. In the middle class, marriage is often still delayed, but imagined scenarios of householding begin to influence goals and the way in which romantic partners are evaluated.

While each try-out partner can fulfill some part of their partner's imagined family scenario, they surely will not fill all parts perfectly. The partner, of course, has a program and a role for them as well. It is important for the individuals to be able to shift their emotional investment from the fantasized "perfect" love of early young adulthood to a real person who is free and ready to enact a relationship in the present. This is a difficult transition in love that requires wisdom and is often imperfectly made. It requires giving up some part of a treasured ideal in return for a life.

As realism replaces grandiosity, young adults may enjoy actually making some of their dreams come true. They may also have a sense of disappointment in that the fantasy of many possibilities is reduced to just a few realities. They may have a new sense of the passage of time when they realize that the "getting ready" of early young adulthood is over.

Mentors—Disillusionment

Later young adulthood may be a time when individuals become disillusioned with their mentors. Just as the ability to idealize was an achievement, the ability to view mentors realistically is a further achievement. This experience can be depressing, however, as the heady feeling of "having the answer" begins to erode. Young adults may feel that their mentors have deceived them and end their relationships in a storm of bitter disappointment. Or they may simply grow away from the mentors, losing interest in their charisma.

As they do, they sometimes view their own fervent, grandiose young adulthoods with some rueful embarrassment. To paraphrase Mark Twain: At 18 young adults may think their parents to be the most ignorant people in the world. At 25, they are amazed at how much those parents have learned in a few short years.

Alcohol and Drugs in Later Young Adulthood

After age 25, many individuals gradually back away from intense drug and alcohol use even if it had been important in their lives. They don't abstain from alcohol entirely but do drink less. The exceptions, of course, are people who have become addicted. During early young adulthood, when so many are using alcohol and drugs excessively, it is difficult to diagnose alcoholism (unless there is a strong preadult and/or family history of drug or alcohol abuse). But in later adulthood, many of the maturational reasons for substance abuse have passed. It can now clearly be seen as a compulsion and addressed as such clinically.

These experiences—the acquisition of real satisfactions, the need to consider the needs of at least one other as well as one's own, the realization that many fantasies cannot be pursued, sobriety itself—are the beginnings of the householder identity, the hallmarks of later young adulthood.

ISSUES FOR THE FAMILY

Parents often anticipate this period with a mixture of relief and dread. As children no longer need daily care, certain chores (particularly for the homemaker) are lightened. When her youngest children (twins) left for college, my sister remarked to her husband, "I cleaned this area yesterday, and it's still clean!… and we've got leftovers!" However, the era also brings a difficult mix of a diminished ability to monitor, influence, and protect children and the feeling (and reality) of continued responsibility for them.

How Financial Support Affects the Relationship

One of the ways in which parents continue to be responsible for children is financially.

In the days when apprenticeship was a standard way of acquiring work skills, children could at least earn room and board in exchange for service from a relatively early age. Now that the need for physical skills is so much less, technical skills are necessary for even many entry-level jobs. Preparation for professional careers requires six to ten years of higher education, and virtually no young adults can support themselves for all that time.

They must be supported by their families, either with cash or room and board until they can reliably produce a living wage. Many young adults find their financial dependence during this period humiliating, especially if attention is drawn to it. Some expect it as their due.

While our technological society thus requires more years of financial dependency, it still puts a very high value on individual freedom of expression. Young adults often manage this built-in contradiction by righteously demanding that all their choices be free from parental influence while ignoring and concealing from themselves their continued financial reliance on parental sacrifice. It is, however, almost impossible to be emotionally independent if one is financially dependent.

Parents may not particularly mind the responsibility in that it is usually one that they expected. However, they may feel that their support entitles them to inquire about, even comment on, their now-grown children's behavior. Those children, trying hard to achieve at least the feeling of independence, may complain that continued parental guidance compromises their aspirations. In affluent families, the education required to reproduce such affluence may require financial support for many years. When a family's limits are reached, parents may have to make hard decisions about how to allocate funds between different children, arousing rivalrous feelings among them.

Continuity versus Innovation

For their adult children, parents usually represent the theme of continuity as well as support. They provide the site for celebration of family life cycle events and the continued observance of family holidays. They communicate their wishes for the adult children to continue to enact the values of the family in their choice of work, friends, religious practice, and cultural style. In return for their support, they hope for loyalty from their children. Because young adults are especially prone to take advantage of their newfound freedom by trying to do things differently, parents are often forced to refine and clarify what they consider to be most important.

This can be a time of real deprivation for parents if they feel that their values are not being carried forward. They may have to turn to each other or to other adults for support. Others may help them to see their legacy represented in the underlying process of their children's independence or creativity rather than focusing only on how their behavior appears so discontinuous with the family from which they just emerged.

If adult children represent the theme of adventure and risk, parents represent the theme of safety. It is very anxiety-provoking for them to bear the necessary try-out activities and mistakes of their children. This anxiety often turns into judgmental exhortations to stop "thrashing around" or "wasting time." Grown children may respond to such criticisms with hurt feelings or lowered self-esteem. They may try to defend themselves by devaluing their parents' wisdom, isolating themselves from all contact so as to avoid criticism, or complying with anxiety-driven parental urging by prematurely committing themselves to a job or field of study about which they are ambivalent. Parents themselves may have recovered from a chaotic, even life-threatening young adulthood. They may find it unbearable to see their children seem to set their feet on the same road.

Family Dynamics

If the departing young adult is a first born, parents may then turn their attention more fully to younger siblings who remain at home. Those siblings may grow into the space vacated by the older, with mixed consequences. A formerly crowded living situation may be relieved if a sibling can move into the now-empty bedroom or even just expand more fully into a formerly shared bedroom. The older child may feel dispossessed, however, and that he or she has lost a home base, even if only as an idea. The older child may be very deliberate about returning at holidays or summer vacations, demanding full reinstatement and creating severe conflict with the now older and stronger usurper.

I have seen this happen in poor families as well. In one family, we discovered that an 8-year-old boy who was having difficulties had recently begun sleeping with his mother. His adult sister had returned home to recover from a horrendous crack episode and took back the couch he usually slept on, which had been hers as an adolescent.

Parents' Relationship

As children move on, parents may turn back to each other as a couple. If reviving the couple relationship is successful, it can fill in the loss of day-to-day parental activities and contact with children. If parental activities have been a welcome distraction from marital discord, these problems may reemerge with disruptive effect. If a marriage that was held together for the sake of child-rearing is now dissolved, young adults may feel that their loyalties must be divided and the continuity of their family is interrupted, leaving them to fend for themselves.

YOUNG ADULTHOOD FOR HETEROSEXUAL MEN

Many writers (Badinter, 1996; Gilmore, 1990) believe that heterosexual manhood is not something that occurs automatically as part of the ordinary development of life. They feel it must be achieved or proven, leaving masculine identity in doubt until it is. Early young adulthood is the era when such proofs are expected—by the young man himself, his family, and society at large.

Michael Kimmel deplores this pressure in *Manhood in America* (1996) when he says, "Every arena becomes a masculine testing ground" (p. 331). Heterosexual manhood is negatively defined in three main ways: A man is not a boy, not a woman, and not a homosexual. A deviation from these standards is strongly censured by shaming and exclusion from the straight male (and often female) community. The narrowness of adult heterosexual sex-role expectations may make men feel that they can never gain adult status without renouncing important parts of themselves (Kilmartin, 1994, p. 100).

Heterosexual manhood can be achieved by independent functioning (both in physical and emotional separation from family), producing displays of strength, risk taking, public drunkenness, willingness to fight other men, dating, and performing sexually with women. Anxiety about success in proving manhood can make young men especially homophobic. One further issue is that such expectations for men are so ubiquitous and unexamined in the straight male community that they are often not even conscious. They are just accepted as the nature of things. They are often not discussed among straight men for fear that such discussion itself implies a questioning that threatens one's manhood. For this reason, it is often useful clinically to explicitly discuss these expectations with young males and their families in therapy. It may be freeing for both to examine their assumptions and develop more positive definitions of straight male adulthood.

Not surprisingly, straight young adult men are the age group and sex that commits the largest number of violent crimes. Of persons arrested for murder and manslaughter, 90 per cent are males and 40 per cent are between the ages of 18 and 24. The largest group of murder victims is males from ages 20 to 24 (U.S. Bureau of the Census, 1996). Being responsible for such a hugely disproportionate share of violent crime, straight young men are understandably the most feared group in any society. Every culture must struggle with the problem of what to do with this highly energetic, highly dangerous group. One strategy is to imprison them, which our society does increasingly every year. Another strategy is to harness their idealism and daring by sending them to kill and be killed in war.

Silverstein and Rashbaum (1994) and Miller (1976) argue strongly that our separation-based theories of development underestimate how much these men "long for an affiliative mode of living" (Miller, 1976, p. 88). Silverstein and Rashbaum present many convincing cases of premature or too extreme separations between mothers and sons that leave sons with feelings of depression and longing that endure well into adult life. Such yearnings also may fuel young men's fantasies of an ideal love that will fill up their feelings of emptiness. Attachment to such fantasies may interfere with attachment to a real, possible woman, prolonging some of the unrealistic idealism of young adulthood inappropriately.

Silverstein and Rashbaum's clinical approach is first to interpret and acknowledge these sometimes as yet unnamed yearnings. They encourage appropriate delays in physical separations and advocate reconciliation between too distant mothers and sons. The title of their book is aimed at mothers in particular, encouraging them not to break with their sons of any age too soon or too extremely.

Straight young men thus face two particular dangers in this era. If they fail to meet society's definitions of courage and independence, they may end their young adulthood with a feeling of defeat and unworthiness. Such a lack of pride may put their marriage and middle adulthood under a cloud of shame and regret.

The opposite danger is that in a misguided effort to prove himself, the young man will prematurely cut himself off from necessary support, creating an emptiness that he may inappropriately expect a wife to fill. Such emptiness may also be expressed in cynicism, a rejection of any values other than immediate pleasures, and a loss of professional and relationship aspirations.

Al, a very successful 53-year-old businessman, called me to help him negotiate an estrangement between himself and his 23-year-old son, Charles. Charles and his 19-year-old sister, Meg, were the product of Al's first marriage to Betty, which had ended in divorce when Charles was 9. "Ended" is not quite accurate, however, because legal battles had endured between Al and Betty for twelve years after the divorce. Al felt that Betty had set Charles against him. He had made a successful second marriage when Charles was 12, and Charles got along reasonably well with Al's second wife.

Charles, a bright and able young man, had gradually stopped attending classes and dropped out of college late in his junior year. He was reluctant to discuss with me his reasons for doing so and certainly had not shared them with his father. Al had been paying his tuition and living expenses and wanted to be more completely informed. Charles

felt that from his early childhood, his father had unfairly high expectations of him and had been less demanding of, and more generous to, his younger sister. Although he appreciated that Al had consistently provided financial support, he felt that Al had been critical and intrusive and expressed far too much anger when Charles disappointed him or was not compliant. Al agreed that he had yelled too loudly and too often at Charles as a young child. He felt that he had realized that when Charles was still young, however, and had gone into extensive psychotherapy to get control of his temper. Charles had lived in a joint arrangement with both of his parents after their divorce. Al felt that his efforts at decreasing his reactivity had been successful and that their disputes during Charles's adolescence had been of normal intensity.

However, Al and Charles had had a very intense verbal argument during Charles' junior year of high school. Charles left Al's home that night, went to his mother's, and had not slept under Al's roof in the six years since. They had maintained a fairly cordial but not intimate relationship until Charles's junior year of college but then had broken bitterly over a car Al had bought for Charles.

Charles had paid for some of his own parking tickets but not all. Al, as the owner of record, had been responsible for the rest. After many arguments, phone messages, and unanswered letters, Al had repossessed the car and sold it, keeping the proceeds. Charles felt that he should at least have received the cash value of the car. Father and son were no longer speaking.

I first met with Al alone a number of times to gather his story of the cut-off and its place in the history and structure of the family. My first meeting with Charles included his mother, Betty, who explicitly and firmly endorsed the idea that she wanted Charles to have a relationship with his father even though she had some residue of resentment toward him.

I met with Al and Charles separately for some months. Al was paying for the sessions. Money was such a toxic issue between them, however, that I advised him to avoid offering any further financial support to his son. I also suggested to Charles that he avoid requesting any. I eventually began to work with each of them on letters to the other about the feelings that led to the estrangement. This was slow going. Their mutual resentment was modified, but the issue of the car remained explosive. Both were still quite reactive to the other's accusations. Charles didn't want to meet face to face with his father until his wishes about the proceeds of the car had been satisfied.

Eventually, a family circumstance eased this impasse. Al's father became very ill, convalesced for a while at Al's home, and then died. Al had a chance to rework some of his antagonistic relationship with his own father and accept some of his father's limitations. He was satisfied with his own behavior toward his father and resolved anew to overcome any limitations in himself with Charles.

Al and Charles met and spoke to each other at the funeral. Perhaps even more important, Betty attended the funeral also, and Charles saw her speaking with Al. The extended family reorganized itself without its patriarch. Charles had inherited some money in a trust from his grandfather, which made him less needful of his father's direct financial support. Al ascended to the position of the senior leader of the family. He was the executor of his father's estate and the trustee for Charles's inheritance. Seeing mother and father speaking together cordially may have made Charles feel that he did not have to choose between them. He may have been eager to know the amount and terms of his inheritance. He may have felt relieved that he now had money of his own (even if in trust) and no longer was dependent on his father. He may have seen that continuing to demand compensation for the car would only block his access to a far greater amount in the trust. At any rate, he now requested a meeting with his father.

Al had always wanted face-to-face sessions. He was now suspicious that Charles was dropping his condition only to gain access to the trust, but he agreed immediately to meet. Each developed agendas, nonprovocative strategies, and ways to avoid reacting to what they anticipated as the other's possible provocations. Al and Charles finally began coming to sessions together. These early sessions were tense and antagonistic. They began to follow their weekly sessions by going out to dinner together. For some months, their weekly session and the subsequent dinner were their only contact. Seeing the danger of their continued reactivity to each other, Al and Charles proposed never to discuss anything at dinner that they had been discussing in therapy. They kept this boundary flawlessly. After

some time, Charles introduced his serious girlfriend to Al at one of these dinners.

Over several months, Al and Charles eventually became less reactive to each other. Charles, with some ups and downs, began to work harder and be more successful at starting up a service business with excellent prospects. Al was an interested advisor but not an investor in it. Eventually, Charles began to visit Al's home for holiday parties and even to sleep over there for the first time since high school. Charles's mother even attended some gatherings at Al's house, and Charles saw them talking together. Two items could still not be discussed fully: whether or not Charles intended to complete his undergraduate degree and the disposition of money from the sale of the car which Al had repossessed. Eventually, even the first of these could be approached, and Charles began to investigate alternatives for completion of his schooling.

This case illustrates characteristic conflicts for each generation. For Charles, the issues of divided loyalties between his father and his mother, his dependency versus his wish to demonstrate his independence through defiance and distancing, his wish to please his father and meet his expectations of him versus his wish to develop self-respect and not be so dependent on his father's approval were all of particular importance.

In the parental generation, Al was struggling with the conflict of wanting to help his child and protect him from frustration versus his wish for Charles to be independent. He had to heal his own conflict with Charles's mother. He had to also resolve some of his own unfulfilled wishes to be approved by his own father. Betty had to continue supporting the father-son relationship, and eventually, she and Al even moved to heal their own antagonisms.

This case was also characteristic in that a lot of the recovery took place in real time; that is, it took place over years and took advantage of maturational changes in both Charles and his parents. It was also characteristic in that the outcome was incomplete. Certain topics were still too explosive for discussion. Relationships between parents and children are not usually fully resolved in young adulthood; nor should we expect them to be.

Charles's dropping out of college could be seen as evidence of some difficulty in traversing his young adulthood. A good part of Charles's ability to become more independent was his renunciation of wishes for revenge on his father and his developing neutrality and emotional distance from his parents' acrimonious divorce. Al's success as the parent of a young adult also required him to give up some of his personal hopes for his son without giving up on him, to help him just enough but not too much, and to focus on the relationship rather then the right or wrongness of Charles's path. This permitted him to draw closer without abandoning his parental standards. Al found a parental role in Charles's adult life as family holiday maker (now even inviting Charles's mother) and business advisor without supplying the direct financial support that he felt had been excessive in the past. Coaching Al and Charles to abandon their vengefulness, clarify their desires, and control their reactivity was still necessary to heal the relationship.

YOUNG ADULTHOOD FOR HETEROSEXUAL WOMEN

Women's lives have been lived more "in relationship" than men's at every stage. For many years, women married out of one household and into another. In the last few decades, however, middle- and upper-class women have experienced a major change. They, like men, often leave home and live alone before marrying. For this reason, young adulthood for these women can be the era of their lives that is least centered on relationships.

Young adult women are not expected to be quite as independent and separate as men, however. They are also not expected to prove their adult gender identity in quite the same way. They are permitted and expected to maintain relatedness. However, they also are more subject to a feeling of continued obligation to family and friends. Society does not expect them to be self-involved, so they receive much more pressure than men to set aside their needs and give service to others. When they can afford it, young women attempt to create a relatively self-involved period in which to develop their skills and their knowledge of themselves.

Kerr (1994) distills from the biographies of eminent women some common characteristics that enabled them to succeed, including the opportunity to have time alone, the chance to be connected to others without losing "separateness," and the ability to know their own feelings. I have encountered many women in midlife who are quite willingly involved in a network of relationships to family of origin, family of procreation, friends, and career. These highly related women look back with relish, however, to a period in young adulthood when they had fewer commitments. During such a period, they may have traveled, had lovers, worked hard, or sowed wild oats. They generally felt free to enact or postpone relationships. Some women who missed such a period say regretfully, "I never lived alone" or "I never did anything just for myself." They wonder whether their adult life might have started at a higher level if they had had a period of self-determination, when they were not so set about by obligations to others.

For women who go to college, it is often assumed by their own families that they will not marry as undergraduates. For professional women taking higher degrees, it is increasingly expected that they will delay marriage even longer. Coontz (1992) contends that for many women, marriage is no longer the "transition to adulthood" it once was. She notes, "The average age for marriage has risen by six years since 1950. More than three-quarters of today's 18-to-24-year-old men and women have never married" (p. 181).

During this era, aspiring professional women often anticipate that they can "have it all," by using a strategy of getting their careers going first and adding a husband and children later. They don't expect to have to choose between work and family. Some women who are currently middle-aged look back at their similar expectations when they were young adults and now consider them naive.

McKenna (1997) feels that young women must hide from themselves the fact that in entering the world of professional work, they are accepting rules created by a male culture. Some may energetically disidentify with the unremunerated work (child care, housework, friendship, partnering) their mothers did. Their mothers may strongly support this, wanting their daughters to have more alternatives than were available to them. Buying into male devaluing of unremunerated domestic work has a price in later life cycle stages for both women and men, but neither sex experiences it as much of a conflict in young adulthood (McKenna, 1997). It is consistent with the ascetic, work-oriented, immortal grandiosity of young adulthood.

YOUNG ADULTHOOD FOR GAY MEN

Most gay men report having had some strong feeling of being gay in early adolescence (Merla, 1996). Looking back, many see signs that occurred even earlier in childhood, but they didn't acquire the organizing concept of a gay identity until adolescence. Such youths often feel quite isolated, both from other gay friends and from a larger gay community, but even if they know that they are gay, few come out as adolescents (Rotheram-Borus, 1995).

Coming out is a many-stage process (Chandler, 1997, p. 126) that continues throughout life, but young adulthood is the time when it is most often begun. While young adulthood holds many challenges for gay men, it may also come as a relief, particularly for those who wish to enact their gay identity at last. They have the freedom to leave home, find a community in which being gay is more accepted, and actively seek the company of other gay men. They are not as concerned with proving their masculinity in the same way as straight men, so they commit less violent crime.

Gay young adults face an extra readjustment in their relationships with their families of origin if they are coming out to them for the first time. They often report having felt like outsiders to their families for some time. It may be a relief from such estrangement to be more authentic and open. Unfortunately, however, they often confront denial, anger, criticism, or rejection from at least some family members. While their families may mellow with time, this can be a period of feeling cut off from one's family of origin with a deep loss of continuity and support.

Some gay men turn toward householding identities in later young adulthood, leading highly related lives with partners and friends. Others stay single well into their middle adulthood. They may live the more work- and self-focused lives of artists, retaining their intense concentration on their aspirations rather than being caught up in the divided lives of householders. A radical interruption in this style is demonstrated by the legions of gay men who have voluntarily nursed their lovers, friends, and even strangers through the throes of HIV-AIDS related illnesses. Far fewer straight men have done such work for their sick wives or close male friends, especially when they could get women to do it.

David was a 23-year-old Master's candidate in graduate school who considered himself a traditional Jew. His parents were not as observant themselves, although they had become more so over the years. His sexual fantasies were almost exclusively about other men. He definitely did not want to be gay, however. Homosexuality was proscribed by his religious beliefs, but this was not his primary resistance to the idea. He had a strongly held ideal to be married to a woman and have a family with her.

During his therapy, he struggled with this contradiction between his ideals and his actual desires. He tried several relationships with attractive women, but these all fizzled out. He entertained in fantasy and rejected the following compromise life-styles: a celibate, solitary life; a marriage to a woman in which they had intercourse for reproductive purposes but were otherwise celibate; a gay marriage in which he and his partner adopted children; a single, celibate life in which he adopted children alone; joining a gay synagogue to attempt to reconcile his sexual desires with his religious morality.

He was adamant about feeling the urge but not wanting to have gay sex, about wanting to be straight but not feeling any urges to have straight sex, and wanting (and deeply enjoying) his practice of traditional Judaism. The incompatibility of these conflicting wishes and life plans left him in despair.

One night, in an especially hopeless mood, he impulsively took a large amount of Tylenol, attempting to reach what he considered to be a lethal dose. After a few hours, he reconsidered and presented himself at a hospital's psychiatric emergency room. He was hospitalized as a medical case but seen by a liaison psychiatrist. This suicide attempt was shocking and unexpected by both of us. David was unharmed physically. He eventually made a full recovery, but the dose was a dangerous one. During this period, I visited him daily in the hospital for a week.

This sobering event had a number of effects. David was very happy that he had not died or harmed himself. During his week in the hospital, he developed the conviction that whatever resolution he made of the contradictions that tortured him, that resolution was going to include his being alive.

Before his suicide attempt, we had discussed David's telling his parents of his concern that he might be gay. He was unwilling to broach the subject with them. After the attempt, we agreed that it was necessary to tell them why he was feeling so bad, but he still recoiled from discussing his gayness. He felt that discussing it would make it too real and that he might have to profess it with a degree of certainty and specificity that he did not feel. He also felt ashamed of it and especially did not want to expose himself to his own idea of his parents' moral judgment, even though they did not have a history of being especially judgmental. After his suicide attempt, however, it seemed that some discussion of his motives was unavoidable. On his posthospital visit home, he did tell them that he felt he might be gay and did not want to be. At the same time, he told them that he wasn't ready to discuss the subject further. They were surprised but accepting and indicated an openness to further discussion if he wanted it. He was comfortable with the limits of his disclosure, and their nonintrusive acceptance of him was a relief to him. He told a very few close friends about his suicide attempt and, for the first time, about his conflicts about being gay. He was much more willing to discuss the issues of gayness with them and did so repeatedly and at some length. He finished his school year successfully, graduated, found a job and planned an adventurous summer vacation. He wanted to live in Israel and found a job there. His leaving the country for summer travel and subsequent work meant an end to his therapy with me. All

his irreconcilable contradictions were still in place, but he was no longer so hopeless.

This case illustrates the difficulty of accepting a socially disapproved identity, especially when that disapproval is internalized. In this case, David's family ideals were a way of maintaining continuity with his family of origin and being consistent with religious beliefs that dictate a great deal about how everyday life should be led. It was hardly a simple matter to accept a sexual identity that was inconsistent with these ideals.

His unexpected, impulsive suicide attempt may be characteristic for gay young men. Several studies find that incidence of suicide attempts is much higher for gay young adults than for the general population (Remafedi, Farrow & Deisher, 1991; Schneider, Farberow & Kruks, 1989). (Remafedi, 1995) also surmises that suicide attempts by gays may not always be preceded by signs of clinical depression.

YOUNG ADULTHOOD FOR LESBIANS

Young lesbians also do not usually come out until young adulthood. They tend to bond earlier into stable couples than gay men do. Because their identity is then partially expressed as a member of a partnership, they want to present themselves as couples to their families (just as married heterosexuals do). Their appearing as a couple makes their homosexuality much more difficult for their families to deny, however. They may wish to visit or attend family rituals with their partners, forcing themselves, their partners, and their families to decide how "out" they want to be. If the partner isn't welcome, the young adult has a hard choice, as does the family.

Families may expect their lesbian daughters to play conventional sex roles (e.g., being bridesmaids) at family rituals and may not recognize life cycle events in their daughter's life. Life markers such as a wedding or a baby shower involving a straight child may bring a family together. The same event for a lesbian daughter may drive the family apart (Slater & Mencher, 1991). As a result, lesbian life cycle events often pass without public family recognition.

Zitter (1987) contends that for lesbians, coming out to their mother poses a special problem. She cites the common idea that mothers expect to lose their sons to another woman but feel that their daughters will never replace them in the same way. When their lesbian daughters bond intimately and exclusively with another woman, however, mothers may feel especially bereft, perhaps even betrayed.

THE POOR GET POORER:
THE LAST TWO DECADES

When low-income African Americans reach young adulthood, they have the same needs as others to increase their personal authority and become more independent. But if the decrease in real wages over the last two decades has made it more difficult for middle-class workers to achieve financial self-sufficiency, the effect has been much more severe for lower-income groups. Income has increased for the upper classes and decreased for the lower ones. For instance, economist Edward Wolfe (1996) reports that between 1983 and 1989, "The top 20 percent of wealth holders received 99 percent of the total gain in marketable wealth, while the bottom 80 percent only got 1 percent." In addition, while labor force participation for young white men has remained the same, it has declined substantially for young black men (Wilson, 1987, p. 82).

Young Adulthood for Lower-Income
African American Men

Because men are still expected to provide financially for their families, not having employment opportunities has serious consequences for them. Entry-level jobs now much more often require a high school diploma. It is much more difficult for lower-income young men, who are less likely to graduate from high school than poor women, to get the jobs that would make them good marriage prospects.

Young men of any race are expected to "prove their manhood" in the young adult era. They are especially vulnerable to humiliation. A great deal

is expected of them, but their power is still very low. Because their job prospects are so poor, it is almost impossible for poor African American men to see young adulthood as a period of preparation for lucrative or even stable employment.

Lower-income young men in this life cycle stage still have the characteristics of young men in general, however. Their idealism makes them proud to identify with those who speak truth to power. These may be "gangsta" rappers, religious leaders, or radical social critics. They may have the same grandiose aspirations and wish to prove themselves as other young men. These sometimes take the form of wanting to exit from poverty through success in professional sports, in which lower-income African American males have been so spectacularly successful. However, in a 1991 article in *Sports Illustrated,* Henry Louis Gates cautions that in all of the United States, only 1,500 African American men are able to support themselves as professional athletes. There are ten times as many African American doctors and ten times as many African American lawyers.

Lower-income young men yearn for and respond to mentors, just as all young adults do. Finding a mentor who can offer a realistic and safe exit from poverty may be a challenge, however. The mentor may himself be a criminal who may use the youth's idealism to make crime seem more justifiable.

The risk of failure and the potential loss of dignity are major factors in the lives of poor young African American men. They may be especially sensitive to moments of disrespect, real or perceived. In such moments, they may feel compelled to make or respond to challenges that expose them to grave physical danger (Canada, 1995). This culture, a result of racism and economic deprivation, makes lower-income young men especially vulnerable to being drawn into violent crime. Young adulthood is the era when more African American men die by accident or violence than in any other decade of their life cycle. African American men age 20 to 24 account for 62 percent of all murder victims of the same age. This is especially striking because they account for only 10 percent of the general population (U.S. Bureau of the Census, 1996).

Because it is so expensive to support oneself in a separate domicile, young men often stay with family in early young adulthood. Lower income African American mothers raise their young boys and girls with equal attentiveness. As their children reach adolescence, however, they sometimes feel that it is harder to sustain their intimate connection with their sons than their daughters. By young adulthood, mothers may feel that they have lost their sons to the world of unruly, unreliable men. If problems arise in the relationship, it is usually because mother and son are underconnected, not overinvolved. In such cases, it is hard to see separation as the primary developmental task of the era. The young man's success is profoundly dependent on his family's support. It is a difficult and subtle task to endorse the young man's fierce pride and strength while insisting that he remain responsive and responsible to the family group. If young men have a job or are in school, they can gain adult status, be regarded respectfully, and be looked to for advice and, eventually, leadership. If they remain unschooled and unemployed, however, they will not be seen as making a contribution to the family. They may be encouraged and tolerated for a while but eventually will receive censure. All young men are proud, so they may show defiance or isolate themselves. Sometimes, they will leave precipitously, staying with another part of the extended family in which there is less authority conflict. For any unemployed young male, this is always an uneasy arrangement. If their activities disrupt the household, they are most likely to be angrily ejected, sometimes to the streets, only to be readmitted in a deteriorated condition.

This group presents a difficult challenge for the clinician because these young men rarely present themselves for therapy as individuals or as parts of families. Their influences on the parts of the family that do come to the clinic must often be discovered by the clinician, sometimes in the face of the family's resistance. An attempt to draw the young men in or at least consider them is usually rewarding and necessary, however, both to their families and themselves.

Young Adulthood for Lower-Income African American Women

If they have not already had children as adolescents, most lower-income African American women have and raise children in this life cycle phase. Because they do not have money to pursue schooling and find it hard to imagine that their socioeconomic opportunities will improve (either by additional schooling or marriage), there is little reason to delay childbearing (Ludtke, 1997). They may even feel that it is dangerous to delay having children (Geronimus, 1992). Geronimus interviewed young women of various races and economic backgrounds about the age at which they felt women should be finished having babies. Poor African American women suggested the earliest cut-off time (age 25 to 30) to stop having children. Geronimus felt that this desire for early timing of birth was due to a number of factors, among them the shorter life expectancy and greater risk of bad health for poor people. She further reasoned that since lower-income African American women often expect to raise their children in partnership with their mothers, they want to have them while the grandmothers are still young enough to be counted on.

Poor young African American women may still have dreams that include a perfect love, but they often don't expect to marry or create a nuclear family. Marriage is seen as creating little advantage for a female and may cause more trouble than it is worth. Williams (1991) interviewed thirty young mothers and wrote, "[They do not] view themselves as having ruined their lives, and they see themselves… as capable of rearing children without marriage or commitment from the father. Few of them expect to marry and nearly all want at least one other child" (p. 51).

While young mothers feel that having and raising children is the most meaningful and promising part of their difficult lives, it does have its costs (see Chapter 24). It makes exit from poverty more difficult and endangers the children who are born into such hard circumstances.

Another cost is that it increases the mother's risk of depression. Depression is a special risk for women as a group, but a particular one for poor young adult women (Brown & Harris, 1978). Another cost of having babies during young adulthood is that these young mothers never have the solitude that can give young women a feeling of self-determination or doing something to develop or cultivate their selves. Their lives are determined by the needs of others without relief. They may understandably become resentful, grudging, or burned out.

Young adult mothers have a more clearly defined role in their extended families (as caregivers to their children) than do jobless young men. As it is more clearly defined, it is also more constricting. They may not be expected to produce cash for the family, but to the extent that they receive help in raising their children, they are (understandably) expected to return such service to others in the family when it is needed. By entering this economy of mutual obligation, they gain adult status and respect. A consequence, however, is that they are rarely free to pursue solitary studies that would permit an exit from poverty and financial self-sufficiency. Separation or even self-sufficiency is not a realistic or even desirable goal for young adult mothers. Without sharing domiciles and child care with their extended family, their lives are simply not viable.

The way in which the extended family is involved in assisting the young adult mother may take on different forms, creating different executive subsystems. Apfel and Seitz (1996) describe four such arrangements: In "parental replacement," grandmother takes on total responsibility for the daughter's child. A "supported primary parent" is a mother who has primary full-time responsibility for child care but is supported by other family members. A grandmother who actively mentors her daughter in parenting by demonstration and in moments of co-parenting views her daughter as an "apprentice mother." The fourth arrangement is "parental supplement," in which several female family members share care of the children.

These arrangements are not mutually exclusive and may vary according to the changing needs of the children, mother, or other caregivers. Watts-Jones (1997) details a method of inquiry that augments the conventional genogram to discover the supportive networks of kin and non-kin characteristic of such families. In a clinical situation, inquiry into such arrangements may be useful in determining the welfare of the family and whether mother is moving toward contributing fully to her own children and the extended family.

Because of the variety and changing nature of these family structures, discovering the executive subsystem is not always a straightforward task. A very useful question for young adult mothers is, "Who helps you?" The answer begins to reveal whom she can or must count on. A follow-up question that addresses the emotional climate of this network is, "Who gets to express their opinion on how you are raising your kids?" This group may include some additional individuals who do not supply care directly, but affect the morale of the mother with their observations.

CONCLUSION

Young adulthood poses a particular challenge for the systems-oriented clinician. It is the era that pulls most to see the individual as an entity separate from societal and family influences. Our separation-based theories of development and our societal expectations about individualism and self-reliance have added to this difficulty. A balanced view of how relatedness continues through this era should help us to understand the conflicts with which our clients struggle at every level of the system.

REFERENCES

Apfel, N., & Seitz, V. (1996), African-American adolescent mothers, their families and their daughters: A longitudinal perspective over twelve years. In B. J. Leadbeater and N. Way (Eds.), *Urban girls:* *Resisting stereotypes, creating identities.* New York: New York University Press.

Badinter, E. (1996). *XY: On masculine identity.* New York: Columbia University Press.

Benjamin. J. (1988). *The bonds of love: Psychoanalysis, feminism, and the problem of domination.* New York: Pantheon.

Bergman, S. (1991). Men's psychological development: A relational perspective. *Work in Progress,* No. 48. Wellesley, MA: Stone Center.

Bly, R. (1997). *The sibling society.* New York: Vintage.

Bowen, M. (1978). *Family therapy in clinical practice.* New York: Jason Aronson.

Brown, G., & Harris, T. (1978). Social origins of depression: A study of psychiatric disorder in women. New York: Free Press.

Canada, G. (1995). *Fist, stick, knife, gun: A personal history of violence in America.* Boston: Beacon.

Chandler, K. (1997). *Passages of pride: True stories of lesbian and gay teenagers.* Los Angeles: Alyson.

Coontz, S. (1992). *The way we never were: American families and the nostalgia trap.* New York: Basic.

Gates, H. L. (1991, August 19). Delusions of grandeur. *Sports Illustrated,* 78.

Geronimus, A. T. (1992). The weathering hypothesis and the health of African American women and infants: Evidence and speculations. *Ethnicity and Disease, 2,* 202–221.

Gilligan, C. (1982). *In a different voice: Psychological theory and women's development.* Cambridge, MA: Harvard University Press.

Gilligan, C. (1991). Women's psychological development: Implications for psychotherapy. (p. 24) In C. Gilligan, A. Rogers, & D. Tilman (Eds.), *Women, girls and psychotherapy: Reframing resistance.* New York: Haworth.

Gilmore, D. (1990). *Manhood in the making: Cultural concepts of masculinity.* New Haven: Yale University Press.

Haddock, R. (1996). The rocky road to adulthood. *American Demographics, 18*(5) 26–56.

Haley, J. (1980). *Leaving home: The therapy of disturbed young people.* New York: McGraw-Hill.

Kerr, B. (1994). *Smart girls: A new psychology of girls, women and giftedness* (Rev. ed.). Scottsdale, AZ: Gifted Psychology Press.

Kilmartin, C. (1994). *The masculine self.* New York: Macmillan.

Kimmel, M. (1996). *Manhood in America.* New York: Free Press.

Ludtke, M. (1997). *On our own: Unmarried motherhood in America.* New York: Random House.

McKenna, E. (1997). *When work doesn't work anymore.* New York: Delacorte.

Merla, P. (1996). *Boys like us: gay writers tell their coming out stories.* New York: Avon.

Miller, J. B. (1976). *Toward a new psychology of women.* Boston: Beacon.

Mogelonsky, M. (1996). The rocky road to adulthood. *American Demographics, 18*(5) 26–56.

Remafedi, G. (1995). Quoted in Chandler, K. (1997). *Passages of pride* (p. 201). Los Angeles: Alyson.

Remafedi, G., Farrow, J., & Deisher, R. (1991). Risk factors for attempted suicide in gay and bisexual youth. *Pediatrics, 87*(6), 869–875.

Rotheram-Borus. M. J. (1997). Quoted in Chandler, K. (1997). *Passages of pride* (p. 130). Los Angeles: Alyson.

Schneider, S., Farberow, N., & Kruks, G. (1989). Suicidal behavior in adolescent and young adult gay men. *Suicide and Life-Threatening Behavior, 19*(4), 381–394.

Silverstein, O., & Rashbaum, B. (1994). *The courage to raise good men.* New York: Penguin.

Slater, S., & Mencher, J. (1991). The lesbian family life cycle: A contextual approach. *American Journal of Orthopsychiatry, 2*(3), 372–382.

Stierlin, H. (1977). *Psychoanalysis and family therapy.* New York: Jason Aronson.

Sum, A., Togg, N., & Taggert, R. (1996). The economics of despair. *American Prospect.* 27, 83–84. Quoted in S. Coontz, (1997), *The way we really are: Coming to terms with America's changing families.* New York: Basic.

U.S. Bureau of the Census (1996). *Statistical abstract of the United States.* (116th ed.) (p. 101). Washington, DC.

Watts-Jones, D. (1997) Toward an African American genogram. *Family Process, 36,* 375–383.

Williams, C. W. (1991). *Black teenage mothers: Pregnancy and childrearing from their perspective.* Lexington, MA: Lexington Books.

Wilson, W. J. (1987). *The truly disadvantaged: The inner city, the underclass, and public policy.* Chicago: University of Chicago Press.

Wolfe, E. N. (1996). *Top heavy: A study of the increasing inequality of wealth in America.* New York: The Twentieth Century Fund. Quoted in S. Coontz, (1997), *The way we really are: Coming to terms with America's changing families.* New York: Basic.

Zitter, S. (1987) *Coming out to Mom: Theoretical aspects of the mother-daughter process* (pp. 177–194). In Boston Lesbian Psychologies Collective (Eds.), *Lesbian psychologies: Explorations and challenges.* Urbana: University of Illinois Press.

CHAPTER 14

BECOMING A COUPLE

MONICA McGOLDRICK

MARRIAGE IN OUR TIMES

The meaning of marriage in our time is profoundly different from its meaning throughout human history, when it was tightly embedded in the economic and social fabric of society. The changing role of women and the increasing mobility of our culture, along with longevity and the dramatic effects of widely available contraceptives, are forcing us to redefine marriage.

The place of marriage in the life cycle has also been changing dramatically. Men and women are having sex earlier but marrying later than ever before. An ever increasing proportion are living together before marriage or even living with several partners before deciding to marry. Indeed, more than half of all marriages now follow cohabitation (Steinhauer, 1995). Marriage used to be the major marker of transition to the adult world, because it symbolized the transition to parenthood; now it often reflects a greater continuity with the phase of young adulthood or even adolescence, since childbearing, especially for the middle and upper classes, is increasingly postponed for a number of years after marriage.

Marriage symbolizes a change in status among all family members and generations and requires that the couple negotiate new relationships as a twosome with many other subsystems: parents, siblings, grandparents, nieces and nephews, and friends (McGoldrick, 1995). In fact, the status changes of marriage may not be fully appreciated by the family until the next phase. It is this transition to parenthood that confronts couples more sharply with the problems of traditional sex roles

and of multigenerational patterns. Women are wanting their own careers and are increasingly resistant to having the primary household and child care responsibilities and to having husbands who are absent from family life. But change comes very slowly.

In most societies, to talk of the choice to marry or not would be almost as relevant as to talk of the choice to grow old or not; it has been considered the only route to full adult status. To marry has been simply part of the "natural" progression through life, part of the inevitable, unless catastrophe intervened. Only recently has our society been modifying its norms on this, as more members of the population do not fit into the traditional patterns and even raise questions about their viability.

Of all dilemmas of the life cycle, the existential dilemma of coupling is probably the greatest. Marriage is the the only family relationship that we swear is forever and the only one that we swear is exclusive; yet it is the one relationship that is least likely to be either exclusive or forever. Just as society has defined "family" as a legally married heterosexual couple with children, "couple" has meant a once-married heterosexual couple in which the man is generally taller, older, smarter, with more income generating power, and in charge of supporting his wife and any children they may have, while the woman was supposed to be physically attractive and ever supportive of her husband in the fulfillment of his dreams while taking care of all other family members, including their children, her parents, his parents, and anyone else in the family who became ill or needed help. All who did not fit into this ideal were judged by its standard and generally found wanting. Yet couples come in many varieties: gay and straight; married and unmarried; tall, ambitious wives and short, nurturing, homebody husbands. The ideal itself costs us all a tremendous amount in terms of our ability to be ourselves and find harmony in our relationships with each other and support the tasks of family life.

A major problem in coupling is that patriarchal rules of male domination in marriage get obfuscated and mystified by the mythology of coupling as a love story of two equals. The patriarchal courtship ideal of Cinderella and Prince Charming gets confused with the ideal of a partnership between two lovers whose souls and bodies will mingle, such that they will think and act as one until death does them part. The contradiction in these two propositions makes marriage a problem for both men and women, but especially for woman, a fact that has only very recently begun to come to our national and international consciousness. Indeed Carolyn Heilbrun (1988) has asked: "Was marriage always in such danger of becoming unappealing to women that the whole society had to contrive to keep the fiction of its desirability alive and intact?" Women increasingly view *traditional* marriage as a bad bargain.

Couple relationships have many dimensions: (Almeida, Woods, Messineo, & Font, 1998):

- Economic.
- Emotional: communication, intimacy, dependence, and so on.
- Power arrangements: from male privilege dominance to partnership and equity.
- Physical power: the continuum from intimidation, abuse, and threats to the belief in the sanctity of each individual.
- Boundaries around the couple in relation to all other connections: to friends, extended family, work, children, and religion. Boundaries may be tight and controlled by one partner or flexible in each area.
- Sexuality: the continuum from sexual intimacy to sexual objectification to rape and exploitation.
- Child Rearing: shared or viewed as women's responsibility.

- Chores and leisure activities: home care, food, priorities for vacation and leisure time.

The complexity of these dimensions should indicate how difficult this life cycle transition is. Abuse may be a part of any these dimensions of a couple's relationship (Almeida, Woods, Messineo, & Font, 1998). However, along with the transition to parenthood, which it has long symbolized, it is seen as the easiest and most joyous. Our society skews us toward a romanticized view of this transition, which adds greatly to its difficulty, since everyone—from the couple to the family and friends—wants to see only the happiness of the transition. The only dimensions that get privileged in the dominant ideology are the emotional and sexual dimensions, and the issues of power even in those dimensions is subtly kept invisible (Almeida et al., 1998). The problems that come with forming a marriage are thus obscured and pushed underground, only to intensify and surface later on.

Furthermore, as Michael Lerner has pointed out (1995), finding a partner, which always used to be a community matter, has become the private problem of individual singles, conducted within a capitalist orientation to coupling, which encourages us to see other people in terms of what they can do to satisfy our needs:

> In the past, relationships were embedded in larger communities of meaning and purpose. The relationship was not about itself, but about some larger shared goal. But today, with those communities of meaning in decline, people increasingly look to their primary sexual relationship to become a compensation for the meaninglessness surrounding them. Yet judged against such standards, very few relationships feel adequate (p. 10).

Marriage, more than any other life transition, is viewed as the solution to life's problems such as loneliness, work/career uncertainty, or extended family difficulties. The wedding itself is seen as terminating a process, though it does not. "And they lived happily ever after" is the myth. Marriage requires that two people renegotiate a great many issues they have previously defined individually or in their families of origin, such as when and how to eat, sleep, talk, have sex, fight, work, and relax. The power aspects of how these issues get negotiated must be kept visible, since the power inequities in most heterosexual couples are highly likely to be obscured by the couple, the extended family, and others in the society (Almeida et al., 1998; Carter, 1996). The couple must decide about vacations, for example, and how to use space, time, and money. Decisions must be made about which family traditions and rituals to retain and which ones partners will develop for themselves. Partners will also have to renegotiate relationships with parents, siblings, friends, extended family, and co-workers in view of the new marriage. It is extremely important that women not be pressured to curtail these relationships, because it isolates them and leaves them vulnerable to abuse in the marriage (Chapter 28; see also Almeida et al., 1998).

The joke that there are six in the marital bed is really an understatement. It has been said that what distinguishes human beings from all other animals is the fact of having in-laws. In the animal kingdom, mating involves only the two partners, who usually mature, separate from their families, and mate on their own. For humans, it is the joining of two enormously complex systems. Some say that if couples could fully appreciate the emotional complexity of negotiating marriage right at the start, they might not dare to undertake the proposition.

For more than a generation, Jessie Bernard raised our consciousness about the fact that marriage produces such profound discontinuities in the lives of women as to constitute a genuine health hazard (Bernard, 1982). In spite of the widespread cultural stereotypes that marriage is something men should dread and fear, all the research supports the opposite—that in every way marriage improves men's mental health while in almost every way, mentally, physically, and even in crime statistics, single women are healthier than married women (Apter, 1985). According to a study by Linda Waite, men appear to benefit from marriage on a great many dimensions. Married men are healthier, have more satisfying sex lives, tend to make more money, and have lower rates of drug,

alcohol abuse, and depression than unmarried men (Steinhauer, 1995). Studies indicate that women get fewer tangible benefits from marriage. They often suffer a wage loss, especially after the birth of children, and tend to be burdened with more housework, and their sexual satisfaction does not appear to improve with marriage (Steinhauer, 1995). Contrary to the popular stereotypes of the frustrated old maid and the free, unencumbered bachelor life, spinsters do very well and bachelors do very poorly (Gurin et al., 1980, p. 42). And statistically, the more education a woman has and the better her income, the less likely she is to marry. The reverse is true for men.

Couples are marrying later and postponing childbearing longer than a generation ago. In 1970, the average age of marriage was 21 for women and 23 for men. Now it is 24 for women and over 26 for men.

More and more couples are passing through a stage of living with one or several partners before marriage, making the transition to marriage much less of a turning point in the family life cycle than it was in the past. Obviously, the meaning of a wedding changes when a couple has been living together for several years and participating jointly in extended-family experiences. Nevertheless, even after a couple has been living together for several years, the transition to marriage can still create great turmoil, especially if the partners have not dealt with their extended family as a couple during the period of living together. Indeed, the parents may have been hoping that the couple would break up and now have to acknowledge the centrality of the relationship for their child. It places no small stress on a family to open itself to an outsider who is now an official member of its inner circle. Frequently, no new member has been added to the system for many years. The challenge of this change can affect a family's style profoundly; the tendency of members to polarize and see villains and victims under the stress of these changes can be very strong.

In any case, there seems to be a timing and a pattern to this phase. Those who marry early often have more difficulty adjusting to its tasks. Women who marry before age 20 (about 25 percent of women) are twice as likely to divorce as those who marry in their twenties. On the other hand, those who marry after 30 (about 20 percent of women) are less likely to divorce, but if they do, they do so sooner than those who marry earlier. Thus it appears that in our culture there is a timing for coupling, and while it seems to be getting later, it appears overall that it is better to marry later rather than sooner. Those who fall too far out of the normative range on either end may have more trouble making the transition. Such people are often responding to family stresses that make the process of coupling more difficult to achieve. In addition to cultural or class issues, which may make earlier marriage a norm among certain cultural groups, such as Latinos or working-class families, those who marry early may be running away from their families of origin or seeking a family they never had. They may leave home by fusing with a mate in an attempt to gain strength from each other. They may have more difficulties later on as a result of their failure to develop an independent identity first. Women who marry late are frequently responding to a conflict between marriage and career and their ambivalence about losing their independence and identity in marriage. An increasing number of men also seem to be avoiding commitment. Some who marry late may also have seen a negative image of marriage at home. They may have been enmeshed in their families and have trouble leaving home, forming outside relationships or developing a secure work situation.

In spite of the trend toward delaying both marriage and pregnancy, most people do marry and have children before age 30. Naturally, those who have children shortly after marriage have relatively little time to adjust to the status changes of marriage and its accompanying stresses before moving on. What is amazing, considering the long-range implications of marriage, is that so many couples spend so little time thinking about the decision. Indeed a number of communities and churches in the United States have been trying to prevent future divorce by requiring premarital counseling courses, a waiting period before marriage, or by providing older couples as mentors for new couples (Marano, 1997). Furthermore, new laws offering two marital options, one harder to dissolve than the the law allows while ostensibly offering a greater level of choice to couples, is in fact part of a backlash movement that pressures couples to accept marital bonds that take us back to an era when a woman could not get divorced unless she could prove adultery.

This concern is limited to heterosexual couples, as gays and lesbians are still denied federal and most religious recognition of their relationships (Glaser, 1996). No state currently allows same sex marriages, although Hawaii may soon be the first to allow them (Purdum, 1996). Interracial marriages were a serious crime in many states until thirty years ago.

It seems that the timing of marital decisions is often influenced by events in the extended family, although most couples are unaware of the correlation of these events and the process that underlies their decision to marry. People often seem to meet spouses or make the decision to marry shortly after the retirement, illness, move, or even untimely death of a parent or after other traumatic family loss. The sense of loss or aloneness can be a strong contributing factor in the desire to build a close relationship. This may blind a person to the aspects of a prospective spouse that do not fit the idealized picture that the other will complete him or her and make life worthwhile. This desire for completion is likely to lead to difficulty accepting the spouse's differentness, which will necessarily show itself in the course of the relationship. As one woman put it,

> My husband and I have always been afraid of the stranger in each other. We keep wanting to believe that the other thought the same as we thought they were thinking, which could never be. We just couldn't appreciate that here was a new and different person, with his or her own thoughts and feelings, who would make life more interesting.

FUSION AND INTIMACY

The basic dilemma in coupling is the confusion of intimacy with fusion. There is a profound difference between forming an intimate relationship and using a couple relationship to complete one's self. Poets have long talked about the difference. Rilke (1954) writes:

Love is at first not anything that means merging, giving over, and uniting with another (for what would a union be of something unclarified and unfinished, still subordinate); it is a high inducement to the individual to ripen…it is a great exacting claim. (p. 54)

There are, of course, sex differences in the way fusion is experienced, since women have traditionally been raised to consider "losing themselves" in a relationship to be normal, and men have been raised to see intimacy as "unmanly." Thus, men more often express fusion by maintaining a pseudo-differentiated distant position in relationships or by possessive demands that their partner conform to their wishes, and women express fusion giving up themselves, their dreams, and their opinions to the relationship.

Recent research comparing heterosexual, lesbian, and gay couples is expanding our understanding of notions of closeness and intimacy in couple relationships. Whereas much of the family therapy literature and research confused notions of closeness, enmeshment, and fusion, which were polarized against differentiation, autonomy, disengagement, and distance, Green, Bettinger and Zacks (1996) offered a clarification of categories that might be useful for understanding intimate coupling partnerships:

- Closeness–caregiving (made up of warmth, time together, nurturance, physical intimacy, and consistency).
- Openness of communication (made up of openness, self-disclosure, and the ability to face conflict and differences without avoidance).
- Lack of intrusiveness (made up of lack of separation anxiety; respecting the other's need for privacy and time alone; lack of possessiveness and jealousy; lack of emotional overreactivity to the other's life problems; lack of mindreading of the other; lack of thinking one knows the other's wishes better than she or he does;

lack of aggressive criticism, hurtful attacks, or attempts to diminish the other, lack of attempt to dominate the other in disagreements.

They found that, contrary to stereotypes that have portrayed lesbian couples as tending toward fusion and gay couples as disengaged, both lesbian and gay couples tend to have more intimate, cohesive relationships than do heterosexual couples—lesbians the most so. Gottman found that the the expression of negativity appears as necessary as positivity in a marriage, though successful relationships need to have the positivity outweigh the negativity in expression (Carstensen, Gottman, & Levenson, 1995; Gottman, 1993). Other research has shown that money and status tend to define relationships of heterosexual couples along power lines. That is, the partner who makes more money and has more status (usually the man) tends to control the relationship decisions, right down to where they will go on vacation and who will clean the toilet. Only lesbian couples seem free to develop their roles and relationships on a basis other than money, power, and status (Blumstein & Schwartz, 1983).

Frequently, others expect a couple to fuse and view the wife as somehow joined to the identity of her husband, thus increasing the difficulties for women in differentiating and maintaining their separate identities. For men, the fear of intimacy and the social expectations of his independence and of his wife's adaptiveness work together to inhibit his development of intimate relationships within which differences necessarily continue to exist. The implication of this is that much of couples therapy requires helping men to learn a new model of human development within which they can develop interdependence and interpersonal relationships and respect for their wives' separate self (see Chapter 2).

Bowen's (1978) theory elucidates the universal tendency to seek some degree of fusion with a partner as related to a person's incomplete differentiation from her or his family of origin. In other words, couples seek to complete themselves in each other to the degree that they have failed to resolve their relationships with their parents, which would free them to build new relationships based on each person's freedom to be himself or herself and to appreciate the other as he or she is. The process whereby people seek to enhance their self-esteem in marriage is based on denying their differentness from their spouse and can result in severe distortions in communication to maintain the myth of agreement (Satir, 1967).

During courtship, couples are usually most aware of the romantic aspects of their relationship. Marriage shifts the relationship from a private coupling to a formal joining of two families. Issues that the partners have not resolved with their own families will tend to be factors in marital choice and are very likely to interfere with establishing a workable marital balance.

It may be that much of the intensity of romantic love is determined by one's family values. From this perspective, Romeo and Juliet might have felt intensely attracted to each other precisely because their families prohibited their relationship. Such obstacles may lead to an idealization of the forbidden person. They, like so many romantic heroes, were conveniently spared a more complete view of their relationship by their untimely deaths, preserving the romance and perhaps obscuring the more pedestrian underlying family dramas that most likely fostered their attraction in the first place. In everyday life, the outcome of such love affairs is often not so romantic, as the following case illustrates.

Susan Feder, the older of two children of a middle-class Jewish family, had known her future husband, Joe, in high school. Her parents, who had themselves been very unhappily married, had invested all their energies in their children's success. Susan planned to go to college, and her brother, who was a "computer genius," was planning to go to M.I.T. A month after her high school graduation, Susan's lawyer father had a heart attack. Her mother, who had always been an anxious person, had been hospitalized for depression when Susan was 10. Ever since then, the mother had been viewed as fragile, and now she seemed quite close to the edge, criticizing her husband continuously, now that he was so dependent. Susan gave up her plans for going away to university and enrolled in the local college. Over the next year, her father recovered, but that summer he had a second heart attack and had to stop work. Shortly afterward Susan began dating Joe, whom she met at her summer job as a secretary, where he was a computer technician. Joe was an only child from an immigrant working-class Puerto Rican family. For him, not only was Susan very attractive, but her family represented social and financial stability, which perhaps appealed to Joe because his own family life had been shaped by his family's poverty, caused by his father's disability in a work accident when Joe was an infant. Joe's mother had to care for her husband while having to care for her own mother as well. There was very little money to support them all. Joe hoped to improve his parents' situation by marrying Susan. He had always felt responsible for his parents' well-being but powerless to make them happy. He was delighted when Susan gave up college and began pushing to marry him. He was threatened by her college pursuits anyway. For Susan, Joe represented the only way she knew to get away from her family's expectations. She had been conflicted about school, since she felt inadequate in comparison to her brother, whose accomplishments were so much the focus of family attention. She had also been receiving mixed messages from her family about continuing her education since her father's heart attack. And since she had grown up not believing that she was really smart, she felt under great pressure about schoolwork. Joe would free her from these pressures. He would not push her to achieve. He accepted her as she was. He had a steady income, which would mean that she would not have to worry about her inability to concentrate on her studies or her fear of failure. She would become Joe's wife, she would raise a family, and her worries about her own identity would be over.

Joe and Susan found each other attractive and saw their relationship as making them feel better than they ever remembered feeling before. Joe's parents disapproved of Susan's not being Catholic and suggested strongly that they wait. Susan's father disapproved of her marrying someone without a college education and thought that she should finish school herself. He also disapproved of her marrying someone who was not Jewish, though the family was not religious. In quiet moments, Susan herself wondered whether she might find someone more educated, but her parents' disapproval pushed her to defend her choice and to reject their "snobbery." Before marriage, Susan and Joe had little chance to be alone together. What time they did have was filled with wedding arrangements and discussion of the families' pressures on them. Almost immediately after the wedding, Susan felt restless. Things with her family had quieted down; they had no more reason to protest. Susan quickly became bored and began to pressure Joe to get a better job. He felt guilty for having "abandoned" his parents, something he hadn't let surface during courtship. To improve their financial situation and to deal with his guilt, he suggested that they move into his parents' apartment, while the parents would move to a smaller apartment upstairs. It would save on expenses and be a good investment. Susan agreed because it meant that they would have much nicer living quarters. Almost immediately, she began to feel pressure from Joe's parents to socialize with them and to have children for them. Having married to escape her own parents, she now felt saddled with two others, with the added burden of not knowing them well. Suddenly, Joe's personality irritated her. Whereas she had initially liked him for his easygoing style and his acceptance of her, she now saw him as lacking ambition. She was embarrassed to have him spend time with her friends, because of his manners and lack of education, so she began to avoid her friends, which left her even more isolated. She tried pressuring Joe to fulfill her dreams and satisfy all her relationship needs. He felt increasingly inadequate and unable to respond to her pressure. She felt that he was a good lover but began to be more attracted to other men at work and began to turn him away. His sense of inadequacy led him to retreat further, and he took to going out in the evening with his own friends, with whom he felt more accepted.

Susan's resistance to parental expectations had now been transferred into the marriage. Joe's hopes for moving beyond his parents' disappointing lives had now been transformed into pressure from Susan for him to succeed, and he resented it. Neither partner had worked out for themselves individually what they wanted in life. Each had turned to the other to fulfill unmet needs, and now each was disappointed.

What began to happen between Susan and Joe is what happens to many couples when the hope that the partner will solve all problems proves to be in vain. There is a tendency to personalize stress and place blame for what goes wrong. At times, one blames oneself; at times, one's spouse. Given enough stress, couples tend to define their problems solely within the relationship. Once this personalizing process begins, it is very difficult to keep the relationship open. Susan began to lay the blame for her disappointments in life on Joe, and he saw himself as responsible for her unhappiness. One major factor that tightens couple relationships over time is their tendency to interpret more and more facets of their lives within the marriage, which is often promoted by the wider social context, which also supports this narrow focus. For example, during courtship, if one partner becomes depressed, the other is not likely to take it too personally, assuming, "There are many reasons one might get depressed in life; this may have nothing to do with me." Such an assumption of not being responsible for the other's feelings permits a supportive, empathic response. After several years of marriage, however, this partner has a much greater tendency to view the other's emotional reactions as a reflection of his or her input and to feel responsible for the partner's depression, or at least responsible to get him or her out of the depression. Once partners begin taking responsibility for the other's feelings, there is a tendency for more and more areas in the relationship to become filled with tension. The more one spouse defines himself or herself by the other, the less flexibility there will be in the relationship and the more their communication will become constricted in areas that are emotionally charged.

These responses are profoundly gendered as well. That is, because women are socialized to take responsibility for others' lives, feelings, and behavior and to consider it selfish to have a life of their own, they are more likely to internalize their problems and feel overresponsible for the marriage. And because men are socialized to define themselves primarily by their ability to provide for their families financially, perform sexually, and handle their emotions without overt emotional dependence, these dimensions will tend to define their feelings of success. Beyond this, they may externalize blame when things go wrong.

In the case of Susan and Joe, neither of them probably had any awareness that Susan was bringing into the relationship a lifetime of being a second-class citizen in relation to her brother. Nor did she ever realize that her mother's depression, anxiety, and frustration may have been related to her having lived a life that disallowed any personal fulfillment, while she was supposed to devote herself to caring for others. She had been a brilliant student herself and in her teens had wanted to go to medical school but was told by her parents that this goal was inappropriate for a woman and would mean she would "never find a man." So she found a man but probably lost herself in the process, and now Susan was perhaps repeating her mistake. Joe could not see that the very life force that attracted him to Susan soon became the problem, as he experienced himself as inadequate compared to her in intelligence and drive. If he hadn't had to measure himself by a yardstick that said that men should be smarter and more successful, he could have enjoyed her strength and intensity. Instead, he saw it as a measure of his failure and tried to stifle or avoid it. Had Susan felt freer of the gender inequities and constraints of our society, she might have appreciated Joe for his sweetness and commitment to his family and used the marriage as a secure base from which to evolve her own life and develop her confidence and skills.

Courtship is probably the least likely time of all phases of the life cycle for couples to seek therapy. This is not because coupling is easy, but because of the tendency to idealize each other and avoid looking at the enormous and long-range difficulties of establishing an intimate relationship. While the first years of marriage are the time of greatest overall marital satisfaction for many, they are also a time of likely divorce. The degree of mutual disappointment will usually match the degree of idealization of the relationship during courtship, as in the case of Susan and Joe. The pull of the relationship during courtship may prevent realization of potential difficulties, which do not show up until farther down the road. On the one hand, as Bowen observed, most spouses have their closest and most open relationship during this period. It is common for living-together relationships to be harmonious and for fusion symptoms not to develop until after marriage. It is as if the fusion does not become problematic as long as there is still an option to terminate the relationship easily (Bowen, 1978). While the demands of marriage frequently tighten a relationship, the fusion may start during courtship, when couples may begin a pattern of pseudo-mutuality, saying that they like everything about each other, expect to share all their free time together, and so on.

On the other hand, it is not uncommon for two people who have been living happily together to find that things change when they do get married, because they and society have now added to the situation the burdensome definitions of "husband" and "wife." These words often bring with them the conceptions of heavy responsibility *for* rather than *to* each other, which living together did not impose. There may also be the burden of having definitely passed beyond youth into "serious" adulthood. Couples may view marriage as such an enormous task that they can never be sufficiently prepared for it. Many couples have the opposite misperception: that marriage will automatically fulfill them regardless of other aspects of their lives. Family attitudes and social myths about marriage filter down from generation to generation, making such transitions proportionately smoother or more difficult.

Couples can become bound in a web of evasiveness and ambiguity, because neither can dare to be straight with the other for fear of things turning out unhappily, as they did in their families of origin. Communication may become more and more covert, the more they define their own worth by the relationship. The content of communication can become totally obscured by the need of both partners to validate themselves through the spouse. It may end with the absurdity of couples spending their time doing things neither wants to do because each thinks the other wants it that way. Or they do things only the way one partner wants, often the husband, because of the way power structures decision making in American couples (Blumstein & Schwartz, 1983), or only the way the wife wants, because the husband takes no responsibility for developing his own relationships.

In some situations, family patterns contribute to the inability of each partner to negotiate successfully the transition to couplehood. In such instances, the concept of marriage has taken on a meaning far beyond the fact of two people sharing their lives with each other. Very often, couples fall into stereotypical roles in which she can think of nothing but marriage and that is the one thing he cannot think about. These patterns reflect the gendered opposite sides of the same lack of differentiation from their families of origin. Men who are not comfortable with their level of differentiation typically fear commitment, whereas such women typically fear being alone.

GAY AND LESBIAN COUPLES

The patterns described here for heterosexual couples may be both simpler and more difficult for gay and lesbian couples (Laird & Green, 1996; Blumstein & Schwartz, 1983; Green et al., 1996; Slater, 1995; Bepko & Krestan, 1985; Nichols & Leiblum, 1986; Roth, 1985). It appears to be an advantage for gays and lesbians that they are less bound by the constricting rigidities of traditional gender roles, which may leave them freer to develop intimate relationships (Green et al., 1996). On the other hand, the stigmatizing of homosexual couples by our society means that their relationships are often not validated by their families or communities and they must cope with prejudice on a daily basis. The AIDS crisis has been a terrible trauma for the gay community, and its impact on gay men at the point of forming a new relationship cannot be underestimated. On the other hand, both partners being of the same gender may increase the couple's understanding of each other. Although some therapists have thought that being of the same gender might increase the likelihood of fusion, recent research indicates that this is not the case. Indeed, both gay and lesbian couples seem to have more cohesive relationships than heterosexual couples, lesbians having the greatest level of closeness (Green et al., 1996). On the other hand, the lack of acceptance that many gay couples experience from their families and from the society at large throughout the life cycle is a serious issue, one that clinicians may often help families to modify (Slater, 1995; Laird & Green, 1996). The price of the secrecy forced on many gay and lesbian couples by society's disapproval is one we need to change. Related to this familial and societal negativity, the lack of normative life cycle rituals is definitely something clinicians can help couples and their families to change (See Chapter 12). It often requires special efforts on the couple's part to receive adequate recognition of their relationship transitions.

> Katherine Moore, a 27-year-old journalist, and Rita Hidalgo, a 30-year-old graphic artist, had been living together for almost two years when they sought help for their relationship problems. Katherine was not sleeping, and Rita was concerned that Katherine was depressed, anxious, and drinking too much. Katherine had been withdrawing from Rita, feeling that Rita was becoming intrusive and bossy. Katherine had struggled since her mid-teens with her lesbianism. In college, she dated men occasionally, hoping that this would release her from her homosexual feelings and the disruption that she felt a homosexual life-style would create for her and her family of origin. In fact, after college, she kept a great distance from her parents, with whom she had always had a stormy relationship. She had been known in her family as the problem child since elementary school. Her conservative Anglo-Irish family operated on the basis of keeping up appearances. Her older sister had always been known as the "good girl" and never went beyond the limits accepted by the family. Katherine was the outspoken one, seen as the rebel. She always argued politics with her father, and he became particularly incensed when she became involved in women's rights. Katherine felt that her mother was sympathetic to her at times, but her mother never dared to disagree openly with her father. After Katherine became involved in women's rights, she had had several lesbian

relationships, but Rita was her first live-in relationship. They had decided to commit to their relationship permanently four months earlier, at which point Katherine's symptoms had increased.

Rita, who came from a Puerto Rican family, had known clearly since high school that she was a lesbian and had socialized with a gay social group from the time she began college. She had not seen her father for years but felt close to her mother and sister. She had never spoken directly of her sexual orientation at home, but she had occasionally brought home female friends and sensed that her mother, who had never remarried after divorcing her father when Rita was 7, might be lesbian herself without knowing it. She suspected that a paternal aunt who had lived for years with another woman was lesbian also.

What precipitated Katherine's turmoil was her announcement to her parents during a visit, which she always made without Rita, that she was lesbian. Katherine said that she had decided to tell her parents about this because she was tired of keeping her life a secret and she and Rita had recently decided to have a commitment ceremony with their friends present to formalize their relationship to each other. Her mother initially seemed not unsupportive, but her father had become extremely angry and told her this was just the last in a series of her "bad judgments" over many years. In several phone calls to her parents over the next weeks, she was greeted with stony silence by both parents. Katherine's symptoms had begun just after this. Rita tried to be supportive, but she had disapproved of Katherine's telling her parents about her homosexuality, believing that "parents never understand and there's no point getting into all that." Rita had become increasingly resentful that Katherine's preoccupation with her parents was destroying their relationship. Katherine had spoken also to a number of her lesbian friends, whose general advice was to forget about her parents because her father sounded like "an insensitive redneck" and why bother.

As Katherine described her relationship with her parents in therapy, it became clear that she was seeking not only greater closeness with them but also their approval for her lesbian choice. Rita was able to see without much effort that she had to let Katherine work out her own relationship with her parents, whatever happened. She agreed to back off and let Katherine figure things out for herself.

The initial therapy sessions focused on helping Katherine sort out her feelings and desires. She struggled to distinguish between her wish that her parents would approve of her lesbianism, her desire to be closer to them in general, and her overall wish for their approval of her behavior. She struggled with how to remain connected with her parents even if they disapproved of her lesbianism and how to let go of her need for their approval. She was coached to write a series of letters to each parent about her years of distancing and rebellion, her criticism of them (for which she now apologized), and her appreciation of how difficult her lesbian choice must be for them. She spoke of her earlier fears that they would cut her off completely and her relief that they had not.

Katherine's letters helped her to clarify that her lesbianism was not a matter for her parents' approval or disapproval. She came to see that discussing her life-style with them came from a deep need to solidify her identity as an adult and end the secrecy of her life that had kept her distant from her parents. Luckily, through her motivation to understand herself and her respect for her parents' limitations, she was able to keep her couplehood with Rita from being overburdened by her hurt. After six months of therapy, Rita decided it was time to speak directly with her own mother, realizing through Katherine's efforts how much could be gained by ending the secrecy, even when, as with Katherine, the response had not been particularly positive. Rita's mother said that she had known for years and was just waiting for Rita to feel comfortable telling her. When, a few months later, they had their marriage ceremony, Rita's mother, sister, and paternal aunt came (though the aunt left her partner at home), but only Katherine's sister attended from her family. While this was not what they might have hoped, Katherine felt reassured that her "good girl" sister had come. Perhaps in the future, when they hoped to have a baby, Katherine's sister would be able to assist the parents in moving toward more acceptance, now that the sisterhood was solidified.

As can be seen from this example, the systemic problems around couple formation are generally similar, regardless of the content of the problems. However, certain patterns are quite predictable for gay and lesbian couples, as they are for religious, class, ethnic, or racial intermarriages.

When the extended family is extremely negative toward the couple, for whatever reason, we encourage couples to take a long view, not trying to turn the acceptance of their relationship into a yes-or-no event but working gradually over time to build bridges for family closeness. Other life cycle transitions, particularly births and deaths, often create shifts in family equilibrium that may allow for redefinitions of family status for the couple.

THE WEDDING

Whether weddings involve jumping the broom, as in African American tradition; standing under a huppa and crushing a wine glass, as in Jewish tradition; or feasting for many days, as in Polish tradition, weddings are among the most interesting family rituals to observe and one of the best times for preventive intervention in family process. As family events, weddings are generally the largest ceremonies organized by families themselves. The organization of the wedding, who makes which arrangements, who gets invited, who comes, who pays, how much emotional energy goes into the preparations, and who gets upset and over which issues are all highly reflective of family process. In general, couples who marry in unconventional ways, in civil ceremonies, or without family or friends present have their reasons, most often family disapproval because of race, religion, class, money, or ethnicity; premarital pregnancy; an impulsive decision to marry; a previous divorce; or the inability or unwillingness of the parents to meet the costs of the wedding (Barker, 1978). From a clinical point of view, the emotional charge of such situations, when it leads to downplaying the marriage as a family event, may well indicate that the family members are unable to make the status changes required to adapt to this new life cycle stage and will have difficulty with future stages. As rituals, weddings are meant to facilitate family transition. As such, they can be extremely important in marking the change in status of family members and shifts in family organization.

Some families may overfocus on the wedding, putting all their energy into the event, losing sight of the marriage as a process of joining two families, and spending more than they can afford. According to a recent survey, the average wedding costs about $16,000, and in the New York area, spending $25,000 is considered near the "lower end" (White, 1997). Such spending reflects the distorted social mythology that make it difficult for couples and families to attend to the true meaning of marriage. Today, with the changing mores, this focus on the wedding may be less intense, but there is still a large overlap of myth associated with marital bliss, which gets displaced onto wedding celebrations in a way that may be counterproductive. Indeed, researcher John Gottman has been making a very strong case for marital success depending on the mundane "mindless moments" of everyday life that create the emotional climate that will make a marriage work in the long run (Gottman, 1994; Marano, 1997).

In addition, marriage may become a toxic issue in a family because of their particular history.

> One couple, Ted and Andrea, had toxic issues on both sides of their extended family. They were able, through premarital coaching, to field stormy reactions in their families so well that they probably prevented years of simmering conflicts that had hampered both extended families over several generations. When they sought help, they said that they were planning to marry in their apartment with only a few friends present unless they could bring their families around to accepting them as they were. Andrea's parents had eloped after her grandparents had refused to agree to their marriage because of religious differences, and her parents had hardly seen their families since. Ted's paternal grandfather had had a heart attack at his son's (Ted's father's) wedding reception and died the next day. Thus, weddings had become dreaded events for both extended families.
>
> Ted and Andrea began their work by contacting extended family members to invite them personally to their wedding. They used these conversations to mention in a casual way the pain of the wedding history for the family. For example, when Ted called his paternal grandmother, who was 85, and who his parents had assured him would never come to the wedding, he told her that his parents were

sure she couldn't make it but that it would mean a great deal to him to have her there, especially since he feared his father might have a heart attack and he needed her support. The grandmother not only made her own arrangements to have a cousin fly with her, but arranged to stay with her son, Ted's father, for the week after the wedding. At the reception, both bride and groom made toasts in verse to their families, in which they ticked off the charged issues with humor and sensitivity and made a special point of spending time with family members.

Surprisingly, few couples ever seek premarital counseling, in spite of the obvious difficulties in negotiating this transition and the fact that preventive intervention in relation to the extended families might be a great deal easier at this time than later in the life cycle. The most that can be said is that it is extremely useful if one has access to any member of a family at the time of a wedding to encourage him or her to facilitate the resolution of family relationships through this nodal event. For example, it is often fruitful to convey to the couple that in-law struggles are predictable and need not be taken too personally. It is important for couples to recognize that the heightened parental tension probably relates to their sense of loss regarding the marriage. When families argue about wedding arrangements, the issues under dispute often cover up underlying systemic issues:

Peter and Martha were in a crisis over their upcoming wedding because of the preoccupation of Martha's mother, Anna Dorsey, with invitations and seating arrangements. Martha's first marriage had been annulled, a fact that her extended family had never been told. Now Martha was furious at her mother for not accepting her new marriage. Mrs. Dorsey was embarrassed to invite her family to the wedding, since they would now know that the first marriage had not worked out. She hoped that with a small wedding, "no one would notice," and over time, her relatives would think that the new husband was the same one the daughter had married at the first wedding. Martha was incensed at what she perceived to be her mother's rejection of her and her new husband. Once she began talking to her mother about how hard this second marriage must be for her mother, the tension diminished consid-

erably. Martha was able to let go of her indignation and move toward showing compassion for her mother's fear of her family's rejection. When she did this, she learned that the issue of family rejection had a long history, back to the mother's own marriage to her father, whose limp had created much family disapproval twenty-five years earlier.

Family members often view others as being capable of "ruining" the event. A useful guideline is for each person to take his or her own responsibility for having a good time at the wedding. It is also useful for the couple to recognize that marriage is a family event and not just for the two of them. From this perspective, parents' feelings about the service need to be taken into consideration in whatever meaningful ways are possible. Martha had always been "Daddy's girl," but through her premarital work on her relationship with her mother, she decided to ask both parents to walk her down the aisle, since, she said, they had both contributed to who she was. Her mother was extremely touched by this gesture, which allowed Martha to make a significant redefining statement about her parents' meaning in her life. The more responsibility a couple can take for arranging a wedding that reflects their shifting position in their families and the joining of the two systems, the more auspicious it will be for their future relationship.

Jim Marcus spent six months in coaching for his wedding, at which he wanted his actively alcoholic mother and the three other mothering figures who had played important roles in his life. His parents had divorced when he was 5. His father remarried for six years when Jim was 8 and again when he was 15. He had grown up in his father's custody, with a family housekeeper involved between his father's marriages. Jim had distanced himself from his alcoholic mother and from both stepmothers for many years. Through coaching, he was able to reverse the process of cut-off for the wedding. He called his stepmothers and his childhood housekeeper to invite them especially to his wedding, discussing with each her importance in his life and how much it would mean to him to have her present at his wedding celebration.

The next problem was the parents of his fiancée, Joan, who were planning an elaborate celebration and wanted everything to go according to the book. This would have made Jim's less affluent family very uncomfortable. Initially, Joan became quite reactive to her mother's fancy plans and her way of making decisions without discussion. At the suggestion of the therapist, Joan arranged to spend a day with her mother, during which she could discuss her feelings about her upcoming marriage and approach her mother as a resource on how to handle things. She discovered for the first time that her mother had been married in a small civil wedding because her Catholic parents disapproved of her marriage to a Jewish immigrant who had no college education. Joan learned how her mother had yearned for a "proper wedding." She realized that her mother's wishes to do everything in a fancy way had grown out of her own unrealized dreams and were an attempt to give Joan something she had missed. With this realization, Joan could share her own wish for a simple celebration to make Jim feel comfortable, especially because of all the problems in his family, which she had never mentioned to her mother before. She asked her mother for advice on how to handle the situation. She told her how uncomfortable she was about the divorces in Jim's family and her fears that her own relatives would disapprove of him, especially if all his mothering figures attended the wedding. Suddenly, her mother's attitude changed from dictating how things had to be done to a helpful and much more casual attitude. A week later, Joan's mother told Jim that if there was any way she could facilitate things with his mother, stepmothers, or other guests, she would be glad to do it.

Friendship systems and extended family relationships frequently change after the wedding. Many couples have difficulty maintaining individual friendships and move, at least in the first years, toward having only "couple friends." We encourage spouses to keep their individual friendship networks, which allow the spouses to maintain their individual interests and preferences.

SEXUALITY

Our society has almost no images of equality in sexuality that would help us in developing sexually gratifying partnership relationships (Carter, 1996).

Helping couples means encouraging them to become pioneers in their sexual relationships, just as it does in other aspects of forming a partnership, as opposed to the traditional couple relationship of a powerful, dominant male and a submissive, responsive female. Helping couples to establish flexible and intimate sexual relationships involves freeing them from the gender stereotypes that are part of their familial and cultural heritage.

From earliest childhood, boys are encouraged to feel positive about their bodies sexually, whereas girls are rarely encouraged even to be familiar with their genitalia, let alone to enjoy them. Boys typically begin to masturbate from earliest childhood, girls not till midadolescence, if then. Women generally have to bear the burden of the repercussions of sexuality in terms of pregnancy or contraception, and in many groups, they are prohibited from using contraception and from refusing sex. All the consequences of sexuality, from pregnancy to sexually transmitted diseases, to women's lack of socialization to be proud of being sexual or even knowing how their bodies work, make it surprising that sex works out as often as it does, not that it so often becomes a problem for a couple.

The current generation has much more sexual experience and knowledge than previous generations did. While the age at marriage has been increasing, the age at sexual maturation and at first intercourse have decreased (Seidman & Reider, 1994). Women as well as men are having sex with more partners than before. The vast majority of young adults (approximately 90 percent) are sexually experienced, and most have sex regularly. They are having sex with more partners and at younger ages than ever before. At the same time, anxieties about AIDs, herpes, and other sexually transmitted diseases are a continuous issue for young couples today.

In the past, as Carter notes, if a husband lost interest in sex, therapists assumed that he was having an affair. Now we ask about recent changes in the wife's income and status, since sexuality seems so clearly linked with power issues in marriage. If the wife is not interested in sex, ask detailed questions about power issues in the couple relationship.

Even when a woman develops a flirtation or affair, explore whether her behavior is an attempt (however misguided) to empower herself through a sexual relationship because as a woman she has felt disempowered overall in the relationship. Our experience is that techniques to enhance sexual enjoyment are only a small part of dealing with a couple's sexual problems. Beyond the use of the techniques of Masters and Johnson and others who have helped to increase our knowledge of men's and women's sexual response, it is important to consider the power dimension in a couple's relationship when they are experiencing sexual difficulty. Sex is at the heart of expressions of intimacy, and the inability to express intimacy is very likely to be related to familial and cultural factors that have made intimacy in this form and most forms almost impossible for men and women in our society. In addition to exploring sexuality in the extended family, using, for example Hof & Berman's (1986) sexual genogram and David Snarch's ideas regarding the "sexual crucible" (1992) to understand the specific messages that partners have been given about their bodies, their own sexuality, and their expectations about what is sexy with a partner, therapists need to pay much more attention than we have to the larger cultural dimensions within which our sexual relationships evolve (Carter, 1996; Heyn, 1992; Schwartz, 1994; Snarch, 1991). That means, primarily, to pay attention to the implicit power dimensions influencing this aspect and all other aspects of a couple's relationship. Given the very high levels of violence against wives in marriage and the trouble our nation is still having acknowledging the concept of marital rape, we must be very cautious about limiting our work with a couple to the interior of their intimate relationship and ignoring the power dimensions.

PATTERNS WITH EXTENDED FAMILY

Women tend to move closer to their families of origin after marriage; men may become more distant, shifting their primary tie to the new nuclear family. In any case, spouses deal with their families in many different ways. Many find marriage the only way to separate from their families of origin, and their enmeshment in the family continues even after marriage. Patterns of guilt, intrusiveness, and unclear boundaries are typical of such systems. Other couples cut off their families emotionally even before marriage. In these situations, the partners may not even invite their parents to the wedding. Parents are seen as withholding and rejecting, and the couple decides to do without them. Another pattern involves continued contact with parents but with ongoing conflicts or tension pushed under the rug. In such families, there is usually involvement of the extended family in the marriage plans but often with fights, hurt feelings, and scenes around the time of the wedding. This pattern is perhaps the most amenable to future resolution of the issues. The conflicts indicate that at least the family is struggling with separating and is not forcing it underground as in enmeshed or cut-off families. The ideal situation, and the one that is very rarely found, occurs when both partners have become independent of their families before marriage and at the same time maintain close, caring ties. In such instances, the wedding would serve for all the family as a sharing and a celebration of the new couple's shift in status.

The second pattern of dealing with parents involves cutting off the relationships in an attempt to gain independence. Many such couples develop restrictive couple patterns that work until later developmental stages destabilize them.

The third common pattern of relationships with extended family involves closeness but avoidance of certain issues. In such families, marriages are excellent opportunities to reopen closed relationships— for example, inviting to the wedding relatives with whom parents are out of touch. It is a good chance to detoxify emotional issues, reviewing marital and family ties over several generations as part of redefining the system. However, the underlying tensions often surface reactively at the time of transition in emotional scenes or arguments around wedding plans, only to go underground again as family members try to act happy and friendly so as not to create unpleasantness. The attempt to smooth things over in itself often creates the likelihood of problems. The fact that all change creates disruption and uncertainty in the system needs to be dealt with in the family if the developmental processes are to move along. For example, it may be easier for the family to move on if they are in touch with their sense of loss at the time of the wedding and if they are a bit confused and uneasy about how to manage the new relationships. Whatever the patterns of difficulty with extended family—conflict, enmeshment, distance, or cut-off—the lack of resolution of these relationships is the major problem in negotiating this phase of the family life cycle. The more the triangles in the extended family are dealt with by an emotional cut-off, the more the spouse may come to represent more than who he or she is, overloading the circuits in time. If the husband's relationship with his wife is his only meaningful relationship, he will be so sensitive to her every reaction, especially to any hint of rejection, that he will overreact to signs of differentness by pulling her to agree with him or blaming her for not accepting him. The intensity will probably make the relationship untenable eventually. Our culture's social mobility and overfocus on the nuclear family to the neglect of all other relationships contributes to this tendency to place more emotional demand on a marriage than it can bear. Once a spouse becomes overly involved in the other's response, both become bound up in a web of fusion and unable to function for themselves.

Some couples transfer parental struggles to the spouse directly. Others choose a spouse who handles their family for them. A man may choose a wife who is totally unacceptable to his parents and then let her fight his battles with them, while he becomes the "innocent bystander." The price that everyone pays in such situations is the failure to achieve any real connection, since issues can never be resolved when other members are brought in to handle one's relationships.

When family members have served a central function in their parents' lives or in the preservation of their parents' marital balance, they may not feel the parents have granted "permission" for them to marry successfully.

IN-LAWS

Among the problematic triangles for the couple, the one involving husband, wife, and husband's mother is probably the most renowned. In-laws are easy scapegoats for family tensions. It is always much easier to hate your daughter-in-law for keeping your son from showing his love than to admit that your son doesn't respond to you the way you wish he would. It may be easier for a daughter-in-law to hate her mother-in-law for intrusiveness than to confront her husband directly for not committing himself fully to the marriage and defining a boundary in relation to outsiders. In-law relationships are a natural arena for displacing tensions in the couple or in the family of origin of each spouse. The converse of this is the pattern of a spouse who has cut off his or her own family and seeks to adopt the spouse's family, forming a warm, enmeshed fusion with the in-laws based on defining his or her own family as cold, rejecting, uninteresting, and so on.

Our society generally focuses blame on the mother-in-law rather than on the father-in-law, who is usually seen as playing a more benign role. Just as mothers get blamed for what goes wrong in families because of their being given primary responsibility for family relationships, so do mothers-in-law get primary blame by extension. Many factors contribute to this process. Just as wives are given responsibility for handling a husband's emotional problems, so are they often put in the position of expressing issues for all other family members and then blamed when things go wrong.

SIBLING ISSUES IN COUPLE FORMATION

Siblings may also displace their problems in dealing with each other onto the intrusion of a new spouse. Predictable triangles are especially likely between a husband and his wife's brothers or between a wife and her husband's sisters. The sisters may see their brother's wife as having no taste, as infusing the brother with superficial values, and so forth. What the system misses in such instances is that the brother probably chose his wife as a protection from his sisters, perhaps to set the limits that he never dared set alone or to allow him to distance himself without the guilt of doing it directly. Often, the brother will get his wife to take over dealing with his family altogether, which usually succeeds only in escalating the tension. Of course, a person may also use the extended family to distance himself or herself from a spouse without taking responsibility for it, under the guise of family duty: "I'd love to spend the day with you, honey, but I have to visit my parents."

Good clues about a couple can be found in the marital relationships of each partner's parents, the couple's primary models for what marriage is about. The other basic model for spouses is their relationship with their siblings, their earliest and closest peers. Couples who marry mates from complementary sibling positions tend to enjoy the greatest marital stability (Toman, 1976). In other words, the older brother of a younger sister will tend to get along best with a younger sister of an older brother. They will tend to have fewer power conflicts, since he will be comfortable as the leader and she as the follower. In addition, they will tend to be comfortable with the opposite sex, since they have grown up with opposite-sex siblings. Those who marry spouses who are not in complementary sibling positions may have more marital adjustments to make in this regard. An extreme case would be the oldest of many brothers who marries the oldest of many sisters. Both would expect to be the leader and would probably have difficulty understanding why the other does not acknowledge their leadership, since they are used to having this at home. In addition, they will be less comfortable with the opposite sex, since they grew up in strongly single-sexed environments (Toman, 1976).

CULTURAL DIFFERENCES

Another arena that becomes problematic in a marriage under stress is the cultural or family style differences. This may be more of a problem in the United States, where people from so many diverse cultural backgrounds marry and find themselves in conflict because each starts out with such different basic assumptions (Crohn, 1994; McGoldrick, Giordano, & Pearce, 1996; McGoldrick & Preto, 1984).

A young couple applied for therapy after a year of marriage because the wife said she was convinced that her husband did not love her and that he had changed after they got married. The wife was the fifth of seven children from a Brooklyn family of Italian extraction. She had met her husband in college and was extremely attracted to his quiet strength and strong life ambitions. He was from a midwestern Protestant family in which as an only child, he was strongly encouraged by his parents to work hard and to live a morally upright life. He had found her vivacious and charming and had also been attracted to her family because of their open affection and because, in contrast to his own "uptight" parents, they always seemed to have a good time.

Under stress, the couple found that the very qualities that had attracted them to each other became the problem. The husband became for the wife "an unfeeling stone." She complained, "He doesn't care about my feelings at all and ignores me completely." For the husband, the wife's vivaciousness now became "hysteria" and he found her "nagging, emotional outbursts, and screaming" unbearable.

As we discussed in therapy their very different family styles of coping with stress, their opposing assumptions became obvious. In the husband's family, the rule was that you should keep your problems to yourself and think them out: with enough effort and thought, most problems could be worked out. The wife's family dealt with stress by getting together and ventilating. The family related intensely at all times but especially when family members were upset. These styles had been turned inward in the marriage and were tightening things even more. The more the wife felt isolated and needed contact, the more loudly she sought attention and the more the husband withdrew to get some space and to maintain his balance. The more he withdrew, the more frustrated and alone the wife felt. Both partners had turned their differences, initially labeled as the source of attraction, into the problem and had begun to see the other's behavior as a sure sign of not caring. Neither had been able to see that their family styles were just different. They were compounding the difficulty by moving further into their own pattern, each blaming the other for the other's response.

Once the family patterns could be clarified in the context of the extended family and ethnic backgrounds, the spouses were able to temper their responses and to see their differences as neutral, rather than as signs of psychopathology or rejection.

ISSUES IN MARITAL ADJUSTMENT

Generally speaking, establishing successful marital partner relationships is more problematic if:

1. The partners come to the marriage with marked differences in power, socioeconomic status, or career options.
2. One spouse is financially dependent on the other because of lack of employment or job skills.
3. The husband tries to isolate the wife from work, friends or family, to control her financially or to intimidate her physically.
4. The couple meets or marries shortly after a significant loss.
5. The wish to distance from one's family of origin is a factor in the marriage.
6. The family backgrounds of the spouses are significantly different (religion, education, social class, ethnicity, the ages of the partners).
7. The spouses come from incompatible sibling constellations.
8. The couple resides either extremely close to or at a great distance from either family of origin.
9. The couple is dependent on either extended family financially, physically, or emotionally.
10. The couple marries early (before age 20) or late (after age 35).
11. The couple marries after an acquaintanceship of less than six months or more than three years of engagement.
12. The wedding occurs without family or friends present.
13. The wife becomes pregnant before or within the first year of marriage.
14. Either spouse has a poor relationship with his or her siblings or parents.
15. Either spouse considers his or her childhood or adolescence to have been unhappy time.
16. Marital patterns in either extended family were unstable.
17. One or both partners believe implicitly or explicitly that men's rights, needs, or privilege should predominate in marriage and that women should serve the needs of others.

Adjustment to marriage is being profoundly affected by the changing role of women in our society, the frequency of marriage of partners from widely different cultural backgrounds, the increasing physical distance from families of origin, and the diminishing role of community in supporting families. Couples are increasingly isolated and expected to manage their lives and families without the community supports that in the past were a primary resource in raising children and meeting family needs. While any two family systems are different and have conflicting patterns and expectations, couples in our present culture are less bound by family traditions and are freer than ever before to develop male-female relationships unlike those they experienced in their families of origin. Couples are required to think out for themselves many things that in the past would have been taken for granted. This applies also to the enormous gap that often exists in our culture between parents and children in education and social status. When there are educational differences between parents and children, it appears better for marital stability when children are more successful than their parents than when parents are more successful than their children. Nevertheless, any large gap is obviously a strain, since parents, siblings, and children will have to adjust to large differences in experience. At the same time, cultural differences add flexibility to the system and stretch the family to become more adaptive.

REFERENCES

Almeida, R., Woods, R., Messineo, T., & Font, R. (1998). The contextual model. In M. McGoldrick (Ed.), *Revisioning family therapy: Race, gender, and culture in clinical practice.* New York: The Guilford Press.

Apter, T. (1985). *Why women don't have wives.* New York: Schoken.

Barker, D. L. (1978). A proper wedding. In M. Corbin (Ed.), *The Couple.* New York: Penguin.

Bepko, C., & Krestan, J. (1985). *The responsibility trap.* New York: The Free Press.

Bernard, J. (1982). *The future of marriage.* New Haven, CT: Yale University Press.

Blumstein, P., & Schwartz, Pepper. (1983). *American couples: Money, work and sex.* New York: William Morrow.

Bowen, M. (1978). *Family therapy in clinical practice.* New York: Jason Aronson.

Carstensen, Gottman, & Levenson. (1995). Emotional behavior in long-term marriage. *Psychology and Aging, 10*(1), 140–149.

Carter, B. (1996). *Love, Honor and Negotiate.* New York: Pocketbooks.

Glaser, C. (1996 September 16). Marriage as we see it. *Newsweek,* 19.

Gottman, J. (1993). The roles of conflict engagement, escalation, and avoidance in marital interaction: A longitudinal view of five types of couples. *Journal of Counseling and Clinical Psychology, 61,*(1), 6–15.

Gottman, J. (1994). *Why marriages succeed or fail.* New York: Simon & Schuster.

Green, R. J., Bettinger, M., & Zacks, E. (1996). Are lesbian couples "fused" and gay male couples "disengaged?": Questioning gender straightjackets. In J. Laird & R. J. Green (Eds.), *Lesbians and gays in couples and families.* San Francisco: Jossey-Bass.

Grohn, J. (1988). In M. McGoldrick (Ed.), *Revising family therapy: Race, culture and gender in clinical practice.* New York: The Guilford Press.

Gurin, G., Veroff, J., & Feld, S. (1980) *Americans view their mental health.* New York: Basic Books.

Heilbrun, C. (1988). *Writing a woman's life.* New York: Norton.

Heyn, D. (1992). *The erotic silence of the American wife.* New York: Random House.

Hof, L., & Berman, E. (1986). The sex genogram. *Journal of Marital and Family Therapy, 12*(1), 39–47.

Laird, J. & Green, R. J. (1996). *Lesbians and gays in couples and families.* San Francisco: Jossey-Bass.

Lerner, M. (1995). The oppression of singles. *Tikkun, 10*(6), 9–11.

Marano, H. E. (1997, May 28). Rescuing marriages before they begin. *New York Times.*

McGoldrick, M. (1995). *You can go home again: Reconnecting with your family.* New York: Norton.

McGoldrick, M. & Preto, N. G. (1984). Ethnic Intermarriage: Implications for therapy. *Family Process, 23*(3), 347–363.

Nichols, M. & Leiblum, S. (1986). Lesbianism as a personal identity and social role: A model. *Affilia,* 48–59.

Purdum, T. S. (1996, September 23). Gay rights groups attack Clinton on midnight signing. *New York Times.*

Rilke, R. M. (1954). *Letters to a Young Poet,* translated by D. M. Hester. New York: Norton.

Roberts, S. (1994). *Who we are: A portrait of America based on the latest U.S. Census.* New York: Times Books.

Roth, S. (1985). Psychotherapy with lesbian couples: Individual issues, female socialization and the social context. *Journal of Marital Therapy, 11*(3), 273–286.

Satir, V. (1967). *Conjoint family therapy.* Palo Alto: Science & Behavior Books.

Schwartz, P. (1994). *Peer marriage: How love between equals really works.* New York: The Free Press.

Seidman, S. N. & Rieder, R. O. (1994). A review of sexual behavior in the United States. *American Journal of Psychiatry, 151*(3), 330–341.

Slater, S. (1995). *The lesbian family life cycle.* New York: The Free Press.

Snarch, D. (1991). *Constructing the sexual crucible.* New York: Norton.

Steinhauer, J. (1995, April 10). Big benefits in marriage, studies say. *New York Times.* p. A10.

Toman, W. (1976) *Family constellation* (3rd ed.). New York: Springer.

White, C. C. R. (1997, July 5). The price a woman pays to say "I do." *New York Times.*

CHAPTER 15

BECOMING PARENTS
THE FAMILY WITH YOUNG CHILDREN

BETTY CARTER

Experiences spiral through the life cycle, presenting the same lessons from new angles: parenthood offers a new view of childhood, so does grandparenthood and so also the roles we are sometimes offered in relation to the children of friends.... It is possible even for childhood to be twice learned, seen from the outside as well as the inside

—Mary Catherine Bateson, *Peripheral Visions* (p. 40)

INTRODUCTION

Let it be stated here at the outset that becoming a parent is one of the most definitive stages of life, a crossing of the Rubicon. Once there is a child, life will never be the same again, for better and for worse. It is certainly true that most parents fall passionately in love with their new babies and consider them fascinating, delightful, and unique additions to the family. However, the roller coaster of the early months and years still comes as a shock to almost all new parents: sleep deprivation, shredded schedules, endless chores, worry about the baby's development or one's own competence, and the need for ceaseless vigilance. This sudden threat of chaos puts enormous stress on new parents and on their relationship, since no amount of doing ever seems enough to get the job done before it needs to be done again. At this stage, the tremendous rewards of parenthood, expressed in all cultures across the ages, can seem largely theoretical.

But still, there is much more mythology and romantic fantasy attached to this transition than there is realistic expectation. Most of the mythology paints a glowing picture, especially of mother

and child, a central icon in cultures and religions from time immemorial. This basic assumption that motherhood—and, by extension, parenthood—is an automatic leap ahead in status, joy, and fulfillment seems not to be much questioned, though the step may be delayed by couples who are concerned with educational and/or career goals. However, it is hard for young couples to make a realistic decision about whether or when to have children because of the tremendous role played by the emotions and by social pressures. A person who remembers a happy childhood and good parents wants to repeat that experience, while someone escaping a terrible childhood often seems impelled to try to do it differently. Women especially seldom escape the culture's view that a childless woman is not a "real" woman. For both sexes, parenthood seems to provide the final ticket for acceptance into adulthood: the woman mothering and the man "providing."

I believe that the transition to parenthood and the care of young children has become even more difficult than it used to be, a situation that is often not appreciated by childless adults or by older parents who raised their children in a less complicated (though not necessarily better) time. So let us learn about the contemporary problems and see how we can help. The need is certainly widespread, since 90 percent of all couples who can have children do so, moving 3,000 couples to parenthood each year in the United States (Belsky & Kelly, 1994).

Expectations versus Reality

As was indicated above, this most romanticized of life transitions creates false expectations in young couples. Society relates only to the pleasures of life with baby, and there is relentless social criticism of any departure from the traditional view of the family that is created by the birth of a child. This criticism is especially virulent in the right-wing discourse on "family values" (Blankenhorn, 1995), which endlessly attacks nontraditional couples, women who choose their legal right to abortion instead of parenthood, mothers who choose or need to go to work, and couples with children who believe that divorce is their best or only option. The impact of these social and economic forces on couples is often outside of the couple's awareness.

In their comprehensive study of the transition of parenthood, Jay Belsky and John Kelly (1994) found that "individuals who entered the transition with fewer romantic and exaggerated expectations are more likely to emerge from the transition happier about their marriages and their spouses than individuals who enter the starting gate wearing rose-colored glasses" (p. 2). They also found that couples and their marriage tended to continue along the trajectory they were on at the time of becoming parents, whether this was a decline in their relationship, an improvement, or no change.

The Emotional System

The new baby is born or adopted into an extended family system that must now make emotional and relationship shifts to make a place for the new member. Many families celebrate the event with a religious ritual: a christening, bris, or naming ceremony, usually followed by a party for family and friends. As with other family transition rituals, issues about how and where the event is celebrated and who gets invited reflect the ongoing extended-family process. Whether there is a ritual or a party or not, the new member in the system is greeted with many differing emotional reactions, depending on its sex, its health, how it is named, how long it was awaited, what kind of relationship its parents have with their various family members, whether the grandparents approved of the marriage, and whether they're all doing their part to shift to adult-to-adult relationships in the parent-grandparent generations.

A first grandchild also creates new grandparents, who often jump into their new role without much planning or discussion with their children, not realizing that there are as many ways to grandparent as to parent. No way is "right," but some ways fit their lives and their children's lives better than others, and it is best when the issue is discussed early on. Complaints about intrusive or indifferent grandparents—or demanding or neglectful adult children—are signs of the need for such discussion.

Whether parents maintain close or distant extended family relationships, they can expect to inherit major unresolved extended family issues and patterns. Multigenerational patterns, triangles, ghosts, and taboo issues are best examined by the parents and dealt with at this time, lest they engulf the new family in emotional problems that they may think they can ignore or evade. On the positive side, this is a good stage of the family life cycle to engage parents in doing family of origin work, even if they have previously resisted or ignored opportunities to continue their emotional differentiation efforts. Parents will do many things for their children's sake that they won't do for themselves, and this fact provides therapeutic leverage for the coaching process (see Chapter 26). It is also a good time for grandparents to give up old grievances and make new efforts to relate positively to their adult children and the children's spouses. I sometimes remind grandparents that in a society with such a high divorce rate, it is wise to be good friends with your daughter-in-law.

Child Care

Child care is the number one practical concern and problem at this phase of the life cycle, and the United States is the only industrialized nation in the world that leaves it to individual families to arrange and pay for child care themselves. According to the latest figures of the U.S. Census Bureau (Casper, 1997), poor families who paid for child care spent 18 percent of their income on it; nonpoor families, although they paid more for child care, spent 7 percent of their income.

Another Census Bureau report (Casper, 1996) states that of the 9.9 million children of working mothers under age 5 in 1993, almost half (40 percent) were cared for primarily by relatives. The interesting breakdowns in this report are as follows:

- 30 percent children in organized facilities (daycare, nursery school)
- 6 percent cared for by mothers working at home
- 16 percent cared for by fathers
- 17 percent cared for by grandparents
- 9 percent by other relatives
- 21 percent by nonrelatives (in-home babysitters or family day care providers)

The report notes that the increase in child care by fathers between 1988 and 1991 was initially thought to be part of a social trend for fathers to become more involved in child care. However, it was reevaluated when the recession of that period ended around 1991 and care of preschoolers by fathers dropped back down from a high of 20 percent to 16 percent. Family daycare in the provider's home also dropped to 17 percent from a high of 24 percent in 1988 following media reports of child abuse and neglect in such settings.

The following are further relevant items in this report:

- Mothers working part-time or evening or night shifts find it easier to arrange for relative and in-home care.
- Black and Latina mothers rely more heavily on relatives for child care than Whites do.

- Children of single parents are more likely to be cared for by grandparents than are children of married couples.
- Relatives provide a great deal of child care for preschoolers in poor families and welfare recipients because of the expense of organized facilities.
- Child care is more expensive in metropolitan areas and most expensive in the Northeast.

Clinically, family therapists should assume that most working mothers feel guilty or anxious about the welfare of their babies and toddlers, whether they are financially required to work or not. Fueling the guilt and anxiety are the steady stream of media reports decrying the poor quality of American child care.

The nation has 97,000 child care centers, of which only 5,000 are accredited by the National Association for the Education of Young Children. One study (Whitebrook, 1997) rated only 61 percent of the *accredited* centers and 10 percent of the nonaccredited centers as good: That's 12,200 "good" centers out of 97,000! Articles frequently criticize care by relatives as less good than care by high-quality child care centers. This, of course, has serious implications for poor and working-class families who rely on child care by relatives and have little or no other choice.

A further source of anxiety are the frequent reports that a baby's intellectual development depends on being spoken to regularly by an attentive, engaged human being during the first year of life. Even the affluent, paying for expensive live-in nanny care in their own homes, are not free from worry about what actually transpires in their absence. And their anxiety peaks during the occasional, but highly publicized, cases of nanny abuse of children.

Lost in all of this highly charged debate is the fact that most studies find that children who attend high-quality daycare centers are found to have better intellectual and social skills than children who have not been to daycare. But the obvious solution to the problem—public funding that will guarantee that *all* American child care centers are high quality—is completely overwhelmed by appeals for a more familiar alternative: It's so much cheaper and easier (for whom?) if mothers simply stay home with their children; never mind that this is economically and culturally impossible. Notice especially that these exhortations are directed only toward women. It remains to be seen whether the funding that some politicians propose periodically can actually be enacted into law and, if so, whether it will be enough to help significantly.

The most important move that clinicians can make regarding this issue is to ensure that it is discussed as a *parental* problem, not a *mothering* problem.

GENDER ISSUES IN PARENTING

The Work-Family Dilemma

Because the two-paycheck family is now the U.S. norm, some parental adjustment in work schedule is necessary when children are born. Seventy percent of U.S. women of working age are currently in the full-time workforce, including more than half of mothers with children under the age of 6. However, it is still assumed in the workplace and by the couple themselves that the dilemma of juggling work and family is solely the mother's dilemma. Depending largely on their economic situation and the mother's career aspirations, she may quit work altogether, cut back to part time, or make whatever child care arrangements she can to keep working full time. If these alternatives are not what she expected to face or don't work out satisfactorily, she may become increasingly resentful and exhausted, probably blaming her husband and envying his single-track pursuit of work. Current job insecurity at all economic levels only adds to the pressure men already feel not to "rock the boat" at work by asking for any special consideration because of family matters. This rigidity of the work system most severely affects working mothers, who are passed over for promotion or raises on the so-called "mommy track." An op-ed article by Danielle Crittenden (1995) in *The New York Times* entitled "Motherhood Lowers Pay" states that young women (age 27 to 33) who remain childless now earn 98 percent of what men of the same age earn, whereas the average pay for all women, which includes working mothers, is only 76 percent.

Following the landmark study done by sociologist Arlie Hochschild, which instantly gave new meaning to the phrase "second shift" (Hochschild, 1989), family therapists became more alert to the unfair share of housework done by women even when both parents worked outside the home. Many of us found that this was confirmed in our clinical practices and we included the issue in books meant to help the general public deal with current family problems (Carter & Peters 1997; Taffel, 1994). In 1994, men were reported doing 34 percent of the work at home, up from 20 percent in 1965 (Pleck, 1994). That still leaves women doing 66 percent and, if both are working full time outside the home, is still unfair. None of this, however, should be interpreted as an excuse to call for women to return home and make it all work out again. In a recent four-year study funded by NIMH (Barnett & Rivers, 1996), the researchers found two-income couples healthier and happier in every way, in spite of long work hours. In addition, they pointed out astutely that the whole conservative push for women to stay home with their children also has the unacknowledged goal of protecting men's jobs in an era of corporate downsizing.

The three unresolved problems of the work-family dilemma remain the unequal participation of men in the work at home, the inflexibility of the workplace, and the growing number of hours of work in the lives of both men and women.

In this regard, Arlie Hochschild has provided us with another provocative study of work and home life (Hochschild, 1997). The sociologist studied a major American company (name disguised), seeking reasons for the fact that even when businesses do offer enlightened programs, such as flextime, part time, and job sharing (and most companies still don't), only a very small percentage of employees use them. For example, in

1990, 88 percent of Fortune 500 manufacturing firms offered part-time work to full-time workers, but only 3–5 percent of employees applied for it. Forty-five percent offered flextime, but only 10 percent of employees used it. The usual reasons given for this are that workers can't afford to work part time; that they fear being laid off if they cut back; that they are poorly informed of company policy; that the policies are really only for "show" and users will be penalized; that even if the company is sincere, middle managers disapprove and are reluctant to cooperate; and finally, that women and minorities have to work more, not less, to prove their competence.

Hochschild agrees that all of these reasons have merit and are often inextricably woven into a corporate culture that frowns on the intrusion of family into work time. However, she adds another, more startling, finding: that home has become such a time-deprived hassle for working parents that women as well as men have begun to seek escape from those pressures by willingly spending more time at the office or the factory, where they have found friends, helping networks, and community. Women and members of minorities who succeed at work also value the respect and heightened self-esteem that comes with their paychecks. Even those who start out hoping to avoid the corporate mold find that as they move up, they are changed by the system far more than they are able to change the company's rules. To be given executive authority and significant raises in salary, employees have to demonstrate that nothing interferes with their acceptance and pursuit of corporate goals. Although generally unspoken, this certainly rules out employees' demands for time, money, or privileges that might benefit family but at corporate cost. The higher the rise, the more unquestionable these priorities must be until the employee hardly recognizes anymore the distinction between what's good for the company and what's good for the family. In any case, a loyal and well paid insider doesn't usually want to lead the fight for subordinates who want to challenge corporate policy.

This total immersion in work has led to more parental guilt, Hochschild found. The higher the workers' income, the more time their children spent in child care; and in a large survey, only 9 percent felt that they were able to balance work and family well. This guilt, Hochschild says, leads to the "third shift," in which parents try, through treats, toys, and "quality time," to do damage control on the emotional consequences for children of such compressed family life.

Hochschild offers suggestions for workplace improvements but also makes it clear that in the presence of global capitalism, the decline of labor unions, and the erosion of civil society, workers' individual solutions will not change the system and may even disadvantage the individuals who use them. To change our society, the real culprit, she calls for the organization of a "Time Movement" to bring us back to the question that was first raised by the women's movement and then, perhaps, detoured by drastic post–Cold War economic and technological changes: "How can women become men's equals in a more child-oriented and civic minded society?" If home and work were nationally restructured to benefit families, and not left up to individual affluence, initiative, and willingness to risk one's job, then men, women and children could only benefit, Hochschild says.

Clinically then, it is very important that family therapists label the work-family problem as a *social* problem, to be dealt with by the *couple,* not a "woman's problem" for her to struggle with alone. Having clients read books, such as those mentioned here, and discussing the issue at length in therapy, should lead to the personal solutions which are what therapy is designed to produce and may also promote social or political action by the client in workplace or community. Whenever a client complains of a social or community problem, it is useful for the therapist to ask, "Is there anything you can do about that?" In my clinical practice, when asked that question, one couple organized their friends to spruce up and repair their dreary child care center, a woman executive lobbied for better maternity and paternity benefits in her father's company, and a young African American man got his church to sponsor a chapter of "Mad Dads" to take back their neighborhood from teen gangs and drug dealers (Carter & Peters, 1997).

The Power Imbalance

All of the above problems usually combine to produce a strong shift of power in the previously equal middle-class "new couple" back toward the traditional arrangement of breadwinner dad and domestic mom. Suddenly, or insidiously, the husband is earning and managing all or most of the money. He feels entitled to cast the deciding vote or veto on expenditures, and his wife does not feel entitled to contest his position nor to demand equal access to their money and equal voice in decisions. She becomes increasingly resentful, while he feels unappreciated. In the absence of an understanding of the failure of current social policy and lack of workplace support for their equal partnership, they blame each other, and their conflict and dissatisfaction with each other rise. Many couples in this predicament contemplate divorce and/or go to couples therapy.

An exception to the tendency of couples to shift back to traditional roles after children are born is couples in which the wife earns more money than her husband. This number, currently estimated at about 25 percent of working wives, continues to grow. It has been my clinical observation that wives who earn more than their husbands don't use that as power over their husbands but continue to minimize or deny the importance of their earnings and often continue to do or manage most of the housework. They do, however, use it as empowerment of themselves, being more willing than lower-earning wives to negotiate assertively with their husbands in decision making. I have sometimes thought that what it takes for gender equality is a higher-earning wife. The small number of wives who make 5 or 10 times more than their husbands are in a different category and, according to an article in the *New York Times,* (Samuels, 1995), often have husbands who quit their own jobs to stay home with the children. Usually, this high-earning wife's job is so all-consuming that, according to Harvard psychiatrist Gerry

Kraines, quoted in the above article, "the marriage can't tolerate two careers" (p. 23).

In light of the severity of the role conflict and socioeconomic squeeze on families with young children, it is not surprising to discover that this is the phase of the family life cycle with the highest divorce rate or that poorer couples have twice the divorce rate of financially comfortable ones (Norton & Miller, 1992.)

In addition to money, the issues of time, isolation, sexual dissatisfaction, and problems with distribution of chores arise out of the power shift that pushes the couple back toward traditional roles (Ault-Riche, 1994; Carter & Peters, 1997). These are often the complaints that resound endlessly in therapy sessions, tempting the therapist to work on practical solutions to specific issues instead of on the power imbalance itself, which, when righted, will enable the couple to negotiate fair resolutions of their own.

The sexual problems that appear at this stage, often arguments over frequency, may be a result of the new mother's exhaustion, especially if she is nursing, but also may become an arena in which to conduct their power struggle. The first is transient and will pass; the second is an ominous threat to the couple's relationship and, if not dealt with at this stage, will do much to corrode their subsequent life together.

Time now becomes a rare commodity, and as the new father buckles down to work and the need for more money, and as the new mother becomes absorbed in the care of her infant, in addition to continuing to work outside the home, their time alone together may virtually disappear. Jay Belsky found that recreational activities for new parents dropped 40 percent during year one, and he reported that in a *Parenting* magazine survey, 81 percent of couples had not spent one weekend alone and 91 percent had had no five-day vacation alone in the past year. Stay-at-home mothers, he reports, suffered most of all from isolation (Belsky & Kelly, 1994).

Shared Parenting

In the United States, as in most of the world, the idea of shared parenting is not new. Until relatively recently, whichever female relatives were around the farm, ranch, or urban development did much of the child care while mothers worked at their many chores—farming, laundry, sewing, cooking, etc.—all of which were much more time consuming than they are today. And nobody worried about the mother-child bond. What *is* new is the idea that fathers should be active, hands-on parents fully participating with their wives in the task that had fallen to mothers alone as the isolated nuclear family replaced the extended family household in the second half of this century.

This novel idea appeared, not surprisingly, in the 1950s, the famous decade of family togetherness. In *Manhood in America* (Kimmel 1996), the author refers to advice given in the 1950s by Dr. Benjamin Spock which made it clear that although no one was suggesting that men let parenthood interfere with their basic role of breadwinning, it was fine for fathers to change a diaper or make the formula occasionally. In other words, working fathers should "help" stay-home mothers parent—a new idea that was tailored to fit the 1950s family structure.

In the 1990s, the "new men" have gotten more involved in household work and child care than any previous American generation. Although their participation doesn't approach 50 percent, many men feel that it does because they are consciously so much more involved than their fathers were. In all surveys on the subject, American men of all ages say that family is the most important facet of their lives and fatherhood their most satisfying accomplishment. However, while the traditional definitions of male success (career achievement, money, and power) are being challenged, they still hold sway in most men's lives. And the new rules for "man the provider" are still very slippery. Is his wife fully committed to being a coprovider for life, or will she suddenly decide that she has to stay home with the children? Will he be penalized at work if he curtails his overtime or travel or takes family emergency leaves? In addition, the male socialization process that few men escape has probably left him cut off from his deepest feelings and somewhat fearful of emotional intimacy. So most

men are still just "helping" at home, even though their wives work outside the home too, many of them at full-time jobs.

Although mothers often ask their husbands for more help, they are usually reluctant to really share the role and decisions of parenting equally. Both men and women are still socialized to believe that mothers have special inborn or intuitive skills related to child care and that all young children need a mother as primary parent. In spite of all of the actual changes in our lives and in our beliefs, the two sacred cows—a "real man's" career and a "real woman's" mothering—maintain a stubborn hold on our emotions.

Family therapist Ron Taffel gave an excellent example of this problem with his description of a young "90's couple" who consulted him because of conflict over child-rearing (Taffel, 1994). Both parents described the housework and child care as divided fairly, with the wife doing a bit more (60 percent) because the husband worked longer hours (40 compared to her 30). Taffel asked each parent to make a separate list of tasks related to the children done by each of them on a given afternoon and evening. At the next session, the parents were rather shaken as the father's list of twelve items was followed by the mother's list of forty-six items. Further analysis revealed that the father's list consisted of talk at dinner, interactions, and direct care of the children, while the mother's, in addition to direct care, contained all of the tasks of planning, arranging, networking, and supervising various events in their lives. In other words, as Taffel puts it, "Mom's responsible; Dad helps out." The consequences of this paradigm, Taffel said, are that the mother feels central but overburdened and the father feels one-down and somewhat defensive. The children turn to mother as the real parent-expert and will someday pass along this paradigm to the next generation. Worst of all, Taffel concluded, mothers and fathers are in danger of leading parallel rather than intersecting lives.

In the book *Kidding Ourselves,* Rhona Mahony (1995) argues that women will never achieve equality with men as long as they insist on, or fall into, primary parenting. To change their part of this ingrained pattern, Mahony says, women must actively resist the pull of tradition and insist on a plan of joint child care from the earliest days. Otherwise, Mahony warns, the head start of mother's prenatal bonding leads inevitably to her gatekeeping on all matters involving the baby, tipping the system back to familiar, but unequal, mommy–daddy roles.

These roles are certainly familiar but they are not inevitable. In a recent study done at Yale (Pruett, 1994), seventeen families were followed in which fathers were the primary caregivers for their children. Nearly all of the fathers expressed the same feelings that new mothers do, such as fear of leaving the baby alone with anyone else, including the baby's mother! In her book about changing fatherhood, Kathleen Gerson (1993) reports that the results of five new studies on the subject show that men become mothers when they do not have wives to do it for them. Furthermore, Gerson found that when men's capacity for nurturing is activated when the child is an infant, men continue to feel competent to be involved in their children's lives.

So, it is not nature that keeps us locked in this dilemma, but rather the powerful grip of centuries-old economic and social arrangements acting on our emotions. The difficulty of really changing a pattern that is so ingrained, even when it needs to be changed and even when men and women want to change it, cannot be overestimated. Nor can the importance of helping parents in therapy deal with this issue in some way.

Child-Rearing and Discipline

The minute a child is born, often before, the nuclear family triangle (parents and child) is ready for potential activation. One of the biggest surprises for new parents may be the degree to which they discover passionate feelings about child-rearing, a subject to which they may have given little previous thought. However, the imprint of their own childhoods, their levels of maturity, and their internalized ideas about their own roles as parents make this a potentially hot issue for many couples.

Gender socialization, leading to unequal participation in child care, as Ron Taffel points out, only makes matters worse. Fathers are cast as "idealists," responsible for preparing the child for the outside world, and mothers as "pragmatists," doing whatever works to get them and the children through each day's "endless list" (Taffel, 1994).

These prescribed roles lead inevitably to the many destructive triangles of family life, especially those which polarize the parents in "too strict—too lenient" positions. "Father knows best" and "angry mommy and the naughty kids" are familiar, unhappy scenarios of family life in which one parent treats the other like one of the children.

Family therapists should help parents to develop age-appropriate, practical approaches to discipline on which both parents can agree. If they can't agree, we should help them to negotiate ways not to interfere with each other's methods, assuming, of course, that the particular methods are not harsh or harmful. Unless there is actual danger, one parent should not intervene at the time the other parent is disciplining a child. If there is disagreement, parents should discuss it in private and then either agree to disagree or shift parental responsibilities so that the parent who cares most about an issue (e.g., table manners) assumes responsibility for dealing with that issue. If the issue has already become a toxic one for parent and child, it will be more helpful to shift responsibility to the less concerned parent. The suggestion of shifting responsibility will usually unmask the underlying problem of the parents' unequal involvement in the role and work of parenting. Clinical approaches that don't address this imbalance will usually not end the disputes over child-rearing and discipline.

Another underlying issue in some conflicts over discipline is the parents' marital problems. If they are engaged in intense power struggles in other areas of their relationship, these will probably spill over into their approaches to child-rearing. Sometimes, when a particular child arouses parental anxiety, for emotional reasons or because of the child's physical or mental problems, parents will triangulate with this particular child and complain of discipline problems or child-rearing disputes that don't exist with the other children. In such cases, usually referred to in the literature as "child-focused families," the issue is not really discipline and has little or nothing to do with the child. Instead, issues with the family of origin or problems in the marital relationship may have created the intense triangle that then displaces the anxiety onto discipline concerns. None of this is to suggest that all or even most child-rearing arguments are a sign of basic marital problems, apart from the usual gender imbalance, or to suggest that such arguments will disappear automatically if parents work on their marital relationship or their families of origin. Even when marital or family problems are primary, it is necessary to first address the problem that brought the family to therapy. As the therapist and couple work on the child-rearing or discipline problems, it will usually become clear whether extensive work on the marital relationship and/or families of origin is essential to changing the presenting problems and maintaining the change.

PROBLEMS

Poor and Teenage Mothers and Children

A survey in 1995 (Bradsher, 1995) reports that poor children in the United States are worse off than poor children in all other industrialized Western nations, except Israel and Ireland. This is because the gap between rich and poor is so wide here and because our child welfare programs are so much less generous than those in Western Europe. The United States ranked eighteenth out of twenty countries in household income of families of poor children and first in household income of families of affluent children. Penelope Leach, the British expert on child development, states that of all the many risks for children in postindustrial societies, poverty puts children at more risk than any other single factor (Leach, 1994).

Although there is much general condemnation of single-parent families, especially the majority that are headed by women, it is very important for family therapists to realize that the structure itself

is not the problem and that single-parent families range across the whole spectrum from highly functional to highly dysfunctional, depending mostly on economics and emotional, family, and community connectedness (see Chapter 19, on poor Black families, and Chapter 24, on single-parent families). Too often, problems of poverty or emotional and social isolation are attributed solely to family structure. Thus, the isolation of the children of overworked, harried two-parent families may be overlooked while we approach every single-parent family from a deficit viewpoint. A useful clinical approach would investigate the status of the mother's family and friendship relationships and the degree to which she is connected to a supportive community, such as neighborhood, church, or temple. Obviously, poverty will exacerbate all of the usual problems of parents, as well as causing many new problems. If the mother is unmarried, she is facing the struggle alone, unless she is rooted in family and community.

Twenty-six percent of U.S. children born in 1994 were born to unmarried women, a percentage approximately equal to births outside of marriage in Canada, France, and the United Kingdom and only half the percentage of such births in Denmark and Sweden (U.S. Census Bureau, 1994). So this is a growing world phenomenon, and we need to develop helpful attitudes toward it. Clearly, the children of a financially stable woman who is emotionally connected to family, friends, and community should be expected to thrive whether their mother is married or unmarried.

Of all births to Black women in the United States in 1994, 66 percent were to unmarried women; of all births to White women, 19 percent were to unmarried women; and of all births to Hispanic women, 28 percent were to unmarried women. Of these, the most problematic category is the 7 percent of unmarried teenagers who bore a child that year (U.S. Census Bureau, 1994). In Western culture in our times, a teenager is, by definition, not ready to be a parent. In any social or economic bracket, a teenager is a child, regardless of intelligence, sophistication, or street smarts. This child needs further time to develop emotionally and intellectually before taking on the adult tasks of earning a living and parenting. Family therapy in this crisis should be aimed at protecting the young mother's development, as well as the baby's. Family therapy should help the teenager and her family come to a joint decision about abortion, relinquishing the baby for adoption, or keeping the baby. Plans should be made to continue the teenager's education if the decision is to keep the baby and for housing with mature family members who can provide assistance with baby care. Involvement of the baby's father, of course, depends on what kind of relationship, if any, he has had with the mother, whether they plan to remain a couple, and whether he can provide financial support. Up to 70 percent of these fathers are adult males (see Chapter 28). This means that these babies are a result of forcible rape, statutory rape, or incest, criminal actions that are seldom prosecuted.

Since a solid majority of American teenagers have had sex by the time they graduate from high school, it is important for the therapist to investigate the level of sex education attained by the teenage mother. The dissemination of birth control and disease control information to teenagers is a sensitive area with some families, and therapists need to approach this discussion diplomatically. The controversial welfare bill of 1996 did provide funds to combat teen pregnancy but, unfortunately, only for programs promoting abstinence from sexual contact. However, all states have applied for these funds, and none, so far, have cut other sex education approaches.

Homeless Families with Children

Of all the families our society neglects, homeless families with children are among the most desperate. Fewer than half of the children attend school, a statistic that is not surprising when we examine the Catch-22 residency regulations in many school districts that bar homeless children from both the school nearest their former home and the school in the neighborhood where they are temporarily residing (Edelman & Mihaly, 1989).

A recent study of homeless families with children (Twaite & Lampert, 1997) examined factors predicting favorable outcomes for 100 families participating in mandated preventive services for truant and homeless children age 10 to 16. They found that the severity of the child's pathology, the intensity of the parental involvement in treatment, parental attendance, and parental understanding of the child's problem were the factors that were related significantly to positive outcomes. This study provided the first empirical evidence of the relationship between the intensity of parental involvement and the effectiveness of such a program. Needless to say, this confirms the family therapy practice of treating children only if their parents or caretakers also participate.

Children with Disabilities

So many hopes and dreams are projected by parents onto their children that a serious illness or disability in the child wreaks havoc. The death of a child—the most untimely event imaginable—doubles the divorce rate (Carter & Peters, 1997).

When a child has a chronic or serious disability (see Chapter 29), it is important for the clinician to help the parents share their grief and sadness with each other and with other family members and friends. It often happens that their perceived need to cope and to "stay strong" for each other makes them fearful of "letting down." It is also essential that very specific plans be made to give respite and encourage other activities for the chief caregiver, usually the mother. She may need help giving herself permission to go to work, go on vacation, or just pursue individual interests and hobbies.

When parents express to the therapist their worry over a young child's functioning, a good first question is whether the child's caregiver or nursery school or other teacher has brought any problem to the parents' attention. Teachers and professional caregivers are used to a wide range of normal functioning and are quick to spot deviations from the norm. Spotting an apparent deviation and correctly diagnosing it, however, are two different things, and family therapists need to watch out for the "diagnosis of the year," in which new diagnoses are defined for school personnel, who then, like medical students, may tend to find them everywhere. At this writing, the favorite informal diagnosis around New York is A.D.D. (attention deficit disorder), but I well remember the years of M.B.D. (minimum brain dysfunction), unspecified "learning disabilities," and plain old "hyperactivity." Since most, if not all, such disabilities of children now come with recommended medications, it is important to help the parents obtain or confirm a correct diagnosis with a second opinion outside of school personnel. Once a diagnosis and treatment plan have been made, possibly including special education, therapists can help the parents not to slip into an adversarial relationship with the school. Such a triangle, fueled by the parents' anxiety, will severely complicate the school's work with the child.

Child Abuse

For a discussion of the dynamics and statistics on physical and sexual abuse of children, see the chapter on violence (Chapter 28). In 1995, federal statistics climbed to over one million abused children. This is a problem at every socioeconomic level in our society, and because so many of the assaults on children are perpetrated by their parents, relatives, caretakers, and family friends, they are all the more shocking. Therapists should be as alert to the signs or hints of child abuse as they are to indications of wife battering. Any suggestion of child abuse is a reason to stop whatever therapy-as-usual we are doing and explore in minutest detail the child's level of risk.

In the old days, a report of suspected child abuse usually resulted in the child's being removed from the home during the investigation. Now, in most states, it is possible to have the suspected perpetrator removed and/or denied access to the child. However, vigilant follow-up by the therapist is often necessary. Under no circumstances should a known child-abusing parent be included in family sessions until he or she has acknowledged the

problem, has agreed to whatever individual treatment and medication are currently recommended, and is ready to apologize in a meaningful way to the abused child and other family members. The leaders of abuser programs are usually good guides to the timing for including the abuser in couple or family sessions. Under no circumstances should it be assumed that abuse will cease as a result of couples or family therapy alone.

Infertility

A client of mine once said to me, "The only thing worse than having a child with problems is not being able to have a child at all." And, in fact, a British study (Kedem, Mikulnicer, Nathanson, & Bartov, 1990) reports that respondents who were asked to rate their most stressful life experiences rated infertility as high as the death of a child or a spouse! Such an experience of loss, of course, generates grief and mourning, which is reactivated with every attempt and failure to conceive, whether through natural means or infertility treatments. The intensity of the negative experience of infertility is often overlooked by the couple's family, friends, or even therapist, and there is danger that the couple will identify themselves as damaged or stigmatized, isolating themselves socially, creating stress, depression, and paralysis. This is especially likely when couples belong to ethnicities that particularly focus on the importance of children or fundamentalist religions that expect couples to produce many children. The director of reproductive endocrinology at New York University, Dr. Jamie A. Grifo, (p. 39) has stated that infertile couples are "traumatized" and have a "higher rate of depression than cancer patients" (Lee, 1996).

In their excellent article "An Infertility Primer for Family Therapists: Medical, Social, and Psychological Dimensions" (Meyers et al., 1995), the members of the Ackerman project studying this subject report that about one out of twelve married couples in the United States are infertile. The causes are 40 percent female, 40 percent male, 10 percent interactive, and 10 percent unknown. However,

Meyers et al. report that, regardless of cause, women exhibit greater emotional distress, probably because of their socialization to become mothers and also due to the fact that women receive the major portion of medical procedures for infertility.

Although White professional couples may form the largest consumer contingent of infertility services (which are extremely expensive), poor people of color with little formal education are more likely to be infertile (Meyers et al., 1995). Adding to the problem, there has been a great deal of controversy about Medicaid programs that might help poor women overcome fertility problems (Beck, 1994). Almost invisible among infertility sufferers are lesbian women who try endless cycles of alternative insemination before giving up the cherished goals of pregnancy and giving birth.

Although reproductive technology has created some dazzling new techniques to help Mother Nature along (at this writing, scientists in Britain have cloned a sheep and some calves, a 63-year-old woman has given birth, and some clinics are selling ready-made embryos for adoption), bioethical discussion and government regulation have not kept pace. Although infertility treatment is a boom industry in which couples spend more than 2 billion dollars a year, often more than $30,000 per couple, most of it not covered by insurance, the vast majority of treatment fails (*U.S. News and World Report,* Nov. 11, 1996). The failure rate appears to be at least three out of four couples (Meyers et al., 1995). In addition, some of the "successes" can be equally problematic, such as the single woman in England who was reported to be carrying octuplets after a course of fertility drugs. Such cases raise the agonizing dilemmas of multiple births following fertility drugs: "selective reduction" (abortion of some fetuses to save the others) or risks of serious birth defects that are much higher in multiple births.

Obviously, all protracted infertility treatments place enormous stress on the couple. Family therapists need to keep informed of the cutting-edge developments and problems of infertility treatments so that we can help couples to determine when it is time to stop such treatments and seek other ways of becoming parents.

ALTERNATE PATHWAYS TO PARENTHOOD

Although infertility treatments such as surgery, drug treatment, alternative insemination, in vitro fertilization, sperm injection, and surrogacy all provide a pathway to parenthood for a small percentage of infertile couples, their current relatively low rate of success and very high cost have kept this new technology from replacing the age-old alternative method of attaining parenthood: adoption.

Adoption

Every year, Americans adopt more than 100,000 children. Another half million people or more— grandparents, siblings, and other relatives—are touched by this process (McKelvey & Stevens, 1994). But the process and the prospects for successful adoption have become more complicated. This is due partially to the scarcity of White infants because of contraception and legal abortion, partially to the fact that more single mothers now feel free to raise their own children, and partially to the problems of the foster care system that was supposed to be part of the solution.

Foster Care

While many parents spend fortunes and travel across the world to adopt children, almost half a million U.S. children are in foster care. Sixty-seven percent of them are Black or of mixed race; two thirds are male; some have learning disabilities or emotional problems; most are between the ages of 5 and 11 (McKelvey & Stevens, 1994). These are the children called "hard to place"; and by the time the foster care system has moved, traumatized, and ignored them for years, many become even harder to place. The challenge for foster parents is to temporarily parent children from troubled families, knowing that they (the foster parents) will have no input into the children's future. The situation has become serious enough to get attention from President Clinton and even the U.S. Congress, which has approved a $5,000 tax credit for nonaffluent families who adopt and $6,000 for adopting a hard-to-place child (*New York Times,* Feb. 15, 1997).

Our society's neglect of poor children remains an outrage. The recent welfare bill has dismantled six decades of antipoverty policy, including welfare for poor children. Scant notice was given to the deletion in the bill of one word ("nonprofit"), which opens the way for profit-making businesses such as managed mental health care corporations or youth care chains that are traded on Wall Street, to compete for Federal welfare payments. The availability of this money guarantees an increase in foster care institutions, even though they have been shown to be detrimental to children's development over the long run. Children's advocacy groups, of course, have decried the use of poor children as a market commodity. This would seem to be an area begging for political action by mental health and child welfare workers, as well as parents of more fortunate children in this, the most affluent country in the world.

Open Adoption

The most revolutionary development in the adoption process is the growing interest in—and controversy over—open adoption. This is an adoption format in which birth parents and adoptive parents meet one another, share identifying and genetic information, and communicate directly over the years. Some may get together regularly and view each other as extended kin; others stick to written or mediated communication until the adoptees are in their late teens. While advocates list many obvious advantages in direct contact, which can break the negative power of the adoption triangle with its cut-offs, fantasies, and loyalty conflicts, critics most fear an invasion of adoptive family boundaries and the possibility that the birth parents may be inconsistent or even drop out of the children's lives (Gilman 1992).

In her excellent discourse on the serious problems produced by personal and institutional se-

crecy in adoption, Ann Hartman reminds us that if we will but listen, they—adoptees, birth parents, and adoptive parents—will teach us what we need to know to be helpful. Hartman points out that open adoption has been the norm in most countries and other times. Outcomes in our society will be known only by researching a generation of adopted children who grew up knowing their birth parents (Hartman, 1993).

Using mediation techniques to help clients design their children's adoptions, with written agreements about the degree of openness, clinician-researcher Jeanne Etter found that after four and a half years, 129 biological and birth parents involved in 56 open adoptions showed 98.2 percent compliance with the adoption agreement, and 93.8 percent satisfaction with having the adoption be open (Etter, 1993). Silverstein and Demick (1994) have proposed a conceptual framework. Grotevant, Elde, and Fravel (1994) report on a spectrum of closed, mediated, and open adoptions, suggesting that open adoptions showed many advantages. The authors wisely concluded with a plea for family therapists to pay closest attention to the individual situation rather then seeking a universal "solution."

It is essential that we help our clients think this through carefully to decide which route they choose to follow, and then help them with its particular challenges. In the end, studies conclude, four out of five of all adoptions are successful (Waldman & Caplan, 1994).

Informal Adoption

Nancy Boyd-Franklin has taught us the importance of understanding the reciprocity of goods and services that has been one of the most important survival mechanisms of African Americans (Boyd-Franklin, 1989). This sharing, she tells us, has produced permeable boundaries around the Black family household that contrast sharply with the rigid boundaries around most White nuclear families. These flexible boundaries have been an integral part of Black community life since the days of slavery, permitting adult relatives or friends of the family to take in children whose parents are unable to care for them for whatever reason. Since original adoption agencies were not designed to meet the needs of Black children, this informal network provided—and still provides—unofficial social services to poor Black families and children.

While the advantages of such sharing of scarce resources are clear now that Black family therapists have pointed them out to us, many early family therapists ignored the difference in poor Black family structure (see Chapter 19) or automatically considered it dysfunctional. Since Black clients understand all too well how their family structure may be judged by White therapists, they may be extremely uneasy if White clinicians do formal genograms early in treatment. It is probably wise for the clinician to simply make mental notes of family and household relationships as they arise naturally in the therapeutic conversation and write these down later. Most important to remember is the simple fact that while some of these structures are dysfunctional, with role and boundary blurring, many are extremely functional (Boyd-Franklin, 1989), as are extended family networks in other cultures. The competent clinician can assess which is which in the usual way: by closely exploring all relationships in each particular family system.

International Adoptions

Although international adoptions are costly, the costs can often be compared favorably to the high costs of infertility treatments. Thus, increasing numbers of Americans, fearful of or burnt out by lengthy treatments and the cost and difficulties of domestic adoption, have turned their sights abroad. This is so especially since the fall of Communism has added the countries of Eastern Europe to the list of the poor countries of Central and South America and Asia that permit foreign adoption. Individuals and couples considering this option should be urged to explore thoroughly the requirements of the foreign country, their particular state, and the Immigration and Naturalization Service (INS). Paperwork and bureaucracy will abound, and it is important to find a U.S. agency that can

help with red tape. Prospective parents should be prepared and willing to make a commitment to embrace the culture of their child and be able to teach the child his or her country's history and culture. In pursuit of this goal, adoptive parents often join American organizations such as Families with Children from China, which offer support and the opportunity to become involved with families with similar intercultural membership.

Gays and lesbians who wish to adopt internationally should be advised to pursue individual rather than couple adoption and to exercise their constitutional right to privacy by omitting mention of their sexual orientation during the application process, even if the U.S. agency is aware of it (Martin, 1993). This is necessary because of the high probability that gay and lesbian applicants will be rejected. Other concerns in international adoption are medical or delays in the child's physical and mental development. These should be explored thoroughly with the helping U.S. agency and with other parents who have adopted from the same country. Some concerns are serious; others are simply cultural differences or short-term lags due to insufficient stimulation or poor nutrition.

Interracial Adoptions

Some international adoptions are also interracial. However, domestic interracial adoptions usually consist of White parents adopting African American children. Some of the issues are similar, especially the need for parental commitment to teaching the child about his or her history and culture and help in developing a positive identity in both the birth and adoptive cultures (Zuniga, 1991). The well-known Black psychiatrists James Comer and Alvin Poussaint (1992) emphasize other issues: the importance of White adoptive parents' examining their motives carefully; the need to discuss racial difference calmly with the child from time to time along with the adoption story; and the need to protect the child from racism without overprotecting him or her. In this regard, Comer and Poussaint point out that although White parents may hear and see more racism even than Blacks do, they do not have the experience of needing to help their children deal with it. Comer and Poussaint warn against continual brooding or outraged reactions to racism, lest these transmit negative messages to the child about being Black. At the same time, it is important to provide a model of constructive ways to fight racism.

These authors also caution against middle-class or upper-middle-class parents' failing to find ways to expose their children to African Americans of their class. It makes sense that exposure only to lower-income status and jobs, and of course, to TV news programs with their selective nightly parade of Black arrests, creates problems for Black children. They need to hear from their parents early and often that they must persist in spite of racism and that they *can* "climb every mountain" (Comer and Poussaint, 1992). They will also learn from the lives of their parents and peers.

During the 1980s, Jerome and Karen consulted me about the acting out of their 12-year-old daughter, Susan. The parents were a White professional couple in their forties; Susan was their African American daughter, adopted in infancy. The family lived in an affluent, all-White Westchester community, where the only Blacks were maids, nannies, handymen, and delivery people. Jerome and Karen, idealistic ex-hippies, complained about Susan's growing rebelliousness and recent behavioral and academic problems in school. They were puzzled, they said, because Susan had previously done excellent schoolwork, was cooperative at home, and had many close friends.

Upon closer examination and conversations with Susan, alone and with her parents, it turned out that the parents had lost touch with Black friends they had known in the 1960s and had not found new ones in their White suburb. Susan's friends were also all White, both in the neighborhood and at school, and they had now started to talk endlessly about the boys, dates, dances, clothes, and romance that awaited them in high school. Although she didn't want to discuss it with me, it was clear that Susan was afraid of what her standing would be once the dating game commenced. I told the parents that the problem seemed to be that they were raising Susan as if she were White, which she wasn't, or as if it didn't matter that she was Black, which it did.

During the next six months, I encouraged the parents to locate community centers and activities both for themselves and for Susan in adjoining towns where there was ethnic, religious, class, and racial diversity. After a short period of defensiveness, they did so enthusiastically, joining a bicycling club, volunteering as parent chaperones at the neighboring town's school events, and joining in PTA discussions and town meetings. As they got to know Black parents whom they liked, they invited them home, along with their usual friends. Susan joined after-school sports and recreation groups at the neighboring town's YWCA. She was encouraged to invite her new friends, Black and White, to their home. Susan's difficulties at her own school diminished as she socialized with the new group of friends. Jerome and Karen reported their enjoyment at breaking out of their own self-imposed segregation. After six months, Karen announced, while Jerome beamed, "We don't know how we fell into this trap, but we did; this isn't 'success,' it's isolation. And now, as soon as Susan graduates from elementary school, we're getting out of it. We're going to move to the next town so that she can go to high school in the 'real world,' and we can pursue our new friendships and activities without all the driving back and forth." When I discussed this case with my colleagues, I called it "the community cure," and it was.

Of course, not all adoptive White parents would be as committed as Jerome and Karen were to doing whatever it took to support their child's racial identification. So it is not surprising that in 1996, when Congress approved a bill that punishes states that prevent or postpone a child's adoption while waiting for parents of the same race, some Black organizations objected and came out against interracial (White–Black) adoptions. President Clinton supported the bill, which did permit race to be considered, but only if there were two or more adoptive families of similar qualification. The purpose was to try to shorten a child's stay in the limbo of foster care, with its well documented failings and abuses.

Single-Parent Adoption

It seems common sense to suppose that a single person who seeks a child by adoption is probably able to carry out the responsibilities of parenting, and this is substantiated in a review of the literature (Shireman, 1995). Because single parents do not have partners to share responsibility, the support of family, friends, and community becomes all the more important. However, indications are that children adopted by single parents are as well adjusted as children adopted into two-parent homes. In fact, single-parent homes may be the placement of choice for some children.

It is extremely important for family therapists to keep an open mind about the strengths of single-parent families (see Chapter 24). Until there is greater flexibility in the adoption approval process and more understanding and respect for alternative family structures, however, some uncertain number of single-parent adoptions will continue to be unidentified lesbians and gay individuals who are not eligible to adopt as openly gay couples. A more promising situation for them is the right—recognized by the highest courts in only three states so far—of a person to adopt his or her unmarried partner's child. (Dao, 1995). This then bestows legal parental rights on unmarried heterosexual partners and gay and lesbian partners.

Lesbian and Gay Parenting

The variables that predict a positive transition to parenthood for lesbian and gay couples are the same (Martin, 1993) as those for heterosexual couples (Belsky & Kelly, 1994).

- Having realistic expectations.
- Having good couple communication.
- The adaptability of each partner to change.
- The ability to tolerate chaos, noise, sleep deprivation, and lack of solitude.

The pitfalls in the parental triangle are also the same: At first, there is the possibility that if there is a primary caretaker, he or she will be closer to the child and the other parent will feel left out. Because this would tend to be exacerbated if the primary parent were also the biological parent, lesbian couples are often especially careful to divide child care equally or, if that is not possible, to shift roles and have the nonbiological parent do the primary caretaking. When children are older and try to use the usual "divide and conquer" strategies on their parents, gay and lesbian parents are somewhat less vulnerable than heterosexual parents because both have received the same gender programming about parenting and are more likely to see eye to eye on child-rearing (Martin, 1993).

What is not the same, of course, is the level of stress caused by social stigma and lack of social, and sometimes familial, support. While it is true in some cases that contact with a child softens negative attitudes in the family of origin toward gay or lesbian offspring, it is also true that the news of an impending child brings all the coming-out issues to the fore again and may bring forth a new level of homophobia as parents who have privately accepted their child's sexual orientation feel threatened by how public a grandchild will be. Questions from family and others center on fears that a child will be hurt psychologically by the social stigma and/or by having parents of only one gender (Martin, 1993). It is hard for heterosexuals to fully own and try to correct the problem of social stigma as their own problem, not that of the gay or lesbian family. Straight people also tend to overlook the benefits such as flexibility, group pride, and multicultural awareness that can accrue to children who have to be raised with the tools to fight discrimination, as children of color are, as children of gay and lesbian families are, as children with disabilities are, and as Jewish children and children of other stigmatized ethnic groups are. It is also important for family therapists to remember that although many families reject their gay and lesbian children, most do not (Laird, 1996).

In this last decade of the twentieth century, referred to jokingly by some homosexuals as "the gay nineties," there has been a dramatic increase in the number and visibility of lesbian and gay couples raising children. In spite of the discrimination that keeps many gay parents from acknowledging their sexual orientation in surveys, estimates of lesbian mothers run up to 5 million, gay fathers up to 3 million, and children of these parents up to 14 million. No estimates fall below 1 million mothers, 1 million fathers, and 6 million children. The largest number of these children were born in previous heterosexual relationships; the second largest to single and coupled lesbians giving birth through known or unknown donor insemination and to surrogates bearing children for gay couples. The third largest group of children come through supposedly single-parent adoptions by lesbians or gay men, most of whom are actually coupled (Patterson, 1992).

In spite of efforts by social conservatives to discredit such families, not a single study has found children of gay or lesbian parents to be disadvantaged in any significant respect relative to children of heterosexual parents (Patterson, 1992). When conservative groups in Hawaii tried to forestall giving gay and lesbian couples the right to legally marry (Goldberg, 1996), they tried to do so by a focus on parenting and the best interests of children. This produced "the most ringing endorsement yet by a court of gay and lesbian parenting," (p. B16) with the judge declaring that the evidence produced by both sides "establishes that the single most important factor in the development of a happy, healthy and well-adjusted child is the nurturing relationship between parent and child" (p. B16).

It is important to remember that since gay and lesbian couples have few role models of specifically gay families, they tend to give much more thought to every step of the way than heterosexuals do:

- Because parenthood is not an assumption, couples discuss thoroughly all the pros and cons involved in the decision.
- Research has revealed that lesbians are more concerned then single heterosexual mothers about their children's having male role models and good relationships with adult men and have thus included male relatives more often in the children's activities (Kirkpatrick, Smith, & Roy, 1981).
- Great attention is paid to building support networks and joining or forming supportive communities to counteract social stigma.
- Idiosyncratic family rituals must be invented for every occasion (See Chapter 12).
- Since division of chores and child care are not based on gender in lesbian and gay families, this issue must be specifically discussed and decided.
- Since matters of inheritance and custody are not protected legally, parents have to make very specific advance arrangements in case of their death or the breakup of the couple—and then hope these arrangements hold up in court if challenged (see sample agreements in Pies, 1988). For this reason, Johnson and Colucci (Chapter 20) urge gay and lesbian parents to get legal advice shortly before or after a child joins the family.

In all clinical work with gay and lesbian families, it is essential to keep the following caveats in mind:

1. Stay carefully informed about the social policy context these families face in all aspects of their lives: They are excluded from the U.S. Census Bureau's definition of family; their civil rights are protected in only eight states; their sexual contact is criminalized in over twenty states (and, of course, in the U.S. military); and they lack the legal protection granted to heterosexuals by marriage, divorce, custody, and inheritance laws (Hartman, 1996).

2. Gay and lesbian couples are both similar to and different from heterosexual couples and from each other. Only accurate personal information will help us to avoid categorizing, essentializing, or overgeneralizing about gay and lesbian couples (Murphy, 1994).

3. If the heterosexual world is open to learning from so-called alternative families, the planned lesbian family is a living laboratory of the partnership model that heterosexuals keep striving to achieve: Both parents are heads of household, each is a primary parent, each is a breadwinner, household chores are divided fairly, and decision making is joint. Participants in one study of planned lesbian families described their families as providing more parental involvement, concern, attention, nurturance, physical affection, expression of feelings, talking, sensitivity, love, caring, and warmth (Mitchell, 1995). That sounds good to me.

CLINICAL GUIDELINES

Evaluation

Whatever the presenting problem is, the entire three- or four-generation family system should be carefully evaluated at five levels:

1. Each individual's development and functioning (see Chapter 2).
2. The couple's relationship and interactions: communication, decision making, time, money, power, intimacy. This includes the nuclear family's handling of life cycle tasks (see Figure 1.1: The Stages of the Family Life Cycle, in Chapter 1), emotional triangles, and issues.
3. The extended Family's current and past patterns of relating and handling loss, secrets, myths, emotional triangles, and toxic issues.
4. The family members' involvement in the community: neighborhood, school, clubs, sports, church, temple, or other community organization. This involves parents' values and beliefs about life, spirituality, social or political action, etc.
5. The applicable rules, norms, and options available in the larger social system depending on the family members' race, ethnicity, class, gender, and sexual orientation.

For a fuller elaboration of these levels, see Chapter 1.

Sharon phoned for a therapy appointment for the couple because of her anger about Gary's long work hours and distant fathering style. In the first session, I ascertained that Gary—a New York City lawyer—and Sharon—a psychologist with a small private practice in Scarsdale—jointly earned over $300,000 a year. They lived in Scarsdale, New York's most affluent suburb, owned a vacation house and two cars, employed a live-in nanny, and paid most of the expenses for the condo owned by Sharon's parents in Florida. Gary worked sixty-five to seventy hours a week, including most Saturdays. He brought work home for Sunday and rarely arrived home on weekdays before 8:00 or 9:00 P.M. Sharon worked about twenty-two hours a week spread over four half-days and two evenings. Gary saw the two young children briefly in the mornings and tried to spend Sunday afternoon with Sharon and the kids. As a couple, they had "no time." Gary vetoed all of Sharon's efforts to get him to cut back his work hours on the grounds of their high expenses and his career goal of becoming a partner in his law firm.

Evaluation

1. Each individual
Each adult and child in the nuclear family appeared to be physically healthy and functioning satisfactorily. No description of extended family members indicated any major physical or mental illness there.

Emotionally, Gary talked about work in a somewhat compulsive, distant way, and Sharon sometimes sounded like a parent, rather than daughter or sibling, in her family of origin.

2. The Couple
- There was no couple time; sex was infrequent.
- The formerly equal couple was imbalanced, with Gary now ignoring or vetoing suggestions he didn't agree with. They had no effective method of discussing or negotiating differences.
- Family tasks were polarized, with Sharon doing or supervising all domestic tasks and Gary earning most of the income.
- Sharon complained of Gary's lack of emotional expressiveness and he of her excessive emotionality. These descriptions seemed consistent with their gender and ethnic differences.

3. The Family Emotional System
- In the nuclear family, father and children spent too little time together; Gary was com-

pletely uninvolved in the household schedules and tasks; Sharon was the only hands-on parent. *Main Triangle:* Sharon and children close and Gary distant.

• Relations with the families of origin were not emotionally functional. Gary was extremely distant from his parents, and they hardly saw him or Sharon. They were minimally involved as grandparents.

• Gary called his father "an uncaring workaholic" but was shocked when Sharon called him (Gary) a chip off the old block. Gary's mother had never complained about his father's work focus and, in fact, had delivered emotionally laden messages to him about the importance of work.

• Sharon was a typical overresponsible oldest daughter who felt obligated to take care of everyone in her family of origin. She contributed money to her sister so that she wouldn't have to move after divorce; she shrugged off her affluent younger brother's refusal to contribute financially to their parents; and she never objected to family members' impositions on her time or money.

Significant Intergenerational Triangles
• Gary–Sharon–their children
• Gary–his father and mother
• Gary's father–Gary–Gary's children
• Gary's family–Gary–Sharon
• Sharon–her mother and father
• Sharon–her parents–her sister Lydia
• Sharon–her parents–her brother Josh
• Sharon's family–Sharon and Gary

Major Emotional Issues
Time, work, money, fathering, caretaking, lack of intimacy, lack of negotiating skills, not living according to their own values.

Major Emotional Threats
• Growing distance and resentment between the couple
• Emotional distance between father and children

4. *Community*
The nuclear family is extremely isolated. Gary and Sharon's schedules had no time for involvement in any community organization whatsoever, except for a half-day once a month that Sharon vol-

unteered at Sophie's nursery school—"so they don't think I'm a bad mother," as she said.

They had no religious affiliation, each having rejected the parents' religion—his Protestant, hers Jewish. Gary felt that the secular culture promoted most of the holidays and traditions he cared about and had grown up with. For Sharon, this was not true. She had thought about joining a synagogue, but Gary always reminded her of their earlier agreement to leave religious affiliation out of their lives.

Occasionally, when Sharon pleaded for weeks, they would go to dinner and the theater. But neither of them felt there was time for any other social event. When Sharon's parents or sister insisted, Sharon took the kids to visit them without Gary.

5. *The Family's Place in the Larger Social System*
This is a White, heterosexual, affluent, educated professional couple. Gary is an Anglo American. By these measures, the family belongs to the most powerful groups in our society. Thus, if they can get psychologically free enough to avail themselves of their options, they have more power to change their situation than the members of any other group would have. The norms of the social system that militate against their getting psychologically free enough to use their options are as follows:

• The socially approved male focus on career and money, reinforced by Gary's parents' example and messages about the "work ethic."
• Gary and Sharon's affluent, consumerist, time-starved life-style, called "success," and envied by their peers.
• The rigidity of the fast-track career path for corporate lawyers.
• Sharon's belief, socially approved and ethnically reinforced, that it is a daughter's "duty" to respond to the wishes and needs of her family of origin regardless of strain on her own emotional and financial resources.
• Gary's belief, consistent with decades of social practice, that young children are fine as long as their mother is available, and fathers need only "provide."

The Therapy

In therapy, Gary and Sharon accomplished the following:

• Gary agreed to come home "early" (by 7:00 P.M.) at least one night a week.

• Sharon stopped giving her sister money (and her sister moved to a house in a town that she could afford). Sharon remained in close contact with her sister.

• Gary's talks with his mother revealed a secret about the issue of work: Gary's maternal grandfather had been an alcoholic with a checkered work history who had once spent several years in jail for forgery, leaving his family on welfare. This had led Gary's mother to preach the value of working hard ever after. Now Gary could see the emotionally programmed aspects of his own work habits. He agreed to come home before 7:00 P.M. two nights a week.

• Sharon worked to restore a relationship with her brother by mail and by phone and eventually requested that he start contributing his share of support to their parents. He agreed and resumed regular contact with them.

• Gary had brief, difficult, but useful talks with his father about work. His father finally acknowledged that he regretted missing Gary's youth. Gary urged him not to miss his grandchildren's youth as well. The number of visits to and from Gary's parents increased from one a year to four, interspersed with calls and gifts.

• Gary and Sharon spent many weeks going over their budget. Sharon said that she would agree to sell their vacation house if Gary would get a less demanding job. He said that he would think about it, and he eventually did, moving to a slower-paced suburban firm at a lower salary. They then sold their vacation house, causing Sharon's family to make other summer plans.

• Sharon joined a synagogue after a long discussion of their religious and ethnic differences, and she participated in the temple's discussion groups and in a social program to help the homeless. Gary joined the men's group I referred him to and became politically active at the urging of other group members.

• After much discussion of "mother guilt," Sharon cut out one evening of work and gave the night off to their nanny so that she and Gary could parent together and then spend a quiet evening alone.

• Gary and Sharon celebrated these dramatic moves as the crowning proof that they could now negotiate very difficult issues. They attributed their agreement to downshift to our discussions, which contrasted their early dreams, values, and ideals with the reality of their current life.

• Gary and Sharon joined a group that met monthly for dinner and theater.

• Gary said that as "daddy time" with his kids got more frequent, it got more enjoyable. "Like sex with Sharon," he added with a smile.

On making the many profound changes that they did, Gary and Sharon had three major advantages: They had an earlier strong, passionate bond and dreams to return to; their families of origin, although problematic in many ways, were essentially free of major dysfunctional patterns; and their privileged positions in the social hierarchies gave them maximum flexibility for change once they decided to go for it. It is important to note here that being in a privileged position does not in itself motivate people to change. In fact, quite the contrary is often true, depending on the degree of importance assigned by the client to maintaining maximum money and power regardless of emotional consequences.

Although this is hardly a typical, everyday case, it does illustrate what can sometimes be accomplished when the clients are motivated and the therapist keeps an eye on the big picture.

Shifting Focus among Levels

Our clinical work does not lend itself to moving in an orderly way from one level of the system to the next, any more than real life does. So, although therapy usually begins with the presenting problem—at this phase, often a child problem—the therapist's work will address the marriage, the family of origin, the community, and the constraints of the larger social system and back again during any phase of therapy or even in any given session. That is how I worked with Gary and Sharon. However, to get a sustained focus and eventual resolution of some issues, it is well to keep mental track of the focus and its shifts.

Be aware of a client's repeated shift away from an uncomfortable area—maybe the marriage—

back to a more "comfortable" problem—maybe the child. When I become aware of this, I might mentally allot the first fifteen minutes to the parents' preferred focus before shifting with some question about the marriage. Or I might work on the marriage indirectly through discussions of parenting roles.

Similarly, if a task to change behavior with a grandparent gets followed in the next session with a child or marital crisis, as sometimes happened with Gary and Sharon, it is important to make mental note of this even if the opportunity to ask about the grandparent is postponed until later, or even the next session. The important point is that the therapist track the process.

On the macro level, I attempt to help a couple achieve some small initial resolution of their presenting problems before introducing the idea of actual work in the family of origin. My first move with Gary and Sharon was to get Gary to agree to come home early one evening a week. However, in any session, I might openly refer to extended family information gathered in the evaluation and connect it to the presenting problem to show that family of origin is a relevant focus. Thus, my questions about Gary's parents and work made it clear that this was an intergenerational issue as well as a problem of the couple.

Questions and comments about community and the rules and norms of the larger social system are usually quite easy to introduce into the discussion, since there is often not as much defensiveness or resistance to talking about these areas as there is to personal and family issues. Of course, it is all connected in the end, as Gary and Sharon discovered when questions about community led to their deeply personal exchange about their religious and ethnic differences.

There is still debate in family therapy about when or whether to include young children in sessions. I believe that changes in children up to adolescence depend on parental intervention on their behalf or on changes in parental attitudes and behaviors. Also, children are too powerless to change the system but sometimes feel responsible if included in problem-focused discussion and complaints. However, I ask detailed questions about their development and try to see them once or twice to verify their parents' observations.

Discipline

Many parental arguments are about disciplining children, and these will spill over into therapists' offices, where we will be called upon to say who's "right." This is the time to have reading material for parents, or to recommend a book for them to buy, rather than step into that triangle ourselves. Harriet Lerner's latest book, *The Mother Dance* (1998) is particularly effective against all of the pitfalls that precipitate discipline problems: parental guilt, anxiety, over-responsibility and uncertainty.

Ron Taffel's book (1994) has a chapter entitled "Everything You Need to Know about Discipline." The chapter helps parents to teach their children that there are consequences for their behavior and limits to parental patience and gives many practical consequences by age of the child.

It is important to remember that ethnicity and class play a strong role in what parents have learned is appropriate discipline, and we should ask clients about their experience and ideas. Comer and Poussaint (1992) remind us that Black parents have often been strict disciplinarians of children because they felt that they had to force their children to obey so that they wouldn't violate racial rules and come to harm. While agreeing with many Black parents who find White middle-class parents too permissive, the authors come out strongly against spanking or shaming and provide useful alternatives by age.

Transition Groups

In their book describing a landmark ten-year study of the transition to parenthood, Cowan and Cowan (1992) describe one of their interventions: They ran a short-term (six-month) group for couples in which the wife was entering the seventh month of pregnancy. For three months before the birth, the couple exchanged expectations; for three months after, they discussed and negotiated problems. The agenda consisted of both items raised by the couples and topics suggested by the leaders. After the birth, the baby was included in the group.

The couples evaluated the experience as very helpful, and no one ever dropped out of a group. The Cowans found that the positive effects of stress reduction lasted a full three years and were especially evident in years 2 and 3. They found that their groups provided the best elements of consciousness-raising groups, support groups, group therapy, and couples therapy. No couple in these groups divorced during the first three years of follow-up, although 10 percent of couples in their study as a whole did.

Helping Parents to Negotiate

The transition to parenthood usually provides the first really hard issues that couples have to learn to negotiate. After they have been helped to restore or enhance their equality, which is the most essential element, the actual process of negotiating is quite simple (Carter & Peters, 1997):

- Know what you want.
- State it clearly and calmly.
- Listen to your partner's position and try to understand his or her emotional investment in that position.
- Work toward a win-win resolution that incorporates something for each partner, such as taking turns or trade-offs.
- Have a viable alternative if negotiations fail.

Helping Fathers to Be More Involved

Ron Taffel (Taffel, 1994) has a lot to say about how he helps men to move more toward child care. He talks with them frankly about their fear of incompetence, fear of their own angry reactions, fear of losing out in their career, and a general sense that they lack the requisite access to their own emotions. I also have such discussions routinely with fathers and find them very productive (Carter, 1993). It is important for the therapist to take a nonblaming stance. After all, you

and the client are up against 5,000 years of more distant fathering, and such a pattern can't be changed overnight. But that's no reason not to start somewhere.

Levine, Murphy, and Wilson (1993) describe many strategies for involving men in early childhood programs. Many of these techniques are generally applicable to encouraging men's participation in family therapy and family life; for example, expect them to be involved, find out what they want, recognize hidden resistance in yourself or the wife, reach out, and recognize men's hidden fears of emotional arenas.

Helping White Parents to Prepare Their Children for a Multicultural World

In about fifty years, this country will have no single majority race or ethnic group. The White population will have to accommodate itself to loss of majority status and learn how to live, work, and relate to people of other races. In some communities, of course, this is already happening, especially in larger cities. However, mostly, it is not happening. But those who are not prepared to embrace or at least accept diversity will be at a severe disadvantage in years to come. There are many White parents who would not wish their children to be among those die-hards, although with the obliviousness of privilege, they may not realize that they need to act now to prevent a later scenario of confusion, disorder, or even violence.

In the excellent book *40 Ways to Raise a Non-Racist Child,* Mathias and French (1996) explore the many ways in which parents can help their children in this regard: Make acquaintances across color lines yourself, trace your family's history of prejudice, begin the lessons early, don't pretend that discrimination doesn't exist, tell the whole story behind the holidays (e.g., Columbus Day, Thanksgiving), choose children's schools carefully to ensure diversity, expand their circle of playmates to include children of other races and cultures, and monitor carefully what they read and watch on TV to check what messages they are receiving on this subject.

Most White parents are surprised to learn that by age 3, a child is aware of and concerned about similarities and differences in skin color and hair (Comer & Poussaint, 1992). This whole subject of multiculturalism is a topic that usually needs to be raised by the therapist, since it is probably not included in popular child care books and White parents may be unaware of its importance to them personally.

Helping Minority-Group Parents to Protect Their Children in an Oppressive Society

Unlike many White heterosexual parents, parents in current minority groups are only too aware of the potential harm to their children of being part of a socially stigmatized group such as people of color and gay and lesbian families. And although all of the items mentioned above also apply here, there are a few in addition: Pay close attention to the child's level of self-esteem, feelings of competence, and positive group identification; and make extra efforts to belong to communities of families like yours both for support and to counteract the negative effects of feeling stigmatized and alienated from the larger society.

Therapists having such discussions with minority group parents, if they are not members of the same group, should prepare themselves by reading carefully, and then recommending books and articles for the clients to read, such as those referred to in this chapter.

Talking to Parents about Values

It is the essence of a parent's job to teach their children what they themselves have learned about how to live a meaningful life. If parents don't think about and articulate their own values, children will infer them from the way their parents live. It is better for us to think about what we want to teach.

Dr. Benjamin Spock, who moved with the times, declared in 1997 that "parental hesitancy" had become the most common problem in childrearing (pp. 123). Dr. Spock strongly emphasized the importance of parental discussion of their principles about crucial topics such as human relations and personal values. He supported the idea of encouraging children to ask questions about everything, including sex, and suggested that parents convey its connection to relationship. He also stated that children need to develop spiritual values and a sense of idealism such as the importance of kindliness, loyalty, and helping others. Children need to see their own parents involved at school, in the community, and in the political process if they are to learn to care about others.

This stage of life is a crucial one at which to help parents look hard at how they are living and ask themselves if this is what they want. In the scramble to make enough money, raise children, and pursue their own careers, parents often fall into one accommodation or another without really meaning to. Because of the complexity of family life at this stage and the paucity of meaningful support from our society, parents deserve an opportunity in family therapy to explore all options and possibilities for a more meaningful family life. Such discussions may lead them to redesign their own roles and relationship regardless of gender imperatives, and/or to realign their relationship to the larger society by redefining "success" in the world to suit themselves (Saltzman, 1991).

CONCLUSION

In spite of all the complexities and difficulties of contemporary family life, I have never actually met any parent who regretted being a parent. Whenever we have done life cycle exercises with trainees, grouping people by life cycle stage and having them discuss the issues, one of the childless participants always says something like, "It's too hard. Why does anyone have children?" At this point, the parents laugh in astonishment and fall all over each other trying to describe the joys, pleasures, and transcendence of parenthood. Maybe it's like talking about sex to a virgin—the problematic aspects of it may be clear, but it's almost impossible to fully articulate the physical, sensory, intellectual, emotional, and spiritual experience of connectedness to another human being through love.

REFERENCES

Ault-Riche, M. (1994). Sex, money and laundry: Sharing responsibilities in intimate relationships. *Journal of Feminist Family Therapy, 6*(1), 69–87.

Barnett, R., & Rivers, C. (1996). *She works/he works: How two-income families are happier, healthier, and better off.* New York: HarperCollins.

Beck, M. (1994). The infertility trap, *Newsweek, 123,* 30–31.

Belsky, J. & Kelly, J. (1994). *The transition to parenthood.* New York: Dell.

Blankenhorn, D. (1994). *Marriage in America: A report to the nation.* New York: Institute for American Values.

Boyd-Franklin, N. (1989). *Black families in therapy.* New York: The Guilford Press.

Bradsher, K. (1995, Aug. 14). Low ranking for poor American children, *New York Times,* p. A9.

Carter, B. (1993). Video: Clinical dilemmas in marriage: The search for equal partnership. Produced by Steve Lerner, distributed by Guilford Publications, New York.

Carter, B. & Peters, J. (1997). *Love, honor and negotiate: Building partnerships that last a lifetime.* New York: Pocket Books.

Casper, L. (1996). *Who's Minding Our Preschoolers?* Report P70–53. Washington, DC: U.S. Bureau of the Census.

Casper, L. (1997). *What does it cost to mind our preschoolers?* Report P70–52. Washington, DC: U.S. Bureau of the Census.

Comer, J. P., & Poussaint, A. F. (1992). *Raising Black children.* New York: Plume, Penguin Books.

Cowan, C., & Cowan P. (1992). *When partners become parents: The big life change for couples.* New York: Basic Books.

Crittenden, D. (1995, August 22). Yes, motherhood lowers pay, *New York Times,* p. A15.

Edelman, M. W., & Mihaly, L. (1989). Homeless families and the housing crisis in the U.S., *Children and Youth Services Review, 11,* 91–108.

Etter, J. (1993). Levels of cooperation and satisfaction in 56 open adoptions." *Child Welfare, 72*(3), 257–267.

Gerson, K. (1993). *No man's land: Men's changing commitments to family and work.* New York: Basic Books.

Gilman, L. (1992). *The adoption resource book* (3rd ed.). New York: HarperCollins.

Goldberg, C., (1996, Dec. 5). Gain for same-sex parents, at least, *New York Times,* p. B16.

Grotevant, H. D., McRoy, R. G., Elde, C. L. & Fravel, D. L. (1994). Adoptive family system dynamics: Variations by levels of openness in the adoption. *Family Process, 33,*(2), 125–146.

Hartman, A. (1993). Secrecy in Adoption. In E. Imber-Black (Ed.), *Secrets in families and family therapy,* (pp. 86–105). New York: Norton.

Hartman, A. (1996). Social policy as a context for lesbian and gay families: The political is personal. In J. Laird & R.-J. Green (Eds.), *Lesbians and Gays in Couples and Families.* San Francisco: Jossey-Bass.

Hochschild, A., with A. Machung (1989). *The second shift: Working parents and the revolution at home.* New York: Viking.

Hochschild, A. (1997). *The time bind: When work becomes home and home becomes work.* New York: Metropolitan Books, Holt.

Kedem, P., Mikulincer, M., Nathanson, Y. E., & Bartov B. (1990). Psychological aspects of male infertility. *British Journal of Medical Psychology, 63,* 73–80.

Kimmel, M. (1996). *Manhood in America: A cultural history.* New York: Free Press.

Kirkpatrick, M., Smith, C., & Roy, R. (1981). Lesbian mothers and their children: A comparative survey. *American Journal of Orthopsychiatry, 51,* 545–551.

Laird, J. (1996). Invisible ties: Lesbians and their families of origin. In J. Laird & R.-J. Green (Eds.), *Lesbians and gays in couples and families: A handbook for therapists,* 89–122. New York: Jossey-Bass.

Leach, P. (1994). *Children first: What our society must do—and is not doing—for our children today.* New York: Alfred A. Knopf.

Lee, F. (1996, Jan. 9). The fertility market, *New York Times,* p. 1.

Lerner, H. (1998). *The mother dance: How children change your life.* New York: HarperCollins.

Levine, J., Murphy, D. & Wilson, S. (1993.) *Getting men involved: Strategies for early childhood programs.* New York: Scholastic.

Mahony, R. (1995). *Kidding ourselves: Breadwinning, babies and bargaining power.* New York: Basic Books.

Martin, A. (1993) *The lesbian and gay parenting handbook.* New York: HarperCollins.

Mathias, B. & French, M. A. (1996). *40 ways to raise a non-racist child.* New York: Harper Collins.

McKelvey, C., & Stevens, J. (1994). *Adoption crisis.* Golden, CO: Fulcrum.

Meyers, M., Diamond, R., Kezur, D., Scharf, C., Weinshel, M., & Rait, D. (1995). An infertility primer for family therapists: Medical, social and psychological dimensions. *Family Process, 34,* 219–229.

Mitchell, V. (1995). Two moms: Contribution of the planned lesbian family to the deconstruction of gendered parenting. *Journal of Feminist Family Therapy, 7,3,*(4) 47–63.

Murphy, B. C. (1994). Difference and diversity: Gay and lesbian couples. *Journal of Gay and Lesbian Social Services, 1,*(2), 5–31.

New York Times (1997, Feb. 15). Clinton urges plan to speed adoptions, p. 12.

Norton, A., & Miller, L. (1992). *Marriage, divorce and remarriage in the 1990's.* Washington, DC: U.S. Bureau of the Census.

Patterson, C. J., (1992). Children of lesbian and gay parents. *Child Development, 63* 1025–1042.

Pies, C. (1988). *Considering parenthood* (2nd ed.). Minneapolis, MN: Spinsters Book Co.

Pleck, J. H. (1994). Family-supportive employer policies and men: A perspective. *Working Paper Series, 274.* Wellesley, MA: Wellesley College Center for Research on Women.

Pruett, Kyle, M. D., cited in *Working Mother,* July 1994. p. 32.

Saltzman, A. (1991). *Down-Shifting: Reinventing success on a slower track.* New York: Harper Perennial.

Samuels, P. (1995, Feb. 12). The executive life. *New York Times,* p. 23.

Shireman, J. F., (1995). Adoptions by single parents. *Marriage and Family Review, 20* (3–4), 367–388.

Silverstein, D. R., & Demick, J. (1994). Toward an organizational-relational model of open adoption. *Family Process, 33*(2), 111–124.

Spock, B. (1997, May). Take charge parenting. *Parenting,* Special Issue, p. 123.

Taffel, R., with Israeloff, R. (1994). *Why parents disagree: How women and men parent differently and how we can work together.* New York: William Morrow.

Twaite, J., & Lampert, D. T. (1997). Outcomes of mandated preventive services programs for homeless and truant children: A follow-up study. *Social Work, 42*(1), 11–18.

U.S. Bureau of the Census, (1994). *The fertility of American women.* Washington, DC: Author.

U.S. News & World Report (1996, Nov. 11). The baby makers, p. 10.

Waldman, S., & Caplan, L. (1994), The politics of adoption, *Newsweek, 123,* 64–5.

Whitebrook, M. (1997, April 20). Study sponsored by the national center for the early childhood work force. *New York Times,* p. 32.

Zuniga, M. (1991). Transracial adoption: Educating the parents. *Journal of Multicultural Social Work, 1,*(2), 17–31. Binghamton, NY: Haworth Press.

CHAPTER 16

TRANSFORMATION OF THE FAMILY SYSTEM DURING ADOLESCENCE

NYDIA GARCIA PRETO

The adaptations in family structure and organization that are required to handle the tasks of adolescence are so basic that the family itself is transformed from a unit that protects and nurtures young children to one that is a preparation center for the adolescent's entrance into the world of adult responsibilities and commitments. This family metamorphosis involves profound shifts in relationship patterns across the generations, and while it may be signaled initially by the adolescent's physical maturity, it often parallels and coincides with changes in parents as they enter midlife and with major transformations faced by grandparents facing old age. There are significant differences in the ways families adapt to these changes depending on the meaning that the family gives to adolescence as a life stage and to adolescent roles and behaviors. Cultural factors and socioeconomic forces greatly affect how families define this stage of development.

As the twenty-first century approaches, families in the United States are more than ever challenged by the risks of living in an increasingly endangered environment and in a society in which, largely for economic reasons, parents choose or are forced to work longer and longer hours, limiting the time they can spend at home with their children. Diminished connections to extended family and community have left parents struggling alone and more dependent on external systems for teaching children and for setting limits on them. At the same time, teenagers are turning more and more to their peers for emotional support and to the pop culture promoted by the media for values and ideas about life. As a result, the family's function as an emotional support system is threatened. The threat is greater for families that are economically disadvantaged and living in poor urban and rural neighborhoods.

This chapter focuses on the overall transformation that families experience as they try to master the tasks of adolescence, keeping in mind that perceptions about adolescent roles and behaviors vary depending on the socioeconomic and cultural context. Most families, after a certain degree of confusion and disruption, are able to change the rules and limits and reorganize themselves to allow adolescents more autonomy and independence. However, certain universal problems are associated with this transition that can result in the development of symptoms in the adolescent or in other family members. Clinical cases will illustrate some of the blocks that families experience during this phase, as well as factors that may contribute to family disorganization or symptomatic behavior and therapeutic interventions that may be effective with these families.

THE SOCIOCULTURAL CONTEXT

The experiences that we have during adolescence in our families, community, and society greatly affect the way in which we teach and guide adolescents later in life. Our cultural values, attitudes about gender, and beliefs about life and death are central factors influencing the formation of their identities. However, the culture in which we live has a tremendous impact on that process.

In the United States, patriarchal values and racism shape relationship patterns between men and women. Men have more political and economic power than women. Whites have more privilege than people of color do. Sexism and racism are sources of social oppression that affect all men and women in this culture and that marginalize and abuse women, people of color, and homosexuals. The media promote and reinforce these values on a daily basis. Adolescents, particularly, are vulnerable to media exploitation. Their values and beliefs about life, their views about gender relationships, the way they dress, talk, and walk are all greatly influenced by what they see on TV and in films and by the music they hear.

The music they listen to, especially, reflects the attitudes of the peer group with which they identify. In most schools and communities in the United States, adolescents, like adults, segregate along racial, cultural, and class lines. Their identity as female, male, lesbian, gay, White, Black, Asian, Latino, rich, poor, smart, or learning disabled is partly shaped by how the media portray those roles. Yet many adolescents cannot identify with the images promoted by the media, nor do they have access to the products being sold. They feel marginalized by society and invisible, and some don't even experience the process of adolescence because they go from childhood directly into adulthood.

In White, middle-class mainstream America, turning 13 "normally" means becoming a legitimate teenager, an adolescent, and symbolizes growth toward physical and emotional maturity, responsibility, and independence. But turning 13 doesn't necessarily have the same meaning for poor African Americans or for Latino and Asian immigrants who are marginalized in this society and have little access to economic resources. Adolescence, for many in these groups, means assuming adult responsibilities as soon as possible. Many have children at age 14, quit school, and go to work as soon as they can be hired. Others stay home to take care of brothers, sisters, or parents who are unable to take care of themselves (Burton, Obeidallah, & Allison, 1996). Some cultures may encourage adolescents to fulfill adult responsibilities, such as caretaking duties, or to contribute financially to the home, yet still expect them to remain obedient to and respectful of parents. Becoming independent, living on one's own, such an important goal in the United States, may not have the same value in other cultures, in which interdependence is preferred (McGoldrick, Giordano, & Pearce, 1996).

DEVELOPING A GENDER IDENTITY

By age 2, children are able to distinguish girls from boys, and by age 4, they begin to identify tasks according to gender. As they develop physically, emotionally, spiritually, and intellectually, distinct differences between boys and girls can be observed. Maccoby (1990) summarizes research findings that show differences in patterns of interaction between boys and girls. For instance, boys tend to be more rough in their play than girls and are more inclined toward dominance. They are also less likely to be influenced by girls, who tend to adopt a style of making polite suggestions. Although this may seem to reinforce the idea that "boys will be boys, and girls will be girls," it is becoming more and more clear that some of our beliefs about gender differences are constructed by culture and society (Mann, 1996). For instance, in *Manhood in America,* Kimmel (1996) writes that "manhood is not the manifestation of an inner essence; it's socially constructed. Manhood does not bubble up to consciousness from our biological constitution; it is created in our culture" (p. 5). In a similar way, girls in this society learn that to become good women, they must be "willing to take care of, or to take on the cares of others, a willingness often to sacrifice oneself for others in the hope that if one cared for others one would be loved and cared for by them" (Gilligan, Lyons, & Hanmer, 1990, p. 8).

Growing up in this context, girls and boys learn that there are different sets of expectations for males and females. It has also been observed that "gender segregation is a widespread phenomenon found in all the cultural settings in which children are in social groups large enough to permit choice" (Maccoby, 1990, p. 414). As they grow, there is an increased emphasis on the separation of genders. The evolution of separate spheres for males and females in this country can be traced back to the mid-1800s (Kimmel, 1996). To become "real men" in the new land, boys had to gain independence from the family as soon as possible. Girls, on the other hand, lost their independence once they matured and married. Being in control was essential for men to compete and be successful, and the presence of women in the workplace threatened that goal. Women became increasingly bound to the home, and their worth was largely measured by their ability to raise children and by their domestic talents. These patterns are intrinsic in patriarchal societies and are not unique to the United States. By observing the adults in their lives and through exposure to television and the media, children learn that men have more power and privilege than women do. Unless children live with adults whose behavior challenges these beliefs, by adolescence they have incorporated into their identities the stereotypes about gender that our culture promotes (Mann, 1996).

Girls growing up in the United States today are perhaps more oppressed than in earlier decades (Pipher, 1994). Even though the women's movement has opened certain doors for females, girls

are coming of age in a more dangerous, sexualized and media-saturated culture. They face incredible pressures to be beautiful and sophisticated, which in junior high means using chemicals and being sexual. As they navigate in a more dangerous world, girls are less protected. America today limits girls' development, truncates their wholeness and leaves them traumatized. (Pipher, 1994, p. 12).

Boys face a different dilemma. As Kimmel (1996) puts it,

they are growing up in a society where the structural foundations of traditional manhood, such as economic independence, geographic mobility, and domestic dominance, have all been eroding. Patterns of self control, exclusion of others, and escape from the home, which in the past had helped males

become successful bread winners and providers, are no longer effective (p. 298).

Yet, rather than looking at how changes in the social structure in this country have affected men and women, a major part of the blame for men's dissatisfactions and limitations continues to be placed on women. For instance, the belief that to find themselves and become true men, boys need to separate from their mothers and bond with their fathers and other men (Bly, 1990; Keen, 1991) perpetuates the problem. Rather than learning to be accountable and responsible to others and to fight against injustice based on difference, they fight for power by excluding and dominating the weaker. And as Gilligan et al., (1990) tell us, "for girls to remain responsive to themselves, they must resist the conventions of feminine goodness; to remain responsive to others, they must resist the values placed on self-sufficiency and independence in North American culture" (p. 10) They must make a commitment to resist and to ask questions about what relationship means to themselves, to others, and to the world.

For African American adolescents, forming an identity goes beyond values and beliefs about gender, since they have to first cope with "society's definition of them as, first and foremost, black" (Hardy, 1996, p. 55). Forming a positive identity as a Black male or Black female in a racist society in which being Black is demeaned poses a dilemma for adolescents. Learning to repudiate society's negative stereotypes and to include their Blackness as positively valued and desired is necessary for Black adolescents to form a positive identity. This is also true for other adolescents of color, such as Latinos and Asians. Living among Whites and facing daily situations based on skin color that are hurtful, humiliating, and devaluing at school and in the street is never an easy experience. The darker the skin, the more difficult it is. Being Black and female means having two strikes against you (Ward, 1990). For Black males, the risk of being killed in the street, incarcerated, or assumed to be involved in criminal activities is much higher than it is for Whites. African American males, especially, have a much lower life expectancy than African American women or Whites of either sex (Hines & Boyd-Franklin, 1996). "Concerns for their children's futures may reactivate parents' sense of powerlessness and rage about racism, sometimes resulting in self-defeating behavior" (Hines & Boyd-Franklin, 1996, p. 76). It is important for parents to help their children cope with the anger and frustration by reconnecting with strategies and stories that have given them strength and sharing them with their children (Hardy, 1996; Hines & Boyd-Franklin, 1996).

These questions are critical, and because during adolescence children acquire the ability to think abstractly, having an adult discussion with them would be possible. Yet the two major forces of adolescence (Wolf, 1991), the onset of sexuality and the mandate that commands adolescents to turn away from parents and childhood, could make such a conversation between parents and children very strained, though perhaps possible with either extended family members or in therapy. These forces are similar for boys and girls. However, there are very distinct differences in the way boys and girls experience the physical, emotional, and sexual changes that adolescence triggers in them and in the way parents tend to react to these changes. Following is a closer look at how boys and girls experience those changes.

Physical Changes

The differences between males and females during this stage of development are clearly visible when it comes to physical changes. Generally, girls tend to grow faster than boys. The experience of having their bodies grow so rapidly elicits reactions of confusion both in them and in their parents. Our little kids begin to turn into adult-looking people. Their features change as their faces become more elongated, and their legs and arms dangle from a trunk that is too small to carry them, especially during early adolescence. Parents are constantly buying new clothes and shoes with mixed feelings of excitement and sadness as they try to keep up with the growth spurts.

The physical growth makes adolescents eat more and sleep longer. Following the growth spurt, their chests expand, their trunks lengthen, and their voices deepen; additionally, shoulders develop in boys and hips in girls. They also seem to have spurts of physical energy, followed by periods of lethargy. This change leads to conflicts between parents and adolescents in most families. Parents become nags in the eyes of their children, and children become inconsiderate, lazy, and disobedient in the eyes of parents.

Outside the home, adolescents have to deal with the pressures of fitting into a peer group. These pressures are, for the most part, gender specific and result from social and cultural expectations based on patriarchal values. For example, although the emphasis on physical attractiveness is strong for both boys and girls, the pressure to be beautiful is enormous for girls. For boys, being physically strong and athletic has more importance. And although being slight in weight and short in stature may cause boys to feel insecurities, girls who don't fit the social ideal of beauty seem to be at greater risk. One reason is that in our culture being beautiful also has negative connotations, as demonstrated by the jokes and caricatures about the "dumb blonde," creating a dilemma for girls. Another is that physical attractiveness means being thin. At an age when their bodies are changing and getting softer and fuller, girls may begin to see themselves as fat.

For many girls, dieting becomes a way to control weight. Bulimia, anorexia, and compulsive eating are conditions that are rarely found in males. Out-of-control eating is often associated with out-of-control emotions. Some studies report that on any given day, half the teenage girls in the United States are dieting, one in five young women has an eating disorder, and 8 million women of all ages have eating disorders (Pipher, 1994). Although clinicians tend to see eating disorders as behavioral manifestations of complex family dysfunction, many see the media as contributing to the problem by setting dangerous standards of beauty and thinness to which girls aspire (Mann, 1996). Some of these standards for thinness are very close to the standards for anorexia (Mann, 1996). An important point here is that although the detection of eating disorders in African Americans and Latinos seems to be increasing, the group that seems to be more affected by this problem continues to be White middle-and upper-class girls.

Sexual Changes

The development of secondary sexual changes ends the growth spurt but not all growth. For girls, this is usually marked by menarche, and for boys by the experience of ejaculations. Most girls reach menarche by age 12 (Males, 1996) and some as early as 9 (Pipher, 1994). Boys tend to reach puberty a year later than girls, usually by age 14 (Males, 1996). Both experience sexual feelings coming to the surface, which is unavoidable because of the biological changes their bodies undergo, and they also feel somewhat awkward and self conscious about their sexually maturing bodies. The implications for girls, however, are different than those for boys. Girls are emotionally unprepared for the sexual harassment they encounter because of these changes (Pipher, 1994).

The reality is that in today's world, girls are at risk, not only for sexual harassment but also for rape and sexual abuse. For instance, the National Women's Study of 4,000 women in 1992 found that one in eight women, a projected 12.1 million in the U.S. population, had been raped. Of the victims, 62 percent were raped before age 18 and 29 percent before age 11. "The survey found that rape in America is a tragedy of youth, with the majority of rape cases occurring during childhood and adolescence" (Pipher, 1994, p. 219). A study by the Alan Guttmacher Institute (1994) asked junior high school girls what they meant by having sex. For 40 percent of girls under age 15 who had had sex, their only experience with sex had been a rape, and the men involved in these rapes were substantially older. This alone is a good reason for parents to feel more protective of daughters and anxious about giving them the same freedom as boys.

The psychological results of rape and sexual abuse of children and adolescents are often depression, eating disorders, suicide, and other emotional disturbances. A major factor in drug and alcohol abuse for both males and females is a history of sexual abuse and rape. The 1992 Rape in America Study (National Victim Center, 1992) found that the age at which a girl's first rape occurred was younger than the age at which she first became intoxicated on alcohol or used drugs. Serious drinking problems were 12 times higher, and serious drug abuse problems 25 times higher in rape victims than in nonvictims. There is also a higher possibility for rape victims to become pregnant than for girls who have not been abused (The Arizona Family Planning Council, 1995). Studies of urban adolescents of color (Smith, 1997) concur with research that points to the interlinking of risk factors in the lives of adolescents, as well as the interlinking of problem behaviors (Ooms, 1995). Sexual abuse, rape, and substance use are clearly linked, as well as the risk for early pregnancy. Teenage boys in the study were more likely to have sex earlier, therefore increasing their exposure to disease. Girls who initiated sex earlier were more likely to become pregnant earlier.

Generally, girls and boys are having sex earlier than in previous generations, and although they are taught at most schools about sexually transmitted diseases, pregnancy, and AIDS, they tend to not use condoms or other forms of protection (Wolf, 1991; Pipher, 1994). Especially for girls, social sanctions against sex have dropped sharply. Behaviors that in the past would have branded a girl a slut among her friends are now more accepted (Wolf, 1991). However, boys are still given more leeway when it comes to sexual behavior. We still live in a society in which "boys, because they are males, have to be aggressive, and they have to use this aggression to prove themselves, not only athletically, intellectually, but sexually as well" (Silverstein & Rashbaum, 1994, p. 120).

For gay and lesbian youths, adolescence is a time when they are more likely to label and understand their sexual orientation. Because of the greater visibility of homosexuals in today's society, there are more possibilities for adolescents to be exposed to role models and to a gay and lesbian culture (Savin-Williams, 1996). The prejudice that adolescents in this situation face is still overwhelming. Coming out to their parents is probably the event that provokes the most anxiety and fear for them, especially for minority adolescents who depend on the family as the primary support system for dealing with the discrimination they experience outside (Savin-Williams, 1996; Morales, 1996).

Generally, gay and lesbian adolescents are more likely to disclose to mothers, fearing more the reaction from fathers. In fact, Herdt and Boxer (1993) found that one in ten youths who disclosed being homosexual to their fathers was expelled from the home. Sometimes, the reaction at home is dangerous and violent. Hunter (1990) found that the majority of violent physical attacks experienced by 500 primarily Black or Latino minority youths occurred in the family and were gay-related. Yet, most adolescents in this situation want their parents to know, and even though initially the relationship usually deteriorates, it tends to improve thereafter (Savin-Williams, 1996).

However, for many, like Horace, a 16-year-old White male of German ancestry, the situation at school and home can lead to suicidal behavior. In therapy, he talked about the loneliness and fear that he experienced.

> My attraction to men is not something I chose. I tried for the longest time to push it out of my mind, and do all the things that boys are supposed to do, but I can't change myself. Sometimes I get scared, especially when I hear about all the gay men who are dying of AIDS. I feel bad for my parents. They love me, but don't understand why this is happening, and are ashamed of me. They also fear for my life. No one else knows in the family, and I hate pretending in front of my grandparents. At school I'm constantly on the look out, worried that they'll find me out and lynch me. I'd be better off dead. I don't see another way out.

Most gay and lesbian adolescents remain closeted, particularly in high school. When there is outside recognition that leads to intense harassment from peers and lack of support at home, emotional problems are likely to emerge. In these cases, there is a high risk of suicide. Some studies have found that 20 to 40 percent of gay and lesbian adolescents have made suicide attempts, half of them have made multiple attempts, and they are two or three times more likely to actually commit suicide than heterosexual youths (Savin-Williams, 1996). However, Shaffer, D.; Fisher, P.; Hicks, R. H.; Parides, M.; & Gould, M. (1995) conducted a psychological autopsy study of 120 of 170 consecutive suicides under age 20 and 147 community, age, sex, and ethnic matched controls living in the greater New York City area that found no evidence that the risk factors for suicide among gays were any different from those among straight teenagers. The data in that study shows that although the experience of establishing a gay orientation may be painful, it does not lead disproportionately to suicide.

Emotional Changes

The emotional immaturity that boys and girls experience during early adolescence is manifested by changeable and intense moods. This instability of feelings leads to unpredictable behavior. Emotional reactions are not always proportionate to the precipitating event, causing confusion for parents and other adults as they try to reason with adolescents (Pipher, 1994). While maturing emotionally, adolescents feel the need to move toward independence, and to do that, they feel compelled to turn away from their childish ways. Implicit in this task is the need to transform the relationship with their parents. As with sexual feelings, it is a process that cannot be avoided. This is complicated, however, because along with wanting to venture out and become independent, there is also a part of them that pulls toward wanting parents to take care of them. They do not want to break the emotional bond they have with their parents. Instead, they want a different balance in the relationship that allows for validation of their changing selves (Apter, 1990). "They want the nurturance without the fuss" (Wolf, 1991). Away from home, they can begin to act mature and responsible, but at home they want to be left alone with no demands and no expectations.

While both girls and boys may go through a similar emotional experience, their patterns for expressing emotion and relating to mothers and to fathers are different. For instance, boys tend to be more withdrawn, going into themselves, and, as in the case of my son, sometimes become clams. Girls don't necessarily stop talking or withdraw; instead, they fight. What I have observed in my clinical practice, and at home with my son and daughter, is that girls are more likely to let parents know what they feel by yelling, while boys are more avoidant and tend to deal with situations by leaving the scene. For boys, engaging in fights with parents may lead to aggressive behavior such as punching holes in walls or breaking furniture, while girls are more likely to scream, cry, and proclaim their hate. These patterns seem to fit cultural and social expectations for gender-specific behavior. For example, boys are usually given more freedom than girls to leave the house, while girls have more permission to express a wider range of emotions (Pipher, 1994). Boys, as Silverstein and Rashbaum (1994) state, learn only to express anger. A similarity between boys and girls, however, seems to be that the more dependent they feel on their parents, the more turbulent this process will be (Silverstein and Rashbaum, 1994; Pipher, 1994; Wolf, 1991).

Another difference between boys and girls is in their pattern of establishing friendships. Girls tend to talk to each other on the phone for longer periods of time and to care more about what one thinks of the other. They spend more energy dealing with relationships and change friendships with greater frequency than boys do. Boys tend to hold on longer to the same friends and to build relationships around activities and sports. However, regardless of these differences, boys and girls are similar in that they are more interested in their friends than in adults. They want to fit in with their peers and, depending on how secure they feel, are easily influenced by group pressures.

CHANGES IN THE FAMILY STRUCTURE

The adolescent's demands for greater independence tend to precipitate structural shifts and renegotiation of roles in families involving at least three generations of relatives. It is not uncommon for parents and grandparents to redefine their relationships during this period, as well as for spouses to renegotiate their marriage, and siblings to question their position in the family. Because these demands are so strong, they also serve as catalysts for reactivating unresolved conflicts between parents and grandparents or between the parents themselves and to set triangles in motion. For instance, efforts to resolve conflicts between adolescents and parents often repeat earlier patterns of relating in parents' families of origin. Parents who have made a conscious effort to raise their children differently by avoiding the same "mistakes" their parents made often have a particularly rude awakening. When their children reach adolescence, they are often surprised to observe similarities in personality between children and parents. Parents in this situation may react with extreme confusion, anger, or resentment or may themselves get in touch with similar needs and, in turn, make the same requests of their own parents or of each other.

Families during this period are also responding and adjusting to the new demands of other family members, who themselves are entering new stages of the life cycle. For example, most parents with adolescents in the mainstream U.S. culture are in middle age. Their focus is on such major midlife issues as reevaluating their marriage and careers. The marriage emerging from the heavy caretaking responsibilities of young children may be threatened as parents review personal satisfaction in the light of the militant idealism of their adolescent children. For many women, this may actually be the first opportunity to work outside the home without the restrictions they faced when the children were young. However, because of the economic situation in this country, there is an increasing need for both parents to work to meet the expenses of raising children and maintaining a home. Especially for working-class families, fathers may have a particularly hard time. Finding that they have reached their limits of earning and advancement or facing layoffs as their place of work no longer needs them makes them feel very insecure.

The normal stress and tension posed to the family by an adolescent are exacerbated when the parents experience acute dissatisfaction and feel compelled to make changes in themselves. At the same time, the grandparents face retirement and possible moves, illness, and death. These stressful events call for a renegotiation of relationships, and parents may be called upon to be caretakers of their own parents or to assist them in integrating the losses of old age. What often forms is a field of conflicting demands, in which the stress seems to be transmitted both up and down the generations. For example, if there is conflict between parents and grandparents, it may have a negative effect on the marital relationship that filters down into the relationship between the parents and the adolescent. Or the conflict may travel in the opposite direction. A conflict between the parents and adolescent may affect the marital relationship, which ultimately affects the relationship between the parents and grandparents.

These patterns may differ depending on factors such as race, class, and ethnicity. For instance, Burton et al. (1996) conducted a study of poor inner-city African American teens and found that in many of the families, there was a narrow age difference between the generations, which tended to blur developmental boundaries and roles of family members. The blurring of intergenerational boundaries in these age-condensed families affected the authority that parents had over children as well as the adolescents' perceptions of appropriate behavior. Consider, for example, a family where the

> child generation included both a young mother (age fifteen) and her child (age one), a young-adult generation, which is comprised of a twenty-nine-year-old grandmother, and a middle-age generation, which includes a forty-three-year-old great-grandmother.
>
> The adolescent mother, as a function of giving birth, is launched into the young-adult role status; however, she remains legally and developmentally a member of the child generation. Similarly, the young-adult female has moved to status of grandmother, a stage typically embodied

> by middle-aged or older women. Further, the middle-aged woman has been propelled to the status of great-grandmother, a role usually occupied by women in their later years." (Burton et al., 1996, p. 406).

The example illustrates the point that as a result of the closeness in generations, chronological and developmental challenges often become inconsistent with generational roles. The result may be that parents and children behave more like siblings, making it difficult for parents to discipline their children. Families may also have difficulty identifying adolescence as a specific life stage.

There are remarkable differences in the rituals that ethnic groups use to handle adolescence. For instance, Anglo Americans (McGill & Pearce, 1996) do not struggle to keep their children at home, as do Italians, Jews, and Latinos. Historically they have promoted early separation of adolescents and the development of an individualistic, self-defined, adult identity. As McGill and Pearce (1996) observe, "if contemporary parents try to promote independence by withdrawing physical, financial, or emotional support too soon, the Anglo American adolescent will probably feel abandoned. The result may be a kind of false adulthood with premature identity foreclosure" (p. 456).

Renegotiating rules and limits is key during this stage of development for most families. "You can't treat me like a baby anymore" may be said in the middle of a "childish tantrum," but the message must be heard and taken seriously. Parents must be ready to let go and yet stay connected to guide, and be protective when necessary. This is much easier said than done. It is true that, adolescents are not babies or little children, but neither are they adults. Even when they fulfill adult roles during early adolescence, such as having children themselves or taking care of ill parents, they are not emotionally mature until later in the process. The family must be strong and able to make its boundaries more flexible. This is usually easier with each successive child but is particularly difficult when parents are unable to support each other, are isolated, and lack the support of extended family or community.

THERAPEUTIC INTERVENTIONS

The Carnegie Council on Adolescent Development (1995), a ten-year national study of adolescence, reported that rates of teen drug and alcohol use, unprotected sexual activity, violent victimization, delinquency, eating disorders, and depression are now sufficiently widespread that nearly half of American adolescents are at high or moderate risk of seriously damaging their life chances. This is true of adolescents across all demographic lines. This finding coincides with the types of problems that are presented in therapy. Parents seeking help for their troubled adolescent in the United States at this point in time are likely to be overworked, overcommitted, tired, and poor and to have little outside support (Pipher, 1994). Many are single parents, mothers in most cases (Sandmaier, 1996). They tend to feel inadequate, see their families as dysfunctional, and expect their children to rebel and to distance themselves emotionally. Viewing these families as dysfunctional is also a widespread tendency among mental health professionals that limits our ability to intervene from a perspective that considers the context in which they live and the effect that culture has on them.

Helping parents to maintain an emotional bond with adolescents in a culture that says that parents are supposed to pull away when a child reaches adolescence is a challenge for most therapists. Yet we all need encouragement to hang in there, listen differently, confront our own limits, and take the necessary measures to earn our child's trust (Sandmaier, 1996). Recent studies find that teenagers who feel close to their families were the least likely to engage in any of the risky behaviors that were studied, which included smoking marijuana or cigarettes, drinking, and having sex, and that high expectations from parents for their teenagers' school performance were nearly as important (Gilbert, 1997). In my clinical practice, I am constantly trying to maintain a balance that respects the parents' responsibility to protect adolescents yet encourages the adolescents' need for independence. At home, I struggle to do the same with my 18-year-old son, and 14-year-old daughter and feel the range of emotions most parents feel when children pull away, keep secrets, and tell us "you don't understand."

Renegotiating Relationships between Parents and Adolescents

What also happens as parents and adolescents try to redefine relationships is that parents often experience a resurfacing of emotions related to unresolved issues with their own parents. In therapy, paying attention to the triangles that operated in the parents' families of origin and coaching them to do so some work with their own parents can be very helpful in furthering their ability to listen and feel less reactive to their children's behavior. Such was the case with Clara and her mother:

Clara, 15, lived with her 39-year-old mother, Mrs. Callahan, her 12-year-old sister, Sonia, and her mother's paternal aunt. Her parents had been divorced since she was ten. Her mother was Puerto Rican, and her father was Irish. He was remarried to an Asian woman. Mrs. Callahan had remained unmarried. She was a professional woman who kept herself isolated from peers and focused her energy on being a good mother. Clara, who had always been very close to her mother, had begun to pull away, stay out late, and show interest in boys. Mrs. Callahan, afraid of the dangers in the street and worried that Clara would become pregnant, restricted her outings. The more Clara challenged the limits, the stricter her mother became. Clara threatened to run away and kill herself. After she spoke to a teacher at school, the referral for therapy was made.

Mrs. Callahan was angry with Clara and unwilling to listen to her daughter's criticisms. She felt rejected by her daughter, for whom she had sacrificed so much. Clara felt bad about hurting her mother but was angry at what she thought was her mother's unfairness. Supporting Mrs. C.'s intention to protect her daughter by validating the dangers that girls are exposed to in this society made it easier for her to listen to Clara's position. Inviting Clara's great-aunt, who lived with them, to the sessions clarified how Clara's adolescence had activated a triangle similar to one that had operated in the previous generation. The triangle, triggered by discipline issues, involved Clara, Mrs. C., and the great-aunt. Clara thought her great-aunt was too old-fashioned and resented her attempts to discipline. Both would complain to Mrs. C., who would try to mediate by explaining cultural differences but was confused about which values to keep and would end up feeling powerless. The aunt would react by moving in to support Mrs. C., and Clara would distance herself, feeling rejected by both.

During her adolescence, Mrs. C. had been involved in a triangle with her mother and this aunt, who was her father's youngest sister. The aunt would try to mediate between Mrs. C. and her mother when they had arguments but would usually end up defending her niece. The mother would then get angry and distance herself from Mrs. C., who in turn would feel rejected. I was able to help shift the triangle by telling them that Clara needed support from both of them but primarily from her mother. I suggested that Clara was as confused as they by the different ways in which the two cultures dealt with adolescence.

Asking them to identify which Puerto Rican values were creating the greatest conflict at home led them to thinking about a compromise. They agreed that dating was the greatest source of conflict, since in Puerto Rico, this practice has very different rules and connotations. Dating does not start until much later, and it is usually in the company of family or friends. I pointed out that for Clara to live in this culture and feel comfortable with her peers, they needed to adapt to some of the values of this culture. As a compromise, they agreed to let Clara go on double dates, but only with people they knew, and to negotiate a curfew with Clara's input.

To make additional changes in the relationship between Clara and her mother, work had to be done with Mrs. Callahan and her mother, who lived in Puerto Rico. Coaching Mrs. C. to share some of her conflicts with her mother through letters and on a visit to Puerto Rico and to ask her advice about disciplining Clara was a way to lessen the emotional distance between them. Mrs. C. became more accepting of her mother's limitations and began to appreciate the attention she gave. This helped her to listen more attentively to her daughter.

Another factor that this case elucidates is the considerable impact that the lack of extended family or other supports has on how families manage adolescence. Some ethnic groups, such as Puerto Ricans, rely heavily on extended family members to help with the discipline of adolescents and the clarification of boundaries. It is common for Puerto Rican parents to send a rebellious adolescent to live with an uncle or godparent who can be more objective about setting limits. This move also provides time for parents and adolescents to obtain enough emotional distance from each other to regain control and reestablish a more balanced relationship. Relying solely on the nuclear family to provide control, support, and guidance for adolescents can overload the circuits and escalate conflicts.

For instance, my home is considered a safe haven for my 17-year-old nephew, my dead brother's son, who lives with his mother. The two of them have a very close relationship, but sometimes they have extremely intense conflict. My nephew was 11 when his father died, and through the years, he has assumed an adult role at times when his mother felt overwhelmed and hopeless. At 17, he challenges her limits, feeling that since she expects him to act as an adult at times, he should be entitled to adult privileges. Not long ago, when I called my sister-in-law to say hello, they were in the middle of a fight. She was desperate, and he had left the house to avoid her screams. He returned while I was on the phone, and I suggested that he come for a visit.

He did, and we talked about the problems at home and about how he misses his father. My husband and I told stories about my brother and how much he had loved the boy. It was easier for him to hear from us that he was not entitled to adult privileges yet and that challenging his mother's limits by screaming and making threats was not helpful or appropriate. I was also able to talk with my sister-in-law after she calmed down about how difficult it is to raise adolescent sons, and how much I respect her for doing it alone without another adult at home. It was good for me to spend time with him. It was good for her to have a break from him and to know that he could talk and reason.

Strengthening the Parental Bond

Whether parents are living together or apart, it is critical for them to agree on rules for adolescents. Adolescents tend to do better in families in which they are encouraged to participate in decision making but parents have rational control and ultimately decide what is appropriate (Henry & Peterson, 1995). Parents who are in control and high in acceptance have adolescents who are independent, socially responsible, and confident (Pipher, 1994). It is also important for parents to resist the impulse to focus entirely on the adolescent's problems and to pay attention to themselves and their own relationship (Carter & Peters, 1996). When parents disagree and one becomes involved in alliances with the children against the other, the problems presented by adolescents escalate. The case of 17-year-old Tom Murphy illustrates some of the shifts that may occur during adolescence when the child is in a triangle with parents who are in a struggle:

> Tom no longer wanted to be an engineer, as his parents were planning for him, but had become interested in lighting and theater. However, his parents, disapproved of his interest and were constantly urging him to go to college. Afraid to cause arguments, he avoided conversations with his parents and refused to go places with them, especially with his mother, to whom he had been a constant companion. At school, he gave up, failing to do assignments that were required for graduation and dropping courses he did not want. His behavior alarmed the teachers enough to ask the psychologist to see him. When his parents were told, they reacted with fear and anger, confused by his behavior, which they experienced as a rejection of their values and efforts to give him a good future.
>
> In therapy, it became clear that Tom was caught in a classic triangle, trying to please his parents and feeling responsible for their arguments. But pleasing one parent meant disappointing the other. Marital problems and arguments in this family had gone on for years. Mrs. Murphy was very dissatisfied with the marital relationship and claimed that Tom, their only child, was the only reason she stayed in it. Mr. Murphy was resentful and tried to minimize the problems, claiming that she and Tom were against him. Mr. Murphy was also involved in a midlife reevaluation of his own work life, which meant coming to terms with disappointments and letting go of unfulfilled dreams. Overwhelmed by conflicts in their marriage and their own midlife struggles, Mr. and Mrs. Murphy had been unable to be objective and supportive of Tom's moves toward independence. Instead they experienced his behavior as Tom's collusive alliance with one parent against the other. His move toward independence represented a threat to the system, especially to the parent's relationship.
>
> The initial focus in therapy was to help the family make decisions about handling the present problem. Mr. and Mrs. Murphy were asked to take a break from making plans for Tom's future, to back off and let him take responsibility for negotiating at school. Instead, they were to make a plan clarifying their expectations of Tom if he did not go to college. Working on this task strengthened their bond as parents and helped Tom to gain confidence about his own choices. As they reviewed their own adolescence and patterns of relationships in their families of origin, they became more objective about each other and were able to make connections between the past and present. Asking them to talk about their plans for the future as a couple enabled them to focus on their relationship and begin to face their problems directly. Tom began to make more responsible decisions about his future.

Building Community

"It takes a village to raise a child" may sound trite, but it is a concept that has deep meaning for any parent who experiences the loneliness and shame of raising adolescents who are troubled. I sit in my office with parents and adolescents and feel their pain as they tell me their stories, sharing their fear as they worry about their children's futures. I worry about my children and pray that the world will heal itself. I don't want them exposed to racism, sexism, violence, and apathy, and yet they are. I see their smiles and know that they have dreams and feel hopeful. I want to extend my heart and give them hope, confidence, strength, and love. In my practice of therapy these have become my most powerful tools.

There is no reason for blame; it accomplishes nothing. It does not heal adolescents or parents. Making connections with other families, other adults, other adolescents and opening our minds and hearts to others who are also struggling are healing. What I can do in my office is limited. I can help them look beyond themselves, at the pressures that affect their lives—our lives. We are in it together. Their children are also mine. I can help parents think about protecting their children, yet be aware of the limits that bound us. I can encourage mothers to defy society by not buying into the belief that boys need to separate from mothers to become "real men." I have become much softer with my son, letting him know that I love him and think that he is a sensitive, caring, and funny young man. I encourage fathers to look inside and outside and get in touch with how sexism limits and isolates them. I try to keep the real self in my daughter alive and look for it in every adolescent girl I meet. Sometimes, it is difficult to look beyond the pain I see in their eyes as they tell me stories of sexual abuse, violence, addictions, and self-mutilation and to consider what there is that is positive in their lives to help them feel strong. I have learned from them that sometimes their only salvation lies in their spiritual beliefs or in their connections to others.

> Tanya, a 14-year-old African American who came in to therapy after reporting at school that her mother's boyfriend had tried to rape her found support and strength in her church. Her mother was angry with her for reporting the boyfriend and blamed Tanya for seducing him. Tanya felt rejected and hurt but knew that she was not responsible for his behavior. She wanted her mother to believe her but had given up hope. In the church, she had found other adults who believed her and encouraged her to ask God's help to forgive her mother. I worked with her mother to help her see her daughter as a 14-year-old girl who did the right thing by reporting an adult man who abused her. I wanted her to feel angry at him and protective of her daughter; instead, she was angry about losing him. I encouraged her to go to church with Tanya, hoping that she would hear God's message and make connections with the adults who supported her daughter. She was not ready, and I had to accept it. Tanya had learned through her faith that there is strength in forgiving, and I was reminded of my limitations and felt grateful to the 14-year-old who was teaching me a lesson.

Establishing support networks with other professionals and working with other systems that may be part of the community in which adolescents live, such as schools, churches, and legal authorities, are crucial. Connecting parents with teachers at schools and with other parents is an essential type of intervention that works toward strengthening natural support systems and lessening the isolation that families experience in our present-day communities (Pipher, 1994; Taffel, 1996) Interventions that take into account the sociopolitical context in which we live and its effect on families and adolescents are critical.

REFERENCES

Alan Guttmacher Institute. (1994). *Sex and America's teenagers.* New York: AGI.

Angelini, P. J. (1995, 17 November). *The relationship of childhood sexual victimization to teenage pregnancy and STDs.* Phoenix, AZ: Arizona Planning Council.

Apter, T. (1990). *Altered loves.* New York: Fawcett Columbine.

Bly, R. (1990). *Iron John.* Reading, MA: Addison-Wesley.

Burton, L., Obeidallah, D. A., & Allison, K. (1996). Ethnographic insights on social context and adolescent development among inner-city African-American teens. In R. Jessor, A. Colby, & R. Shweder (Eds.), *Essays on ethnography and human development.* Chicago: University of Chicago Press.

Carnegie Council on Adolescent Development. (1995). *Great transitions: Preparing adolescents for a new century.* New York: Carnegie Corporation.

Carter, B., & Peters, J. K. (1996). *Love, honor, and negotiate: Making your marriage work.* New York: Pocket Books.

Gilbert, S. (1997, September 10). Youth study elevates family's role. *New York Times.*

Gilligan, C., Lyons, N. P., & Hanmer, T. (1990). *Making connections.* Cambridge, MA: Harvard University Press.

Hardy, K. (1996, May/June), Breathing room. *The Family Networker,* 53–59.

Henry, S., & Peterson, G. W. (1995). Adolescent social competence, parental qualities, and parental satisfaction. *American Journal of Orthopsychiatry, 65* (2) 249–262.

Herdt, G. L., & Boxer, A. M. (1993). *Children of horizons: How gay and lesbian teens are leading a new way out of the closet.* Boston: Beacon Press.

Hines, P., & Boyd-Franklin, N. (1996). African American families. In M. McGoldrick, J. Giordano, & J. K. Pearce (Eds.), *Ethnicity and family therapy.* (pp. 66–84). New York: The Guilford Press.

Hunter, J. (1990). Violence against lesbian and gay male youths. *Journal of Interpersonal Violence, 5,* 295–300.

Keen, S. (1991). *Fire in the belly: On being a man.* New York: Bantam.

Kimmel, M. (1996). *Manhood in America: A cultural history.* New York: The Free Press.

Maccoby, E. (1990). Gender and relationships: A developmental account. *American Psychologist, 45,* (4), 513–520.

Males, M. A. (1996). *The Scapegoat generation: America's war on adolescents.* Monroe, ME: Common Courage Press.

Mann, J. (1996). *The difference: Discovering the hidden ways we silence girls–Finding alternatives that can give them a voice.* New York: Warner Books.

McGill, D., & Pearce, J. (1996). American families with English ancestors from the colonial era: Anglo Americans. In McGoldrick, M., Giordano, J., & Pearce, J. K. (Eds.), *Ethnicity and Family Therapy.* (pp. 451–466) New York: The Guilford Press.

McGoldrick, M., Giordano, J., & Pearce, J. K. (Eds.). (1996). *Ethnicity and family therapy.* New York: The Guilford Press.

Morales, E. (1996). Gender roles among Latino gay and bisexual men: Implications for family and couple relationships. In J. Laird & R.-J. Green (Eds.), *Gays and lesbians in couples and families.* (pp. 272–297) San Francisco: Jossey-Bass.

National Victim Center. (1992). *Rape in America.* Washington DC: Author.

Ooms, T. (1995). Strategies to reduce non-marital childbearing. In K. A. Moore (Ed.), *Report to Congress on out-of-wedlock childbearing* (pp. 241–265). Hyattsville, MD: U.S. Department of Health and Human Services.

Pipher, M. (1994). *Reviving Ophelia.* New York: Ballantine Books.

Sandmaier, M. (1996 May/June.). More than love. *The Family Networker,* 21–33.

Savin-Williams, R. C. (1996). Self-labeling and disclosure among gay, lesbian, and bisexual youths. In J. Laurd & R.-J. Green (Eds.), *Lesbians and gays in couples and families,* (pp. 153–182), San Francisco: Jossey-Bass.

Shaffer, D., Fisher, P., Hicks, R. H., Raudes, M., & Gould, M. (1995). Suicide and life threatening behavior. *American Association of Suicidology, 25* (Supplement) pp. 64–71.

Silverstein, O., & Rashbaum, B. (1994). *The courage to raise good men.* New York: Penguin Books.

Smith, C. A. (1997). Factors associated with early sexual activity among urban adolescents. *Social Work, 42*(4) 334–346.

Taffel, R. (1996 May/June). The second family. *The Family Networker,* 36–45.

Ward, J. V. (1990). Racial identity formation and transformation. In C. Gilligan, N. P. Lyons, & T. Hammer (Eds.), *Making connections.* (pp. 215–232). Cambridge, MA: Harvard University Press.

Wolf, A. E. (1991). *Get out of my life but first could you drive me and Cheryl to the mall?* New York: The Noonday Press.

CHAPTER 17

THE LAUNCHING PHASE
OF THE LIFE CYCLE

LYNN BLACKER

OVERVIEW

Myths of Midlife

"Launching children," "empty nest," "midlife crisis"—These phrases conjure up the widely held image of midlife and beyond as the end of meaningful life, a period of decline, depression, and death. Women are pictured as being worse off than men, their primary role of child-rearing completed. They are thought to be rattling around their empty homes or frantically attempting to make a life for themselves. Men are viewed more optimistically, since they have a longstanding career as their primary focus and source of self-esteem. They are disconnected from their unfulfilled wives, but if they want, they can always have one last fling. Given these divergent paths, marriages are assumed to be at their low point of satisfaction. In the 1960s, this constellation of negative images was named the "empty nest syndrome" (Shapiro, 1996).

This is a dramatic scenario and might make a good film script, but it does not match reality. First, midlifers who have launched their children report more enjoyment of life and more happiness in their marriages than do people the same age who have children at home (White & Edwards, 1993). A study of 3,000 adults found that empty nesters were actually less depressed than adults living with children or those who never had children (Shapiro, 1996). Second, women anticipate and welcome the departure of their children from the home (Mitchell & Helson, 1990) and cope even better than men do with this stage of the life cycle

(Bergquist, Greenberg, & Klaum, 1993). Women say that they have a better quality of life at midlife than at any other time (Mitchell & Helson, 1990). Third, men go through a period of reassessment at midlife, and most of them experience an increase in their capacity for relationship skills and an interest in connecting with family members (Levinson, 1978). The concept of the launching stage as a period of depressed women, distant, workaholic men, and the nadir of marital happiness has been refuted in study after study, so that by now the term "empty nest syndrome" has been minimized to the point of irrelevance (Dowling, 1996; Shapiro, 1996).

How do we explain these counterintuitive results of studies of parents whose children have left the home? The launching phase must be understood in terms of the life stage in which it occurs: midlife. Although the terms "launching" and "midlife" overlap, they are not synonymous. Launching is just one of many life cycle tasks that must be accomplished during the midlife years. Like launching children, the other midlife tasks involve a significant realignment of family roles. These other tasks of midlife include becoming a couple again; developing adult relationships with adult children; accepting new family members through marriage and birth; and resolving issues with, providing care for, and finally burying their parents. Once again, the popular view of midlife is characterized by negative stereotypes and misconceptions. Rather than worrying about declining health and diminished energy and feeling generally demoralized about the idea of impending mortality, most midlifers are in excellent health, feel young and vigorous and are excited by the many choices they have before them (Bergquist et al., 1993).

Middle Age: A New Life Cycle Stage

Like "empty nest syndrome," "middle age" is a relatively new term. It is the most recently identified phase of the life cycle, having first been described in 1978 by Levinson (Dowling, 1996). The newness of the construct reflects the fact that we are living longer; therefore, life cycle tasks have a new normative timetable. In 1900, when people died by age 49 (Pogrebin, 1996), life cycle tasks were compressed. Launching and marrying off children, burying parents, becoming grandparents and becoming widows commonly occurred concurrently in one decade. But now, this phase may last 20 years or more and is currently the longest phase in the life cycle. Midlife is commonly defined as spanning the ages of roughly 45 to 65, encompassing the period from launching the first child to retirement. Because of better health and increasing longevity, it may get expanded even more in the future. Of course, a significant number of men and women are beginning new families at midlife rather than launching them. For more information about the varied lifestyle options available to men and women at midlife, see Chapters 6, 15, and 21.

The Graying of America and the Midlife Stage

The "graying of America" is one of the most significant new features of contemporary society. Not only are we living longer, but also the large cohort of post–World War II baby boomers is now entering middle age. Their faces are everywhere, from television advertisements to the President of the United States. They have higher expectations of their own productivity and expect more of their middle years than previous midlifers. Intact midlife households have the highest mean income of any age group (McCullough & Rutenberg, 1989), and services are popping up continually to address this huge market, which has not yet even peaked. The impact of the aging of America is related to and compounded by other significant phenomena of the latter part of twentieth century: the reduced size of families, more women in the workforce, higher divorce rates than in the past, more elderly surviving parents, and more middle-aged single women (McCullough & Rutenberg, 1989).

Taken together, this means that families, having fewer children, will finish the launching task at an earlier age than past generations and will experience a longer postlaunch period until retirement. This provides many midlife women with an opportunity to expand their part-time work or even begin careers outside the home for the first time and provides men with a new opportunity for reassessment. The high midlife divorce rates mean that for many people, especially women, being in the workforce will be a necessity. Finally, during this elongated postlaunch period, their parents are also living longer, so midlifers, especially daughters, will be involved in their care. All in all, as midlifers gradually make the transition through this lengthy period, they will be making significant reassessments of their roles in their families, their marriages, their work lives, their support systems, and their life expectations to adapt to the dramatic changes they experience over this twenty- to twenty-five-year period.

Awareness of Mortality

Before the identification of midlife as a life stage, it was thought that human development stabilized in early adulthood. Then, Erik Erikson in the 1960s and Daniel Levinson in the 1970s developed frameworks that describe life cycle stages and accompanying developmental tasks that occur throughout life. Both of these theorists suggest that the developmental tasks of midlife must include an attentiveness to developing meaning and purpose in one's life, which Erikson calls "generativity" (Julian, McKenry, & McKelvey, 1992). Therefore, it is not coincidental that the concept of reassessment permeates the family tasks of the midlife/launching stage. A key impetus for this reassessment is the realization that time is running out. As Bernice Neugarten (1968) notes, individuals at midlife begin to measure their position in the life cycle in terms of time left to live rather than time since birth. With this new perspective, priorities change. People may choose to no longer put aspirations and dreams on hold. The loss of some hopes and plans may also need to be mourned. However, as will be seen throughout this chapter, people tend to experience midlife not as an end, but as a time of great potential.

The Impact of Class and Culture

Although many people consider the stage of midlife to be the prime of life (Gallagher, 1993; Mitchell & Helson, 1990), this rosy picture applies mainly to the middle and upper socioeconomic classes. For the less economically secure, the outlook is very different. The lower socioeconomic classes can anticipate decreasing job opportunities, especially with the massive downsizings and closings of industrial sites in the last decade and the increasingly technological work environment. Furthermore, working-class and poor women typically anticipate being both homemakers and employees throughout their adult lives, working in jobs that may not be particularly fulfilling (Bergquist et al., 1993). Working-class men, who often depend on physical strength for their jobs, may be considered middle aged in their thirties, and with their poor access to health care, they may not expect to live beyond retirement. This is particularly true of African American men, who have high mortality rates due to heart disease. For these men and women, having little economic autonomy, the midlife tasks of reevaluating the life course and developing new plans and dreams are not realistic. In fact, it has been suggested that the very idea of a midlife crisis is a cultural construct that is relevant only to the middle and upper classes (Gallagher, 1993).

Cultural and ethnic identification is another consideration in understanding the way families approach the tasks of the midlife stage. For example, in Anglo American or Polish families, children are expected to establish their independence with less parental assistance or involvement than is seen in Italian or Brazilian families. Dutch families tend to have greater acceptance of adult children continuing to reside in the home than German families do. Greek families may have a greater adherence to the traditional value of women not seeking employment out of the home than Jewish families do. Poor African American families, which place a high value on interconnectedness between family members, may never actually have an "empty nest," as elderly family members are likely to be active members of their expanding households and family systems (McGoldrick, Giordano, & Pearce, 1996). These intergenerationally transmitted influences contribute to the family's ease or difficulty in moving through this phase.

GENDER ISSUES: MEN AND WOMEN AT MIDLIFE

Baby Boomer Values

Although every generation must go through approximately the same life cycle transitions and accomplish the same tasks, each cohort brings its own unique historical experience. Those who are now entering midlife are baby boomers. This is the generation born just after World War II and raised in the 1950s and 1960s with traditional values and gender role expectations, namely, to be heterosexual, find a spouse, marry early, and, if female, stay home. Male entitlement strongly permeated their socialization. Then, in 1963, Betty Friedan published *The Feminine Mystique,* and the baby boomers, then in their midteens, were introduced to the sexual revolution. They became the generation that transitioned between postwar traditional values and the changing social climate that followed. Many baby boomers, especially the women, responded to the new prescription for social change. For the first time in great numbers, women attended college, entered the full-time workforce, and got divorced in great numbers. Although they attempted to create more egalitarian marriages, they still struggled with two conflicting sets of values, and even the most "liberated" couples tended to revert to traditional marriages after their children were born. Nonetheless, the values of individual entitlement, self-fulfillment, and gender equality oriented this group to the massive social changes of the last quarter century, and these values continue to be relevant as they face the challenges and demands of midlife. However, some baby boomers entered adulthood with traditional values still intact. For them, the tasks of midlife collide with these values, and the dissonance of role expectations or the stress of having partially changed values creates another layer of adjustment as women and men redefine their roles at midlife with each other, within the family, and in society (Carter & Peters, 1996).

Middle-Aged Women: Postmenopausal Zest

According to the popular depiction in the mass media, the physical changes associated with menopause are unbearably uncomfortable, and the loss of fertility is thought to trigger a preoccupation with mortality that may lead to depression. Actually, although women do experience changes and may feel a sense of discomfort and/or loss, the most commonly expressed feeling about the cessation of menstruation is relief (Shapiro, 1996). Current research indicates that most women anticipate and welcome the arrival of menopause and find the transition uneventful (Mitchell & Helson, 1990). Ninety percent of menopausal women report no significant changes in anger, anxiety, depression, or self-consciousness related to menopause (Gallagher, 1993). In fact, fewer menopausal women are depressed than women with young children (Apter, 1995). Nonetheless, 75 percent of menopausal women do notice some physical changes related to menopausal hormonal shifts, such as hot flashes, vaginal dryness, weight gain, increased vulnerability to osteoporosis, and changes in cognitive processing (Leiblum, 1990; Warga, 1997). These women may find hormone replacement therapy helpful. While hormone replacement therapy is now the focus of considerable media coverage, women are advised to consult their physicians to assess the risk factors of using or not using the treatment.

Contrary to the negative stereotype of menopause as a time of constriction, many women actually experience it as a catalyst for change and growth. Women describe themselves as feeling more assertive, confident, energetic, and sexually freer. Margaret Mead dubbed this phenomenon "postmenopausal zest," which she defined as "that creativity and energy released when we no longer need to care for children" (Apter, 1995, p. 201). Menopause is not credited with physically causing postmenopausal zest; instead, it creates the conditions for women to experience freedom and the opportunity for change.

The Male Midlife Crisis

Unlike women, whose postlaunch wake-up call leads to an energized zest for life, men's experience of mortality is a lengthy, internal process. By age 40, men begin to experience a gradual series of physical changes that do not really bring them much below their maximal level of functioning; however, these changes are significant enough to notice, such as baldness, paunchiness, and wrinkles. Levinson (1978) theorizes that every man must grieve and accept the symbolic death of the youthful hero in himself and then work through a process of reevaluation and reassessment, which Levinson views as a normative task for all men in their forties. However, according to the popular conceptualization of the midlife crisis, this process of reassessment is traumatic. The stereotype suggests that men, feeling that they have squandered their dreams and have nothing to live for, suddenly quit their jobs, dash out of their marriages, and begin a spending spree on high-ticket items to bolster their self-esteem. Again, research indicates that the overwhelming majority of men accomplish the developmental tasks of reevaluation and regrouping through a long, introspective process rather than an acute acting-out crisis. Although they will be making adjustments in their relationships and in their worklives, relatively few men experience the process as catastrophic (Gallagher, 1993).

Men and Women Out of Sync

It is clear that the actual experience of men and women as they pass through midlife turns several stereotypes on their heads. It also leads to an interesting conclusion: Men and women become decidedly out of sync as they pass through midlife. Women get energized before the launching phase, generally around the age of 40. They begin by anticipating their children's leaving the home several years before the children actually leave—often fueled by the tumult of the teenage years. During this anticipatory period, women begin to envision new plans for themselves. By the time their children are being launched, women feel that there is a big world outside waiting for them. They are excitedly going back to school, beginning new jobs, or returning to full-time employment. By their fifties, midlife women are well on their way in their new or resumed jobs, careers, or personal pursuits.

Meanwhile, during the decade of their forties, usually while their children are still in the home, men begin a very gradual process of reevaluation. This process may be prompted by their noticing changes in their marriages as their wives begin looking outside the home for their new focus. However, men still remain focused primarily on their careers. Feeling that they have a last chance for success, they may actually develop a greater investment in work. It is not until later in midlife, some time in their fifties, that they begin to think differently about the meaning of work in their lives. Slowly, they become more introspective as they seriously reassess their lives. For some, this process is triggered by gradual physical signs of the aging process. For others, a specific incident—a promotion or failure at work, a retirement package, a personal or family illness, or death—may be the catalyst. Some may react to a feeling of being abandoned by their wives, or they may feel regret for not having spent more time with their children. Whatever the impetus, men begin to explore their inner selves, seeking greater meaning in life. However, it is usually not until the latter half of the launching stage, some time in their mid- to late fifties or perhaps early sixties, that men become noticeably less focused on work. They are finally willing to slow down and accept their current level of achievement at work, even if this level does not match their early dreams. They experience an increased awareness of relationships and interests that

they may have previously suppressed. They tend to become less competitive and aggressive and more willing to listen and learn (Better Carter, personal communication, January, 1998).

Thus, during midlife, men and women are moving past each other in different directions and at different paces. As women develop autonomy and move toward outside commitments, men want more time for leisure and/or travel and expect their wives to be free to join them (Carter & Peters, 1996). These gender contradictions are often confusing and unsettling to the partners and may lead to significant shifts in the marriage, including a redefinition of what constitutes a good husband or wife. As women become more independent, there may be a change in the balance of power in the marriage and a renegotiation of marital expectations, plans, and dreams—or the viability of the marriage itself.

Launching Children: What It Feels Like

All in all, launching children is a very individual experience for both mothers and fathers. Some women cry for a week or two; some are surprised by how quickly they adjust. Some women feel worse with the departure of the first child; some, with the last. They may feel that the house is too quiet, especially if they are single parents. There may be mixed feelings of happiness and sorrow at the loss of active parenting. But what most mothers have in common is that after a short time, they may feel relieved, revitalized, and ready for their own launching. Men also feel the loss, especially if they have missed much of the child-rearing because of their earlier focus on work. Now, as their children are leaving, fathers are beginning to be ready to spend less time at work and more time with their families. Thus, men may actually find their adjustment to the launching experience more problematic than women do, since men often find themselves without either their wives or children at home when they want them.

Gail (age 49), a single parent, entered treatment when her only child, Dana (age 18), left for college. Gail could not get through a day without repeated bouts of crying. She initially used treatment to mourn the loss of her early pictures of what her life would be like when Dana was launched—images that did not match her current financially constrained single life-style. Gail was also assisted in maintaining appropriate parental contact with Dana without drawing her daughter in as a confidante or caretaker. Recognizing that the loss of the full-time parenting role is particularly stressful for single women, Gail agreed to utilize her support system by reaching out to close family members and friends. Together, they planned a "mother's liberation ritual" to mark this life cycle passage. Like many women, Gail was adept at relationship skills, and she responded well to this intervention. She also found keeping a journal to be a useful tool for identifying neglected and new interests, not to be used as time fillers but as expressions of her own authentic self, which she now had the freedom to explore.

MIDLIFE MARRIAGES

Research has presented two contradictory facts about midlife marriages: (1) Midlife is the period of the peak of marital happiness (White & Edwards, 1993), and (2) midlife is the period during which two out of the three most dramatic divorce peaks of the life cycle occur (Shapiro, 1996). A number of interrelated factors account for the findings of both high marital happiness and high divorce rates at midlife, including launching children, women going into the workplace, and men's increased introspection and reassessment process. However, of all the factors related to the status of midlife marriages, the launching of children is the single most significant one.

Marital Happiness at Its Peak

Studies of the impact of launching children leave no doubt that launching children is good for marriages and good for the partners' general feeling of well-being. In fact, the presence of children in the home has not been found to correlate with marital happiness in any age group (White & Edwards, 1993). Therefore, marital happiness is described as having a first peak after the marriage, dropping off during the child-rearing phase, and peaking again in the launching stage, producing a U-shaped

model. Although stress in the home is reduced as each child leaves, the full beneficial effect of the launching process occurs only after the last child moves out (Shapiro, 1996).

What are the reasons for this boost in marital happiness at the launching stage? The removal of stress and the simplification of household routines are certainly key factors. Partners are no longer so focused on their children and can think more about and spend more energy on their marriages; and with the awareness that time is moving on, partners expect more from their relationships. At the same time, women's new outward focus takes some of the pressure off marriage as the primary source of gratification after the children leave. Then, too, midlife partners have been together for many years and have developed the relationship skills with which they weathered the stressful child-raising years. Finally, the very nature of marriage tends to change during midlife. Relationships are increasingly characterized by friendship, companionship, equality, tolerance, and shared interests (Dowling, 1996).

White and Edwards (1993) identify two qualifiers to the positive correlation between launching children and marital happiness. First, it appears that the timing of the launch is critical. When children leave too early or too late, parents tend to remain child focused, question their parental effectiveness, and do not experience that marital boost. Second, parents need to stay closely connected to their children to experience the improvement in well-being. Without frequent telephone or personal contact, parents tend to feel that their parenting role has ended, and they actually report feeling worse than they did when the children were home. These two qualifying conditions usually indicate that other transitions were not adequately resolved and are resurfacing during the launching phase. Often, marital issues and conflicts are buried during the tumult of the child-rearing years and are revisited after the children leave.

Midlife Sexual Love

Midlife presents men and women with physical changes that will require adjustments in their sexual lives. Beginning some time in their fifties and continuing into their sixties, men's sexual responses gradually slow down. They experience decreased frequency and intensity of orgasm, less ease in achieving erection, and a longer refractory period. The men's reactions to these changes depend on their self-esteem and how well they can acknowledge their emerging need for tenderness. Women may notice physical changes in their sexual responses somewhat earlier in the life cycle than men, perhaps as early as 35, or with the onset of menopause, which generally occurs during the mid-forties to mid-fifties. Changes in sexual functioning during menopause may include decreased vaginal lubrication, painful intercourse, and changes in the appearance of the genitalia (Leiblum, 1990).

The bodies of both partners are showing obvious signs of age. Fortunately, because of the developmental and logistical shifts of this period, the partners are well-equipped to make the necessary adjustments. First, the children are launched. With the children out of the home, both partners, especially the woman, feel less inhibited and preoccupied, and they may become more responsive and passionate. The cessation of menstruation also has a disinhibiting effect. Men's increased expressiveness and vulnerability and women's greater willingness to express their needs further contribute to this positive outcome. Interestingly, midlifers tend to still perceive their bodies as more youthful than they are, so they are not significantly inhibited by the physical signs of aging bodies (Bergquist et al., 1993). Also, after so many years together, most partners find that they are more patient with and tolerant of each other (Apter, 1995). They also may bring a more mature sense of self to their sex lives, which can enhance their sexual potential (Schnarch, 1997).

MIDLIFE DIVORCES

The High Divorce Rate at Midlife

While divorce is increasingly prevalent in all age groups, the increase is particularly noticeable in midlife: One dramatic divorce peak occurs after fifteen to eighteen years of marriage and another after twenty-five to twenty-eight years (Shapiro, 1996). According to the U.S. Census Bureau, the number of Americans who divorced between the ages of 40 and 54 in 1995 represents almost 14 percent of the population, up 11 percent from a decade ago (Rubin, 1997). In the 1950s, only 4 percent of divorces involved marriages of more than fifteen years. In the 1980s, the divorce rate for this group rose to 25 percent. This represents a very large group of unmarried people. In 1970, there were 1.5 million people in the United States who were divorced and not remarried. In 1991, the number had risen to 6.1 million (Dowling, 1996). However, despite the high divorce rate, it is important to bear in mind that 75 percent of midlifers are still in married or partnered relationships (Gallagher, 1993).

Why After All Those Years?

Sometimes the empty nest does not lead to the solidification of the marriage or to the acceptance of a familiar relationship. After many years of not dealing with differences, but instead burying feelings or distancing from each other or turning elsewhere, some couples realize that what is empty is the marriage. Some marriages simply cannot survive without the children present. Some couples hold onto their children to retain them as buffers; others decide to divorce. Two significant factors contribute to the timing of these midlife divorces. First, there is a change in the structure of the family and a freedom that comes with the end of the day-to-day responsibility for children. The couple has a newly available ration of time, finances, and emotional focus, which provides the opportunity and resources for change. Second, one or both of the spouses is motivated to seek a divorce by the unpleasant prospect of being left alone with a stranger or an adversary for the remainder of life. Both of these factors are magnified by the realization that time is running out.

Interestingly, 85 percent of divorces are initiated by women (Apter, 1995). Because women today are better educated than they were in the past, they are more marketable for employment. Sometimes, as women begin to experience their independence and develop their competence, they are less willing to remain in a relationship that they recognize as dead. The sense of empowerment that comes with making the decision to end an unsatisfying relationship helps to enhance women's self-confidence and their capacity for assertiveness. Though some women may be terrified of being alone and of handling finances, the emotion that most often accompanies the decision to divorce is relief (Apter, 1995). Despite their fears, women rarely regret their decision to divorce (Dowling, 1996).

When women turn outward, men take notice. They may experience a sense of confusion, vulnerability, and abandonment. Some men, as they go through the midlife process of reassessment, develop a renewed appreciation of their marital relationship, or at least they decide that remaining in the marriage is preferable to leaving, while some men respond to the questioning of an unhappy marriage by seeking a new, exciting romance. This decision may be fueled by their developing awareness of mortality and a desire for that last chance for happiness. However, a decision to end a long marriage is usually a protracted and painful one. People who are now at midlife were socialized in a time when divorce was less prevalent, and they are likely to experience their divorces as personal failures. This is especially true for women, as women tend to assume that it is their responsibility to make relationships work.

After twenty-five years of marriage, Tina (age 47) and Ed (age 49) launched their second child from the home. Tina had returned to graduate school two years before this event and was deeply absorbed in her studies, while Ed was focused on his legal career. Despite these distractions, Tina found the silence between them to be a painful indicator of their long-term estrangement. She told Ed that if they did not enter marital therapy, she did not want to remain in the marriage. Ed then agreed to enter treatment. After completing the initial assessment, the couple's therapist suggested a nine-month plan: Both Tina and Ed would agree to put their maximum effort into being the best partners they could be for the next nine months; after that, they would reevaluate their relationship. During

that period, in addition to couples work, each partner was individually coached to strengthen their own support systems and to identify and pursue their individual interests and needs. Despite this work, Ed and Tina remained disconnected. After five months, Ed disclosed that he was involved in a longstanding affair. With what she described as relief, Tina stated that she had had enough—The marriage was over. Both Tina and Ed agreed to remain in treatment for three months to handle the separation process as constructively as possible. They were given the names of local divorce mediators so that the separation and divorce process would be collaborative rather than adversarial. Individual therapeutic work with Tina focused primarily on her learning to manage her finances, while work with Ed primarily addressed developing plans to maintain contact with his children. Tina returned to treatment several months later to address the feelings of loss and failure that followed the initial sense of relief and hopeful expectation.

Women on Their Own

There is no question about it—although men have higher incomes and greater opportunity to find new mates, women do better on their own. As Terri Apter notes, "Whereas divorcing women are likely to discover their capacity for independence, divorcing men are likely to discover their dependence." (1995, p. 178) Divorced men have three times the mortality rate of married men and are more prone to stress-related alcoholism and suicide. By contrast, women tend to experience a wide range of psychological growth after divorce, including an increase in such qualities as self-esteem, assertiveness, and humor (Dowling, 1996). This is not to say that divorce is not a crisis; it is always a series of crises and disillusionments. There is usually an initial confusion, a feeling of "not knowing who I am" or of no longer being part of a family or part of a couple. But women recover more quickly than men and are more likely to use the experience as a jump start for personal growth, especially when they are the initiators of the divorce.

One of the reasons that midlife women do so much better after divorce is that they have more friends and close family ties. With their larger support systems, they are not as lonely as they had feared they would be. They are also not as frantic as men to enter new relationships, although the prospect of dating after so many coupled years can be as frightening as it is exciting. However, since midlife women have a more limited dating pool than midlife men, their potential for remarriage is dramatically lower. Therefore, it is functional that women tend to develop what Apter (1995) calls "a growing understanding that love is not a woman's whole existence, but an important part of a different whole" (p. 244). Women learn to challenge the assumption that they can be happy only by having a man, being married, and being a mother. However, this role shift is made more difficult by the fact that our society is organized around the status of couplehood, so much so that many singles complain of a feeling of invisibility. At first, women who have remained close to home tend to feel self-conscious eating alone in restaurants and are reluctant to travel alone; however, once they have experienced going off on their own, most find independence to be enriching and enjoyable (Anderson & Stewart, 1991). More problematic is the difficulty in finding ways to manage their need for physical affection and sexual gratification and the profound sense of deprivation they feel. This is one of the postdivorce losses that women talk about frequently with friends and in therapy. Some women pursue opportunities to meet eligible men, some engage in recreational sex, and some find gratification through masturbation. However, for many midlife single women, there is a grudging acceptance that they do not have a sexual partner now, and this reality may not change in the future. Therapists can provide useful support in helping women process this loss, while at the same cautioning them against using rebound relationships or hasty remarriages as a solution to this problem.

In their book *Flying Solo,* Anderson and Stewart (1991) state that the tasks midlife women are least prepared to master are those related to the ultimate indicator of power: money. Many women say that they are terrified to spend money after

their divorce. This may be a realistic concern, as most women's standard of living goes down after divorce, while that of their ex-husbands goes up. Therefore, the authors suggest that dealing responsibly with money, especially making long-term financial plans, is the "final frontier" of women's independence (p. 265).

MIDLIFERS AT WORK

Women Finding Meaning at Work

Current midlife women were socialized to expect that family life would be a higher priority than work. Nonetheless, changing social forces have led women into the workforce, so by age 50, over 67 percent of women are employed outside the home (U.S. Bureau of the Census, 1996). As they launch their children, women increasingly say that their career is what gives them a sense of meaning and pleasure (McCullough & Rutenberg, 1989), and this is not just true for professional women (Anderson & Stewart, 1991). Women who reenter the work force as their children begin to move out may initially just want to fill a void or address a financial need. However, they soon begin to change their perceptions and to see themselves as women with talents and opportunities, rather than as mothers without children at home. They also shift their view of work from just providing financial security to being a source of autonomy and independence. Work also provides midlife women with a new sense of community, and especially if they are single, work may become the center of their social lives (Bergquist et al., 1993; Hochschild, 1997). Furthermore, McQuaide (1998) identified a number of factors which contribute to the well-being of midlife women that are related to their working outside the home. These factors include an income above $30,000, a sense of effectance, and high self-esteem.

Sexual and Age Discrimination at Work

This positive picture of midlife women at work is clouded by the endurance of sexual discrimination in the workplace. Women were not a presence in the workforce until the 1960s and 1970s. During that time, the salaries of women stabilized at rates much lower than those of men's salaries. From 1960 to 1979, the median earnings of women working full-time stabilized at approximately 59 percent of the earnings of men (Bergquist et al., 1993). Then, from 1979 to 1993, women's median earnings rose from 62 percent to 77 percent of men's (Lewin, 1997). However, a troubling new study indicates that after twenty years of a steadily narrowing wage gap, it is now widening again: The median earnings are now just under 75 percent of men's (Lewin, 1997). Women also continue to be underrepresented in power positions. For example, only 2 percent of chief executive officers of major corporations and fewer than 10 percent of corporate board members are women (Bergquist et al., 1993). Furthermore, as midlife women enter the workforce and attempt to develop their careers by changing jobs, they find that age discrimination limits their ability to be hired or to move into new positions (Pogrebin, 1996). Thus, women remain about ten years behind their male cohorts in job development (Ackerman, 1990). This is indicative of the double discrimination that mature women face: first for being women and second for aging. Youthful appearance is not just about looks; it is about power. And when it comes to youth and power, there is a gender gap. While midlife women experience a sense of invisibility as they show signs of aging, men are considered to have character or wisdom. Nonetheless, some positive changes are occurring. Corporations are making accommodations to women who took the "mommy track." Corporate women who chose flexible work arrangements to raise their children are able to get back on track and are accepted by co-workers when they return to full-time employment (Shapiro, 1996).

Men Reassessing Priorities

Men in their forties are still strongly career focused, but by their early to mid-fifties, some men begin to reprioritize marital satisfaction as a central factor to their happiness (Julian et al., 1992). However, work remains important, and it is not until they approach 60 that they realistically assess what they have accomplished in their careers. As part of this reevaluation, men often decide that the price of their occupational success was too high. However, this does not necessarily mean that they willingly initiate a process of relinquishing or reducing the power and money that accompany their success. In a study of 4,000 male executives, 68 percent admitted they had neglected their families for their careers, and 50 percent said that they would have done it differently (Bergquist et al., 1993). When this realization occurs, it is usually hypothetical, but it may become very functional for the many midlife men who lose their jobs when companies reorganize. Some men report that the experience of being downsized pushed them into developing more balanced and fulfilling lives (Bergquist et al., 1993; Carter & Peters, 1996).

Regrouping after the Pink Slip

The numerous reorganizations in the corporate world have significantly affected midlife men and women through early retirement packages and layoffs. These job terminations may result in an initial sense of betrayal, disillusionment, and confusion, especially for men who had viewed themselves as good company men and fear that they may now be unemployable because of their age, type of experience, and high salary level. For women, the restructurings may mean that the middle management jobs that they had hoped to find have disappeared. For many men and women, the response to these challenges is a mobilization of their resiliencies and resources. For some, this may mean retraining or additional education, especially in the increasingly technological marketplace, and opportunities to meet new people and gain new perspectives and skills. For others, this may be an opportunity to start their own business. Entrepreneurship is a major phenomenon of the 1990s, with women-owned business representing the fastest growing segment of the economy (Bergquist et al., 1993). For those who remain employed, benefits such as medical plans, vested retirement plans, or profit-sharing plans provide the "golden handcuffs" that keep people employed at jobs that may be less than satisfying. This has particular significance for midlifers because the economic reality, especially for single women, is that they may be working past the age of 70. Even among married women, economic pressures may lead to a lengthening of the period of employment. Indeed, a new study indicates a shift in gender patterns of older married midlifers in the workplace. While the percentage of working married men age 55–64 has declined in the last fifteen years, the percentage of working married women in that age range has sharply increased. The study suggests that women, who lack the Social Security credits or pension savings of men their age, are continuing in the workforce after their husbands retire to secure their economic survival (Uchitelle, 1997). The stress of adjusting to changes in work status frequently motivates individuals and families to seek clinical assistance. In addition to attending to practical matters, such as budgetary concerns and reassignment of household chores, clients will need to address maintaining their support systems and reassessing the meaning of productivity at this stage in their lives.

REDEFINING FAMILY RELATIONSHIPS AT MIDLIFE

The Sandwich Generation

Contrary to the image of aging parents being packed off to the nursing home, most elderly people are healthy enough and financially stable enough to live independently throughout their lives. Most of those who develop infirmities or illness are cared for by their children. Because people are living longer, the period of providing care for aging parents has moved from the forties to the fifties. Also, because child-bearing has been delayed and children are older when they leave home, midlifers may be caring simultaneously for aging parents and young adults—and perhaps for returning children and grandchildren as well. The

group of adults caught in this competition of roles is called the "sandwich generation." Typically, the caregivers are midlife daughters and daughters-in-law, not sons. Women provide the day-to-day care for their aging parents and sometimes their in-laws, while their husbands and brothers provide financial support and supervise property and other assets. It is not that men do not care, but the tasks of caregiving have traditionally been distributed differentially between the sexes.

Fortunately, this system overload occurs when adults are at their peak of competence, control, and ability to handle stress (Gallagher, 1993). If the family views caregiving as normal rather than burdensome, the phase will be less stressful. These caregiving expectations are strongly influenced by ethnic values. For example, Latino, Asian American, African American, and Native American families tend to normalize the caregiving role, while Irish and Czech families are less likely to do so. Anglo Americans, who value independence and self-sufficiency to the extreme, tend to find provision of care to the elderly particularly problematic for both generations (McGoldrick et al., 1996). However, even in families in which caregiving is culturally supported, women caregivers are at high risk for stress-related illnesses and are sometimes called the hidden patients in the health care system. Greene (1991) has identified the following issues for midlife caregivers:

- *A shift in intimacy:* Caregivers become aware of personal details, and that breaks down generational boundaries.
- *A shift in power and responsibility:* Caregivers, who now give rather than receive nurturance and advice, feel like parents to their parents.
- *Financial burden:* The financial demands of caring for parents occurs around the same time midlife women are launching children, starting new careers, and/or going to school.
- *Role competition:* Caregivers may also be mothers, partners, employees, homemakers, and/or students.
- *Emotional ambivalence:* Caregivers feel anger and embarrassment about providing their

parents with intimate physical care, but also guilt and responsibility. As a result, they may have difficulty setting limits on their level of participation.

- *Confrontation with one's own aging and mortality.*

As a result of these pressures and the potential for burnout, caregivers may need assistance with identifying their own needs and setting appropriate limits. This is particularly true for single midlife women, who are the most isolated but who are assumed to be free of other responsibilities and are the most overwhelmed. The more resilient caregivers are able to view this period as an opportunity to resolve old issues with parents that have persisted through previous life cycle phases. For those who had managed their intergenerational issues as they occurred and moved more smoothly through earlier life cycle transitions, the postlaunch phase provides an opportunity for both generations to continue to adjust their relationship in ways that are mutually satisfying.

Meryl (age 48) and Steve (age 50) called for an appointment in response to Meryl's complaint of depression. At intake, it was apparent that Meryl was worn out. According to the couple, her main problem was the pressure of visiting her widowed mother five times a week, doing all the shopping and household chores, and chauffeuring her mother to her medical and other appointments. Meryl had not complained until the previous fall, when the couple's youngest child, Amy (age 18), had gone off to college. At that point, Meryl's resentment spilled over, and she complained that Steve was not supportive. Steve stated that he held up his end by being the family's sole wage earner, and now he was doubly burdened by bills for Amy's tuition and for his mother-in-law's home health aide. Upon further probing, it became apparent that Meryl's sense of isolation was a long-standing marital issue that had surfaced with such urgency only when their daughter was no longer in the home. The first phase of treatment addressed the couple's presenting problem: Meryl's urgent sense of burden, burnout, and isolation. As a typical oldest daughter, Meryl had assumed the over-responsible role in her family of origin. She was coached to call her younger sister and brother to express her need for them to assume a more equitable role in caring for their mother. With some prodding, both siblings agreed to increase their visits and phone contacts with their mother. Meryl was also coached to begin setting limits on her unconditional availability to her mother. These interventions began to challenge Meryl's previously unquestioned assumption that she alone was responsible for the smooth running of the family.

Just as midlifers have the opportunity to redefine their relationships with their parents, they may also feel able to establish a more comfortable relationship with in-laws if they are not caught up in old conflicts with them. With their recognition of their own mortality, midlifers may now see themselves as peers with in-laws. Feeling on a more equal footing, midlifers' constraints of surface politeness or resentment may drop away, and they are better able to express their own wishes.

The Death of Parents

Dealing with the death of parents is now considered a normative task of midlife. However, normative does not mean easy. The death of a parent at any time is a major loss, but at midlife, there are special developmental tasks that are related to, and may have an impact on, the resolution of their grief. As described by Scharlach and Fredricksen (1993), these tasks include the following:

- *Acceptance of one's own mortality:* This is seen as the critical task of this life cycle phase. Midlifers are aware that they are now the executive generation and can no longer look to their parents for guidance. They may become more attentive to their own health, draft their wills and make their own funeral arrangements. Along with freedom from child care, this awareness of mortality is a prime trigger for the life reassessment process.
- *Redefinition of family roles and responsibilities:* Midlifers are now the heads of the family. The role of maintaining family contacts, continuing family rituals and values, and guiding

the next generation now falls to them. This redefinition also includes attending to unresolved issues with siblings without the impetus of the older generation to prod them.

- *Change in self-perception:* Midlifers who experience the death of a parent may become more self-reliant and autonomous, while at the same time more responsible toward others. This flowering of autonomy and emotional connectedness is viewed as an indicator of midlife maturity.

Unresolved grief following the death of a parent is usually related to longstanding unresolved issues, such as feelings of dependency, criticism, guilt, or ambivalence. The experience of death and mourning rituals may provide an opportunity to readdress these issues, even after the parent's death. As with all unresolved issues, if they are not addressed now, they will find ways of resurfacing later in life.

Redefining Relationships with Adult Children and Boomerang Kids

It is one thing to have children move out of the home. It is another to view them as adults and relate to them accordingly, and still another for young adults to see their parents as people with a history, life, and concerns of their own. Fortunately, parents and children tend to stay closely connected after launching, often speaking several times a week (White & Edwards, 1993). This validates the parental role and makes the launch less wrenching. If they see that their children are becoming more and more independent in their new roles as young adults both inside and outside the family, parents feel that their job was well done and are able to relinquish some of their parental oversight. If the young adults are not harboring major unresolved issues, then parents and children are increasingly able to interact on an adult, mutually supportive basis. In fact, parent-child relationships have been found to become more affectionate and close after the children leave home (Troll, 1994), and parents often come to view their children as

close friends (Shapiro, 1996), especially after the children marry and have children of their own.

More and more frequently, young adult children, especially sons, remain home or return home after a brief period on their own. This may be due to financial concerns, lengthened years of education, delayed marriage plans, or marital breakups. The phenomenon of adult children, and perhaps grandchildren, residing at home is most likely to occur under three conditions: if the parent-child relationship has been positive, if the family has positive attitudes about continuing to provide children with support, and if the family is "intact," rather than being a step-family or a single-parent household. Another factor that encourages adult children to reside with parents is the tendency of couples in unhappy marriages to triangulate their children and hang onto them as a source of emotional support or as a means of maintaining equilibrium in the home. Additionally, parents may want to maintain an immature adult child in their home because of their concern about that adult child's ability to function independently (Aquilino, 1991).

Parents, especially middle-class parents, anticipate the freedom that comes after children leave. Therefore, having adult children in the home produces stress. This is related partly to the frustration of their expectations, but also to the fact that the household is simply more complicated with children present. However, the crucial factor in the parents' response is the way in which they interpret the children's presence. Parents view the situation more negatively if their children are unemployed or move back after a marital breakup than if the children remain home while working or going to school or if they never had been married. The more autonomous and less dependent their children are, the better the parents feel about having adult children in the home. Here again, class and ethnicity influence the family's responses. For example, because of their beliefs about adult development, upper-middle-class parents may find their children's presence worrisome (Aquilino, 1991). By contrast, poor or working-class African American midlifers are more accepting of the tradition, born of necessity, of having their adult children reside in their homes and/or assuming the role of parenting their grandchildren (McGoldrick et al., 1996).

Redefining parent-child relationships as adult-to-adult personal relationships does not happen automatically when grown children leave home, or even when they marry and have children. It is quite common for unresolved emotional issues or differences in the wish for close involvement to create situations of polite, dutiful distance instead of a warm and eager sharing of lives between generations. Resolving old issues is the central emotional task of the younger generation, but parents can help or hinder the process. Their shift from hands-on direction of adolescents to on-call consultant to young adults may not be easy. Some parents also find it difficult to be more open and personal with "children" whom they have always shielded from "adult" problems. For specific interventions in helping either generation change their relationship at this juncture, see Chapter 26 on coaching.

Accepting the Expansion of Family through Marriage and Grandchildren

While midlife is a period of family contraction because of the launching of children and the illness or death of aged parents, it is also a time of expansion and regeneration through marriage and the birth of grandchildren. Families must change their usual relationships with their grown children and also learn to incorporate their children's new spouses and their families. Although some families experience antagonism with in-laws, parents often form close relationships with sons-in-laws and/or daughters-in-law (Bergquist et al., 1993). This process is facilitated if children have chosen spouses who are compatible with their parents' ethnic, class, and religious values or, alternately, if the family is flexible and open to differences. Family of origin traditions and beliefs regarding the appropriate degree of inclusion of in-laws also govern the melding process. On the other hand, if the choice of a marriage partner is seen as a reactive challenge to the parents or if the spouse is selected as a way for the child to distance from the parents, the blending of the two families will be more problematic. Conflicts may develop around such issues as holiday plans or acceptable terms of address. Parents may feel unwanted and attempt to be either overinvolved or underinvolved with the young couple or, in extreme cases, cut them off. In general, these difficulties are actually displacements for unresolved family issues that are reenacted through the children's marriage. Because women are typically assigned the role of being responsible for the family's emotional life, the most difficult of these problems usually involve the women in the family: sisters-in-law, mothers with their sons or daughters, and mothers-in-law with daughters-in-law. Betty Carter and Joan Peters (1996) note that the target of mother-in-law jokes is invariably the husband's mother. In this drama, the son is caught in the middle as family history is repeated. Carter and Peters advise that the players who are responsible for handling the problem be the family members, not the in-laws.

Joan (age 54) and Frank (age 55) prided themselves on their close Italian Catholic family and were disappointed when their son Perry (age 24) married Kathy (age 24), a German Methodist. Nonetheless, Joan continued her daily calls to Perry and still prepared large Sunday dinners, which the new couple increasingly began to miss. A crisis occurred when Perry spent Thanksgiving and then Christmas Eve with his wife's family. Joan reacted angrily with Perry. Their distress and bewilderment about the ensuing estrangement led Joan and Frank to seek therapy. At intake, it was apparent that Joan's intensity was balanced by Frank's affable distancing. Their traditional roles—homemaker and wage earner—had worked well when the children were home, especially since Joan's overresponsible parental role was culturally sanctioned. After first normalizing their dilemma in the context of their life cycle stage and ethnic expectations, the therapist challenged the couple to refocus on their marital relationship (a normative midlife task) and suggested that they get "remarried." They were coached to begin dating and eventually to invite Perry and Kathy out on a double date. They were cautioned to avoid making demands on the younger couple or to refer to past disappointments. Joan was also encouraged to re-examine her expectation of daily contact with her son and her lack of acknowledgment of his married status. This proved to be extremely challenging for Joan until Frank recalled his feeling of being dis-counted by Joan's mother when he and Joan were newlyweds.

One of the supreme rewards of midlife is grandparenthood. Grandparents say that the plea-sure of seeing their own children parent the next generation is a joy that defies description. Family identity is solidified as the family reenacts mean-ingful life cycle rituals and ceremonies. Grandpar-ents have an opportunity to revisit and perhaps redo their experience as parents without the day-to-day responsibility of child care. On the other hand, Bergquist et al. (1993) have identified the following potential problems of grandparenthood:

- If grandparents are divorced, conflict may arise around who gets invited to parties or, if they are remarried, who are the "real grandparents."
- If adult children divorce, custody agreements may need to include grandparents' visitation rights. This may be a potentially critical issue if the relationship between the two adult gen-erations, especially with the in-laws, has not been good.
- If the adult children are incapacitated by drug abuse or illness, grandparents may be re-cruited to raise their grandchildren.

Relations with Siblings and Other Kin

The sibling relationship is the family relationship of longest duration—longer than with parents, spouses, or children. While levels of closeness vary at different periods, the sibling relationship tends to be sustained throughout life. Despite dis-tances or differences, siblings often come together to share holidays and special occasions. Midlife siblings draw together as aunts and uncles, parents, and grandparents become ill and die, leaving them to assume their place as the older generation. They also face the stressor of distributing the tasks of providing care to their aging parents. Typically, a sister, either the oldest or the closest, will assume the role alone if a family therapist has not been in-volved to help the sister get support from her sib-lings. After a parent's death, the primary caregiver may feel resentment with her siblings for their lesser involvement. As part of the grief process, siblings should be encouraged to address this issue and find a way to adequately express their appreciation to the caregiver. Failure to do so may lead to a disrup-tion of relations. There also may be other issues that have been chronic sources of conflict through other life phases. After the parents' deaths, if there is no outside help, siblings may distance them-selves or cut off rather than work at resolving these conflicts. If the discord persists, the siblings risk losing a significant source of practical and emo-tional support that they may need in later life.

FRIENDSHIPS AT MIDLIFE

Friendships take on new importance at midlife. During the child-raising years, friendships were often diluted by the omnipresence of children at most social gatherings, but at midlife, they matter again in a profound and personal way. Midlifers are reinventing themselves. Their families look different. They may be suddenly single. For all the special concerns of midlife, long-term friends are there to provide a sense of belonging and continu-ity, while new friends are needed to address new interests and realities. With their heightened aware-ness of life's fragility, midlifers consciously value and appreciate their friends.

For single women in particular, friends are needed to provide a sense of connection and com-munity. Just after divorce or widowhood, women tend to turn to their married friends. This soon shifts, and single women find that they need to de-velop a network of single friends. Developing this network requires exploring new depths of self-confidence and assertiveness, but the effort pays off. Friends function almost like a new extended family that provides resources, support, and oppor-tunities for developing purpose and meaning in life through connection. The connection between fe-male friendships and the well-being of midlife women has been supported by research (McQuaide, 1998). Therefore, clinicians should offer treatment to midlife women that helps them enhance their social networks.

For men, forming or maintaining friendships may be a new experience, since they were not socialized to develop relationship skills, and their wives had performed that role during earlier life stages. Now, it is more important than ever for men to take responsibility for the work of maintaining relationships, including friendships. However, men's friendships continue to conform to the cultural norms of "masculinity," which prescribes superficial and competitive connections, rather than the more intimate, disclosing friendships of women (Julian et al., 1992). Friendships do become more important to men at midlife, especially if they are divorced or widowed; however, true to their upbringing, which emphasized financial and work success, men still tend to rely primarily on the close partnership of a one-to-one relationship with a woman, who is expected to make it work out. The emotional isolation of men at this stage of life should be treated by therapists as a serious crisis waiting to happen. A good place to help men start to learn how to maintain relationships is to coach them on relating to their grown children.

> When John (age 55) was told by his wife that she was leaving him, he moved into a condo and began dating, but he still felt unremittingly lonely. At the urging of his sister, John entered therapy. His lack of relationship skills was indicated by his humorous yet poignant expression of surprise at his wife's decision to end the marriage: "I didn't know we were unhappy until she told me!" An exploration of his support system revealed superficial relationships with his children and friends. John reported that he had not yet disclosed to his closest friends at work that he was living on his own. His difficulty with emotional closeness was normalized in the context of the socialization of men in our culture. The therapist suggested to John that before he could develop a truly intimate relationship with a woman, he must first learn to connect with family members. The therapist began by coaching him to schedule dinners with his son Dan (age 31), who lived locally, and to maintain phone

contact with his daughter Emily (age 28), who was away at graduate school. John was cautioned to take care not to attempt to put his children in a caretaking role, but rather to reconnect around his desire to know more about their lives, interests, and memories.

GAYS AND LESBIANS AT MIDLIFE

The tasks of midlife are egalitarian. Gays and lesbians, bisexuals, and heterosexuals are all challenged by the same developmental and life cycle issues. However, gays and lesbians have unique midlife concerns that require special attention, some of which are addressed below. A full discussion of a family life cycle model for gays and lesbians can be found in Chapter 20.

Midlife Gay and Lesbian Parents

There has always been a minority of gays and lesbians—often an invisible minority—who have parented and launched children. There is no single route to this role. Sometimes when heterosexual couples divorce, one of the partners identifies him or herself as homosexual. Other gays and lesbians become parents after coming out by using alternative means of insemination, surrogacy, sexual intercourse, or adoption. Gay males who are parents overwhelmingly became fathers during an earlier heterosexual marriage, while deciding to become parents after coming out is primarily a lesbian phenomenon and has been called the "lesbian baby boom" (Patterson, 1996).

Gays and lesbians who leave marriages at midlife are influenced by the same life reevaluation process experienced by midlife heterosexuals who decide to divorce, including the sense of time running out and the postlaunch boost. The timing of their decision to leave their marriages and begin living openly as homosexuals is also frequently due to the sensitivity of these parents to their children's needs. Most children of homosexuals are nonreactive about their parents' sexuality until they reach adolescence. At that time, because of their own developmental issues, some adolescents may experience anger and embarrassment at having a parent who is "different" and stigmatized. Therefore, many gay parents wait to come out until their children reach young adulthood, with the expectation that their children will then be more able to accept their sexual orientation. Parents may also delay their decision to live openly as gays or lesbians because of the ongoing homophobia of the court system and the possibility of losing visitation rights with their children during divorce proceedings (Bigner, 1996).

> Cheryl (age 46) had been married for eighteen years to Stan (age 49), a successful businessman, and their daughter Jill (age 17) was starting to plan for college. Cheryl had given up a teaching career to be a stay-at-home mom and was involved in several volunteer activities in her upper-middle-class community. Before her marriage, she had experienced romantic feelings for women but never acted on them. When she married Stan, she immersed herself in her roles as wife and mother and put those feelings out of mind. Then, after fifteen years of marriage, she met Elaine (age 42) at a tennis game and felt drawn to her. The two women developed a close friendship and eventually became romantically involved. Because of Stan's frequent business trips, Cheryl was able to keep the relationship a secret. As devoted as she came to feel to Elaine, Cheryl felt equally committed to her family's stability and could not leave her marriage. Feeling torn between two lives and becoming increasingly depressed about her struggle to maintain the pretense of stability, Cheryl entered therapy. Cheryl stated that she had no intention of leaving her family, but she needed help with her depression. Treatment initially addressed the stress of managing the logistics of her situation. As Cheryl felt more relaxed about talking about her dilemma, her therapist helped her look at her own homophobia—at stereotypical images she held of gay people, her early concepts of homosexuality, and her family's attitudes. Cheryl was then able to identify her own sense of shame that added to her need to maintain the secret. Cheryl was then encouraged to look at her social network to identify those friends who would accept her as a gay woman. She was coached to firm up those relationships and then to slowly share her dilemma. She was also assisted in moving closer to her daughter, as that relationship was most important to her. When her level of comfort was clearly established, Cheryl was assisted in preparing to disclose her relationship to her husband and daughter through extensive use of role play.

The process of simultaneously launching children, divorcing, and coming out complicates three processes that are already major life transitions when experienced separately. Each of these transitions requires major role shifts and life-style changes, with feelings that range from liberation to loss. Furthermore, gay parents and their children are engaged concurrently in the processes of individuation and the development of new adult identities. However, for the parents, there is an additional issue of developmental lag. Bigner (1996) notes that gay men who come out at midlife are off-time in terms of their development of a stable, positive homosexual identity compared with gays who come out earlier in life. These men may prematurely seek to replicate the exclusive, committed relationship model of heterosexual marriages, which may complicate their integration into gay culture.

Aging Bodies and Confronting Mortality

Coming to terms with aging is a key developmental task of midlife. Among gay men, concern about body image is particularly strong, as they fear that signs of aging will mean that they are less sexually desirable. The critical midlife task of accepting one's own mortality is also drastically heightened among gay men. A large proportion of men living with HIV/AIDS are now in midlife; some of these men have been HIV-positive for ten years or more. In addition to their acute personal awareness of mortality, gay men have buried and grieved for numerous friends and partners. Therefore, rather than just beginning to confront mortality at midlife as heterosexuals typically do, gay men have been living with a heightened awareness of death on a daily basis for many years.

Midlife lesbians are more tolerant of the body changes that come with age than midlife gay men. Women in general tend to focus more on the emotional than the physical aspects of intimacy. Therefore, with two women in a relationship, the partners are much less prone to equate desirability and beauty with youth, thinness, or any of the other usual male criteria of female beauty (Cole & Rothblum, 1990). However, women in lesbian partnerships may find the transition of menopause to be more problematic than heterosexual women do. Human sexuality researcher Sandra Leiblum (1990) suggests that the couple's adjustment to the physical and psychological effects of menopause may be exacerbated by their experiencing menopause together, as both women's sexual interest and performance may decline at the same time. Furthermore, lesbian partners undergoing menopause at the same time may respond more acutely to their mutual cessation of fertility if they were prevented from having children because of their lack of access, as lesbians, to donor insemination or adoption options. In this case, the association between menopause and loss will be compounded for lesbian partners (Slater, 1995). Nonetheless, it has also been reported that lesbian women complain much less of menopausal symptoms than do heterosexual women (Pogrebin, 1996).

As with midlife heterosexual couples, midlife gays and lesbians are more companionable and less passionate. At this stage of life, both gays and lesbians report that while they remain sexually active, sex does not have the urgency it did in their youth. This is particularly true of lesbians, who are typically less sexually active (though not less affectionate or expressive) than either gay male or heterosexual couples (Green, Bettinger, & Zacks, 1996; Leiblum, 1990). However, while sex may be less frequent, gays and lesbians report sex to be more satisfying in midlife (McWhirter & Mattison, 1984; Tully, 1989). Johnson and Keren (1996) note that gay couples are much less likely than heterosexual couples to view infrequent sex with their partners as an indicator of a relationship problem.

Support Systems

Gays and lesbians who are now in midlife were raised in an even more homophobic society than today's younger generation and may not have felt able to disclose their sexual orientation or their partnerships to family members; or if they did disclose, they may have been rejected or kept at a distance. Therefore, friends are overwhelmingly important sources of support and come to serve as more accepting quasi-families. These "families of choice" may include homosexual friends, heterosexual friends, co-workers, children from former marriages, and selected family members. As gays and lesbians age, especially those without children, the expectation is that they will be turning to members of their families of choice to care for them in sickness or old age (Tully, 1989).

SUMMARY

Midlife, the longest phase of the life cycle, is a time of major family restructuring. The family shrinks when children are launched from the home or when parents of midlifers are lost through the death. Additionally, many families experience loss through midlife divorce or the death of a spouse. Women also "leave" voluntarily by joining the workforce or other outside involvement, while midlife men may suddenly experience the loss of employment if their company is restructured. On the other hand, the family expands through the marriage of adult children and the birth of grandchildren. Families may also expand when launched children return home, some with their own children, or if aged parents join the household. Any one of these events is a stress point that might motivate families to seek a family therapist for help.

With or without treatment, families will need to adjust to the realignments and redefinitions of roles that result from these restructurings. While women typically lead the way toward change, men frequently join the process by being jolted into an awareness that they are at risk of losing relationships they had taken for granted. Making a decision about working on or ending unsatisfying relationships or reconnecting with estranged family members becomes more urgent when an individual is aware of being closer to death than birth. Accomplishing these shifts requires midlifers to reexamine and alter the rigid role definitions that have defined their relationships during the child-rearing years. Admittedly, this is a tough job in a culture that still supports traditional gender roles, but midlifers know that it is "now or never." There-fore, they may be more accessible to clinical intervention than at earlier stages in their life cycle. Thus, rather than being a time of winding down, midlife is a long life cycle stage that can be a fertile time for new options, growth, and change.

REFERENCES

Ackerman, R. (1990). Career developments and transitions of middle aged women. *Psychology of Women Quarterly, 14,* 513–530.

Anderson, C. M., & Stewart, S., with Dimidjian, S. (1991). *Flying solo.* New York: W.W. Norton.

Apter, T. (1995). *Secret paths: Women in the new midlife.* New York: W.W. Norton.

Aquilino, W. S. (1991). Predicting parents' experience with coresident adult children. *Journal of Family Issues, 12,* 323–342.

Bergquist, W. H., Greenberg, E. M., & Klaum, G. A. (1993). *In our fifties: Voices of men and women reinventing their lives.* San Francisco: Jossey-Bass.

Bigner, J. (1996). Working with gay fathers: Developmental, postdivorce parenting, and therapeutic issues. In J. Laird and R.-J. Green (Eds.), *Lesbians and gays in couples and families: A handbook for therapists,* (pp. 370–403). San Francisco: Jossey-Bass.

Carter, B., & Peters, J. K. (1996). *Love, honor and negotiate: Making your marriage work.* New York: Pocket Books.

Cole, E., & Rothblum, E. (1990). Commentary on "Sexuality and the midlife woman." *Psychology of Women Quarterly, 14,* 509–512.

Dowling, C. (1996). *Red hot mamas: Coming into our own at fifty.* New York: Bantam Books.

Friedan, B. (1963). *The feminine mystique.* New York: W.W. Norton.

Gallagher, W. (1993, May). Midlife myths. *The Atlantic Monthly,* 551–568.

Green, R.-J., Bettinger, M., & Zacks, E. (1996). Are lesbian couples fused and gay male couples disengaged? Questioning gender straitjackets. In J. Laird and R.-J. Green (Eds.), *Lesbians and gays in couples and families: A handbook for therapists,* (pp. 185–230). San Francisco: Jossey-Bass.

Greene, C. P. (1991). Clinical considerations: Midlife daughters and their aging parents. *Journal of Gerontological Nursing, 17,* 6–12.

Hochschild, A. (1997). *Time binds: When work becomes home and home becomes work.* New York: Metropolitan Books.

Johnson, T. W., & Keren, M. S. (1996). Creating and maintaining boundaries in male couples. In J. Laird and R.-J. Green (Eds.), *Lesbians and gays in couples and families: A handbook for therapists,* (pp. 231–250). San Francisco: Jossey-Bass.

Julian, T., McKenry, P. C., & McKelvey, M. (1992). Components of a man's well-being at midlife. *Mental Health Nursing, 13,* 285–298.

Leiblum, S. (1990). Sexuality and the midlife woman. *Psychology of Women Quarterly, 14,* 495–508.

Levinson, D. J. (1978). *The seasons of a man's life.* New York: Ballantine Books.

Lewin, T. (1997, September 15). Women losing ground to men in widening income difference. *New York Times,* pp. A1, 12.

McCullough, P. G., & Rutenberg, S. K. (1989). Launching children and moving on. In B. Carter & M. McGoldrick (Eds.), *The changing family life cycle: A framework for family therapy* (2nd ed.) (pp. 285–309). Boston: Allyn and Bacon.

McGoldrick, M., Giordano, J., & Pearce, J. K. (Eds.) (1996). *Ethnicity and family therapy.* New York: The Guilford Press.

McQuaide, S. (1998). Women at midlife. *Social Work, 43,* 21–31.

McWhirter, D. P., & Maattison, A. M. (1984). *The male couple: How relationships develop.* Englewood Cliffs, NJ: Prentice-Hall.

Mitchell, V., & Helson, R. (1990). Women's prime of life: Is it the 50's? *Psychology of Women Quarterly, 14,* 451–470.

Neugarten, B. (1968). The awareness of middle age. In B. Neugarten (Ed.), *Middle age and aging: A reader in social psychology,* (pp. 93–98). Chicago: University of Chicago Press.

Patterson, C. J. (1996). Lesbian mothers and their children: Findings from the Bay Area Families Study.

In J. Laird and R.-J. Green (Eds.), *Lesbians and gays in couples and families: A handbook for therapists,* (pp. 420–437). San Francisco: Jossey-Bass.

Pogrebin, L. C. (1996). *Getting over getting older.* New York: Berkley Books.

Rubin, N. (1997, December 7). In middle age and suddenly single. *New York Times,* Westchester Regional Section, pp. 1, 8.

Scharlach, A. E., & Fredricksen, K. (1993). Reactions to the death of a parent during midlife. *Omega, 27,* 307–319.

Schnarch, D. (1997). Passionate marriage. *Family Therapy Networker, 21,* 42–49.

Shapiro, P. G. (1996). *My turn: Women's search for self after children leave.* Princeton, NJ: Peterson's.

Slater, S. (1995). *The lesbian family life cyle.* New York: The Free Press.

Troll, L. (1994). Family connectedness of old women: Attachments in later life. In B. F. Turner & L. E. Troll (Eds.), *Women growing older,* (pp. 169–201). Thousand Oaks, CA: Sage.

Tully, C. T. (1989). Caregiving: What do midlife lesbians view as important? *Journal of Gay and Lesbian Psychotherapy, 1,* 87–103.

Uchitelle, L. (1997, December 14). She's wound up in her career, but he's ready to wind down. *New York Times,* Section 3, pp. 1, 13.

U.S. Bureau of the Census. (1996). *Statistical abstract of the United States.* Washington, DC: U.S. Government Printing Office.

Warga, C. L. (1997, August 30). Estrogen and the brain. *New York Magazine,* 26–31.

White, L., & Edwards, J. N. (1993). Emptying the nest and parental well-being: An analysis of national panel data. *American Sociological Review, 55,* 235–242.

CHAPTER 18

FAMILIES IN LATER LIFE
CHALLENGES AND OPPORTUNITIES

FROMA WALSH

*For age is opportunity no less
than youth itself, though in another dress,
and as the evening twilight fades away
the sky is filled with stars invisible by day.*
—Longfellow

The major demographic changes over the coming decades concern the aging of societies worldwide. What passes unnoticed is that families are aging as well, as they are also becoming more diverse. This chapter examines the emerging challenges and opportunities for families in later life associated with retirement and financial security; grandparenthood; chronic illness and caregiving; and death, loss, and widowhood. Clinical guidelines are offered to encourage the many possibilities for personal and relational resilience and growth and for meaningful connection, reconciliation, and transformation of intergenerational relationships.

THE GRAYING OF THE FAMILY

Declining birth rates, health care advances, and increasing longevity are contributing to the rise in the number and proportion of elderly people in the United States, as in other parts of the world (Kausler, 1996). Family networks are becoming smaller and top-heavy, with more older than younger family members. Life expectancy has increased from 47 years in 1900 to over 76 at present. The baby boom generation, now entering its fifties, will soon swell the over-65 population to record levels: 13 percent of our population by the year 2000, up from 8 percent in 1950. By 2040, over one in five Americans will be over 65 (one in four people in most of the Western world). With medical advances and healthier life-styles, a growing number of people are living into their 80s, 90s, and even past 100. Later life is being redefined in terms of the "young old," persons age 65 to 85 who are mostly healthy and vibrant, and the "old old" or "fourth age" of elders over 85, the fastest-growing segment of older people and the group most vulnerable to serious illness and disability.

The Varying and Extended Family Life Cycle Course

As societies age, the family life course is becoming ever more lengthened and varied (Hareven, 1996; Walsh, 1993). Four- and five-generation families add complexity in balancing members' needs and family resources. With fewer young people to support the growing number of elders, threats to Social Security and health care benefits will likely fuel greater insecurity and intergenerational tensions. More "young old" people at retirement age, with diminishing resources, are involved in caring for their elderly parents. At the same time, the trend toward having few or no children will leave elders with fewer intergenerational connections. The declining proportion of younger people and increasing workforce involvement of women exacerbate family strain in providing financial and caretaking support. New technologies prolonging life and the dying process pose unprecedented family challenges. With impersonal, inadequate health care systems and the loss of community in our society, the family is more important than ever in providing not only caregiving, but also a sense of worth, lasting emotional ties, and human dignity at life's end.

Pathways through later life are increasingly varied. Our aging population is becoming more racially and ethnically diverse (Johnson & Barer, 1990). Changes in family life-styles also present new challenges with aging. The growing number of single older adults (Anderson & Stewart, 1994) and couples who are unmarried or without children forge a variety of significant kin and friendship bonds. With greater life expectancy, couples may have thirty to forty years ahead after launching children; increasing numbers are celebrating fifty and sixty years of marriage. Although nearly 50 percent of marriages end in divorce, remarriage is becoming the most common family form. Two or three marriages over a long lifetime, along with periods of cohabitation and single living, are likely to become increasingly common, creating enlarged and complicated family networks in later life. As Margaret Mead (1972) noted, it's difficult for one relationship to meet the changing developmental priorities of both partners over a lengthened lifetime. In view of these challenges, perhaps it's remarkable that over 50 percent of couples do *not* divorce.

The family and social time clocks associated with aging are also becoming more fluid. As many become grandparents and great-grandparents, others are beginning or extending parenthood. With new fertility methods, women in middle age are bearing children. Men, whose remarriages are often to women many years younger than themselves, are increasingly starting second families in later years.

Aging gay men and lesbian women meet needs for meaning and intimacy in varied ways (Berger, 1996; Reid, 1995), with developmental challenges strongly influenced by their present life circumstances and social environment (Cohler, Hostetler, & Boxer, 1998). In the context of the current HIV/AIDS epidemic, many experience their life course as doubly out of time from the social norm (Hagestaad, 1996): Not only do they confront mortality and loss earlier than most others, but also it is difficult to plan for an uncertain future. Concerns of middle and later life tend to be compressed in a present focus, with a foreshortened sense of time (Borden, 1992).

To be responsive to the growing diversity in society, our view of "family" must be expanded to the lengthened and varied course of the life cycle and therapeutic objectives must fit the challenges and preferences that make each individual and family unique. We will need to learn how to help family members live successfully in complex and changing relationship systems, buffer stressful transitions, and make the most of their later life course.

Ageism and Gerophobia

As a society, we are not readily confronting the challenges of later life or seeing the opportunities that can come with maturity. Our gerophobic culture holds a fearful, pessimistic view of aging as decay. The trajectory theory of human development depicts an upswing during the early years, with gains in competency and achievements. Aging is seen as unmitigated deterioration, decline, and loss, until the downslope ends in death. The elderly have been stereotyped as old-fashioned, rigid, senile, boring, useless, and burdensome. In a culture that glorifies youth, we cling to it, strive to recapture it, and face aging with either dread or denial. As Letty Cottin Pogrebin (1996) observes, many people continue to think of themselves as "thirty-something" until they realize that's what their children are.

The clinical literature on aging has been predominantly a discourse on illness, disability, and declines in functioning, neglecting the positive changes that can occur with maturity. The prevailing biomedical view pathologizes later life, focusing on disease and treatment. The mental health field has given scant attention to the later phases of life other than noting that adults over age 65 are the group most vulnerable to mental illness, particularly organic brain disease and functional disorders such as depression, anxiety, and paranoid states (Butler & Lewis, 1983). Suicide rates also rise with age, the highest rate being among elderly white men. A grim picture of later life is indeed portrayed. Institutionalized forms of ageism and sexism make it especially difficult for women to thrive and prosper.

Pessimistic views of the family hold that most elders either have no families or, at best, have infrequent, obligatory contact; that adult children don't care about their elders and dump them in institutions; and that families in later life are too set in their ways to change long-standing interaction patterns. In fact, family relationships continue to be important throughout later life for most adults (Hughson, Christopherson, & Bonjean, 1996). Contrary to popular belief and stereotype, families provide most direct caregiving assistance, psychological support, and social interaction for elderly loved ones (Brody, 1985; Cohler, 1995; Sorenson, 1977; Sussman, 1976). The vast majority live with spouses or other relatives, including children, siblings, and aged parents.

Couples who weather the storms that are inevitable in longlasting relationships and childrearing report high marital satisfaction in their postlaunching years, as they have more time and resources for individual and shared pursuits. In later life, needs for companionship and caregiving come to the fore. Although sexual contact may be less frequent, intimacy can deepen with a sense of shared history and connection over time.

The importance of sibling relationships often increases over adulthood (Cicirelli, 1995). The centenarian Delany sisters, born into a southern African American family, pursued careers and lived together most of their lives, crediting their remarkable resilience to their enduring bond. They watched over each another and saw their differences as balancing each other out. They also shared enjoyment in conversation and laughter. When Dr. Bessie Delany, who lived to the age of 103, was asked how she accounted for their longevity, she quipped, "Honey, we never married; we never had husbands to worry us to death!" (Delany & Delany, 1993, p. 24).

Although most older Americans and their adult children prefer to maintain separate households, they sustain frequent contact, reciprocal emotional ties, and mutual support in a pattern aptly termed "intimacy at a distance" (Blenkner, 1965; Spark & Brody, 1970). Research finds a strong link between social contact, support, and longevity. Elders who visit often with friends and family and maintain a thick network of diverse relationships are likely to live longer than those with few kin and social resources (Litwin, 1996). The proximity of family members and contact by telephone are especially important to those who live alone, 80 percent of whom are more elderly women, typically widowed. Adult children and grandchildren also benefit in many ways from frequent contact and support. However, in our mobile society, uprooting for jobs or retirement can bring enormous strain in the ability to provide mutual support and caregiving in times of crisis.

Negative stereotypes of older people and their families have led clinicians to pessimistic assumptions that they are less interesting than younger clients, a poor investment for therapy, and too resistant to change. Elders are most often treated custodially, given a pat on the hand and a medication refill, or expected to fit into programs geared to younger adults. Functional problems may be discounted as merely a natural, irreversible part of aging and deterioration. In a social context of gerophobia, it is perhaps not surprising that a recent survey of family therapy literature over the past decade found a paucity of journal articles on family issues in later life and the concerns of older adult members (Van Amburg, Barber, & Zimmerman, 1996), concluding from this lack of attention that the family therapy community is still engaged in "coming of age."

A normal life course perspective of family development and aging is needed, emphasizing the potential for growth and meaning as much as negative aspects of change. The family as a system, along with its elder members, confronts major adaptational challenges in later life. Changes with retirement, grandparenthood, illness, death, and widowhood alter complex relationship patterns, often requiring family support, adjustment to loss, reorientation, and reorganization. Many disturbances are associated with difficulties in family adaptation. Yet such challenges also present opportunities for relational transformation and growth.

LATER-LIFE TRANSITIONS AND CHALLENGES

Each family's approach to later-life challenges evolves from earlier family patterns. Systemic processes that develop over the years influence the ability of family members to adapt to losses and flexibly meet new demands. Certain established patterns, once functional, may no longer fit changing life cycle priorities and constraints.

For most families in the dominant culture, launching of children from home sets the stage for relationships in middle and later life. With the structural contraction of the family from a two-generational household to the marital dyad or single parent alone, parent-child relationships are redefined and parental involvement shifts to refocus on individual and couple life pursuits. Most parents adjust well to this "empty nest" transition (Neugarten, 1991) and are more likely to have trouble when children return to the nest for financial considerations. When a child has filled a void in a marriage or a single parent's life, it can complicate a family's subsequent ability to deal with later-life challenges, as in the following case:

Luis (age 66) was brought by his wife, Maria, for treatment of serious alcohol abuse since his retirement. Living with the couple was their 42-year-old son Raul, who had never left home. Longstanding close attachment between the mother and son had stabilized a chronically conflictual marriage over the years, when Luis had worked long hours outside the home. Retirement shifted the balance as Luis, now home all day, felt like an unwanted intruder. Lacking job and breadwinning status as sources of self-esteem, he felt like an unworthy rival to his son for his wife's affection at a time in his life when he longed for more companionship with her. Competitive struggles fueled Luis's drinking, erupting into angry confrontations. His wife sided protectively with the son.

In Latino families, as in many ethnic groups, ties between a mother and her children are commonly stronger than the marital dyad (see Chapter 8). However, in this family, a pattern that provided a workable balance over many years became a dysfunctional triangle when retirement disrupted the relationship system.

Retirement

Retirement represents a significant milestone and adjustment for individuals and couples. For the retiree, particularly for men in our society, there is a loss of meaningful job roles, status, productivity, and relationships that have been central to traditional male standards for identity and self-esteem throughout adult life. Whether retirement was desired or forced will affect adjustment. Loss of a role as financial provider along with income reduction may bring significant stress. Residential change, a common occurrence at retirement, adds further dislocation and loss of connectedness with nearby family, neighbors, and community. A successful transition involves a reorientation of values and goals and a redirection of energies and relationships (Atchley, 1992).

For women in the workforce, retirement can be a financial disaster. A recent survey (U.S. Department of Labor, 1994) found that 40 percent of employed women over age 55 have no pension plan and 34 percent have no health insurance. Furthermore, divorced women may find that they have no rights to their former spouse's pension benefits at his death. For such reasons, many women continue working past retirement age. As our society grapples with the coming crisis in Social Security and retirement benefits, the retirement age for most workers is likely to rise from 65 to 70, which will require a major shift in expectations and later-life plans.

In traditional marriages, couples may have difficulty with the husband's retirement, accompanied by losses of his job-related status and social network, especially if they have repeatedly been uprooted from kin and social networks to accommodate career moves. Another challenge involves the retired husband's incorporation inside the home, with a change in role expectations, time together, and the quality of interaction (Szinovacz & Harpster, 1994). It can be problematic if the husband tries to take over the household, making the wife feel displaced or under his thumb. At the other extreme, if a retired husband feels that he has earned full leisure while his wife is expected to continue to take care of the household, her resentment is likely to build. For successful adaptation to retirement, couples need to renegotiate their relationship to achieve a new balance. With needs and concerns shared through open communication, relational resilience is strengthened as partners pull together to reshape their lives, plan financial security, and explore new interests to provide meaning and satisfaction together and on their own.

Grandparenthood

As people live longer, increasing numbers are becoming not only grandparents, but also great-grandparents. The experience can hold great significance, as Margaret Mead (1972) remarked on her own response to becoming a grandparent: "I had never thought how strange it was to be involved at a distance in the birth of a biological descendant…the extraordinary sense of having been transformed not by any act of one's own but by the act of one's child" (p. 302). Grandparenthood can offer a new lease on life in numerous ways. First, it fulfills the wish to survive through one's progeny, thereby assisting in the acceptance of mortality. As Mead (1972) experienced, "In the presence of grandparent and grandchild, past and future merge in the present" (p. 311). Grandparenthood also stimulates the reliving of one's own

earlier child-rearing experiences. Such reminiscence and new perspective can be valuable in coming to accept one's life and one's parenting satisfactions and achievements as well as any regrets or failure.

Grandparenthood is a systemic transition that alters intergenerational relationships (Spark, 1974). When adult children become parents, this can be an opportunity for reconnection and healing of old relational wounds with their parents, as they begin to identify with the challenges inherent in parenting and develop more empathy for their parents' positions.

Grandparents and grandchildren may enjoy a special bond that is not complicated by the responsibilities, obligations, and conflicts in the parent-child relationship. A common saying is that grandparents and grandchildren get along so well because they have a common enemy. Such an alliance can become problematic if a grandchild is triangulated in a conflict between parent and grandparent, as in the following case.

After the death of her father and her own divorce, Sharleen (age 32) and her son Billy (age 8) moved in with Sharleen's mother to consolidate limited resources. The family was seen in therapy when Sharleen complained that Billy was behaving badly and was disrespectful to her. At the first session, Billy went to his grandmother for help in taking off his boots. The grandmother quickly took over the discussion while Sharleen seemed passive and helpless. Billy, sitting between them, glanced frequently to his grandmother for cues. Each time Sharleen and her mother started to argue, Billy drew attention to himself. Sharleen's attempts to quiet him were ineffectual, whereas Billy responded immediately to a raised eyebrow from his grandmother.

The grandmother complained that she was overburdened by having to take care of "both children." Sharleen felt that her mother undercut her efforts to assume more responsibility by criticizing everything she did as "not right," meaning not her way. We explored how the grandfather's sudden death from a heart attack had left the grandmother feeling devastated by the loss and uncertain how to go on with her own life. Taking charge to help her daughter raise Billy filled the void. Therapy focused first on family losses—both the death and the divorce—for all three generations. Then attention was directed to work out more balanced relationships so that Sharleen could be a more effective mother to her son while the grandmother's role as head of the household was redefined from a position of control to honored-elder status. Sharleen agreed to respect her mother's wishes about how she wanted her home kept. Her mother agreed to respect Sharleen's ways of child-rearing and support her parental leadership.

While most grandparents are relieved not to have primary caretaking demands, expectations to be a resource and yet not an interference can be burdensome (Cherlin & Furstenberg, 1986). As Mead (1972) asserted, "I think we do not allow sufficiently for the obligation we lay on grandparents to keep themselves out of the picture—not to interfere, not to spoil, not to insist, not to intrude" (p. 303). When a widowed parent moves in with adult married children, conflicts of loyalty and primacy can erupt in triangles involving both partners and the parent/in-law.

In poor and minority communities with high rates of early pregnancy, grandparenting typically occurs early. Grandmothers, often only in their thirties and forties, and great-grandparents provide care for the children, particularly when single parents must work. While this provides a vital lifeline for the youngsters and their parents, it often takes a toll on their own health, when combined with other heavy job and family responsibilities or increasing frailness (Burton & Dilworth-Anderson, 1992; deToledo, 1995).

Foster grandparenting can enrich later life, serve as a resource for single and working parents, and provide connectedness across the generations, especially where more informal connections are lacking in age-segregated living arrangements. Seniors can also be encouraged to volunteer in child care centers. Youngsters benefit from the attention, companionship, and wisdom of their elders.

Chronic Illness and Family Caregiving

As our society ages, the number of people with chronic conditions is increasing dramatically and those impaired are living longer with disabilities than ever before. Even though most elders do maintain good health, fears of loss of physical and mental functioning, chronic pain, and progressively degenerating conditions are common preoccupations. Health problems and severity vary greatly. Among seniors age 65 to 84, arthritis, high blood pressure, and heart disease are most prevalent. For people over 85, the risk of cancer and the extent of disabilities increase, combined with intellectual, visual, and hearing impairment. Physical and mental deterioration may be exacerbated by depression and helplessness, reverberating with the anxiety of family members.

Because our society lacks a coherent approach to caring for people with disabling chronic conditions, growing numbers live with deteriorated health and lack access to appropriate and affordable services. Families in poverty, largely members of minorities, are most vulnerable to environmental conditions that heighten the risk of serious illnesses, permanent disabilities, and caregiver strain, as well as early mortality (Lockery, 1991). Diseases such as asthma, diabetes, high blood pressure, and heart disease are most prevalent among the poor.

Family caregiving is a major concern. The increasing numbers of frail elderly people over 85 pose growing demands for long-term care and financial coverage (Baltes, 1996). By 2020, there will be twice as many elderly (14 million) needing long-term care as today. In 1970, there were twenty-one potential caregivers (defined as people age 50 to 64) for each person 85 or older; by 2030, there will be only six such potential caregivers, severely straining intergenerational relations. As average family size decreases, fewer children are available for caregiving and sibling support. With more people marrying and having children later, those at midlife—the so-called sandwich generation—are caring simultaneously for children and adolescents, as well as for aging parents, grandparents, and other relatives. Finances can be drained by college expenses for children just as medical expenses for elders increase. Adult children who are past retirement and facing their own declining health and resources must assume responsibilities for growing numbers of infirm parents. The likelihood of being caregivers for one or more aging family members is rapidly increasing.

Growing numbers of elders with chronic conditions are receiving care at home, producing a crisis in caregiving. Only 5 percent of the elderly are maintained in institutions, yet chronic health problems require increasing hospitalizations, medical costs, and home-based care for daily functioning. Family and friends are the front lines of support. Nearly three quarters of disabled people over 65 rely exclusively on these informal caregivers. As the pool of caregivers diminishes, caregivers themselves are badly strained by multiple pressures.

Women at midlife are especially burdened, as job demands are juxtaposed with expectations to maintain traditional responsibilities for homemaking, child-rearing, and elder care. Caregiving responsibilities have been almost exclusively the domain of women, mostly daughters and daughters-in-law; three out of four primary caregivers are women. Their average age is 57, but one fourth are 65 to 74, and 10 percent are over 75. As women have become fuller participants in the workforce and their income essential in two-parent as well as single-parent families, rebalancing of work and family roles is needed. Yet few employers offer schedule flexibility or consider men to be caregivers.

Prolonged caregiving takes a heavy toll. Eighty percent of caregivers provide help seven days a week, averaging four hours daily. In addition to housekeeping, shopping, and meal preparation, two thirds also assist with feeding, bathing, toilet, and dressing. The lack of useful management guidelines by most medical specialists adds to the confusion, frustration, and helplessness family members commonly experience. Some aspects of chronic illness are especially disruptive for families, such as sleep disturbance, incontinence, delusional ideas, and aggressive behavior. One symptom and consequence of family distress is elder abuse, which is most likely to occur in overwhelmed families, stretched beyond their means and tolerance.

Among the most difficult illnesses for families to cope with are dementias, progressive brain disorders. Alzheimer's disease, accounting for 60 percent of dementias, is one of the most devastating illnesses of our times. It affects one in ten people over 65 and nearly half of those over 85. The disease is often not correctly diagnosed; cognitive losses are erroneously assumed to be a natural part of aging. The irreversible course of the disease can last anywhere from a few years to twenty years or more, becoming an agonizing psychosocial and financial dilemma for families. Over time, Alzheimer's disease strips away mental and physical capacities in gradual memory loss, disorientation, impaired judgment, and finally loss of control over bodily functions. People with Alzheimer's may repeatedly ask the same questions, forgetting earlier answers, or prepare a meal and forget to serve it. They may get lost easily and forget where they live. With impaired memory and judgment, they may forget entirely about a boiling pot or a child under their care or make disastrous financial decisions. It is most painful for loved ones when they are not even recognized or are confused with others, even with those long deceased.

Since medical treatment of the illness is limited, a custodial bias has prevailed in its management. Individuals who are kept at home on low-dose or drug-free regimens do not show as severe decrements as those in institutions, where they tend to be highly medicated and isolated from familiar people and surroundings (Zarit, Anthony, & Boutselis, 1987). Adult daycare can partially relieve family burden. Family psychoeducation and support networks are helpful in meeting caregiving challenges, coping with stress, and dealing with confusion and memory lapses. Useful illness-related information and management guidelines reduce the risk of caregiver depression, particularly with ambiguity in the illness course (Bonjean, 1989; Boss, 1991; Henderson & Gutierrez-Mayka, 1992; Light, 1994). Family members can be helped in grieving for the loss of a loved one's family roles and relationships.

In approaching all serious illness in the elderly, clinicians and researchers need to expand the narrow focus on an individual female caregiver to encourage the involvement of all family members as a caregiving team. It is important for clinicians not to assume that family distress indicates a family causal role in deterioration of a chronic illness. Family intervention priorities should include (1) stress reduction; (2) information about the medical condition, functional ability, limitations, and prognosis; (3) concrete guidelines for sustaining care, problem solving, and optimal functioning; (4) linkage to supplementary services to support family efforts. To meet caregiving challenges, communities must support families through a range of services, from day programs to assisted living and commitment to full participation of elders, including those with disabilities, in community life (Pinkston & Linsk, 1984).

Family dynamics also require attention. For couples, chronic illness and disability can skew the relationship between the impaired partner and caregiving spouse over time (Rolland, 1994; see also Chapter 29). In some cases, a caregiving partner may overfocus on the other's disability to avoid facing his or her own vulnerability, anxiety, or longings to be taken care of. Couples therapy can help each to gain empathy for the other's position, address such issues as guilt and blame, and rebalance their relationship to live and love as fully as possible.

Intergenerational dependency issues come to the fore as aging parents lose functioning and control over their bodies and their lives. Handling increased dependency of aging parents is not a parent-child role reversal as some imply. Even when adult children give financial, practical, and emotional support to aging parents, they do not become parents to their parents. It should be kept in mind that despite childlike appearance or functioning, the aged parent has had over fifty years of adult life and experience (Spark & Brody, 1970). Family therapists can open conversation about dependency issues with sensitivity and a realistic appraisal of strengths and limitations. An elderly father may be driving with seriously impaired vision, unwilling to admit the danger or give up his autonomy to be driven by others. Older parents often fail to tell their adult children that they are fi-

nancially strapped because of the shame and stigma of dependency in our society, with its ethos of the rugged individual. Adult children can be coached on ways to develop a filial role (Blenkner, 1965), taking responsibility for what they can appropriately do for aging parents and recognizing their own constrains (Boszormenyi-Nagy & Spark, 1973; Brody, 1974).

If an aging parent becomes overly dependent on adult children, who become overly responsible through anxiety or guilt, a vicious cycle may ensue: The more the children do for the parent, the more helpless the parent may become, with escalating neediness, burden, and resentment. Ambivalent overattachment and dependence are common (Kahana & Levin, 1971). Siblings may go to opposite extremes in meeting filial responsibilities, as in the following case:

> Mrs. Z., a 74-year-old widow, was hospitalized with multiple somatic problems and secondary symptoms of disorientation and confusion. She complained that her two sons, Tim (age 46) and Roger (43) didn't care whether she lived or died. The sons reluctantly agreed to come in for a family interview. On the phone, Roger offered his belief that his mother's hospitalization was merely a ploy for sympathy, to make him feel guilty for not being at her beck and call as Tim was. He said that he had learned years ago that the best relationship with her was none at all. In contrast, Tim had become increasingly responsible for his mother, particularly since she had been widowed. Yet the more helpful he was, the more helpless she became in managing her own life. He felt drained by his mother's growing neediness.
>
> The overresponsible son was coached to be more helpful by challenging his mother to function maximally rather than doing for her. The underinvolved son was encouraged to join his brother and to relieve him of some limited, specific burdens. Both sons were helped to communicate their feelings and concerns directly with their mother and to be patient in listening to her. They were advised not to be put off if their mother initially resisted the changes. With anxiety in the system reduced and the family working together, Mrs. Z.'s thinking and functioning improved markedly.

Caregiving challenges can be burdensome; yet they can become opportunities for healing strained relationships and forging new collaboration as a caregiving team, building relational resilience. When family conflict has been intense and persistent, where ambivalence is strong, or when relationships have been estranged, caregiving for aging parents is more likely to be complicated. Life-and-death decisions become more difficult, as in the following crisis situation:

Joellen, a 38-year-old single parent, was deeply conflicted when her father, hospitalized for long-term complications from chronic alcohol abuse, asked her to donate a kidney needed to save his life. She felt enraged to be asked to give up something so important when he had not been there for her as a father over the years. He had been a mean drunk, often absent and many times violent. She was also angry that he had brought on his deteriorated condition by his drinking and had refused to heed his family's repeated pleas to stop. Further, she was hesitant to give up a vital organ when she had to think about caring for her children and their possible future needs. Yet, a dutiful daughter and a compassionate woman, she also felt a sense of obligation and guilt. She did not want her father to die because she denied him her kidney.

When I suggested that Joellen talk with her mother about her dilemma, she learned that her father had also asked her siblings for the kidney donation. Estranged from them, Joellen feared that old rivalries would be stirred up as to who would be seen as the good giving child or the bad selfish ones. I encouraged her to overcome her reluctance to meet with her siblings to grapple with the dilemma, and to persevere when the meeting proved hard to schedule. When the siblings finally met, they were surprised to learn how torn each of them felt. Old rivalries shifted as they began to reach out to one another.

I suggested that they begin to plan together about how they might collaborate to share the many challenges likely to come up in caring for both of their aging parents. As each envisioned taking a part of future responsibilities, the elder brother, who was healthy and had no plans for a family of his own, volunteered his kidney for their father. The decision was less conflictual for him because he had ex-

perienced better times with his father in earlier years before the problem drinking. As the others offered to support him and agreed to contribute to their parents' future well-being in ways that fit their abilities and resources, a new solidarity was forged.

The point at which failing health requires consideration of nursing home placement is a crisis for the whole family (Tobin & Kulys, 1981). Contrary to myth, placement is usually turned to only as the last resort, when family resources are stretched to the limit, and most often in later stages of mental or physical deterioration. Nevertheless, feelings of guilt and abandonment and notions of institutionalization can make a placement decision highly stressful for families, particularly for adult daughters, on whom the caretaking expectations typically concentrate.

Mrs. Arletti called for help, stating that she felt helpless to control her teenage son and feared that he needed to be institutionalized. A family assessment revealed that the problems had developed over the past eight months, since Mrs. Arletti's mother had been brought into their home. She wept as she described her mother's Parkinson's condition and her difficulty in providing round-the-clock attention, on top of a full-time job. She was alarmed by her mother's occasional loss of balance and falling, especially since finding her on the floor one morning. Her worry about institutionalization concerned her mother: At her father's deathbed, a year earlier, he had asked Mrs. Arletti to promise that she would always care for her mother. She felt alone with her dilemma, her husband preoccupied by his work.

This case underscores the importance of inquiry about elderly family members even when problems are presented elsewhere in the system, which may express concerns of the family crisis. It's also crucial to attend to a spouse's distancing and lack of support, in this case due to the husband's lingering guilt over having left the care of his dying mother to his sisters.

Family sessions can be helpful in assessing needs and resources, weighing the benefits and costs of options, and sharing feelings and concerns before reaching a decision together. Often, through discussion, new solutions emerge that can support the elder's remaining in the community without undue burden on any member. Organizations such as the Visiting Nurses Association can provide home services and inform families of community backup. Respite for caregivers is crucial to their well-being. When placement is needed, therapists can help families to see it as the most viable way to provide good care and help them to navigate through the maze of options.

We must also re-vision chronic care, which is often thought of narrowly in terms of medical services and nursing home placement. A report commissioned by the Robert Wood Johnson Foundation (Institute for Health and Aging, 1996) takes a broader view to address chronic care challenges for the twenty-first century. The report envisions a system of care: a spectrum of integrated services—medical, personal, social, and rehabilitative—to assist people with chronic conditions in living fuller lives. A continuum of care is needed to ensure that individuals receive the level and type of care that fit their condition and their changing needs over time and to support independent living, optimal functioning, and well-being as long as possible.

Dealing with terminal illness is perhaps the family's most painful challenge, complicated by agonizing end-of-life decisions. The rising rate of suicide among the elderly involves not only a desire for control over their own dying process but also is a response to unmet needs for pain control and palliative care and worries about laying financial and emotional burdens on loved ones. Clinicians need to work with families to reduce suffering and make the best arrangements to keep the seriously ill person comfortable and comforted, while balancing the needs of family members.

Family adaptation to loss involves shared grieving and a reorganization of the family relationship system (Walsh & McGoldrick, 1991; see also Chapter 11). Avoidance, silence, and secrecy complicate mourning. When patient and family hide knowledge of a terminal illness to protect one another's feelings, communication barriers create distance and misunderstanding, prevent preparatory grief, and deny opportunities to say goodbyes. Therapists can assist family members with feelings of helplessness, anger, loss of control, or guilt that they could not do more. It may be easier for younger family members to accept the loss of elders whose time has come, than for elders to accept the loss—and their own survival—of siblings or their own children who die first. The death of the last member of the older generation is a milestone for a family, signifying that the next generation is now the oldest and the next to face death. It is important, also, to address the impact of an elder's death on grandchildren, often their first experience with death and loss.

Widowhood

Widowhood is a highly stressful transition, with a wide diversity of responses in adaptation. Women are four times as likely as men to be widowed and are widowed at an earlier age with many years of life ahead. Those in traditional marriages, who are more dependent on their husbands, begin in midlife to anticipate the prospect of widowhood (Neugarten, 1991). Research finds that 5 percent of bereaved spouses become severely depressed; 10 to 17 percent become depressed to a clinically significant degree. The initial sense of loss, disorientation, and loneliness contributes to an increase in death and suicide rates in the first two years, especially for men. Social contact is often more disrupted for men, since wives traditionally link their husbands to the family and community, especially after retirement. Yet the long-term hardships for widowed women tend to be greater, with more limited financial resources and remarriage prospects. Widows over age 75 are at highest risk of poverty; currently, over 50 percent have incomes of $10,000 or less.

Despite initial problems with the challenges in daily living, most older surviving spouses are quite resilient over time. The profound loss may even be accompanied by positive feelings associated with pride in coping. Most widows view themselves as having become more competent and independent;

only a small portion view the changes entirely neg-atively (Lopata, 1996). Older people are at highest risk when adult children have moved away and when they have lost most of their friends and sib-lings through death or relocation.

The psychosocial challenges in the transition to widowhood involve grief over the loss and rein-vestment in future functioning (Lieberman, 1995; Lopata, 1996). A realignment of relationships in the family system also occurs (Walsh & McGold-rick, 1991; see Chapter 11). The initial task is to take in the fact of death, transforming shared expe-riences into memories. Encouragement of expres-sion of grief with family members and through meaningful rituals is most helpful. Attention must also turn to the reality demands of daily function-ing and self-support. Wherever possible, clinicians and adult children should help both partners to an-ticipate widowhood, preparing for the challenges each would face. Many need to acquire new skills for independent living, such as managing finances, returning to the job market, or arranging household maintenance. The adjustment to being physically alone, in itself, may be difficult.

Within one to two years, adjustment shifts to new activities and interest in others. The label of "widow" can be harsh, defining a person in terms of spousal loss. This identity can interfere with the process of reengaging in life. Reentry is also im-peded by distancing of family and friends who have not faced their grief or come to terms with their own mortality or possibility of widowhood. Further dislocation may occur if one's home is given up or if financial problems or illness block independent functioning. In such cases, widows are likely to move in with adult children, siblings, or even very aged parents. One woman prepared for the imminent loss of her husband by reassuring herself that she could go home to her mother. Her mother's death shortly after the death of her hus-band was devastating.

Remarriage is becoming an increasingly com-mon option for older adults, although less so for women. Economic and legal constraints lead many elderly couples to live together without formal marriage. Critical to the success of remarriage is the relationship with adult children and their ap-proval of the union. Problems can arise when a child views remarriage as disloyalty to the de-ceased parent. Adult children may be shocked by remarriage of an aged parent—especially when they cannot conceive of the elderly as attractive or sexually active—and may assume that the new spouse is interested only in money. Concerns about a will may arise, particularly if children view in-heritance as compensation for earlier disappoint-ments or as evidence that they will still come before the new partner.

Cross-Generational Interplay of Life Cycle Issues

Within every family, the later-life challenges of the elderly interact with salient concerns of children at their own concurrent life phases. With increasing diversity in family patterns and the tendency to-ward later marriage and child-rearing, different pressures and conflicts may be generated. The is-sues that come to the fore between an older adult parent and young adult child will likely differ from those that arise between a parent, a middle-aged child, and an adolescent grandchild. Tensions are heightened when developmental strivings are in-compatible, as in the following case:

> Julia, in her mid-twenties, was beginning a social work career and engaged to be married when her 63-year-old mother, who lived 2000 miles away, developed cardiovascular disease, with a long and painful deterioration. Julia, who had always been close to her mother, felt torn. Her sense of obliga-tion was countered by reluctance to put her own new job and marriage plans on hold indefinitely. The situation was complicated by Julia's recently emerging separation and identity issues. She had always been close to her mother and dependent on her direction and support. The geographic distance from home that she had established bolstered her self-reliance. Like many of her peers, she had ab-sorbed the cultural ethos confusing differentiation with distancing and disconnection. Now, just at the time her social world pushed her to be independent and self-directed, her mother needed her most; and Julia feared losing her.

Phone contact became increasingly strained. Julia's mother saw her failure to return home as uncaring and selfish. Deeply hurt, she struck back: "What kind of social worker can you be if you can't even care about your own mother?" Julia made a brief visit home, feeling guilty and upset. The uncertain course of the prolonged illness made it difficult to know how long her mother would live or when to plan trips. Julia sent her mother gifts. One, picked with special care and affection, was a leather-bound book for her memoirs. On her next visit, Julia discovered the book, unopened, on a closet shelf. Deeply hurt, she screamed at her mother to explain. Her mother replied, "If I wrote my memoirs, I'd have to write how much you've let me down." Julia cut her visit short. When she returned to her own home, conflict erupted with her fiance, and the wedding plans were canceled. Deeply upset by the breakup, Julia phoned her parents for consolation. Her mother expressed her own disappointment, saying that she now had nothing to live for. A few hours later, she had a stroke. Julia's therapist interpreted this as her mother's narcissism and manipulation. Furious, Julia did not return home again before the long-anticipated call came one night from her father informing her, "Mom is dead."

Julia scarcely grieved. She got married within weeks to someone she hardly knew. It was not until the marriage broke up that tremendous grief at the loss of her mother surfaced, with guilt and regret over the final alienation and the fact that it was too late to change the past. Working with a family therapist, she determined to learn from that experience to repair her strained relationship with her father—whom she had not visited since her mother's death—before it was too late. With the therapist's coaching, she also initiated new connections with her mother's family, learning more about her mother's life and coming to understand her more fully as a person. She also learned that her mother's own mother had cut her off because of disappointment with her shortly before Julia's grandmother's death. With new compassion and emotional reconnection, Julia arranged a memorial service to honor her mother on the anniversary of her death.

The mother's developmental needs at the end of life occurred "off-time" from the perspective of the daughter's developmental readiness and out of sync with her age peers. Terminally ill, the mother needed to draw her family close and to feel that she had successfully fulfilled her role as a mother. The young adult daughter was threatened by the closeness and dependency at a time of impending loss, when she was not yet secure in her own personhood and felt her culture's pressure for autonomy. In this case, cross-generational anniversary reactions complicated the picture as unresolved issues from the mother's relationship with her own mother were revived, adding fuel to the conflict, disappointment, and estrangement at life's end.

As Erikson (1959) noted, young adults in our culture are emerging from the search for identity into issues of commitment. The fear of ego loss in situations calling for self-abandon may lead to isolation and self-absorption. This may heighten preoccupation with making initial choices and commitments, especially marriage, career, and residence, that define one's place in the adult world. Responding to caregiving needs and threatened loss of aging parents at this life stage may be fraught with conflict. Clinicians need to help young adults offset the cultural push for family disconnection and prioritize relationships with their elders at the end of life.

SUCCESSFUL AGING

The aging process is more variable and malleable than was long believed (Posner, 1995). Elders can enhance their own successful development in their approach to their challenges and by making the most of their options. Baltes and Baltes (1990) have posited that successful aging is accomplished by "selective optimization with compensation" as a means of coping with reduced functioning. They cite the example of the pianist Arthur Rubinstein, who described how he dealt with the weaknesses accompanying aging. First, he selectively reduced his repertoire, playing a smaller number of pieces. Second, he practiced them more often (an optimizing strategy). Third, he slowed down the speed of his playing just before the fast movements, producing a contrast effect that heightened the impression of speed (a compensating strategy). By these means, he sustained a successful concert career into old age.

Studies of normal adult development and family functioning indicate that a variety of adaptive processes, rather than one single pattern, contribute to successful later-life adjustment (Bengtson, 1996; Birren & Schaie, 1995; Schulz & Heckhausen, 1996). This diversity reflects differences in family structures, individual personality styles, gender roles, and ethnic, social class, and larger cultural influences (Gelfand, 1982; Gibson, 1982). Traditional gender role distinctions of earlier adulthood tend to shift as older men show increasing passivity and accommodation in response to environmental challenges and greater needs for nurturance and affiliation, whereas older women become more assertive and active in meeting their own needs (Gutmann, 1997). The development of more androgynous modes of response, of aspects of life that were earlier constrained, can enable a greater role flexibility that may be related to longevity and greater life satisfaction in old age.

Likewise, successful family functioning in later life requires flexibility in structure, roles, and responses to new developmental needs and challenges (Caspi & Elder, 1986; Walsh, 1993). As patterns that may have been functional in earlier stages no longer fit, new options must be explored. With the loss of functioning and death of significant family members, others are called upon to assume new roles, responsibilities, and meaning.

Strengths That Have No Name

Betty Friedan's (1993) analysis of international studies reveals that older adults may actually integrate problems at a higher level than the young, in particular attending to ethical and contextual issues. Also, the degree of mental acuity varies depending on the environment: The more autonomy, the more acuity. In discovering "strengths that have no name," from a number of studies of different populations, Friedan concludes that women experiencing the most profound change and discontinuity were the most vital in later life. The women who were most frustrated, angry, and depressed were those who held on most rigidly to the early roles—or had been forced to stay in or repeat the "cluttered nest" past its time and thereby were kept from moving on (p. 143). In the anthology *If I Had My Life to Live over I Would Pick More Daisies* (Martz, 1992), women reflect on the choices they have made and wish to make from childhood to old age, their alternatives both extended and limited by personal belief systems, ethnic and cultural identity, class and economic status, age, and gender. Personal choices are never simple; more often, they are complex, conflictual, and intertwined with the decisions of others because of their strong relational orientation. Friedan found that what distinguished women who were vital was not which roles they played in earlier adulthood, but whether or not they had developed a quest, creating a sense of purpose and structure for making life choices and decisions.

In contrast to the redefinition of self that many women must move through with menopause, widowhood, or divorce, most men's identities continue to be based in career and sexual potency. As these paths to self-expression close off, aging men who continue to invest in these two "proofs" of masculinity experience uncertainty, decline, and a void. Friedan proposes that men choose meaningful work, not give up and retire as we've been taught to do. Intimacy can become more basic and ultimately more rewarding than sexual intercourse, as an emotional intercourse that is shared in more authentic ways than in gender games of youth.

Heilbrun (1997) approaches maturity with celebration, finding possibilities in aging for enrichment and unexpected pleasures. For her, the greatest reward of parenting has been delight in her fully grown progeny, considering them to be friends with an extra dimension of affection. She finds it powerfully reassuring at this time to think of life, and each day, as borrowed time to be fully savored. As May Sarton wrote in her essay *At Seventy,* this can be the best time of life because we are more ourselves than ever: We have less conflict and are more balanced; we are better able to know and use our powers; we are surer of what counts in life and have less self-doubt to conquer.

Wisdom of the Elders

The notion that the later years may have a significance of their own is scarcely considered. In Erikson's theory of human development, old age is viewed as a critical period, during which resilient individuals may review earlier life experiences and their meaning in the quest to achieve integration and overcoming despair at the end of life's journey. In this process, the new adaptive strength of wisdom may be gained. The task of achieving integration is challenging, as older adults are faced by the finiteness of life and knowledge of past imperfections. More recent extension of Erikson's work (Erikson, Erikson, & Kivnick, 1986) emphasizes the importance of vital involvement in the present for the ultimate achievement of integration. Interviews with octogenarians revealed many pathways for integration and reconciliation of earlier life issues. Some look for models of aging in parents or grandparents; others look to friends or even media personalities. Some achieve a sense of integrity from displaying such attributes as humor, compassion, continual growth, and commitment. For the most resilient aged people, past traumas and inescapable missteps are ultimately put into perspective. Even those who have not achieved integration are actively involved in attempts to reach some resolution. A priority for clinicians is to recognize the sources of meaning in late life and understand how older adults integrate the varied experiences of a lifetime into a coherent sense of self and life's worth.

What is notable about this life stage is the search for life's transcendent meaning. A common thread that emerges through the accounts of study participants is the dynamic portrait of older people, not as victims of life forces but as resilient, possessing the capacity to shape as well as to be shaped by events. Transcendence involves the freedom to risk, with courage, seeing aging as a personal and spiritual evolution and, instead of focusing on limits, seeking new horizons for learning, adventure, and change.

Spiritual faith, participation in religious services or activities, and congregational support are wellsprings sustaining resilience for most elderly people (Walsh, 1998; in press). Medical studies suggest that faith, prayer, and spiritual rituals can actually strengthen health and healing by triggering emotions that influence the immune and cardiovascular systems. One study of elderly patients after open-heart surgery found that those who were able to find hope, solace, and comfort in their religious outlook had a survival rate three times higher than those who did not. What matters most is drawing on the power of faith to give meaning to precarious life challenges.

The search for identity and meaning is a lifelong process. Individuals and their families organize, interpret, and connect experiences in many ways. We must be sensitive to the culture and time in which individuals have lived and the contribution of structural sources of meaning. At the same time, we need to recognize the diverse ways in which people are influenced by common background. For some, religion is salient in making meaning of their experience; for others, it might be ethnic heritage or the education that enabled them to rise out of poverty. Many elders show enormous potential for continual self-renewal. They are vital and potent as they create their own meanings by interpreting and reformulating experiences, values, structural forces, and elements of their own particular contexts.

CLINICAL CHALLENGES
AND OPPORTUNITIES:
A RESILIENCE-BASED APPROACH

A resilience-based approach to practice (Walsh, 1996, 1998) engages elders collaboratively, affirms their strengths and personhood, encourages their optimal functioning, and builds social network resources to support independent living to the fullest extent possible. This orientation rebalances the traditional clinical focus on patient deficits, which too often leads professionals to objectify the elderly, become unduly pessimistic, underestimate their resourcefulness, and make plans for them, based on what professionals think is best, as in the following case:

Rita, a 78-year-old widow, was admitted to a psychiatric unit with a diagnosis of confusional state and acute paranoia after an incident in which she accused her landlord of plotting to get rid of her. Rita's increasing blindness was making independent living more difficult and hazardous. Her apartment was in disarray, and she had trouble managing simple daily tasks. She was socially isolated, stubbornly refusing assistance from "strangers." Her only surviving family member was a sister who lived in another state. The hospital staff, doubting that Rita could continue to function independently, worked out a nursing home placement for her. Rita vehemently objected, insisting that she wanted only to return to her own apartment. Hospitalization was extended to "deal with her resistance" to the their plan.

A family therapist's strength-based interviews with Rita led to a new appreciation of her as a person and to a plan that was reached collaboratively with her. When asked what most distressed her, Rita replied that it was her failing vision. Asked how she felt about living alone, she responded, "I'm not alone; I live with my books." Rita had been a teacher, happily married, without children, until her husband's death sixteen years earlier. Her beloved father died the same year. After those painful losses, she withdrew from family and friends, determined never to become dependent on anyone again. Rita centered her life on her work; she was known as a "tough cookie," respected by colleagues for her perseverance with challenging students. Since retirement, she had immersed herself in her books, which became a vital source of her resilience. They enhanced her knowledge, imagination, and pleasure, transporting her beyond her immediate circumstances. The books held special meaning because she had inherited many of them from her father, a scholar. They revived her close childhood relationship, when he had spent countless hours reading to her. Now Rita's loss of vision was cutting her off from her most valued connections.

In Rita's strong identification with her father was an intense pride in his part-Indian heritage, carrying a sense of hardiness in adversity, a toughness, and a will to survive and adapt. These strengths were found in the therapist's visit with Rita to her apartment. At first glance, all appeared chaotic: piles of books, clothing, and food containers everywhere. However, a closer inspection revealed that Rita had carefully ordered her environment in a system that made sense to adapt to visual impairment. With a magic marker, she had color-coded food containers; clothes were arranged according to function; books were stacked by subject. Almost blindly, she could easily locate everything she needed.

Rita's stubborn "resistance" had been viewed as a pathological denial of dependency needs. Yet self-reliance had served Rita well over many years. It was the breakdown of her primary mode of adaptation—her vision—that brought confusion and anxiety. Still, realistically, Rita would require some assistance to maintain independent living. Her reluctance to become dependent on caretakers made her reject any aid with one exception: She herself had contacted a religious organization that sent Brothers to read to her whenever she called. She could allow help when she took initiative and had some control in determining the nature and boundaries of the relationship. This positive experience became a model for building a social resource network to support Rita's objective of independent living. Her ability to take responsibility for herself and her determination to function as autonomously as possible were reinforced. She was encouraged to select, and initiate contact with, a few neighbors and shopkeepers she trusted who could provide occasional backup service. Setting up a routine of weekly phone contact with her sister became a source of meaningful touchpoints for both.

Applying the concept of resilience to the family as a functional unit, a family resilience approach affirms the potential in all families for healing and growth, by tapping into their strengths and building resources as they confront life challenges (Smith et al., 1995; Walsh, 1998). Multigenerational and couple relationships in later life encompass a variety of situations that are potentially stressful and may benefit from this approach, as illustrated above. Given the potentially destructive impact of unresolved conflicts and cut-offs (Bowen, 1978), the fallout of hurt, misunderstanding, anger, alienation, sense of failure, and guilt may accompany children and grandchildren into their future relationships. Strains can be prevented and repaired by helping multiple family generations to redefine and reintegrate their roles and relationships as they age and mature.

Family Life Review

I have found the application of life-review therapy (Lewis & Butler, 1974) to couples and families to be of great benefit in later life. It extends the process of the aging person's reminiscence, which facilitates acceptance of one's life and approaching death, to include the perceptions and direct involvement of significant family members who are central to such resolution. Hearing and sharing the varied perspectives on life experiences and relationships enlarge the family story, build mutual empathy, and can heal old wounds for all family members.

> In the case of Mrs. Z. and her sons Tim and Roger (described earlier in the chapter), the mother and sons were encouraged to share reminiscences of their family life history. They were helped to explore developmental periods of particular emotional import, evoking crucial memories, responses, and new understanding. The brothers' longstanding rivalry was put into perspective. Roger's cut-off became better understood in recalling a late adolescent conflict over autonomy that he handled by leaving home in anger, severing contact, and vowing to remain self-sufficient. His relationship with his parents had become frozen at that point but now could be brought up to the present. Mother and sons shared their grief at the death of the father for the first time together. Most important, a healing reconciliation among the surviving family members was achieved.

The resolution of later-life issues rests on the foundation of all earlier life stages. Conflicts or disappointments in earlier stages that may have resulted in cut-offs or frozen images and expectations can be reconsidered from a new vantage point and from the many viewpoints of family members. People in later life are often able to be more open and honest about earlier transgressions or shame-laden family secrets. Past mistakes can be more readily owned and forgiven. Misunderstandings and faulty assumptions about one another can be clarified. Successive life phases can be reviewed as relationships are brought up to date. Family albums, scrapbooks, genealogies, reunions, and pilgrimages can assist this work. Precious end-of-life conversations can be videotaped and preserved. The transmission of family history to younger generations can be an additional bonus of such work (Myerhoff, 1992).

Looking Ahead

Families should be encouraged to consider and prepare together for such challenges as transitional living arrangements and end-of-life decisions, discussions that are commonly avoided. Future-oriented questions can also open up new possibilities for later life fulfillment. One son carried concern about how each of his parents would manage alone on the family farm if widowed, but he dreaded talking with them about their death. Finally, on a visit home, he got up his courage. First he asked his mother, tentatively, whether she had ever thought about what she might do if Dad were the first to go. She replied, "Sure, I've thought about it for years. I know exactly what I'd do: I'd sell the farm and move to Texas to be near our grandkids." Her husband shook his head and replied, "Well if that isn't the darndest thing! I've thought a lot about it too, and if your mother weren't here, I'd sell the farm and move to Texas!" This conversation led the couple to sell the farm and move to Texas, where they enjoyed many happy years together.

Making the Invisible Visible

The invisibility of the elderly and ageism have contributed to the unresponsiveness of mental health services to the needs of older adults and their families. Clinical training programs must expand from preoccupation with early developmental stages and offer greater exposure to elders and their families. I once assigned a group of medical students to interview a couple in later life about their life course. The students looked stunned. One acknowledged that he had never had a real conversation with an older person, including his parents. This led us to a valuable discussion of age segregation in our society and professional ageism stemming largely from avoidance of the personal reality of our own aging, losses, and death. Clinicians need to develop awareness of our apprehensions, a perspective on the whole life course, and appreciation of what it is like to be old.

Developmental models for understanding growth and change in later life are needed, for example, to include wisdom and integrative understanding. Current theory, research, and practice are biased to the extent that they fail to include values and meanings that are salient to elders. Clinical services must be flexible to fit the diversity of older people and their significant relationships and to support optimal functioning and integration in the community. Clinicians can foster a growing sensitivity to people who are attempting, with courage, to adapt to losses and challenges of later life in ways that fit needs for identity, connectedness, and meaningful experience.

Problems involving family relationships with elderly members are often hidden. Older adults are more likely to present somatic problems than emotional or relational problems (Qualls, 1991). In a medical assessment, such functional problems as depression, confusion, and anxiety may not be detected or may be assumed to be merely part of old age. Even in cases of organic disease, family relationships can exacerbate or alleviate suffering. The stressful impact of chronic illness on the family also requires attention to family needs for support, information, caregiving guidelines, respite, and linkage to community resources. Clinicians have an ethical responsibility to ensure that interventions respect the developmental needs of all family members. Families are our most valuable resources in treating serious illness. Our clinical interventions can strengthen their resilience in coping with persistent stress. We must encourage their collaboration, understand their caregiving challenges, and support them in our social policies and provision of health care.

The complexity and diversity of family networks in later life require careful clinical assessment. Clinicians shouldn't mistakenly assume—or accept an older adult's initial claim—that there is no family or that the family is not important in later life. Given the prevalent pattern of intimacy at a distance, we must look beyond the sharing of a household to identify significant relationships. Emotionally meaningful bonds with siblings, a daughter-in-law, a nephew, cousins, or a godchild can be valuable resources. The very statement that one has "no family left" may indicate continuing emotional significance of recent deaths or unresolved losses. Longstanding cut-offs may hold potential for repair. Drawing a genogram with an elder can be particularly useful in identifying those who are significant and or could be drawn upon for support.

Another problem of visibility occurs when younger generations present themselves or their children for treatment. Problems involving elderly family members may be hidden behind complaints or symptoms elsewhere in the system. Diagnostic evaluation commonly includes past family-of-origin history with little or no mention of current ongoing extended family relationships or recent changes that may be connected to distress. Whatever the age or problem of the symptom bearer, it is important to inquire about elder members and relationships in the extended family.

Clinicians who are trained to view families from a model based on early developmental stages, with family structure, roles, and functioning geared to child-rearing imperatives, must be careful not to transfer assumptions to families in later life. Moreover, reification of the nuclear family model has pushed the extended family to the margins, much to the detriment of us all. Family assessments should explore how each family, given its particular composition, modes of adaptation, and needs of its members, has responded to later-life challenges. When it has broken down, we need to consider the options for reorganization and transformation of relationships to fit each family situation. Clearly, the later-life challenges and the diversity in family networks require that we develop new, more flexible conceptualizations and approaches to understand and strengthen family functioning to master challenges and seize opportunities for enriched relationships.

CONCLUSION

The diversity, complexity, and importance of family relations in later life can be expected to become even greater in the coming years. Because more people are living longer than elders did in the past, we lack role models for later-life family relations, just as we lack appropriate labels and role definitions. The term "adult children" is loaded with attributions of dysfunctional childhood families. The term "postparental" is unfortunate, as parents never cease to be parents. Instead it is the *nature* of parent-child relationships that changes over the years. We need to explore and expand possibilities for growth in that transformation. Elders can be encouraged to draw on their rich history and experience to inform both continuity and innovation, as society's futurists. The wisdom of our elders, linked with the energy and new knowledge of the young, can be the basis for rich interchange and planning for the future. Important in the resilience of our society is a sense of pride in age, the value of history and life experience, and the capacity to adapt courageously to change.

More people today are living longer than at any time in history, generating a shift in the population that some regard as the "aging revolution." What will we do with this gift of long life? How can we contribute to people's ability to live with vitality and meaning into advanced old age? Our society and all helping professionals will need to prepare for these challenges. Clinicians' interface issues with our aging families—and with our own aging and losses—may contribute to anxiety, avoidance, overresponsibility, or empathic difficulties with elders and their adult children. As we reach out to become better acquainted with the elders in our own families, as we attempt to resolve our own losses and grievances, and as we explore new relational possibilities with growing maturity, therapeutic work with families in later life will take on new meaning and possibilities for growth.

REFERENCES

Anderson, C., & Stewart, S (1994). *Flying solo: Women at midlife and beyond.* New York: Norton.

Atchley, R. C. (1992). Retirement and marital satisfaction. In M. Szinovacz, D. J. Eckert, & B. H. Vinick (Eds.), *Families and retirement.* Newbury Park, CA: Sage.

Baltes, M. M. (1996). *The many faces of dependency in old age.* New York: Cambridge University Press.

Baltes, P. B., & Baltes, M. M. (1990). Psychological perspectives on successful aging: The model of selective optimization with compensation. In P. B. Baltes & M. M. Baltes (Eds.), *Successful aging: Perspectives from the behavioral sciences* (pp. 1–34). New York: Cambridge University Press.

Bengtson, V. (1996). *Adulthood and aging: Research on continuities and discontinuities.* New York: Springer.

Berger, R. (1996). *Gay and gray: The older homosexual man* (2nd. ed.). New York: Haworth.

Birren, J., & Schaie, K. W. (1995). *Handbook of the psychology of aging* (4th ed.). San Diego: Academic Press.

Blenkner, M. (1965). Social work and family relationships in later life with some thoughts on filial maturity. In E. Shanas & G. Strieb (Eds.), *Social structure and the family: Generational relations.* Englewood Cliffs, NJ: Prentice-Hall.

Bonjean, M. (1989). Solution focused psychotherapy with families caring for an Alzheimer's patient. *Journal of Psychotherapy and the Family, 5,* 197–210.

Borden, W. (1992). Narrative perspectives in psychosocial intervention following adverse life events. *Social Work, 37,* 153–141.

Boss, P. (1991). Ambiguous loss. In F. Walsh & M. McGoldrick (Eds.) *Living beyond loss.* New York: Norton.

Boszormenyi-Nagy, I., & Spark, G. (1973). *Invisible loyalties: Reciprocity in intergenerational family therapy.* Hagerstown, MD: Harper & Row.

Bowen, M. (1978). *Family therapy in clinical practice.* New York: Jason Aronson.

Brody, E. (1974). Aging and family personality: A developmental view. *Family Process, 13,* 23–37.

Brody, E. (1985). Parent care as normative family stress. *Gerontologist, 25,* 19–29.

Burton, L. M., & Dilworth-Anderson, P. (1992). The intergenerational family roles of aged black Americans. *Marriage and Family Review.*

Butler, R., & Lewis, M. L. (1983). *Aging and mental health: Positive psychosocial approaches* (3rd ed.). St. Louis: Mosby.

Caspi, A., & Elder, G. (1986). Life satisfaction in old age: Linking social psychology and history. *Journal of Psychology and Aging, 1,* 18–26.

Cherlin, A. J., & Furstenberg, F. F. (1986). *The new American grandparent: A place in the family, a life apart.* New York: Basic.

Cicirelli, V. (1995). *Sibling relationships across the life span.* New York: Plenum Press.

Cohler, B. J. (1995). The family in the second half of life: Connecting theories and findings. In R. Blieszner & V. Hilkevitch Bedford (Eds.), *Handbook of aging and the family.* (pp. 59–94). Westport, CT: Greenwood Press.

Cohler, B. J., Hostetler, A., & Boxer, A. (1998). Generativity, social context, and lived experience: Narratives of gay men in middle adulthood. In D. McAdams & E. de St. Aubin (Eds.), *Generativity and adult development: Psychosocial perspectives on caring and contributing to the next generation.* Washington, DC: American Psychological Association Press.

Delany, S. & Delany A. E.(1993). *Having our say: The Delany sisters' first 100 years.* New York: Dell.

deToledo, S. (1995). *Grandparents as parents: A survival guide for raising a second family.* New York: The Guilford Press.

Erikson, E. H. (1959). *Identity and the life cycle.* New York: International Universities Press.

Erikson, E. H., Erikson, J. M., & Kivnick, H. (1986). *Vital involvement in old age: The experience of old age in our time.* New York: Norton.

Friedan, B. (1993). *The fountain of age.* New York: Simon & Schuster.

Gelfand, D. (1982). *Aging: The ethnic factor.* Boston: Little, Brown.

Gibson, R. (1982). Blacks at middle and late life: Resources and coping. *The Annals of the American Academy,* 79–90.

Gutmann, D. (1997). *The human elder in nature, culture and society.* Boulder, CO: Westview.

Hagestaad, G. (1996). On-time, off-time, out of time? Reflections on continuity and discontinuity in an illness process. In V. Bengston (Ed.), *Adulthood and aging* (pp. 204–222). New York: Springer.

Hareven, T. K. (Ed.). (1996). *Aging and generational relations over the life course: A historical and cross-cultural perspective.* New York: Aldine de Gruyter.

Heilbrun, C. (1997). *The last gift of time: Life beyond sixty.* New York: Dial Press.

Henderson, J. N., & Gutierrez-Mayka, M. (1992). Ethnocultural themes in caregiving to Alzheimer's disease patients in Hispanic families. *Clinical Gerontologist: Special Issue on Hispanic Mental Health, 11,* 59–74.

Hughson, G. A., Christopherson, V. A., & Bonjean, M. J. (Eds.). (1996). *Aging and family therapy: Practitioner perspectives on Golden Pond.* New York: Haworth.

Institute for Health & Aging, University of California, San Francisco. (1996). *Chronic care in America: A 21st century challenge.* Princeton, NJ: Robert Wood Johnson Foundation.

Johnson, C. L., & Barer, B. M. (1990). Families and networks among older inner-city blacks. *The Gerontologist, 30,* 726–733.

Kahana, R., & Levin, S. (1971). Aging and the conflict of generations. *Journal of Geriatric Psychiatry 4,* 115–135.

Kausler, D. L. (1996). *The graying of America: An encyclopedia of aging, health, mind, and behavior.* Urbana: University of Illinois Press.

Lewis, M. I., & Butler, R. N. (1974). Life review therapy. *Geriatrics, 29,* 165–173.

Lieberman, M. (1995). *Doors close, doors open: Widows, grieving, and growing.* New York: Grosset/Putnam.

Light, E. (1994). *Stress effects on family caregivers of Alzheimer's patients: Research and interventions.* New York: Springer.

Litwin, H. (1996). *The social networks of older people: A cross-national analysis.* Greenwood, CT: Praeger.

Lockery, S. (1991, Fall/Winter). Family and social supports: Caregiving among racial and ethnic minority elders. *Generations,* 58–62.

Lopata, H. (1996). *Current Widowhood: Myths and realities.* Thousand Oaks, CA: Sage.

Martz, S. H. (Ed.). (1992). *If I had my life to live over / I would pick more daisies.* Watsonville, CA: Papier-Mache Press.

Mead, M. (1972). *Blackberry winter.* New York: William Morrow.

Myerhoff, B. (1992). *Remembered lives: The work of ritual, storytelling, and growing older.* Ann Arbor: University of Michigan Press.

Neugarten, B. (1991). Successful aging in 1970 and 1990. In E. Pfeiffer (Ed.), *Successful aging: A conference report.* Raleigh, NC: Duke University.

Pinkston, E., & Linsk, N. (1984). *Care of the elderly: A family approach.* New York: Pergamon.

Pogrebin, L. C. (1996). *Getting over getting older.* New York: Little, Brown & Company.

Posner, R. A. (1995). *Aging and old age.* Chicago: University of Chicago Press.

Qualls, S. H. (1991). Resistence of older families to therapeutic intervention. *Clinical Gerontologist, 11,* 59–68.

Reid, J. D. (1995). Development in late life: Older lesbian and gay lives. In A. D'Augelli & C. Patterson (Eds.), *Lesbian, gay, and bisexual identies over the lifespan.* (pp. 215–245). New York: Oxford University Press.

Rolland, J. R. (1994). *Families, illness, and disability.* New York: Basic Books.

Schulz, R., & Heckhausen, J. (1996). A life span model of successful aging. *American Psychologist, 51,* 702–714.

Sorensen, E. M. (1977). Family interaction with the elderly. In P. Watzlawick & J. Weakland (Eds.), *The interactional view.* New York: Norton.

Smith, G., Power, P., Robertson-Tchabo, E., & Tobin, S. (1995). *Strengthening aging families.* Thousand Oaks, CA: Sage.

Spark, G. (1974). Grandparents and intergenerational family therapy. *Family Process, 13,* 225–238.

Spark, G., & Brody, E. M. (1970). The aged are family members. *Family Process, 9,* 195–210.

Sussman, M. (1976). The family life of old people. In R. Binstock & E. Shanas (Eds.), *Handbook of aging and the social sciences.* New York: Van Nostrand Reinhold.

Szinovacz, M., & Harpster, P. (1994). Couples' employment/retirement status and the division of household tasks. *Journal of Gerontology: Social Sciences, 49,* 125–136.

Tobin, S., & Kulys, R. (1981). The family in the institutionalization of the elderly. *Journal of Social Issues, 37,* 145–157.

Van Amburg, S. M., Barber, C. E., & Zimmerman, T. S. (1996). Aging and family therapy: Prevalence of aging issues and later family life concerns in marital and family therapy literature (1986–1993). *Journal of Marital and Family Therapy, 22,* 195–203.

Walsh, F. (1993). Conceptualization of normal family processes. In F. Walsh (Ed.), *Normal family processes* (2nd. ed.). New York: Guilford Publications.

Walsh, F. (1996). The concept of family resilience: Crisis and challenge. *Family Process, 35,* 261–281.

Walsh, F. (1998). *Strengthening family resilience.* New York: Guilford Publications.

Walsh, F. (Ed.)(In press). *Spiritual resources in family therapy.* New York: Guilford Publications.

Walsh, F., & McGoldrick, M. (1991). *Living beyond loss: Death in the family.* New York: Norton.

Zarit, S., Anthony, C., & Boutselis, M. (1987). Interventions with caregivers of dementia patients: Comparison of two approaches. *Psychology and Aging, 2,* 225–232.

CHAPTER 19

THE FAMILY LIFE CYCLE OF AFRICAN AMERICAN FAMILIES LIVING IN POVERTY

PAULETTE MOORE HINES

> *Well, you were born...and though your father and mother and grand-mother, looking about the streets through which they were carrying you, staring at the walls into which they were carrying you, had every reason to be heavy hearted, yet they were not. For here you were: Big James, named for me—to be loved. To be loved, Baby, hard, at once, and forever, to strengthen you against a loveless world. Remember that. I know how black it looks today for you. It looked bad that day too. Yes, we were trembling. We have not stopped trembling yet. But if we had not loved each other, none of us would have survived. And now you must survive, because we love you, and for the sake of your children and your children's children.*
>
> —Letter from James Baldwin to his 15-year-old nephew

James Baldwin's touching letter to his nephew evokes the importance of our kinship network, of hope in the face of so little, of remembering our history and our connectedness and our strength to survive—all that poor African American families need so desperately in our times. Nowhere is the need for a life cycle framework more urgent than in work with poor African American families. Nowhere is it more crucial that we attend to the importance of people's connections to their history, communities, and hope for a future.

About 13 percent of the total U.S. population are African American (33 million people). The dominant discourse is that African Americans are responsible for their position in society and have

equal opportunities to achieve the American Dream. But the truth is this group's struggle for basic freedoms and opportunities has continually been thwarted by the pernicious and pervasive effects of racism at every level of our society. Poverty adds its own pain. Individuals who are poor and African American (approximately 2.1 million) must contend with systematic efforts to disconnect, invalidate, and crush dreams on a daily basis. They are three times as likely as White to live in poverty (31 versus 11.6 percent) (U.S. Census Bureau, 1996). Racial differences are not erased with increased education; Blacks are poorer than Whites even when they have a high school diploma or college degree (U.S. Census Bureau, 1996).

A growing number of family theorists, researchers, and practitioners have countered deficit-focused perspectives about the poor and have brought much-needed attention to the strengths of the culture. These include Harry Aponte (1994),

The author gratefully acknowledges Monica McGoldrick for her patience and assistance in bringing this paper to fruition. Recognition is also due Waymon Benton and J. C. Williams who provided consultation and background material to support the formulation of this paper.

Andrew Billingsley (1992), Nancy Boyd-Franklin (1989), Brown and Parnell (1990), Linda Burton (1990, 1995, 1996a, 1996b), Ken Hardy and Tracy Laszloffy (1998), Robert Hill (1972, 1993), Hines and Boyd Franklin (1996), Lewis and Looney (1983), Jayne Maboubi and Ashburn Searcy, (1998), Vanessa Mahmoud (1998), Elaine Pinderhughes (1982, 1989, 1998), and many others. They assert that the lives of poor African Americans can only be understood within a framework that acknowledges the far-reaching interactive effects of African culture, slavery, racism and its residuals (e.g., internalized racism), and social, economic, and political disenfranchisement.

What is essential to our efforts as therapists is to focus on African Americans' resourcefulness and ability to survive and even thrive under oppressive circumstances throughout history in this country. It is a true testament to the resilience of the human spirit and nothing short of a miracle that African Americans have survived and made such significant gains in the educational, economic, political, and many other arenas (Collins, 1996; Roberts, 1995). Countless uncelebrated poor African Americans lead invisible lives distinguished by a defiant spirit of hope, an exceptional capacity for problem solving, and a commitment to transcending the odds (Hines, 1998).

The purpose of this chapter is to dispel the notion that family therapy is a futile endeavor with poor African American families and reinforce the value of working from a proactive framework that situates families within their cultural and life cycle context and links them with the rich resources of their heritage.

FACTORS INFLUENCING DIVERSITY, FUNCTIONING, AND RESILIENCE THROUGH THE LIFE CYCLE

As we approach the twenty-first century, the reemergence of conservative political agenda in the United States is drastically reducing the safety net that was previously available to the poor of all backgrounds. There is an increasing gap between the haves and have-nots. There has been a collapse of the low-wage economy in the ghetto (Wilson, 1997). Jobs are no longer available for people who do not have technical skills, a situation that pushes African Americans who, in the past, were working at low-wage jobs or looking for work into the underclass. The Urban League's hidden unemployment index measured African American unemployment at 23.2 percent (Jacob, 1994). In many inner-city communities, fewer than one in four adults are employed at any time (Wilson, 1997). Residential areas, particularly in urban areas, are increasingly segregated by class and mass flight of businesses and the middle class are leaving an insufficient tax base and lack of political power to rebuild decaying physical environments. There is strong evidence that once work disappears from a community and people grow up without even the hope of working, drug use and crime intensify dramatically, and the disorganization of the social community becomes overwhelming (Wilson, 1997).

These circumstances have extensive consequences for adolescents and young adults, in particular, who have had little or no opportunity to develop a job history or skills. Schools remain inferior and increasingly racially segregated. Far too many students are poorly prepared to compete in a society that requires ever more technical skills from its workers. Nevertheless, recently passed welfare reform legislation requires able-bodied adults to work for nonprofit entities to maintain their cash subsidies. Even so, assistance will be limited to five years whether or not individuals are successful in securing work. Meanwhile, budgets for health care, social services, and education and training are being slashed.

The media and professional literature construct and reinforce a negative identity for African Americans, and perpetuate the inaccurate notion that the poor are a homogenous population, doomed to be dysfunctional. The overfocus on negative elements in the lives of poor African Americans leaves many therapists feeling hopeless and frustrated. They are inclined to overlook the fact that the characterization as "poor" simply does not convey the variation in life that low-income individuals experience any more than it does for middle- or upper-class families. Family income does not equate with family competence. Poor families vary in structure, coping styles, and levels of resilience. Some live in single-family units; others reside with members of their kin network. Some are working poor; some are temporarily unemployed. Some are downwardly mobile; others are slowly improving their economic status. Some (38 percent) live in families in which the only source of income is government assistance; others (25 percent) make do with what they can generate through their meager earnings and by exchanging resources within their family support system ("Status of African-American Children under Three Living in Poverty," 1992).

Numerous factors mediate the effects of adverse economic, environmental, and social conditions on family functioning, including the number of generations they have been embedded in poverty, the level of their connection with their larger family systems, their religiosity, and the nature of their response to their oppression (Pinderhughes, 1982). Another variable that is hypothesized to be of major import is level of acculturation, that is, the extent to which the family maintains traditional African American practices, values, beliefs, and preferences (Barbarin, 1993).

CHARACTERISTICS OF THE FAMILY LIFE CYCLE

Despite their heterogeneity, African American families living in poverty are uniformly apt to face innumerable barriers to transcending their concrete circumstances on a daily basis. Their life cycle is distinguished by at least four characteristics.

Condensed Life Cycle

Progression through the various life cycle phases is generally more accelerated for poor African Americans than for their working- and middle-class counterparts. Individuals have children and become grandparents at far earlier ages (Burton, 1996a, 1996b). When families have a condensed, overlapping intergenerational structure, family roles are chronologically and developmentally out of sync with generational position (Burton, 1996b). Acceleration for one person creates acceleration for others throughout the family system. For example, the adolescent mother, by giving birth, is launched into young adult status (parenthood), and her young adult mother becomes a grandmother, often being forced to assume the role responsibilities of surrogate parent. The potential for role overload in such life cycle patterns is tremendous. The abrupt assumption of new roles and responsibilities often means that they have inadequate time to resolve their developmental tasks. Facing so many pressures, adults may be overwhelmed, inconsistent, or too busy to pay sufficient attention to their own or their children's needs. Outcomes depend on the extent to which transitions are anticipated, the level of support available from extended family, and the extent to which the development of caretakers is stalled (Burton, 1996a, 1996b). Families adapt better when there is clarity regarding the logistical, emotional, behavioral, and relational shifts that must be made at all levels of the system to support positive evolution of the family and its individual family members through the life cycle.

Female-Headed Households

The percentage of African American family households headed by a married couple with children declined dramatically from 59 percent to 32 percent between 1970 and 1990 (Henderson, 1994; U.S. Bureau of the Census, 1997). Some parents are separated or divorced, while others were never legally married. The trend toward motherhood without marriage reflects not a cultural devaluation of marriage (Staples, 1985), but rather an adaptation to circumstances that limit the availability of mates as well as of hopes and dreams for other life possibilities. Poor young girls may come to think of pregnancy and motherhood as offering the hope of love and increased status in their families. Most single-parent households are female headed, but many share parenting functions with others in their kinship network and are part of multifamily residences.

Chronic Stress and Untimely Losses

Frequently embedded in large, extended family networks that span the life cycle continuum, African

American families living below the poverty threshold experience frequent shifts in household membership as a result of job loss, illness, death, imprisonment, and alcohol and drug addiction. It is not uncommon for families to move several times a year, and children may experience a great many different family constellations. The contrast of living in a society of plenty in which they must struggle constantly to meet basic needs breeds frustration. Their capacity to work around obstacles and be hopeful about life are stretched continuously. Ordinary problems—such as transportation or a sick child—easily become crises because of a lack of resources to solve them. Men and women, young and old, may assume an outward facade of apathy that is merely armor intended to protect them from further disappointment, pain, and degradation. Persistent stress is likely to affect their spiritual as well as their physical and emotional health.

Reliance on Institutional Supports

In 1987, approximately 54 percent of rural and 64 percent of urban low-income African American families sought public assistance to meet their basic needs (Jones, 1994). Stigmatization and the need to comply with numerous regulations, which barely allow them to survive, can push an already stressed emotional system over the edge. Mutual aid has always been a prominent feature of African American culture. The strongest institution in the natural support system has been churches. Many other civic organizations, such as Urban Leagues and community development corporations, also provide a critically needed safety net for those whose needs far surpass their resources.

ASSESSMENT AND TREATMENT CONSIDERATIONS

A family life cycle framework is totally congruent with African values, the most widely held being a deep sense of family or kinship, including both the vertical (the living, the dead, and those yet unborn) and the horizontal, encompassing all persons living in the tribe, even those in different family units

(Mbiti, 1970). A life cycle approach counters the pervasive narrow, individualist focus that characterizes so much of the social science literature, promoting a deficit approach, which has amounted to blaming the victim (Billingsley, 1968; Hill, 1993). For example, most discussions of teen mothers and their children have focused narrowly on the maternal grandmother and the young teenage mother as they provide for the child. This myopic focus ignores the caregiving responsibilities and practices of the young father, grandfather, great-grandparents, siblings, and other kin in such situations. It also ignores the needs of other family members, such as the frail elderly, which influence the quality of life for a teenage mother and her child as well as others in the family (Burton, 1995).

The family life cycle approach becomes even more powerful when fortified by a connection with principles of living and adaptation that have promoted African American survival and transcendance through many generations of slavery and oppression. A growing number of theorists/practitioners have formulated prevention and treatment approaches based on Afrocentric values (Hines & Sutton, 1998; Phillips, 1990; Rowe & Grills, 1993; Nobles, 1974, 1986; Williams, 1997 and many others). Undergirding these perspectives is the premise that healthy functioning of African Americans is closely linked to principles drawn from African culture that define what one stands for and how one behaves within a bicultural and oppressive context. There is also a common belief that the first task of transformative healing is to confront and dismantle the misguided presumption of White superiority and that the solutions to understanding and resolving the problems of today are rooted in the past.

African principles, for example, form the basis of the celebration of Kwanzaa, an African American holiday that was developed in 1965 to celebrate and reinforce African American values (Karenga, 1988). Row & Grills (1993) described an approach for treating drug addicted clients that they call the Seven Intentions of Transformative Healing that is based on a related but different formulation of traditional African values. Williams

(1997) advocates a family therapy model that she has named Tarajia based on the promotion of specific guidelines for behavior drawn from commonly embraced African principles. Hines and Sutton (1998) have developed a violence prevention program for adolescents and parents that emphasizes traditional African values. The program is called SANKOFA, named for an African bird that has become an important symbol for many African Americans, because it flies forward while looking backward. While there are commonalities and variations in the principles that are highlighted and in their interpretation across models, the dictates contained in each model reverberate deeply and richly for African Americans. They resound repeatedly in homes and pulpits and can be found in African American literature and music of all types.

Drawing on this earlier work, the author conceptualized an approach to assessment and intervention with African American Families that has proven particularly helpful to those living in the context of poverty. The model incorporates seven traditional African principles:

1. *Consciousness* pertains to having a clear awareness of our feelings, thoughts, beliefs, principles, purpose, family, cultural heritage, and potential, as well as obstacles to self-actualization and group actualization, including racism.

2. *Connectedness* pertains to unity (*umoja* in Swahili) or sticking together, a sense of belonging (Rowe & Grills, 1993), and regard for the well-being of our people and all other living systems. It is reflected in the African adage "I am because we are" and reflects the idea that our self-definition depends on our fundamental interrelationships with our family and our people (Nobles, 1986; Rowe & Grills, 1993) as well as mutually supportive links within our kin network and community.

3. *Caring* pertains to the ability to nurture, protect, support, and show concern for the safety of our family and the larger group. Africans have always had a strong mutual-aid orientation (Nobles, 1974) and a belief in giving back

(*rudisha* in Swahili). Caring reflects the essential interdependence of African Americans, the belief that "If I don't care for you, I don't care for myself" (Rowe & Grills, 1993). It requires collective work and responsibility or unity (*ujima* in Swahili) to build and maintain our community together, to make our sisters' and brothers' problems our problems, and to solve them together (Karenga, 1988).

4. *Competence toward our purpose* involves commitment to self-actualization and group actualization, developing ourselves, our families, our communities, and our culture to their fullest potential (Rowe & Grills, 1993). It pertains to self-determination (*kujichagulia* in Swahili), the right to define ourselves, name ourselves, create for ourselves, and speak for ourselves, instead of being defined and spoken for by others (Karenga, 1988). It requires achieving the skills to cope with and even modify or transcend our circumstances.

5. *Conduct* pertains to accepting our reciprocal responsibility to engage in right behavior and to teach others how to do so. It requires that African Americans do the right thing simply because they know that it is right, regardless of what others do. It involves the ability to forgive and resolve past injustices with one another (Williams, 1997).

6. *Creativity* (*kuumba* in Swahili) involves using our God-given talents to help our families and community not only to survive but to transcend adversity, to use our originality, inventiveness, imagination, intuition, and artistic abilities to transform pain into meaning and hope and leave the world better and more beautiful than it was when we inherited it (Karenga, 1988).

7. *Courage* pertains to demonstrating the spiritual strength to withstand adversity to achieve one's goals; to live up to the examples of one's ancestors. It requires having hope and "faith [*imani* in Swahili] to believe with all our heart in our people, our parents, our teachers, our leaders, and the righteousness and victory of our struggle" (Karenga, 1988).

This evolving Afrocentric life cycle framework allows therapists to assess families' competence in fulfilling life cycle tasks within the context of values drawn from their heritage. It helps therapists to predict the key developmental tasks that may be stalled when families must focus so extensively on external conditions. The framework promotes awareness of the relationship between the behavior of family members across generations (vertically) in relationship to current sociopolitical/economic conditions (horizontally). Family members can be empowered to participate in their own healing and to search for wisdom in their own cultural and family heritage.

The initial task of understanding the presenting problem(s) within the context of the family's life cycle phase, family functioning, and the larger ecology must be undertaken with care. Many practitioners (Hines & Boyd-Franklin, 1996) have suggested that taking a genogram history requires diplomacy and should be gathered gradually as the family comes to trust that the therapist will not treat them as institutions have typically treated them in the past—in demeaning, disrespectful, and racist ways. Therapists can assess families' actual and ideal functioning in relation to the seven principles of African American family and individual competence that are highlighted in this chapter.

The power of relating to principles for living is connected with the growing need for African American families to critically examine the myriad of messages they receive about how to survive in a society in which there is a push to assimilate at the same time that basic rights and opportunities are still denied. Socialization about how to survive in an oppressive context is more haphazard than it was in the past, so it is all the more important that therapy help to recontextualize families in relation to the larger context. Questions to help achieve this aim include the following:

- Does your family have any information about its origins (i.e., tribal connections) in Africa?
- What is the story of your family's journey from slavery through the present?
- What keeps you going in spite of ongoing adversity?

- Do you have a mission or calling, something that you think you are meant to do?
- What has been the impact of racism, poverty, and other forms of oppression on your family's functioning?
- Do you believe there is a higher being, deity, or divine force?
- How do you nourish your spiritual side?
- How would your ancestors have solved this problem?
- What wisdom would they pass on to you if they could consult with you regarding your current concern(s)?
- Were any sayings or stories passed down to you that have special meaning for you when you face difficult circumstances?
- What do you believe are the basic responsibilities that individuals in your family/ethnic group have to each other?
- What constitutes right, ethical, moral, responsible behavior in this situation?
- Are there any cut-offs within the extended kin system that relate to internalized racism (e.g., skin color), institutionalized racism, or other socioeconomic and political circumstances?
- Do you think you or other family members have allowed yourselves to be enslaved by how others see you?
- What do you do to avoid giving up your power and dreams?
- How can you connect with the spirit and wisdom of the higher power that guided your ancestors through the Middle Passage and slavery?
- As a trailblazer, managing the complexities of living in two worlds, what skills have you needed to develop?

Work with multiproblem poor African American families requires creativity, attentiveness to their idiosyncrasies, and validation of their potential, regardless of where they are in the family life cycle. Families need orientation to therapy and to know the nature of the therapist's connection to other service agencies. Convening family members to communicate and problem solve without their usual distractions can be invaluable in and of itself. Flexibility in time, place, family member participation, and use of a therapeutic team makes an enormous difference (Brown & Parnell, 1990). It is important to clarify reality constraints (e.g., conflicting work schedules) that may hamper family members' participation in therapy (Hines & Boyd-Franklin, 1996) and to offer them some help during the first session, however minor. There is nothing sacred about the typical one- or even two-hour session; half- and full-day sessions may be more effective and may enable therapists to mobilize key family members, who may not otherwise be available for appointments. Extended sessions also make it easier to engage and mobilize families before they are distracted by new stresses. In addition, the flexibility offered by a diverse therapeutic team counters burnout and maximizes therapeutic creativity (Hines, Richman, Hays, & Maxim, 1989).

Therapists must strive to empower family members by helping them to understand the ways in which the social system may undermine their functioning as individuals and a family, sorting out the factors in their predicament that belong to external systems and those that belong to them. This helps them to avoid assuming blame for systemic influences while taking responsibility for ways in which they may collude in reinforcing their own powerlessness (Pinderhughes, 1982). The author recommends the use of culturally congruent strategies—oral history interviews, daily reading of scriptures or meditations, participation in rites of passage, use of videos and readings based on the lives of African Americans—to help families connect with their family and group history, their potential, and their hope about overcoming their current challenges (Hines, 1998).

STAGES OF THE FAMILY LIFE CYCLE

The life cycle of the poor can be loosely divided into three basic life cycle phases, which are frequently overlapping. It is common for families to be in several stages simultaneously, given their extended kin and intergenerational context.

Stage 1: Adolescence/Unattached Young Adulthood

African American youths are at risk for many life difficulties because of the combined effects of racism, poverty, and the general vulnerabilities of adolescence. In addition to the ordinary tasks of adolescence, they have the added burden of developing a sense of efficacy in the face of persistent racism and other oppression. Their environment is full of minefields, and there is little room for error; actions such as dropping out of school or being argumentative when stopped by the police may have lifelong consequences. The jobless rate of Black teenagers age 16 to 19 doubled to 50 percent between 1969 and 1983 (Hill, 1993), twice as high as the rate for Whites (Wright Edelman, 1997). Even Black students who graduate from college are nearly twice as likely to be unemployed as White high school graduates with no college (Wright Edelman, 1997). Pregnancy is usually high on parents' worry list for their adolescent daughters; indeed, a high number of girls miss this stage almost completely through early pregnancy, which catapults them into premature adulthood and parenting (Ventura, Taffel, Mosher et al. 1992). For sons, parents fear for their safety and lives, knowing that authorities are quick to arrest them for minor offenses, book, remand them for trials, and give them harsh dispositions (Roberts, 1995; U.S. Bureau of the Census, 1997). Their neighborhoods are often drug and crime ridden, and there are constant pulls to engage in illegal activity. Violence is an everyday occurrence in their schools and neighborhoods. In fact, homicide is now the leading cause of death for African Americans of both genders between the ages of 15 and 44 (U.S. Bureau of Census, 1997). Many youths feel compelled to carry weapons for self-protection (Hines, Macias, & Perrino, in press). AIDS is the fourth leading cause of death in African American females aged 15 to 24. It is the fifth leading cause of deaths among their peers.

At every life cycle phase, families need to provide family members with a balance of separateness and attachment that will promote their adaptive success (Lewis & Looney, 1983). During adolescence, this balance becomes especially difficult to work out. While yearning for independence, acknowledgment, and respect, many poor youths learn to protect themselves emotionally by turning off to the rules of the dominant society that devalues and excludes them. The infiltration of "street values" into youth culture and the media's preoccupation with this subculture has heightened negative sentiments about youths everywhere they turn. Most African American youths learn to project an external demeanor that masks the disappointment, hopelessness, and helplessness that flow from their economic, racial, gender, and age-based oppression. Their creative and distinctive use of nonstandard language and attraction to nontraditional clothes, music, and hairstyles might be viewed as an effort to reject rejection and to exercise some power in their lives (Franklin, 1989). The schism between societal expectations and what they are able to achieve puts these youths at high risk for depression, anxiety, physical problems, rage, and a host of other problems. Staying connected with their dreams and not compromising their priorities require extreme determination.

Burton (1990) has suggested that young males in particular tend to become invisible at this phase of the life cycle, disappearing from school and church, not appearing in the work system, and even disconnecting from their families. In some communities, boys begin to disappear from their families as early as age 10, being socialized beyond that point primarily outside the house by peers and older men in the community, who instruct them in the ways of survival.

Hale-Benson (1986) suggests that Black children across social classes are at risk in the traditional educational process, needing to master at least two cultures, and Black males must master three: the larger context, African American culture, and the African American male subculture. Kunjufu (1985) contends that there are several critical periods in Black youths' development: fourth and fifth grade when Black children, especially boys, seem to experience a slump in their achievement; adolescence, which appears particularly turbulent; and the young adult years, which offer

critical opportunities that may determine the quality of later life.

Some youths try to fend for themselves in spite of their difficulties making financial ends meet; others remain in their families' household, whatever inner or interpersonal conflict this entails. Some deal with pressure to strike out on their own by breaking away in anger; others get married and/or have children with the assumption that this new status will force others to acknowledge them as adults. Some try to resolve the dilemma by relocating to another geographic area but can afford to do so only if they live with relatives, which may create other relationship problems.

Learning to cope with racism and other oppression is an unenviable challenge. It is most difficult for parents to help their children approach school and the world of work with optimism. Even a high school degree now carries little guarantee that a person will find work, and training beyond high school costs money that they do not have. Both in school and in the larger community, African American teens are exposed to ongoing macro- and micro-assaults and treated as if they are either invisible or dangerous (Franklin, 1993). Even more than their elders, they need the skills to operate in a bicultural context. Young adults encounter far more subtle racism than their parents and grandparents experienced growing up. The curricula that they are taught on a daily basis remain largely Eurocentric in focus. Parents have the complex task of teaching their children to cope with racism without overfocusing or underfocusing on the issue, a challenge at any life cycle phase but especially at this time when rebelliousness and the value teens place on the opinions of their peers interfere with their receptiveness to learning from their parents anyway. The adoption of African-centered ideas may be critical to counter the dominant ideas, which are bound to undermine African Americans' conceptions of themselves and their place in the world. Obviously, youths are particularly vulnerable if their parents are absent or dysfunctional and other adults are not available to provide positive role modeling and active guidance. The best protection is having parents or caretakers and mentors who acknowledge and openly communicate regarding the harsh realities of their world while conveying clear principles for living, high expectations, and monitoring the youths' activities without being overprotective.

Financial limitations and family obligations can make it difficult for young adults to fulfill key tasks of this stage: to establish intimate relationships and a work identity and to self-differentiate. Many poor Black youths are growing up not seeing anyone in their family network who has the opportunity to work. This keeps them from believing that they can become a part of the American Dream and makes it hard for them to remain hopeful and motivated to resist giving up or becoming part of a counterculture of drug dealing and other illegal and dangerous activities that offer financial reward and status, though incarceration or early death are also likely outcomes. If they are in a position to work, they are likely to feel compelled to provide caretaking or resources to other needy family members, compromising their own interests and needs.

Key Therapeutic Tasks.   Parents and youths often need to have both separate and joint sessions to sort out their beliefs, feelings, and concerns. Parents may need to be coached to communicate clear, specific guidelines for children's conduct and to help their children appreciate the difference between being responsible for a situation and being accountable for how they respond to the situation. That is, while they may encounter ongoing situations in life that are externally imposed, unfair, and oppressive, they must still be accountable to themselves, their families, and their community for their *conduct*—whether they choose to use constructive or destructive strategies to cope with adversity.

Given the time and energy that are dedicated to surviving each day, we should not underestimate the value of simply creating a forum where family members allow each other to have a voice. Therapists must be able to sit through family members' expression of their pain, disillusionment, and rage while reminding them of the values they hold, which may be different from the choices they are

making daily. Therapists must also be willing to label destructive behaviors, even while acknowledging their positive intent. Families may benefit from participating in structured dialogue and problem-solving sessions. It may be useful to facilitate discussion between parents and adolescents about differences in the challenges that they have faced. Getting adults to tell relevant stories is an excellent tool for (re)connecting everyone with the legacies that can serve as road maps for coping with current struggles. (This is part of the principle of *connecting* described in the list of African-centered principles.) At times, for example, children may not appreciate that their fathers, having no resources, may leave their families or become invisible so that the family can be eligible for medical benefits and financial assistance (McCall, 1984).

Parents may become immobilized in their ability to set limits on their children out of their own frustration or hopelessness about their children's chances of finding a meaningful place in society. Therapists can be of great service in getting parental figures to come up with a clear position or to at least avoid sabotaging each other in setting limits. Anxieties need to be channeled into activities that do not exacerbate the youth's inclination to invalidate parental feedback. Respected older male relatives and community members may be brought in to help young men reexamine their definitions of manhood and free themselves of the limitations that their peers and larger society may impose. Videotapes can be a powerful stimulus for conversations about courage and conduct and help family members to make emotional as well as cognitive shifts.

It is critical for the executives in families to impress on their adolescents the necessity of having a plan of action to accompany their dreams. In the words of an African proverb, they must convey that "The hand that knocks you down is not likely to be the hand that picks you up." Young adults require knowledge and a toolbox of life skills, including anger and stress management, conflict resolution, safer sex negotiation, and time management skills to effectively negotiate the demands they will face in life. Therapists should not assume that parents or adolescents possess these skills or the confidence to apply them. It is preferable to link clients with opportunities for culturally sensitive skills training (Hines & Sutton, 1998) in their school, work, and community settings whenever these opportunities are available.

Stage 2: Coupling, Bearing and Raising Children

Many African Americans grow up and face adulthood living in poverty, even when they work. A related and significant factor, influencing male/female relationships and hence, family life is that between the ages of 20 and 40, Black females outnumber African American men in that group (U.S Bureau of the Census, 1997).

Couple Relationships.   Couple relationships can be extremely difficult to develop and sustain in the context of poverty and racism. Stress is persistent, and conflicts arise easily. In 1994, 38 percent of African American women and 42 percent of African American men were married, down from 45 percent and 49 percent, respectively, in 1980 (Collins, 1996). The divorce rate for Blacks is 1.5 times the rate for Whites, and this does not include those who have ended their relationship without legal divorce (U.S. Bureau of the Census, 1995). The media provide a constant inducement for couples to compare their lives and relationships to those of the rich and famous, whose resources are dramatically better than their own. Housing tends to be substandard and overcrowded, with no physical space or money for recreation or cooling off when conflicts arise. There is a tendency for the many frustrations of living in a context of oppression to get misdirected into male-female relationships. As in most other cultures, women are socialized to be the nurturers in their families and are particularly inclined to ignore or sacrifice their own needs. Within the culture, individuals are seen as having intrinsic worth irrespective of their level of academic achievements or economic success in life. There is widespread recognition of the special oppression that impedes Black men's capacity to live

up to their role demands. This increases the risk that women will accept role overload as a way of life.

Young African American males, who are the most direct focus of the larger society's racism, are reluctant to make a commitment to a relationship when they are unable to meet their financial obligations. Wilson (1997) has been documenting the long-term decline in the proportion of Black men, especially young Black men, who are in a position to support a family and has shown the obvious and overwhelming relationship between joblessness and female-headed households. He asserts that marriage is an "opportunity structure" that no longer exists for large numbers of Black people. Men are at high risk for acting out their disappointment and frustrations through drinking or drug use, womanizing, or becoming chronically angry, withdrawn, and absent from the families they cannot support.

Taking on Parental Roles.   While some African American mothers are mature working women, many are unmarried teenagers. When adolescent sexual experimentation leads to pregnancy, young women frequently reject abortion and adoption, choosing to have and keep their babies. They may quickly feel overburdened and depressed. Particularly if their education is interrupted, their role can become constricted to that of caretaker. If they attempt to enter the job market, child care and transportation costs can be prohibitive. Many are forced to obtain public assistance to ensure housing, food, and medical benefits.

The role of young fathers with children born outside of marriage is often vaguely defined. If they still identify with their adolescent peer group, they may be slow to accept shared responsibility for their children. Mothers may actually restrict fathers' involvement to protect their children from the possibility of broken promises. In time, children expect their fathers' absence, though it may bother them. Boys, in particular, are handicapped by this concept of maleness, but there has been a concerted effort to reverse this trend. An increasing number of young men are getting involved in parenting education and support programs. Burton (1995) found about 25 percent of the fathers in her research sample and their families were participating in caregiving to their children.

Parents can easily become overburdened with too many responsibilities and too few resources and emotional reserves. Often, several children are close in age, and it is not uncommon for children to span the range from infancy through adolescence. An older child may take on responsibility for helping to reduce the parental load, helping with child or elder care, household maintenance, or working to contribute to the family's meager cash resources. Parents tend to be authoritarian and use physical punishment to ensure that children quickly learn and abide by lessons that are intended to protect them from dangers in their harsh surroundings. Coaching parents to change their discipline strategies, when this is necessary, requires tact and an understanding of the extreme pressures they face (Denby & Alford, 1996).

Realigning Relationships with Extended Family.
The birth of children hastens couples' need to integrate new spouses or mates into extended-family networks. They often live with or near parents and other family members. While the extended-family network is likely to provide child care and a much needed cushion of emotional if not financial support, a high level of connection leaves room for some predictable problems. Couples may struggle with issues of loyalty between their newly created family and one or both extended-family systems. Families often include children and/or grandchildren as well as other relatives of one or both partners, creating the challenge of fitting together disparate and changing relationships. Furthermore, poverty tends to mean an extremely high family mobility, so parents and children must continually adjust to relatives moving in and out, and they themselves tend to change living quarters and schools very frequently.

Single-parent family structures are not inherently dysfunctional, but they are particularly vulnerable because of poverty, task overload, and a lack of resources. More relevant than the structure of the single-parent family are the availability of other resources and the family's ways of functioning. Family adaptive strategies, when pushed too far, can become a vulnerability. For example, parental children can provide critical support to siblings, while developing self-esteem, and an enhanced sense of their own potential, if parents ensure that they assume only responsibilities that are within their capacity (Hines & Boyd-Franklin, 1996; Watson, 1998). But when parents abdicate responsibility to children who have inadequate skills, support, and power to meet the challenge, these children can easily become the object of their siblings' rage. The effort to take care of others may divert attention from their own developmental needs, leaving them ripe for frustration. Adaptive strengths are maximized when adults show sensitivity to the unique characteristics and needs of each child, avoid cutting children off from their fathers and paternal families, are clear about unacceptable behavior, and use positive, consistent discipline strategies.

Key Therapeutic Tasks.
Given the likelihood of role overload and isolation at this phase, helping parents and other caretakers to maintain supportive, reciprocal connections with family, fictive kin, friends, and community supports is extremely important. This is even more critical when aging grandparents assume parental responsibilities, especially when children have special needs stemming from parental drug addiction and AIDS. Sibling relationships, which are especially important in African American culture, should be validated and nurtured as an extremely important part of the relationship network (Watson, 1998; see also Chapter 9). It is important to maximize the involvement of fathers and the paternal extended family if this is at all possible. Therapists can help to strengthen family systems by linking them with community organizations that can provide concrete resources and supporting their capacities to advocate on their own behalf. Schools do not validate or reward children who have relational cognitive styles as African Americans typically do from growing up in fluid, shared-function families.

Therapists need to advocate for poor families with school systems and empower parents to take an active role in their children's education because of the likelihood of racist disempowerment of children, which contributes to their acting-out behavior.

Many parents and caretakers require assistance to increase their focus on caring for self and reducing the level of their overfunctioning. This is likely to involve setting limits on relationships in which there has been little or no reciprocity in terms of emotional or concrete support. For others, it will involve reducing their role overload by negotiating to share family tasks. Discussion of family legacies that that have contributed to the roles that family members have assumed over time can help families to see the dangers of fostering overdependence on one person. Families can lose a great deal if no one is in training to assume critical tasks. By assisting families to learn about their heritage, therapists help them to gain a sense of hope and connectedness to something larger than themselves.

Parents may need coaching about how to provide children with age-appropriate details regarding imminent changes in the living situation, family member absences, and about how to avoid triangling children into their conflicts.

Families are far less likely to be overwhelmed, depressed, or frustrated when they participate in at least some pleasurable activities. Most are socialized to understand that their lives will involve ongoing struggle and sacrifice. Adults will generally be more comfortable planning pleasurable activities for the sake of the children than for themselves. Therapists must be willing to acknowledge the obstacles that families face even when the intention is to challenge some of the premises that lead clients to give up on their dreams. Reference to sayings or proverbs that have evolved in the African American community over the generations may have a richness of reverberation that families can connect with. For example, a saying such as "It is accomplishments that inspire others, not merely our dreams" (Riley, 1993) might trigger discussion of specific efforts families need to organize when

their sense of being overwhelmed is impeding their efforts for action (Hines, 1998).

Stage 3: Families in Later Life

The life expectancy of an African American is 69.2 years, six to eight years less than for other Americans. Among the aged, 31 percent of Black women, and 21 percent of Black men live below the poverty line, compared to 5 percent of White men and 13 percent of White women. (U.S. Bureau of Census, 1997). Families in later life are likely to consist of a child generation, a young adult parent generation, a middle-aged grandparent generation, and one or even two elderly great-grandparent generations. In contrast to middle-class families, this phase of the life cycle does not signify retirement or a lessening of daily responsibilities for poor African Americans. Many continue working to make ends meet in spite of poor health. Even when they do retire, it is unlikely they will have "empty nests." Instead, they are likely to be active members of expanding households and family systems, frequently providing care to grandchildren, adult children, and other elderly kin. Although women in this stage are likely to be in bad health and have extremely low incomes, it is they who are most likely to provide stability for children when the system is threatened with dissolution because parents cannot fulfill their roles. Grandfathers and grandfather surrogates also help to provide intergenerational care (Burton, 1995). More typically, grandparents' role is to provide child care assistance, while their adult children retain primary responsibility for child-rearing. But as the drug and HIV epidemics have grown, increasing numbers of adult children are dysfunctional and rely on their elders for housing and other support (Boyd-Franklin, Steiner, & Boland, 1995). The increase in single-parent-headed families has also influenced the roles that grandparents play in these families.

Illness is likely to be disregarded by the elderly until their functioning is seriously impaired. This is often related to a belief that idleness hastens age-related symptoms and death and the conviction that the family will suffer if elderly members do not provide the usual assistance. They do not seek to adapt but to overcome the problems associated with aging.

Elderly family members are great sources of human wisdom and strength by virtue of their survival. They not only provide financial assistance and physical care for children and sick family members; they also serve as family advisors, mediators, convenors of the kinship system, and transmitters of the culture. Grandparents often have relationships with their grandchildren that are as close as, if not closer than, the relationships they have with their own adult children. They may have spent more time nurturing their grandchildren, nieces, nephews, and other kin than they were able to devote to their own children. Their homes are usually the gathering place for the kin system.

It is common, particularly for those who were teenage parents, to assume greater responsibility in their nuclear and extended families as they mature and as aging family executives decline in health. There may be unresolved intergenerational issues connected with co-parenting and surrogate parenting arrangements that therapists may have to help family members work through. Individual and subgroup meetings may be required to uncover issues (e.g., shame about drugs, crime, or sexual behavior) that family members feel inhibited about discussing. Disregarding these issues can mean that children are caught in the middle.

Life for poor African Americans typically involves repeated loss because of the size of their kinship system alone, but poverty contributes conditions that make loss a tragically, frequent experience. The repeated experience of loss can both facilitate and complicate family members' adjustment to the issues they confront as family members age and begin to decline in health. The loss of a family member who is central to a family's functioning may be the stimulus that results in the other members' feeling overwhelmed, depressed, deserted, hopeless, angry, and/or bitter about life. Such emotional states obviously retard the progression of the family unit as well as its individual members. For others, their spirituality and family

support give them strength and resilience to transcend their losses.

The assistance that individuals are able to provide to others, particularly in later life, can help them to retain a sense of purpose. However, one area for clinical assessment is whether they can do so without compromising their own needs. The stress of managing child care responsibilities, providing emotional and financial support to adult children and other kin, and contributing to the care of other elderly family members can be overwhelming. The situation is further complicated when their health is failing or retirement is not financially feasible.

Denial about a decline in functioning, illness, or ultimately death may result in disturbed family communication around issues that are critical to maintaining family stability, resulting in faulty problem solving. Efforts to protect the elderly from the realities of their failing health can, in fact, add to their distress in that they are less likely to feel free to openly discuss the major life transition they are undergoing and their concerns about how others in the family will be affected.

Key Therapeutic Tasks. When family members become ill because they did not take care of their health, therapists can ease the family's pain by normalizing their frustration with the aging person. Family members may also need coaching to plan a confrontation with an elderly family member about the need for medical treatment or restrictions on his or her activity. Conflicts about the failure of various family members to shoulder their share of responsibility are common. Elderly family members are often catalysts for gathering family members to address the need for a changing of guards so that continuity of family functioning is maintained. When family members are ambivalent about or closed to participation in therapy sessions, it can help to appeal to their concern that their elderly family members experience greater peace of mind from knowing that all is in order. In return, therapists can motivate the elderly to participate in sessions by emphasizing the need for family members to access the wisdom of their elders and avoid unhealthy dependency that will leave them unprepared to function effectively when the elderly person can no longer do caretaking.

Older family members are sometimes ambivalent about dealing with certain topics (e.g., drugs, illicit sex, or criminal behavior) if they have not resolved their own guilt and/or confusion about choices made when they were younger. But their advice may be even more credible because of their life experience and it may be helpful for them to speak openly about information they may have long avoided or kept secret. Exploring individual and family legacies often results in reconnecting with stories, images, and the fortitude of ancestors and mobilizes family members to move forward with tasks they have magnified to the status of undoable.

Those in the middle generation, burdened by providing assistance to older and younger family members, are at particularly high risk for symptoms. Given the cultural emphasis on being strong and the common interpretation that this means "keep moving," men and women are challenged to grant themselves time to rebound from physical and emotional depletion. It may help to ask what wisdom their ancestors would share with them about managing this situation.

Case Illustration

The Long family was referred for treatment by school authorities to address the excessive school absences and suspected drug use of 16-year-old Raheem. In fact, they represented a family at all three family life cycle stages. The immediate family consisted of Raheem's parents, Isabella (age 46) and Ralph (age 48) and a 13-year-old sister, Rachel. The previous year, the oldest son, Lashan, at age 19 had been accidentally run over by a police car that had been chasing someone else, as he was walking to evening classes at a local college. The paternal grandmother, 65-year-old Caroline, lived several blocks away with her 29-year-old son Larry and her 12-year-old grandson Andre, who had been with her since infancy, when his father, Michael, had been incarcerated. Caroline was suffering from diabetes and high blood pressure. Most of the aunts, uncles, and cousins lived in the local community.

Raheem's problematic behavior had begun after his brother's death. Lashan had been the first in his immediate family to attend college. Ralph had always worked two jobs to make ends meet. But shortly after Lashan's death, he lost his job as a painter because of new regulations, which blocked the employment of those without union credentials. Since then, he could find only occasional odd jobs. Isabella had given up her job as a school crossing guard because of a painful arthritic condition. Also within the past year, Ralph had agreed to "disappear" from the household to allow his family to qualify for medical benefits and food stamps, and he was now staying with his mother, a situation that was increasing the stress in her small household. He had also increased his drinking from occasional binges to daily drinking until he was drunk.

Raheem refused to speak or listen to his father and dismissed his mother's efforts to set limits. Initially, Ralph reacted to Raheem's "disrespectful behavior" with rage and threats to put him out of the household. Isabella was furious with her husband. She confronted him almost daily, expressing disgust about his drinking and his "failure as a husband and as a father." She was also feeling hopeless about Raheem's "refusal to live up to his potential." Recently, Rachel had started to violate her curfew and angrily accused her mother of being overprotective with her but permissive with Raheem. Isabella repeatedly shielded her children's transgressions from their father and her ailing mother-in-law. The grandmother, whose own health was failing, was feeling frustrated and overwhelmed by the needs of her grandson, whose grades had gone down in school. Her son Larry was also a problem, coming home only when he needed something, and she feared that he was involved with drugs.

The family reflected the three patterns typical of the life cycle of the poor that we have discussed earlier: They had a condensed life cycle, Andre having been born when his father was a teenager; female-run households, as the grandmother's was and now briefly the mother's was; and finally the multiple stresses so common in poor families. Over time, the therapy team focused work on life cycle tasks at several levels of the system: (1) consistent child-rearing for the youths in the family, all three of whom (Raheem, Rachel, and Andre) were having problems, (2) the couple relationship, since long unresolved problems in Isabella and Ralph's relationship had now escalated and were intensified by Ralph's drinking and the anger they were directing at each other; and (3) the overburdening and burnout of the grandmother caretaker.

First, the therapists arranged a long session in which all family members were invited; only Larry refused to attend. The therapists attempted to expand the family's consciousness about how they had arrived at their current dilemma, pointing out that they had been pushed to their limit by the senseless death of Lashan, the dramatic decline in the family's meager financial underpinnings, and the deterioration of Isabella's and Caroline's health. The therapist outlined the various stressors that were beyond the family's control (e.g., crime in the neighborhood, illness, unanticipated job loss, negative peer pressure, housing and school problems). Though there were clear racial preferences in effect, Mr. Long had no way to fight the situation that led to his job loss. Isabella and Ralph had discussed but not followed up on seeking legal aid to explore the wrongful death of Lashan. Each family member had handled the feelings of loss, anger, hopelessness, and helplessness with behaviors that were destructive to their individual and family functioning. The members of the executive system of the Long family, connected in their pain and concern, were divided in their awareness of each other's needs, hope, and ideas about how best to counter the circumstances that threatened their family.

To reawaken and expand their consciousness and empower the family, the therapists encouraged the grandmother, father, and mother to tell their family history while Raheem, Rachel, and Andre listened. They told stories of the extraordinary challenges their family had overcome over the generations. Themes of family togetherness, faith, perseverance, and creativity were threaded in each. At the therapist's urging, Ralph agreed to end his cut-off with his brother Michael and took Raheem and Andre with him to see Michael at the prison for the first time in nine years. The therapists facilitated a dialogue between the adults about differences in their expectations and the messages they were giving to the children in the family. The therapists discussed with them how to hold the youths in the family and each other accountable and what shifts were necessary in their co-parenting to foster their

child-rearing goals. Mr. Long, initially very angry that his two brothers had caused his mother so much pain, was highly skeptical about Michael's embracing the Muslim religion. But Michael proved to be an important agent of change. He was able to penetrate Raheem's armor and impress upon him the inaccuracy of his peers' visions of prison life. He spoke candidly to Raheem and Andre about the devastating ways in which drugs had affected not only him but his son and his mother as well, and now probably his younger brother Larry. He challenged both to avoid turning over key life decisions to their peers.

In subsequent individual sessions with Ralph, the team urged him to call upon the courage that had brought him through the Vietnam War and the wisdom passed on by his father to confront his alcohol abuse, his children's need for a positive role model, and his own need to be responsible as a father and husband. Isabella was coached to communicate her distress to her husband without resorting to yelling and put-downs that typically resulted in angry exchanges, distancing by Ralph, and overfunctioning on her part. Ralph was able to articulate his disappointment that his wife never seemed to appreciate his effort to be a good husband and father. Until his recent drinking, he had maintained his commitment to himself, from boyhood, to be different from the men he grew up around, who dealt with their blues by cheating on their wives, being physically abusive, drinking, gambling, and wasting their lives doing nothing. Ralph and Isabella discussed the kinds of contributions that Ralph could make to demonstrate his caring for his wife and family in spite of his joblessness. The therapists engaged the couple as well as their teens in practice sessions to improve their competency in the art of negotiation. The therapists used the one-way mirror and bug-in-the-ear device to coach the couple to renegotiate their roles in their home. Similarly, Raheem and Rachel rehearsed ways to negotiate for privileges with their parents. Ralph began to take a more active role in the family and coordinated the meetings to help Raheem reestablish his academic standing.

The therapists then turned their attention to the grandmother's health in a second long family session. The family members spoke about their love and caring for her and confronted her about her repeated violation of her diet and inconsistent use of her medication. She spoke to her family about her belief in not giving in to her aches and pains. Discussion ensued about how she could acknowledge her illness by taking her medication and continue to support herself and her grandchild but give up the overtime cleaning and home health care jobs she regularly accepted. She insisted that the family join her in attending church services on Lashan's birthday, which had proven to be a difficult anniversary for the family ever since his death. Acknowledging the innumerable demands and circumstances that impeded their social activity, the therapist asked the executives in the family system to explore the down-side of allowing themselves to become totally depleted, given the enormous importance of the work involved in rearing children in their community. The themes of courage, caring, and doing the right thing by each other reverberated for the adults and youth in the family system.

The therapist articulated the family's unspoken concern that these efforts, without new opportunities, would still fall short of helping the family reduce their level of dependence on government assistance. Mr. Long made a connection with a cousin who owned a small business and was able to secure a part-time position, which had the potential of becoming full time, contingent on his continuing with weekly AA meetings. The therapist was resourceful in linking the family with a new community development corporation, which assigned a mentor and tutor for Andre. Isabella enrolled in their adult education program, where she would be a candidate for further training after attaining her GED. Raheem and Rachel had very grudgingly attended the first session of a rites of passage program that the organization had initiated for young men and women. Isabella reported that neither would admit to liking the program but complaints about going somewhere to be "preached at" had not resurfaced since their first visit. Unfortunately, Larry remained a serious concern, but the grandmother was no longer allowing him to come home whenever he wanted, disrupting the household.

AVOIDING THERAPIST BURNOUT

It is understandable that therapists experience burnout in working with poor families that have multiple problems. Services may be delivered in neighborhoods in which safety is a constant concern (Markowitz, 1997). In most instances, they are working across racial/ethnic differences and socioeconomic lines as well. It is not unusual for families to arrive for therapy with ambivalence if not outright annoyance about the process. Although therapists may understand why this is so, it can still be difficult to accept family members' display of such negative sentiments.

To minimize burnout, we as therapists need to explore where we fall on the continuum of racial, ethnic, gender, sexual orientation, and socioeconomic privilege and assess our personal beliefs about poverty and coping with adversity. It is helpful to stay in regular, active consultation with colleagues who can help us step out of the minefield of guilt or do-gooder behavior that does not benefit our clients or ourselves. African Americans are particularly attuned to indications of genuiness; if our posture is negative, hopeless, or patronizing, we are unlikely to be successful or gratified (Hines, 1998; Hines & Boyd-Franklin, 1996). Humility and active commitment to collaboration are essential therapist skills. The value of our work does not reside in our ability to provide answers to our clients' problems, but rather in helping them to define their options, however limited; take responsibility to reduce the stressors that are affecting them negatively; and improve their handling of circumstances beyond their control. Family therapists are also constantly challenged to redefine the roles and boundaries we were taught to abide by during our training. Families may request assistance with issues that are not related to the presenting problem or planned session goals. Families may leave treatment without termination interviews, only to reappear after another crisis. This revolving-door phenomenon represents an opportunity to help families reach higher levels of functioning as they progress through the family life cycle rather than treatment failure.

Work with multiproblem poor African American families requires significant time, creativity, energy, and clarity. Those who do this work need to be able to schedule appointments flexibly. Caseload assignment policies and performance evaluations should not include a major emphasis on the number of cases that are seen. Flexibility in session timing and team consultation are definitely cost efficient when we consider the cost of no-shows for scheduled appointments, therapist burnout, staff turnover, client dropout, alternative use of emergency services, and the cost of hospitalization. Managed care companies are currently aggressively targeting low-income populations to join their plans. There is is both a challenge and an opportunity to advocate for policies that promote high quality and efficient service delivery. The paperwork and certification process alone are major deterrents to families' receiving the treatment they require.

Most therapists who work with multiproblem families have a genuine commitment to assisting the population and often ignore the need to retreat and replenish their own energy, even to take lunch away from the office. We need to refuel our own tanks, as we so often caution families. A key process, essential to this outcome, is staying connected with our respective wellsprings of energy and spiritual renewal. In our experience, therapists can also gain valuable insights, contacts, and a renewed energy for work in the the clinical arena by using our knowledge and skills to help reengineer

the human service system; design and deliver school-, work-, and community-based interventions; and promote policies that create opportunities and foster healthy environments.

CONCLUSION

There is much for us to learn about how to assist families living in the context of poverty and institutionalized racism. Even though the larger issues of oppression require societal intervention, our current knowledge is sufficient to use family therapy as a tool that can help multiproblem poor families. An Afrocentrically oriented family life cycle perspective provides a useful framework for assessment and intervention, since it does not focus solely on the impact of context and external stresses but permits an understanding of how these exacerbate the stress of normal developmental needs and unresolved family issues. Most important, it provides direction for intervention. It encourages therapists to validate clients' experiences within a context of societal oppression while empowering them, in the spirit of their ancestors, to take whatever steps they can to counter the forces that would undo them.

REFERENCES

Aponte, H. (1994). *Bread and spirit: Therapy with the new poor.* New York: W. W. Norton.

Barbarin, O. (1993). Coping and resilience: Exploring the inner lives of African American children. *Journal of Black Psychology, 19,* 478–492.

Billingsley. A. (1968). *Black families in white America.* Englewood Cliffs, NJ: Prentice Hall.

Billingsley, A. (1992). *Climbing Jacob's ladder: The enduring legacy of African-American families.* New York: Simon & Schuster.

Boyd-Franklin, N. (1989). *Black families in therapy.* New York: The Guilford Press.

Boyd-Franklin, N., Steiner, G., & Boland, M. (1995). *Children, families & HIV/AIDS.* New York: The Guilford Press.

Brown, D. B. & Parnell, M. (1990). Mental health services for the urban poor: A systems approach. In M. Mirkin (Ed.) *The social and political contexts of*

family therapy. (pp. 215–236). New York: The Guilford Press.

Burton, L. M. (1990). Teenage childbearing as an alternative life-course strategy in multigeneration Black families. *Human Nature, 1*(2) 123–143.

Burton, L. M. (1995). Intergenerational patterns of providing care in African-American families with teenage childbearers: Emergent patterns in an ethnographic study. In V. L. Bengtson, K. W. Schale, & L. M. Burton (Eds.), *Adult intergenerational relations: Effects of societal change,* (pp. 79–125) New York: Springer.

Burton, L. M. (1996a). Age norms, the timing of family role transitions and intergenerational caregiving among aging African American women. *Gerontologist, 36*(2), 199–208.

Burton, L. M. (1996b). The timing of childbearing, family structure and the role responsibilities of aging

Black women. In E. M. Hetherington & E. A. Blechman (Eds.), *Stress, coping and resiliency in children and families.* (pp. 155–172). Mahwah, NJ: Lawrence Erlbaum Associates.

Collins, L. V. (1996). *Facts from the Census Bureau for Black History Month.* Washington, DC: U.S. Bureau of the Census. http://www.census.gov/ftp/pub/Press-Release/blkhisl.htm/

Denby, R., & Alford, K. (1996). Understanding African American discipline styles: Suggestions for effective social work intervention. *Journal of Multicultural Social Work, 4*(3), 81–99.

Farley, R., & Allen, W. (1987). *The color line and the quality of life in America.* New York: Russell Sage Foundation.

Franklin, A. J. (1989). Therapeutic interventions with urban black adolescents. In R. Jones (Ed.), *Black adolescents,* (pp. 309–337). Berkeley, CA: Cobb & Henry.

Franklin, A. J. (1993, July/August). The invisibility syndrome. *Family Therapy Networker,* 33–39.

Hale-Benson, J. E. (1986). *Black children: Their roots, culture and learning styles.* Baltimore: Johns Hopkins University Press.

Hardy, K. V., & Laszloffy, T. A. (1998). The dynamics of a pro-racist ideology: Implications for training family therapists. In M. McGoldrick (Ed.), *Revisioning family therapy: Race, culture and gender in clinical practice.* New York: The Guilford Press.

Henderson, L. (1994). African Americans in the urban milieu: Conditions, trends, and development needs. In B. Tidwell (Ed.), *The state of Black America.* (pp. 11–26). New York: National Urban League.

Hill, R. B. (1972). *The strengths of Black families.* New York: National Urban League.

Hill, R. B. (1993). *Research on the African-American family: A holistic perspective.* Westport, CT: Auburn House.

Hines, P., (1998). Climbing up the rough side of the mountain. In M. McGoldrick (Ed.), *Revisioning family therapy: Race, culture and gender in clinical practice.* New York: The Guilford Press.

Hines, P., & Boyd-Franklin, N. (1996). African American families. In M. McGoldrick, J. Giordano, & J. Pearce (Eds.), *Ethnicity and Family Therapy* (2nd ed.), (pp. 66–84). New York: The Guilford Press.

Hines, P., Macias, C., & Perrino, T. (in press). Implementing a violence intervention for inner-city adolescents: Potential pitfalls and suggested remedies. *Journal of Prevention and Intervention in the Community.*

Hines, P., Richman, D., Hays, H., & Maxim, K. (1989). Multi-impact family therapy: An approach to working with multi-problem families. *Journal of Psychotherapy and the Family, 6,* 161–175.

Hines, P. & Sutton, C. (1998). *SANKOFA: A violence prevention curriculum.* Piscataway: University of Medicine and Dentistry of New Jersey.

Jacob, J. (1994). Black America, 1993: An overview. In Tidwell, B. (Ed.), *The state of Black America.* New York: National Urban League.

Jones, S. (1994). Silent Suffering: The plight of rural Black America. In Tidwell, B. (Ed.) *The state of Black America.* New York: National Urban League.

Jones, D., & Harrison, G. (1994). Fast facts: Comparative views of African American status and progress. In Tidwell, B. (Ed.), *The state of Black America,* (pp. 213–236). New York: National Urban League.

Karenga, M. (1988). *The African American holiday of Kwanzaa: A celebration of family, community and culture.* Los Angeles: University of Sankore Press.

Kunjufu, J. (1985). *Countering the conspiracy to destroy black boys.* Chicago: African American Images.

Lewis, J. & Looney, J. (1983). *The long struggle: Well-functioning working-class Black families.* New York: Brunner/Mazel.

Maboubi, V., & Searcy, A. (1998). Racial unity from the perspective of personal family history: Where black or white entered our families. In M. McGoldrick (Ed.), *Revisioning family therapy: Race, culture and gender in clinical practice.* New York: The Guilford Press.

Mahmoud, V. (1998). The double bind dynamics of racism. In M. McGoldrick (Ed.), *Revisioning Family Therapy: Race, culture and gender in clinical practice.* New York: The Guilford Press.

Markowitz, L. (1997, November/December). Ramon Rojano won't take no for an answer. *Family Therapy Networker,* 24–35.

Mbiti, J. S. (1970). *African religions and philosophies.* New York: Anchor.

McCall, N. (1984). *Makes me wanna holler: A young Black man in America.* New York: Random House.

Nobles, W. W. (1974). Africanity: Its role in Black families. *Black Scholar, 5,* 10–17.

Nobles, W. W. (1986). *African psychology: Towards its reclamation, reascension and revitalization.* Oakland, CA: Institute for the Advanced Study of Black Family Life and Culture.

Phillips, F. B. (1990). N. T. U. psychotherapy: An Afrocentric approach. *The Journal of Black Psychology, 71*(1), 55–74.

Pinderhughes, E. (1982). Afro-American families and the victim system. In M. McGoldrick, J. I. Pearce, & J. Giordano (Eds.), *Ethnicity and family therapy.* (pp. 108–122). New York: The Guilford Press.

Pinderhughes, E. (1989). *Race, ethnicity and power.* New York: The Free Press.

Pinderhughes. E. (1998). Black genealogy revisited: Restorying an African American family. In M. McGoldrick (Ed.), *Revisioning family therapy: Race, culture and gender in clinical practice.* New York: The Guilford Press.

Riley, D. (1993). *My soul looks back. "Lest I forget": A collection of quotations by people of color.* New York: HarperCollins.

Roberts, S. (1993). *Who we are: A portrait of America based on the latest U.S. Census.* New York: Times Books.

Rowe, D., & Grills, C. (1993). African centered drug treatment: An alternative conceptual paradigm for drug counseling with African-American clients. *Journal of Psychoactive Drugs, 25*(1), 21–33.

Staples, R. (1985, November). Changes in black family structure: The conflict between family ideology and structural conditions. *Journal of Marriage and the Family* 1005–1013.

Status of African-American children under three living in poverty. (1992). *Child Poverty News, 2*(3). http://ciat.cpmc.columbia.edu:88/news/childpov/new:0054.html

U. S. Bureau of the Census. (1995). *The black population in the United States: March 1995.* Washington, DC: Government Printing Office.

U.S. Bureau of the Census (1996). Annual Demographic Survey, March Supplement. Revised September 26. Contact (pop@census.gov).

Ventura, S. J., Taffel, S. M., Mosha, W. D., et al, (1992). Trends in pregnancies and pregnancy rates: Estimates for the United States: 1980–1992. *Monthly Vital Statistics Report 43*(11).

Watson, M. (1998). African American Siblings. In M. McGoldrick (Ed.), *Revisioning family therapy: Race, culture and gender in clinical practice.* New York: The Guilford Press.

Williams, J. C. (1997). Introduction to the Tarajia Saba: Values to promote family healing. Paper presented at the Association of Black Psychologists 29th Annual Convention, Washington, DC.

Wilson, J. (1997). *When work disappears.* New York: Vintage.

Wright Edelman, M. (1997). An advocacy agenda for Black families and children. In H. P. McAdoo (Ed.), *Black families* (3rd ed.), (pp. 323-332). Thousand Oaks, CA: Sage.

CHAPTER 20

LESBIANS, GAY MEN, AND THE FAMILY LIFE CYCLE

THOMAS W. JOHNSON
PATRICIA COLUCCI

This disease will be the end of many of us, but not nearly all, and the dead will be commemorated and will struggle on with the living, and we are not going away. We won't die secret deaths anymore. The world only spins forward. We will be citizens. The time has come.

—Tony Kushner (1992)

Popular culture has historically portrayed lesbians and gay men as denizens of a subcultural world divorced from "the family." Few images exist of lesbian daughters or gay sons sitting on a family porch sipping iced tea with Mom and Dad or walking a daughter down the aisle on her wedding day. Lesbians and gays are more typically painted as eternally single adults cruising from one failed relationship to another or as underground couples coming into the light only in the "gay ghettoes" of the Castro District, Provincetown, or Northampton, Massachusetts (dubbed "Lesbianville" by the TV show *20/20*). Fortunately, popular stories and images of lesbian/gay life (or, more exactly, "lives," as there really is no prototypic lesbian/gay community) are changing and becoming less marginal. For example, two recent popular-run movies show lesbians and gays in the American mainstream and also in the context of family: *Home for the Holidays* (1995) offers a gay male character who maintains close attachments to a family of origin, to a male lover, and to a family of choice. Likewise, in the *Incredibly True Adventures of Two Girls in Love* (1996), two lesbian adolescents are portrayed in the contexts of family of origin, fam-

ily of choice, and their newly discovered romantic relationship with each other. Given cultural evidence like these films, clearly, the word is out that family is as integral a component of lesbian or gay life as it is for a heterosexual one. However, even though the construct of "family" is being applied more often to lesbian/gay life, dominant opinion maintains that their structures and norms are idiosyncratic and strikingly different from those of heterosexual family life. For example, from a lesbian/gay perspective, clinicians such as Slater (1995) and Siegel and Lowe (1994), claim that the families created by lesbians and gays are invented or reinvented entities, inconsistent with heterosexual family institutions.

It is our premise, like that of Laird (1993) and Lukes and Land (1990), that lesbians and gays are bicultural. They are reared in the same dominant culture as heterosexuals and have internalized the same sets of norms, values, and beliefs. They belong to mainstream families and use some of the same premises of family life as their heterosexual kin. But at the same time, lesbians and gays add a unique spin to this heritage because of their experiences with homophobia and with the special circumstances created by same-sex pairing. Following this track, we believe that gays and lesbians are part of a complex multigenerational family system consisting of a family of origin, a multigenerational lesbian/gay community, and/or a family of choice that consists of friends, partners, and/or children.

The family life cycle notion (Carter & McGoldrick, 1980, 1988) and the multicontextual framework (Carter, 1992) are useful heuristic constructs for charting a three- or four-generational family's movement across time and across the overarching space of culture. These constructs can be applied usefully to the lives of lesbian and gay people in relation to the families in which they were raised. This will, in part, be the focus of this chapter. However, it is also useful to explore how the same-sex couple relationship, the lesbian/gay parenting system, or the family of choice are integrated or not integrated in the multigenerational extended family across all stages of the family life cycle.

Some lesbian/gay family clinicians and researchers (Siegel & Lowe, 1994; Slater & Mencher, 1991) argue that the popular family life cycle models do not apply to lesbians and gays. Because these mainstream models are based on heterosexual experience and traditional Judeo-Christian values, they have a number of serious validity problems relative to the lesbian/gay context. Slater (1995) outlines the problems. First, she claims that these models assume that child-rearing is the *raison d'etre* of family life. Although there is a current lesbian/gay baby boom, parenting is not a cornerstone of homosexual family life. For many lesbians and gays, the couple relationship or the network of relationships with close friends constitutes a complete family unit. We suspect that this is also the case for many heterosexual people.

The second problem that Slater notes appears in the definition of what constitutes family in these popular models. The criteria usually revolve around blood and legal ties. The research of anthropologist Kath Weston (1991) indicates that lesbians and gay men use broader criteria to define their families. Often, close friends are enumerated as family members and compose a "family of choice" or a "family of creation."

A third problem mentioned by Slater is that the dominant family life cycle models assume that a key function of intergenerational relationships lies in the transmission of norms, rituals, values, prescriptions, and folk wisdom from one generation to the next, all in the service of promoting continuity of the family over time. This applies in part to lesbians and gays, for they are also members of blood families that persist across time. However, no assistance and guidance are provided through biological or adoptive family legacies about how to survive and flourish in the world as a lesbian or gay person. As Martin (1982) notes, lesbians and gays belong to a minority group of which their families are usually not members. This also applies to lesbian and gay parents when they do not share a minority group identity with their heterosexual children.

A fourth problem that Slater sees occurs in the importance of rituals in the family life cycle (Imber-Black & Roberts, 1992). Family rituals and traditions often serve as points of punctuation that note and celebrate life passages in the context of family. The repertoire of rituals in any given family frequently excludes important life transitions for lesbians and gay family members. For example, it is a rare extended-family system that holds a shower or a wedding for a gay or lesbian family member (Imber-Black & Roberts, 1992).

A fifth problem with the dominant family life cycle models, as noted by Slater, appears in the lack of language and norms for various aspects of lesbian and gay life in the context of the family of origin. For example, there is no formal name for the relationship between a mother and her lesbian daughter's life-partner. Similarly there is no consensus on the name for the daughter's partner in her couple relationship: Is she a girlfriend, a lover, a life-partner? In addition, when a lesbian couple moves into parenthood through the alternative insemination of one of its members, what is the name for the non-birth mother? What is the name for the relationship between the second mother's parents and her child? In this situation, the absence of norms (and, of course, homophobia) might allow the second mother's family to take a position of marginalization or nonrecognition of her child. A marginalizing dominant culture might view this second mother as an unattached single adult who has no relational claims upon her but those of her family of origin.

The critique of the dominant family life cycle model offered by clinical researchers such as Slater has great usefulness. However, we are not ready to discard the model, but rather seek to amend and extend it to make a better fit with a lesbian or gay life.

We will use the family life cycle format devised by Carter and McGoldrick (1980, 1988) and look at each stage in turn with two lenses: (1) a lesbian/gay lens that looks at the unique lesbian/gay cast to the experiences and issues involved for persons at each stage of the family life cycle and (2) a family system lens that looks at the multigenerational impact of the life cycle experiences of lesbian and gay members. Putting the lesbian/gay family member in the subject position, we will use the following life cycle sequence: adolescence, leaving home: single young adulthood, coupling, parenting, and mid-life/later life.

ADOLESCENCE

Adolescence is confusing and destabilizing enough for most families, but when a child discovers that she or he is lesbian or gay, the tumult becomes even more acute for the adolescent and also for the family if they learn of their child's identity. The upheaval for the child revolves around the anxiety, shame, and disorientation they face when they recognize that a stigmatized and devalued sexuality is a part of their own personal repertoire of feeling and experience (Martin, 1982). Often, the lesbian/gay child must master this challenge on his or her own because of fears about the reactions of family and friends. The isolation, stigmatization, and confusion may account for the high rate of suicidal behavior among lesbian/gay youngsters. Various studies (Herdt, 1989; see also the summary in Savin-Williams, 1996) report that 20 to 40 percent of lesbian/gay youths make suicide attempts and that these youths are two to three times more likely to kill themselves than are their heterosexual counterparts.

Lesbian and gay identity development is a complicated process that entails cognitive, behavioral, and affective shifts, not necessarily in a clear, continuous order. The identity development process can commence at any age, given that some people do not experience homosexual desire or affiliation until adulthood or even in later life. A number of models have been developed to chart this process (see Scrivener & Eldridge, 1995, for a summary), but the most popular is the model developed by Australian psychologist Vivienne Cass (1979). Cass maintains that lesbians and gay men pass through six stages of an increasingly consolidating lesbian/gay identity. Cass's model has been subject to social constructionist critique (Laird, 1993; Sophie, 1985–1986), given that many postmodern theorists have trouble with the continuous, progressive, ahistorical, noncultural nature of development models (Gergen, 1982; Hoffman, 1993). There is also considerable diversity by gender, class, race, and culture in how lesbian/gay identity develops. For example, adolescent lesbians typically recognize homosexual desire and experiment with homosexual activity later than gay male adolescents do (Boxer, Cook, & Herdt, 1989, cited in Savin-Williams, 1996). In terms of race, class, and culture, some minority lesbian and gay adolescents may give racial or cultural identities greater importance and put homosexual identity in the background (Morales, 1990).

Lesbian and gay adolescents face the same individuation tasks as heterosexual ones, but they have less assistance from the family in rehearsing and planning for an adult life in that the family cannot help in figuring out how to live a lesbian/gay life. Adolescent dating rituals such as planning for the prom and going steady become meaningless activities for the lesbian/gay adolescent who is forced to pass as heterosexual. Group identification becomes a source of pain for the lesbian/gay adolescent who is struggling to find a place to belong.

If a lesbian/gay adolescent discloses either consciously or inadvertently to the family, all hell often breaks loose. Families may immediately become disoriented and alienated from their child (Fairchild & Hayward, 1979; Johnson, 1992), and litanies of self-blame and guilt emerge as parents scan the past to figure out "where we went wrong." Numerous studies report a high frequency of violence, threats, and expulsion after a family learns of the homosexuality of an adolescent son or daughter (Herdt & Boxer, 1993; Martin & Hetrick, 1988; Savin-Williams, 1994). It is estimated that 50 percent of homeless teens are lesbian/gay (*20/ 20*, 1992). One way to understand the family's strong reactions is to look at the influence of the larger homophobic and heterosexist culture that stigmatizes a lesbian/gay child and explains the source of the identity as failed and defective parenting. Even when families are more even-tempered, there is still a tremendous anxiety about the child's safety in relation to an antagonistic dominant culture and a lesbian/gay community that is perceived as predatory. Parents of homosexual adolescents struggle with anxiety about their child's foray into the world, but the world is perceived as even more dangerous and unknown for lesbian/gay teens. Normal parental anxiety about an adolescent becomes even more acute for parents of lesbian/ gay teens. Many of the lesbian/gay teens we have worked with experience overprotectiveness from their families, and they are blocked from important adolescent experiences that prepare them for adult lesbian/gay life. Parents seem particularly anxious about allowing their children to join lesbian/gay adolescent support groups because of worries about recruitment, exploitation, and exposure to HIV. However, these groups are critical in helping a lesbian/gay adolescent to develop a sense of normalcy and belonging. Given all of this strong reactivity in a family, it is wise for a therapist to tread very slowly and carefully around the issue of adolescent disclosure to the family.

> Katie's family placed her in a psychiatric hospital at the age of 13 after a period of depression in which she began to experience academic decline, social withdrawal, and suicidal urges. She was given a diagnosis of major depression and borderline personality disorder and placed on medications. After discharge from the hospital, she confided in her outpatient therapist that she thought she might be a lesbian. During the months

she became depressed, she had developed a crush on a female schoolmate. She explained that they had been dating—spending time at the movies and shopping mall. But at the same time, she was afraid that if her mother found out, she would be disappointed, and that if her large network of aunts and uncles found out, they would think she was crazy. She had often heard her family make disparaging remarks about homosexuality. The therapist focused on creating an atmosphere of safety for Katie—a place where her homosexual desires were normalized and she could examine the complexity of all of her sexual feelings, including attraction to boys. In addition, the therapist met with the family to alleviate their anxiety about Katie and to work out how they could best support their daughter. Katie made the decision not to disclose her sexual orientation issues at this time. The therapist agreed that because of her age and her own lack of comfort with her emerging sexual orientation, it made sense for Katie to postpone disclosure to her parents until a more appropriate stage in her own development.

LEAVING HOME/SINGLE YOUNG ADULTHOOD

According to Carter and McGoldrick (1980, 1988), the tasks faced by an emancipating young adult in the "leaving home" phase of the life cycle revolve around the development of emotional and financial responsibility for self, the establishment of a beginning vocational identity, the initiation of adult intimate relationships, and the commencement of a process of differentiation of self. The second-order changes experienced by the family include renegotiation of the parenting system, movement toward adult-to-adult relationships with grown children, and adjustment to the entrances into and exits from the system relevant to later life. For the young adult lesbian or gay person, the tasks of this developmental stage, as in adolescence, can become even more complicated as they continue to handle simultaneously the normative demands of young adult identity development, the intricacies of lesbian/gay identity development, and the stresses of living in a stigmatizing larger culture. Lesbian and gay identity clearly affects the dating experience, but it can also color the choices the young adult makes in terms of work and friendship. Some lesbian/gay adults may opt for a split-self adaptation (straight to the world but gay to the self) and appear to adjust well to the demands of young adulthood. However low-level anxiety may persist under the competent veneer that relates to feelings of fraudulence or to fears of being found out. Identity conflicts may also have a significant impact on attempts to explore couple relationships.

> Eve is a 30-year-old woman who presented for therapy with confusion about her sexuality. She had just recently ended a three-year relationship with a woman. Although saddened by the loss, Eve was relieved because she felt that it was much easier to be heterosexual than to be a lesbian. Eve was not out at work, nor was she out to her family. At work, she worried that she would be looked over for promotions or she would lose her job if her homosexuality were discovered. With regard to her family, Eve wondered whether they knew at some level about her relationship with her ex-lover, but she was determined that she would never confirm their suspicions. She was not worried that her parents would cut her off if she came out to them, but she was anguished over the probability that they would feel they had failed as parents. She stated, "Why should I put them through any unnecessary pain?" In terms of friendships, Eve had a few lesbian friends, but she never felt able to discuss her struggle around accepting her sexuality.

Eve's singlehood allowed her to pass as a heterosexual woman, for there was no other person to account for within her family and in her relationships with co-workers. Moreover, there was no other person to push her to move further with her identity struggle.

Schwartzberg, Berliner, and Jacob (1995) maintain that regardless of sexual orientation or gender, singlehood affects a person's place in society as well as in the family. For example, singles are often seen as eternal young adults who are still not fully functioning adults. Thus, it may be easier for families to ignore their son or daughter's homosexuality when they are not coupled. The family may take the position that their child is "just going through a phase" or hasn't met the right opposite-sex partner who will help the person "straighten out." Singlehood and nondisclosure to the family allow the system to continue to assume that the child is straight.

Dating in the lesbian/gay world is as wild, wonderful, and horrible an experience as it is in the straight world. However, there are different norms about parity, about sex, and about gender role functioning in the lesbian/gay world that the young adult needs to learn. There are no resources for this knowledge other than the lesbian/gay communities, given that parents certainly cannot help here. Dating and coupling can also be confounding when coupling partners are at different stages of identity development. In these situations, it is helpful to encourage the couple to access support and social connections in order to normalize some of the problems and to reality-test about some negative assumptions about the lesbian/gay communities. It is also helpful for the therapist to remind the couple that the "enemy" is the larger homophobic culture that colors their emotional relational functioning, and not each other.

Conflict over a young adult child's homosexuality can have second-order effects on the family. Parents may become so absorbed in their reactivity that they lose track of other important processes such as the renegotiation of their own relationship, the recognition of the shifting roles and functioning of older relatives, or reevaluation of their priorities for the next stage of life. In some cases, lesbian/gay young adults are forced out of the system because of unremitting conflict, and they are deprived of participation in the restructuring of the family and in the relevant rituals of families in later life (such as retirement, the birth of grandchildren, or second-career decisions of midlife parents). The reactivity typically faced by parents of young adult lesbians and gays is fairly similar to the experiences of lesbian/gay adolescents. The only difference is that the parents' ability to exert control over the child's life has diminished, and at this point of life, their child is fairly able to survive with or without their blessing. Fortunately, many families are able to move through this process and find a way to accept and adjust to their child's homosexuality; but some parents do not, and denial remains a persisting stance (Cramer & Roach, 1988; Griffin, Wirth, & Wirth, 1986; Johnson, 1992; Robinson, Walters, & Skeen, 1989).

COUPLING

Coupling is a life endeavor that is filled with complexity for all couples, straight or lesbian/gay. But there are issues that are unique to lesbian and gay couples that derive from the special nature of same-sex pairing and from the adaptation that lesbian/gay couples make to a devaluing larger culture. Specifically, there are no legal protections for lesbian/gay couples and no set of socially prescribed rituals to support and guide couple functioning. However, there are couple issues that lesbians and gays face in common with straight couples: the influence of the family of origin, the impact of other external systems such as minority cultures and dominant culture, the prescriptions supplied by gender socialization, and the decision about whether or not to have children.

Like all couples, lesbians and gays are subject to the effects of family of origin relationships. Very rarely, however, do we speak, read, or hear about lesbians or gay men in an extended family context (Laird, 1996). We believe that the family of origin is the most powerful emotional system in a lesbian/gay life as it is in a heterosexual one. In terms of couple relationships, the family of origin provides a blueprint for life and sets the stage for the ways in which people connect and relate (Carter & Orfanidis, 1976).

According to Bowen systems theory (Bowen, 1978), the ability of partners in all couple relationships to develop and maintain authentic relationships with the family of origin is crucial for the well-being and satisfaction of the couple. This is no less important for lesbian and gay couples. Iasenza, Colucci, and Rothberg (1996) write, "disclosing and integrating one's lesbian identity into one's family of origin is necessary for an individual to develop authentic, differentiated relationships with family members" (p. 125). Obviously, this also applies to gay men.

However, this is easier said than done, given a family's reactivity. The way in which a family responds to a daughter or son's homosexuality is multiply determined. Variables such as the history of a system's management of difference, the level of systemic openness/closedness, and the degree of differentiation of the members of the extended system all affect the system's response. The family reaction to a lesbian daughter or gay son's disclosure and to her/his couple relationship is informed by all of these variables as is the daughter or son's response. In terms of couplehood, there are many parents who are genuinely happy about a lesbian/gay child's finding a relationship and participate in the celebration of the joining of the couple. For other families, their daughter or son's couplehood may serve as a living and breathing reminder of their child's homosexuality, which forces the family to move out of a position of denial or distance and wrestle once again with their reactivity. Some families take ultimatum positions and standoff positions such as not allowing their child's partner in their home. In extreme cases, some families may utilize a cut-off. Bowen (1978) maintains that the family response will have an effect on the couple relationship. For example, a cut-off may create tension and conflict around separation in a couple, as the disengaged member "puts all their eggs in the basket" of the couple relationship.

> Nadine and Lee had been together for about two years when they presented for couples therapy. Nadine reported that Lee would become anxiety-ridden whenever Nadine was involved in separate activities or would ask for "space" for herself. Lee explained that Nadine was her prime source of relationship in that she had left her home in the suburbs to live with Nadine in the city. She also explained that she had not seen her siblings or her mother in about fifteen years because of conflicts over her homosexuality. Lee's three young adult sons had also become enraged at her for moving in with Nadine, and she stopped speaking with them.

It is important to note that many of Bowen's premises have been subject to a feminist critique (Laird, 1993; Lupenitz, 1988), which claims that his ideas are gender-biased. Unfortunately, Bowen never discussed the fact that women are socialized to be adaptive and deferential to others, not considering their own needs and values first. This, of course, is the very definition of lack of differentiation. Similarly, Laird (1993) and Green, Bettinger, and Zacks (1996) challenge the notion that family of origin adaptations make or break couple relationships for lesbian couples. However, as Laird notes (1993, 1996), the family of origin relationship certainly represents an important theme in the stories of lesbian and gay couples and an important source of stress for these couples to master.

The external system of the larger dominant culture also wields considerable importance in lesbian/gay coupling. Stories about the impact of harassment, anti-lesbian/gay violence, and exclusion from key legal protections and entitlements (e.g. domestic partner benefits) are unfortunately abundantly available. The discriminatory practices and threats influence the couple process in a number of ways. For example, Krestan and Bepko (1980) noted that these dangers bring a couple closer in a "two-against-the-world" adaptation that leaves them at risk for fusion. Other clinicians (Mencher, 1990) maintain that this cohesion is a functional response that shores up couple survival and strength. Other clinicians contend that societal homophobia has a divisive effect and serves as an undermining force that can drive couples apart (Johnson & Keren, 1996; Krestan & Bepko, 1980).

Surrounding lesbian/gay communities also plan an important part in lesbian/gay coupling. Some literature underscores the supportive function of the surrounding lesbian/gay community (Weston, 1991); other literature indicates that the lesbian/gay communities may have shifting positions about sexually exclusive couple relationships that may be antagonistic to committed coupling (Johnson & Keren, 1996; Krestan & Bepko, 1980). Some of the norms of the lesbian/gay community also affect couple process. For example, there have been varying norms in the gay community about monogamy (Green et al., 1996; Johnson & Keren, 1996) that affect the contracts that male couples establish around sexual openness or exclusivity.

These norms are discussed in the literature (Blasband & Peplau, 1985; Kurdek & Schmitt, 1985–1986) but are not well known, especially by straight therapists. Naturally, a reactive response by the therapist to non-monogamous contracts would have a negative impact on the clients, so it is important for the clinician to be open to the couple's viewpoints regarding monogomy, and to reflect critically on his or her own biases and values.

Many lesbians and gays belong to other minority communities aside from the homosexual one. For example, lesbians and gays of color manage multiple loyalties and may not necessarily hold their lesbian/gay identity as primary. Other cultures may have strong prohibitions about homosexuality that at times place the lesbian or gay man of color in a difficult bind: Does she or he affiliate with lesbian or gay communities and run the risk of losing family support which represents the loss of an important lifeline when living in a hostile dominant culture? This dilemma may arise dramatically in a couple relationship, particularly in an interracial relationship, when the couple must struggle with the issue of how visible/invisible to be in the context of the extended family and the minority community.

Gender socialization also plays a part in lesbian and gay couples. Blumstein and Schwartz's (1983) landmark study of homosexual, lesbian, and gay couples and how they handle the core issues of couple life—money, work, and sex—points to the influence of gender scripts in all relationships. For example, there is a marked difference between lesbian couples and gay male couples in terms of power distribution. Lesbian couples depart from the dominant culture formula for couples that "money = power," which historically has given authority to heterosexual men because of their higher wage-earning privilege. Blumstein and Schwartz found that the balance of power in lesbian couples is not determined by either woman's income, since the female couples strive for equality in their couplehood. Roth (1989) reports that lesbian couples make all sorts of creative and intricate financial arrangements to avoid power imbalances in decision making and planning. However, further study with a more contemporary sample is warranted to determine whether these findings still hold up.

Stacey and Maureen have lived together in a committed relationship for ten years. Theirs had always been a two-income household until recently, when Maureen decided to go back to school. The agreement was that Stacey would financially support the household until Maureen completed her studies. Upon earning her degree, Maureen would work and Stacey would leave her teaching position to pursue a career in writing. Although both women had access to a joint account, Maureen felt compelled to ask Stacey for money and had a difficult time doing so. She often found herself "without a dime." This was very stressful for Maureen, and the couple began to argue. Upon learning the source of Maureen's stress, the couple set up a "cookie jar" system. There was always enough money in the cookie jar if either member of the couple ran short throughout the week. This allowed Maureen to go to their pooled assets instead of to Stacey, which decreased her anxiety tremendously.

Money and power are also a source of tension for gay men. Men are accustomed to earning their own income, controlling their own purse-strings, and making their own decisions (Blumstein & Schwartz, 1983). In fact, as in heterosexual couples, in male couples, the higher income earner often holds more power in the system.

James and David had been in a committed relationship for seven years. David was not out to his family, while James was out and accepted by all family members. The couple decided to buy a house six years into their relationship. Up to that point, David's family thought that he lived alone. Upon buying the house, trouble emerged in the couple. David began having sex with other men, in spite of their agreement on monogamy. The arguing and tension between the couple escalated to the point at which they came into therapy, feeling confident that the relationship would probably end. Eventually, David revealed that he had made a "big mistake" in purchasing the home with James. He wanted to buy James out, and maintain the relationship as the sole owner of the home, with James

continuing to live with him. He felt that co-owning property was too complicated. He also was at a loss in terms of explaining to his family who James was. If he was the sole proprietor of the house, he would feel more in control of himself and his family. He felt he could then run his life the way he wanted to.

In their findings about sex, Blumstein and Schwartz (1983) reported that sexual frequency and compatibility were not important factors in relationship satisfaction for lesbian and gay couples, in comparison to heterosexual couples. Norms regarding sex were different. For example, outside sexual encounters were not associated with relational difficulties in male couples. Kurdek and Schmitt (1985–86) as well as Blasband and Peplau (1985) supported Blumstein and Schwartz's findings that nonmonogamy in male couples was not necessarily a signal of couple dysfunction. Blumstein and Schwartz offer the following explanation: For gay men, like all men following traditional gender scripting, sex can be recreational as well as relational, and "outside sex" may not necessarily have the same negative valence and be threatening to a couple relationship from a male perspective. Similarly, Blumstein and Schwartz found that lesbian couples had a lower rate of sexual frequency compared to the other couples, but this was not associated with couple dissatisfaction. A critique of Blumstein and Schwartz's research (Frye, 1987; Loulan, 1987) maintains that the examiners used phallocentric criteria to measure sexual functioning and that perhaps nongenital intimacy was an important but unmeasured aspect of sexual functioning for the female couples in the study. However, Blumstein and Schwartz's premise for this finding was again, as for male couples, a gender socialization perspective: that women in our culture are not socialized to be sexual initiators and that this effect is potentiated when two women couple. It is important to note here that Blumstein and Schwartz collected their data in the 1970s; the results may be quite different now, a situation that argues for the importance of a replication of their study with a 1990s sample.

PARENTING

There are up to 5 million lesbian mothers and up to 3 million gay fathers in the United States (Patterson, 1992). This figure includes children born to mothers and fathers who had previously been in heterosexual relationships. Over the past ten years, however, more and more lesbians and gay men are choosing to have children either as single parents or within the context of their couple relationship. This recent baby boom poses new challenges for lesbians and gay men.

The challenge commences for lesbian/gay couples, as for heterosexual ones, during the initial negotiation and decision-making period of having children. However, there are some issues that are unique to the lesbian/gay couple. For example, numerous options are available for expanding one's family either as a single adult or as a couple: alternative insemination with a known or an unknown donor, conceiving with a donor who will or will not assume a co-parenting role, domestic or foreign adoption, and developing a contract with a surrogate. Selecting a method from a wealth of alternatives for bringing a child into a family is a challenge that most heterosexuals do not encounter, except for couples dealing with infertility and single heterosexuals. Lesbians who choose the route of alternative insemination, with the aid of a physician, must be very careful in selecting a fertility specialist, since there are many physicians who still discriminate against lesbians having children.

Mary and Jean had been together for ten years before deciding to have a child. They decided to consult a fertility expert in their community who had an excellent reputation in terms of medically assisting women to achieve pregnancy. In the initial consultation, when they identified themselves as a same sex couple, the doctor questioned whether the couple had really thought this through. She lectured that it was okay for them to be in a committed relationship, but was it fair to bring a child into it? Mary and Jean were devastated. They had worked hard and long to achieve a positive identity as individuals and as a couple and had been able to develop positive extended-family relationships over the years. While Jean was able to externalize

her anger at the doctor, Mary began to think that perhaps they were making a mistake.

There are physicians who will work with lesbian couples only if they choose to use frozen sperm from a sperm bank. These conditions place lesbians in a disempowered position, with the physician superimposing her or his ethics and morals on the couple.

Some lesbians and gay men decide to conceive a child together (through a variety of methods) as an opposite-sex pair and to share the experience of parenting together. There are no role or relational prescriptions for such family constellations, leaving the process open for the parenting team to develop their own personally constructed family of creation system (Weston, 1991). However, the families of origin of the parenting team need extensive support, information, and space for emotional ventilation in integrating this alternative family constellation. The families may lag behind their lesbian/gay family members in appreciating the validity of revised and reconstructed norms for family life.

In terms of adoption, there is also considerable work for pre-parents in contending with cultural homophobia. For example, many adoption agencies will not work with lesbian or gay individuals. Some are overtly homophobic, and others will discourage lesbians and gay men from applying to their agency.

Judy and Shelly had tried for several years to have a child. Shelly was unable to carry children for medical reasons, and Judy, after several months of alternative insemination, was not able to conceive. The couple decided that they would let go of the idea of Judy getting pregnant and adopt a child. They decided to apply for international adoption. Judy and Shelly thought that it made sense to work with the same adoption agency as Shelly's brother and sister-in-law, who had adopted a child three years earlier. The director of the agency was very warm and inviting when Shelly made the initial call. When Shelly informed the director that she and her partner were lesbians, the director immediately discouraged Shelly from applying to the agency. She said that the agency did not work with lesbians and hung up on Shelly.

Couples choosing to adopt must also decide who will be named by the courts as the legally adoptive parent. In 1995, New York became only the third state, after Vermont and Massachusetts, whose highest court recognizes the right of unmarried homosexual and heterosexual couples to adopt children.

Selecting the parenting method is only the first step in the lesbian or gay man's parenting journey. Other relational complexities need to be addressed. For lesbian couples who choose alternative insemination there are options in terms of who will become pregnant. For many couples, the decision is influenced by the age of each partner, the health care benefits, the career development and income level of each partner, and each partner's health status. Some couples choose for both partners to become pregnant at the same time (Martin, 1993) or sequentially. For couples choosing the surrogacy route, there are relational tasks to tackle. For example, a major decision for the male couple choosing this route revolves around deciding whose sperm to use. Like lesbian couples choosing pregnancy, gay couples must sort through each partner's personal investment in conception. In addition, practical factors such as the morphology and motility of the sperm have to be considered.

The reaction of a family of origin to the news of a grandchild is usually a joyous moment for all, but this is not always the case in lesbian and gay families. A baby can bring up concerns about increased visibility for the lesbian/gay member or for the extended family. For some families, this is the first time they talk out loud about their child's homosexuality and thus have to negotiate from square one about their unresolved reactivity to their child's stigmatized sexuality. Many families embrace their child and her/his partner but do not have a clue about how and what to tell friends and neighbors in terms of the baby. And of course, there are families that will accept their child and her or his partner openly and lovingly and look forward to the arrival of their grandchild.

It is important to note here that the coming-out process for lesbians and gays is not a one-time "let people know and be done with it" kind of affair. Families often need time to integrate their child's homosexuality into the system. Therefore, for lesbians and gay men, coming out to the family should precede expanding one's nuclear family. Ideally, this will prepare families to embrace their new granddaughter or grandson with more open arms.

In terms of second-order family process, the role of the biological or adoptive parent is clear. However, the nonbiological or nonadoptive parent's role is often blurred. Slater (1995) writes that the lack of legal protection and the lack of roles and language leave lesbian and gay families vulnerable to intrusion and invalidation. For example, there is no universal language in the lesbian/gay community for figuring out what to call the nonbiological or nonadoptive parent, or determining how to refer to the co-parent's family of origin. Each family unit is unique in how they refer to their family and what the child will call them. For example, one family may choose "Daddy" and "Papa"; another family may choose to have the child call both parents by their first names. Couples may select a name that is symbolic to the individual or couple. Grandparents might also experience confusion in how to refer to themselves in relation to the grandchild and knowing what, in fact, their role to the child is. They may struggle with what to call themselves if they are the parents of the nonbiological or nonadoptive parent. The nonbiological grandparents may fear that they will not have access to the child if the couple separates, and may distance themselves as a means of protection.

Given all of this complexity, it is very important that all lesbian and gay individuals seek legal counsel before or shortly after a child arrives in their lives. As Martin (1993) maintains, it is not illegal for lesbians and gay men to have families with children; however, they are not legally recognized as families. Children are still removed from their lesbian/gay parents' homes because of their parents' sexuality. And there is no built in legal protection for the nonbiological or nonadoptive parent. However, lesbian and gay couples can take measures to safeguard their families legally. For example, in some states, second-parent adoption rights are being pursued through court decisions. Consultation with a local lesbian/gay community center can provide information about lawyers who are well prepared for these judicial undertakings.

Because there are so many potential stresses and strains for lesbian/gay families, a great deal of anxiety wells up in the dominant culture about the welfare of the children raised in these homes. Patterson (1996) studied child development in lesbian families, and her results indicate that child development proceeds normally in lesbian households. Only recently have researchers begun to study the parenting styles of gay fathers and their relationships with their children (Bigner, 1996; Dunne, 1987).

Because of the potential for stress and strain due to cultural homophobia and heterosexism, it is important that lesbians and gay men who either have children or are thinking about having children join community support groups composed of other lesbians and gay men who have the same goal. In addition to providing of support to one another, these networks also serve as a valuable source of information.

It is crucial to recognize here that infertility is as compelling an issue in the lesbian/gay community as it is in the heterosexual world (Brown, 1991). However, there are issues that are unique to lesbians and gay men dealing with infertility, such as the lack of support from the family as well as from the larger system because of cultural resistance to lesbian/gay parenthood. In addition, because of the novelty of the lesbian/gay baby boom, resources and support in the lesbian and gay communities around this issue may be limited. Support groups for lesbians and gay men with fertility problems need to be developed.

MIDLIFE/LATER LIFE

Walsh (1988) provides a thorough picture of the tasks that lie before a multigenerational system dealing with the aging of its members. She indicates that families meet the following challenges at this point in life: (1) launching young adult members; (2) recasting family process and norms as young adults leave home, as various members age, and as other members dies; (3) re-visioning the self to suit the vicissitudes of midlife and later life; (4) adapting to changes regarding work and income for aging family members; (5) adjusting to loss; and (6) addressing concerns about generativity and legacy, which include adaptation to grandparenthood in many families.

Some of these tasks and processes are less relevant for or are handled differently in various families because of diversity in terms of race, culture, and class. For example, a poor or working-class older adult may not have the luxury of addressing the re-visioning of self because his or her time and energy are spent in making ends meet or in helping younger generations with financial pressures. In other families, launching may not be as dramatic a point of family punctuation as it is in white European families. In other cultures, role prescriptions are so defined and compelling that there really is no role or task negotiation process. Considerable research has been published about this cross-cultural perspective on aging (see Johnson, 1995 for a review). There is also variation in family's adaptation to the aging process when a family member is lesbian or gay. Four themes are important in understanding the unique lesbian and gay issues.

The history of the lesbian/gay person's relationship with the family is a key theme. Families and their gay and lesbian members adapt to each other over time with a broad variety of arrangements (Johnson, 1992). Some lesbian/gay family members split their lives into the gay life and the straight life and never disclose their true sexuality to family. Included in this group are married lesbians and gays who maintain underground homosexual lives. Other lesbian/gay members disclose fully, but their families never adjust or accept beyond an adaptation of denial and cut-off. Still other lesbians and gays are fortunate enough to have families that accept and accommodate. And many lesbians and gay men maintain relationships with families that are somewhere between the last two styles of adaptation.

History on a broader sociocultural level also plays an influential part in the family history of the older lesbian/gay member. For example, before the lesbian/gay liberation marker of the Stonewall Riots in 1969, many lesbians and gays led "lives of quiet nonconformity" (Kimmel & Sang, 1995, p. 190), in which there were numerous dangers and hurdles in disclosing one's sexuality to family, friends, and co-workers. Most midlife and older lesbians and gays in the 1990s reached sexual maturity before Stonewall, so their lesbian/gay narratives may be more colored by secrecy and privacy about their sexuality, especially in terms of family relationships, than those of their younger counterparts.

The family of choice also is an important variable in understanding a gay son or lesbian daughter's historical relationship with the family of origin. Literature on lesbian/gay aging reports that many midlife and older lesbians and gays rely heavily on a network of close friends when it comes to providing and receiving instrumental and emotional assistance (Friend, 1991; Kehoe, 1989; Kimmel & Sang, 1995; Reid, 1995; Tully, 1989). Weston (1991) refers to this network as the "chosen family." This system may serve as the figure in a midlife lesbian or gay man's life while the family of origin remains as the ground. However, it is important to recognize that figure/ground relationships are not static; they can shift back and forth over a lifetime.

Chosen families may exert as much claim upon a lesbian or gay man's loyalty as the family of origin, and they may supply resources and support that are missing from traditional family relationships. The frequency with which chosen families have been primary caregivers to gays and lesbians with serious illness such as AIDS or breast cancer offers a striking example of this point.

One possible net effect of the complexity of negotiating family acceptance when the support provided by the family of choice may be so much easier to obtain is the development of distance and formal relatedness in family of origin relationships. However, the aging process may disrupt this stable distant family functioning. For example, a gay man, long accustomed to an emotionally and geographically separate life from his family, may face disorientation and anxiety when called upon to help in the care of an elderly parent with Alzhe-

imer's disease. A longstanding distance is violated with the intimacy that is required in this kind of caregiving. Or an older lesbian might not think of accessing family support after a diagnosis of cancer if she is used to counting on her friends for care rather than her siblings. Renewed contact with the family may stir up unresolved battles and wounds for everyone in the family.

> Max, a gay man in his late seventies, had never disclosed his sexuality to anyone over the course of his life. He worked in a large urban area but lived in the country with his elderly parents until they died. His experience with the gay world consisted of anonymous sexual encounters with men, and his life revolved around work and caring for his immigrant parents. In later life, his brother and his nephew began to pursue a closer relationship with him. This intensified after he suffered a heart attack in that they wanted to help him more with his day-to-day burdens. Max was used to independence and self-sufficiency, and with some guilt, he resisted his family's overtures. His primary physician pressured him to give up some of the chores he performed in his large old farmhouse and to allow the family to help. Unresolved anxiety and shame about his homosexuality emerged.

Max's self-sufficiency and independence are consistent with what the literature describes about lesbians and gays in midlife and later life (Friend, 1991; Reid, 1995). However, the same literature also suggests that lesbians and gays who have managed to achieve a positive identity fare better as they age. Max's rigidity and anxiety probably relate in large part to his continuing internalized homophobia.

A second theme with regard to lesbian/gay aging in the family context is the invisibility of milestones in the lesbian/gay family member's life. Given the marginalization of homosexuality by the larger culture and the frequency with which de facto segregation occurs between the heterosexual and lesbian/gay communities, the family of origin may have little understanding of the importance of some of the events that typically occur in lesbian/gay later life. Lesbian/gay loss and widowhood stand as striking examples of this point. Families may have little appreciation of the enormity of loss faced by a middle-aged gay man who has buried scores of friends throughout the AIDS crisis. One of us (TJ) worked with a gay man in his forties who had lived in a stable triad relationship for many years. Both lovers died from AIDS, and the man was immobilized with grief. However, his family was unable to provide emotional support. Even in the more traditional situation of couple relationships, many gay men report the absence of family of origin members at funeral services and memorial services for deceased lovers. Stories are legion in the lesbian/gay communities about families marginalizing a lesbian or gay lover when a family member dies.

> Lily had lived with her lover Eileen for twenty years. When Eileen died, her siblings took charge of the funeral arrangements and assumed that they would be the executors of her estate. Lily and Eileen had never formally spoken of their relationship in either of their families, and the families categorized the relationship as "close friends" or "roommates." Lily felt paralyzed when Eileen's family began to talk about identifying which of the couple's furniture and artwork belonged to Eileen and would be part of their inherited estate.

A third theme is intergenerational responsibility. Caregiving is the key issue here. As was noted earlier, when an elderly parent becomes frail and in need of closer support, the family's stable distance regulation patterns may begin to shift. For example, an older sister who has been the primary caregiver of an elderly father who was severely disabled by a series of strokes may need her younger lesbian sister to provide respite help. The younger sister may have maintained distance from her family because of unresolved conflict about her homosexuality. The request for her assistance may stir up anxiety not only in the younger sister, but also in the rest of the family. In other families, a lesbian or gay member is assumed to be an unattached single adult no matter who is in their life and no matter how old they are. Families may assume that this member is always available for caregiving crisis.

Tony had always been the most responsible of the three sons in his family. He and his lover of ten years were typically the hosts of family celebrations and holidays. When his father suffered a heart attack and underwent coronary bypass surgery, his mother became profoundly depressed and unable to help her husband in his recovery. The family elected Tony to move in temporarily to help the parents. Their rationale was that his brothers were married and had families to look after and that Tony really had no other claims on him. Tony felt frustrated with the relentless burden of his overresponsible position in the family but also became infuriated at the family's disqualification of his couple relationship.

The fourth theme—legacy—applies to both the family and the lesbian/gay member. Because families may be unaware of the circumstances of a lesbian/gay member's life, or because they may devalue that member's life, there may be considerable worry for elderly parents about what will happen to their lesbian/gay children after their deaths. If the son or daughter is seen as eternally unattached, the parent may not appreciate the level of support provided by a chosen family or by a lover. Some parents also feel anguish over the issue of the continuity of the family beyond the current generation. This issue has probably been allayed for some parents because of the recent lesbian/gay baby boom. However, many lesbian and gay people still choose not to have children, and generativity issues may emerge for these individuals in midlife as well as for their parents in later life.

Related to the generativity issue, Laird (1993), Siegel and Lowe (1994), and Slater (1995) talk about the multigenerational nature of the lesbian/gay community and how generativity needs may be met through mentorship to younger lesbians and gays as well as through the community. The lesbian/gay member may also leave behind an important legacy for future generations in the family of origin: Her or his survival may serve as a touchstone for future family members who feel "different" or "other" in various ways. Her or his life gives a map and a set of narratives in charting how a family handles otherness in both functional and dysfunctional ways. The lesbian/gay aging literature suggest that lesbians and gay men have a fairly high rate of successful aging (Friend, 1991; Kehoe, 1989; Kimmel & Sang, 1995). Confronting the strictures of homophobia and heterosexism leaves the lesbian/gay person with considerable flexibility, self-determination, creativity, independence, and crisis competence (Friend, 1991). The older lesbian/gay family member may stand not only as an emblem of survival in the face of prejudice and adversity, but also as a model for successful aging.

CONCLUSION

Lesbians and gays have always been members of families—whether the families in which they were reared or the families that they created. And lesbians and gays, like all people, have filled their lives with connection. However, in the past, their rela-

tionships took place invisibly, and families rarely spoke out loud about their members' homosexuality. Now the emotional and familial connections maintained by lesbians and gays are no longer located underground. There is greater visibility about their couple relationships, their parenting experiences, and their struggle to integrate within their families of origin. The stories of lesbian/gay adolescents, the midlife same-sex couple, or the older lesbian woman or gay man are more public as are the stories of their many families. However, the mental health establishment must run to catch up with these people, and the task of becoming competent and informed in helping them is an arduous one for it involves reevaluating and recasting some cherished norms about family and relational life while holding onto some others. But herein lies the joy and suffering of postmodern life: When the truth is up for grabs, life can be terrifying but also simultaneously liberating.

REFERENCES

Bigner, J. J. (1996). Working with gay fathers: Developmental, postdivorce parenting, and therapeutic issues. In J. Laird & R. Green (Eds.), *Lesbians and gays in couples and families: A handbook for therapists* (pp. 370–403). San Francisco: Jossey-Bass.

Blasband, D., & Peplau, L. A. (1985). Sexual exclusivity versus openness in gay male couples. *Archives of Sexual Behavior, 14,* 395–412.

Blumstein, P., & Schwartz, P. (1983). *American couples: Money, work, and sex.* New York: Morrow.

Bowen, M. (1978). *Family therapy in clinical practice.* New York: Jason Aronson.

Boxer, A. M., Cook, J. A., & Herdt, G. (1989, August). First homosexual and heterosexual experiences reported by gay and lesbian youth in an urban community. Paper presented at the Annual Meeting of the American Psychological Association. San Francisco.

Brown, L. (1991). Therapy with an infertile lesbian client. In C. Silvertein (Ed.), *Gays, lesbians, and their therapists: Studies in psychotherapy* (pp. 15–30). New York: Norton.

Carter, B. (1992). *A multicontextual framework for assessing families.* (Available from the Family Institute of Westchester, White Plains, N.Y., or on

Videotape: *Clinical dilemmas in marriage,* available from Guilford Publications, NY.)

Carter, E., & McGoldrick, M. (1980). *The family life cycle.* New York: Gardner.

Carter, B., & McGoldrick, M. (1988). *The changing family life cycle: A framework for family therapy* (2nd ed.). New York: Gardner.

Carter, E., & Orfanidis, M. (1976). Family therapy with one person and the family therapist's own family. In P. Guerin (Ed.), *Family therapy: Theory and practice* (pp. 193–219). New York: Gardner.

Cass, V. (1979). Homosexual identity formation: A theoretical model. *Journal of Homosexuality, 4*(3), 219–237.

Cramer, D. W., & Roach, A. J. (1988). Coming out to Mom and Dad: A study of gay males and their relationship with their parents. *Journal of Homosexuality, 15*(3/4), 79–91.

Dunne, E. J. (1987). Helping gay fathers come out to their children. *Journal of Homosexuality, 14,* 213–222.

Fairchild, B., & Hayward, N. (1979). *Now that you know: What every parent should know about homosexuality.* San Diego: Harcourt Brace Jovanovitch.

Friend, R. (1991). Older lesbian and gay people: A theory of successful aging. In J. A. Lee (Ed.), *Gay midlife and maturity* (pp. 99–118). New York: Haworth Press.

Frye, M. (1987). Lesbian sex. In, *Willful virgin: Essays in feminism,* (pp. 109–119). Freedom, CA: The Crossing Press.

Gergen, K. (1982). *Toward tranformation in social knowledge.* New York: Springer-Verlag.

Green, R., Bettinger, M., & Zacks, E. (1966). Are lesbian couples fused and gays couples disengaged? Questioning gender stereotypes. In J. Laird & R. Green (Eds.), *Lesbians and gays in couples and families: A handbook for therapists* (pp. 185–230). San Francisco: Jossey-Bass.

Griffin, C. W., Wirth, M. J., & Wirth, A. G. (1986). *Beyond acceptance: Parents of lesbians and gays talk about their experiences.* Englewood Cliffs, NJ: Prentice-Hall.

Herdt, G. (Ed.). (1989). *Gay and lesbian youth.* New York: Harrington Park Press.

Herdt, G., & Boxer, A. M. (1993). *Children of Horizons: How gay and lesbian teens are leading a new way out of the closet.* Boston: Beacon Press.

Hoffman, L. (1992). A reflexive stance for family therapy. In S. McNamee, & K. Gergen (Eds.), *Therapy as social construction* (pp. 7–24). London: Sage.

Hoffman, L. (1993). *Exchanging voices: A collaborative approach to family therapy.* London: Karnac Books.

Iasenza, S., Colucci, P. L., & Rothberg, B. (1996). Coming out and the mother-daughter bond: Two case examples. In J. Laird & R. Green, (Eds.), *Lesbians and gays in couples and families: A handbook for therapists* (pp. 123–136). San Francisco: Jossey-Bass.

Imber-Black, E., & Roberts, J. (1992). *Rituals for our times: Celebrating, healing, and changing our lives and our relationships.* New York: HarperCollins.

Johnson, T. W. (1992). Predicting parental response to a son or daughter's homosexuality (Doctoral dissertation, Rutgers University, 1992). *Dissertation Abstracts International.*

Johnson, T. W. (1995). Utilizing culture in work with aging families. In G. C. Smith, E. A. Robertson-Tchabo, & P. W. Power (Eds.), *Strengthening aging families: Diversity in practice and policy* (pp. 175–202). Thousand Oaks, CA: Sage.

Johnson, T. W., & Keren, M. S. (1996). Creating and maintaining boundaries in male couples. In J. Laird & R. Green (Eds.), *Lesbians and gays in couples and families: A handbook for therapists* (pp. 231–250). San Francisco: Jossey-Bass.

Kehoe, M. (1989). *Lesbians over sixty speak for themselves.* New York: Haworth Press.

Kimmel, D. C., & Sang, B. E. (1995). Lesbians and gay men in midlife. In A. R. D'Augelli, & C. J. Patterson (Eds.), *Lesbian, gay, and bisexual identities over the lifespan: Psychological perspectives* (pp. 190–214). New York: Oxford University Press.

Krestan, J., & Bepko, C. (1980). The problem of fusion in the lesbian relationship. *Family Process, 19*(3), 277–289.

Kurdek, L. A., & Schmitt, J. P. (1985–1986). Relationship quality of gay men in closed or open relationships. *Journal of Homosexuality, 12,* 85–99.

Kushner, T. (1992). *Angels in America: Part 2: Perestroika.* New York: Theatre Communications Group.

Laird, J. (1993). Lesbian and gay families. In F. Walsh (Ed.), *Normal family processes* (4th ed.), (pp. 282–328). New York: The Guilford Press.

Laird, J. (1996). Invisible ties: Lesbians and their families of origin. In J. Laird & R. Green (Eds.), *Lesbians and gays in couples and families: A handbook for therapists* (pp. 89–122). San Francisco: Jossey-Bass.

Loulan, J. (1987). *Lesbian passion: Loving ourselves and each other.* San Francisco: Spinsters/Aunt Lute.

Lupenitz, D. A. (1988). *The family interpreted: Feminist theory in clinical practice.* New York: Basic Books.

Lukes, C. A., & Land, H. (1990). Biculturality and homosexuality. *Social Work, 35,* 155–161.

Martin, A. (1993). *Lesbian and gay parenting handbook: Creating and raising our families.* New York: Harper Perennial.

Martin, A. D. (1982). Learning to hide: The socialization of the gay adolescent. *Adolescent Psychiatry, 10,* 52–65.

Martin, A. D., & Hetrick, E. S. (1988). The stigmatization of the gay and lesbian adolescent. *Journal of Homosexuality, 15,* 163–183.

Mencher, J. (1990). Intimacy in lesbian relationships: A critical examination of fusion. (Works in Progress No. 42). Wellesley, MA: Wellesley College, Stone Center for Developmental Services and Studies.

Morales, E. (1980). Ethnic minority families and minority gays and lesbians. In F. Bozett & M. Sussman (Eds.), *Homosexuality and family relations* (pp. 217–239). Binghamton, NY: Haworth Press.

Patterson, C. (1992). Children of lesbian and gay parents. *Child Development, 63,* 1025–1042.

Patterson, C. (1996). Lesbian mothers and their children. In J. Laird and R. Green, (Eds.), *Lesbians and gays in couples and families: A handbook for therapists* (pp. 420–437). San Francisco: Jossey-Bass.

Reid, J. D. (1995). Development in late life: Older lesbian and gay lives. In A. R. D'Augeli & C. J. Patterson (Eds.), *Lesbian, gay and bisexual identities over the lifespan: Psychological perspectives* (pp. 215–242). New York: Oxford University Press.

Robinson, B. E., Walters, L. H., & Skeen, P. (1989). Response to learning that their child is homosexual and concern over AIDS: A national study. In F. W. Bozett (Ed.), *Homosexuality and the family* (pp. 59–80). Binghamton, NY: Harrington Park Press.

Roth, S. (1989). Psychotherapy with lesbian couples: Individual issues, female socialization and the social context. In M. McGoldrick, C. M. Anderson, & F. Walsh (Eds.), *Women in families: A framework for family therapy* (pp. 286–307). New York: Norton.

Savin-Williams, R. C. (1994). Verbal and physical abuse as stressors in the lives of sexual minority youth: Associations with school problems, running away, substance abuse, prostitution, and suicide. *Journal of Counseling and Clinical Psychology, 62,* 261–264.

Savin-Williams, R. C. (1996). Self-labeling and disclosure among gay, lesbian, and bisexual youths. In J. Laird & R. Green (Eds.), *Lesbians and gays in couples and families: A handbook for therapists* (pp. 153–182). San Francisco: Jossey-Bass.

Schwartzberg, N., Berliner, K., & Jacob, D. (1995). *Single in a married world.* New York: Norton.

Scrivner, J. R., & Eldridge, N. S. (1995). Lesbian and gay family psychology. In. R. H. Mikesell, D. Lusterman, & S. H. McDaniel (Eds.), *Integrating family therapy: Handbook of family psychology and systems theory* (pp. 327–345). Washington, DC: American Psychological Association.

Siegel, S., & Lowe, E., Jr. (1994). *Uncharted lives: Understanding the life passages of gay men.* New York: Dutton.

Slater, S. (1995). *The lesbian family life cycle.* New York: Free Press.

Slater, S., & Mencher, J. (1991). The lesbian family life cycle: A contextual approach. *American Journal of Orthopsychiatry, 61,* 372–382.

Sophie, J. (1985–1986). A critical examination of stage theories of lesbian identity development. *Journal of Homosexuality, 12*(2), 39–51.

Tully, C. (1989). Caregiving: What do midlife lesbians view as important? *Journal of Gay and Lesbian Psychotherapy, 1,* 87–103.

Walsh, F. (1988). The family in later life. In B. Carter & M. McGoldrick (Eds.), *The changing family life cycle: A framework for family therapy* (2nd ed.), (pp. 311–332). New York: Gardner.

Weston, K. (1991). *Families we choose: Lesbians, gays, kinship.* New York: Columbia University Press.

CHAPTER 21

THE SINGLE ADULT AND THE FAMILY LIFE CYCLE

KATHY BERLINER
DEMARIS JACOB
NATALIE SCHWARTZBERG

Although most people marry at some point in their lives, the numbers of those who do not are increasing. In the 1970 adult (over age 18) population of the United States, 19 percent of men and 14 percent of women had never been married. By 1994, these percentages rose to 27 percent and 20 percent, respectively (U.S. Bureau of the Census, 1995). Even when marriage does occur, factors such as delayed marriages, a close to 50 percent divorce rate and longer life expectancy mean that more people than ever before live singly during the course of their life. The 1994 census indicates that about 40 percent of adults (over 18) were either unmarried, divorced, or widowed. Singlehood has generally been regarded as a transitional period between families, and we lack well-developed notions of the different requirements of living on one's own at different phases of life. We need a sense of the emotional and developmental flow of the lives of people (and their families) who are single for long periods of time.

We must find a way to think about singlehood that is not about the failure to marry but validates the single experience as what it is—one way to live life. Our culture has a distinct bias toward marriage. The media, for example, often continue to portray single people as silly (as in *Seinfeld*) or vulnerable (as in *Single White Female*) (see Schwartzberg, Berliner, & Jacob, 1995, Chapter 2). Pressures on men to demonstrate maturity through marriage and on women to believe that no self-definition should take precedence over that of wife or mother are very real.

When single people describe their lives as fulfilling, then, it is often with surprise or in the face of subtle disapproval. One impediment in thinking about single life as good is the notion that accomplishing marriage is itself a life task. While marriage is one of life's big milestones, problems arise when people regard marriage as *the* next step necessary for the unfolding of adult life. If not getting married is seen as evidence of deviance, then marital status becomes the pivotal definer of normalcy. The single person may become frozen, waiting for marriage, not moving forward with the business of life. Our framework attempts to remove marriage as the centerpiece of adulthood but at the same time recognizes the impact of living a life that deviates from the socially prescribed path.

We have tried to grasp the experience of living life singly, without children or a live-in romantic partner, and validate the experiences of those who may marry at some later time, those who choose to be single, those who may rear children without partners, and those who simply happen to find themselves single at times in their lives when they had not imagined they would be. Most of what we present is relevant to gay and lesbian single people. The intense homophobia of our society has such a profound impact, however, that additional emotional issues and developmental phases overlay those that heterosexual single people deal with.

SETTING THE CLINICAL STAGE

In working with clients who are distressed by their single status, therapists must recognize the impact of the dominant cultural, therapeutic, and family messages that divide single people from the community of adults. The therapeutic frame needs to include an understanding of the contexts that elevate marriage and denigrate singlehood. The main contexts influencing people's judgments about singlehood are messages from the larger society, multigenerational themes in the family, ethnicity, and gender. Because the impact of gender on the experience of singlehood varies with age, gender differences are included within each life cycle phase.

Marriage as Social Empowerment

Marriage is an empowering institution that creates an automatic status change for both men and women in the family of origin, in religious and societal organizations, and in the perception of self. It provides public acknowledgment of movement to responsible adulthood and participation in the ongoing history of family and society. Not being part of that institution is often experienced as loss of social legitimacy. As one 50-year-old divorced Jewish woman put it, "I became a second-class citizen overnight."

The importance of marriage, and conversely societal discomfort with singlehood, varies with political climate. The emotional power of the code phrase "family values" gives a clear message today that those who live outside a heterosexual marriage are outside the fabric of American life itself. We haven't come all that far; this is reminiscent of life in the 1950s, when the postwar culture also elevated marriage, the family, and family consumerism (Coontz, 1992).

Furthermore, community and religious life is structured to a great degree around passages of life created by marriage and parenthood. A christening, a Bar or Bat mitzvah, confirmation, graduations— these are the events that are celebrated. Single people participate, but the main story will always be about someone else's family.

Marriage and the Family of Origin

Marriage has important functions in the structure of the family of origin. It is the way to perpetuate names, rituals, and family lineage. In the ongoing life of the family, marriage initiates the realignment of relationships between parent and child (Carter & McGoldrick, 1989). It signals a successful end to the rearing of children and defines new boundaries between generations. When marriage doesn't occur in the expected time frame, a gridlock in the unfolding of family life may occur, leaving parents and the single adult struggling to find other ways to mark adulthood. This process has historically been more difficult for daughters, who only recently are being raised to have an adult role outside of marriage (McGoldrick, 1989).

Multigenerational Themes.   The meaning of marriage and singlehood in each family is best viewed from the perspective of at least three generations. The highly conflictual or abusive marriage of an emotionally important ancestor, for example, may continue to ripple its "marriage meaning" through time. Marital events such as divorce are also pertinent. Parents may worry that their divorce is influencing their child's ability to wed, or unresolved issues from the divorce may perpetuate a reactivity that either romanticizes or damns marriage. Lastly, what have been the role models for living a satisfying single life? How have single people been viewed?

When reactivity around marriage/singlehood interlocks with other generational legacies, the impact will be even more powerful (Carter & McGoldrick, 1989). Family sensitivity to a theme of underresponsibility in men, for example, may greatly intensify pressure on sons to demonstrate responsible manhood through marriage.

Ethnic Variations.   A family's attitude toward singlehood is also shaped by ethnicity (the converging threads of economic, religious, and racial history). The Irish have had a greater tolerance for singlehood than almost any other group (McGoldrick, 1996). Marriage was viewed not as a framework for self-fulfillment but rather for parenting, often bringing economic hardship in the wake of increasing numbers of children (Diner, 1983). For women, the church—not the family— had historically been the center of community life (McGoldrick, 1996).

In the American Black community, economic disadvantage, the high mortality and incarceration rates of men, and continued oppression have had a profound effect on marriage rates (Staples, 1988). According to 1994 data, Black Americans have the lowest rate of marriage of any American cultural group. 42.4 percent of adult Black men and 36.2 percent of Black women report themselves never married (U.S. Bureau of the Census, 1995). While an expansive notion of kinship and connection to wider community (Franklin, 1988) creates more roles for a single person, marriage continues to be preferred to singlehood as a way of embracing legitimacy in the mainstream society (Heiss, 1988).

When life's core is the family, pressure to marry intensifies. Jews, for example, have a religious imperative to "be fruitful and multiply." Their history of genocide increases the urgency for marriage and family (Rosen & Weltman, 1996). One Jewish saying goes: "There is no such thing as being single, just not-yet-married."

Understanding your client's legacies regarding marital status (e.g., the available roles for unmarried men and women, the flexibility of pathways to adulthood, the meaning of marriage as a rite of passage and of family continuity) is essential. Therapists will be less likely to impose their own cultural biases, and clients can approach family of origin issues in new ways. Clients who are fixated on marriage may see these explorations as digressions; therapeutic finesse lies in respecting clients' perceptions while making larger perspectives relevant.

THE SINGLE PERSON'S LIFE CYCLE

Single people often have difficulty locating themselves in the flow of "normal life"; they (and their families) are unclear what the next step is when marriage and/or childbirth don't occur. Our life cycle phases and tasks are based on life's chronological milestones and the shifts in issues, possibilities, and relationship to family and future that getting older brings. Our intent is to provide pathways for growth and movement in a relatively uncharted land.

At each phase of adulthood, single people still need to confront the expectation of marriage, because it remains the norm; cope with having an unrealized goal if marriage is desired; and understand the impact of living a life that deviates from the norm. There will be considerable variation in individual timing of negotiating issues, in the overlap of some issues from one age to the next, and in the fact that not all issues emerge for all people.

The stages of the single adult life cycle are as follows:

The twenties

1. Restructuring interaction and boundaries with family from dependent to independent orientation.
2. Finding a place for oneself in the world outside the family—in work, friendships, and love.

The thirties

1. Facing single status.
2. Expanding life goals to embrace possibilities in addition to marriage, including child-rearing.

Midlife (forties to midfifties)

1. Addressing the "ideal family" fantasy to accept the possibility of never marrying and the probability of never having biological children.
2. Redefining the meaning of work.
3. Defining an authentic life that can be established within single status.
4. Establishing an adult role within the family of origin.

Later life (fifties to when health fails)

1. Consolidating decisions in work life.
2. Enjoying the freedom and autonomy of singlehood.
3. Acknowledging and planning for the future diminishment of physical abilities.
4. Facing increasing illness and death of loved ones.

The Twenties: Not Yet Married

The complex emotional work of the young adult launching from the family of origin and finding a place for herself or himself in the world is presented elsewhere; here, we will highlight the issues and experience of singlehood.

People usually assume that marriage will take place and that finding a mate is part of the "work" of the twenties. The young adult's gender, class, ethnicity, and sexual orientation will shape the vision each young adult has of what can lie in store.

When the central emphasis of the young adult period is on preparing for a career and developing a sense of self, concern about finding a mate will be low. In cultures in which universal and early marriage is expected, however, or when career opportunities are limited and/or young people do not have the money for prolonged career preparation, a focus on marriage or child-rearing as the next step may arise earlier.

Gender Differences.   The largest gender difference at this phase is the perception of the impact of achievement on marriageability. Men know that increased status will only be an enhancement, while women believe that achievement will diminish their chances for marriage (Faludi, 1991). When messages from society and family equate concentrating on career with lowering one's marriageability, singlehood anxiety and conflict about the next life step can become intense by the late twenties. These feelings are illustrated in Betsy Israel's article in *Mirabella* (1996), in which she writes:

> My symptoms (loss of purpose in life, loss of interest in career, crying continuously) could have indicated any number of depressive states. Yet I came to view them all in one highly particular way: I had failed completely to become a couple. (p. 69)

Black women may feel less in a bind; while White parents (especially working-class ones) continue to view marriage for daughters as a route to financial stability, Black parents place much more emphasis on preparing daughters to work (Higgenbotham & Weber, 1995) and tend not to see marriage as a replacement for the need to earn money (Staples & Johnson, 1993).

Young women who lack the possibility of fulfilling jobs move toward marriage or procreation as the next step earlier than do those preparing for a career. Conversely, young men with limited job opportunities whose ability to assume the economic mantle of husband is minimal may avoid marriage.

Marriage as a Premature Solution.   Young adults may enter marriage as a premature solution to the central emotional work of negotiating an adult self within the family of origin or as a way to escape intense intergenerational conflict in the home. When children cannot afford to leave and establish their own territory or when parents expect their children to live at home until marriage, the conflict between generations can escalate greatly.

Therapy may involve helping the young client and his or her family postpone a precipitous marriage that only detours or triangulates the emotional work of negotiating an adult self through the spouse. Renegotiating new boundaries without marriage is difficult work, however, when positions are rigid and conflict is intense.

Establishing Relationships outside the Family.
Friendships and love relationships outside the family supply the emotional foundation for emerging independence and the development of an adult self. When friendships are taken seriously, as they should be—not viewed as transitional to marriage—there is less tendency to invest all one's emotional energy in finding "Mr(s). Right." We need to inquire about the meaning, depth, and extent of friendships in all people's lives, but particularly so for single people. Finding a path that places equal emphasis on the development of work skills and the capacity for close relationships is important for the healthy growth of both sexes. Stein (1981) underscores the fact that a one-sided emphasis may be seriously debilitating for those who remain single for a long time. The treatment of Bob illustrates the problems a man may have with investing in friendships (see Figure 21.1 on page 366):

Bob (age 28) entered therapy depressed and demoralized because he had been unable to find a new girlfriend after the breakup of a three-year relationship. Bob was very successful at work but was lonely and isolated. He had trouble making friends on his own and counted on girlfriends to provide emotional anchorage. His neediness was pushing women away.

Rather than focusing exclusively on his difficulties in romantic relationships, the therapy addressed the crucial task of creating social networks. For Bob, looking at multigenerational themes was particularly relevant. He came from a middle-class Midwestern Protestant family. The older of two boys, he described his mother as emotionally distant and his father as warm but weak. His mother, to whom he looked for the moral leadership of the family, had never sought friends. She thought the need for friends indicated a weakness of character. When Bob was coached to find out more about his mother's family, it emerged that her own mother had been orphaned at birth. Although Bob's grandmother was raised by a caring relative, she feared becoming emotionally attached. The lesson she taught her daughter, Bob's mother, was that one should act as if one didn't need people.

Tracking the generational messages about the meaning of friends was key for Bob in opening up awareness of his needs for affiliation. Having friends would make for a more enjoyable life and take the intensity off finding a mate. Bob's work in exploring his parents' history allowed him to approach his family differently. He now began to have more personally revealing conversations with his mother, broaching previously taboo subjects such as her "self-sufficiency" compared to his own neediness."

If the young adult can keep anxiety about finding a spouse low enough, the process of dating can be helpful in learning about the self in relationships and in experimenting with adult gender and

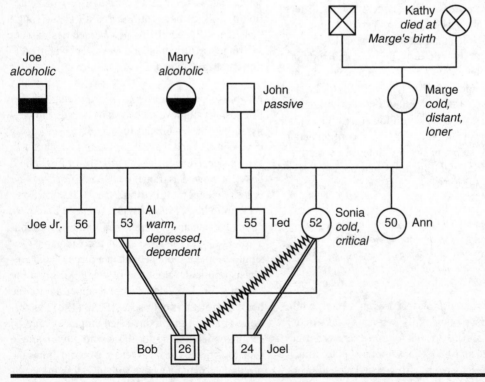

FIGURE 21.1 Bob Smith's Genogram

social roles. Dating that is fraught with intensity about latching onto a mate can only become tedious and painful.

Owning an adult self also includes finding ways to validate one's sexuality. This means either dealing with the complexities of being sexual outside of marriage (including the specter of AIDS in each encounter) or, if celibacy is valued, acknowledging the absence of sex as a healthy choice.

The Thirties: The Adult Crisis

At 30, there is an urgency to getting one's act together; the age of experimentation is supposed to be over (Levinson, 1978; Stein, 1981). The realization that many of one's peers are now married propels many single people to intensify their search for a mate. Seeing others proceed with the "real" business of life (having children and juggling child-rearing and work), single people begin to feel out of sync. Anxiety around getting married can intensify so greatly at this age that one's experience of self and one's development can be almost totally eclipsed. Women usually experience this "singlehood panic" at a younger age than men, partly because of the pressure of the biological clock and partly because of the societal judgment that says that men may choose to remain single but women should do so only involuntarily.

This increased anxiety means that requests for therapy often focus on enhancing marriageability. Rather than trying to move clients off this goal, it's better to stay relevant to the client's vision of the purpose of treatment, since the desire to be married is an important adult goal. Getting married is a legitimate—but incomplete—frame for therapy. An initial dilemma is how to honor a client's desire for marriage and still address issues in a context that doesn't make marriage the end product of successful treatment. Moving ahead with work on the developmental tasks of this phase can lower anxiety and increase self-respect. But moving too exclusively—not acknowledging the validity of a desire for marriage or the real problems a single client might have with intimacy—can be experienced by the client as

the therapist's judgment that the client really *is* "unmarriageable."

To remain open to the possibilities for marriage yet not be taken over by this pursuit, the single person and his or her family need to make a major shift: attaining the belief that there is more than one way to lead a healthy life. This shift is fundamental to the emotional work of this period and sets the stage for later years, should the client remain single.

Working on life cycle tasks does not rule out marriage but simply facilitates the experience of growing as an adult. It takes into account the reality that the client is now single, whatever the future brings. Coming to grips with singlehood means looking at the ways the single person may be putting his or her life on hold, such as postponing financial planning, setting up a home, even buying kitchen utensils. Not doing these things helps to maintain the presumption that important aspects of life proceed only after marriage.

What is put on hold are usually the things a future mate is supposed to take care of. Traditional gender training does not lend itself well to single status, and members of each sex need to develop skills in areas that are assumed to be the province of the other. For a woman, this means that career has to be taken seriously to provide both financial stability and a sense of identity—something that women (particularly lower-middle-class White women) have not been socialized to consider (Adams, 1981). For a man, it means learning how to develop networks and friendships (Meth & Pasick, 1990). For both, it means making one's home feels like a home.

Friendships need to accommodate what Peter Stein (1981) called their "patchwork" quality. This is a time when friends move into and out of romantic relationships or marry and therefore are not consistently available. A large circle of friends to share celebrations and life together can help to decrease the sense of abandonment when good friends shift primary emotional loyalty to another.

Helping single clients to articulate aspects of an adult self in the family of origin is a key aspect of coaching in this phase. Acknowledging sexual maturity outside marriage is one of the most anxiety-provoking areas for both client and parents.

> Joan, a 35-year-old systems analyst, was struggling to grow up in her role as daughter. She had been coached to invite her parents to *her* home for dinners, reduce the number of weekends visiting home, tell her parents what she did with her free time, and share her work successes. Joan was encouraged by the positive responses she received and felt increased respect.
>
> Then a further opportunity presented itself. She had gone on a cruise with friends and had brought in the pictures. One was of herself in a sexy dress, looking very happy. When asked whether she had shown it to her parents, Joan said, "Of course not!" We talked about why not—what the impact would be if she did and how it might change things. We recognized that here was a chance to present an aspect of her adult self, her sexuality, that all family members had colluded to deny. When she did share her pictures, she got the uncomfortable silence that we had predicted, but she still felt that she had conveyed an important message about her maturity.

Toward their midthirties, most women and some men (and their families) experience heightened concern over potential childlessness. The thought of missing out on one of life's most profound experiences surfaces and may keep reverberating for years. When combined with parental distress over not having grandchildren, this sadness can develop into a dense web of reactivity. It is important to truly hear this concern without trying to change or fix it.

The painful intensity of these feelings can lead to closing off discussion about marriage or childlessness to maintain a pseudo-calm in the family. When family colludes to deny important realities, however, relationships and personal growth suffer.

> Susan, a 39-year-old Jewish woman, no longer discusses her childlessness with her parents. When she had divorced ten years earlier, she had apologized to her mother about not giving her a grandchild. Her mother then had been very reassuring, telling her that parenthood wasn't all it was cracked up to be and not to worry. She was totally taken aback when now, ten years later, her mother relayed an anecdote of meeting a friend who had recently become a grandmother. Susan asked the name of the baby, to which her mother replied, "I didn't ask. It made my heart ache."

Susan's own pain about her lack of children, which she had hidden from her family, and her high reactivity to her mother's similar feelings led her to close off this toxic issue, thereby freezing the development of their mother-daughter relationship.

The Forties to Mid-Fifties: Developing Alternative Scripts

A fortieth birthday ushers in the realization that time is running out. The emotional weight of closing options falls most heavily on women. Women have a procreative time limit and usually continue to feel social and personal pressure to marry "up" (taller, richer, older). Men can have children much later in life and many continue to have a wide range of acceptable partners from which to choose. Even so, the men we interviewed described feeling uncomfortable with the isolation and the increasing social approbation of remaining single.

A drift toward segregation between single and married people, begun in earlier years, is typically firmly in place by midlife. There are powerful reasons for this divide, among them differing demands for time and commitment, perceptions of single people as a threat to married life, and single people's avoidance of married life and child-focused celebrations to bypass painful feelings of loss. This segregation contributes greatly to feelings of isolation from mainstream life as well as to idealized fantasies of married life. Work on diminishing this gap can help a great deal.

An issue for people at this age is the probability of never achieving the family they expected to have. If marriage does happen, it will likely be with a divorced or widowed spouse. If child-rearing is in the picture, it will likely be with someone else's children or as a single parent.

Helping clients to disentangle the main loss—spouse, child, or "package"—is important. It opens up consideration of alternatives. Those whose primary distress centers on child-rearing, for example, can explore other options for bringing children into their lives, including the difficult step of single parenthood, rather than remaining mired, awaiting a spouse.

The pain of these losses around expected family and particularly around childlessness may wax and wane throughout life, getting retriggered by changes in circumstance and priorities.

Gender Differences.   Connecting with a viable social network becomes increasingly difficult for single men as they get older. Only about 8 percent of men remain never married after age 45 (U.S. Bureau of the Census, 1995), and Bernard (1982) found that at midlife, the average never-married man is significantly less educated and earns less money than his female single counterpart. In addition, unmarried men report much higher rates of problem drinking and substance abuse than do either married men or women, regardless of marital status (Waite, 1995). The author speculates that marriage benefits men by supplying emotional connection and caretaking.

On the other hand, Anderson, Stewart, and Dimidjian (1994) fill a vacuum by recounting the stories of midlife women who feel happy about their lives and who they are. Based on in-depth interviews of ninety women—unmarried, divorced and/or single mothers—these stories reflect the sense of competence, satisfaction, and pleasure in life that these women feel—contrary to continuing stereotypes.

Defining an Authentic Life as a Single Adult.
Societal emphasis placed on marriage and children as the primary vehicles for mature love may leave some single adults feeling that their relationships and loves are less valuable. This is a notion that must be challenged. Holland (1992) writes,

> We need to stay open to the simple possibilities of loving. We were told in youth that the whole point and purpose of love, the only possible excuse for it, was to set up a traditional household that becomes a working part of the social machine. Just maybe,

> though, love comes in other shapes usable by us, the non-traditional unfamilied legion. (p. 252)

Disentangling love from marriage allows single people to legitimize their loving experiences, whatever their form, and not feel that they are, as Anderson et al. (1994) put it, "make do" substitutes for the real thing.

Another aspect of feeling authentic involves forging a connection with future generations. This helps people to feel a sense of continuity with history and meaning beyond individual achievement and personal satisfaction. Single people will need to create their own connections; they are not automatically provided by marriage and the family package. Single people often don't realize that connection to the future is important. One woman who chose to become a Big Sister said, "I don't know why I waited so long to bring a child into my life."

Feeling authentic also means accepting that friends are family, not a poor substitute. Inquiries about friendships are particularly important with men; their single cohort is vastly diminished by this age, and they may have focused on other life areas rather than building networks for themselves (Meth & Pasick, 1990).

Redefining the Meaning of Work.   The workplace is usually the central organizing hub of daily life for single people, and the connection of work life to personal satisfaction cannot be overestimated. Work is more than earning money; skills and talents must be used in a meaningful way in one's job or in other arenas. Clients themselves may not realize the importance of work to their feelings. The following example illustrates how work issues can be detoured into a fixation on finding love:

Janet, a 44-year-old woman working as a salesperson for a swimsuit company, was intensely focused on her difficulties with men. Marriage was her goal, and she was frustrated and anxious. While she was beginning to get some intellectual perspective, her obsession with marriage ran her life. Exasperated, one day she exclaimed that if she could get any pleasure in other parts of her life, she might be able to be less depressed.

When we explored her work, she acknowledged that she found it so boring that she was frequently behind in billing, which, in turn, got her angry with herself about being a failure at even this "nothing" job. Janet had never considered her work day important; it was just a way to fill time until evening dating began. She had no awareness of how her dissatisfaction with work was increasing her anxiety about dating. Shifting the focus of therapy to meaningful use of her talents and skills brought new energy to sessions.

Taking work seriously goes hand in hand with taking responsibility for one's financial future. This is a necessity in the forties and fifties. Men may have anxiety about how they are managing their money, but they don't usually doubt their need to do it. Women, on the other hand, may have been brought up to believe that this is man's territory and might also need to learn about finance along with the therapy. This endeavor can be filled with anxiety; many women associate it with giving up on the possibility of ever being taken care of through marriage.

Family Work.   Feelings of anxiety or failure as parents can resurface at this time, as it sinks in that their "child" really may never marry. When parental emotionality meshes with a the child's reactivity around the same issues, the potential for explosivity and possible cut-off is high. Work may need to begin with relationships with siblings, in which emotionality is usually less intense. Developing a nonperipheral role, building separate relationships with nieces and nephews, and hosting events rather than being perennial guests are some ways in which single people can decrease distance in the family-of-origin.

The Fifties to Failed Health: Putting It All Together

This phase may extend two decades or more—encompassing "second life" goals and plans, job shifts, retirement, and the death of parents—until

failed health signals the last years. Single people who have faced earlier life tasks are positioned to reap the fruits of single status: freedom and autonomy. Unencumbered by financial and/or emotional responsibility toward adult children, single people can devote more time and energy to shaping personally meaningful work or just pull up stakes and move into new areas. Issues of this later life phase reflect this inner duality: a yearning to slow down and savor life coupled with a sense of urgency about getting goals accomplished in the time that is left (Bergquist, Greenberg, & Klaum, 1993).

By age 65, only 54 percent of women are living with a spouse, compared to 80 percent of men (U.S. Bureau of the Census, 1995). Single women moving through the later-life phase, then, find themselves to be less statistically deviant than do single men. The majority of a single man's peers live a very different life. The inescapable conclusion from current data is that the older single man has the poorest physical and emotional health (Bernard, 1982; Waite, 1995). Schaie and Willis (1986) report that single White men over the age of 70 are three times more likely to commit suicide than are same-aged White women, Black men, or Black women.

Consolidating Decisions about Money and Work, Planning for the Future.   Emotional intensity about using one's life fully tends to increase as that inner voice says, "If I don't do it now, I never will." Single people may have an advantage in making major shifts because they do not have to adjust plans around spouses and children. Exploring options for even partial realization of goals and dreams that have been put on the shelf is always useful. Even if money is limited and jobs cannot be changed, life can include these dreams. One 55-year-old factory worker saved for ten years for a trip to a distant country. Accomplishing this enabled her to feel like an an adventurous woman instead of a factory drudge.

Planning for the future is critical at this juncture. It includes thinking about a home base that feels financially and physically secure and may mean considering joining forces with others to pool resources. If a client strongly resists addressing these issues, examining multigenerational themes may help.

> Lauren, a 54-year-old never-married woman, had derived a lot of satisfaction from her work and great enjoyment in her life. Now, however, she found herself almost paralyzed with anxiety about her future. She had put no money aside and was frightened about the coming years. At the same time, she strongly resisted saving money. She hosted expensive dinners and took lavish vacations, which only increased her panic.
>
> When multigenerational themes were explored, it emerged that both her mother and grandmother had died before the age of 60. Both had had lives of hard work and little luxury. Her paralysis about planning for a future was fueled by her unconscious belief that she wasn't going to have one. Her vision of life's cycle included death within the next five years. Bringing this powerful template into conscious awareness was crucial in freeing Lauren from her "inexplicable" terror.

A final piece of planning is the making of one's will. This is more than a duty; it is a profound emotional experience. Looking at possessions and deciding how and with whom you want them to be valued after your death can change a client's entire perspective. People retrieve memories that have been pushed aside and rediscover priorities and attachments that have faded. Communicating decisions directly to the people involved can shift relationships in one's current life:

> John had always had an affectionate and fun-filled relationship with his nieces; he was the one who took them to concerts, the theater, and dinner. When John decided to tell them about their inheritance from him, his lawyers and his own family tried to talk him out of it. He went ahead anyway, on the grounds that his nieces should have this information in planning their own futures. For the first time, his nieces realized the depth of his love for them and came to see him as a second parent.

Family Work. As parents age and become infirm, family relationships often need realignment. Parental anxiety around singlehood may resurface after years of dormancy as parents struggle to feel their children "settled" before they die. Family of origin work with parents is particularly poignant now, since this may be the last opportunity for the adult child to resolve his or her own feelings about single life and communicate some reassurance to aged parents.

The need to care for aged parents often puts strain on sibling relationships, which may have stayed frozen in time at the point when each child left home. Allen (1989) found that unmarried women are called upon to be primary caretakers significantly more often than widowed daughters are. Implicit in this selection is the judgment that the lives of single women are more expendable than those of married women. Family of origin work with siblings can be very difficult, if not impossible, when there is little emotional glue between them and reactivity is high. The cost of nonresolution, however, may be the dissolution of family connections after the parents' death.

Enjoying the Freedom. Personal freedom is one of the great benefits of singlehood, and using it well gives richness to the single experience. People whose lives have centered on duty or responsibility may need help in giving themselves permission to spend time and money in personally satisfying ways.

Successful aging for us all lies in maintaining the activities and attitudes of earlier years for as long as possible (Schaie and Willis, 1986) and in gaining a wide perspective (wisdom) while keeping a vital investment in old pleasures and new experience (Erikson, 1982).

REFERENCES

Adams, M. (1981). Living Singly. In P. Stein (Ed.) *Single Life,* (pp. 221–234). New York: St. Martin's Press.

Allen, K. R. (1989). *Single women; family ties.* Newbury Park CA: Sage.

Anderson, C. M., Stewart, S., & Dimidjian, S. (1994). *Flying solo.* New York: Norton.

Bergquist, W. H., Greenberg, E. M., & Klaum, G. A. (1993). *In our fifties: Voices of men and women re-inventing their lives.* San Francisco: Jossey-Bass.

Bernard, J. (1982). *The future of marriage.* New Haven, CT: Yale University Press.

Carter, B., & McGoldrick, M. (1989). *The changing family life cycle: A framework for family therapy* (2nd. ed.). Boston: Allyn & Bacon.

Coontz, S. (1992). *The way we never were.* New York: Basic Books.

Diner, H. (1983). *Erin's daughters in America: Immigrant women in the 19th century.* Baltimore: Johns Hopkins Press.

Erikson, E. (1982). *The life cycle completed.* New York: Norton.

Faludi, S. (1991). *Backlash.* New York: Crown.

Franklin, J. H. (1988). A historical note on Black families. In H. P. McAdoo (Ed.), *Black families* (2nd ed.), (pp. 23–26). Newbury Park, CA: Sage.

Israel, B. (1996, January). Happiness and the single woman: What's good and what's not about being unattached in America. *Mirabella,* 68–73.

Heiss, J. (1988). Women's values regarding marriage and the family. In H. P. McAdoo (Ed.), *Black Families* (2nd ed.), (pp. 201–214). Newbury Park CA: Sage.

Higginbotham, E., & Weber, L. (1995). Moving up with kin and community: Upward social mobility for black and white women. In M. L. Anderson & P. H. Collins (Eds.), *Race, class & gender: An anthology* (2nd ed.), (pp. 134–147). Belmont, CA: Wadsworth.

Holland, B. (1992). *One's company.* New York: Ballantine.

Levinson, D. (1978). *The seasons of a man's life.* New York: Ballantine Books.

McGoldrick, M. (1989). Women through the family life cycle. In M. McGoldrick, C. M. Anderson, & F. Walsh (Eds.), *Women in families: A framework for family therapy* (pp. 200–226). New York: Norton.

McGoldrick, M. (1996). Irish families. In M. McGoldrick, J. Giordano, & J. I. Pearce, (Eds). *Ethnicity and family therapy* (2nd ed.) (pp. 544-566). New York: The Guilford Press.

Meth, R., & Pasick, R. (1990). *Men in therapy.* New York: The Guilford Press.

Rosen, E., & Weltman, S. (1996). Jewish families: An overview. In M. McGoldrick, J. Giordano, & J. I. Pearce (Eds.), *Ethnicity and family therapy* (2nd ed.) (pp. 611–630), New York: The Guilford Press.

Schaie, K. W., & Willis, S. L. (1986). *Adult development and aging.* Boston: Little, Brown & Company.

Schwartzberg, N., Berliner, K., & Jacob, D. (1995). *Single in a married world.* New York: Norton.

Staples, R. (1988). An overview of race and marital status. In H. P. McAdoo (Ed.), *Black families.* (2nd ed.), (pp. 187–189). Newbury Park, CA: Sage.

Staples, R., & Johnson, L. B. (1993). *Black families at the crossroad: Challenges and prospects.* San Francisco: Jossey-Bass.

Stein, P. (1981). Understanding single adulthood. In P. Stein (Ed.), *Single life: Unmarried adults in social contexts* (pp. 9–20). New York: St Martin's Press.

U.S. Bureau of the Census (1995). *Statistical Abstract of the United States,* 115th Edition. Washington, DC: U.S. Government Printing Office.

Waite, L. (1995, November). Does marriage matter? *Demography, 32*(4), 483–507.

CHAPTER 22

THE DIVORCE CYCLE
A MAJOR VARIATION IN THE AMERICAN FAMILY LIFE CYCLE

BETTY CARTER
MONICA McGOLDRICK

The largest variation of the traditional family life cycle consists of families in which divorce has occurred (see Chapter 23). In the 1980s, divorce reached the status of a normative event with a rate of 50 percent for first marriages and 61 percent for subsequent marriages (Glick, 1984). Thus, statistically, the divorce cycle consists of marriage, divorce, remarriage, and redivorce. Although that rate dipped somewhat during the 1990s, to 46 percent, the United States still has the highest divorce rate in the industrialized world. We also have the highest marriage rates (90 percent first marriage, 70 percent remarriage), which reflect the American belief in marriage and family as the structure of choice. We attribute the difficulties on the journey towards this goal to our failure to redefine marriage to include gender equality and women's economic independence (see Chapter 14). It is no coincidence that a majority of divorces are initiated by women. The lack of social support for an equal-partnership marriage is reflected in concrete obstacles such as the lack of affordable child care and workplace demands for primacy, as well as old, unrealistic, gendered expectations that men and women still bring to marriage. This struggle to live out new roles while still playing by the old rules undermines marriage and remarriage and will continue to do so until we define and support new rules in emotional and concrete ways (Carter & Peters, 1996). In our experience as clinicians and teachers, we have found it useful to conceptualize divorce and its aftermath as an interruption or dislocation of the traditional family life cycle, which produces the kind of profound disequilibrium that is associated throughout the entire family life cycle with shifts, gains, and losses in family membership.

Although a few researchers and many conservative spokespersons still see divorce as a source of major family pathology (Wallerstein & Blakeslee, 1989) we agree with mainstream researchers and clinicians who have recognized that divorce is a transitional crisis that interrupts developmental tasks (Ahrons & Rodgers, 1987; Hetherington, 1993). Because marital separation causes major practical as well as emotional readjustments, short-term distress is normal even when it is severe. As in other kinds of family crisis (e.g., death, serious illness, job loss), the key that determines whether the crisis is transitional or has permanent crippling impact is whether it is handled emotionally in an adequate way within the family system in spite of lack of social support. If it is well handled emotionally (and financially), family members, including children, may exhibit temporary symptoms and behavioral manifestations of high anxiety over a period of months or a few years. But several years after the divorce, if the developmental tasks of divorcing and those of settling into the postdivorce "binuclear" family are satisfactorily accomplished, there are few, if any, observable or testable differences due to having been part of a divorced family.

Note that the transitional crisis of divorce has two overlapping phases: the separation and legal divorce and the settling into the so-called single-parent form in two households. For 35 percent of divorced women, this is the end of the divorce crisis. Their once highly stigmatized household of mother and children has now become part of a growing category of permanent American family forms. Paradoxically, the stigma that was once associated with divorced mothers has now largely moved to unmarried mothers, so being a divorced parent is no longer in itself a stressful label. For 65 percent of divorced American women and 75 percent of American men, a second transitional crisis will ensue when either or both spouses remarry.

Thus, if we visualize a family traveling the road of life, moving from stage to stage in their developmental unfolding, we can see divorce as an interruption that puts the family on a "detour"—an additional family life cycle stage—in which the physical and emotional losses and changes of divorce are put into effect and absorbed by the three-generation system. The family (now in two households) then rejoins the "main road" and continues its forward developmental progress, though in a more complex form. If either spouse remarries, a second detour occurs—a second additional family life cycle stage—in which the family must handle the stress of absorbing two or three generations of new members into the system and struggle to define their roles and relationships to existing family members. When this task of merging in midjourney with another three-generation system has been completed, the new, highly complex system rejoins the "main road," and individual and family development continues.

GENDER ISSUES IN DIVORCE

Men and women inevitably have made different kinds of investments in marriage and will thus have different emotional experiences as they seek to disengage (Carter, 1988). Until very recently, women have been socialized to invest their entire identity in marriage and have been given the major responsibility for its success. Thus, regardless of the facts in the case, women may see divorce as a personal failure. It is crucial that the therapist not assume that remarriage is the chief solution to her problems, but rather be able to help her connect to her strength, competence, and emotional ability to go it alone unless or until she chooses otherwise.

For divorcing men, there is the serious possibility that they will lose their children in one way or another. Unless fathers take concrete steps to stay connected with their children, most of the social and emotional forces that are at play during divorce and remarriage will increase the emotional distance between fathers and children. Men also need help in acknowledging the degree of their emotional dependence on their former wives before they can begin to mourn their losses, handle their guilt at leaving their children, and start to see what part they played in the marital breakup. It is urgent to explore the man's social network for support and counsel him to deal with the issues rather than escape to another intense relationship.

We believe that the crisis of divorce can be used in therapy for both women and men as an opportunity to do now the developmental work that was skipped in the usual gendered socialization process. Thus, women should be helped to develop financial competence and to take responsibility for their lives and future, whether they remarry or not. Men need to learn the skills that will enable them to relate fully to their children, develop intimate friendships with men as well as women, and learn to conduct their own emotional, domestic, and social life so that they need not remarry unless they choose to. Such a goal—divorce therapy as resocialization process—would, of course, call for coaching the client in work with the family of origin, as well as the ex-spouse and children (see Chapter 26).

TIME

Our experience supports that of others who have found that it takes a minimum of two or three years for a family to adjust to its new structure—and that's if there are no cut-offs and all the adults are working at it full tilt. Families in which the emotional issues of divorce are not adequately resolved can remain stuck emotionally for years, perhaps for generations. (See Table 22.1 for an outline of the phases in the stage of divorce.)

TABLE 22.1   An Additional Stage of the Family Life Cycle for Divorcing Families

PHASE		EMOTIONAL PROCESS OF TRANSITION: PREREQUISITE ATTITUDE	DEVELOPMENTAL ISSUES
Divorce	The decision to divorce	Acceptance of inability to resolve marital tensions sufficiently to continue relationship.	Acceptance of one's own part in the failure of the marriage.
	Planning the breakup of the system	Supporting viable arrangements for all parts of the system.	a. Working cooperatively on problems of custody, visitation, and finances. b. Dealing with extended family about the divorce.
	Separation	a. Willingness to continue cooperative co-parental relationship and joint financial support of children. b. Work on resolution of attachment to spouse.	a. Mourning loss of intact family. b. Restructuring marital and parent-child relationships and finances; adaptation to living apart. c. Realignment of relationships with extended family; staying connected with spouse's extended family.
	The divorce	More work on emotional divorce: overcoming hurt, anger, guilt, etc.	a. Mourning loss of intact family; giving up fantasies of reunion. b. Retrieval of hopes, dreams, expectations from the marriage. c. Staying connected with extended families.
Post-divorce Family	Single parent (custodial household or primary residence)	Willingness to maintain financial responsibilities, continue parental contact with ex-spouse, and support contact of children with ex-spouse and his or her family.	a. Making flexible visitation arrangements with ex-spouse and family. b. Rebuilding own financial resources. c. Rebuilding own social network.
	Single parent (noncustodial)	Willingness to maintain financial responsibilities and parental contact with ex-spouse and to support custodial parent's relationship with children.	a. Finding ways to continue effective parenting. b. Maintaining financial responsibilities to ex-spouse and children. c. Rebuilding own social network.

THE DIVORCE AND POSTDIVORCE FAMILY EMOTIONAL PROCESS

Our concept of the divorce and postdivorce emotional process can be visualized as a roller-coaster graph, with peaks of emotional tension at all transition points:

1. At the time of the decision to separate or divorce.
2. When this decision is announced to family and friends.
3. When money and custody/visitation arrangements are discussed.
4. When the physical separation takes place.
5. When the actual legal divorce takes place.
6. When separated spouses or ex-spouses have contact about money or children.
7. As each child graduates, marries, has children, or becomes ill.
8. As each spouse is remarried, moves, becomes ill, or dies.

These emotional pressure peaks are found in all divorcing families—not necessarily in the above order—and many of them take place over and over again, for months or years. A more detailed depiction of the process appears in Table 22.1.

The emotions released during the process of divorce relate primarily to the work of emotional divorce, that is, the retrieval of self from the marriage. Each partner must retrieve the hopes, dreams, plans, and expectations that were invested in this spouse and in this marriage. This requires mourning what is lost and dealing with hurt, anger, blame, guilt, shame, and loss in oneself, in the spouse, in the children, and in the extended family.

FAMILY EMOTIONAL PROCESS AT THE TRANSITION TO REMARRIAGE

The predictable peaks of emotional tension in the transition to remarriage occur at the time of serious commitment to a new relationship; at the time a plan to remarry is announced to families and friends; and at the time of the actual remarriage and formation of a stepfamily, which take place

simultaneously as the logistics of stepfamily life are put into practice.

The family emotional process at the transition to remarriage consists of struggling with fears about investment in a new marriage and a new family: one's own fears, the new spouse's fears, and the fears of the children (of either or both spouses); dealing with hostile or upset reactions of the children, the extended families, and the ex-spouse; struggling with the ambiguity of the new family structure, roles, and relationships; rearousal of intense parental guilt and concerns about the welfare of children; and rearousal of the old attachment to the ex-spouse (negative or positive). Table 22.2 depicts the process in somewhat greater detail, as does Chapter 25.

Our society offers stepfamilies a choice of two conceptual models, neither of which works: families that act like the intact family next door that is glorified in TV situation comedies and the wicked stepparents of the fairy tales. Our first clinical step, then, is to validate for stepfamilies the lack of social support and clarity in the paradigm of family they are offered. Clinicians can offer them the challenge of helping to invent a new form of family structure, with the following guidelines making good systems sense: giving up the old model of family and accepting the complexity of a new form; maintaining permeable boundaries to permit shifting of household memberships; and working for open lines of communication between all sets of parents, between grandparents, and between them and their children or grandchildren (see Chapter 25).

In our experience, the residue of an angry and vengeful divorce can block step-family integration for years or forever. The rearousal of the old emotional attachment to an ex-spouse, which characteristically surfaces at the time of remarriage and at subsequent life cycle transitions of children, is usually not understood as a predictable process and therefore leads to denial, misinterpretation, cut-off, and assorted difficulties. As in the case of adjustment to a new family structure after divorce, step-family integration seems also to require a minimum of two or three years before a workable

TABLE 22.2 Remarried Family Formation: A Developmental Outline*

STEPS	PREREQUISITE ATTITUDE	DEVELOPMENTAL ISSUES
1. Entering the new relationship	Recovery from loss of first marriage (adequate emotional divorce).	Recommitment to marriage and to forming a family with readiness to deal with the complexity and ambiguity.
2. Conceptualizing and planning new marriage and family	Accepting one's own fears and those of new spouse and children about remarriage and forming a step-family. Accepting need for time and patience for adjustment to complexity and ambiguity of: 1. Multiple new roles. 2. Boundaries: space, time, membership, and authority. 3. Affective issues: guilt, loyalty conflicts, desire for mutuality, unresolvable past hurts.	a. Work on openness in the new relationships to avoid pseudomutuality. b. Plan for maintenance of cooperative financial and co-parental relationships with ex-spouses. c. Plan to help children deal with fears, loyalty conflicts, and membership in two systems. d. Realignment of relationships with extended family to include new spouse and children. e. Plan maintenance of connections for children with extended family of ex-spouses.
3. Remarriage and reconstruction of family	Final resolution of attachment to previous spouse and ideal of "intact" family; acceptance of a different model of family with permeable boundaries.	a. Restructuring family boundaries to allow for inclusion of new spouse-stepparent. b. Realignment of relationships and financial arrangements throughout subsystems to permit interweaving of several systems. c. Making room for relationships of all children with biological (noncustodial) parents, grandparents, and other extended family. d. Sharing memories and histories to enhance step-family integration.

*Variation of a developmental schema presented by Ransom et al. (1979).

new structure permits family members to move on emotionally.

Table 22.2 describes the developmental steps required for remarried family formation. It is similar in some respects to that described by Ransom and co-workers (1979). Their outline was particularly apt in addressing the need to conceptualize and plan for the remarriage. Although it is certainly true that more advance planning would also be helpful in first marriages, it is an essential ingredient for successful remarriage because of the different conceptual model required and because of the number of family relationships that must be renegotiated at the same time. We have added to the framework dealing with children and extended family as well as the new spouse because as Ransom et al. themselves have observed, "the presence of children at the earliest stages prevents the establishment of an exclusive spouse-to-spouse relationship which pre-dates the undertaking of parenthood" (p. 37).

It is our opinion that the emotional tasks listed in column 2 of Table 22.2 are key attitudes in the transition that permit the family to work on the developmental issues of column 3. If as clinicians, we find ourselves struggling with the family over developmental issues (column 3) before the pre-requisite attitudes (column 2) have been adopted, we are probably wasting our efforts. For example, it is very hard for a parent to help children remain connected to ex-in-laws who were never close or supportive unless the parent has fully embraced the ideas of the new model of family. Much education and discussion may be required before a client can put into effect ideas that may seem counterintuitive, aversive, or time consuming. See further discussion of these and other issues in Chapter 25.

When they came for marital therapy, Josh Steiner and Susan Watson had been married for 14 years. They had a 12-year-old son, Sam and a 10-year-old daughter, Karen. Susan's complaint was that Josh was a workaholic, like his father and hers, and now that Sam was approaching his teens, "he needs his father." Josh, a surgeon, and a senior administrator at the hospital, worked over sixty hours a week, often more. Susan, also a physician, had for years kept her hours strictly part-time to allow for child care. Their relationship had veered from distance to periods of conflict "about the kids and me, not about *us*," Josh said. As marital therapy seemed to go in circles, the therapist inquired closely into their past relationship and future commitment, causing Susan to admit that she had "given up on him" some years ago and "could not imagine growing old with him." She agreed to "try" to help put the marriage back together, but consistently "forgot" between-session assignments, "didn't notice" that Josh was coming home earlier, and so on. Both she and Josh resisted the therapist's suggestions that they put some energy into their family of origin relationships.

After six months of stalling, Susan said that she wanted a divorce; she had decided this years ago, had hoped to be able to postpone it until the children were older, but now could not tolerate the wait. Josh flew into a rage, quit therapy, hired an aggressive divorce lawyer, and told Susan that he planned to sue for custody of the children. The therapist phoned Josh, convincing him to come back to therapy "for the sake of the children—whether it's marital or divorce therapy, they need you to re-build or dismantle your marriage in an orderly way."

It turned out quickly to be divorce therapy, and although he was even further enraged, Josh made several steps "for the sake of the children": he stopped threatening to sue for custody and agreed to continue divorce therapy until the family was living separately and the separation agreement was signed. On her part, Susan agreed to forgo any claims of alimony and let the lawyers negotiate about child support. She was interested in the therapist's suggestion that they go to divorce mediation, but Josh refused, and she decided not to press the point with him.

At this point, the therapist saw each of them separately for several sessions, inquiring in detail about Susan's financial plans (she hadn't "really thought about that") and Josh's plans for staying in close touch with his children ("You mean I should cancel my plan to get a studio apartment?"). For several months, the therapist saw Josh, Susan, and their two children separately and in various combinations as the couple first planned how to tell their children ("no blaming"), then told them, then arranged for the children to help Josh move to his new two-bedroom apartment and put some of their things there. Along this path, the therapist helped each of them to resist destructive suggestions from their lawyers (e.g., Josh should refuse to move out of the house; Susan should refuse to permit Sam's bar mitzvah planning to proceed). As the early logistics were put into place and family grieving over the changes came into focus, Josh suddenly fell in love and left therapy to make a new life, in spite of the therapist's warnings about timing.

Susan remained in therapy but wanted to focus on her reactions to Josh's girlfriend and her children's reactions to the woman, who was divorced with a daughter Karen's age. Susan made several fairly superficial moves with her family of origin, mostly making more contact with her father and brother, but couldn't think of specific issues with them except for a global sense of being the outsider. Susan was able to follow the therapist's coaching suggestions that she not get into conflict with Josh's girlfriend but rather tell Josh that she preferred to make visitation arrangements with him, not the girlfriend. She felt a huge sense of relief that the marriage was over and even acknowledged that Josh had not been a bad guy at all, except for always being away, "but then, I didn't really want him around all the time anyway." She recognized but couldn't identify the reasons for this ambivalence. When their separation agreement was declared satisfactory and signed by both of them, Susan expressed a mixture of sadness and relief and left therapy. She said that the kids were moody, but they had all survived Sam's bar mitzvah, which Josh had "ruined" by insisting on bringing along his now live-in girlfriend, even though Sam and even Josh's mother had objected. "But now it's almost over," she said as she thanked the therapist and left.

Less than a year later, Susan was back because of Sam's behavior at school—fights, failing grades, and disrespecting the teachers. He was now over 14 years old. Meanwhile, Josh and his girlfriend had broken up, and Josh was angrier and less available to the children than ever. Susan now had a housemate, an artist and writer, who "helps with the mortgage and helps with the kids. Karen loves her and Sam will too when he straightens out." After a few questions from the therapist, Susan burst into tears and acknowledged that the housemate was actually her lover. She said, "I *didn't* want to be gay; I *don't* want to be; but I never dreamed you could feel this way about someone." However, she said, no one else knew. "Can you imagine what Josh would do?" She told several stories of custody lost because of a parent's homosexuality and of gays and lesbians who had lost their careers and their families when their sexual orientation was discovered. As the discussion proceeded, she told the therapist that if this secret was behind Sam's bad behavior, she'd just have to give up her relationship with the woman she loved; she couldn't tell. The therapist urged her to go very slowly on any move, because society's attitude was a very big item here, and they should talk and think it through very carefully in therapy before she did anything. Susan agreed.

The first move the therapist suggested was that Susan locate a town in the area that had a legally established precedent of *not* changing custody because of a parent's homosexuality and that she keep that in mind as an "insurance policy" if Josh or anyone threatened legal moves against her. Then, when Susan decided that, more than anything, she wanted to continue her relationship with her lover, Alice, she and the therapist worked out the following plan, which Susan put into effect over the next two years:

- Susan told Alice to back off the kids, not discipline them or act like a parent, but to spend some separate time occasionally with each, talking or doing something fun.

- Susan came out to her children, who were first upset, especially Sam ("You're more disgusting than Dad and Cheryl"), but then interested. They agreed to let their mother tell anyone else she decided to.

- Therapy sessions then included various combinations of Susan, Alice, and the children to process the children's reactions and to help organize their family, which had the same structure as a heterosexual remarried household. They agreed to speak to the children's teachers and to participate in gay and lesbian social groups after Josh had been told so that they wouldn't have to live a secret life.

- Susan came out to Josh, who went into an uproar. Having predicted this and been coached not to react to it, Susan stayed calm and suggested that he return to therapy "for the sake of the children."

- After this, Susan and Josh were seen separately—and occasionally together—for coaching in their families of origin and to review the marriage in light of this new information. Josh had to get over his "wounded masculinity" because Susan had left him for a woman. He couldn't answer the therapist's question as to how it would feel better if she'd left him for another man. Slowly, their empathy for each other returned. Josh survived meeting Alice and even admitted that he rather liked her. Sam's acting out ceased, and both children became involved in their schoolwork and social activities, including those at a local center for gay and lesbian families.

- Both did a little more work in their families of origin. Josh came to see that his position in his parental triangle, blaming his mother for the conflict with "poor dad," had set him up to repeat his father's pattern and be impatient with women's "demands." Susan knew that she would never be able to know whether her feeling left out related to her unrecognized sexual orientation or her mother's favoritism toward her younger sister—or which came first. But she made sure she wasn't left out of current contact and gatherings.

- Susan came out to her family, using it as an opportunity to deal differently with each member. Josh also used this revelation as an opportunity to open up to his family members and improve those relationships.

- Susan told her closest associate at work and was relieved to find her colleagues supportive and unconcerned.
- Josh requested sessions for himself and a new, serious, woman friend, Sheila, because they were thinking of getting married but were concerned about the reaction of Sheila's two teenagers. They were also concerned that her ex-husband, who was extremely distant and paid only sporadic child support might use this opportunity to just cut off from his sons and invest his time and money in his own stepsons. Josh was also concerned about Sam and Karen's reactions to another major change.

CONCLUSION

The preceding case shows the extreme complexity of the emotional and structural issues that follow divorce. The divorce-specific issues interact with issues from the families of origin, issues from the family's current life cycle stage (e.g., adolescence), and issues created by social attitudes (e.g., homophobia). This family worked on their relationships over a period of more than five years before all the pieces fell into place. But when they did, the results were impressive: Susan, Alice, and the children all attended Josh's wedding, mingling pleasantly with the bride, her sons, and her family. And as Sam left for an excellent college, he said that he expected "all of my parents" to write, visit, and send goodies. Two years later, Karen graduated from high school with several honors at a ceremony attended by all of them.

What is most striking about their story are the many, many opportunities along the way to fall into conflict and cut-offs, most of which, with the help of the therapist, they resisted, while setting a course aimed always at maintaining and improving their significant relationships.

REFERENCES

Ahrons, C., & Rodgers, R. (1987). *Divorced families: a multi-disciplinary developmental view.* New York: W. W. Norton.

Carter, B. (1988). Divorce: His and hers. In M. Walters, B. Carter, P. Papp, & O. Silverstein, *The invisible web: Gender patterns in family relationships* (pp. 253–271). New York: The Guilford Press.

Carter, B., & Peters, J. (1996). *Love, honor & negotiate: Building partnerships that last a lifetime.* New York: Pocket Books.

Glick, P. (1984). Marriage, divorce and living arrangements. *Journal of Family Issues 5,* 7–26.

Hetherington, M. (1993). An overview of the Virginia longitudinal study of divorce and remarriage. *Journal of Family Psychology, 7,* 39–56.

Ransom, J., Schlesinger, S., & Derdeyn, A. (1979). A stepfamily in formation. *American Journal of Orthopsychiatry, 49,* 1.

Wallerstein, J., & Blakeslee, S. (1989). *Second chances: men, women, and children a decade after divorce.* New York: Tichnor and Fields.

CHAPTER 23

DIVORCE
AN UNSCHEDULED FAMILY TRANSITION

CONSTANCE R. AHRONS

Although divorce is a common occurrence of family life today, our society still tends to view it as an abnormality that will go away if only we can find out how to make it do so. But the realities are that divorce and remarriage are unscheduled life transitions that will affect large numbers of families and alter their developmental life course. In this chapter, divorce will be examined from a normative perspective, and the process will be discussed as a multidimensional series of predictable transitions that affect families intergenerationally.* Although all divorces have some common denominators, where divorce occurs in the developmental life cycle of the family will alter the family's pattern of the process, their developmental path and their present and future interactions. How divorce affects the family is also altered by diverse sociocultural factors. Ethnic and religious groups may differ in the way they perceive divorce, and these different perceptions influence how a family copes with divorce. Clinicians working with families need to understand the process so that they can help families move through the divorce process and reorganize as healthy family systems.

THE CONTEXT OF DIVORCE

Historical and Legal Perspectives

History demonstrates that, despite our belief in the newness of divorce, our society evolved ways of dissolving marriages in tandem with ways of making marriages. Divorce is as firmly woven into the fabric of society as marriage is. Even the most cursory societal examination clearly reveals patterns that show us that divorce is here to stay.

Divorce rates have been on the rise for the past three centuries, reaching their peak in the late 1970s. However, in each decade, there have been fluctuations; divorce rates tend to decline during hard times and rise in times of prosperity. Between 1965 and 1980—the prosperous years—divorce rates more than doubled. In the late 1980s, the economy dipped, and the divorce rate declined slightly; with minor fluctuations, it has leveled off at our current rate.

The first recorded divorce in America happened back in 1639, in a Puritan court in Massachusetts, when James Luxford's wife asked for a divorce because her husband already had a wife. The divorce was granted. Public and legal debates about the high divorce rates and how liberal or restrictive divorce laws should be occurred as early as the late 1700s. These early debates were very similar in tone and content to the discussions we hear these days about whether we should make divorces more or less difficult. The pattern of liberalizing divorce laws and then tightening them, seesawing from honoring the individual to honoring the society and back again, is one that we see throughout Europe and the United States.

Today, every state has some form of no-fault divorce law. Waiting periods are short, and mandatory reconciliation counseling is virtually absent. These liberalizations occurred during the 1970s.

*Most of this chapter is based on and contains excerpts from Constance R. Ahrons, *The Good Divorce,* HarperCollins, 1994, and Constance R. Ahrons and Roy H. Rodgers, *Divorced Families,* W.W. Norton, 1987.

As we have moved into a more conservative political climate in recent years, new legislation is being proposed to tighten the divorce laws again by limiting the parameters of no-fault legislation and once again requiring mandatory counseling.

Demographics and the Probability of Divorce

The probability of divorce is associated with a number of demographic factors. Age is the strongest predictor. Couples who are 20 years of age or younger when they marry have the highest likelihood of divorce. People with less income and education tend to divorce more than those with higher education and incomes. An important exception to this principle relates to women: Well-educated women (five or more years of college) with good incomes have higher divorce rates than do women who are poorer and less educated.

Geographically, there are some differences as well. People in the Western part of the United States have higher divorce rates than those in the Northeast. This may be due partly to the fact that the average age is lower in the West. Also, there is a higher concentration of Catholics in the Northeast.

There are also significant racial differences. Divorce rates for the Black population are two times those of Whites or Hispanics. Although the explanations for the higher divorce rate among African Americans vary, socioeconomic differences seem to play a part. On the average, Blacks are less educated, poorer, and more often unemployed than Whites.

Religion also plays a part. Catholics and Jews have a lower divorce rate than Protestants. Since Catholicism is the religion of traditional Hispanics, part of the explanation for the racial differences in divorce rates may be attributed to religious affiliation. Although Catholics have a lower divorce rate, their rates have risen just as rapidly as those of the general divorce population (Ahlburg & DeVita, 1992; Guttmann, 1993).

A sixfold increase in cohabitation since 1970 has also affected divorce rates. In some European countries, a recent decline in divorce rates can be attributed to the increase in informal cohabitation arrangements. In Sweden, for example, this increase in cohabitation has decreased the marriage rate as well as the divorce rate. Breakups of these informal unions, of course, are not included in the divorce rate. It has been suggested that cohabitation may actually be pruning the divorce rate (Kirn, 1997). These "preventive divorces" are not officially recorded.

At present, 45 percent of all first marriage in the United States end in divorce (Lamb, Sternberg, & Thompson, 1997). Demographic trends suggest that the current divorce rates in the United States are now fairly stable. Demographers predict that 40 to 60 percent of all current marriages will eventually end in divorce. Those who predict the lower rates say that the divorce rate will decline as the baby boomers age; that boomers who wish to divorce have already done so, and those that haven't are past the stage of life when the odds of divorce are the highest (Glick, 1990). Those who predict an increase, whether large or small, say that women's and men's roles will continue to change. That change, plus the increasing financial independence of women—historically the less satisfied party in marriage—will continue to push the rates upward (Bumpass, 1990).

Ethnic and Life Cycle Variations

A serious weakness of the current state of divorce research is that almost all of the research is based on White, middle-class samples. Because our interest in divorce has been on its effects on children, most of the research has focused on young children and their mothers (Lamb et al., 1997). A growing body of research based on information collected from both parents, using court records rather than clinical data, is gradually beginning to provide important data on the entire family system (Ahrons, 1994; Hetherington, 1993; Maccoby & Mnookin, 1992; Stewart, Copeland, Chester, & Malley, 1997). These studies tend to be small, in-depth studies based on in-person interviews, often conducted at two or three different times periods in the divorced family life cycle.

Larger studies, utilizing national samples, provide comparative information on divorced and married families. These studies usually focus on school-age children and their primary parent, most frequently the mother. These studies are often part of a larger study, and although they contribute greatly to our general knowledge of the effects of divorce, they provide less family interactional data than do the smaller, more intensive studies.

Unfortunately, there is a paucity of research on divorce in midlife and later life and on the effects on older children and young adults. Also lacking from the research are data on different ethnic groups and what, if any, variations exist in process or outcome.

Most of what is presented in this chapter is based on the existing research, with particular emphasis on the author's own longitudinal study.[*] When information is available in the literature on ethnic and life cycle variations, the findings will be noted.

The Social Context

Divorce is usually thought to be symptomatic of family instability and synonymous with family dissolution. This view is reflected in the terms used to describe the divorced family: "broken home," "disorganized," "fractured," "incomplete." A review of the divorce literature over the past two decades makes it clear that divorce is generally regarded as pathological and an index of social disorder. Most research has been designed to search for problems created by divorce and often relies on clinical or problem identified populations. Not only is divorce viewed that way in the professional literature, but it is quite common to find divorce labeled in the media as the cause of all sorts of social problems, such as drugs, delinquency, and family

violence. The stories presented in the media are usually the worst-case scenarios, which, unfortunately, then tend to be viewed as the norm.

This view has given rise to a distorted perception of divorce, leading investigators and practitioners to focus primarily on pathology. For example, the term "single-parent family" implies that a family contains only one parent; however, in most divorced families, although mothers are usually the primary caregivers, both parents continue to function in parental roles (Stewart et al., 1997). Divorce creates new households with single parents, but it results in a single-parent family only when one of the parents, usually the father, has no further contact with the family and does not continue to perform a parental function. More appropriate terminology would distinguish between these two circumstances and would describe the former as a "one-parent household" (Ahrons, 1980a, 1980b).

Although the loss of the father-child relationship is an all too common outcome for many children in divorced families, innovative custody arrangements such as joint custody and the increased involvement of fathers in child-rearing roles have also created postdivorce family arrangements in which the children continue to be reared by both parents. The majority of postdivorce families have evolved continuing and well-functioning relationships that do not appear to be at all pathological (Lamb et al., 1997). In such cases, divorce has not terminated family relationships; rather, it has been a process whereby the form of these relationships has changed.

DIVORCE AS A MULTIDIMENSIONAL PROCESS

From a legal and social status perspective, divorce is an event; it moves individuals from the condition of being legally married to that of being legally divorced. When the divorce decree is final, the partners are free to remarry. However, looked at from a family dynamics standpoint and not a legal standpoint, divorce is best regarded as a multidimensional process of family change. It has roots somewhere in the past, before the legal act

[*]The Binuclear Family Study is a longitudinal study of 98 families interviewed at three points in time. Funded by the National Institutes of Mental Health and the University of Wisconsin, this research began in 1979 and examines the reorganization process of families at one, three, and five years after divorce. A twenty-year follow-up study of the 201 children (now ages 21 through 45) is in progress.

transpired, and carries with it effects that extend into the future. Each family member will be profoundly affected by it; as members of a postdivorce family, individuals will be forced to learn new ways of coping and of relating to the society at large, as well as to each other.

The Binuclear Family

The process of divorcing culminates in a complex redefinition of relationships within the family. Although the structure of postdivorce families varies, some basic tasks must be accomplished in all separations. Once a family has established the ground rules for living separately (for example, where the children will reside or how visitation will be arranged), the family needs to clarify rules for relating within and across the various subsystems within the family system, for example, the parental subsystem or the parent-child subsystem.

The multidimensional divorce process can be viewed as a series of transitions that mark the family's change from married to divorced status. This process involves disorganizing the nuclear family and reorganizing it into a binuclear family. The binuclear family consists of two households or subsystems, maternal and paternal, which then form the nuclei of the child's family of orientation (Ahrons, 1979, 1980a).

Binuclear families are similar to extended kin or quasi-kin relationships. In many families, for example, the marriage of a child marks the beginning of a quasi-kin relationship between the families of the newly married couple. In this quasi-kin structure, two families are bonded through the marriage of their children. Jewish families have institutionalized this nonblood familial relationship. The Yiddish term *"machetunim"* means "relatives through marriage," referring specifically to the relationship between the family of the bride and the family of the groom (Rosten, 1989). Many Jewish families frequently spend holidays and special events with their "machetunim." These two families may or may not like each other, but amicability is not the primary reason for their gathering. They gather not as intimates, but as "blood" relations.

The bonds created by families joined through marriage are similar to the bonds of the divorced family. In both types of families, a child gives rise to the continuing bond. In the family joined through marriage, the relationship between the two sets of in-laws usually determines the interrelationships within the extended family system. The style of relationship within the divorced family is usually based on the nature of the relationship between the divorced spouses.

Transitions of the Divorce Process

Transitions are turning points, uncomfortable periods that mark the beginning of something new while signifying the ending of something familiar. Although the changes may be anticipated with puzzlement and foreboding, they may also be approached with exhilaration. During transitional periods, families are more personally vulnerable, but paradoxically, these are also the times when personal growth is most likely to occur.

Usually, when we think of transitions, we think in terms of the biological developmental clock: adolescence, midlife, or aging. In defining biological developmental transitions, in outlining typical themes, common feelings, and experiences, we normalize situations that otherwise would feel, and appear to be, abnormal. When people know what to expect, it doesn't take away all the upheaval, but it does help them to cope better with the difficult changes that the transition inevitably brings. People experience great relief when they can place themselves within a natural progression that has a beginning and an end. Although we usually define transitions within developmental frameworks (e.g., birth of a first child, retirement), some life transitions are unrelated to developmental or social time clocks.

Unlike other transitions that occur more or less on predictable chronological timetables, divorce can occur at any time during the family life cycle. Unlike expected transitions in the life cycle, divorce has a greater potential to cause disequilibrium that can result in debilitating crises. And unlike family crises of sudden onset, the divorce process begins long before the actual decision to obtain a legal divorce. Divorce is an internal crisis of relationship, a deliberate dissolution of the primary bond in the family, and the family's identity appears to be shattered. For most people, ending a marriage is the most traumatic decision of their life. The usual ways of coping are unlikely to work. People often act in ways that no one around them can make sense of. Abigail Trafford (1982) refers to this period as "crazy time."

Stress, crisis, and adaptation are three concepts that are often used in understanding how families cope with a myriad of life's distressful events, such as chronic illness, death of a loved one, and unemployment (Boss, 1987; McCubbin & Patterson, 1983; Rodgers, 1986). Stress occurs when there is an imbalance (perceived or actual) between what is actually happening—the stressors—and what family members feel capable of handling. Crisis occurs when the stress exceeds the ability of individuals in the family to effectively handle the stressors. All families have different levels of tolerance—breaking points—beyond which they are no longer able to cope with the situation. When too many things hit all at once, when stressors pile up, system overload sets in. When the family's reservoir of coping behaviors becomes depleted or outmoded and they do not know what to do, they are in a crisis.

Divorce is ranked at the top of the list of stressful life events. Many stressors overlap in the divorce transitions. All of the normal coping abilities are taxed by complex personal and familial changes. Add the lack of adequate role models of good divorces, the absence of clear-cut rules or rituals for managing this new and unfamiliar stage of life, and the lack of external resources, such as community support and positive social sanctions, and crisis is certainly a predictable outcome.

Ambiguity is a big contributor to stress (Boss, 1983; Boss & Greenberg, 1984). For divorcing parents and their children, the knowledge that their family will continue to be a family, restructuring from a nuclear to a binuclear form, reduces some of the debilitating ambiguity associated with divorce. Understanding that divorce is a process with predictable transitions of disorganization followed by structured transitions of reorganization helps to at least reduce the intensity and duration of the crisis. When families have knowledge of what to expect with adequate role models to assist them, they can better identify which decisions need to be made—and when—and can then decide upon what kind of new rules need to be established. The knowledge and ability to plan facilitate their capacity to cope more effectively during the crisis and manage the mass of overwhelming feelings. In effect, they move the divorce process toward "normality."

The lack of adequate norms, knowledge, and role models has been detrimental for divorcing families. Clinicians working with them have also lacked the knowledge and skills to help these families move through the transitions and emerge as healthy binuclear families. New strategies for assisting families through the divorce process, such as mediation, psychoeducational workshops, coparenting seminars, and divorce therapy, that incorporate normative models are emerging and creating healthier outcomes for families.

THE TRANSITIONS FRAMEWORK

Breaking down the very complex process of divorce into transitions—common developmental steps—allows us to then explore the ways people adapt at each of the stages. Developed from my longitudinal research on divorcing families, five overlapping transitions, each with distinct role changes and tasks, were identified (Ahrons, 1980a, 1994; Ahrons & Rodgers, 1987). The first three transitions—individual cognition, family metacognition, and systemic separation—form the core of the disorganizing emotional separation process. The last two transitions—systemic reorganization and systemic redefinition—form the family reorganization process.

Although they are presented sequentially in their ideal developmental order, the transitions usually overlap. Each transition includes social role transitions encompassing a complex interaction of overlapping experiences. There is no neat rule for when a particular transition will occur in a particular person or couple or for how long the transition will last. What we do know, from studies in the United States and from cross-national studies, regardless of cultural or national differences, is that it takes most people between one and a half and three years after the initial separation to stabilize their feelings (Cseh-Szombathy, Koch-Nielsen, Trost, & Weda, 1985). Each transition is heralded by increased stress. At the end of the transition, the stress tends to plateau or to decrease.

Individual Cognition: The Decision

The decision to end a marriage is usually far more difficult and prolonged than the decision to marry. The dread of negative repercussions, of an uncertain future, and of painful losses all combine to make the transition a wrenching and internally violent one. The first step toward divorce is rarely mutual. It begins within one person, often starting as a small, amorphous, nagging feeling of dissatisfaction. The feeling grows in spurts, sometimes gaining strength, sometimes retreating, flaring up, and again moving forward. For some people, this private simmering of unhappiness goes on for years. For others, a few months of depression may be more they can bear. The hallmark of this transition is ambivalence, accompanied by obsession, vacillation, and anguish. It is not uncommon for the individual in the throes of this process to have an affair and/or seek out a therapist.

When an individual begins to seriously question feelings for his or her mate, a passage of emotional leave-taking takes place. This "erosion of love" starts slowly and may be barely noticeable at first. Behaviors that were acceptable for years become annoying; habits that were tolerated become intolerable. More and more "evidence" is collected as a case is built to justify the decision to leave.

Characteristic of the coping mechanisms in this transition is the denial of marital problems. Spouses also resort to blaming to obtain respite from a situation that is perceived as intolerable. Marital conflicts usually escalate the search for fault in the other spouse and often result in his or her being labeled the culprit. This time can be a

highly stressful one, especially for the children, who often become pawns in the marital strife. Conflict-habituated marriages are less threatening to some families than the uncertainty and change that accompany separation and divorce. In other families, instead of open conflict, there are a distancing and withdrawal of emotional investment, both in the marriage and often in the family. In families with dependent children, it is not uncommon to make a decision—albeit often not adhered to—to stay in the marriage until the children are grown. The dissatisfied partner may decide to invest emotional energy in extramarital interests while attempting to maintain the facade of an intact family. These patterns usually result in family dysfunction. When marital relationships are highly conflictual or cold and distant, it is not unusual for a child living in that household to develop symptoms, which in turn may prompt the family to seek therapy. In this way, the "secret" may become exposed.

Another very common pattern that clinicians see is the couple who come in for therapy with two different—but not openly stated—agendas. Although both may come in for marriage counseling, one partner has already emotionally disengaged from the relationship and comes to therapy as a way to relieve his or her guilt. She or he can then say, "I've tried everything to make this marriage work, even marriage counseling." Or the disengaged partner, fearful of the other partner's reaction to the planned leave-taking, may seek out a therapist who can become the caretaker/rescuer of the soon-to-be left partner. In both cases, the therapist has the difficult task of trying to help the couple to honestly face their issues before any treatment contract can be arrived at.

Although a divorce often ends up being a mutual decision, at the early stages there is one person (the initiator or leaver) who harbors the secret desire to leave and one person who is initially unaware of that desire (the opposer or the left). In some cases, both partners may have had similar fantasies, but one person usually takes the first step and begins the process.

Leavers and lefts have very different feelings at the outset. The leaver has had the advantage early on of wrestling with his or her emotions, has already started grieving, and has already detached to some degree. The person being left is perceived to be the victim. This person's immediate reactions range from disbelief and shock to outrage and despair. The partners have unequal power at this point. The person being left is more vulnerable. Having had no time to prepare—to adapt to the overwhelming threat—the one being left is more likely to experience crisis at this point.

Who takes the role of leaver and who takes the role of left often relate to gender. In the United States and most European countries, it is estimated that between two thirds and three quarters of all divorces are initiated by women. One of the biggest factors leading to this statistic is the increase in women's economic independence. It is not that women used to be happier in marriage than they are today, but they often believed that they could not survive outside of marriage without their husband's money. Even today, the lowest divorce rate occurs in traditional marriages with breadwinner husbands and full-time homemaker wives. Not only have women's economic opportunities expanded, so have their social opportunities. Even though we are still a very coupled society, it is much easier today than it was even 20 years ago to live a full life as a single woman. Even so, many women say that they left because they had no choice. Stories of years of abuse, betrayal, or absenteeism by their husband are common.

Family Metacognition: The Announcement

Proclaiming one's desire to separate from one's partner is no easy task. But for some couples, the announcement is as far as their marital crisis will go. Sometimes, the moment of confrontation creates an opportunity to actually improve a marriage. For other couples, the announcement is the first step in a tangled escalating series of confrontations and reconciliations. For still others, one day they're married and the next day they're not; the announcement can also be a clear, direct, and sometimes almost instant path to separation and divorce.

Denial often follows any major shock. One common reaction is for the spouse to call the leaving partner's reasons frivolous. It is not uncommon, in the early phase right after the announcement occurs, to think that a few minor changes—becoming more attentive or more attractive—will help what seems to be an anomalous outburst to blow over. Although it is rare, sometimes a new wardrobe, flowers, extra telephone calls, and other efforts do help temporarily, especially when the potential leaver is still very ambivalent.

Leavers almost always portray a long, painful process of leave-taking. The one being left is coping not only with rejection but also with having to develop an account after the fact. In the first two phases of the process, the leaver commonly feels guilty; the left feels angry. Rarely is the process symmetrical, let alone rational or mutual.

In many cases, the announcement seems spontaneous, as much a dreadful surprise to the leaver as to the left. In these cases, the discomfort is often so severe that the leaver (either consciously or unconsciously) resorts to setting up a situation that will bring the issue into the open without anyone having to accept responsibility. The leaver may get forgetful and leave a lover's letter on the dresser, stay out all night, or arrive home with the proverbial lipstick on the collar. Once discovered, the objects or events provoke a crisis, and it's over. Creating a crisis makes it possible to shift the blame. The couple can then fight about whatever issue got raised in the crisis, rather than dealing with the long-term issues of their distressing marital relationship.

Betrayal and Blame. Statistics on extramarital affairs are very varied and highly unreliable, owing to the unwillingness of many people to disclose them (Brown, 1991; Spring, 1996). But they are quite common to marital separations. What is worse than the affair itself, more difficult to cope with, is the protective web of lies. As each lie gets uncovered or explodes during a battle about the affair, the betrayed spouse begins to question the entire history of the relationship. The betrayed person questions the betrayer closely, even obsessively, trying to separate truth from fiction. The betrayer and the betrayed rarely see eye to eye on how much talking is needed.

For a myriad of reasons, it is difficult for the betrayer to be truthful. Perhaps he or she wants to hold onto both the spouse and lover, wants to protect against possible legal ramifications, or does not want to inflict more pain. The betrayed senses that there is more and keeps pressing, trying to get to the bottom of things. The betrayer may comply for awhile, then usually grows impatient with the constant focus and repetition. The betrayer thinks that the betrayed spouse is "carrying this too far." Blame then shifts to the betrayed spouse for not letting go (Brown, 1991; Lerner, 1993; Spring, 1996). This common and very predictable pattern, unfortunately, lays the groundwork for a highly acrimonious and destructive divorce process. If a clinician is brought into this process at this transition, she or he may be able to help the couple to sort out the issues and to understand the power struggle that pervade this process. However, all too often, the betrayer is unwilling to commit to therapy, and the issue of "the affair" pervades the rest of the divorce transitions. Although divorce is legally no-fault and adultery is no longer needed to show cause, blame often plays a big role in the emotional divorce process.

Rage, prejudicial myth making, depression, and impulsive desires to retaliate are normal reactions for the partner who is being left. Anger plays an important role when there is a bad blow to the ego. It temporarily shields the betrayed spouse from facing devastating emotions: grief, rejection, even self-hatred. If, over the course of the marriage, mutual anger has been buried, the anger can easily erupt in this transition. All the past injustices that went unconfronted are replayed. Both the earlier denial and the current anger help the one who has been left to cope with a life that is swinging out of control.

Loss.   Divorce is marked by severe losses. Not only are the losses related to the present life-style, but there are also losses of future plans and fantasies. Even for the couple in the early stages of marriage, there are powerful feelings of loss. Their whole dream of married life may be shattered; the children they had planned for and the house they were going to buy remain unrealized dreams. The couple with young children have to face that their future plans will never materialize: the wonderful skiing vacations they were planning to take in a couple of years or the camping trip to the Grand Canyon. The midlife couple who divorces after a long marriage may have had retirement plans that will never come to fruition: the long awaited trip to Europe after the children were grown or that secluded house at the lake.

Unresolved grieving for losses is a major deterrent to a making a healthy adaptation to divorce. Clinicians need to be aware that when anger is the major coping mechanism of a divorcing spouse, uncovering the grief may need to be a very slow process. Otherwise, the depression may be so overwhelming that the spouse, especially if she or he is the primary parent, may not be able to function in the parental role.

This transition is key to the rest of the transitions. Family therapy at this time can be very productive. Sometimes, even a few sessions can help to clarify how to deescalate the anger whenever it occurs during the divorce process. Additional sessions can help both children and adults to defuse their terror about the major changes that divorce brings; they can start to plan. To avert a serious crisis requires that both partners show considerable patience, maturity, and honesty. Leavers need to understand their partner's angry reaction and give him or her time to deal with it. Being able to talk about some of the changes that can be expected during the next transitions as the marriage is being dismantled is important, as frustrating and difficult as such talk may be. The more responsibly couples plan for a timely separation, the less likely it is to break down into debilitating crisis. For couples, being rational during such emotional times is often impossible without the help of a therapist.

Systemic Separation: Dismantling the Nuclear Family

Most people remember the day they separated—not the day their divorce was legally awarded—as the day their divorce began. Separation day is one of those marker events that divorced people never forget. For children, this is when they realize the enormity of what is going on, even though they may have suspected or feared the prospect of some time.

Some couples and children feel a great sense of relief at the separation transition, especially when the marriage had become highly stressful. Other families are overwhelmed with fear and anxiety. For still others, it is the worst crisis point of all. Everyone experiences this transition as a time of major disorganization, when the routines of daily life go up in smoke. It's a time of anomie—normlessness. Old roles disappear; new ones have yet to form. The future of the family is unknown.

There are no clear-cut rules for separating. Who moves out? How often should spouses continue to see one another? When (and what) should they tell family and friends? Who will attend the school conferences next week? Who will get the season tickets for the theater? Who will attend the wedding of a mutual friend next month? These types of questions, seemingly trivial but deeply resonant, plague newly separated people at all stages of the family life cycle.

Orderly and Disorderly Separations. Separations fall on a continuum from orderly to disorderly, from the anticipated to the utterly shocking. Orderly separations are the least destructive. They are most likely to occur if there has been time for some preparation and planning before the actual physical separation. Disorderly separations usually occur when the earlier crisis points have not been worked through. Separation involves major life changes, and it requires careful planning, especially when there are children. Children have the right to know what's going on, and they need to have adequate time to process it with both parents. Even couples with grown children need to prepare their adult offspring—and grandchildren—for the changes that separation entails.

Abrupt departures usually create severe crises for those left behind. It's the ultimate rejection—abandonment. The abandonment leaves one feeling totally helpless and frequently culminates in a severe debilitating family crisis, such as a suicide attempt by one partner or a major clinical depression requiring hospitalization. Abandoned children regress, get depressed, or act out. The rejection is too great and too sudden to cope with.

Orderly separations have two common factors: good management and firm relationship boundaries. Good management requires knowing about and preparing for the transitions of divorce, averting crises by defusing tension at marker points, and giving the process enough time for everyone to adjust.

Boundaries are simply rules for how separated spouses will interact—and not interact. To construct good boundaries, spouses need to recognize how their roles have changed. To keep the boundaries firm, new rules and rituals need to be developed.

Role changing after divorce has two distinct stages: coping with role losses and establishing new roles. When someone retires, he or she loses the worker's role; when a parent dies, people may find themselves missing being someone's child. When divorce occurs, there is the loss of the role of spouse to mourn and cope with.

For women in particular, the two roles of wife and mother traditionally provide a central core of identity. Often, the two roles become enmeshed. It is not unusual to hear an ex-wife say "he left *us.*" The more a woman's identity is tied to a combined wife/mother role, the more likely she is to experience this stress of role loss.

Men's role loss after divorce may seem less pronounced than women's. Even though gender roles are shifting, men are still more likely than women to define themselves by work and to define their roles as spouses more narrowly. The more demanding and compelling his work, the more a man can throw himself into it to fill up his time and thoughts, anesthetizing the pain of the separation.

Even for the couple that divorces in the early stages of marriage, the discomfort of role loss is felt. Losing the role of being coupled and returning to singleness are fraught with feelings of failure and loss of status. For the longer-married couple, the extent of the role losses are more complex and severe. Their lives have usually been defined by their married status: friends, neighbors, community, and family all view them as a couple. Returning to a single existence that they have not experienced for twenty or thirty years requires a totally new self-definition.

Rules are needed for any system to function. When one household becomes two, many of the rules that are built into the marital system become instantly obsolete. New rules will be needed to define a new relationship. Separated couples need to find ways to reduce the intimacy and appropriately increase their distance. Until the actual separation, a couple is usually unaware of how interdependent their lives have become. Trial and error may be necessary until they establish a new comfort level.

Rituals mark important transitions and events. They solidify, solemnize, and publicize our values. They also quell our anxiety by showing us how to behave in the face of the unknown (Imber-Black & Roberts, 1992). Although plenty of rituals exist that help people to enter a marriage, welcome a newborn, start a new job, or retire from one, there are no socially accepted rituals to mark the end of a marriage, the announcement of a divorce, the construction of a binuclear family, or the acceptance of new and sometimes instant members into a family of remarriage. No rites of passage exist to help mourn the losses, to help healing, or to help solidify newly acquired roles. Unlike other important transitions, divorce lies in a zone of ritual ambiguity (see Chapter 12).

While leaving its participants in a void with respect to public rituals, divorce also affects the private rituals that are so central to family life. Daily rituals such as opening the mail together over coffee or walking together to get the newspaper are seamlessly woven into the texture of family life; the more elaborate rituals that many families construct around birthdays and holidays will also disappear or change, leaving gaping wounds. When the nuclear family is dismantled in the wake of divorce, it is also necessary to dismantle what seemed like a permanent point of view of a portion of the past, present, and future.

What roles, rules, and rituals each family chooses to establish will vary depending on individual preferences, sometimes on ethnic background, and certainly on the particular life stage of the family.

Reconciliations are common during the separation transition. The pain of separating, the continuing bonds of attachment, the distress of children and extended family, and the realities of divorce can cause couples to reunite. When the reconciliation is based on these reasons and not on a basic understanding and correction of the marital problems, it is likely to be brief. In some families, parents separate and reconcile briefly, perhaps several times, increasing and prolonging the stress of the separation. In the most common divorced family form, the mother and children remain as one unit while the father moves out and functions as a separate unit. The mother-headed household faces a dilemma: Should it reorganize and fill roles that had been enacted by the physically absent father, or should it maintain his psychological presence in the system by not reorganizing. If the mother-child subsystem tries to reassign roles, the father's return will be met with resistance. On the other hand, if they deal with him as psychologically present, they perpetuate family disequilibrium and stress. These children face a difficult and very stressful transition with the family in a constant state of disequilibrium characterized by boundary ambiguity (Boss, 1987) created by the father's intermittent exit and return. This "on again, off again" marital relationship often continues for years as the spouses resolve their ambivalence and make the transition to reorganization. This type of cyclical pattern is evidenced more in highly dysfunctional families, and family violence tends to be more prevalent in them (Kitson, 1992).

As the marital separation is shared with extended family, friends, and the community, the tasks of the economic and legal processes begin. These mediating factors can help or hinder the transitional process. The couple usually encounters the legal system at this time and faces additional stress as they confront economic hardship and child-focused realities. This may escalate the crisis, since spouses now need to divide what they had previously shared.

Legal Issues. Although no-fault divorce legislation reflects changing social attitudes, the legal system still operates on an adversarial model. Based on a win-lose game, the legal divorce frequently escalates the spousal power struggle, adding additional stress to the already disorganized system. If a couple chooses to mediate their differences instead of using the traditional adversarial model requiring different legal representation by each spouse, they are less likely to escalate the familial stress. Although mediation has only recently been introduced as a conciliatory method of resolving divorce disputes, it has the most promise for helping couples to reach an amicable solution to the complex issues of custody, support, and property settlement. As a method that encourages couples to be responsible for their own family decisions, it also teaches them problem-solving techniques that will be useful throughout their post-divorce family life. Couples that choose litigation over mediation are more likely to continue to resort to litigation whenever they encounter inevitable postdivorce conflicts.

Economics and custody are two arenas in which gender differences clearly emerge. Mothers are more likely to carry the major responsibilities for children, whether they get full custody or share custody in a joint legal custody arrangement. Although it differs by state, well over 80 percent of mothers have either full custody or primary physical custody. In terms of economics, women tend to end up with less money and men with more. Although studies differ in the percentages they report, there is agreement that women's income is reduced by 15 to 30 percent, while men's income often remains the same or increases or decreases slightly.

These first three turbulent transitions form the core of the emotional divorce process. The lingering feelings of attachment, ambivalence, and the ambiguity of the future combine in complex ways to make this a time of deep soul searching, anxious discomfort, and vacillating but intense desires. For couples with children, whether young or older, it is a process of letting go while still holding on. They have to begin the most difficult task of terminating their marital relationship while redefining their parental one.

Systemic Reorganization: The Binuclear Family

The presence of children, at any stage in the family life cycle process, requires that divorced parents restructure their lives in ways that allow children to continue their relationships with both parents. The nuclear family is now dissolved, and the highly complex and varied process of reorganizing needs to begin.

How a family reorganizes is crucial to the health and well-being of its family members. Research clearly identifies several major factors that contribute to the healthy adjustment of children:

1. Children need to have their basic economic and psychological needs met.
2. They need support for maintaining the familial relationships in their lives that were important and meaningful to them before the divorce. That usually means not only parents but extended family, such as grandparents.
3. They benefit when the relationship between their parents (whether married or divorced) is generally supportive and cooperative.

The reorganization into a binuclear family in which these three major factors are present provides children with the opportunity to survive divorce without long-term psychological damage. In most binuclear families, the children divide their living time—in a wide range of patterns—between the households. Some children divide their time fairly equally, either splitting the week or spending one week or longer in each household. Other children spend a majority of their time in one household, and still others alternate between households on a flexible, irregular pattern. The importance of the binuclear family model is that the family remains a family, although the structure is very different than it was before the divorce. Giving divorced families a name that acknowledges that families continue to be families even after divorce encourages the development of new, more functional role models for divorcing families. It also gives them a legitimate status and removes from them the stigma of social deviancy.

The Former Spouse Relationship.   To maximize the potential for these three factors requires a major transformation in the former spouse relationship. Each parent must find new ways of relating independently with the child while they simultaneously develop new rules and behaviors with each other. This co-parenting relationship is central to the functioning of the binuclear family in much the same way as the relationship between married spouses is central to the function of the nuclear family.

In the past, there was some disbelief that divorced partners could have an amicable relationship. The lack of language to describe the former spousal relationship, except in terms of a past relationship (e.g., "ex" or "former"), is an indication of the lack of acceptance of it as a viable form. The general distrust of a continuing relationship after divorce is reflected in the prevailing stereotype that former spouses must, of necessity, be antagonists—otherwise, why would they divorce? This stereotype is reinforced by a bias in the available clinical material. Clinicians tend to see only difficult or problematic former spousal relationships, while well-functioning divorced families are less apt to seek professional intervention.

Unlike the popular stereotype that former spouses are, of necessity, mortal enemies, the realities are that there is as much complexity and variation in these relationships as there is in married spouses relationships. Former spouse relationships form a continuum with the very angry and hostile relationships at one end and the very friendly at the other. There are a multitude of relationship variations between the two extremes (Ahrons, 1981; Ahrons & Wallisch, 1986).

Co-Parenting Relationships.   In analyzing the relationships between former spouses in the Binu-

clear Family Study, five typologies emerged: perfect pals, cooperative colleagues, angry associates, fiery foes, and, dissolved duos. Perfect pals are a small group of divorced spouses who remain close friends. If they have children, they are almost always joint custody parents who, equitably sharing child-rearing responsibilities, are good problem solvers with few conflicts.

The cooperative colleagues are a larger group who would not call each other friends but who manage for the most part to have an amicable relationship. They are child-focused, and although they have conflicts, they are able to separate their marital from their parental roles, not allowing the former to contaminate the latter. When they are unable to resolve a conflict, they are likely to choose a mediator or therapist to help them rather than to resort to litigation. Some have shared custody; others elect to have a primary parent, but both fathers and mothers remain important and involved in their children's lives. A number of studies have found that about half the divorced parents fit into this broad category (Ahrons, 1994; Goldsmith, 1980; Maccoby & Mnookin, 1992; Wallerstein & Kelly, 1980).

Angry associates are quite similar to cooperative colleagues in some ways; parents in these groups continue to interact and have involvement in their children's lives. The major difference between the cooperative colleagues and the angry associates is that the latter group cannot separate their parental and marital issues. When there is conflict about the children, it quickly fuses with an old marital fight. Power struggles are common to this group; their separation and divorce battles often involved custody disputes and long legal battles over financial matters. Fiery foes are hostile and angry all the time; the ex-spouse is their mortal enemy, and they are unable to co-parent. Like conflict-habituated married couples, they are still very emotionally attached to each other, although they would be quick to deny it. Their divorces tended to have been highly litigious, involving extended family and friends, with legal battles continuing for many years after the divorce. With both angry associates and fiery foes as parents, children usually suffer from devastating loyalty conflicts and often lose significant relationships with extended kin.

In the dissolved duos, ex-spouses have no further contact with one another, and one parent assumes totally responsibility for the children. Of the five groups, these families are the only ones that fit the "single-parent" category.

Establishing Boundaries.   While in the earlier transitions, the absence of clear boundaries and the high ambiguity create most of the stress, in this reorganization transition, the clarification of the boundaries generates the distress. Boundaries are hot issues in all intimate relationships, not just divorce. They touch off unresolved conflicts or crash into opposing strongly held values. Among ex-spouses, money and new loves often are the touchiest issues, bound to set off escalating battles. Often, an old repetitious fight that the couple has engaged in for years continues, masked in the details of living separately. One major arena for these power struggles to flourish in relates to the children.

All divorcing parents know how important it is to make decisions on the basis of their children's best interests. But the worst arguments can happen over what exactly these interests are. Which school Johnny should attend, although couched in an argument over his best interests, usually boils down to a pitched battle about which parent has more authority, more power, more control over Johnny's life. In reality, although "the best interests of the child" is a concept that is commonly accepted and heavily relied upon by judges, lawyers, mediators, and therapists, there is little consensus about the criteria (Kelly, 1997).

All parents, whether married or divorced, have parenting conflicts. How they affect children is determined by how the parents resolve their conflicts. In binuclear families, it is necessary to more specifically construct firm boundaries—between households, in each parent-child relationship, and between ex-spouses. To co-parent effectively requires a contract that sets out the rules and roles in the binuclear family. This contract—what I call a limited partnership agreement—assumes that par-

ents are partners, but the kind of limits that are set on that partnership are determined by their relationship. Perfect pals can have a very flexible and often unwritten type of contract because they are able to negotiate easily. Most cooperative colleagues find that they need to have a more structured agreement, outlining children's living schedules, how holidays will be spent, who goes to what meetings, who pays for what needs, and so on. Angry associates need an even more structured agreement, often stating specifics about what a parent can and cannot do with children. Fiery foes usually have everything possible written in a legal contractual form, although they are most likely to violate their contracts.

In the perfect pal and cooperative colleague families, ex-spouses often choose to spend some holidays together, attend children's events together, and share information about children's needs. In angry associate and fiery foe families, parallel parenting is the norm. They operate independently as parents, not sharing information or events.

Even midlife and later-life couples with adult children need to have some agreement about how their postdivorce family will function. Will both parents attend the child's wedding? Will they sit at the same table for the celebration dinner? Will both grandparents attend their grandchild's birthday party or graduation? Establishing clear boundaries is important across all stages of the family life cycle.

Family Redefinition: The Aftermath

A family's redefinitional process frequently includes remarriage and the introduction of stepparents into the postdivorce family. Remarriage creates a series of transitions that are beyond the scope of this chapter (see Chapter 25) but are part of the ongoing transitions of family redefinition. For some families, a potential remarriage partner or spouse-equivalent may become part of the family system before the legal divorce and at the early phases of the reorganization transition. Some unnamed (e.g., the relationships between mothers and stepmothers) and thus unsanctioned relationships within the binuclear family structure take on an importance in the redefinitional process. They are kin or quasi-kin relationships in the context of the binuclear family (Ahrons & Wallisch, 1987).

Relationships between parents and stepparents in the binuclear family provide an important emotional continuity for both parents and children. It facilitates this transition by redefining the divorced family so that the amount of relationship loss experienced by children and parents is minimized.

Family values and structures of many African American families provide a helpful model for binuclear families. The African American family is centered on the children, the family unit often being defined as including all those involved in their nurturance and support. Encouraging extended family relationships for the benefit of the children allows for continued responsibility regardless of changes in marital relationships. Unlike the traditional family structure favored by most White American families, the African American family structure is less based on the legal relationship between spouses; hence, divorce is less likely to interfere with the child's familial ties (Boyd-Franklin, 1989; Crosbie-Burnett & Lewis, 1993). If the assumption of parental responsibility is not based on blood kin, then divorce is less likely to be as disruptive to the child's family relationships.

One important and frequently overlooked strength that many ethnic families have when divorce occurs is their bicultural socialization. Children in these families usually have to learn to live in two cultures simultaneously—that of their ethnic community and that of the wider society (Crosbie-Burnett & Lewis, 1993). This acculturation process could be a very helpful model for a child in learning to live in the two household cultures of the binuclear family. If one parent remarries and there are children from another family (step-siblings), being bicultural could facilitate their being better able to accommodate the different family cultures that ordinarily create considerable stress for stepfamilies

Although we have no research data, it is likely that gay and lesbian families, who operate outside of the legal marital system, have kinship structures similar to those of the African American family. For children, the family structures that incorporate extended family, fictive and quasi-kin, and family relationships by choice are more likely to remain intact if the primary love relationship wanes. Because family roles are more ambiguous in gay and lesbian families, they may also prepare children better to accept the ambiguity that is inherent when families change their structure.

Lesbians, who are socialized, as most women are, to value emotional connectedness, often try to remain friends or family after the breakup of a love relationship. Their subsequent connection may take various forms: focusing on co-parenting children, celebrating holidays or vacations together, or remaining friends within a close circle. As with postdivorce heterosexual couples, the transformation from lovers to friends takes a lot of work, but many women are committed to the process (Shumsky, 1997). In married and divorced heterosexual relationships, women tend to be the kinkeepers of the family, whether nuclear or binuclear. In the Binuclear Family Study, the findings show that the relationship between mothers and stepmothers was much more emotional and interactive than was the relationship between fathers and stepfathers (Ahrons & Wallisch, 1987).

Gay men, on the other hand, like most men, often lack the vocabulary or emotional access to their feelings of loss after a breakup. This is especially true of the sometimes ambiguous relationships that occur in gay male culture, in which open contracts may permit casual or transient affairs to coexist with long-term relationships (Shernoff, 1997).

Of course, HIV and AIDS also have a profound effect on gay male relationships, in which there may be fear of a partner's HIV-positive status, guilt if one's own status is negative, or a tendency to stay together when both partners are negative, largely because it is safe (Remien, 1997). In all of these circumstances, it is extremely important for the therapist to help those who want to break up to do so in the least destructive and most caring way, helping them to remain connected if that is desirable. The gay community, Remien reminds us, is full of stories of ex-lovers who are at their ex-partners' bedside and who maintain a bond that nourishes them both.

The struggle to define all of these relationships and transitions for themselves—coupling, parenting, breaking up—is made both more difficult and more creative by the fact that they exist outside of society's social and legal rules. Where children are concerned, however, the nonlegal standing of a nonbiological, noncustodial parent can create devastation for someone who may for years have been a co-parent or even a primary parent of her or his partner's children (Sundquist, 1997). Interestingly, when a remarriage ends in a divorce, this same dilemma holds true for a step-parent, who has emotional but no legal, biological, or custodial ties to the child.

Many agonizing dilemmas arise about holding on or letting go and trying to figure out "the best interests of the child" as adult relationships shift. Karen Sundquist's article (1997) on this subject ends with a statement about her relationship with her ex-partner's children that holds true for all of us: "I am convinced that these bonds of family we form are not disposable and should not be easily broken."

CLINICAL OVERVIEW

A model of divorce, characterizing it as a normative process rather than evidence of pathology or dysfunction, has been presented in this chapter This is aimed at helping clinicians transcend prevalent stereotypes and myths, thereby creating clinical guidelines for treating families of divorce. Within this model, clinicians can recognize the transitions of the divorce process and help client families cope more effectively during this very painful and complex process. They can then identify what differentiates divorces that are successful or "good" from those that are unsuccessful or "bad."

Quite simply, a good divorce has three major objectives: (1) The family remains a family; (2) the negative effects on children are minimized; and

(3) both ex-spouse integrate the divorce into their lives in a healthy way. Although the structure of the family has been altered, parents continue to enact their parental roles, and the process of socializing and being responsible for their children's emotional and economic needs continues.

Bad divorces are those in which spouses are unable or unwilling to settle their marital related conflicts without enmeshing the children in their divorce drama. Children in these divorces often lose a relationship with one parent (usually the father), are caught in painful loyalty conflicts about their parents, and suffer irreparable emotional damage.

By understanding the normal transitions of the divorce process, clinicians can help their clients to better understand and cope with the emotional, legal, and practical tasks they need to complete. By providing information and knowledge, clinicians can help divorcing couples to make decisions based on their children's best interests. And by learning and teaching important conflict reduction techniques, they can assist parents to make the many complex decisions that will need to be addressed.

Because divorce is a legal decision with economic repercussions, clinicians need to be aware of how the legal process works in their state. Even though all states now have no-fault legislation, many divorces continue to be adversarial. Learning which lawyers in your community are open to collaboration with a therapist and which lawyers' styles are more mediative than adversarial will be very helpful to the clinician's continuing work with the divorcing family. For the divorcing couple, as well as the therapist working with them, the impact of the legal system on the emotional process is complex and has the potential to be counterproductive to the therapist's goals. It is best to encourage the divorcing couple to make as many decisions together as possible before engaging the legal system. As was noted earlier, mediation is a very helpful way for divorcing couples to settle their differences in a mutual problem-solving approach.

The economics of divorce filter into every aspect of the divorce process. It is important for the clinician to understand how money was managed during the marriage. In a more traditional marriage, the wife frequently knows little about the financial picture. In such cases, the husband has more power in the discussion of finances. Although a therapist should never give financial advice or try to settle the overall economic distribution (unless formally trained and acting as a divorce mediator), it is important to have an understanding of how money is used in the negotiation of the divorce.

In marriages with dependent children, financial issues are entwined with custody decisions. When a wife has been the primary caretaker of the children and the husband has been the primary breadwinner, the most common scenario is that the children represent power for the mother and money represents power for the father. This gets played out in the emotional terrain, often in very subtle and complex ways.

In marriages with older or adult children, women often have less power in the negotiations than men do. These midlife divorces are frequently the ones that result in women becoming "displaced homemakers." The common situation is that of the wife, who either has left a job to take care of children and home or is less educated than her husband, finding herself at midlife having to seek a job without adequate experience, education, or training. Her earning potential is often much less than that of her husband. The law often does not provide adequate repayment to women for the years they devoted to caring for the family. A woman of 50 may find herself without retirement or Social Security benefits. Therapists need to be aware of these gender inequities and educate women about their rights.

Another area in which women may be at a disadvantage is that they are frequently not as comfortable in negotiations or dealing with lawyers, accountants, and other professionals. When women have not been actively employed outside the home or have worked in jobs with considerably less compensation than their husbands, they are less likely to understand the economic world to which their husbands may be more attuned. Women often are overwhelmed by the legal and economic decisions they face. The way they may want to cope with their lack of knowledge is to allow others to decide for them. They may also be so uncomfortable with the process that they are willing to settle and compromise too quickly to avoid continuing to function in an arena in which they feel powerless. This may cause them to agree to an economic settlement that does not give them the future financial security that they will need. Women, socialized to be nice, often have a difficult time holding their own in a conflictual situation. The therapist has an important role in helping a women in that situation to understand her own dynamics about money and to help her learn to cope with negotiating in a conflictual dispute.

Finally, it is important for the clinician to remember that divorce affects the entire family system. Parents and siblings of the divorcing couple usually become very involved in the process. When there are children, the grandparents, aunts, uncles, and cousins are all part of the kinship network. In good divorces, the kinship network continues satisfying relationships with the children and frequently with the divorcing in-law. In angry divorces, kin often take biological sides, creating breaches in relationships with the children as well. Clinicians would be wise to ask about extended family relationships and be open to bringing relatives into the sessions to help them sort out their issues.

Working with divorce requires a complex multilevel approach (Ahrons, 1996). Clinicians need to be aware of their own biases and stereotypes, and they need to correct for them by gaining adequate knowledge of the emotional, legal, and economic divorce processes. They need to look through a wide-angle lens and incorporate both spouses' families of origin. Ethnic, racial, and gender differences need to enter into the therapeutic equation, as do the family's developmental life cycle transitions. A therapist who chooses to work with divorcing families will need to tolerate high level of conflicts and cope with complex painful emotions.

Therapy with divorcing families is a challenging and difficult process for both the therapist and the family. Working with a family and taking them through the process, helping them to emerge as a healthy, functioning binuclear family, is a goal worth striving for.

REFERENCES

Ahlburg, D., & DeVita, C. (1992). New realities of the American family. *Population Bulletin, 47,* 15.

Ahrons, C. (1979). The binuclear family: Two households, one family. *Alternative Lifestyles, 2,* 499–515.

Ahrons, C. (1980a). Divorce: A crisis of family transition and change. *Family Relations, 29,* 533–540.

Ahrons, C. (1980b). Redefining the divorced family: A conceptual framework for postdivorce family systems reorganization. *Social Work, 25,* 437–441.

Ahrons, C. (1981). The continuing coparental relationship between divorced spouses. *American Journal of Orthopsychiatry, 51,* 315–328.

Ahrons, C. (1994). *The good divorce: Keeping your family together when your marriage comes apart.* New York: HarperCollins.

Ahrons, C. (1996) *Making divorce work: A clinical approach to the binuclear family* [videotape]. New York: The Guilford Press.

Ahrons, C., & Rodgers, R. (1987). *Divorced families: A multidisciplinary developmental view.* New York: W. W. Norton.

Ahrons, C., & Wallisch, L. (1986). The relationship between former spouses. In S. Duck & D. Perlman (Eds.), *Close relationships: Development, dynamics, and deterioration* (pp. 269–296). Beverly Hills, CA: Sage.

Ahrons, C., & Wallisch, L. (1987). Parenting in the binuclear family: Relationships between biological and stepparents. In K. Pasley & M. Ihinger-Tallman (Eds.), *Remarriage and Stepfamilies.* New York: The Guilford Press.

Boss, P. (1983). Family separation and boundary ambiguity. *The International Journal of Mass Emergencies and Disasters, 1,* 63–72.

Boss, P. (1987). *Family stress.* Beverly Hills, CA: Sage.

Boss, P., & Greenberg, J. (1984). Family boundary ambiguity: A new variable in family stress theory. *Family Process, 24,* 535–546.

Boyd-Franklin, N. (1989). *Black families in therapy: A multisystems approach.* New York: The Guilford Press.

Brown, E. (1991). *Patterns of infidelity and their treatment.* New York: Brunner/Mazel.

Bumpass, L. (1990). What's happening to the family? Interactions between demographic and institutional change. *Demography, 27,* 483–498.

Crosbie-Burnett, M., & Lewis, E. (1993). Use of African-American family structures and functioning to address the challenges of European-American postdivorce families. *Family Relations, 42,* 243–248.

Cseh-Szombathy, L., Koch-Nielsen, I., Trost, J., & Weda, I. (Eds.). (1985). *The aftermath of divorce—Coping with family change: An investigation in eight countries.* Budapest, Hungary: Akademiai Kiado.

Glick, P. (1990). American families: As they are, and were. *Sociology and Social Research, 74,* 139–145.

Goldsmith, J. (1980). Relationships between former spouses: Descriptive findings. *Journal of Divorce, 2,* 1–20.

Guttmann, J. (1993). *Divorce in psychosocial perspective: Theory and research.* New Jersey: Lawrence Erlbaum Associates.

Hetherington, E. M. (1993). An overview of the Virginia Longitudinal Study of Divorce and Remarriage with a focus on early adolescence. *Journal of Family Psychology, 7,* 39–56.

Imber-Black, E., & Roberts, J. (1992). *Rituals of our times: Celebrating, healing, and changing our lives and our relationships.* New York: HarperCollins.

Kelly, J. (1997). The best interests of the child. *Family and Conciliation Courts Review, 35,* 377–387.

Kirn, W. (1997, August 18). The ties that bind: Should breaking up be harder to do? *Time,* 48–50.

Kitson, G. (1992). *Portrait of divorce: Adjustment to marital breakdown.* New York: The Guilford Press.

Lamb, M., Sternberg, K., & Thompson, R. (1997). The effects of divorce and custody arrangements on children's behavior, development, and adjustment. *Family and Conciliation Courts Review, 35,* 393–404.

Lerner, H. (1993). *The dance of deception: Pretending and truth-telling in women's lives.* New York: HarperCollins.

Maccoby, E., & Mnookin, R. (1992). *Dividing the child: Social and legal dilemmas of custody.* Cambridge, MA: Harvard University Press.

McCubbin, H., & Patterson, J. (1983). The family stress process: The double ABCX model of adjustment and adaptation. In H. McCubbin, M. Sussman, & J. Patterson (Eds.), *Social stress and the family: Advances and developments in family stress theory and research* (pp. 7–37). New York: Haworth Press.

Remien, R. (1997). Three portraits of how HIV and AIDS can complicate a break-up. *In the Family,* 18–19.

Rosten, L. (1989). *The joys of Yinglish.* New York: Penguin Books.

Rodgers, R. (1986). Postmarital reorganization of family relationships: A prepositional theory. In S. Duck & D. Perlman (Eds.), *Close relationships: Development, dynamics, and deterioration* (pp. 239–268). Beverly Hills, CA: Sage.

Shernoff, M. (1997). Unexamined loss: An expanded view of gay break-ups. *In the Family,* 10–13.

Shumsky, E. (1997). Making up the rules: Lesbian ex-lover relationships. *In the Family,* 14–15.

Spring, J. (1996). *After the affair: Healing the pain and rebuilding trust when a partner has been unfaithful.* New York: HarperCollins.

Stewart, A., Copeland, A., Chester, N., Malley, J., & Barenbaum, N. (1997). *Separating together: How divorce transforms families.* New York: The Guilford Press.

Sundquist, K. (1997). She gets the kids: Becoming an every-third-weekend and -Tuesday ex-co-mom. *In the Family,* 20–21, 27.

Trafford, A. (1982). *Crazy time.* New York: Harper & Row.

Wallerstein, J., & Kelly, J. (1980). *Surviving the breakup: How children and parents cope with divorce.* New York: Basic Books.

CHAPTER 24

SINGLE-PARENT FAMILIES
STRENGTHS, VULNERABILITIES, AND INTERVENTIONS

CAROL M. ANDERSON

When there is a commitment to living and loving together, there is family.
—Joan Anderson, *The Single Mother's Book*

Most single parents provide the structure, values, and nurturance that their children need, despite the hardships they experience and the bad press they receive. Their homes are not "broken," their lives are not miserable, and both parent and children thrive while managing the added tasks required of them. Unfortunately, rather than focusing on these strengths, we consistently concentrate on the problems: the breakdown of traditional family values, the deleterious effect of divorce on children, the irresponsibility of teen parents. If single parents are overwhelmed by the tasks of raising children on their own, they lack organization, determination, or parenting skills. If they work, they are neglecting their children; if they do not, they are no doubt lazy "welfare moms" getting rich off the federal deficit.

If it takes a village to raise a child, it's easy to understand the difficulties of single parents who are attempting to maintain healthy families, raise their children, and have some semblance of a life for themselves in the context of unsupportive communities. They have an overload of child care and household chores, limited time and energy for their own interests, and frequently insufficient money to cover their basic needs. Our society could respond to these families in two ways: It could make policies and develop programs that would provide single mothers with a living wage, better child care, and more supportive communities; or it could make divorce more difficult and single parenting close to impossible by failing to enforce the payment of child support, eliminating welfare, neglecting the needs of the children of the working poor, and then blaming mothers for the problems that result. Unfortunately, we seem to have chosen the second alternative.

Society's failure to provide single parents with financial, social, or psychological support not only contributes to their distress, but requires that each single-parent family individually address and conquer problems that could be better addressed collectively. Our critical attitudes are also reflected in a vast but flawed literature that clearly documents the problems of children and parents in single-parent families (Acock & Demo, 1994; Arendell, 1986; Furstenberg & Cherlin, 1991; Hetherington, Cox, & Cox, 1978; Kalter et al, 1985; Shaw & Emery, 1987; Simons & Johnson, 1996; Wallerstein & Blakeslee, 1989) but contains few attempts to study the many single women and single men who are actually successfully raising children. Too often, the goal seems to be proving an ideological point rather than genuinely increasing our understanding of why some are capable of responding well to the unique problems, needs, and tasks of single parenthood.

We are told that children who grow up in a household with only one biological parent are worse off, on average, than children who grow up in a household with two, regardless of the parents' race or educational background (McLanahan & Sandefur, 1994). But this and other studies documenting higher rates of dysfunction in the children of single mothers fail to sort out the relative impact of poverty (Edin & Lein, 1997), a history of living in a dysfunctional or abusive family (Furstenberg & Cherlin, 1991; Demo & Acock, 1988), or the family's stage of adjustment to divorce. Yet poverty is associated with many factors beyond single parenthood. Poor parents have less education and fewer resources, frequently have less helpful networks, and live in more troubled communities (Hall, Gurley, Sachs, & Kryscio, 1991; Simons, 1996), all factors that influence the development of children. Poverty is such a strong determinant of well-being that it accounts for about half of the disadvantage in children's lower achievement; and when its influence is factored out, the differences between the adjustment of children in one- and two-parent families all but disappear (Demo & Acock, 1988; McLanahan & Booth, 1989; Simons, 1996). In addition, divorce is associated with a history of marital conflict, family tensions, alcoholism, and chronic abuse, all factors that can be devastating for child development…(see Chapters 27 & 28). Finally, there is already evidence that the short-term negative impact of divorce on children does not always hold in the long term, especially if the children are cared for by a supportive adult (Amato, 1993; Blechman, 1982; Elder, Van Nguyen, & Caspi, 1985; Friedman & Andrews, 1990; McLanahan & Booth, 1989). These three factors—family dysfunction, the possibly temporary trauma of divorce, and above all poverty—may account for more of the variance in child outcome than single parenthood.

CHANGING PREVALENCE AND PATHWAYS

Addressing the needs and problems of single-parent families is crucial, since their numbers have increased more than threefold in the last twenty years (Gringlas & Weinraub, 1995), currently making up over one third of all American families with children under the age of 18 and over 61 percent of African American families (Children's Defense Fund, 1997). Today, there are over 15 million single-parent households, over 14 million of them headed by mothers. The category of single-parent household is an increasingly heterogeneous one. It includes an increasing number of poor never-married minority women who are struggling to raise two or three children on welfare, but it is also growing across all socioeconomic groups, the greatest increase being among the affluent and well educated. There are never-married career women with six-figure incomes who can afford private schools and full-time child care, gay and lesbian parents, a small but increasing number of single fathers, and a large group of divorced women who have exchanged marriage for going it alone with their children (Gottfried & Gottfried, 1994; Malson, 1986; Okun, 1996). Even though high rates of remarriage cause life in divorced single-parent households to be temporary, over half the children born in the 1990s will spend all or some of their childhood in a single-parent household (Furstenberg & Cherlin, 1991; Lamb, Sternberg, & Thompson, 1997).

The issues of single mothers differ significantly from those of single fathers. Single mothers are more likely to be poor or on welfare; single fathers are more likely to be financially secure (Barber & Eccles, 1992). Single mothers tend to be criticized; single fathers tend to be seen as noble. On the other hand, single mothers are also more likely to have an available network to provide psychological and practical support; single fathers are likely to be more isolated. Because it is by far the most prevalent form of single-parent family, this chapter will emphasize the issues of single mothers and their children. Therapists will be urged to counter the negative social forces that make up the social context of single-parent families by taking a longitudinal perspective that emphasizes the capabilities of parents and children for resilience and adaptation. Using this perspective, therapists can help parents to overcome the immediate challenges they face by affirming their ability to parent their children and helping them to mobilize a supportive community. Effective management of immediate challenges will also help to increase the self-esteem of parents and children, give them the skills and courage to reach out to extended family and friends, and build bridges of competence to the future. It is a challenge for many therapists to work effectively with single-parent families because societal views are reinforced by the pervasive focus on pathology in clinical training. Many therapists find it difficult to accept the fact that the presence of problems in single-parent families is not necessarily evidence of individual inadequacies, moral weaknesses, or intrapsychic turmoil. Even so, there are very real individual problems within many of these families, and our caseloads contain a disproportionate number of single parents requesting help. But these parents and children also have strengths and resilience, both of which must be appreciated and acknowledged before we can see their lives in perspective and help them to address the challenges they face, whatever the causes.

THE ADAPTATION OF CHILDREN IN SINGLE-PARENT FAMILIES THROUGH THE LIFE CYCLE

The impact of being raised in a single-parent family on children's well-being is significant and complex, though there is considerable disagreement as to exactly what it is and whether it is lasting (Allison & Furstenberg, 1989; Demo & Acock, 1988; Hetherington 1989; Holloway & Machida, 1992). All children need supportive adults who are functioning well enough to provide consistent nurturance, values, and limits. All children also want a "normal" family, one that's just like everyone else's. Children whose parents have divorced, whose parent has died, or whose parents never married are less likely to experience their families as either predictable or normal, but they can and do adjust to their circumstances. Those who are raised by poor single parents from infancy may have to cope with more financial stresses and often a fragmented or chaotic household, but even these children can learn how to get their needs met within

their networks. Similarly, while the immediate post-divorce years are particularly stressful (Garfinkel & McLanahan, 1986; McLanahan and Sandefur, 1994), this painful reality also is often temporary (Ahrons, 1994; Emery, 1988). Even children who serve as message carriers or pawns in the marital wars, deal with a series of cut-offs from previously significant adults and other children, or manage their grandparents' disapproval of the single parent's new lifestyle tend to overcome these stressful experiences, particularly if they are nurtured by a supportive adult or, in the case of divorce, if their parents are able to work out some sort of cooperative contract (Ahrons, 1981; Emery, 1988; Friedeman & Andrews, 1990).

Nevertheless a substantial minority of the children of single parents have more than their fair share of problems, and it is these children who are most likely to be seen by therapists, particularly those working in the mental health centers of inner cities. A variety of problems are common, including poor academic performance, low self-esteem, acting out, or difficulties with peers (Amato & Keith, 1991; Conger et al., 1992; Hetherington, Cox, & Cox, 1978; Furstenberg, Brooks-Gunn & Morgan, 1987; Gringlas & Weinraub, 1995; Hetherington, Cox, & Cox, 1978; McLanahan & Sandefur, 1994; Samuelsson, 1994; Simons, Beaman, Conger, & Chao, 1992; Simons, Johnson, Beaman, & Conger, 1993; Wallerstein, 1987; Zill, 1990). Of those whose parents are divorced, these are probably the children who are more likely to have irregular contact with their noncustodial parent and his or her network or to have parents who cannot agree on visitation arrangements. It is up to therapists to learn about the impact of these factors and help single-parent families to use their strengths and their network of family and friends to manage these problems.

VALIDATING THE HISTORY AND PRESENT OF SINGLE-PARENT FAMILY EXPERIENCES

Contrary to the cries of alarm from some quarters, there is no real evidence that marriage is going out of style. Most women want to be mothers in the context of a marriage or at least in the context of a long-term loving relationship. While they can and do create satisfying lives on their own, their status as single parents is usually achieved by default: A relationship has not worked, or a marriage has ended, usually for very good reasons. Whether their past relationships involved abuse and abandonment or simply unresolvable conflict, single mothers almost certainly have had to deal with the fallout of loss, disappointment, and the opinions of those around them that they have failed at a woman's prime mission, maintaining her family. With this personal and social baggage as a backdrop, both never-married and divorced women entering single motherhood must shift to lives of constant responsibility and of managing their families alone. The lives into which these mothers move also can be expected to be stressful. Compared to their married counterparts, they work longer hours, face more stressful life changes, have more economic problems, and are less supported emotionally and in their parent role. It is not surprising that they are more psychologically vulnerable (Burden, 1986; Compas & Williams, 1990; Gringlas & Weinraub, 1995; McLloyd & Wilson, 1990; Stack, 1989; Travato & Lauris, 1989; Tschann, Johnston, & Wallerstein, 1989).

ENGAGING SINGLE-PARENT FAMILIES IN THERAPY

Given what we know about their history and their current reality, it would seem obvious and inevitable that when therapists see single mothers, their well-being would be made a major target of assessment and intervention. It is not. In part, this may be the result of society's apparent assumption that all mothers should meet needs, not have them, but it also may be because mothers frequently do not seek or accept help for themselves (Dover, Leahy, & Foreman, 1994). In the context of busy schedules and task overload, they may view therapy as just one more time-consuming burden and may believe that they wouldn't be so stressed if only their children would be better behaved. However, like a

perverse game of dominoes, a mother's coping influences her child's adjustment, and if a mother's needs are not addressed, there is a negative impact on her child's mental health and response to therapy (Dover et al., 1994; Hall et al., 1991; Holloway & Machida, 1992; Shear, Anderson, & Greeno, 1997).

It is important to emphasize that the significance of maternal well-being is not raised here to blame mothers yet again, but to emphasize the importance of addressing their needs. If a mother suffers from depression, low self-esteem, or simply task overload, it certainly isn't her fault, and the demoralizing impact of these forces must be countered before she can provide for the needs of her children. Therapists can facilitate this process by working with her to create webs of support, recognizing and reinforcing her strengths, and reinforcing her role as family executive. Family therapists are in a unique position to help single mothers. Unfortunately, when mothers bring their families for help, too often their ambivalent or negative feelings about therapy are exacerbated by therapists who try to ingratiate themselves with children at the mother's expense, getting caught in a triangle between the parent and child or even between the parent and her family of origin. More behaviorally oriented family therapists limit their interventions to advice on better parenting, stressing charts and token economies that are often unrealistic, given the mother's daily life and resources. Even worse, therapists of many theoretical models implicitly blame single mothers for their children's problems. These therapist behaviors are all the more problematic because single-parent families are most likely to come for help at three very sensitive points in time. They come immediately after a divorce, as the family works to manage reactions to loss and create a new structure (Kissman & Allen, 1993); when parent coping has been compromised by depression or overwork (Downey & Coyne, 1990); and, most frequently, as children encounter academic and behavioral difficulties (Westcot & Dries, 1990). To engage a single mother at these times, therapists should pay special attention to the experiences she has had on the journey to their current status and acknowledge her current struggles to succeed at the hard job of raising children without the sanction of a marriage or in the face of a marriage that was not viable. Such acknowledgment and recognition lay the groundwork for an approach to single-parent families that emphasizes their social context, structure, and longitudinal development.

THE SIGNIFICANCE OF THE SOCIAL CONTEXT: KIN AND NONKIN NETWORKS

Single-parent families are profoundly influenced by the social context in which they spend their lives, whether this is a supportive network of family and friends or an isolated existence in a judgmental community. Many single-parent families are unusually well connected outside the home, contain other adult family members within the household, and/or have a live-in primary partner (Simons, 1996). This is fortunate because single-parent families that are embedded in a fabric of social support are less vulnerable than those that are isolated (Belsky, 1990; Edin & Lein, 1997; Gladov & Ray, 1986; Koeske & Koeske, 1990; Malson, 1986; Stack, 1974). Consistent with a "tradition that has no name," African American households contain a high percentage of other relatives, and beyond the household, active family networks provide frequent contact, social support, and mutual aid (Hatchett, Cochran, & Jackson, 1991). These provisions are often vital to single-parent survival (Hatchett et al., 1991; Malson, 1986; McAdoo, 1980; Taylor, Jackson, & Quick, 1982; Thompson & Wilkins, 1992). However, even within this richness of connectedness, it is the mothers who need them most (those with lower income and lower education) that tend to have smaller networks and to receive less help from them (Caldwell, 1996; Hatchett et al., 1991).

Since the context of single-parent households is so vital, an assessment of the number and quality of supports available to single parents forms one of the cornerstones of treatment. It prevents us from missing the problems of those who most need our support to broaden their sense of connectedness. Determining the existence of a large kin and non-kin network, however, is not enough. The quality

of these contacts is important (Olson, Kieschnik, Banyard, & Ceballo, 1994) and must be assessed and cultivated. Single mothers who do have intense and frequent contact with their families, for instance, report mixed blessings. Extended-family members may be the source of increased stress through their disapproval, triangling with children, split loyalties caused by divorce, or requests for help with a variety of other family troubles. For instance, 18-year-old Karma, who works hard to support her 9-month-old daughter in community daycare, prefers to turn to her family of friends rather than her crack-addicted sister and alcoholic mother, both of whom ask for money and criticize her for neglecting her child by not going on welfare. And while the support received by remaining in their parental household is particularly useful to many teen mothers (Thompson & Wilkins, 1992), three-generation households also have complicated relationship and generational boundary issues. The addition of a new generation to an existing family household requires fundamental changes in the way the whole family is structured and the way roles are defined, with an ongoing need to sort out child care tasks and adult responsibilities. The time when a teen parent wants to move toward independence becomes a time when she needs increased support from her parents to help with her child, a time when she must defer authority to her own parents in some areas while taking charge of her child and maintaining credibility as the child's parent in others. At the same time, her parents must continue the life cycle task of launching and letting go, one that is more difficult if they must also provide continued financial and emotional support to a daughter they do not see as responsible. Many parents find it particularly difficult to allow the ongoing involvement of the baby's father with their daughter, her baby, and their family life. Often, they resent him and consider his participation to be either irrelevant or troublesome. Still, they must learn to support his involvement, not only to maintain the important bond between father and child, but also because his presence usually contributes to the psychological well-being of the adolescent mother (Thompson & Wilkins, 1992) and the maintenance of family ties. Work with the Brown family demonstrates how a therapist helps a family to maintain a life cycle perspective as they wend their way through the ambiguous developmental process of helping a child raise a child while growing up herself:

> The Browns, a middle-class African American family, sought therapy when their 13-year-old middle daughter, Colleen, became pregnant. The parents were devastated and mystified by the daughter's pregnancy but never even considered not taking responsibility both for her and for their coming grandchild. Coaching them to handle the ambiguities of supporting Colleen, who gave birth at 14, through her adolescence while encouraging her to take some level of responsibility for her son, Darien, was a challenge. The parents had to be encouraged repeatedly to make openings for their grandson's father to become involved in a parental role, so angry were they about his behavior with their daughter. At 17, Colleen became pregnant again, by a different boyfriend. This further challenged her parents, who at this point pressed her to take more responsibility for parenting both of her children, though they still supported her in continuing school. In therapy, they were helped to set increasing limits with her and to increase their expectations of her responsibility while still fostering her own development. On follow-up, when Colleen was 21 and planning a move to a different state with both children, she had matured into a responsible and articulate parent, able to tell her own father about the disappointments she had felt with him in earlier years and to coach him to deal with problems he was having with her younger brother, now 14 himself.

The somewhat older single parent who returns to her family of origin after a divorce is able to receive child care and financial help, but often at the cost of her independence. These once independent mothers commonly find it frustrating when they become caught in conflicts with their own parents over how to manage their children and struggle to maintain a sense of themselves as competent adults in the face of increased parental involvement and control. When intergenerational conflicts can be minimized, these arrangements can provide an enriching opportunity for all family members. Grandparents can have stronger connections with their grandchildren, single parents can have times of genuine respite knowing that the children are being cared for by family members who love them, and children can have a variety of adult caretakers and siblinglike relationships with cousins. In fact, such expanded families can provide a sense of clanlike belonging that transcends that provided by many intact but more isolated nuclear families.

Single mothers who live independently often suffer greater financial and child care strains and sometimes greater social isolation. One common "solution" that mothers choose for these problems, in part out of fear of being alone, is to bring a romantic partner into their household, even when they are less than certain that he is an appropriate choice. In effect, they barter with him to provide for some of their needs in a quid pro quo arrangement with or without real companionship. When the relationship can develop into a loving, supportive, and lasting one, such support has been noted to protect adult women from depression in the face of stressful life events (Brown, Harris, & Copeland, 1972; Brown & Harris 1978). But the contributions of live-in partners are not always totally positive. Many compete with the children for the single parent's time and attention, undermine maternal authority, or get intensely involved, only to leave precipitously. Additionally, men who do not have a biological bond to a child are more likely to be physically and sexually abusive (Margolin, 1992). Complicated negotiations may be needed when live-in boyfriends expect (because of their gender) to establish family rules when they have neither the mandate nor the credibility to make them and contribute little practical or financial help. Since some single mothers have trouble standing up for their rights, or even knowing that it is appropriate to do so, they may need the therapist to help make it clear to male partners that their role is not that of parent, but that of a support for the mother in her efforts to care for and discipline her children. Negotiating differences between mothers who are not particularly authoritarian and boyfriends who believe in firm rules creates tensions of its own. Single mothers who are psychologically or financially insecure often find themselves struggling with conflicting loyalties to their children and to their partner and find it difficult to establish the boundaries necessary to protect their children from these partners for fear that the partners will leave them without the support they desperately need. These women may be in the greatest need of help to expand their adult support network.

Therapists can also help to alleviate problems in single-parent household life by facilitating a web or support beyond the household, encouraging a range of positive connections for both parent and child, an interrelated archipelago of individuals and groups that provide a context of reciprocal and mutual responsibility. Network interventions should be planned with a wide-angle lens, addressing the needs of each family member for both a sense of belonging and concrete assistance. As has already been indicated, the therapist helps single parents to begin to mobilize their network by first attending to others who may actually be living in the home, moving to those close family and friends outside the home who are actively involved in important aspects of family life, adding those network members who might be available if they were to be asked, and finally working to build new strands of support as needed. Once it is determined which friends and members of the extended family might be available, moves can be made to facilitate connections and, if necessary, to devise interventions to decrease the tension in relationships that have been primarily stressful. Coaching middle-class single parents on their relationships with members of their family of origin (see Chapter 26) may be especially important because single parenthood is often a hard choice for parents and siblings to accept and understand. Helping women from poor multiproblem families sometimes means coaching them on how to set limits on what they can and will do for their family members without totally severing ties.

All women who are just becoming single parents may need help addressing how their new status changes their relationship with friends and family. Unless reassured that the single parent wants to be included, some friends assume that they would be uncomfortable in gatherings of couples or intact families, and others may be uneasy about seeming to choose one partner's side over another in the divorce. Recently divorced single mothers may also be seen as a threat to intact marriages (perceived as a loose cannon on the deck of suburban affairs). Thus, the friends they had when they were married may no longer be available to them. It is possible to sort out, maintain, and strengthen most of these ties with effort, but single mothers may need to be strongly encouraged by the therapist to tolerate the risk of rejection or the discomfort of going alone.

There are times when a woman's network cannot provide the right kind of help or support. Ties may have been weakened or disrupted by divorce or relocation; existing network members may be insensitive to the problems of single parents and their children; the single parents who need them most may not have the skills to develop and maintain helpful relationships; and many single parents find it exceedingly difficult to ask available extended family or friends to pitch in with practical, financial, or emotional support. Their pride, fear of becoming a burden, fear of rejection, or even fear of loss of custody makes it hard to ask for help. Developing new strands of support can also seem like just one more chore to an overextended, overstressed mother. Most single mothers would rather collapse on the couch after a trying day than take the initiative to connect, especially with people they don't know well. Again, it takes the therapist, serving as a temporary cheerleader and coach to get network development off the ground.

When the right help or the right amount of help is not available from the family's existing informal sources, at least two formal sources can be exploited: established community groups or organizations and groups that are formed to meet the specific needs of particular types of families. For a single parent, connections with such groups as "mother's day out," craft classes, or church groups can help her to develop new relationships while meeting some of her needs for activities and respite. To address the particular need for relationships with other women in similar circumstances, it may be necessary to create a group especially for single mothers, since such groups often do not exist in a given community. Such groups are inherently supportive, providing mothers with the opportunity for activities and discussions that can make them feel less isolated and stigmatized. The groups can, however, meet more than the psychological needs of parents, since they can also provide opportunities for maternal respite through trade-offs of child care responsibilities, transportation to children's activities, or information about community resources. In the following case, Mary asked for help for her son, which she received. She also was helped to strengthen her network by reconnecting with her family of origin and joining a group of other single mothers:

Mary, a 35-year-old Polish American divorced mother of three, did not have much of an available network when she requested therapy for her 8-year-old son. Her mother had died when she was a teenager, her remarried father had consistently responded to her requests for help by telling her she had made her bed, so she should lie in it, and her siblings lived 2,000 miles away. Five years ago, her husband had left her to take a construction job in the Middle East, and when he returned to this country, he relocated to another state. Neither he nor his family has been available to provide support since then. Now, with no husband and no child support, Mary felt that she never had enough money to meet her children's needs, much less provide them with the Air Jordans or Doc Martens that they claimed were essential for social survival. Frequently frazzled and exhausted, she put her own needs so far down the agenda that she didn't even know she had them. With society's help, she felt guilty for not being able to hold onto the ideal all-American family. She knew that marriage is no guarantee of happiness or support, but she still resented and envied her married friends when they complained about financially supportive spouses who didn't do equal child care.

Despite the stresses that dominated Mary's life, she would not have come to therapy if her son's teachers had not complained that he was underper-

forming and acting out in class. The fact that her children were constantly fighting, her discipline was admittedly inconsistent, and their home was chaotic seemed to her to be par for the course. Finding the time to get the kids together to come to the clinic were major and exhausting tasks, and initially, the family's attendance was sporadic. However, as Mary began to feel supported by the therapist, she began to feel better about herself, and she more easily mobilized the kids. She found it helpful to talk about the challenges of single parenting without having to feel that she was inadequate. In family sessions, she and her children worked out a list of rules, chores, and consequences. She successfully delegated increased responsibilities to her 12-year-old daughter for dinnertime and after-school chores and somewhat less successfully to her sons for cleaning their own rooms. Combining efforts to help her reconnect with her family and develop new ties, the therapist encouraged her to get the courage to write to a sister whom she had not contacted in several years. Mary was surprised when her sister not only responded, but offered an invitation to visit. The therapist gave Mary the name of a local church, which provided a tutor and Big Brother for her son, and also helped Mary to identify and gather together several single mothers for regular Friday night potluck dinners with videos for the kids to free up time for the mothers to talk. Over time, this group strengthened and became a source of ongoing and mutual coverage for a variety of tasks and emergencies. At follow-up, she reported that she had visited her sister and felt good about their contact. Mary continues to describe her life as difficult but is proud of her ability to make it as a single parent.

Support networks for single parents are important, but the networks of children also need attention. They need a variety of connections to balance the inevitable intensity of the single parent-child relationship and to fill the gaps in what any one parent, however competent, cannot provide. Even though we now know that divorce also has positive effects (Ahrons, 1994; Arditti & Madden-Derlich, 1995; Barber & Eccles, 1992), there is no denying that loss of contact with a father and his network has ramifications and causes pain (Amato & Keith, 1991; Furstenberg et al., 1987;

Gringlas & Weinraub, 1995; Hetherington, Cox, & Cox, 1977; Zill, 1990). It has been suggested that as much as 70 percent of the social network may be disrupted in a divorce, so the loss experienced is beyond that of loss of a parent (Hetherington et al., 1978). If possible, therapists should work to involve the child's father as an ongoing part of the child's network. When the relationship between ex-spouses is conflictual, continued involvement of the father may make things more difficult for the mother, and she may prefer not to spend her limited energies making the necessary arrangements, particularly if the father is unpredictable. His comings and goings can be stressful for the child, and mothers often end up having to deal with the emotional fallout on their children. It isn't surprising that mothers often complain not that they are single parents, but that they are not quite single enough. Mothers may need support in allowing the father access to the child, tolerating the unfairness of those times when the father is idealized or they are blamed for his failures.

Still, father involvement in the child's network is important enough to work hard to find ways not only to maintain it, but to ensure that it is of substance. When contacts between child and father are often brief and unnatural, fathers may need help in behaving as a parent, not a friend (Arendell, 1986; Furstenberg & Nord, 1985; Simons & Beaman, 1996; Whitbeck, Simons, & Kao, 1994), particularly since it is clear that children tend to do better if their father continues to actually participate as a parent (Simons, Whitbeck, Beaman, & Conger, 1994) but little evidence that visitation per se has any impact at all (Amato, 1993; Emery, 1988; Furstenberg & Cherlin, 1991; Simons & Beaman, 1996). The bottom line is that a child needs both parents, so both parents should be coached to cooperate in the best interests of their child (Ahrons, 1994; Lamb et al., 1997). Divorced single parents who can both maintain active parenting roles with their children without becoming overly combative with each other provide children with the possibility of two loving homes and parents with welcome periods of respite. Whether of not the father continues to be involved, it is important to strengthen the child's network by minimizing the loss of extended family members and family friends, and increasing the involvement of community supports. Teachers, soccer coaches, Big Brothers and Big Sisters, and activity group leaders can be considered as possible network resources for children. Males in this wider network of adults can be recruited to provide contacts and activities to minimize the impact of the loss of those fathers who do not stay involved. Even if no individual is able to make a major or permanent commitment to the child, each can offer a piece of what is needed.

RECOGNIZING AND MOBILIZING STRENGTHS

All single-parent families have strengths that can be mobilized to solve the problems of family members, even the most troubled ones. Effective problem identification and solving should begin by helping family members to identify strengths and resources, emphasizing what they can control and minimizing or accepting what they cannot. A consistent effort should be made to help mothers feel that they are competent, that they have all the skills necessary to take care of their families, and that the problems associated with single-parent family life need not be permanent or insurmountable. It was easy to help mobilize some of Annie's strengths, which involved determination, a good job, and a strong network:

> Annie says that she got married at 21 in part because she liked her husband's sarcastic sense of humor but mostly because she had finished college and thought it was the thing to do. The meanness of his humor quickly wore thin, and the relationship that evolved was never particularly wonderful or nurturing. The process of leaving probably began ten years before it occurred, when she began to ask herself, "Would I like to grow old with this man?" and the answer was a definite no. In her late thirties, she realized that she was in a dead-end job and a dead-end marriage and burned out on both. She took a risk and returned to graduate school. Finishing school and getting a new job made a massive contribution to her self-esteem. Feeling

valued for the first time because she was good at her work probably dealt a death blow to her psychologically abusive marriage. She finally gave up during a summer that had been a bad one in many ways: Her mother had died, the job she loved was overwhelming, and her husband had become psychologically missing in action. She took a deep breath and left, refusing to get sidetracked by her husband's increasingly conservative and critical views. She sought coaching to help her through the process and used it well to keep her eye on the ball: She committed herself to finishing the task of raising her two children, then ages 10 and 5, while simultaneously working on her career and her personal development.

She came out of the chute fighting and has spent the last nine years as a single parent of two children, now ages 19 and 14. Parenting adolescents is stressful, but her children are doing well, even though her daughter is in the eye-rolling, black nailpolish, mom-is-uncool stage of development. Annie works long hours and seldom dates (in part because her children have never approved of the men she brings into her life). Although she still occasionally fantasizes about the "perfect relationship," she considers herself to be lucky to be on her own. As she puts it, "Some women never get over the fact that they need a man to be whole." She is most definitely whole. Being single has helped her to develop herself and has exposed her to different ways of thinking and coping. She has managed to survive and bring up her children with determination, the help of her strong faith, and her extended network of family and friends dating back to junior high, a network that she carefully nurtures.

Mobilizing strengths often requires the therapist to tackle the issue of the single mother's self-esteem head-on, since it is critical to the mother's ability to accomplish the tasks at hand (Holloway & Machida, 1992). Although good self-esteem contributes to good parenting, many women become single parents without much of a credit balance in the self-esteem department. Some originally chose their partners because they had little esteem, some lost their sense of self in a neglectful or abusive relationship, and some never lived on their own long enough to develop an independent sense of self-

worth. For very young single mothers, increasing self-esteem may require practical help in discovering who they are, how to care for their child, and how to manage their ambivalence about the loss of their teenage freedoms without neglecting their responsibilities, becoming bitter, or feeling bad about themselves. For newly divorced single mothers, increasing self-esteem sometimes involves coaching them to feel less responsible for the failure of their marriage, helping them to see they do not need the ticket to an automatic social life that marriage provides, and cultivating in them a view of themselves as capable of flying solo. Self-esteem for women who tend to be self-sacrificing can be increased by helping them to avoid neglecting their own needs completely, even when they want to do so. They must be encouraged to focus a little of their energies on nurturing themselves even when their initiative is low, if not for their own good then for the good of their children.

Helping a mother to put what she is going through into cultural and developmental perspective is another way of beginning to help her cope more effectively (Holloway & Machida, 1992). Pointing out the prevalence of single parenthood and the lack of support from society for all single parents lets her know that she is not alone. The idea that there are benefits in addition to problems in single parenthood (Arditti & Madden-Derdich, 1995) can be woven into discussions of her history and current circumstances. Information provides her with distance from her daily struggles and lays the groundwork for the development of specific strategies to combat any vulnerabilities she or her children might have.

In attempting to affirm a single parent's strengths, it is important to avoid moving too rapidly, or she will feel dismissed. Only after listening to a woman's story should the therapist make an effort to affirm the resilience and courage that she generates on a daily basis. Only after she has been assured that the therapist understands the difficulties of going it alone should she be reminded that she can be happy and fulfilled even without a spouse and should feel proud of her accomplishments in raising her children. Discussion of the risks, and especially the benefits, of single parent-hood can help her to see that many of the things they are now being forced to learn will in time become valued strengths. This includes the increased closeness that occurs between single parents and their children, the accelerated growth and development of children who function in helping roles, the early acquisition of independence and a wide range of survival skills, including the ability to cope with loss and adapt to change, the increased appreciation of the need for connections with people resulting in links to a rich, diverse, and flexible network of friends, neighbors, extended family, and religious groups. The effective coping of children also should be affirmed, since many come to grips with issues that would challenge adults, and they make important contributions to the family's well-being.

REINFORCING THE MOTHER'S AUTHORITY

Forming a new family requires that the new single parent gain credibility and assume power as the sole executor of a family system that once was ruled by two, a task that may be particularly difficult for women who have never lived independently, who have tended to rely on their spouses to provide discipline and limit setting, and/or who are temporarily immobilized by depression or loss. Because this new family structure must be created at a time of high stress when the new single parent may feel least prepared to do so, a significant amount of support may be necessary. The biggest problem for many divorced women becomes too great a tolerance for a child's negative behaviors, a tendency to become overly permissive as mothers attempt to make up for the losses and disadvantages they think their children have experienced, or inconsistency based on the unpredictable stresses in their own lives. The biggest problem for teen mothers is taking responsibility consistently. When it isn't clear who is in charge, the teen or her parents, children either become confused or learn to play one adult off against another to get what they want.

All children need the security of structure, predictability, and stability, and distressed children who are experiencing serious life transitions need these qualities more. The clear boundaries and limits that are key elements in maintaining family structure are also important for maintaining maternal sanity. At the most basic level, it is important to define who is in and who is out of the family, who comes to sessions, and who has the right to make household rules. For single mothers living in their own parents' homes or women who have men living with them for relatively short periods of time, the answers to these questions are not always easy. Helping the single parent to negotiate issues of power, rules, and responsibilities, whether with her parents, her lover, or her children, is sometimes the most important task of therapy, since it lays the groundwork for how everyone can live together.

Many single parents don't seem to know how to set effective limits except when a crisis is in progress, so they frequently find themselves exhausted by unproductive standoffs with their children (Herz, 1988; Hetherington & Clingempeel, 1992; Morawetz & Walker, 1984). Although they know that a healthy family is no democracy, single parents can treat their children more like friends to meet their own needs for companionship or to avoid energy-depleting conflict. Alternatively, they can make some pretty extreme rules in attempts to control disasters before they occur. Worse yet, they can try to do both: be a friend and then, when things become chaotic, make extreme rules that cannot be enforced. Therapists can help by sorting out what is and is not reasonable depending on the child's age and family circumstances, by serving as a model, by repeatedly reinforcing the mother's authority in front of her children, and by helping her to encourage her family and the other adults in her life to support her efforts. Because there are some data that suggest that low income and fewer resources are associated with an increase in maternal violence (Margolin, 1992), it is also crucial to carefully draw the line between the need for firm limits and overly negative parental reactions.

The mother's ability to be in charge of her family is complicated by the need for her to require that older children take some responsibility for their younger siblings and household chores. In some families, mothers allow children to have so much authority that their own is compromised. Therapists can help mothers to retain their status as ultimate authority and keep a direct line to each child even as they delegate more than the usual number of responsibilities to their older ones.

Family stability and parental authority can also be reinforced by maintaining family routines and rituals that ensure predictability and structure. Some single parents with multiple responsibilities are so overwhelmed by day-to-day survival issues that they neglect the need for these routines and family rituals, forgetting the comfort, structure, and sense of continuity that they provide. In fact, after a death or a divorce, some parents abandon even the most basic rituals such as regular family dinners, not to mention Sunday outings or birthday and other holiday celebrations. Some even say that they feel rituals are less relevant since they are no longer a "real" family. Reestablishing this important aspect of family life can reassure children, reinforcing the feeling of a normal family and diminishing the need to challenge their mother's authority to find out whether she is really in charge.

ADDRESSING SPECIAL LIFE CYCLE ISSUES OF SINGLE-PARENT FAMILIES

Single-parent families can come into being at almost any stage of the family life cycle, their formation becoming superimposed on the tasks and issues of other phases and interacting with them in complex ways. Whether a single-parent household is created through death, divorce, adoption, or even birth, members must mourn the loss or partial loss of the mother's partner/child's parent, the loss of a child's biological family, and everyone's dream of what the family could have been but now will not be. Women may become single parents when they are 14 and their child is an infant, when they are 45 and their children are teens, and at all phases in-between. Whenever it occurs, it is a high-stress time, and depression, anxiety, and sleep disorders are not uncommon. It is difficult even for those single parents who also feel relief at being out of a bad

relationship. Common tasks include mourning, establishment of a new or revised family identity, and maintaining or increasing supportive network connections.

Mourning is particularly important for the divorced single-parent family, since it provides a basis for members to create a new workable structure. Mourning losses may be less of an issue for families that are created by one parent from the outset, but even some of these mothers need to mourn the loss of a dream family. The ambiguity of the loss and the ambiguity of the family boundary make the process of mourning in single-parent families more difficult (Boss, 1983). It's hard to mourn the loss of a parent who is still seen on weekends and Wednesday nights, the loss of the fantasy of a father or a partner who never was, or simply the loss of a sense of family. It is particularly hard when there are no prescribed rituals to accomplish this process. Old losses may be kept alive in many ways: Parents may discourage children from talking of loss to protect the child from pain or to avoid having to deal with their own sadness; children may hide their sadness and anger or take on functions of the absent parent to avoid increasing their mother's burden; unspoken family rules may maintain the status quo and discourage direct discussion of events and feelings; children may act out or fail to perform in school in attempts to distract or reinvolve a mother who is preoccupied with her need to support the family; children may act out at home to bring a psychologically absent depressed mother back into contact. For young children, an angry, frazzled parent is less frightening than a sad one, particularly when there is no other adult to provide a sense of security.

Single Parents with Young Children

For single parents without another adult in the household, raising children is hardest when they are young and require constant supervision, guidance, and nurturance. As they get old enough to go to school or help around the house, parental life becomes a little easier. On the other hand, a single-parent family identity becomes more of a problem for many school-age children, particularly those who live in communities of predominantly two-parent households where they are regarded as different at a time when it is vital to be just like everyone else. Young boys in particular appear to be at risk for behavioral problems during this phase (Clark, Sawyer, Nguyen, & Baghurst, 1993; Hetherington et al., 1978; Shaw Emery, & Tuer, 1993).

These issues of feeling different are also problematic when a single-parent family has been created through adoption. Single-parent adoptions often involve older children, often from other countries, often troubled, and often of another race (Groze, 1991). The lack of fit between the child and the parent in temperament, abilities, and values can have a pervasive influence on all stages of the family life cycle and requires work and compromise from all family members. These single parents must create a family identity that incorporates racial and ethnic diversity. They also must establish ways of operating with a child who could have considerable history and baggage from a dysfunctional family and/or an institution. Frequently, this means coping with a child's insecurity about parental commitment, attachment problems, teaching the most basic rules about acceptable behavior, and managing community prejudice. Single parents must deal with these issues while working out an altered relationship with their own family and finding a way to integrate the child's memories of his or her family of origin. Therapists should make these highly charged issues overt and discussable, preparing mother and child for the extended time it takes to become a family (often at least two years) when it must be formed midstream in the lives of the members.

Single Parents with Adolescents

When the children in single-parent families are older, they are likely to take on and be granted more authority over their younger siblings and the household. It is important to remember that these so-called parental children are often essential, not pathological, for the survival of single-parent households. This role becomes a problem only when children are required to totally sacrifice their childhood to chores and responsibilities, when parents fail to retain ultimate responsibility for the rules of family life, or when children (frequently an oldest or one of the opposite gender) actually assume the role of the absent parent. These factors make it difficult for the single parent to retain credibility and set limits effectively and for the child to actually have a childhood.

Single parenthood becomes harder yet in the teen years, especially when normal adolescent obnoxiousness dominates the household and children begin to overtly challenge parental rules and values. Even when mothers are comfortable setting limits and when children present no more than the usual problems testing them, adolescence is a trying time for single parents, who can get worn down by teenage random acts of rudeness. The universal parental dilemma of finding the right balance between allowing age-appropriate rules and freedoms is complicated by the single mother's awareness that it is up to her alone to get it right and that there is no real guarantee that she will be spared tragedy even if she does it right. Girls who are raised in single-parent families present special worries during these years, since they are at risk for getting overinvolved in romantic relationships looking for the father they have not had or to compensate for unhappiness at home. If the mother is isolated and bitter, they run a greater risk of problems with intimacy. If there is an unrelated male partner in the home, there is an increased risk of sexual abuse with a young girls' emerging sexuality.

Boys often develop more than the usual distance from their mothers, in part because they are warned by society about being "mama's boys" and they are led to believe that they cannot become men unless they cut the apron strings. Olga Silverstein, in her book *The Courage to Raise Good Men* (1994), suggests that we help mothers by challenging both the message to boys about being attached to their mothers and the message given to mothers that they must distance themselves emotionally from their sons to protect the son's "autonomy needs." Family therapists at this phase should pay careful attention to the relationships of mothers and sons, since boys are particularly likely to challenge maternal authority during adolescence (Hetherington et al., 1978). Some boys feel that they must compensate for their father's absence by becoming the "man of the house" and trying to take care of their mother. Mothers may become disempowered, and sons may be particularly resistant to their authority and even monitor their free time and dating. Mothers, therefore, may need support to maintain their parental role and not give it up prematurely.

Special attention should be given to all adopted children as they enter their teens, since a disproportionate number require therapy (Okun, 1996) as they struggle with reemerging questions about their identity ("Who am I? Why was I given away?"). An even higher percentage of those from single-parent adoptive homes may need assistance reworking their identity with an additional twist ("If I had to be given away, why couldn't I have been given to a two-parent family?"). Resentment at not having the ideal family, complicated by the seemingly endless testing of the limits of parental commitment with anger, depression, acting out, and even substance abuse, brings many of these families for therapy. Single parents may need a therapist's help to draw in network members to help provide controls, to avoid personalizing the teen's messages, to find ways to continue to support the child, and to tolerate the often unusually rocky moves toward emancipation.

Single Parents of Young Adults

Eventually, children grow up and leave, and the single-parent family is transformed again. Although almost all families become single-parent families sooner or later, most do not become so until late in life. While, as Lillian Rubin says, most women respond to their children leaving home with a decided sense of relief (Rubin, 1979), gracefully accomplishing this developmental task can be a problem for single parents, who may find it more difficult to let go because they do not have the support and comfort of a marriage to provide a continuing sense of belonging or family. The welcome freedom, relief, and sense of accomplishment is counterbalanced by sadness that they are unable to share yet another of their child's developmental steps with a partner who cares as much as they do and the need to reevaluate their own priorities to make an independent life for themselves. This is more difficult for single mothers who have not maintained an active social or work life during the child-rearing years. Awareness of parental anxieties increases the child's guilt about leaving and stimulates anger if children think they are being smothered or constrained by the implicit demands of their parents' needs. Therapists can help single mothers to prepare for their child's emancipation by encouraging mothers to develop interests and networks of their own before the child is ready to leave.

CONCLUSION

Effective single parenting is hard work and requires more support for families than tends to be provided in today's mobile and fractured communities. Nevertheless, single parents can take care of themselves, raise healthy children, and contribute to society. Single mothers can survive and complete the tasks assigned to them, providing their children with structure, nurturance, and values while meeting their own needs for intimacy, companionship, and community. Children can grow strong and make good use of the unusual and enriched diversity of experiences provided to them, including strong connections with extended family and friends. Many single-parent homes are less "broken" or troubled than those of intact families. It helps neither families nor our communities if we disparage or neglect single parents and their children.

It is time for our society to accept and support single-parent families. There is no way to preserve the way we never were. Today's increased emphasis on the future of the family implies that there once was or is now such a thing as *the* family, but families have always come in many forms and are likely to become even more diverse in the future. Single parenthood is becoming more common, not less so. The emphasis on so-called family values has little to do with families and a lot to do with enforcing a conservative version of what is seen as socially acceptable behavior. The opinions of former Vice President Dan Quayle notwithstanding, today's families are as much "Murphy Brown" and "Grace under Fire" as they are "Ozzie and Harriet" and "Father Knows Best." In our efforts to help, we must provide support and validation and take special care to challenge the assumption that single-parent families are always problem infested. As one single parent who had successfully raised three children vehemently stated, "I may have been divorced, but there was nothing broken about my home."

REFERENCES

Acock, A. C., & Demo, D. H. (1994). *Family diversity and well-being.* Thousand Oaks, CA: Sage.

Ahrons, C. (1981). The continuing coparental relationship between divorced spouses. *American Journal of Orthopsychiatry, 51,* 315–328.

Ahrons, C. (1994). *The good divorce: Keeping your family together when your marriage comes apart.* New York: HarperCollins.

Allison, P. D., & Furstenberg, F. F. (1989). How marital dissolution affects children: Variations by age and sex. *Developmental Psychology, 25,* 540–549.

Amato, P. R. (1993). Children's adjustment to divorce: Theories, hypotheses, and empirical support. *Journal of Marriage and the Family, 55,* 23–38.

Amato, P. R., & Keith, B. (1991). Parental divorce and the well-being of children: A meta-analysis. *Psychological Bulletin, 110,* 26–46.

Arditti, J. A., & Madden-Derlich, D. (1995). No regrets: Custodial mothers' accounts of the difficulties and benefits of divorce. *Contemporary Family Therapy, 17*(2), 229–248.

Arendell, T. (1986). *Mothers and divorce: Legal, economic, and social dilemmas.* Berkeley, CA: University of California Press.

Barber, B. L., & Eccles, J. S. (1992). Long-term influence of divorce and single parenting on adolescent family- and work-related values, behaviors, and aspirations. *Psychological Bulletin, 111*(1), 108–126.

Belsky, J. (1990). Parental and nonparental child care and children's socioemotional development: A decade in review. *Journal of Marriage and the Family, 52,* 885–903.

Blechman, E. (1982). Are children with one parent at psychological risk? A methodological review. *Journal of Marriage and the Family, 44,* 179–198.

Boss, P. (1983). Family separation and boundary ambiguity. *The International Journal of Emergencies and Disasters, 1,* 63–72.

Brown, G., & Harris, T. (1978). *Social origins of depression: A study of psychiatric disorder in women.* London: Tavistock Press.

Brown, G., Harris, T., & Copeland, J. (1972). Depression and loss. *British Journal of Psychiatry, 130,* 1–18.

Burden, D. S. (1986). Single parents and the work setting: The impact of multiple job and homelife responsibilities [Special Issue]. *Family Relations, 35,* 37–43.

Caldwell, C. H. (1996). Predisposing, enabling and need factors related to patterns of help-seeking among African American women. In H. W. Neighbors & J. S. Jackson (Eds.), *Mental health in Black America* (pp. 146–160). Thousand Oaks, CA: Sage.

Children's Defense Fund (1997). *Status of America's children yearbook.* Washington, DC: Children's Defense Fund.

Clark, J. J., Sawyer, M. G., Nguyen, A.-M., T., & Baghurst, P. A. (1993). Emotional and behavioural problems experienced by children living in single-parent families: A pilot study. *Journal of Paediatric Child Health, 29,* 338–343.

Compas, B. E., & Williams, R. A. (1990). Stress, coping, and adjustment in mothers and young adolescents in single and two-parent families. *American Journal of Community Psychology, 18,* 525–545.

Conger, R. D., Conger, K. J., Elder, G. H., Lorenz, F. O., Simons, R. L., & Whitbeck, L. B. (1992). A family process model of economic hardship and influences on adjustment of early adolescent boys. *Child Development, 63,* 526–541.

Demo, D. H., & Acock, A. C. (1988). The impact of divorce on children. *Journal of Marriage and the Family, 50,* 619–648.

Dover, S. J., Leahy, A., & Foreman, D. (1994). Parental psychiatric disorder: Clinical prevalence and effects on default from treatment. *Child: Care, Health & Development, 20*(3), 137–143.

Downey, G. & Coyne, J. C. (1990). Children of depressed parents: An integrative review. *Psychological Bulletin, 108,* 50–76.

Edin, K., & Lein, L. (1997). *Making ends meet: How single mothers survive welfare and low-wage work.* New York: Russel Sage Foundation.

Elder, G. H., Van Nguyen, R., & Caspi, A. (1985). Linking family hardship to children's lives. *Child Development, 56,* 361–375.

Emery, R. E. (1988). *Marriage, divorce, and children's adjustment.* Beverly Hills, CA: Sage.

Friedeman, M. L., & Andrews, M. (1990). Family support and child adjustment in single-parent families. *Issues in Comprehensive Pediatric Nursing, 13,* 289–301.

Furstenberg, F. F., Brooks-Gunn, J., & Morgan, S. P. (1987). *Adolescent mothers in later life.* New York: Harvard University Press.

Furstenberg, F. F., & Cherlin, A. J. (1991). *Divided families: What happens to children when parents part.* Cambridge, MA: Harvard University Press.

Furstenberg, F. F., & Nord, C. W. (1985). Parenting apart: Patterns of child-rearing after marital disruption. *Journal of Marriage and the Family, 47,* 893–904.

Garfinkel, I., & McLanahan, S. S. (1986). *Single mothers and their children: New American dilemma.* Washington, DC: The Urban Institute Press.

Gladov, N. W., & Ray, M. P. (1986). The impact of informal support systems on the well-being of low income single parents. *Family Relations, 35,* 113–123.

Gottfried, A. E., & Gottfried, A. W. (Eds.). (1994). *Redefining families: Implications for children's development.* New York: Plenum Press.

Gringlas, M., & Weinraub, M. (1995). The more things change…Single parenting revisited. *Journal of Family Issues, 16,*(1) 29–52.

Groze, V. (1991). Adoption and single parents: A review. *Child Welfare, 70*(3), 321–332.

Hall, L. A., Gurley, D. N., Sachs, B., & Kryscio, R. J. (1991). Psychosocial predictors of maternal depressive symptoms, parenting attitudes, and child behavior in single-parent families. *Nursing Research, 40*(4), 214–220.

Hatchett, S. J., Cochran, D. L., & Jackson, J. S. (1991). Family life. In J. S. Jackson (Ed.), *Life in Black America* (pp. 46–83). Newbury Park, CA: Sage.

Herz, F. B. (1988). The post divorce family. In B. Carter & M. McGoldrick (Eds.), *The changing family life cycle* (pp. 372–398). New York: Gardner Press.

Hetherington, E. M. (1989). Coping with family transitions: Winners, losers, and survivors. *Child Development, 60,* 1–14.

Hetherington, E. M., & Clingempeel, W. G. (1992). Coping with marital transitions. *Monographs of the Society for Research in Child Development, 57* (2–3, Serial No. 227).

Hetherington, E. M., Cox, M., & Cox, R. (1977). Beyond father absence: Conceptualizations of the effects of divorce. In E. M. Hetherington & D. Parke (Eds.), *Readings in child psychology* (pp. 308–314). New York: McGraw Hill.

Hetherington, E., Cox, M., & Cox, R. (1978). The aftermath of divorce. In J. Stevens & M. Mathews (Eds.), *Mother/child father/child relationships* (pp. 149–176). Washington, DC: National Association for the Education of Young Children.

Hetherington, E. M., Cox, M., & Cox, R. (1979). Family interaction and the social, emotional, and cognitive development of children following divorce. In V. Vaughn & T. Brazelton (Eds.), *The family: Setting priorities* (pp. 89–128). New York: Science and Medicine.

Holloway, S. D., & Machida, S. (1992). Maternal child-rearing beliefs and coping strategies: Consequences for divorced mothers and their children. In. I. E. Sigel, A. V. McGillicuddy-DeLisi, & J. J. Goodnow (Eds.), *Parental belief systems: The psychological consequences for children* (2nd ed., pp. 249–265). Hillsdale, NJ: Lawrence Erlbaum Associates.

Kalter, N., Riemer, B., Brickman, A., & Chen, J. W. (1985). Implications of parental divorce for female development. *Journal of the American Academy of Child Psychiatry, 24,* 538–544.

Kissman, K., & Allen, J. A. (1993). *Single parent families.* Newbury Park, CA: Sage.

Koeske, G. F., & Koeske, R. D. (1990). The buffering effect of social support on parental stress. *American Journal of Orthopsychiatry 60*(3), 440–451.

Lamb, M., Sternberg, K., & Thompson, R. (1997). The effects of divorce and custody arrangements on children's behavior, development, and adjustment. *Family and Conciliation Courts Review, 35,* 393–404.

Malson, M. R. (1986). The black working mother as role model. *Radcliffe Quarterly, 72,* 24–25.

Margolin, L. (1992). Child abuse by mothers' boyfriends: Why the overrepresentation? *Child Abuse & Neglect 16*(4), 541–551.

McAdoo, H. P. (1980). Black mothers and the extended family support network. In L. F. Rodgers-Rose (Ed.), *The Black woman* (pp. 125–144). Newbury Park, CA: Sage.

McLanahan, S. S., & Booth, K. (1989). Mother-only families: Problems, prospects, and policies. *Journal of Marriage and the Family, 51,* 557–580.

McLanahan, S. S., & Sandefur, G. (1994). *Growing up with a single parent.* Cambridge, MA: Harvard University Press.

McLoyd, C. C., & Wilson, L. (1990). Maternal behavior, social support, and economic conditions as predictors of distress in children. *New Directions for Child Development, 46,* 49–69.

Morawetz, A., & Walker, G. (1984). *Brief therapy with single-parent families.* New York: Brunner/Mazel.

Okun, B. F. (1996). *Understanding diverse families: What practitioners need to know.* New York: The Guilford Press.

Olson, S. L., Kieschnick, E., Banyard, V., & Ceballo, R. (1994). Socioenvironmental and individual correlates of psychological adjustment in low-income single mothers. *American Journal of Orthopsychiatry, 64*(2), 317–330.

Rubin, L. B. (1979). *Women of a certain age: The midlife search for self.* New York: Harper & Row.

Samuelsson, M. A. K. (1994). Associations between the mental health and social networks of children and parents in single-parent families: A comparison between a clinical group and a control group. *Acta Psychiatrica Scandinavica, 90,* 438–445.

Shaw, D. S., & Emery, R. E. (1987). Parental conflict and other correlates of the adjustment of school-age children whose parents have separated. *Journal of Abnormal Child Psychology, 15,* 269–281.

Shaw, D. S., Emery, R. E., & Tuer, M. D. (1993). Parental functioning and children's adjustment in families of divorce: A prospective study. *Journal of Abnormal Child Psychology, 21*(1), 119–134.

Shear, M. K., Anderson, C. M., & Greeno, K. (1997). *Psychiatric illness in mothers who bring children for mental health care.* Paper presented at Improving the Condition of People with Mental Illness: The Role of Services Research. Washington, DC.

Silverstein, O., & Rashbaum, B. (1994). *The courage to raise good men.* New York: Penguin Books USA.

Simons, R. L. (1996). *Understanding differences between divorced and intact families: Stress, interaction, and child outcome.* Thousand Oaks, CA: Sage.

Simons, R. L. & Beaman, J. (1996). Father's parenting. In R. L. Simons (Ed.), *Understanding differences between divorced and intact families: Stress, interaction, and child outcome* (pp. 94–103). Thousand Oaks, CA: Sage.

Simons, R. L., & Beaman, J., Conger, R. D., & Chao, W. (1992). Childhood experience, conceptions of parenting, and attitudes of spouse as determinants of parental behavior. *Journal of Marriage and the Family, 55,* 91–106.

Simons, R. L., & Johnson, C. (1996). Mother's parenting. In R. L. Simons (Ed.), *Understanding differences between divorced and intact families: Stress, interaction, and child outcome* (pp. 81–93). Thousand Oaks, CA: Sage.

Simons, R. L., Johnson, C., Beaman, J., & Conger, R. D. (1993). Explaining women's double jeopardy: Factors that mediate the association between harsh treatment as a child and violence by a husband. *Journal of Marriage and the Family, 55,* 713–723.

Simons, R. L., Whitbeck, L. B., Beaman, J., & Conger, R. D. (1994). The impact of mothers' parenting, involvement by nonresidential fathers, and parental conflict on adjustment of adolescent children. *Journal of Marriage and the Family, 56,* 356–374.

Stack, C. (1974). *All our kin.* New York: Harper & Row.

Stack, S. (1989). The impact of divorce on suicide in Norway, 1951–1980. *Journal of Marriage and the Family, 51,* 229–238.

Taylor, R. J., Jackson, J. S., & Quick, A. D. (1982). The frequency of social support among black Americans: Preliminary findings from the National Survey of Black Americans. *Urban Research Review, 8*(2), 1–4.

Thompson, M. S., & Wilkins, W. P. (1992). The impact of formal, informal, and societal support networks on the psychological well-being of black adolescent mothers. *Social Work, 37*(4), 322–328.

Travato, F., & Lauris, G. (1989). Marital status and mortality in Canada: 1951–81. *Journal of Marriage and the Family, 51,* 907–922.

Tschann, J. M., Johnston, J. R., & Wallerstein, J. S. (1989). Resources, stresses and attachment as predictors of adult adjustment to divorce: A longitudinal study. *Journal of Marriage and the Family, 51,* 1033–1046.

Wallerstein, J. S. (1987). Children of divorce: A ten-year study. In E. M. Hetherington & J. D. Arasteh (Eds.), *The impact of divorce, single parenting and stepparenting on children* (pp. 197–214). Hillsdale, NJ: Lawrence Erlbaum Associates.

Wallerstein, J. S., & Blakeslee, S. (1989). *Second chances, men, women, and children a decade after divorce.* New York: Ticknor & Fields.

Westcot, M., & Dries, R. (1990). Has family therapy adapted to the single-parent family? *American Journal of Family Therapy, 18*(4), 353–372.

Whitbeck, L., Simons, R., & Kao, M. (1994). The effects of divorced single mothers' dating and sexual atti-tudes on the sexual attitudes and behaviors of their adolescent children. *Journal of Marriage and the Family, 56,* 615–621.

Zill, N. (1990). *U.S. children and their families: Current conditions and recent trends.* Report of the Select Committee on Children, Youth and Families, U.S. House of Representatives, Washington, DC.

CHAPTER 25

REMARRIED FAMILIES

MONICA McGOLDRICK
BETTY CARTER

As the first marriage signifies the joining of two families, so a second marriage involves the interweaving of three, four, or more families whose previous family life cycle courses have been disrupted by death or divorce. So complex is the process of forming a remarried family that we have come to think of this process as adding another whole phase to the family life cycle for those involved.

More than half of Americans today have been, are now, or will eventually be in one or more stepfamilies during their lives (Larson, 1992). Indeed, stepfamilies are becoming the most common family form and estimates are that there will soon be more binuclear families than nuclear families in the United States (Bernstein, 1989). Approximately 35 percent of children will live in one by the age of 18 (Glick, 1989). Half of the marriages that occur each year are remarriages. By the year 2010, they say, stepfamilies will be the most prevalent type of family in the United States, since almost 50 percent of first marriages are expected to end in divorce and approximately 70 percent of divorced individuals (more men than women) remarry (Norton & Miller, 1992; Visher & Visher, 1996).

Yet our society still does not recognize this family form as normal. The process of forming a remarried family has remained inadequately understood, the redivorce rate remains high—about 14 percent higher than the first-marriage rate, and about half of remarriages terminate in less than five years (Norton & Miller, 1994).

Most family research has focused on intact first families. The emerging norms for forming a remarried family have only recently begun to be defined. The built-in ambiguity of boundaries and membership defies simple definition, and our culture lacks any established patterns or rituals to help us handle the complex relationships of acquired family members. The kinship terms that our culture does provide, such as "stepmother," "stepfather," and "stepchild," have such negative connotations that they increase the difficulties for families that are trying to work out these relationships. Constance Ahrons (Chapter 23) calls postdivorce families "binuclear," a term that is descriptive and nonstigmatizing. We have chosen to use the term "remarried" to emphasize that it is the marital bond that forms the basis for the complex rearrangement of several families in a new constellation, though increasing numbers of these families are not actually marrying, or at least not marrying for a while. Still, it is the couple's bond that makes them take the trouble to go through the complexities of family formation. Nevertheless, we frequently use the term "stepfamily" to indicate the presence of children from past relationships as part of the remarried system.

A NEW PARADIGM OF FAMILY

Many of the stepfamily's difficulties in life and in therapy can be attributed to attempts by the family or therapist to use the roles and rules of first marriage families as a guideline. Such attempts to replicate the "intact" nuclear family lead to severe problems. An entirely new paradigm of family is required for remarried families. Pasley, Rhodes, Visher, and Visher (1996) have shown that negative or undesirable outcomes are associated with therapists who are not knowledgeable about the special processes and structure of stepfamilies.

Although it is extremely hard for everyone to give up the idea of the "nuclear family," drawing a tight loyalty boundary around household members, excluding outside biological parents or children, is neither realistic nor appropriate. Instead, families need to develop a system with permeable boundaries around the members of different households to allow children to belong in multiple homes, moving easily and flexibly between households. Families need to allow for open lines of communication between ex-spouses and between children, their biological parents, their stepparents, their grandparents, and other relatives. Indeed, extended family connections and outside connectedness may be even more important for children's well-being than they are in first families (Gorell Barnes, Thompson, Daniel, & Burchardt, 1998).

Because parent-child bonds predate the marital bond, often by many years, and are therefore initially stronger than the couple bond, stepparents tend to compete inappropriately with their stepchildren for primacy with their spouse, as if the couple and parent-child relationships were on the same hierarchical level. Instead, functional remarried families must allow for the built-in ambiguity of roles and relationships and the differential ties based on historical connections and the nature of the various relationships. In particular, each parent needs to accept parental responsibility for his or her own children while accepting the spouse's feelings without trying to combat or compete with the other's parent-child attachments.

Forming a remarried family requires revisioning of traditional gender roles. This model overturns completely the notion that the stepmother, just because she is a woman, should be in charge of the home, the children, or the emotional relationships throughout the system. It suggests instead that the parent with the historical relationship with the child should be the primary parent. Traditional gender roles, requiring women to take responsibility for the emotional well-being of the family, tend to pit stepmother and stepdaughter against each other and place the ex-wife and the new wife in adversarial positions, especially concerning the children. Indeed, traditional roles, rigidly applied, are one of the most serious flaws in the currently unstable structure of first marriages. And if the old rules that called for women to rear children and men to earn and manage the finances are not working well in first-marriage families, which they are not, they have absolutely no chance at all in a system in which some of the children are strangers to the wife and the finances include sources of income and expenditure that are not in the husband's power to generate or control (e.g., alimony, child support, earnings of the ex-wife or current wife). These issues, in addition to the primacy of children's bonds to their biological parents, make stereotypical gender roles completely inadequate to the tasks required for remarried families.

In a functional remarried system, child-rearing responsibilities must be distributed in ways that validate the bond to biological parents. Each spouse must take primary responsibility for raising and disciplining his or her own biological children. The relationship of the children and stepparent remains to be defined and worked out as their connection evolves. Stepparents then gradually assume their role in whatever friendly relationship evolves with the child: godparent, aunt or uncle, or friend. Unless the children are young at the time of the remarriage, the parent-and-child paradigm may not apply. This is a reality, not a failure on anyone's part.

This model of family rests on the assumption that ex-spouses are responsible adults who can learn to cooperate with each other for the sake of their relationships with their children. Contraindications to postdivorce arrangements of joint or shared custody would obviously include the following:

- Mental illness in one or both parents.
- A history of violence and/or child abuse or neglect.
- Alcohol or drug abuse.

In our experience, this is one of the most difficult developmental transitions for families to negotiate. This is because of the wish for premature closure to end the ambiguity and pain and because of the likelihood that the previous stage (mourning a death or working out the emotional complexities of divorce) has been inadequately dealt with and will, in any case, be emotionally reactivated by the new family formation. Indeed, Montgomery, Anderson, Hetherington, and Clingempeel (1993) found in their longitudinal study that living together before remarriage provided a beneficial in-between stage of adjustment that reduces the trauma of remarriage. Much therapeutic effort must be directed toward educating families about the built-in complexities of the process so that they can work toward establishing a viable, open system that will allow them to get back on their developmental track for future life cycle phases.

It is easy to understand the wish for clear and quick resolution when one has been through the pain of a first family ending. Unfortunately, however, the instant intimacy that remarried families may hope for is impossible to achieve. The new relationships are harder to negotiate because they do not develop gradually, as intact families do, but begin midstream, after another family's life cycle has been dislocated. Children's sibling position frequently changes, and they must cope with variable membership in several households. Naturally, second families carry the scars of first-marriage families. Neither parents, children, nor grandparents can forget the relationships that went before and that may still be more powerful than the new relationships. Children never give up their attachment to their first parent (biological or adoptive), no matter how negative the relationship with that parent was or is. Having the patience to tolerate the ambiguity of the situation and allowing each other the space and time for feelings about past relationships are crucial to the process of forming a remarried family. However, the "battle fatigue" of family members quite naturally leads to a tendency to seek comfort, often resulting in the characteristic pseudomutuality (Goldstein, 1974) that denies difficulties and prevents their resolution.

We believe that information that normalizes the experience is one of the most powerful clinical tools in helping families to negotiate the complexities of remarried families. Some of the most clinically useful research findings on remarried families come from the work of Hetherington, Clingempeel, and their colleagues (Hetherington, 1989, 1990, 1991, 1993, 1995; Hetherington, Cox, & Cox, 1977, 1985); Visher and Visher (1979, 1988, 1991, 1996); Ahrons and Rodgers (1987); Ahrons (1994); Furstenberg and his colleagues (1983, 1991); Sager et al. (1983); Ann Bernstein (1989, 1994); and Pasley and her colleagues (Pasley & Ihinger-Tallman, 1987, 1994; Pasley, Rhodes, Visher, & Visher, 1996) and from the *Stepfamily Bulletin,* published quarterly by the Stepfamily Association of America in Baltimore, Maryland.

The following trends and principles concerning remarried families have been suggested by research over the years:

- The more effectively custodial parents can function, the better will be their children's adjustment (Furstenberg & Cherlin, 1991).
- The less parental conflict children are exposed to, the better will be their adjustment (Furstenberg & Cherlin, 1991).
- The more regularly children visit their noncustodial parents, the better will be their adjustment (Furstenberg & Cherlin, 1991).
- Cordial or courteous, low-intensity relationships with the ex-spouse and the ex-spouse's new marital partner work best (Dahl, Cowgill, & Asmundsson, 1987). It takes stepfathers almost two years to become comanagers of their stepchildren with their wives. They first need to become friends of the children and can only gradually move into the role of active parenting (Visher & Visher, 1996).
- Experience with and valuing of nontraditional gender roles increase the flexibility necessary for stepfamily organization. Families not of the dominant culture, such as African Americans, have much to teach families of the dominant groups about adaptive strategies necessary for the complexities of remarried families: the complexity and ambiguity of roles and relationships, the permeability of roles and household boundaries, and the fact of being peripheralized by the dominant culture (Crosbie-Burnett & Lewis, 1993).

- Family integration is most likely when extended family approves of or accepts the marriage, next best when they disapprove or are negative, and worst when they are cut off or indifferent (Duberman, 1975). Cut-offs are more common with the paternal extended family, and connections are more often strong with maternal relatives in remarried families, but relationships with extended family don't always work out smoothly. While children are quite prepared to have multiple sets of grandparents, uncles, and aunts, the middle generation can get caught up in conflicts, and managing relationships with so large a network of kin can be complicated (Furstenberg & Cherlin, 1991; Barnes, Thompson, Daniel, & Burchardt, 1998).

- Family integration is easier if the previous spouse died rather than divorced and even harder if the new spouse has never been married before (Duberman, 1975).

- Family integration is more likely, the longer the new family has together as a unit and harder when there are adolescents (Duberman, 1975). Both boys and girls in early adolescence (beginning at age 11½) seem to have a particularly difficult time adjusting to their parents' remarriage (Hetherington, 1990).

- Family integration is more likely if children are not left behind by one partner and if partners have a child together (Duberman, 1975).

- Women in stepfamilies (mothers, stepdaughters, and stepmothers) experience more stress, less satisfaction, and more symptoms than men (Bernstein, 1994). Stepmother-stepdaughter relationships are the most difficult of all stepfamily relationships (Duberman, 1975). Daughters, who are often closest to mothers in divorce, tend to have a lot of difficulty with stepfathers, no matter how hard the stepfather tries. Girls' stress probably reflects the fact that they feel more responsible for emotional relationships in a family and thus get caught between loyalty toward and protection of their biological mothers and conflicts with

their stepmothers (Bray, 1986). While divorce appears to have more adverse effects for boys, remarriage is more disruptive for girls (Hetherington et al., 1985; Anderson, Hetherington, & Clingempeel, 1989).

- Boys, who are often problems for a single mother, may settle down after the entry of a stepfather (Hetherington & Clingempeel, 1992).

- It helps if therapists think of all parental figures as potentially enriching the children's support network. In earlier times, when families lived in larger extended family and community enclaves, children had a whole network of adults who cared for them and helped to raise them. That is the model that helps here—not making choices about who is the better parent (Visher & Visher, 1996).

- Childhood experiences in a large family may be helpful in dealing with the complexities of a remarried family (Dahl et al., 1987).

- Children do better if they have regular contact with both parents (Hetherington, Stanley-Hagan, & Anderson, 1989). Such contacts increase rather than decrease the likelihood that strong and positive relationships will develop between children and their stepparents.

- Men tend to remarry sooner and more often than women. Whereas their first wives are on the average three years younger, their second wives are on the average six years younger than they are.

- The more income and education a woman has, the less likely she is to remarry. The reverse is true for men: The more income and education they have, the more likely they are to remarry, and the sooner.

- The incidence of violence and abuse is vastly greater in stepfamilies than in traditional families.

- About 65 percent of remarrying couples have children (Stepfamily Association, 1997).

- The sense of belonging in a remarried family takes three to five years for most of its members, longer if there are adolescents (Dahl et al., 1987).

- Families may move or do extensive redecorating in the first year or so to avoid the feeling of living in someone else's house (Dahl et al., 1987).
- Finances and children from prior marriages are the major contributors to adjustment problems of remarried families (Pasley et al., 1996). And remarriage often leads to a renewal of financial and/or custody difficulties in the prior relationships (Hetherington et al., 1977).
- Serious discipline issues and visitation arrangements for children are best handled by the biological parent (Dahl et al., 1987).
- Families with stepchildren are much more complicated and twice as likely to divorce. Marital satisfaction is correlated with the stepparent's connection to stepchildren (Dahl et al., 1987). Although the remarriages themselves might be quite congenial, the presence of stepchildren often creates child-related problems that lead the couple to separate). Interestingly, one study found that 15 percent of stepparents did not list their stepchild as part of the family, even when the child lived with them. Stepchildren were even more likely to exclude a live-in stepparent (31 percent) (Bernstein, 1989; Furstenberg, Nord, Peterson, & Zill, 1983). Stepchildren appear to be much more likely to change residence or leave home early than children who lived with both biological parents.
- Children in stepfamilies may appear to have more power than children in first families (Bray, 1992), although they may experience a decrease in autonomy compared to their status in the preceding single-parent phase, when they typically have more adult privileges and responsibilities.
- Many families do not withstand the early stages of family reorganization required by remarriage. About one fourth of them divorce within the first five years, a rate much higher than that for first marriages. The most complex remarried families, in which both spouses have been married before and both

have children, have the greatest difficulty establishing stability (Furstenberg & Cherlin, 1991).
- The instability of remarried families shouldn't be overstated. Remarried partners do not wait as long to leave an unhappy situation as partners in first families, and those who manage the early years have no greater likelihood of divorcing than in first marriages (Furstenberg & Cherlin, 1991).
- Remarriage of either spouse tends to decrease contact between fathers and their biological children. One study found the level of contact between a divorced father and his children to be twice as high if he did not remarry and even greater if the mother did not remarry. If both parents remarried, only 11 percent of the children had weekly contact with their fathers, compared with 49 percent of the children when neither parent had remarried (Furstenberg & Cherlin, 1991).
- In 70 percent of divorcing couples, one of the spouses was involved in an affair, but only 15 percent of them later married this person (Hetherington et al., 1977).
- Remarriage of a former spouse tends to be accompanied by a reactivation of feelings of depression, helplessness, anger, and anxiety, particularly for women (Hetherington et al., 1977). Men, possibly because it may release them from financial responsibility and because they are usually less central to the emotional system, tend to be less upset by the remarriage of an ex-wife (Hetherington et al., 1977).
- Conflicting role expectations set mothers and stepmothers into competitive struggles over child-rearing practices (Hetherington et al., 1977).
- It appears better for stepmothers to retain their work outside the home for emotional support and validation (Visher & Visher, 1996). In addition to contributing needed money, it makes the stepmother less available at home for the impossible job of dealing with her husband's children.

STEPFAMILY FORMATION
FOLLOWING DEATH

Some different issues arise in stepfamilies that are formed after the premature death of a parent. There are gender issues: A new stepfather may be perceived as rescuing the family from poverty after the death of the primary wage earner, whereas children tend to view their mother as completely irreplaceable and resent any efforts to function in her role. However, young children will eventually accept a stepparent, including a stepmother, if the remaining parent can help the children to grieve for their loss before confronting them with a stepmother. When the father does remarry, he must help the children to see and accept the new person in her own right rather than collude with the children in wanting the family to continue in exactly the same way it did when their mother was alive. On the other hand, if insufficient attention is paid to the children's grief work, they may never accept a stepmother. (For a videotape with commentary of a family dealing with these issues, see McGoldrick, 1996.)

Although there are certain advantages in forming stepfamilies after a death in that the ex-spouse is not around to "interfere," ghosts can be even more powerful, especially given people's tendency to idealize someone who is lost prematurely. All of the family triangles will occur predictably but may be harder to recognize and deal with when one of the people in the triangle is a dead person. Talking, remembering, and acknowledging the dead person's human failings and foibles help to exorcise the ghost, but none of this can be done without the active leadership of the remaining biological parent. Late adolescents or older children generally resist attempts to "replace" their dead parent, and the wise stepparent will honor that position.

GAYS AND LESBIANS IN STEPFAMILIES

Although they are not permitted to marry legally, a significant number of postdivorce families consist of a gay or lesbian couple with the children of one or both of them from a previous heterosexual marriage. These systems have all of the problems of heterosexual remarried systems in addition to the burdens of secrecy and isolation that may be caused by social stigma (Laird & Green, 1996).

In extreme cases, the adults may feel that they have to try to remain closeted, even to their children, for fear of repercussions in custody or employment. There is almost always anxiety about the consequences of coming out to the extended family, the children's teachers and friends, co-workers, neighbors, and acquaintances. Therapists can be most helpful if, in addition to the usual therapy for remarried systems, they can help the couple in sifting through their various networks to dismantle the secrecy and isolation. Connection to supportive community groups and access to supportive literature and studies are extremely important.

MONEY IN REMARRIED FAMILIES

Finances are a major area of conflict in remarried families. The complications regarding finances in remarried families flow mostly from assumptions of traditional gender roles, which completely disregard contemporary economics and the experience of generations of poor and working-class families. They also ignore the fact that either or both parents usually enter the remarriage with significant financial obligations to the first family. Failure to pay or be able to collect alimony and/or child support wreaks havoc in postdivorce families. A husband who is the sole wage earner in a remarried family often has to decide which set of children has top priority—his own or the stepchildren he lives with. These priorities are also influenced by his relationship with his ex-wife; if it is bad, his visitations and child support payments tend to lag or even cease. A new wife may complain about the money her husband gives to his children, particularly if she doesn't receive child support owed for her own children. Overall, children do tend to lose out financially when their parents remarry; that is, children from intact first families tend to receive more from their parents (White, 1992). In affluent families, problems also surface around how wills should be made and how much financial assistance should be given to which adult children. Where money is concerned, blood may suddenly seem thicker than relationship.

PREDICTABLE EMOTIONAL ISSUES IN REMARRIAGE

The basic premise of family systems theory is that we all carry into our new relationships the emotional baggage of unresolved issues from important past relationships. This baggage makes us emotionally sensitive in the new relationships, and we tend to react in one of two ways: We become self-protective, closed off, and afraid to make ourselves vulnerable to further hurt, putting up barriers to intimacy, or we become intensely expectant and demanding that the new relationships make up for or erase past hurts.

Either of these stances complicates the new relationships. In first marriages, the baggage we bring is from our families of origin: our unresolved feelings about parents and siblings. In remarriage, there are at least three sets of emotional baggage:

1. From the family of origin.
2. From the first marriage.
3. From the process of separation, divorce, or death and the period between marriages.

To the extent that either or both remarried partners expects the other to relieve him or her of this baggage, the new relationship will become problematic. On the other hand, to the extent that each spouse can work to resolve his or her own emotional issues with significant people from the past, the new relationship can proceed on its own merits.

Complex, Conflicting, and Ambiguous New Roles and Relationships

This complexity is reflected in our lack of positive language and kinship labels, the shifting of children's sibling position in the new family, and the lack of differentiation of parenting and stepparenting functions.

Stepparent Roles

Our model of stepparents is a deeply blaming one. A stepmother's unhappiness with her new spouse and ambivalence about her parenting role are particularly acute when the stepchildren are young and remain in the custody of her husband's ex-wife. In this common situation, the stepmother feels less emotionally attached to the children; she feels disrupted and exploited during their visits and has to deal with the fact that her husband's co-parenting partnership is conducted more with his ex-spouse than with her (Ambert, 1986). Stepfathers are frequently caught in the double bind of rescuer versus intruder, called upon to help discipline the stepchildren and then criticized by them and their mother for this intervention. Overtrying by the new parent is a major problem in remarried families, often related to guilt about unresolved or unresolvable aspects of the system.

Complex and Ambiguous Boundaries of the System

Boundary difficulties include issues of membership, space, authority, and allocation of time. An additional boundary problem arises when instant incest taboos are called for, as when several previously unrelated teenagers are suddenly supposed to view each other as siblings.

Affective Problems: Wishing for the Resolution of Ambiguity

Intense conflictual feelings, or their denial, are predictable problems of remarried families. These may include guilt about the previous spouse and/or children. One of the injunctions most harmful to remarried families is that a person must love another's children as much as his or her own.

The Tendency toward Pseudomutuality or Fusion

Remarried families are formed against a background of loss, hurt and a sense of failure. This often leads to a desire to not "rock the boat" this time, which suppresses doubt, conflicts, and differences that should be dealt with.

Loyalty Conflicts

One of the greatest strains on parents is to let their children have and express the full range of negative and positive feelings toward all of their parents and stepparents. Often, parents want the child's whole allegiance. Children feel caught, afraid that if they don't love a new stepparent, they will hurt and anger one parent, but if they do love the stepparent, they are disloyal and will hurt or lose the love of the other.

THE PROCESS OF REMARRIAGE

The emotional issues of remarriage go back at least to the disintegration of the first marriage. The intensity of emotion unleashed by the life cycle disruption of divorce must be dealt with over and over again before the dislocated systems are restabilized. Seen in this way, it should be clear that no amount of "dealing with" the emotional difficulties of divorce will finish off the process once and for all before remarriage, although it appears clinically that the more emotional work is done at each step, the less intense and disruptive the subsequent reactivations will be. Failure to deal sufficiently with the process at each peak may jam it enough to prevent remarried family stabilization from ever occurring, a problem that is reflected in the high rate of redivorce.

THE IMPACT OF REMARRIAGE AT VARIOUS PHASES OF THE FAMILY LIFE CYCLE

In general, the wider the discrepancy in family life cycle experience between the new spouses, the greater the difficulty of transition will be and the longer it will take to integrate a workable new family. A father of late adolescent and/or young adult children with a new, young wife who was never previously married should expect a rather strenuous and lengthy period of adjustment, during which he will have to juggle his emotional and financial responsibilities toward the new marriage and toward his (probably upset) children. His wife, looking forward to the romantic aspects of a first marriage, will encounter instead the many stresses of dealing with adolescents who probably resent her, whether the children live with the couple or not. If either spouse tries to pull the other exclusively into a life-style or attitude that denies or restricts the other spouse's family life cycle tasks or relationships with children from previous relationships, difficulties will expand into serious problems. If the husband expects his new wife to undertake immediately a major successful role in his children's lives or to be the one who always backs down gracefully when her interests and preferences clash with those of the children, there will be serious trouble in the new marriage, as the formation of the new couple bond is continuously given second priority. On the other hand, if the new wife tries, overtly or covertly, to cut off or drastically loosen the tie between father and children or takes on the role of mother to them, or if she insists that her claims always have his prior attention, thus forcing him to choose between them, there will also be serious trouble. Variations in which the new wife claims to support her husband but embarks on a battle with his ex-wife as the source of the difficulties are equally dysfunctional.

Since it is not possible emotionally either to erase or to acquire experience overnight, it is useful to conceptualize the joining of partners at two different life cycle phases as a process in which both spouses have to learn to function in several different life cycle phases simultaneously and out of their usual sequence. The new wife will have to struggle with the role of stepmother to teenagers before becoming an experienced wife or mother herself. Her husband will have to retraverse with her several phases that he has passed through before: the honeymoon, the new marriage with its emphasis on romance and social activities, and the birth and rearing of any new children of their own. Both need to be aware that a second passage through these phases automatically reactivates some of the intensity over issues that were problematic the first time around. Attempts to "make up for" past mistakes or grievances may overload the new relationship. The focus needs to be on having the experiences again, not on undoing, redoing, or denying the past. With open discussion, mutual support, understanding, and a lot of thoughtful planning, this straddling of several phases simultaneously can provide rejuvenation for the older spouse and experience for the younger spouse that can enrich their lives. If the difficulties are not understood and dealt with, they will surface as conflict or emotional distance at each life cycle transition in any subsystem of the remarried family.

SPOUSES AT SAME LIFE CYCLE PHASE

When the remarried spouses come together at the same phase of the family life cycle, their greatest difficulties will tend to be related to whether they are at a childbearing phase. Obviously, spouses with no children from previous marriages bring the least complexity to the new situation. Families with grown children and grandchildren on both sides are complex systems with long histories and will require some careful thought to negotiate successfully. Neither of these circumstances, however, is likely to provide anything like the degree of strain involved at phases including either young or adolescent children, in which the roles of active parenting and stepparenting must be included in the new family. Unfortunately, the advantage of having similar tasks, responsibilities, and experiences is frequently swamped in a competitive struggle that stems from the overload of these tasks and concern (six children are not as easy to raise or support as three), the intense emotional investment in good parenting ("My methods are better than your methods"), and the need to include both ex-spouses in the many arrangements regarding the children ("Why do you let your ex dictate our lives?").

STEPFAMILIES AND YOUNG CHILDREN

Children's struggles with the predictable issues may surface as school and/or behavior problems, withdrawal from family and peers, or acting-out behavior, any of which complicates or may completely obstruct the process of stepfamily reorganization. There are indications that preschool children, if given some time and help in mourning their previous loss, adjust most easily to a new stepfamily and that the adjustment is most difficult for stepfamilies with teenagers. Children of latency age seem to have the most difficulty resolving their feelings of divided loyalty (Wallerstein & Kelly, 1980) and benefit from careful attention to their need for contact with both parents. Clearly, children of all ages suffer when there is intense conflict between their biological parents and benefit when their parents maintain civil, cooperative, co-parental relationships (Ahrons & Rodgers, 1987; Ahrons & Wallisch, 1986). Ahrons's research (1981) indicates that if parents cannot be cooperative, structuring the relationships is the next best alternative.

STEPFAMILIES WITH ADOLESCENTS

Since the difficulties that most American families have with adolescents are legendary, it is not surprising that the additional complications of this phase in stepfamilies can push the stress level beyond manageable bonds. We have found the following common issues in stepfamilies at this phase.

1. Conflict between the need for the remarried family to coalesce and the normal concentration of adolescents on separation. Adolescents often resent the major shifts in their customary family patterns and resist learning new roles and relating to new family members when they are concerned with growing away from the family.
2. Particular difficulty for a stepparent in attempting to discipline an adolescent.
3. Adolescent attempts to resolve their divided loyalties by taking sides (Wallerstein & Kelly, 1980) or actively play one side against the other.
4. Sexual attraction between stepsiblings or stepparent and stepchild, along with the adolescent's difficulty in accepting the biological parent's sexuality.

THE IMPACT OF REMARRIAGE IN LATER LIFE CYCLE PHASES

Although there is not the daily strain of living with stepchildren and stepparents, remarriage at a post-child-rearing phase of the life cycle requires significant readjustment of relationships throughout both family systems, which may now include in-laws and grandchildren. It is probable that grown children and grandchildren will accept a remarriage after a death of a parent more easily than one after a late divorce. There will often be great relief throughout the family if a widowed older parent finds a new partner and a new lease on life, whereas a later-life divorce usually arouses concern and dismay throughout the family. A frequent problem for older remarried couples is negotiating about money. The strength of children's reactivity to a parent's remarriage, even after the adult child believes that she or he has long ago resolved the loss or divorce of the parent(s), may be overwhelming to them. They may need coaching to find a way to incorporate a new love of their parent into their lives.

Clinically, we find that the major factor in three-generational adjustment to remarriage in late middle or older age is the amount of acrimony or cooperation between the ex-spouses. When the relationship is cooperative enough to permit joint attendance at important family functions of children and grandchildren and when holiday arrangements can be jointly agreed upon, family acceptance of a new marriage tends to follow.

FAMILY THERAPY WITH REMARRIED FAMILIES: CLINICAL PROCEDURES AND ILLUSTRATIONS

Whatever the presenting problem in a remarried family, it is essential to look laterally as well as back to previous generations and to evaluate the current and past relationships with previous spouses to determine the degree to which the family needs help to work out the patterns required by the new structure. Ongoing conflict or cut-offs with ex-spouses, children, parents, and grandparents will tend to overload the relationships in the remarried family and make them problematic.

We will summarize several major predictable emotional issues in remarriage.

In first-marriage families, the major problematic triangles involve the parents with any or all of the children and each parent with his or her own parents and in-laws. In the more complex structures of remarried families, we have identified six of the most common triangles and interlocking triangles commonly presenting in the binuclear family. In no way do we mean to suggest by this focus that the triangles with the extended family and grandparental generation are unimportant to the understanding and the therapy of remarried families. In fact, we consider genograms, a basic tool for exploring structure and tracking process in all families, to be particularly essential in work with remarried families, because of the structural complexity that so influences the predictable triangles that exist in these situations (McGoldrick, 1995; McGoldrick, Gerson, & Schellenberger, 1998). In our clinical work with remarried families, coaching of the adults on further differentiation in relation to their families of origin proceeds in tandem with work on current family problems (see Chapter 26). The extended-family aspect of the family therapy in these cases has been mostly deleted from the following examples because of the space limitations of this chapter.

One final caveat: The brief case stories are meant to illustrate possible clinical moves. They fail to convey the enormous intensity aroused by attempts to shift these relationships; the extreme anger and fear that block change; the many, many slips back; and the recycling of old conflicts that accompany each move forward. Our experience indicates that families that are willing to work on relationships with their families of origin do better than those that do not.

KEY PRESENTING TRIANGLES IN REMARRIED FAMILIES

The Husband, the Second Wife, and the Ex-Wife, or the Wife, the Second Husband, and the Ex-Husband

When this triangle is presented as the main difficulty, usually around financial issues or sexual jealousy, it is likely that the ex-spouses have not accomplished an emotional divorce. The first step in this most tricky clinical work is for the therapist to establish a working alliance with the new spouse, who will otherwise sabotage efforts to focus on the first marriage. Efforts to work on the resolution of the divorce by seeing either the ex-spouses alone or all three in sessions together will probably create more anxiety than the system can handle. We have found that such work goes most smoothly when a spouse is coached in the presence of the new spouse to undertake steps outside of the therapy sessions that will change the relationship he or she currently maintains with the ex-spouse. Along the way, the new spouse will have to learn to acknowledge the past importance of that bond to his or her spouse and to accept the fact that some degree of caring will probably always remain in the relationship, depending on the length of time the first marriage lasted and whether there were children.

Catherine and John Blackman, both in their mid-thirties, came for marital therapy after two years of marriage because of "endless money conflicts" regarding John's support of his ex-wife, Agnes, and their two daughters, ages 8 and 10, who lived with their mother. John felt guilty about having left his first wife, who had been depressed and drinking and had no social life since their divorce. Catherine felt that John put the needs of his ex-wife over hers and gave in to Agnes's every demand for extra money. John defended his ex-wife's need for money and her refusal to work on the grounds that the children needed her. He said that he could not "kick her while she was down" and that he barely responded to his first wife's frequent phone calls and never saw her alone. After several sessions, Catherine understood that John could not be free to plan a life with her until he had resolved his guilty attachment to his first wife, which would not be resolved, but exacerbated, by Catherine's urging him to fight or cut off all contact with his ex-wife. With Catherine's somewhat ambivalent support, John arranged several meetings with Agnes during which they discussed the limits of his future financial support of her and he offered to keep the children temporarily while she reorganized her life.

Agnes's angry accusations about the divorce had been predicted in a therapy session, so John was able to hear them out fairly well without counterattacking. In joint sessions with Catherine alternating with outside meetings with Agnes and his children, John slowly rode out Agnes's angry tirades about the past, responded to the children's questions about the divorce, took responsibility for his part in their marital problems and his decision to divorce, and became firmer in his insistence that Agnes work out a plan with him for the financial and emotional care of the children. Eventually, when her attacks on him provoked neither counterattacks nor guilty withdrawal, Agnes accepted the reality of the divorce and turned her attention to improving her life and the children's. With continued effort on John's part, their contact became both more friendly and less frequent. By the time they left therapy, Agnes phoned John only when necessary and had ceased criticizing Catherine to the children, who were now less hostile to Catherine. During their joint sessions and in sessions with John's children, Catherine had heard John express his sorrow at the failure of his first marriage and had learned to accept that part of his past without reacting personally. She moved very cautiously with the children, leaving all disciplinary decisions to John and Agnes. Most difficult of all, Catherine really accepted that part of their income would need to go to John's children and that she could share in that commitment.

The Pseudomutual Remarried Couple, an Ex-Spouse, and a Child or Children

In this triangle, the presenting problem is usually acting out or school problems with one or more children or perhaps a child's request to have custody shifted from one parent to another. The remarried couple presents itself as having no disagreements and blames either the child or the ex-spouse (or both) for the trouble. Although the request in therapy will be for help for the child or for managing the child's behavior, the background story will usually show intense conflict between the ex-spouses, the new spouse being totally supportive of his or her spouse in conflicts with the stepchild. The first move in sorting out this triangle is to put the management of the child's behavior temporarily in the hands of the biological parent and get the new spouse to take a neutral position, rather than siding against the child. This move will probably calm things down, but they will usually not stay calm unless the pseudo-mutuality of the remarried couple is worked on, permitting differences and disagreements to be aired and resolved and permitting the child to have a relationship with his or her biological parent that does not automatically include the new spouse every step of the way. Finally, work will need to be done to end the battle with the ex-spouse and complete the emotional divorce, the lack of which is perpetuated by the intense conflict over the child or children.

Bob and Nora Bergman came to therapy for help in dealing with Bob's son, Larry (age 14). They had been married for one year, during which Larry lived with his mother and visited on weekends. Nora Bergman's daughter from her first marriage, Louise (age 9), lived with the couple. Nora's first husband had died of cancer when Louise was 5. The Bergmans reported that their marriage was extremely harmonious and that Louise was bright, cheerful, and pleasant and had an excellent relationship with both her mother and her stepfather. They thought that Larry was becoming "seriously disturbed." His school grades had dropped dramatically, he was increasingly truculent and withdrawn on weekend visits, he provoked endless fights with Louise, and he refused simple requests from Nora to pick up his belongings. Since Larry's mother, Susan, was "an unbalanced person" who used every opportunity to "harass" them, they thought that Larry was "also becoming mentally ill."

Bob worked long hours and left the management of the household and children to his wife, who, he reported, dealt pleasantly and impartially with both children. Nora agreed, saying that she loved Larry "as if he were my son" and devoted herself entirely to the welfare of her "new family of four." She tried her best to be polite to the ex–Mrs. Bergman but found her rude and almost impossible to deal with and thought that she was a harmful influence on Larry, treating him inconsistently and occasionally leaving him alone when she went on dates. Larry reported that both Bob and Nora "hated" his mother, and he could not stand to hear them talk about her. He said that his mother phoned to check on his welfare only because she knew that his father left everything to "that woman."

In therapy, Bob agreed to be the liaison to his son's school and was put in total charge of Larry's behavior during visits to the remarried household. He was also encouraged to take Larry on occasional trips alone. He admitted, after a lot of encouragement, that he and his new wife had some different ideas on raising boys but that he had not wanted to argue with her, since she was doing such a great job generally. Nora finally admitted that it was difficult to be a part-time mother to a stranger. She was encouraged to rethink her role, since Larry already had a mother. When Larry's behavior improved, the couple agreed to work on their relations with "crazy" Susan. As they stopped their end of the battle, Susan's "crazy" behavior diminished, although Bob was not willing to go very far toward resolving the old issues between himself and his ex-wife. Nora, however, did considerable work on resolving her mourning for her first husband and was able for the first time to start telling her daughter about him and to share old picture albums with her. This work, she said, made it easier for her to enjoy her second family and not to try so hard to make everyone happy.

The Remarried Couple in Conflict over the Child or Children of One of Them: The Husband, the Second Wife, and the Husband's Children or the Wife, the Second Husband, and the Wife's Children

The first of these triangles, although not the most common household composition, is the most problematic because of the central role the stepmother is expected to play in the lives of live-in stepchildren. If the stepmother has never been married before, and if the children's mother is alive and has a less than ideal relationship with her ex-husband, it may be an almost impossible situation. The stepmother should be helped to pull back long enough to renegotiate with both her husband and the children as to what her role realistically should be. Rather than leave the stepmother and children to fight it out, the father will have to participate actively in making and enforcing such rules as are agreed upon. When their immediate household is in order, the husband will have to work on establishing a cooperative co-parental relationship with his ex-wife, or the conflict with her will set the children off again and inevitably reinvolve his new wife. If the first wife is dead, he may need to complete his mourning for her and help his children to do so in order to let the past go and not see his second wife as a poor replacement of his first.

Sandy and Jim Burns came for marital therapy on the verge of divorce. Jim's first wife, Susie, had died of cancer when Jim's daughters were ages 3 and 4. He had married Sandy a year later, and she had moved into their house, which Susie had decorated with exquisite taste. Although uncomfortable to be so thoroughly surrounded by signs of Susie, Sandy rationalized that it would be wasteful to redecorate the house and settled into it. She listened carefully while Jim explained the girls' routines and likes and dislikes and tried to keep their lives exactly as they had been. As the years went by, with Jim criticizing every departure from "the way Susie did it," Sandy's nerves began to fray and she became, in her own words, "a wicked stepmother." She screamed at the girls and at Jim, and they exchanged glances and whispered about her. Once, she threatened to redecorate the house but backed down under Jim's anger. Now, with both girls teenagers and increasingly rude to her and Jim withdrawn and sullen much of the time, she thought that perhaps she should admit failure and leave the marriage.

The first turning point in therapy came when Jim realized that in his grief for his first wife and his concern for his children's welfare, he had never really made a place for Sandy in the tightly knit bereaved system of himself and his daughters. He had never supported her authority with them and had continued to join them in their rebellion against her. He now willingly took charge of the girls' behavior and insisted that they treat Sandy with courtesy.

This move, which we call the "gatekeeper intervention" is designed to hold the biological parent responsible for making room in the system for the new spouse. When a stepmother is involved, the father needs to deliver two messages to his children:

1. Be courteous to my spouse (not "your" anything).
2. "You are answering to me. You haven't lost both your mother and me."

When Jim and Sandy's relationship was in better shape and the girls' behavior had improved, the therapy focused on the incomplete grief work of Jim and the girls, who visited Susie's grave several times together. On their third visit, Jim invited Sandy to join them. After that, Sandy redecorated the house and hung a picture of Susie with their other family pictures. Throughout this period, Sandy worked on relationships in her family of origin, particularly with her mother, who had spent most of her life resisting Sandy's father's attempts to "tell her what to do."

The Pseudomutual Remarried Couple, His Children, and Her Children

This triangle presents as a happily remarried couple with "no difficulties except that their two sets of children fight constantly with each other." The children are usually fighting out the conflicts denied by the remarried couple either in the marriage or in the relationship with the ex-spouse(s). Since direct confrontation of the pseudo-mutuality stiffens resistance, and since the presenting request is made in regard to the children, it is wise to begin with an exploration of the triangles involving the children and ex-spouses, focusing on the welfare of the children.

Blake and Sally Brown requested family therapy because of the endless fighting between their children whenever Blake's children visited. Blake and Sally were in their thirties and had been married for less than a year. Their relationship had begun as an affair while Blake was still married, a fact that they believed was not known by Blake's ex-wife or children, ages 8 and 6. Sally had been divorced two years before the affair began and had custody of her two children, a boy of 8 and a girl of 5. The couple said that they supported each other on all issues related to their ex-spouses; in fact, Blake frequently arranged the visits of Sally's children to their biological father, since it "upset Sally to argue with him." Blake's ex-wife was a "disturbed person," whom he could hardly deal with, but, again, they worked together not to let her cause trouble for them. Sally had assured Blake that if his ex-wife's "irrationality" became too disturbing for his children, she would support him in attempts to gain custody and raise them with her own children.

Neither Blake nor Sally saw any connection between their problems dealing with their ex-spouses and their children's battles with each other, so the therapist spent several sessions educating them about children's loyalty conflicts in divorce and remarriage and the time required for them to accept stepparenting. When this registered on Blake, he began efforts to improve his relationship with his ex-wife. Blake and Sally's pseudo-mutual cover was blown as Sally collapsed in tears, threatening separation, termination of therapy, or anything else that might deter Blake's change. In subsequent sessions, she confessed strong feelings of guilt and insecurity because of the affair, fearing that she had "taken him away from his wife, who would therefore be justified in trying to take him back." Eventually, Sally came to recognize that the hidden agenda in her offer to raise Blake's children was the wish that they both had to eliminate contact with Blake's ex-wife.

With the issues now out on the table, Blake and Sally were responsive to the therapist's suggestions that each take on the jobs of dealing with their respective ex-spouses and managing their own children. When they did this, the conflict between the two sets of children abated. The work of each of them in relationship to their ex-spouses was long and intense, and they threatened to give it up or divorce each other many times during the process. The lack of time between Blake's marriages made his struggles with his guilty attachment to his ex-wife particularly intense, which triggered Sally's guilt and insecurity. Only after some period of work in their families of origin were they able to understand and take responsibility for their own contributions to the failure of their first marriages. Feeling less like victims, they were able to reduce their tendency to huddle together helplessly against the "outside."

A Parent, the Biological Children, and the Stepchildren

As in the previous case, this triangle may present as simple household conflict with the parent caught in the middle between his or her biological children and stepchildren. It is, in fact, quite complex, always interlocking with the triangle involving the remarried couple (who may have either a pseudo-mutual or a conflictual relationship) and the triangles with both ex-spouses.

Florence Green sought a consultation to help her resolve a battle that she was involved in with her 18-year-old-son, Donald, who was threatening not to go to college at all if he couldn't go to the expensive school of his choice rather than the moderately priced college Florence preferred for him. Florence said that she wanted to clarify her own position on this issue, which, she said, kept shifting. When she argued with Donald, she pointed out the sensible choices and good work habits of her stepson, Phil, also 18; yet, in frequent and bitter battles with her husband, Adam, she accused him of always favoring "his" son over "hers." Florence reported that in their fifteen years of marriage, they had not yet become a family. The main reason she stayed in the marriage, she implied, was that she and her second husband had a son together who was only 13.

The Green family is an example of a remarried family that has not achieved integration and restabilization even after the passage of many years. They had married within a year of their previous divorces. Florence had cut off her ex-husband, who, she said, only disappointed and neglected their son, Donald. Adam Green, a wealthy physician, had engaged in a series of bitter custody battles with his ex-wife, which continued to the present day. Florence was heavily invested in obtaining a "good father" for Donald and both pushed and criticized her husband in his relationship with her son. In an attempt to make things work out, she made extra efforts to get along with her husband's son, Phil, which then aroused Donald's resentment. On his side, Adam Green's emotional energies went into the custody battles with his ex-wife and his professional practice, which was extremely demanding. He could not understand his wife's failure to appreciate the financial security he gave her and her son and had become increasingly resentful of Donald's antagonism toward him and Phil. The family alliances were perfectly reflected in Adam's recently drawn will, which left the major share of his estate to his son, Phil; a secondary legacy to Alex, the son he and Florence had together; a smaller amount to Florence herself; and nothing to Donald. Florence worried that the uneven inheritance would continue the family feud in subsequent generations, pitting her own two biological sons, Donald and Alex, against each other and destroying any relationship between Donald and Phil.

Family therapy in this complex situation required motivation on Florence's part to go back to the unresolved tasks of fifteen years ago and pull herself out of the triangles involving her husband and Donald, on the one hand, and Donald and Phil, on the other. Better progress would have been made initially if her husband had agreed to be involved in the treatment and been persuaded to give up the battles with his ex-wife. Eventually, Donald requested help in extricating himself from the scapegoat position and reconnecting with his biological father. Since the marital bond was in question, Florence had to find the motivation to initiate these changes for her own sake and that of her children. Only after she had confronted her husband about the negative effects his will would have and had convinced him that both their family relationships and the terms of his will must change did she decide that it was worth working toward stabilizing her second marriage.

The Remarried Spouses and the Parents of Either

This triangle features the in-laws as part of the presenting problem, but it should be remembered that relationships with the grandparents' generation are as crucial in remarried families (Gorell Barnes et al., 1998) as they are in all other families, and their exploration should be a part of a routine evaluation. The presentation of the older generation as part of the current problem is most likely to occur if they have disapproved of the divorce and remarriage or have been actively involved in caring for their grandchildren before or during the remarriage.

Mr. and Mrs. Hendrix had been married for two years when they appeared for marital therapy. Eric was a businessman in his middle forties and had been previously married. His ex-wife had custody of his three sons, the oldest of whom now lived with Eric's parents "because of the excellent high school in their town." Joan Hendrix was fifteen years younger than her husband and had not been married before. Eric said that their major problem was that Joan constantly fought with his mother and put him in the middle. Joan stated that Eric's mother had never accepted Eric's divorce or their marriage and that she talked and acted as if Eric were still married to his ex-wife, Ethel, with whom the older Mrs. Hendrix retained a very close relationship. Further, Joan complained, she had not yet had a honeymoon, and every weekend was devoted to entertaining Eric's children either in their small New York apartment or, worse, at Eric's parents' home in the suburbs. On the latter occasions, Joan said, her mother-in-law was cold and hostile toward her, interfered with every move she made toward Eric's children, and spoke constantly of Ethel's loneliness and financial difficulties. When Eric and Joan stayed overnight, Eric's mother insisted that the younger children share a room with them rather than "mess up" the living room. Eric never called his mother to task for any of this but expected Joan to "understand that she means well."

Since both Eric and Joan wanted their marriage to work, they negotiated a deal whereby Eric would clarify the boundary of his new marriage with his parents, his children, and his ex-wife and Joan would stop criticizing and arguing with her mother-in-law. For openers, Eric and Joan took a belated honeymoon trip over the objection of his mother that he should not leave his children for such a long period. Thereafter, however, Eric's part of the bargain was easier said than done. During the extended period that he spent renegotiating his visitation arrangements, resolving his guilty attachment to his first wife, and reworking his relationships with his parents, there were many eruptions throughout the system. One of his children started failing in school, the older boy returned to live with Eric's ex-wife, his father had a heart attack, and his ex-wife was hospitalized briefly for depression. With each upsurge of tension, Joan was pulled back into conflicts with her mother in-law. These occasions lessened considerably when she started serious work in her own family of origin, from whom she had been estranged since her marriage. Although very pleased with the outcome after several years of intensive work, Joan said that she had "aged ten years trying to work out a marriage to a whole family instead of just to a person." During the course of treatment, the therapist involved all of the family subsystems in sessions: the remarried couple alone, with Eric's children, and with Eric's parents; Joan and her parents; Ethel and the children; Ethel alone; Ethel and her parents; and once, Ethel, Eric, Joan, Eric's mother, and the oldest son.

We routinely contact an ex-spouse and invite him or her to meet alone or with the children to hear our opinion of the children's problems that have been brought to our attention by the remarried family. When we inform the family of our intention to do this, we are frequently warned that the ex-spouse in question does not care, won't respond, or is crazy. Nevertheless, such a phone call frequently locates a concerned parent who is perfectly willing to come in, although warning us that our client is crazy. These ex-spouses can frequently be engaged in subsequent sessions alone or with the children.

CONCLUSION

The most frequent parental mistakes in remarried families are:

1. Parents' preoccupation with themselves and neglect of their children's experience (which follows from the juxtaposition of conflicting life cycle tasks: parenting and courtship).
2. Treating the remarriage as an event, rather than a complex reformation of the family, which takes years.
3. Trying to get children to resolve the ambiguities of multiple loyalties by cutting off one relationship to create clarity in the others.

Our general goal in working with remarried families is to establish an open system with workable boundaries and to revise traditional gender roles.

This goal requires:

- A working, open, coparental relationship between former spouses.
- Working through the emotional divorce between former spouses. (We assume this is not resolved if they are not speaking or have continuous conflicts.)

- Children should never have the power to decide on remarriage, custody or visitation, although children's input into decisions obviously increases with age.
- Parents need to help children have the full range of feelings for all parents—accepting the divided loyalties.

Our recommended guidelines include the following:

1. Take a three generational genogram and outline previous marriages before plunging into current household problems.
2. Keep in mind particular difficulties related to family members being at different life cycle stages, the emotionally central role of women in families and the special difficulties for them in moving into a new system, and their trying to maintain the myth of the intact family.
3. Beware of families struggling with developmental tasks before they have adopted the prerequisite attitudes for remarriage: for example, a parent pushing a child and stepparent to be close without accepting that their relationship will take time to develop.
4. Help the family gain patience to tolerate the ambiguity and not "overtry" to make things work out. This includes accepting that family ties do not develop overnight. Encourage stepparents to understand that a child's negative reactions are not to be taken personally and help them tolerate guilt, conflicted feelings, ambivalence, divided loyalties, and so on.
5. Include the new spouse in sessions in which you coach the client to resolve his or her relationship with an ex-spouse, at least in the beginning—or you will increase their paranoia.
6. Take the frequent characterization of an ex-spouse as "crazy" with a grain of salt. The list of the ex-spouse's outrageous behavior may reflect the client's provocations and/or retaliations.
7. When the remarriage ends a close single-parent/child relationship, the feelings of loss,

especially for the child, have to be dealt with and the shift to a new system will take time.

8. If the child is presented as the problem, try to involve all parents and stepparents as early as possible in therapy. If joint sessions are held, the discussion should be directed toward cooperative work to resolve the child's difficulties. We do not permit discussion of marital issues at these meetings.

9. In problems involving child-focused uproar, put the natural parent in charge of the child temporarily. When the uproar subsides, coach the natural parent on ways to "move over" and include his or her spouse in the system—first, as a spouse only. Warn the family that the shift to active stepparenting may take several years

and will require the active support of the natural parent. In the case of older adolescents, it may not be appropriate to expect the shift to occur to any great degree at all.

10. Look at the "hidden agenda" in sudden proposals to rearrange custody, visitation, or financial arrangements.

11. Include work on the spouses' families of origin as early in treatment as possible.

12. Work to get parents to define predictable and adequate plans for visitation and to keep up relationships with the ex-spouse's extended family.

13. Regarding the predictable patterns and processes in remarriage, educate and normalize, normalize, normalize.

REFERENCES

Ahrons, C. (1981). The continuing coparental relationship between divorced spouses. *American Journal of Orthopsychiatry, 51,* 315–328.

Ahrons, C. (1994). *The good divorce.* New York: HarperCollins.

Ahrons, C. R., & Rodgers, R. H. (1987). *Divorced families.* New York: Norton.

Ahrons, C., & Wallisch, L. (1986). The relationship between former spouses In S. Duck & D. Perlman (Eds.), *Close relationships: Development, dynamics and deterioration* (pp. 269–296). Beverly Hills, CA: Sage.

Ambert, A. M. (1986). Being a stepparent: Live-in and visiting stepchildren. *Journal of Marriage and the Family, 4814,* 795–804.

Anderson, E. R., Hetherington, E. M., & Clingempeel, W. G. (1989). Transformations in family relations at puberty: Effects of family context. *Journal of early adolescence, 9*(3), 310–334.

Bernstein, A. C. (1994). Women in stepfamilies: The fairy godmother, the wicked witch, and Cinderella reconstructed. In M. P. Mirkin (ed.), *Women in context: Toward a feminist reconstruction of psychotherapy.* New York: The Guilford Press.

Bernstein, A. C. (1989). *Yours, mine, and ours: How families change when remarried parents have a child together.* New York: Norton.

Bray, J. H. (1986). Reported in *Marriage and Divorce Today,* 12(9).

Bray, J. H. (1988). Children's development in early remarriage. In E. M. Hetherington & J. Arasteh (Eds.), *The impact of divorce, single-parenting, and step-parenting on children.* Hillsdale, NJ: Lawrence Erlbaum Associates.

Bray, J. H. (1992). Family relationships and children's adjustment in clinical and non-clinical stepfather families. *Journal of Family Psychology,* 6, 60–68.

Brody, J. (1998, January 28). Genetic ties may be a factor in violence in stepfamilies. *New York Times,* pp. C1, C4.

Carter, B. (1988). Remarried families: Creating a new paradigm. In M. Walters, B. Carter, P. Papp, & O. Silverstein (Eds.). *The invisible web: Gender patterns in family relationships.* New York: The Guilford Press.

Carter, B. (1996). *Love, honor, and negotiate.* New York: Pocket Books.

Cherlin, A. J. (1992). *Marriage, divorce, remarriage* (rev. and enlarged ed.). Cambridge, MA: Harvard University Press.

Cherlin, A. J., & Furstenberg, F. F. (1994). Stepfamilies in the United States: A reconsideration. *Annual Review of Sociology.* 20, 359–381.

Clingempeel, G. W., Coylar, J. J., & Hetherington, E. M. (1994). Toward a cognitive dissonance conceptualization of stepchildren and biological children loyalty conflicts: A construct validity study. In K. Pasley & M. Ihinger-Tallman (Eds.), *Stepfamilies:*

Issues in theory, research and practice (pp. 151–174). Westport, CT: Greenwood.

Crosbie-Burnett, M., & Helmbrecht, L. (1993). A descriptive empirical study of gay male stepfamilies. *Family Relations, 42,* 256–262.

Crosbie-Burnett, M., & Lewis, E. A. (1993). Use of African-American family structures and functioning to address the challenges of European-American postdivorce families. *Family Relations, 42,* 243–248.

Dahl, A. S., Cowgill, K. M., & Asmundsson, R. (1987). Life in remarriage families. *Social Work, 32*(1), 40–44.

Duberman, L. (1975). *The reconstituted family: A study of remarried couples and their children.* Chicago: Nelson-Hall.

Furstenberg, F. F., & Cherlin, A. (1991). *Divided families: What happens to children when parents part.* Cambridge, MA: Harvard University Press.

Furstenberg, F., Nord, C. W., Peterson, J. L., & Zill, N. (1983). The life course of children of divorce: Marital disruptions and parental contact. *American Sociological Review,* 656–668.

Glick, Paul C. (1989). Remarried families, stepfamilies and stepchildren: A brief demographic profile. *Family Relations, 38,* 24–27.

Goldstein, H. S. (1974). Reconstituted families: The second marriage and its children. *Psychiatric Quarterly, 48*(3), 433–441.

Gorell Barnes, G., Thompson, P., Daniel, G., & Burchardt, N. (1998). *Growing up in stepfamilies.* New York: Oxford University Press.

Hetherington, E. M. (1989). Coping with family transitions: Winners, losers, and survivors. *Child Development, 60*(1), 1–14.

Hetherington. E. M. (1990, March 23). *Remarriage, lies, and videotape.* Presidential address to the Society for Research on Adolescence, Atlanta.

Hetherington, E. M. (1991). The role of individual differences and family relationships in children's coping with divorce and remarriage. In P. A. Cowen, & E. M. Hetherington (Eds.), *Family transitions.* Hillsdale, NJ: Lawrence Erlbaum Associates.

Hetherington, E. M. (1993). An overview of the Virginia longitudinal study of divorce and remarriage with a focus on early adolescence. *Journal of Family Psychology, 7*(1) 39–56.

Hetherington, E. M., & Clingempeel, W. G. (1992). Coping with marital transitions: A family systems per-

spective. *Monographs of the Society of Research in Child Development, 57*(2–3, Serial No 227).

Hetherington, E. M., Cox, M., & Cox, R. (1977). The aftermath of divorce. In J. H. Steven & M. Matthews (Eds.), *Mother-child relations.* Washington, DC: NAEYC.

Hetherington, E. M., Cox, M., & Cox, R. (1985). Long term effects of divorce and remarriage on the adjustment of children. *Journal of American Academy of Psychiatry, 24*(5), 518–530.

Hetherington, E. M., Stanley-Hagan, M., & Anderson, E. R. (1989). Marital transitions: A child's perspective. *American Psychologist, 44*(2), 303–312.

Laird, J., & Green, R. J. (1996). *Lesbians and gays in couples and families.* New York: Jossey-Bass.

Larson, J. (1992). Understanding stepfamilies. *American Demographics, 14,* 360.

McGoldrick, M. (1995). *You can go home again: Reconnecting with your family.* New York: Norton.

McGoldrick, M. (1996). Living beyond loss [Videotape]. New York: Newbridge Communications.

McGoldrick, M., Gerson, R., & Schellenberger, S. (1998). *Genograms in family assessment* (2nd ed.). New York: Norton.

Montgomery, M. J., Anderson, E. R., Hetherington, E. M., & Clingempeel, W. G. (1993). Patterns of courtship for remarriage: Implications for child development and parent-child relationships. *Journal of Marriage and the Family, 54,* 686–698.

Norton, A. J., & Miller, L. F. (1992). *Marriage, divorce and remarriage in the 1990s* (U.S. Bureau of the Census, Current Population Reports, Series P-23, No. 180). Washington, DC: U.S. Government Printing Office.

Pasley, K., & Ihinger-Tallman, M. (Eds.). (1994). *Stepparenting: Issues in theory, research and practice.* Westport, CT: Praeger,

Pasley, K., & Ihinger-Tallman, M. (1987). *Remarriage and stepparenting: Current research and theory.* New York: The Guilford Press.

Pasley, K., Rhodes, L., Visher, E. B. & Visher, J. S. (1996). Successful stepfamily therapy: Clients' perspectives, *Journal of Marital and Family Therapy, 22*(3), 343–357.

Ransom, J. W., Schlesinger, S., & Derdeyn, A. (1979). A stepfamily in formation. *American Journal of Orthopsychiatry, 49*(1).

Sager, C. J., Brown, H. S., Crohn, H., Engel, T., Rodstein, E., & Walker, L. (1983). *Treating the remarried family.* New York: Brunner/Mazel.

Stepfamily Association of America. (1997). Some facts about stepfamilies. Internet: *http://www.stepfam. org/facts.htm* (1/26/98).

Visher, E. B., & Visher, J. S. (1979). *Stepfamilies: A guide to working with stepparents and stepchild.* New York: Brunner/Mazel.

Visher, E. B., & Visher, J. S. (1988). *Old loyalties, new ties: Therapuetic strategies with stepfamilies.* New York: Brunner/Mazel.

Visher, E., & Visher, J. (1991). *How to win as a stepfamily* (2nd ed.). New York: Brunner/Mazel.

Visher, E. B., & Visher, J. S. (1996). *Therapy with stepfamilies.* Ner York: Brunner/Mazel.

Wallerstein, J., & Kelly, J. (1980). *Surviving the breakup.* New York: Basic Books.

White, L. (1992). The effect of parental divorce and remarriage on parental support for adult children. *Journal of Family Issues, 13*(2), 234–250.

Whiteside, M. (1982). Remarriage: A family developmental process. *Journal of Marital and Family Therapy, 8,* 59–68.

CHAPTER 26

COACHING AT VARIOUS STAGES OF THE LIFE CYCLE

BETTY CARTER
MONICA McGOLDRICK

This paper will outline Bowen's method of coaching and discuss common triangles and coaching interventions that we have developed at various life cycle stages to suggest a way to orient oneself clinically to individuals and families throughout the life cycle. We offer this summary because we consider this theoretical framework to be powerful for assessing and intervening with families at each point in the life cycle, using Bowen's multigenerational and our multicontextual framework. The increasing multiculturalism in the United States makes the work of emotional connectedness and social inclusiveness more important than ever (McGoldrick, 1998).

Family systems therapy is based on the idea that the family is, except in rare circumstances, the primary emotional system to which we ever belong that shapes and continues to determine the course and outcome of our lives. As in any system, relationships and functioning (physical, social, emotional, and spiritual) are interdependent, and a change in one part of the system is followed by compensatory changes in other parts of the system. Such primary impact makes the family our greatest potential resource as well as our greatest potential source of stress.

The ultimate goal of family systems work is to get a person-to-person relationship with each living person in your current nuclear and extended family. The process of working out personal relationships occurs at different levels, including genealogical research, and the work on each level depends on the client's internal clock.

The basic idea of coaching is that if you can change the part you play in your family problems and hold it despite the family's reaction, while keeping in emotional contact with family members, you maximize the likelihood (not a guarantee!) that they will eventually change to accommodate your change (Bowen 1978a). Coaching is a method of therapy based on the theoretical concepts of Dr. Murray Bowen (1978b; Papero, 1990; Kerr & Bowen, 1988) and elaborated by his students Carter, Fogarty, Friedman, Guerin, Kerr, Lerner, McGoldrick, Titleman, and others. The term "coaching" refers to the stance of the therapist as being like a coach, on the sidelines of a game, keeping the big picture in mind, advising on strategy, and noting reactions, strengths, and weaknesses. The coach cheers players on, but the work and the responsibility to reach the goal remain with the players. The word "coach" also, of course, describes a teacher or mentor helping a student to master a difficult task.

Bowen family systems theory provides a way of thinking about and intervening in the full spectrum of emotional and social functioning. It is based on the idea that if one person changes, all others in emotional contact with him or her will have to make compensatory changes. Family therapy is thus not defined by or restricted to any particular number of family members' attending therapy sessions and sometimes family therapy with one person is the better choice (Szapoczynik et al., 1983).

In this approach, discussion focuses on overall patterns in the network of relationships rather than just the individual's intrapsychic processes. The work focuses on the most motivated and functional family member, rather than the "sickest," because this is the person who is most able to take action to change his or her part in the family process. The emphasis in coaching is on the who, what, when, where, and how of family patterns and themes, rather than on the why of individual motivation. The main work of the therapy is conducted outside of therapy sessions in the relationships with actual family members, rather than during sessions in the relationship with the therapist. Teaching, thinking, planning, and other intellectual processes leading up to actual relationship change are given priority in the therapy process over interpretation and insight, which may otherwise substitute for action, or emotional catharsis and support which might eliminate the anxiety that drives motivation to change. Emotional functioning is viewed in the context of universal reciprocal processes varying in degree from family to family. Feelings are related to family emotional patterns, rather than being dealt with primarily in the therapeutic relationship. The therapist encourages the development of a calm atmosphere, diminishing emotional intensity, as best for the therapeutic endeavor.

The goal is to establish a climate in which a thoughtful response, rather than emotional reactivity, is predominant, both in the therapy and in the process of changing family relationships. The theory emphasizes the importance of knowing the distinction between thinking and feeling and calls for applying each appropriately, for example, thinking through your plans for life or the status of your marriage and feeling intensely in the actual conduct of your relationships and life events that naturally produce emotional responses. Most of us do the opposite much of the time: reacting emotionally at crucial decision-making moments and letting intellectualization and rationalization block or dampen our emotional lives. Internal and external systems are seen as having significant reciprocal influence on each other, and the internal system is not seen as the most relevant to psychological functioning. Indeed, the assumption is that external systems such as relationships frequently determine internal feeling states, rather than vice versa.

In this approach, transference phenomena are actively discouraged. Therapists, standing on the sidelines of the client system and serving as consultants, try to keep themselves from being pulled into the family emotional field or from entering it intentionally, while developing a reality-oriented, open, and, one hopes, warm and respectful relationship with the individual who is consulting them (Carter & McGoldrick Orfanidis, 1976).

SYSTEM INTERACTIONS

Family relationships tend to be highly reciprocal, patterned, and repetitive and to have circular, rather than linear, motion. In other words, cause-and-effect thinking, which asks why and looks for someone to blame for a problem, is not as useful as identifying patterns and tracing their flow, since all family patterns, once established, are perpetuated by everyone involved in them, although not all have equal power or influence. But, of course, family systems do not exist in a vacuum. Rather, their members are also embedded in the systemic patterns of the larger context of their community and society and limited by the structure of these larger systems in profound ways. Thus, in a family that is embedded in a patriarchal social system, women and children have decidedly less power to influence the structure than do men; and in a hierarchically organized racist, classist, and homophobic system, the poor, people of color and gays and lesbians have little freedom to challenge existing social structures. While there is a reciprocal aspect to all relationships, and it is a person's individual participation in any system that is all he or she can change, the analysis of the system must include also the unequal power distribution to members of a system. This does not mean that the relationships are not reciprocal, but rather that one must factor in the dimension of power to think clearly how to change them and what the consequences will be of attempting change from a less powerful position.

In a family, if any person changes, his or her emotional input and reactions also change, interrupting the predictable flow. Other family members will be jarred out of their own unthinking responses and, in the automatic move toward homeostasis that is inherent in all systems, will react by trying to get the disrupter back into place again. In two-person subsystems, such as married couples or parent-child relationships, the element of reciprocity of emotional functioning can be striking, as in the enduring marriages of the sinner and the saint, the master and the slave, the dreamer and the doer, and the optimist and the pessimist or the intense involvement between the nagging mother and the dawdling child. This is obviously not to say that the power of both partners to change such relationships is equal.

FUSION VERSUS DIFFERENTIATION

The emotional forces of interdependence tend to lead to a kind of fusion, or stuck-togetherness, of family members within a system. This togetherness should not be confused with emotional closeness. Family members may fail to develop themselves or give up part or most of their autonomy out of anxiety that their self-assertion will cost them the love or approval of other family members. Indeed, women in our society are raised to give up self in this way. The measure of differentiation or emotional maturity is thus that individuals are able to distinguish between thinking and feeling and able to think, plan, know, and follow their own beliefs and self-directed life course, rather than living reactively to the cues of those close to them. They do not have to spend their life energy on winning approval, attacking others, or maneuvering in relationships to obtain emotional comfort. They can move freely from emotional closeness in person-to-person relationships to self-direction in pursuit of their personal life goals and back. Then can freely take "I-Positions," which are calm statements of their beliefs or feelings, without having to attack others or defend themselves. In their personal relationships, they can relate openly, without needing to talk about others or focus on activities or impersonal things to find common ground.

TRIANGLES

The basic unit of an emotional system is the triangle, which typically stabilizes two-person systems under stress. Few people can relate personally for very long before running into some issue that makes one or both anxious, at which point it is common to triangle in a third person or thing as a way of diverting the anxiety from the relationship of the twosome. Triangles are always dysfunctional in the sense that they offer stabilization through diversion, rather than through resolution of the issue in the twosome's relationship. It is also harmful to those who are pulled into the middle or onto one side of a conflict. Thus, a couple having relationship issues, instead of dealing with the issues, may focus on a child, whose misbehavior gives them something to come together on in mutual concern. Repeated over time, triangling becomes a chronic dysfunctional pattern, preventing resolution of differences in the couple and making one or more of the three vulnerable to physical or emotional symptoms. Such dysfunctional stabilization, although problematic, may be experienced as preferable to change.

In a triangle, the three relationships are interdependent; they are not three separate person-to-person dyads. Any dyad in a triangle is a function of the other two. Detriangling is the process whereby one individual frees himself or herself from the enmeshment of the triangle and develops separate person-to-person relationships with each of the other two. Involvement in triangles and interlocking triangles that span the generations is one of the key mechanisms whereby patterns of relating and functioning are transmitted over the generations in a family. Usually, the most emotionally significant triangle in a person's life is the one with his or her parents, and subsequent triangles often replay those unresolved issues. Since the concept of triangles is so crucial and methods of detriangling are often counterintuitive, the reader is referred to the full clinical treatise by Guerin, Fogarty, Fay, and Kautto (1996).

DISTANCING AND CUT-OFF

The concepts of fusion and reactive distance or total cut-off are central to systems theory. The pull for togetherness in a relationship can be pictured as exerting a force like that of two magnets. When the pull becomes too strong and threatens to engulf individuality and blur separateness, there will be a reactive pulling away on the part of one or both. Much of the emotional interaction between spouses and between parents and children consists of the jockeying of each for an optimal position in relation to the other, in which the emotional bond will be felt as comfortable, rather than too close or too distant. Since each person is highly likely to have a different comfort range, the shifting back and forth is continuous. When the emotional intensity in the system is too great, the pull toward fusion too strong, family members frequently try to cut off the relationship entirely.

Cutting off a relationship by physical or emotional distance does not end the emotional process; in fact, it intensifies it. If one cuts off relationships with parents or siblings, the emotional sensitivities and yearnings from these relationships tend to push into one's other relationships, with a spouse or with children, becoming all the more intense in the displacement. The new relationships will tend to become problematic under this pressure and lead to further distancing and cut-offs.

DIFFERENTIATION

Bowen's concept of differentiation describes a state of self-knowledge and self-definition that does not rely on the acceptance of others for one's beliefs but encourages one to be connected to others without the need to defend one's self or attack the other. Ironically, although Bowen's is the only early family therapy theory that gives equal weight to autonomy and emotional connectedness as characteristics necessary for the differentiation of adult maturity, he is widely misunderstood in the field. Bowen's term "differentiation," which he equated with "maturity," is commonly misused and misquoted as if it meant autonomy, separateness, or disconnectedness. And because Bowen emphasized the necessity of distinguishing between thinking and feeling, he has been criticized by some feminists for elevating "male" attributes of rationality over "female" relationality. Actually,

Bowen was addressing the need to train one's mind to control emotional reactivity so that, unlike animals, we can control our behavior and think about how we want to respond, rather than be at the mercy of our fears, phobias, compulsions, instincts, and sexual and aggressive impulses. This does not in any way mean suppressing authentic and appropriate emotional expressiveness, which is part of the primary goal of Bowen therapy. Grounding oneself emotionally and learning to connect emotionally by developing a personal relationship with every member of one's family are, indeed, the blueprint for all subsequent emotional connections.

Dan Goleman (1997), in his book *Emotional Intelligence,* discusses this same process of mind over emotional reactivity, crediting Aristotle with defining the original proposition: "Anyone can become angry, that is easy. But to become angry with the right person, to the right degree, at the right time, for the right purpose—this is not easy (Aristotle, *The Nicomachean Ethics*)," (p. ix). The question, Goleman says, is "How can we bring intelligence to our emotions and civility to our streets and caring to our communal life?" (p. xiv).

The blind spot in Bowen theory (1978b), as we see it, is that it does not account for the fact that women and minorities have experienced a socialization that actually proscribes the assertive, self-directed thinking and behavior that are necessary for differentiation. Failure to acknowledge these disparities mystifies those within our society who are raised in oppressive ways and are not starting on an even playing field. Girls in this society are expected to put the needs of others before their own. Even to define their own values, wishes, or opinions is generally seen as selfishness. People of color are raised to be deferential to Whites and to accept the fact of the privileges Whites have in this society. They must fight harder for any opportunities they get in the society and accept, in most situations without resistance, the prejudice and need to stifle their resentments of slights on an everyday basis. Gays and lesbians are told by official U.S. military policy and by social attitudes and laws, "don't tell" us who you are. A White male who tries to differentiate will generally be responded to with respect; a woman, a person of color, or a homosexual who tries to differentiate may be sanctioned, ostracized, or even harmed by the community. Thus, our assessment of a person's development must include assessment of social obstacles to their accomplishing the tasks leading to maturity.

THE ROLE OF THE COACH

Bowen's concept of the role of the coach seems remarkably similar to the Buddhist idea of a master teacher. The Buddhist nun Pema Chodron has described her mentor, Trungpa Rinpoche, as a master of not confirming: "Talking to him was like talking to a huge space in which everything bounced back—you had to be accountable for yourself." She believes that the teacher's role is to wean students from dependency, from the parent-child view of life, the theistic view:

> Theism implies that you can't find out for yourself what's true. You take Buddhist teachings—or any teachings—and try to fit yourself into them, without really grappling with them in a way that could transform your being. You're just trying to live up to some ideal. You're still looking for the security of having someone else to praise or blame. Accountability, on the other hand, doesn't offer that kind of support. There is no hand to hold. No matter what other people say, when it comes down to it, you are the only one who can answer your own questions. (p. 11)

Coaching generally focuses on helping the client to define a self in the family of origin. This is a long-term effort by the client to increase his or her functional and emotional level of maturity. Except in rare circumstances, the most important triangle is that of the client and his or her parents. Detriangling from that and staying detriangled from multigenerational family patterns make up the core of the work of becoming a more mature self, autonomous and emotionally connected.

However, a person may become enmeshed in many other intense triangles in the original family, the nuclear family, or the current relationship system at work, with friends, or in the community. And coaching may mean helping a client to deal with any of the above, whether the client has previously done the basic work with parents or not. We believe that all intense emotional triangles interlock with the parental triangle or are in some ways displacements of unresolved issues with parents. Thus, other emotional triangles are much more easily dealt with if the basic work has been done. However, relatively mature and highly motivated clients can often be coached to change their behavior and emotional functioning in other current triangles before or even without any particular effort with the family of origin. Every presenting problem should be conceptualized in terms of a triangle. The client can then be taught how triangles work and coached to change his or her input into problems in the triangles of relationships, marriage, divorce, remarriage, or workplace as a way of untying the knot that brought him or her into therapy. When this initial work has achieved some relief, it is the therapist's job to review the ways in which the client's emotional reactivity was connected to triangles and issues in the family of origin and suggest that the client continue the work. The decision is up to the client, and if the decision is not to continue, the therapist should express willingness to continue in the future if the client has a change of heart or mind.

A basic assumption of systems thinking is that if one person changes her or his emotional functioning in the family, the system will change. The only exception might be in couple relationships, which are the only "optional" relationships in all family relationships—the only ones that are not necessarily forever. If one partner really changes and the other remains inaccessible or unchanging, it means that the couple system is not viable and the first partner probably has no option but to move on. Thus, the wife of an alcoholic who differentiates may precipitate her husband into AA, or she may learn that her husband is too caught up in his addiction to respond, no matter what she does. If he chooses his addiction over the marriage, her only real choice eventually is to leave. In general, however, the systems assumption is that if one person changes her or his role, the system will be altered and the person will be able to function more freely in current and future relationships, whether family, social, or professional. A person's ability to change his or her emotional functioning will depend, of course, on a number of factors. Children and people of any age who are not financially independent will have limited ability to take a position of emotional independence in a family. Furthermore, there are situations in which family members are so locked into their addiction or other dysfunctional pattern that a differentiating move only clarifies that the system is too rigid, disengaged, or immature to move beyond reacting.

Any change involves a minimum of three steps: (1) the change, (2) the family's reaction to the change, and (3) dealing with the family's reactions to the change. These three steps could, of course, take years. Murray Bowen was fond of remarking that most of us do a two-step much of the time: We attempt to change, but when someone says "change back," we do it. Successful change involves going beyond this, by planning how to deal with the predictable reaction of the system to the initial effort.

HUMOR

This intense and automatic reaction of the system to maintain homeostasis and resist change has led to the development of various direct and indirect strategies, including the ability to laugh at yourself and gain a certain lightness with regard to your own emotional reactivity. Indeed, humor is one of the most effective ways to detoxify a situation. Part of the very power of triangles, ruts, labels, and rigid patterns is that we feel stuck and take the situation too seriously. Surprise and gently humorous redefinition of a situation by the therapist may jostle that inflexibility in such a way that the challenge is softened. After a long story about mother's "unbelievable intrusiveness," for instance, a coach might smile and ask, "How come you don't appreciate her great love for you?" Or, as Bowen remarked to a man who had had a lot of previous therapy, describing having slept with his mother

until he was 8: "If you hadn't had a course in the horrors of sleeping with your mother (in your previous years of therapy), how would you have evaluated it?"

Carrying a situation to the point of absurdity may often help people to gain perspective on their overly intense involvement in a rigid position and reduce what was threatening and serious to triviality. After long complaints about a wife's conversational style at a party, the coach might say, "It sounds like you shouldn't take her anywhere until she learns how to behave right."

Furthermore, the very act of sharing a laugh can help to reduce the tension and restore some of the commonality that has been cut off by bitterness. By suddenly disorganizing the established social situation, humor creates a surprising new arrangement and opens new possibilities. "Just think," one coach remarked, "of the wonderful opportunity that 'impossible woman' is giving you to learn patience." Humor relabels a situation and may allow us to gain power over a system in which we have previously been caught. It also enables the therapist to play "devil's advocate." The idea here is that the coach challenges the client to concentrate on his or her own values and wishes rather than remaining stuck and helpless about another person's behavior, rejection, or definition of the relationship.

DETRIANGLING

Detriangling is shifting the motion of a triangle and unlocking the compulsory loyalties so that three dyadic relationships can emerge from the enmeshed threesome. Reversals use the recurring pattern in the triangle but place the speaker in a different position in it. For example, a son who has an enmeshed relationship with his mother and a distant relationship with his father might begin to detriangle by going to his father with the confidences his mother has inappropriately shared with him and say, "Mom seems terribly upset, and I'm sure you will be able to help her out. I don't know why, but she came to me with her worries and said...." To prevent a two-step, the original plan would have to include a way to deal with mother's anger and sense of betrayal after father confronts her with the son's report.

A reversal is essentially an attempt to change a habitual pattern of relating by saying or doing the opposite of what you usually say or do in response to someone else. Although a client may at first call this "lying," the reversal actually expresses the unspoken and unacknowledged other side of an issue and tends to break up rigid, predictable, repetitive communication patterns. A wife who ordinarily gets angry when her husband gets sick and calls him a hypochondriac reverses her pattern and plays Florence Nightingale; a man who usually can't talk to his father because he is so dictatorial asks for advice.

It is important to realize that strategies such as reversals are not to be undertaken lightly. They succeed only when the person doing them has the emotional control to edit his or her feelings of hurt, anger, sarcasm, and vengeance out of the communication and when it conveys a respect for the other. Such techniques are not a substitute for, or part of, person-to-person intimacy. In disciplined hands, they can substitute for the destructive emotional games and repetitive interchanges that tend to be part of our relationships and thus reduce some of the distance or repetitious conflict that stands in the way of intimacy.

OPENING UP A CLOSED SYSTEM

In trying to open up important but buried issues, there are several ways to proceed. Sometimes, it can be done merely by contacting family members who have been cut off from the family or by carefully raising emotionally loaded issues with various family members. A more complex operation for a system that is not in current crisis is what Bowen called setting up "a tempest in a teapot": magnifying small emotional issues in such a way that old dormant triangles are activated and can be dealt within a new manner. Family members may be stuck emotionally in the same life cycle phase as when the family got derailed in previous generations, and opening up

these issues may promote healing and change. Tactics that stir up, without attacking, an emotional system that is not currently in a state of tension are necessary because emotional patterns tend not to be clear when the system is calm. The triangles and other dysfunctional patterns are dormant, available for use in the next family crisis.

It might be necessary to activate a dormant triangle, for example, if a son cannot move directly toward his father without the father's withdrawing. In such a case, it may be necessary to talk to those people with whom the father has relationships, perhaps the father's siblings or his parents. Such moves can not only provide a wealth of information and perspective on the father, but if carefully selected bits of the information are told to the father, it may also activate the triangle between the father, his sibling, and their mother. Once the father realizes that his brother is giving family information, he may feel impelled to open up with his side of the story. If the father felt like the outsider in the relationship with his mother and brother, he is likely to fear being the outsider again if his own child moves toward his brother. If the direct contact with the uncle is not enough to create a shift, the son may want to raise a toxic issue with the uncle, on the theory that the uncle may then take a different move with the father and thus open the system. If the system is very closed, the son may have to magnify a small issue with the uncle to push the system to react. It is important to distinguish such a push from destructive and hurtful threats or unleashed secrets.

ENGAGEMENT AND SYSTEM MAPPING

Engagement consists of helping the client shift focus from the self or others to an overview of self-with-others. Coachees frequently portray themselves as victim or rescuer, with very little attempt at objective, nonjudgmental reports of emotional or behavioral transactions among family members. They also tend to accept uncritically the view of the parent with whom they are aligned, failing to consider the subjectivity of each perspective.

At this stage, we find it useful to broaden the perspective on the presenting problem or the central relationships by asking about similar issues at various levels of the system, inquiring about various members' views of central issues, and gradually introducing systems concepts such as triangles and automatic reactive processes into the discussion. This standard Bowen technique was subsequently reinvented and relabeled "circular questioning." Whatever you call it, it is a very useful way to interview individuals. We have found it helpful to recommend systems readings including personal family stories, to help orient clients to a family systems perspective. (See the bibliography at the end of this chapter.)

The first real step in coaching is to ask the person to draw a genogram (McGoldrick, 1995; McGoldrick, Gerson, & Schellenberger, 1998), showing factual and relationship information for the family over at least three generations—names, births, deaths, marriages, divorces, geographical location, and all significant physical, social, and psychological changes or dysfunction. Family history is mapped through discussion of the genogram, which should not be treated like a form to fill out. Questions or comments that highlight the connection between the presenting problem and the family system enhance the client's engagement.

We also ask for a family chronology, which is like a time map, as the genogram is a structure map. It shows in chronological order the major family events and stresses and is especially useful for understanding the motion of family patterns over time and the intersection of the client's life with these patterns. This is important because the connections among major family events tends to be obscured within a family by the anxiety these events create.

During the initial phase of engagement and history taking, it is important to set a calm, matter-of-fact tone to help defuse the intensity of emotion aroused by a current crisis or by opening up anxiety-producing material. It is also useful to introduce family systems concepts as soon as the anxiety is low enough for them to be heard, including ideas about emotional interaction, reciprocity, triangles, changing self, effects of sibling position

on relationships, and the transmission of relationship patterns from one generation to the next.

PLANNING: LEARNING ABOUT THE SYSTEM AND ONE'S OWN ROLE IN IT

Planning is usually an indistinct continuation of the initial stage of engagement; it is reached when the coachee's anxiety has diminished to the point at which she or he can discuss how personal thoughts and feelings fit into family patterns and give some consideration to possible changes and their effects. She or he may ask, "If I were to try to get to know my father better, how would I go about it and how would that help me with my current problem?" Understated questions from the coach that are designed to elicit in detail the tone and history of this relationship and the main triangles in which it is embedded are better at this point than suggestions for concrete actions, which may increase anxiety again. However, gathering genogram information and the very process of looking at the family in this way shift the focus from guilt and blame to a more objective "researcher" position. As the coachee begins to observe and listen at a family gathering, instead of participating as usual, shifts in thinking and relating may occur; these should be carefully noted and incorporated in the planning.

Gaps in the genogram or family chronology are obvious places to start. The assumption is that the more facts you know, the better position you are in to evaluate what has happened in your family and thus to understand your own position and to change it if you wish. In terms of gaining a preliminary focus on the family patterns, for example, one could look at the similarity between the central triangles over three generations: self, mother, father, and each parent with his or her parents; the effects of sibling position on the family process (McGoldrick, 1989; 1995; Toman, 1976; Chapter 9) and triangling in each generation; and the stress on the family at crucial points in the family history, such as just before the marriage, and around the birth of each child. Other patterns that may be examined are the reciprocity in the marriages in the family:

Who overfunctions and who underfunctions? Who tends to move in and who tends to move out? What toxic issues in the family tend to be avoided? All of these are of primary importance.

We favor holding off on concrete moves in a family at least long enough for the person to get a general notion of how the emotional system operates, what the central issues are, and what the client's own agenda and motivations are. If one wants to make someone else happy, save someone, change someone, tell someone off, get someone's approval, or justify and explain oneself, the effort will likely fail. In any case, it will not be worth the struggle, since either it will present no change or it may even reverse positions, as when the victim becomes the bully.

REENTRY

The process of differentiating can be rather simply defined: It consists of developing personal and authentic relationships with each member of the family and changing one's part in the old repetitious, dysfunctional emotional patterns to the point at which one is able to state, calmly and nonreactively, one's personal view of important emotional issues, regardless of who is for or against such a view. It involves learning to see your parents as the human beings they are or were, rather than as your "inadequate parents." This sounds so simple that it is difficult to convey the anxiety that is aroused at each step of the way, even for the people who are most committed to the work. The first moves to be recommended by the therapist will depend on what kinds of relationships the client currently maintains with family members and what objectives she or he has for changing these relationships. A relationship that has been intense and conflictual will require a more gentle reapproach than one that is characterized by distance.

If the person is involved in a conflictual win/lose relationship with a parent and the issue has been displaced onto some specific concrete explosion, such as a falling out over some long-past insult or onto some abstract issue such as religion or politics, we frequently recommend as a first step

that the person "let go of the rope" in this tug-of-war so that the personal emotional issues can have a chance to emerge. By this, we mean not only stopping the argument or cut-off but actually acknowledging the parent's point of view in some way so that the relationship can move on to more important personal matters.

John Martin, a fourth-year medical student, sought coaching with M. M. after hearing a lecture on systems ideas. He had been cut off from his father since beginning medical school because his father, a widower who had recently remarried, had, unbeknownst to John, taken all John's savings for medical school and used it for his own honeymoon. John had been so outraged that he had refused to speak to his father since that time but now felt challenged and intrigued by the idea of bridging cut-offs.

John's mother had died of cancer when he was 16, leaving behind two younger children as well, Peter (age 14) and Susan (age 12). John's father had maintained great distance from all three children, burying himself in his work and leaving them with one housekeeper after another. John became the functional parent to both younger siblings, went to the local state university, and worked hard each summer, saving his money because his father had told him that four years of college was all he could afford to pay for. He was totally shocked when he went to take out money for his first medical school payment to discover that his father had cleaned out the account for a honeymoon to Hawaii. He managed somehow to begin medical school anyway, without missing a beat, and was now a fourth-year student. The coaching task was to help John see himself as powerful enough to forgive his father to set himself free. The therapist suggested that the father sounded like he was operating under the delusion that he was the child and John the adult, or else he would never have done such an absurd thing as to steal his son's money for his own enjoyment. It was suggested that there seemed to be a grain of truth in this, since John had in fact managed much more successfully and maturely than the father for many years. It was suggested the possibility that he could forgive his father and let him know that he was looking for a connection and would welcome a reconciliation because he needed a father and was missing him. John rose to the occasion and wrote his father a most touching letter about his love for him, how much he missed his mother, how happy he was for his father that he had found love again, and his hopes for his brother and sister. His father's response was positive, though not apologetic, and John felt, when seen later that year, that he had "gotten a father back."

If someone has maintained routine, dutiful contact with the family through general letters addressed to both parents or phone conversations with only the mother, who acts as the central switchboard relayer of family news, the person is coached to establish direct contact with the father and other family members. This shift alone may bring many buried issues to the surface.

Harold, a 40-year-old mechanic, described his family as "friendly and close." He saw no connection between the state of his family relationships and the problem for which he sought help: dealing with the effects of his wife's serious physical illness. He called his mother weekly for an exchange of general family news. He saw his father, brother, and sister at holiday get-togethers a few times a year. Initially, he maintained that he would have no difficulty talking directly with each family member but that it would make no real difference. However, once he started to do it, he found that he became intensely nervous after a few minutes of talk with his father, because he could find nothing to say. His brothers quickly turned the phone over to their wives, and his sister responded to a letter from him with an angry attack about his having left responsibility for their aging parents entirely to her. These responses in himself and his family enabled him to recognize that he had been emotionally pulling away from his wife in her illness as he had pulled away from his family and their concerns. He embarked on restoring his family relationships with the initial motivation that they could offer each other support.

If the person has a fused relationship with one or both parents that is not overtly conflictual, a first step might be to break off routine patterns such as daily phone calls or weekly visits on a certain day, making contacts less ritualized and more unpredictable.

Such initial contact steps are usually followed up by brief visits, during which the person's main task is to observe and listen to family interaction in a new way. This information is then incorporated into the further planning sessions, during which tentative hypotheses are developed about the role the person plays in the family process and what role he or she would like to have. Predictions are made about the reactions of others to any changes in posture or behavior on his part.

The following sections discuss some typical triangles and coaching suggestions for various life cycle phases.

THE SINGLE YOUNG ADULT

The basic triangle at this phase is usually with parents, though the presenting problem may be about uncertainties in relationships with boyfriend or girlfriend or anxiety about educational or occupational decisions. Asking the question "What do your parents think about this?" will usually elicit the problematic triangle.

All theories of adult development, including ours, consider this to be the stage in which the young person leaves childhood dependency behind and moves out into his or her own life apart from the family of origin. Nevertheless, this process is context bound and varies considerably, depending on the larger society. Parents of 20-something adults are usually astounded to learn that the average age of the signers of the U.S. Constitution was about 25. But let us remember that that was "middle age" in 1776.

Closer to our own time, parents in their fifties and sixties remember leaving the parental home shortly after high school or college to work and live on their own if they were male or to marry if they were female. They think that something is wrong with a son or daughter who remains or returns home. Yet adult children are doing that in record numbers, more males than females. They may move out and then back again; they may move from job to job or be unable to find any suitable job; they may move in with a boyfriend or girl-friend; or they may go to graduate school through their late twenties. Above all, they do not marry until much later in the decade. Parents often don't realize that contemporary society, with its eco-nomic uncertainty, its requirement of protracted education and skill training, and the acceptability of late or no marriage or childbearing, tends to keep the young in an adolescent or barely post-adolescent mode until they are in their thirties.

Financial dependence breeds emotional de-pendence, and the level of emotional dependency must be carefully assessed in planning the therapy of a single young adult. Certainly, emotional issues with the family of origin are paramount, since the basic task of this phase is to get a good start on the process of differentiation. However, this can be a difficult idea for young Americans who imagine that the past is unimportant and they can invent themselves by willpower or through geography—moving far away from the family.

A further complication at this stage is the widespread belief, shared by many therapists, that autonomy is the major goal and that autonomy means separateness. Emotional connectedness is largely overlooked, if not openly rejected, although it might be more tolerated for young females. It is extremely important for clinicians to realize that both autonomy and emotional connectedness are necessary characteristics for maturity in both males and females and that autonomy does not mean be-ing separate in the sense of being disconnected; it means being self-directed, self-supporting, and able to choose and pursue one's course through life. Young women of recent generations have begun to insist on their right to autonomy, but few voices clamor for men's right to learn the skills of connect-ing emotionally (Silverstein & Rauschbaum, 1994).

Some young adults may be mature enough to be coached in the same way as other adults. For those who are not ready, there are useful adaptations.

We have found that coaching young adults in groups is an excellent way to engage and motivate them. When the therapist brings several single young adults together for coaching, there is almost always someone who begins to do the tasks with his or her family and reports progress and exhila-ration to the group, thereby inspiring others to try. Therapists using this approach believe it to be the method of choice for clients in their twenties. There is one big caveat. Coaching is not group therapy. The pull of group process must be resisted by the therapist, who should work with the clients one at a time in the group, limiting comment from the group regarding anyone else's work.

If a group is not available or feasible, we gener-ally work with the young adult clients alone through the engagement and planning phases. However, if the client seems to be unwilling or unable to carry out tasks with his or her parents, we suggest bring-ing one or both parents into the session and doing the tasks directly. It is made clear that the young adult will have to take the lead in bringing up what-ever issue she or he has planned in a nonattacking, nondefensive way. This forestalls the experience we have all had of young clients introducing their par-ents to us and then sitting back and waiting for us to do the work for them. The therapist's role in this ses-sion is to monitor the traffic and block attacks or counterattacks from anyone.

After a family session, the therapist can meet again with the young adult alone for as many ses-sions as are needed to debrief and to absorb the les-sons of the joint session and to plan for the next issue or the next family member to be invited to a session.

The positive aspect of this format is that it al-lows a young client to take personal responsibility and yet still feel supported as she or he learns to speak about difficult issues with parents. It doesn't push the client back into an adolescent position, which would happen if all sessions were family sessions. It also demonstrates the importance of family emotional issues, which the young client might deny if all sessions were individual sessions.

THE YOUNG COUPLE

Typical triangles at this phase involve spouses and their in-laws; spouses and partners or friends from previous days; and spouses and work, money, division of labor, how to spend leisure time, etc. Couple problems in this life cycle phase as at other phases typically lead back to each partner and his or her family of origin. Couple problems are never solely dyadic problems. Conceptualizing and treating them as such tend to intensify the couple's negative fusion or lead to the wife's feeling more responsible for the problem.

In coaching work with couples, it is usually advantageous to see them together as each works on his or her own family. Seeing a spouse so vividly in the context of the family of origin and hearing the details of the spouse's socialization and struggle to surmount the inevitable problems with parents not only increase a partner's understanding and empathy toward the spouse, but also help significantly to diminish blame for current marital problems. If spouses are so locked in bitter conflict that they harden their hearts against the other's struggle, or if they use information revealed to buttress their own accusations or interrupt with unhelpful comments, then the spouses should be seen separately for coaching, in this or any phase of the life cycle.

As in the previous stage, the influence of issues from the family of origin is extremely important but will tend to be minimized by the couple, who are usually focused on their disappointments with each other and may see family of origin work as irrelevant to their specific problems.

With young couples, the therapist can alternate the focus between their relationship and their families of origin in any given session. It is essential that the therapist track the presenting complaints through both families of origin early on to provide evidence that connects the complaints to longstanding family issues and triangles. It is not enough to point out these connections in one genogram session. The therapist must refer to the connections frequently to expand the couple's focus from themselves. This process of making connections also tends to reduce blame as problems are expanded beyond the spouse's personal ill-will. Tacking a large genogram up in the therapy room or handing out copies of each partner's genogram

in sessions may help to keep the whole family system in everyone's mind.

An important clinical question is asking how each member of the couple left home. Did they leave in a calm, planned way and spend enough time alone to become a functioning self? Or did they explode out in conflict, distance themselves from the family, or marry immediately? Leaving home is like a fingerprint or footprint, providing an indication of the degree of differentiation (i.e., maturity) that each partner achieved personally before their coupling. Current relationships with parents also indicate the relationship issues that sooner or later will play out in the couple relationship.

Given the growing number of young couples who live together without marriage or before marriage, it is important to give some thought to the clinical implications of this. When there is no permanent commitment, couples therapy tends to focus on superficial complaints and disappointments or the argument about whether to marry or not.

We believe that a couple's failure to make a public commitment to each other has meaning, and the therapy format should reflect the fact that they are as much singles as they are a couple. We may set up a format whereby we see each partner individually in succeeding weeks and then, in the third week, see them as a couple. This gives ample space for each to consider calmly whether to stay in the relationship or leave and to work on their own part of the problem without losing face. This also gives the therapist an opportunity to try to engage each partner in the family of origin work, which usually reveals and helps to resolve the couple impasse, if you can get them to do it.

Because of its connection to power and to love, analyzing how a family deals with money is an important issue in coaching. If a young person (or a traditional wife) has no access to the money necessary for survival, he or she remains functionally dependent on others which will certainly affect his or her ability to freely disagree or differentiate from those who control the means of survival. It is important to ask who controls the money; whether there have been conflicts regarding wills; and whether the family believes in financially assisting grown children.

The therapist should look for gender differences in handling money because if a husband controls a couple's money, they will not be able to negotiate as equals. When a family business or a will has left family money unequally divided among siblings, relationships are likely to be impaired or even cut off, often for generations. Coaching family members about redoing such arrangements before they happen or, if necessary, after they happen for the benefit of their relationships may be the best way around such difficulties.

FAMILIES WITH YOUNG CHILDREN

Typical triangles involve (1) each spouse and a child (or the children as a group); (2) either or both spouses, a child, and a grandparent or grandparents; (3) in-law triangles; (4) each spouse and the husband's work; or (5) each spouse and an affair. This stage has a very high divorce rate. If the couple doesn't present with marital problems, the state of the marriage should be explored and evaluated in connection with any or all of the above triangles.

If the presenting problem concerns a child, as it often does, it is important to attend to that problem to some degree before attempting to engage the parents in family of origin work. Once the crisis has receded, both parents should be engaged in coaching if possible. The motivation of clients in this stage of life is noticeably better than that in previous stages. Becoming parents themselves usually allows the younger generation finally to see the relevance of family. Also, parents are often willing to do things for the children that they find too difficult to undertake for themselves. Although this motivation will need to shift to the self, doing it for the children's sake is a reason to begin.

Including the couple's marital work, concerns about children, and the families of origin of both spouses in the process of therapy requires therapist flexibility in shifting focus and the ability to keep track of the macro and micro levels (see Chapter 15).

If the client is an unmarried or postdivorce single parent, there are some special areas of focus and other typical triangles in coaching work, which we will consider below.

FAMILIES WITH ADOLESCENTS

Because of the major physical, social, and psychological changes that adolescents go through, the most common triangles at this phase concern the adolescent and his or her peer group. Parents may become polarized in response to adolescent behavior, or adolescents may act out in response to parental triangles involving work, affairs, or grandparents.

Clients at this stage may present with marital crises or concerns about adolescent acting out. Again, the acute crisis should be dealt with before full-scale coaching begins, but a carefully elaborated genogram will undoubtedly shed much light on the antecedents of the couple's or adolescent's problems.

Parents at this phase of the life cycle, usually in their forties, may be the most highly motivated coaching clients of all. They usually understand quite well the importance of emotional connectedness to the family of origin and may feel guilty themselves about their teenagers' problems. Their parents are getting older and perhaps ill, and they know that they don't have forever to resolve their own issues with them.

THE COUPLE AT OR PAST THE LAUNCHING STAGE

Couple problems at this stage usually reflect long-standing marital conflict or distance and are likely to be embedded in multiple interlocking triangles of the couple and their parents, siblings, children, work, affairs, or visions of the future.

At the launching stage, the intergenerational balance of power shifts, and the relationship between parents and their launched or launching young adult children is no longer mostly in the hands of the parents. At this stage, coaching involves helping these parents deal with the increased independence of the generation below as well as the growing dependence of that above.

The parents of these parents are either elderly and quite possibly in failing health or they are already deceased. Nevertheless, clients at this stage of life can be rather easily engaged in discussion of the intergenerational issues. The usual objection to actually raising difficult issues with their elderly parents is that they are "too old" to be upset. Our experience is that parents are never too old or even too ill to benefit from whatever their adult children want to communicate, assuming that it is communicated in a nonattacking manner. After all, it is the elderly person's developmental task to bring closure to life's storms, and when the family system is not too rigid, efforts by their adult children are usually accepted in this framework.

We have encouraged midlife adults to speak to dead parents at their gravesites; to write letters to dead parents; to say "I love you" or "I want to forgive you" to elderly parents who are drunk, drugged, or in a coma; or to say, "Tell me that you love me" to a senile parent. These dramatic moves are culminations of the work conducted in discussion with surviving or unimpaired family members who knew the parent and by genealogical exploration, which usually reveals issues, triangles, and ghosts that shed light on current generations.

Even a formerly abusive, now ill elderly parent can be sent a letter about the abuse that is not attacking: "I used to think I could never forgive you for the abuse, which had such a lasting negative impact on my life, but now I am trying to believe that these actions on your part were the result of something terribly wrong in your own life. I want to believe that you didn't mean to harm me to such a degree, but that you were swept up in some emotional storm that you didn't know how to control." And so on. The letter should be followed up by a visit or phone call in which the topic is pursued, assuming always that the parent is not mentally ill or addicted.

In terms of their own launched or launching young adults, parents should be coached to shift gears from "boss" to "fellow adult." Parents not only need to let go, but also need to conduct their half of a changed adult-to-adult relationship with their grown children. This may mean ceasing or curtailing financial support, accepting the young adult's choices regarding work or mate, changing inputs into their lives from directive to suggestive, maintaining a flexible pattern of visits and phone calls in both directions, and, most of all, being willing to conduct open discussions, stripped of the need to shield "the children" from the parents' real concerns, and expressing interest but not intrusion in their lives.

Remembering the old adage "A son is a son till he gets him a wife, but a daughter's a daughter for all of her life," therapists should pay extra attention to parents' expectations of and relationships with their grown sons. This is especially important for mothers of sons, whose relationships are socially invalidated (Silverstein & Rauschbaum, 1994). The older generation should be coached to avoid conflict with their children-in-law, to take up issues or problems that arise between families with their own child, and to give up blaming difficulties on the in-law. Needless to say, "problem grandparenting" is something grandparents can be helped with in coaching and, if feasible, in joint sessions with their adult child (initially without the child's spouse). At issue here are the unarticulated expectations of all concerned about the proper degree of involvement of grandparents. These differences are usually quite negotiable once automatic reactivity is stopped.

If grown children are involved in ongoing conflict with their parents, it is wise to suggest inviting the younger generation to participate in therapy, since they have most of the power. Since you will be seen as the parents' therapist, it is a good idea to see the younger ones alone first to hear their uncensored version of events and to assure them by word or deed of your generational neutrality. The best outcome would be for one or more of them to be willing to be coached so as to assume responsibility for their part of the problem and to use the power they have to restore the relationship.

If members of the younger generation are already in their own therapy and want the parents to see their therapist, we agree to this as long as they are seeing a family therapist. If they agree to join the parents' therapy, we see the various individuals, couples, and generations both separately and to-gether, depending on issues and clinical timing. In general, joint sessions accomplish less if neither generation has been coached to present a changed position, but they do provide the therapist with an invaluable picture of the family's approach to handling differences for evaluation purposes.

When grown children use extreme distance or cut-off to try to deal with parents, the latter can do a lot of wrong things but can't end the cut-off until the adult child is ready to do so. Helping parents to see the cut-off as multigenerational process instead of the child's personal meanness is a first step. Then all the details of the issue that caused the final rupture must be discussed so that the therapist can put himself or herself into the child's position and guess his or her probable feelings and interpretations of parental words and actions. Finally, the parents should be coached to communicate carefully worded messages to the child. Such letters may convey a change of position or apology, if those seem appropriate, or may simply express the parents' desolation at the loss of contact. The therapy consists largely of getting parents to the point of readiness to write such letters. Each parent should write separately to eliminate the typical problem of their presenting themselves and being reacted to as a unit instead of as two separate people.

ELDERLY CLIENTS

The most common triangles at this phase are between the elderly couple and a middle-aged child; an elderly woman, her daughter, and her grandchild; or an elderly parent, his or her doctor, and the middle-aged children.

In private practice, we are more likely to hear about than to meet elderly parents or grandparents. However, they should always be present in the genogram in the therapist's mind, because they are often the key to nodal events of the past, as well as the gateway to change for the next generation, as described in the previous section.

Many therapists do direct clinical work with the elderly through agency outreach or in nursing homes. The majority of such clients are women,

because women live longer and because they never give up their concern about relationships. If the family relationships are in poor shape or, in the case of older men, if they feel they didn't succeed at work, depression can be a problem. Men mellow as they age and as they leave their competitive struggles behind them. This natural process can make the most belligerent man into a more empathic, relationship-oriented person. Consider the remarkable turnaround of Governor George Wallace of Alabama; the deathbed apology of Lee Atwater, the publicist who was responsible for the racist "Willy Horton" political ads; the end-of-life admission by French Premier Valéry Giscard d'Estaing of his Nazi connections; and the apparently agonizing quest by Robert McNamara, former Secretary of Defense, for exculpation for his role in the Vietnam War.

We recommend encouraging the elderly in their life review, urging them to approach the task with compassion for self and to share their story with family members. It is the family task at this phase to care for the elderly and to receive their story and their wisdom. If family members don't seem to be doing their part of the job, we recommend getting in touch and, again, proceeding with both individual and joint sessions as needed, coaching both generations to resolve their issues with the other.

COACHING SINGLE PARENTS

Never-Married Single Parents

The most common triangles involve a single mother, her child, and her parents or the mother, her child, and the child's father.

With such clients, it is important to learn the client's family's reaction to the unmarried parenthood. A woman's unmarried pregnancy carries more stigma than a single-parent adoption, although concerns will also exist about that situation because of our society's devotion to the traditional family as the "correct" one. It is extremely important in this, as in any other controversial situation, that the client understand and accept her parents' disapproval as almost inevitable in our society before she initiates conversation with them about it.

In all situations that involve strong parental disapproval, it is necessary to coach the client, first to try to understand the source of the disapproval apart from parental ill will and second to realize that to become a mature adult, it is necessary to give up the need for parental approval, although most people never give up wanting it.

In addition to coaching single parents in the context of their families of origin, it is extremely important to coach them toward joining a meaningful community. An isolated parent and child are at risk; a single parent and child connected to a caring group at church or temple, or a close-knit group of friends, can be expected to thrive.

Divorcing and Postdivorce Parents

The most common triangles involve divorced or divorcing spouses and each of their children; a divorced spouse, his or her children, and the parents and family of the ex-spouse; the divorced spouses and a new love interest of either; or the interlocking triangles of a divorced spouse, the ex-spouse, the new love interest, and the children.

At the time of divorce, coaching can play an invaluable role in the current situation:

1. See each parent separately if possible, and coach each to minimize destructive, vengeance-seeking behavior. If only one parent will come to coaching, help that one to understand the rewards to self and children of "unilateral disarmament," refusing to respond in kind to the partner's provocations.
2. Help each or either parent to understand the importance of keeping the children out of the battle.
3. Focus on money and financial matters with the wife, helping her to plan a return to work if necessary or feasible.
4. Focus on the children with the husband, helping him to gain the skills necessary to conduct his own relationship with his children, and to abide by his financial commitments to them.

If the divorce is in the past and most of the above has not occurred smoothly (and it usually hasn't), coaching can help either parent to undo his or her part in the ensuing conflict or cut-off with the ex-spouse. To rework the relationship of the ex-spouses into one of co-parental cooperation, the client must be helped to stop blaming the divorce or failed marriage on the ex-spouse and examine closely his or her own role, however large or small, in the debacle. This is the work of the "emotional divorce," which requires giving up as finished the hopes and dreams invested in the marriage, and re-investing in one's own future course (see Chapter 22).

The clinician must, of course, also track the issues of the failed marriage and divorce in relation to the extended family from very early in therapy. And early on, the client is coached to discuss the divorce in some meaningful way with parents and to deal with their reactions to the divorce.

As the current struggle with the ex-spouse or focus on adaptation to postdivorce realities recedes to the point at which something other than the divorce can be attended to, coaching shifts to other multigenerational themes, issues, and triangles. And at the stage at which the client is able to look to the future, the coaching becomes like a resocialization process, helping men to develop relationship skills they need and women the autonomy and self-sufficiency they will need.

At the close of this work, the client should be free to have a cooperative co-parental relationship with the ex-spouse (assuming that the ex-spouse is sane and not violent or addicted). The client should also feel free to pursue a single life until such time as he or she may choose to remarry, and then with the expectation of a different kind of marriage.

COACHING REMARRIED FAMILY MEMBERS

In addition to tracking the issues in the family of origin of a spouse in a remarried family, it is necessary to get information on the family of the ex-spouse or the deceased spouse. It is also important to get the details of the divorce or the death to determine whether they were handled adequately or are unresolved and intruding into the current family. If they are unresolved, the client should be coached to redo the mourning or the emotional divorce. In either case, it is important to include the second spouse in the sessions in which a client is being coached to resolve the death or the divorce. If left out of these sessions, the second spouse has a tendency to become paranoid, wondering whether the therapy will undermine the second marriage. When included, the second spouse tends to become a staunch ally of the therapist, understanding that unresolved issues from a first marriage take up emotional space in the present.

Both the biological parent and the stepparent usually need help in distinguishing their roles (see Chapter 25). If the stepparent and stepchildren are in an uproar, with the biological parent caught in the middle, direct coaching of the couple to detriangle will be necessary.

Special attention should be given to the situation of the stepmother in a remarried family, since she is usually in the most vulnerable position. Coaching in the families of origin helps to strengthen both partners for a most complex family situation. It is also important to coach a biological parent to maintain contact with the family of the deceased or divorced spouse, since these are the children's grandparents.

COACHING MINORITY-GROUP CLIENTS

All clients have very specific issues and triangles related to their stage of the family life cycle and to the particular history and circumstances of their families of origin. Additionally, most problematic issues and triangles in minority-group families will be directly related to their lack of power and stigmatized status in the larger society. The most important clinical intervention is to help family members to get on the same side against the social problem instead of letting it divide them. It is essential to evaluate carefully the consequences for such clients of changing their role in any system, emotional or social, and to incorporate these caveats in the planning. It is very important that the therapist understand that disadvantaged social status reduces the options available for personal

change. The difficulties of changing in the face of social obstacles and stigma should not be attributed to lack of client motivation or maturity.

GUIDELINES FOR THE THERAPIST

1. Expect intense resistance to the idea of dealing with parents and family in real life instead of complaining in private to an understanding therapist. Discuss the advantages for the client in doing so. Suggest readings and tell stories of colleagues' and other clients' success and satisfaction, including personal stories, when clinically appropriate (see bibliography below).

2. When the anxiety level is low, educate the client in the major elements of systems theory. In addition to material written for the general public, clients also benefit from reading various professional books and chapters written for therapists, if the material relates to the client's specific problems or circumstances, or to the client's ethnicity, race, gender, class, sexual orientation, or culture.

3. Advise the client to expect a surge of anxiety symptoms with each new move, and normalize this. We sometimes ask what symptoms the client experienced during adolescence as a way of indicating the intensity of the emotional reactions that are ahead.

4. Once the client has agreed to work, emphasize the need for planned, not reactive or impulsive, moves in the family system.

5. Resist the pull to see the individual as the unit of dysfunction or treatment. Resist the pull to accept the client's descriptions of family members and their motivations as "truth." Keep the multigenerational family and its cultural context in mind as the client speaks. Put yourself mentally in the position of family members the client is complaining about. And be aware of your own family issues.

6. Be prepared to help the client prioritize and strategize throughout the work. Keep in mind the gender, racial, and cultural context of the client and family when making suggestions.

7. Remember that a coach also cheers from the sidelines and provides encouragement and appreciation. This is not the same as emotional support, approval, reassurance, or pity, all of which are condescending and disabling to the client. The therapist should convey the belief that the client can deal with his or her own family. If there are exceptional circumstances to the contrary, the client shouldn't be in the coaching format.

8. Remember that if you haven't worked on differentiating yourself in your own family, you will probably be prone to misjudge the intensity of systemic reaction to your client's moves and also prone to accept the client's resistance. For work that is beyond the initial reconnecting or reduction of conflict, you may want to refer the client to an experienced coach. You might also consider working in your own family.

9. When the client is concurrently in another type of therapy, remember that "too many cooks spoil the broth," especially if the other therapist appears to be having a real impact on the client. Suggest that the client put one of you on hold until the other therapy is completed. Also, consider that if the client is paying more for the other therapy (because of more frequent sessions or a higher fee), then he or she is likely to be more influenced by that relationship.

10. Resist the client's tendency, especially if he or she has been in psychodynamically oriented therapy, to try to make you the "good parent" or intensify the emotional climate between you and the client. Explain openly coaching therapy's different rules.

11. If the client is of a different race, ethnicity, religion, gender, sexual orientation, or social class, you have a responsiblity to educate yourself about the issues involved for that client (McGoldrick, 1998; Laird & Green, 1996; McGoldrick, Giordano & Pearce, 1996; Walters, Carter, Papp & Silverstein, 1988).

12. If your personal or religious beliefs or your emotional reactivity do not permit you to have an understanding position regarding any client's issues or status, you have a responsibility to refer the client to a therapist who does.

REFERENCES AND SELECTED BIBLIOGRAPHY

Bowen, M. (1978a). On the differentiation of self. In M. Bowen, *Family Therapy in Clinical Practice* (pp. 467–528). New York: Jason Aronson.

Bowen, M. (1978b). *Family therapy in clinical practice.* New York: Jason Aronson.

Carter, E. A., & McGoldrick Orfanidis, M. (1976). Family therapy with one person and the family therapist's own family. In P. J. Guerin (Ed.), *Family Therapy* (pp. 183–219). New York: Gardner.

Chodron, P., & hooks, b. (1997, June). Beyond right or wrong: A conversation between Pema Chodron and bell hooks. *The Sun,* 258, pp. 11–14.

Goleman, D. (1997). *Emotional intelligence.* New York: Bantam.

Guerin, P., Fogarty, T., Fay, L., & Kautto, J. G. (1996). *Working with relationship triangles: The one-two-three of psychotherapy.* New York: Guilford Press.

Kerr, M., & Bowen, M. (1988). *Family evaluation: The role of the family as an emotional unit that governs individual behavior and development.* New York: Norton.

Laird, J., & Green, R. J. (Eds.). (1996). *Lesbians and gays in couples and families.* San Francisco: Jossey-Bass.

McGoldrick, M. (1989). Sisters. In M. McGoldrick, C. Anderson, & F. Walsh (Eds.), *Women in families.* New York: Norton.

McGoldrick M. (1995). *You can go home again: Reconnecting with your family.* New York: Norton.

McGoldrick, M. (1998). Belonging and liberation: Finding a place called "home." In M. McGoldrick (Ed.), *Revisioning Family therapy: Culture, Class, Race, and Gender* (pp. 215–228). New York: The Guilford Press.

McGoldrick, M., & Gerson, R. (1995). *Genograms in family assessment.* New York: Norton

McGoldrick, M., Gerson, R., & Schellenberger, S. (1998). *Genograms in family assessment* (2nd ed.). New York: Norton.

McGoldrick, M., Giordano, J., & Pearce, J. K. (1996). *Ethnicity and family therapy* (2nd ed.). New York: The Guilford Press.

Papero, D. (1990). *Bowen family systems theory.* Boston: Allyn & Bacon.

Silverstein, O., & Rauschbaum, B. (1994). *The courage to raise good men.* New York: Viking.

Szaporcznik, J., Kurtines, W. M., Foote, F. H., Perez-Vidal, A., & Harvis, O. (1983). Conjoint versus one-person family therapy: Some evidence for the effectiveness of conducting family therapy through one person. *Journal of Consulting and Clinical Psychology, 51,* 889–899.

Titleman, P. (1987). *The therapist's own family.* New York: Jason Aronson.

Toman, W. (1976). *Family constellation* (3rd ed.). New York: Springer.

Walters, M., Carter, B., Papp, P., & Silverstein, O. (1988). *The invisible web: Gender patterns in family relationships.* New York: The Guilford Press.

The Family Therapist's Own Family Stories

Bowen, M. (1978). On the differentiation of self. In M. Bowen, *Family therapy in clinical practice* (pp. 467–528). New York: Jason Aronson.

Carter, B. (1991). Death in the therapist's own family. In M. McGoldrick, C. Anderson, & F. Walsh (Eds.) *Living beyond loss.* New York: Norton.

Colon, F. (1998). The discovery of my multicultural identity. In M. McGoldrick (Ed.) *Revisioning family therapy.* New York: The Guilford Press.

Folwarski, J. (1998). No longer an orphan in history. In M. McGoldrick (Ed.) *Revisioning family therapy* (pp. 239–252). New York: The Guilford Press.

Friedman, E. H. (1987). The birthday party revisited. In P. Titleman (Ed.) *The therapist's own family.* New York: Aronson.

Hall, C. M. (1987). Efforts to differentiate a self in my family of origin. In P. Titleman (Ed.) *The therapist's own family.* New York: Aronson.

Maboubi, J., & Searcy, A. (1998). Racial unity from the perspective of personal family history. In M. McGoldrick (Ed.) *Revisioning family therapy.* New York: The Guilford Press.

Pinderhughes, E. (1998). Black genealogy revisited. In M. McGoldrick (Ed.) *Revisioning family therapy.* New York: The Guilford Press.

Family Systems Readings for Clients

Ahrons, C. (1994). *The good divorce.* New York: HarperCollins.

Bepko, C. S., & Krestan, J. (1985). *The responsibility trap.* New York: The Free Press.

Carter, B., & Peters, J. (1996). *Love, honor and negotiate.* New York: Pocketbooks.

Imber-Black, E., & Roberts J. (1992). *Rituals for our times.* New York: HarperCollins.

Imber-Black, E. (1998). *The secret life of families.* New York: Bantam Books.

Lerner, H. G. (1985). *The dance of anger.* New York: Harper & Row.

Lerner, H. G. (1989). *The dance of intimacy.* New York: Harper & Row.

Lerner, H. G. (1993). *The dance of deception.* New York: HarperCollins.

Lerner, H. G. (1998). *The mother dance.* New York: HarperCollins.

McGoldrick, M. (1995). *You can go home again.* New York: Norton.

Rosen, E. J. (1998). *Families facing death.* New York: Lexington Books.

Schwartzberg, N., Berliner, K., & Jacob, D. (1995). *Single in a married world.* New York: Norton.

Silverstein, O., & Rauschbaum, B. (1994). *The courage to raise good men.* New York: Viking.

Taffel, R. (1994). *Why parents disagree.* New York: Morrow.

Walsh, F., & McGoldrick, M. (Eds.). (1991). *Living beyond loss.* New York: Norton.

CHAPTER 27

ALCOHOL PROBLEMS AND THE FAMILY LIFE CYCLE

JACQUELINE HUDAK
JO ANN KRESTAN
CLAUDIA BEPKO

Conservative figures estimate that 14 million Americans are alcoholic. Every alcoholic directly affects the lives of at least four to five other people. Half of those who receive treatment will relapse in two to four years. In 1991, drinking was a factor in over 17,000 fatal automobile accidents and 197,000 injury crashes. Traffic accidents are the greatest single cause of death for every age between 6 and 33. Alcohol is involved in nearly half of these (Eigen, 1992). Alcohol and other drugs are associated with up to 50 percent of spousal abuse cases, 68 percent of manslaughter charges, and 52 percent of rapes (Center for Substance Abuse Prevention (CSAP) 1994). Given the sobering realities of the effects of alcohol in our culture, clinicians have been advised to assume the existence of an alcohol problem in a family until thorough assessment proves otherwise (Bepko & Krestan, 1985).

Working with families that are affected by alcoholism presents special challenges to the family therapist. The work is often confrontative, with clients embedded in strong denial systems. Families often do not see the presenting problem as being related to drinking behavior. It is the clinician's task to rule this out. The ability to see the alcoholism is an important issue. The fact that alcohol consumption is sanctioned in our culture, is indeed considered a rite of passage during certain life cycle phases, contributes to solidifying the denial system. Denial becomes a defense against acknowledging the increasing loss of control that typically occurs, on both emotional and functional levels. Denial may be considered one of the major symptoms of the alcoholism itself and may extend to denial of both the problematic drinking and the impact of that drinking on other family members (Vaillant, 1983). If the clinician is in denial about alcohol issues in his or her own life, it may be difficult to address this issue with a family. Often, the family therapist will need partnership and consultation with an addiction professional.

ADDICTION IN CONTEXT

Alcoholism is hard to define. On any given day, we are besieged with different messages about alcohol use and addiction in our culture. The debate continues about the medical use of marijuana, a young college freshman dies from alcohol poisoning, a woman is arrested for public drunkeness while pregnant, and crack-addicted babies are abandoned in hospitals nationwide. We cannot decide as a culture whether to treat or incarcerate drug addicts. Yet the media tout the many wonders of the substance that can make you feel cool, sexy, or like a "real man." The images are everywhere and convey messages about fun, belonging, and achievement. In so many ways, our society promotes the use of alcohol, yet it cannot contend with the consequences.

Jacqueline Hudak would like to dedicate this chapter to her sister Peggy on the occasion of her tenth sober birthday.

Zinberg and Bean (1981) urged clinicians to develop a more comprehensive definition of alcohol addiction that specified the relationship of the alcoholic to his or her social context. This comprehensive model would recognize that it is the society that defines and labels the phenomenon of addiction and the culture that contributes to its development or inhibition. Thus, what is considered alcoholism, or even problem drinking, can vary from one culture or ethnic group to another, as well as from one period of history to another.

In this chapter, we will address alcohol problems through the family life cycle. Although we focus primarily upon alcohol as a psychoactive substance, it should be noted that different cultural groups use different drugs. Indeed one's substance of choice is closely tied to one's race, gender, sexual orientation, and class. For example, while alcoholism rates for men of color may be lower than those for White men at various life cycle stages, the rates of cocaine addiction may be quite high. It is not within the scope of this chapter to address all mood-altering substances for all groups, but it is important not to obscure the larger picture. There is perhaps no disorder more a product of its social setting than addiction to mood-altering drugs.

The lack of a universally agreed-upon definition of alcoholism complicates clinical assessment and frequently results in misdiagnosis of or failure to identify addiction in families. We have found it useful to consider alcoholism within the context of disease and view it as a true biopsychosocial illness, since physiological, psychological, and social factors all contribute to one's vulnerability. In this chapter, we use the National Council on Alcoholism's definition of alcoholism: "The person with alcoholism cannot consistently predict on any drinking occasion the duration of the episode or the quantity that will be consumed." (The National Council on Alcoholism, 1976).

The clinician should be aware that an alcoholic likes almost nothing better than to argue about definitions of alcoholism rather than stop drinking. This relates to the denial embedded in our cultural thinking about alcoholism as well as the alcoholic's personal denial. It is wise, however, to reserve discussions of definitions and disease for colleagues.

THE FAMILY LIFE CYCLE: A LONG-TERM PERSPECTIVE ON ALCOHOL USE

Most studies of alcoholism capture the characteristics of the alcoholic at certain points in their lives but reveal little about how they got to that point or what will happen thereafter. In *The Natural History of Alcoholism Revisited,* Vaillant (1995) addresses this issue in a longitudinal study of 600 men. Although the sample is limited in terms of gender and race, it does provide a way to think about the illness over the course of the life cycle.

Alcoholism has been viewed as a progressive disease, proceeding from stage to stage in fixed sequence, and ending in either abstinence or death. Using the data from his study, Valliant (1995) suggests that the course of alcoholism can be viewed as generally comprising of three linked stages:

> *The first stage is heavy "social" drinking—frequent ingestion of two to three ounces of ethanol a day (three to five drinks) for several years. This stage can continue asymptomatically for a lifetime; or because of a change of circumstances or peer group it can reverse to a more moderate pattern of drinking; or it can "progress" into a pattern of alcohol abuse (multiple medical, legal, social and occupational complications) usually associated with frequent ingestion of more than four ounces of ethanol (eight or more drinks) a day. At some point in their lives, perhaps 10–15 percent of American men reach this second stage. Perhaps half of such alcohol abusers either return to asymptomatic (controlled) drinking or achieve stable abstinence. In a small number of such cases…the alcohol abuse can persist intermittently for decades with minor morbidity and even become milder with time. Perhaps a quarter of all cases of alcohol abuse…will lead to chronic alcohol dependence, withdrawal symptoms, and the eventual need for detoxification. (p. 379)*

For the majority of alcoholics, the journey from the first drink to an inability to control one's consumption is a process of habit formation that takes from five to thirty years. Indeed, for some, alcohol abuse can be a lifelong career. However, the degree to which one's social environment accepts or denies alcohol abuse is an important determinant in helping someone to realize that his or her drinking is out of control.

Vaillant cites four components as essential in treating alcoholism: (1) offering the patient a nonchemical substitute dependency for alcohol, (2) reminding the patient ritually that even one drink can lead to pain and relapse, (3) repairing the social and medical damage that the patient has experienced, and (4) restoring the patient's self-esteem. Self-help groups, such as Alcoholics Anonymous (AA), offer the simplest way to provide the alcoholic with these four components. In Vallaint's study, more recovered alcoholics began stable abstinence while attending AA than while attending alcohol treatment centers.

SELF-HELP GROUPS

Sensitivity to context is important in referring to AA or related groups for families of alcoholics, such as Al Anon. Concepts of AA and Al Anon need to be adapted for different groups. For example, the concept of powerlessness is central to such recovery programs. In AA, powerlessness refers to the alcoholic's lack of control over the amount of alcohol she or he drinks. Feminists believe that the term "powerlessness" undermines the very empowerment that women and other disenfranchised groups need. Therefore, many recovering women use the term "surrender." The shift in one's belief system about powerlessness and the shame that is attached to it is, we believe, critical to sustained sobriety itself.

Another term that is central to the AA program is "Higher Power." The confusion about this term continues to plague AA's attempt to encourage a spiritual component to one's recovery from alcoholism. The often sexist and noninclusive language of such programs can also be offensive to clients. The recovering Jewish community has established Jewish Alcoholics and Chemically Dependent (JACS), which borrows many AA tenets

without using the often recited Lord's Prayer in meetings. However, the effectiveness of AA and Al Anon programs and their availability at no cost in virtually every city in the United States and every country worldwide are indisputable. We encourage clinicians to talk with clients and to help them work through real issues about the content of these programs while blocking any attempts to turn these issues into excuses not to attend meetings.

Other groups that are gaining recognition include the the Rational Recovery Movement (Trimpey, 1996) and Recovery in Moderation (Kishline, 1996).

BIAS AGAINST THE ALCOHOLIC

It is important to note that despite the gains made in defining and treating alcoholism, alcoholics and addicts continue to be viewed as too morally deficient or weak to stop using alcohol. The medical profession, the gatekeeper to medical services to this population, has been found to harbor a strong bias in this area. A panel of experts found that most doctors do not try to identify severe alcohol and drug habits. When doctors do find evidence of dependency, they do not know how to respond. Doctors tend to view alcohol problems as the result of personal shortcomings. The medical profession tends to hold doctors who treat these patients in low esteem. Clinicians need to be sensitive to the stigma that still exists about women who abuse substances and are thus viewed as "out of control." Women's addictions tend to remain hidden, unlike those of male addicts, whose arena for drinking and drug use is much more social and external. Women's shame about addictive behavior is more intense than that of men and is a major block to their seeking treatment. Another significant obstacle is inadequate family support and lack of child care.

Class and racial status also affects attitudes toward female substance abusers. Women of color who are poor are much more likely to be indicted by the legal system for the use of alcohol and drugs during pregnancy than are White, upper-class women according to the Center for Reproductive Law and Policy.

Women are still overmedicated in this culture, and many women become addicted to drugs that are prescribed by doctors, who are often unaware of the women's alcohol use. It is chilling to note that 82 percent of prescriptions for antidepressants are written for women (Lerner, 1997).

Women substance abusers are more likely than men to have grown up in families disrupted by divorce, death, or other trauma. Nearly 70 percent of women substance abusers in treatment were sexually abused as children (CASA, 1996). Almost as high a percentage suffer from corresponding eating disorders. Addicted women tend to suffer high rates of depression and are viewed as sicker than male addicts (Forth-Finnegan, 1991).

Substance abuse among women is often a response to oppressive role expectations and class constraints and to the ongoing devalued status of women in this culture. A whole self-help industry has evolved around designating women who relate to addictive family members as "co-dependent," another form of cultural blaming of women (Krestan & Bepko, 1991). Yet statistics show that men are more likely to leave alcoholic women than women are to leave alcoholic men and that a female spouse is much more likely to participate in a husband's treatment than he in hers. Women at either extreme of the life cycle, in adolescence and later life, are most likely to go untreated for addiction.

THE IMPACT OF RACE AND CULTURE

Drugs depend both for their desirability and for their effect on the environment in which they are taken. Although this chapter deals primarily with alcohol problems, we should not obscure the fact that for certain populations, alcohol use may be low at points in the life cycle, but use of illicit drugs may be high. Some cultures have a heightened physical vulnerability to addiction, and further information is useful in helping the clinician to think about the issue for various ethnicities across the life cycle. Drinking among Blacks has sometimes been characterized as representing two extremes: abstinence and abuse (Herd, 1990). Church attendance, family history of alcohol prob-

lems, household density, and socioeconomic status were all found to affect the development of alcoholism in this population (Herd, 1990). Black and White men tend to have similar drinking patterns, although Black men have higher abstention rates than Whites (Grant et al., 1991). The same pattern was found with women. Heavy drinking peaked among younger Whites and decreased with age. Heavy drinking among Blacks peaked in middle age before decreasing in later life. Young Blacks may be more likely to abuse illicit drugs. Among the population age 35 and older, Blacks were more likely than Whites or Hispanics to use illicit drugs. Black women are more likely than women in any other racial/ethnic group to have used crack cocaine (National Institute on Drug Abuse, 1990). The link to institutionalized racism and poverty for this group must be studied further, as well as the propensity to incarcerate rather than offer drug treatment. The lack of access to treatment facilities is a well-known impediment to recovery for these families.

Latino males are more likely to experience drinking problems than African American or white males (Caetano, 1989). They seem especially susceptible to alcohol-related violence (Goodman, Istre, Jordan, Herndon, & Kelaghan, 1991). Hispanic men drink more than Hispanic women. Drinking increases with income and education for both sexes (Caetano, 1989). Alcoholism among Hispanic men peaked at ages 30 to 44. Among Hispanic women, it peaked at ages 18 to 29, with a progressive decrease thereafter (Committee on Cultural Psychiatry, 1996).

The rates of alcoholism for the Native American Indian population can be understood only in the context of annihilation imposed by those who sought to eradicate their very culture and traditions (Tafoya & Del Vecchio, 1996). The death rate from alcoholism among American Indians and Alaska Natives is 5.4 times higher than the U.S. death rate for all races (Indian Health Service, 1992).

Vaillant (1995) demonstrates further the dramatic effect of parental and cultural background on lifetime patterns of alcohol use. Men whose parents had grown up in Mediterranean cultures were far less likely to develop alcohol dependence. Italian culture permits childhood drinking but forbids drunkenness and encourages drinking low-proof alcohol with food in the presence of family members. Valliant contrasted this with the Irish, who prefer drinking in pubs, where alcohol intake is separated from the family and from food intake. The Irish forbid their youths to learn how to drink but praise men who consume large quantities of high-proof alcohol.

ADDICTION: STAGING AND LIFE CYCLE ISSUES IN ASSESSMENT

The presence of addiction in a family—in whatever generation—complicates differentiation for all family members. Family boundaries are often too rigid or too diffuse; roles are frequently reversed or otherwise inappropriate, and triangles are activated and shift, depending on whether the alcoholic is drinking. At advanced stages of alcoholism, families tend to be cut off, and isolation from both the extended family and the community are prevalent. The alcoholism is frequently a secret, as are violence, incest, and other potential complications of the alcohol.

Family assessment should include standard questions about the drug and alcohol use of all family members, including grandparents, aunts and uncles, and extended-family members. However, the most revealing question to ask may be "How much pain has been caused by the drinking?" Alcohol problems at any point within at least a three-generation time frame of the family presenting for treatment significantly affect behavioral and emotional patterns evolving within the family. Symptoms such as disturbances in job performance, marital conflict and infidelity, problems in children's school functioning, depression, social isolation, abuse of prescription drugs, or a host of physical disorders may follow from alcohol problems Young adults presenting typical problems of separation may be reflecting the influence an alcoholic grandparent has had on family interactions.

The family's developmental stage and the progression of the disease within the individual inter-sect to become a context in which a life cycle assessment must take place. Two interacting sequences occur simultaneously: the progression of the alcoholism within the individual and the developmental progression within the family itself. Alcoholism both influences and is influenced by the movement through the family life cycle. For example, alcoholism can emerge as a response to launching a child, or a child may be delayed or disrupted as a result of alcoholism. The role of the family therapist before the addicted family member gets sober is to encourage entrance into AA. Intervening with the family of the alcoholic, without the alcoholic's even entering therapy, is often highly effective and can be supported by referral to Al Anon.

Over time, alcoholism distorts patterns of behavior and communication within the family system and affects all family members. Treatment of other family problems may stop or alleviate the drinking behavior in some families, in which the drinking is more situational; but when it has become an addiction, it assumes such central importance that it becomes the fulcrum of interactional sequences. In such cases, abstinence from drinking is a necessary, although insufficient, goal. The distorted patterns of behavior and communication must also be treated if abstinence is to be maintained. Historically, these families have been referred to as "alcoholic systems" (Steinglass, 1987). Such families become organized around the alcohol, and change must address these patterns to build on the family's strengths, resiliency, and coping mechanisms (Berenson, 1976).

THE FAMILY WITH ADOLESCENTS

The intensely demanding nature of adolescent behavior and the emergence of separateness and difference in families all serve to make adolescence a tumultuous time for families. Issues around response to authority, autonomy, and sexuality begin to dominate family life during this phase.

Recent survey data reveals that the age at which children are beginning to smoke cigarettes daily, drink alcohol, and use marijuana and other illegal drugs, including cocaine and hallucinogens such as LSD, is the youngest ever (CASA, 1997). The percentage of 12-year-olds who have a friend or classmate who has used illegal drugs such as acid, heroin, or cocaine jumped by 122 percent from 1996 to 1997. For all teens age 12 to 17, there was an increase of 44 percent from 1996 to 1997.

Among 12- to 17-year-olds with no other problem behaviors, those who used three "gateway" drugs (cigarettes, alcohol, and marijuana) in the past month were almost 17 times likelier to use another drug such as cocaine, heroin, or acid— boys more than girls (CASA, 1997). Many baby boomer parents appear to be resigned to such widespread drug use by their teens. Forty-six percent expect their teens to try illegal drugs. And 65 percent of boomer parents who regularly used marijuana in their youth believe that their teens will try drugs (CASA, 1996).

However, alcohol remains the drug of choice among teenagers, the one that they use and abuse most frequently, and the drug most associated with risky behaviors such as drunk driving, teen pregnancy, suicide, and violence. The percentage of teens who have tried alcohol has remained steadily high since 1990, and the percentage of eighth graders who are binge drinking is increasing (CASA, 1997). Male high school seniors had a markedly higher incidence of heavy drinking than female high school seniors, but this gap has narrowed during the last decade (Johnston, O'Malley, & Bachman, 1991). Alcohol and drug use is associated with the leading causes of death and injury (e.g., motor vehicle crashes, homicides, and suicides) among teenagers and young adults.

The influence of peers is the most powerful predictor of alcohol use among young people, but the family is an important preventive agent. Teenagers who feel close to their families are the least likely to engage in risky behaviors, including smoking marijuana or cigarettes, having sex, and drinking. Parents' high expectations regarding school performance are nearly as important (Gilbert, 1997).

Diagnosing adolescent alcohol problems is much more difficult than it is for other age groups.

Ultimate treatment depends on the parents' level of denial, the solutions that were previously attempted, and the consequences already suffered by the adolescent as a result of the addiction. Family therapists must help the parents to decide when to back off to leave the responsibility for consequences of drinking to the adolescent and when to take responsibility themselves for the adolescent's abuse, including forcing him or her into in-patient treatment.

The recovery process is much more complex if one or both parents are also addicted. The clinician must then assess which family member has the least amount of denial about the problem. If sobriety is not achieved at this phase of the life cycle, the consequences are serious. As the disease progresses, the addict will function less and less. Developmental tasks, such as education and career choice, will be severely compromised. The person may become involved with the law. He or she will be unable to participate in their family and will miss significant life events, such as graduations or a sibling's marriage. Through the years, these unrecovered family members become like family ghosts. They are so impaired and have such a long history of disappointments with their families, that it is difficult even to maintain contact. Families need to protect themselves against the symptomatic behaviors of addicts, such as lying and stealing. Long-term alcoholics are written out of family wills. It is important in such cases for the family therapist to contextualize the problem as addiction (not that the person is "bad") and encourage family members to gain support in programs such as Al Anon.

If a family enters treatment at this phase of the life cycle, with concern about drinking, the the addiction is likely to be severely progressed. However, as adolescents develop, they become more vocal and more likely to speak out about a parent's drinking, often with great hostility and anger. Therefore, the clinician should carefully track alcohol and drug use on the part of the parents and assess potential impact on the presenting problem, which is usually the behavior of the adolescent. Often, when an adolescent is intensely scapegoated, alcoholism or drug addiction of a parent is a factor. Precipitating a crisis often gives such children a sense of control in what can otherwise be an unpredictable and chaotic environment.

And what of the adolescent whose addicted parent(s) do not recover at this phase? Such a child would probably be either overfunctioning or underfunctioning, depending on gender and birth order. An overresponsible child may have difficulty with separation and individuation. Launching would be complex as the adolescent struggles with intensely mixed feelings: I want to leave this home but am so afraid someone will get hurt or die if I do.

THE UNATTACHED YOUNG ADULT

The primary developmental task for the young adult, differentiation of self from family of origin, is severely impaired by alcoholism in the family. If the young adult manifests the disease at this age and does not get sober, future life choices will be severely compromised, and he or she may have developed the skills to survive within the family system without having the skills to separate from it.

Young adults can be cut off from their family emotionally, particularly if sobriety or recovery has not been achieved by either parent or any other family members. Treatment during this particular life phase may help to restore the individual's capacity to negotiate the developmental stages that follow. Adult children of alcoholics are often unaware of the significant influence alcoholism has had on their own lives. Denial, pride, and defensiveness, the defenses that enabled the adult child to survive, eventually block the accomplishment of adult relational tasks.

The clinician has much to consider regarding alcoholism when treating a young adult. Heavy use of alcohol is considered a rite of passage by many; therefore, the diagnosis of a problem is particularly difficult. It is important to track carefully the drinking habits of young adults and educate them about their vulnerabilities to developing alcohol problems at some point in their lives.

Alcohol abuse and dependence are most likely in late adolescence and young adulthood, more for men than for women. Whites tend to abuse alcohol more, while people of color are more likely to use other drugs. For this age group, 20 percent of women have alcohol problems, compared to 33 percent of men (Grant et al., 1991).

The risk of alcohol dependence is determined by a complex interplay of genetic and environmental factors. Younger male relatives of male alcoholics are at particular risk for the disease. The risk for developing alcoholism has been found to be seven times greater among first-degree relatives of alcoholics than among controls (Merikangas, 1990).

Research on homosexual and heterosexual populations has established an association between alcohol use, drug use, and high-risk sexual behavior (U.S. Department of Health and Human Services, 1990). The correlation is significant enough to merit discussion with clients at this age and make them aware of the risks.

There are widespread and harmful consequences of heavy episodic, or "binge" drinking on college campuses, not only for students who abuse alcohol, but also for others in their immediate environment (Wechsler, 1996).

NEW COUPLES

Alcohol abuse powerfully interferes with tasks at this phase of the life cycle. The interactional sequences that form around alcohol use set the stage for the inability to resolve later issues of difference, power, and intimacy. Some major pitfalls for heterosexual couples may be the expectation of Utopia, boundary problems with extended families, and a tendency to triangle to stabilize the relationship by focusing on a third person or issue, including alcohol.

COUPLES AT ANY STAGE

Alcohol use is a frequent regulator of closeness and distance in a couple. Marriages that are affected by alcoholism may present with intense symmetrical conflict, competitiveness, a high degree of overt/covert dependency on the part of both spouses, or an extreme role imbalance, that is, one partner overfunctions while the other underfunctions. Similar dynamics may occur in marriages in which one or both partners were children of an alcoholic parent, even if no drinking problem exists in the marriage.

Treating a couple with an alcohol problem is complex. The primary goal is the drinker's achieving abstinence. A critical factor would be the time lapse between the onset of early warning signals of alcoholism and the couple's presentation for treatment. For example, was someone caught driving under the influence? If so, did the person participate in treatment? Who sees the drinking as a problem? The person with the least intense denial is the one who is more open to treatment. If this is the drinker, the clinician can request a period of abstinence, usually 90 days, with attendance at a self-help program. If the client breaks the contract for abstinence, this further supports the supposition of alcoholism, and a discussion must ensue with the alcoholic and his or her family about the need for more structured treatment, such as day or in-patient hospitalization. If the client has been drinking heavily for some years, in-patient detoxification may be necessary.

If the alcoholic rigidly denies having a problem, his or her spouse may be the one who is more open to defining the problem as alcoholism. A key component of treatment in this case is referral to Al Anon, a self-help program for family members of alcoholics. Involvement in this program will educate nondrinking clients about the disease of alcoholism, help them to give up overfunctioning for the alcoholic, and help them to keep a strong self-focus.

Infidelity is a typical problem. An affair is often perceived as more threatening than a drinking problem. Sexual problems for the male, such as impotence, loss of libido, and inability to ejaculate, have long been associated with drinking. Alcohol has deleterious effects on the endocrine system and reproductive function (Adams & Cicero,

1991). Thus, the presentation of infertility or sexual problems merits a detailed assessment of the past and present use of alcohol and drugs.

DOMESTIC VIOLENCE

Caution is needed when the referral is made for the partner of the alcoholic spouse. The clinician must carefully track the presence of domestic violence. If the alcoholic has engaged in threatening or intimidating behavior toward his or her spouse or there has been a violent incident, referral must be made to a batterers program. The couple should not be seen together. Al Anon is not appropriate until the partner is safe. Again, context is important. The message of Al Anon, couched in terms of "giving up control" is dangerous to battered women. Instead, the woman should be seen alone, informed of her legal rights, and referred to a women's group.

Alcohol is present in more than 50 percent of all incidents of domestic violence and thus merits further discussion (Permanen, 1991). The cause-and-effect thinking that has dominated research in this area is potentially dangerous to families. It supports the false belief, prevalent in much addiction treatment, that if the drinking stops, so will the violence. Further, it ignores the entire continuum of power and control and associated behaviors in which the perpetrator of violence will continue to engage (Almeida, Woods, Messineo, Font, & Heer, 1994). The clinician working with a family struggling with addiction must be well versed in these dangerous and complex issues. Men who batter need to be referred to a treatment program that addresses the specific issues of power and control in conjunction with their treatment for addiction. This view is in opposition to the long-held notion in addiction treatment that the addiction must be treated before any other issue and not doing so places the addict at great risk for relapse. While there may be some merit to the relapse argument, the option of ignoring the violence and placing a partner or children at continued risk is not tenable.

If clinicians find no evidence of domestic violence, they may proceed with coaching the spouse to gradually give up functioning for the alcoholic and to take positions with the alcoholic that foster sobriety. Encourage the spouse to stop serving alcohol at home and to avoid situations in which drinking is present. The spouse may move out of the bedroom until the drinking stops. Couples need to acquire a vision of an alcohol-free marriage, and a significant portion of therapy time should be devoted to this. The couple should be educated about any family predisposition for alcoholism via a genogram. People in their extended families who are sober and in recovery can provide excellent sources of support.

AFTER SOBRIETY

If the alcoholic stops drinking, the clinician should be prepared for, and inform the family of, the fact that early sobriety can be a most difficult time. This is often surprising, since the long-awaited event—sobriety—has finally occurred. Sobriety can provide a clear picture of just how alcoholic drinking has affected the family. Other family members may manifest symptoms such as depression. Treatment should focus on stabilizing the system and educating family members about the significant role alcohol played in their daily interactions. Issues regarding transmission to the next generation should be addressed. Relapse prevention needs to be addressed through frank discussion and cognitive and behavioral training and support for the couple while encouraging a strong focus on self.

If the alcoholic continues to drink, the clinician must be prepared to predict drinking's impact on the couple as they move through the life cycle. Complementarity of the overfunctioning and underfunctioning roles will become more rigid and extreme, and the ability to parent will be compromised.

GAY AND LESBIAN COUPLES

Gay and lesbian couples also experience problems with alcohol use. The rate of substance abuse problems in the gay community has been reported to be three times as high as that in the heterosexual population (Anderson, 1966). Perhaps this is because, until very recently, bars were the only venues available for socializing and connecting with other gay people.

Gay and lesbian couples live in a heterosexist environment that stigmatizes their life-style choices and sexual preferences. Frequently, their families of choice are not acknowledged and their families of origin are rejecting and alienating. Substance abuse may be a response, as it is for women, to cultural oppression and shaming. Outreach to gays and lesbians with substance abuse problems is negligible, and attention to their special needs is rare. Yet their families are no less damaged by abuse, and there is a great need for nonhomophobic alcoholism treatment.

Life cycle phases for gay and lesbian families involve some additional stages that do not apply to heterosexuals, and the stress of these stages is often associated with heavy substance use. Gay people struggle with self-acceptance. Work with the family of choice may be more critical than work with the family of origin. The heterosexual family struggling with a gay child needs to know that being gay does not "cause" addiction but is an important part of the context in which it occurs.

NEW PARENTS

Young adults who used illegal drugs or alcohol as teenagers tend to cut down or quit when confronted by the responsibilities of marriage and family (Bachman, Wadsworth, O'Malley, Johnston, & Schulenberg, 1997). A study of more than 33,000 young adults at two-year intervals up to fourteen years, found that substance abuse goes up when adolescents break free of parental restraints but then goes down again once they mature and accept new responsibilities such as love and marriage. Those who give up drugs and alcohol after using them as teenagers are more likely to return to them after personal setbacks, such as divorce.

This is important information for the clinician treating a family at this phase of the life cycle. Family history and the history of drug and alcohol use by each parent are vital in understanding their propensity toward addiction. Research suggests that alcohol and drug use should decline at this phase of the life cycle. If this is not what the family is reporting, it may indicate a problem. The family therapist needs to be aware of such vulnerabilities toward addiction and should have frank discussions with the parents about it.

CHILDREN IN ALCOHOLIC FAMILIES

More than 15 million school-age children are affected by parental alcoholism. The alcoholic family with young children may be referred for treatment because of school problems, learning disabilities, delinquency, or evidence of neglect or abuse. Perhaps they come voluntarily for help with marital issues or behavioral problems with their child.

The role of maternal alcoholism in the etiology of intellectual, physical, and academic disabilities in children has been well documented as fetal alcohol syndrome (FAS) (Streissguth, 1976). FAS has been identified only in children born to women who drank heavily while pregnant. Exposure to alcohol in utero can produce deleterious effects ranging from gross morphological anomalies to mental impairment (including retardation) to more subtle cognitive and behavioral dysfunctions (U.S. Department of Health and Human Services, 1990). Diagnosis is difficult because only the most severe cases are identifiable at birth.

EARLY WARNING SIGNS FOR CHILDREN AT RISK

Recent studies that examine risk factors for alcoholism have found interesting links between temperament and the eventual shift in later life to drinking problems. For example, hyperactive children are more likely than other children to have an alcoholic biological father (Cantwell, 1975). In fact, paternal alcoholism appears to be prevalent even when hyperactive children are raised by adoptive parents. This has led to the suggestion that alcoholism and hyperactivity may have a common genetic basis that places a person at increased risk for both disorders (Tarter, Alterman, & Edwards, 1985.) Male children of alcoholic fathers appear to be at particular risk (Tarter, Babene, Escallier, Larid, & Jacob, 1990). Short attention span and low task persistence may also mark vulnerability to alcoholism (Pihl and Peterson, 1991). Such tendencies may become more severe with parental divorce and neglect. Clinicians who are presented with a family exhibiting such behaviors need to be aware of the potential for alcoholism in one or both parents and alert the parent to their child's increased susceptibility.

One of the functions of family life is to provide children with emotional and physical safety and an environment within which normal developmental tasks can be completed. Addiction distorts normal family processes, skews family roles, and creates a climate in which fear, anger, mistrust, guilt, and sadness prevail. Such families tend to be alcohol focused rather than child focused. Normal dependency needs of children go unmet, and the child may experience a sense of chronic grief and loss that manifests itself in depression and a sense of being different or isolated from others.

Various authors have identified roles that children assume: the hero, lost child, adjuster, scapegoat, and mascot (Black, 1981). Each role generally identifies either an overresponsible or underresponsible pattern of behavior that represents the child's attempt to address the disorganization and inconsistency of the family environment. The assumption of a role appears to be based on one's birth order and gender, although it can change over time. While an understanding of such family roles is useful, the clinician should view each child's response as his or her attempt to cope with a traumatic situation. Adaptive behaviors were skills that were necessary to survive their childhood and can be quite useful in a later life cycle phase.

The presence of addiction places children at risk for a variety of abusive and neglectful situations, which must be carefully assessed. Sexual abuse, battering, and neglect are common experiences for the child in an alcoholic home. Over 70 percent of incest victims lived in alcoholic homes, and 69 percent of reported cases of battering and neglect were related to alcohol abuse (CASA, 1996).

WHEN A PARENT GETS SOBER

When parents achieve sobriety at this phase of the life cycle, there may be some interesting consequences for the family. A precocious 8-year-old once said, with much frustration, "There never used to be any rules in my family. Now, my Dad has stopped drinking, and there's rules all over the place!"

The impact of a parent becoming sober is powerful for all family members. In early sobriety, the family may experience the physical loss of the drinking parent, through either hospitalization or intense participation in AA.

If parents become sober while the children are young, the children may later have difficulty understanding that their parent is alcoholic, since they may not have a memory of him or her drinking. Children with memories, often traumatic, require thorough and repeated discussions over time about how the disease affected them. It may take a long time to rebuild the trust between family members and heal the often deep wounds left by drinking. Again, AA can be a vital support. For example, a tradition in AA and similar programs is to recognize time by celebrating at anniversary meetings, which family members are invited to attend. This is a powerful tool for healing in families, particularly at one- and two-year anniversary dates. Attendance by family therapists at such celebrations is a valuable learning experience and a supportive act on behalf of the client.

LAUNCHING CHILDREN AND MOVING ON

This phase typically takes place when parents are in their mid-forties to mid-sixties, and is commonly referred to as the "empty nest" phase. It is a stage that begins when the children start to leave home and ends with the couple living alone in preretirement. Huge changes are seen in the family during this time, with some members leaving and new members entering.

The impact of addiction is significant in this period because, in reestablishing themselves as a marital dyad, a couple is forced to face issues that perhaps were unresolved earlier in the marriage. Addiction may represent an attempt to avoid these issues. It may replace the children in the family triangle, or it may be that, although once tolerated, drinking now becomes a focus of concern for the nondrinking spouse. Changes in the expectations of or needs to avoid intimacy often occur at this stage. The equilibrium that evolved in the relationship changes dramatically. Midlife also forces most couples to cope with the loss of parents and extended family supports.

Midlife is the time when men and women are most likely to seek help for alcohol problems. Husbands of alcoholics rarely seek help for the wife's drinking. This tendency to deny the problem or to act protectively toward the wife is more typical of husbands than of the wives of alcoholic husbands. If the drinking spouse does not achieve sobriety at this time, divorce is often the result. Relationships with their grown children can be unpredictable at this time, since the alcoholic must now function for himself or herself after the divorce and often cannot.

The marriage may still be precarious even if sobriety is achieved. If the drinking had an early onset, the nondrinking spouse may feel that too much damage has occurred. The sober alcoholic may be like a totally new person to the nondrinking spouse. In the early sobriety phase of treatment, a total restructuring of the marriage is taking place. Again, the use of AA and Al Anon is critical in providing tools to such couples.

THE FAMILY IN LATER LIFE: ADDICTION AND THE ELDERLY

The 65 and over age group is the fastest-growing group in the United States as longevity increases and the effects of the baby boom birth rates become more apparent. In this life phase, both the adult and other family members must adapt to the shifting of power from older to younger family members. Loss is a concurrent and equally important theme.

The American Medical Association predicts that by the year 2000, 20 percent of the elderly population will be addicted to a substance. This means that if the alcoholism rates remain constant, there will be 50 percent more elderly alcoholic patients at the turn of the century than there were at the end of the 1970's. Currently, 83 percent of the elderly population takes some kind of medication, and 50 percent of those take some form of sedative (Allen, 1996).

Several aspects of aging may interfere with the detection of alcohol use problems among the elderly (Caracci & Miller, 1991). These include attitudes on the part of the patient, the physician, and the family, often dominated by denial and long-standing beliefs that alcoholism is a moral weakness or character defect. Further, symptoms of alcoholism at this life cycle phase, such as memory loss, bone fractures associated with falls, isolation, and depression, may be misdiagnosed as signs of the aging process.

In general, a growing isolation from family and peer supports tends to characterize the elderly, and this isolation could be defined as the major problem affecting the older person's adjustment to this life phase. Drinking may first become problematic for the person in retirement, it may become exacerbated during this phase, or it may recede as a problem. It is useful to classify alcoholism of the elderly into two subgroups: early onset, defined as that beginning before age 65 and having progressed since, and late onset, which began after age 65 (Maletta, 1982). Factors that contribute to the development of late-onset drinking problems include increased biological sensitivity to alcohol, late-life stresses, more free time, and pressure from peers in some retirement communities to increase alcohol intake (Alexander & Duff, 1988). The late-onset group is thought to be larger and is viewed as having a better prognosis. Drinking in this group is considered to be related more specifically to the stresses of aging and is seen as more responsive to therapeutic attempts to relieve those stresses.

The most distinctive feature of the early-onset drinker is the almost total social isolation that has occurred by age 65. The therapist should attempt to decrease isolation by helping the family to evolve solutions for providing the person with contact and support. The issue of who is responsible for what or whom must be dealt with, as should be the emotional factors in the family related to loss, grief, and unresolved anger. Both the family and the older person need to make productive use of community supports, and it should never be assumed that referral to AA or Al Anon is an unproductive suggestion because of the person's age. Some individuals may require detoxification and medical treatment for the physiological consequences of abusive drinking.

ASSESSMENT

Appropriate assessment of alcoholism and the staging of treatment should include a clear understanding of the following points (Bepko & Krestan, 1985):

1. Where is the addiction? Who uses, and with whom? When, and under what circumstances? How much do they use, and what changes occur as the result?
2. Who is most affected by the drinking or drug use? Is a son or daughter more anxious than a spouse? Is one parent more upset by a child's drug use?
3. Is it really an addiction? This question is always in the back of the family's mind, and while only the alcoholics/addicts themselves can make that determination, the clinician must also make this assessment and use the decision strategically. Diagnosis is critical, and if the clinician has a problem with this, he or she should seek help from a colleague or addiction professional.
4. In what phase is the drinking behavior? How long the person has been using, and how much? Assess whether the client can stop using without medical consequences.
5. In what life cycle stage is the individual who is drinking? An adolescent drinker represents different family dynamics and requires dif-

ferent treatment approaches than an elderly drinker.

6. In what generation of the family is the individual who drinks, and in what stage of the life cycle is the family this drinker is affecting? What developmental tasks have been accomplished by the drinker/family, and which seem to be arrested by the drinking?

7. What is the time lapse between the onset of the early warning signals of alcoholism and the presentation of the family for treatment? How many life cycle phases have occurred since the drinking began, and how have they been or not been resolved?

8. How does the family think about the drinking or drug use? Do they deny that it is a problem or think that it is the only problem?

9. How has the family adjusted to the drinking, and what solutions have already been tried?

10. Assess the degree to which the family has isolated itself.

11. What is the family history of both addiction and recovery?

12. Make a detailed and careful assessment of the patterns of overresponsibility and underresponsibility in the marriage or family.

There are several guidelines that the clinician should employ in treating families with addiction at any phase of the life cycle. First, remember that there is a range of drinking patterns that could constitute alcoholism; focus more upon the consequences of that person's drinking behavior and the ways in which other people in their lives describe it as problematic. In an illness such as alcoholism, an individual's pattern of heavy use, abstinence, and controlled drinking can vary greatly depending on personality, environment, and culture.

As part of the assessment, consider asking the active alcoholic to limit himself or herself to two drinks a night. Construct a clear contract around this whereby all parties understand that if the contract is broken and the person drinks more (even on a special occasion), the drinking will be viewed as problematic and not under the person's control. Similarly, a contract can be made not to drink for a period of time, usually 90 days, with the same stipulations. A clear part of the contract should be attendance at AA if the contract is broken. Encourage attendance at multiple AA groups. It would be wise for the clinician to educate himself or herself about the local AA community by attending open meetings and having the meeting book available in the office.

SUMMARY AND CONCLUSIONS

Alcoholism is a highly treatable disease. It is the task of the family therapist to keep this concept at the forefront of his or her work with families. A life cycle perspective is critical in providing the context for the clinician and family to begin to navigate through the complex interplay of factors that comprise this disease. We have attempted, through research data and clinical example, to provide the therapist with a map, relevant questions, tools, and a long-term vision.

We agree with George Vaillant (1995), who states, "The first step in treatment is hope…the second…is diagnosis" (p. 362). We thus encourage hope and an aggressive pursuit of a diagnosis that will frame the problem as an illness, not a moral weakness or personal shortcoming.

There are some significant problems in need of redress in the field of alcoholism research. First, most studies to date are of White men and thus cannot be generalized to women or other populations, who we know have different drinking patterns. Further, the field lacks any longitudinal studies, other than Vaillant's, which is again, of White men. We need to understand more fully the relationship between the development of this disease and gender, race, sexual orientation, and socioeconomic status. Many questions remain unanswered: Why does alcoholism peak at different phases of the life cycle, depending on one's race? What is it about being a Black or Hispanic man in middle age that contributes to alcohol dependence? What of the correlation in some groups between a rise in income and education and the development of alcoholism? How does poverty affect this?

Our hope is that the clinician will come to view addiction as an illness with serious, long-term, life-threatening consequences. Our challenge as family therapists is to remind families of the potential threat to their well-being that addiction represents, while simultaneously helping them to maintain a vision of recovery. Further, we must remind both ourselves and our clients that the alcoholic is more than a person with a disease: He or she is a mother, daughter, father, child, or grandparent who is loved despite the painful consequences of drinking.

REFERENCES

Adams, M. L., & Cicero, T. J. (1991). Effects of alcohol on beta-endorphin and reproductive hormones in the male rat. *Alcoholism: Clinical and Experimental Research, 15*(4), 685–692.

Alexander, E., & Duff, R. W. (1988). Social interaction and alcohol use in retirement communities. *Gerontologist, 28,* 632–638.

Allen, R. (1996). Alcoholism in the elderly. *Journal of the American Medical Association, 275*(10), 797–801.

Almeida, R., Woods, R., Messineo, T., Font, R., & Heer, C. (1994). *Violence in the lives of the racially and sexually different: A public and private dilemma in expansions of feminist theory through diversity.* New York: Hayworth Press.

Anderson, S. (1966). Substance abuse and dependency in gay men and lesbians. *Journal of Gay and Lesbian Social Services, 5*(1) 59–76.

Bachman, J. G., Wadsworth, K. N., O'Malley, P., Johnston, L. D., & Schulenberg, J. E. (1997). *Smoking, drinking and drug use in young adulthood: The impacts of new freedoms and new responsibilities.* Mahwah, NJ: Lawrence Erlbaum Associates.

Bepko, C., & Krestan, J. A. (1985). *The responsibility trap: A blueprint for treating the alcoholic family.* New York: Free Press.

Berenson, D. (1976). Alcohol and the family system. In P. Guerin (Ed.), *Family therapy: Theory and practice.* New York: Gardner Press.

Black, C. (1981). *It'll never happen to me!* New York: Ballantine Books.

Caetano, R. (1989). Drinking patterns and alcohol problems in a national sample of U.S. Hispanics. In D. L. Spiegler, D. A. Tate, S. S. Aitken, & C. M. Christian (Eds.), *Alcohol use among U.S. ethnic minorities: Proceedings of a conference on the epidemiology of alcohol use and abuse among ethnic minority groups* (pp. 147–162) (NIAAA Research Monograph No. 18. DHHS Pub. No. (ADM)89–1435). Washington, DC: U.S. Government Printing Office.

Cantwell, D. P. (1975). Genetic studies of hyperactive children: Psychiatric illness in biologic and adopting parents. In R. R. Fieve, D. Rosenthal, & H. Brill (Eds.), *Genetic research in psychiatry.* Baltimore: John Hopkins Press.

Caracci, G., & Miller, N. S. (1991). Epidemiology and diagnosis of alcoholism in the elderly: A review. *International Journal of Geriatric Psychiatry, 6*(7), 511–515.

Center for Addiction and Substance Abuse at Columbia University. (1996). Boomer parents appear resigned. *Columbia University Record, 22*(3).

Center for Addiction and Substance Abuse at Columbia University. (1997, August 13). *Substance abuse and the American adolescent.* [Press release].

Center for Reproductive Law and Policy. *Punishing women for their behavior during pregnancy.* New York: Reproductive Freedom in Focus.

Center for Substance Abuse Prevention (1994). *Violence.* Alcohol, tobacco and other drugs resource guide. U.S. Department of Health and Human Services.

Committee on Cultural Psychiatry. (1996). *Alcoholism in the United States: Racial and ethnic considerations.* (Report No. 141). Washington, DC: American Psychiatric Press.

Eigen, L. D. (1992). *Estimating and controlling the cost of alcohol-related injuries at the local level.* Paper presented to the Secretary's National Conference on Alcohol-Related Injuries, Washington, DC.

Forth-Finegan, J. L. (1991). Sugar & spice and everything nice: Gender socialization and women's addiction—A literature review. In C. Bepko (Ed.), *Feminism and Addiction* (pp. 19–48). New York: Hayworth Press.

Gilbert, S. (1997, September, 10). Youth study elevates family role. *New York Times,* p. 10.

Goodman, R. A., Istre, G. R., Jordan, F. B., Herndon, J. L., & Kelaghan, J. (1991). Alcohol and fatal injuries in Oklahoma. *Journal of Studies on Alcohol, 52*(2), 156–161.

Grant, B. F., Hartford, T. C., Chou, P., Pickering, R., Dawson, D. A., Stinson, F. S., & Noble, J. (1991). Epidemiologic Bulletin No. 27: Prevalence of DSM-III-R alcohol abuse and dependence: United States, 1988. *Alcohol Health & Research World 15*(1), 91–96.

Herd, D. (1990). Subgroup differences in drinking patterns among black and white men: Results from a national survey. *Journal of Alcohol Studies, 51*(3), 221–232.

Indian Health Service. (1992). *Trends in indian Health, 1991.* Rockville, MD: Indian Health Service.

Jellinek, E. M. (1960). *The disease concept of alcoholism.* New Haven, CT: College and University Press.

Johnston, L. D., O'Malley, P. M., & Bachman, J. G. (1991). *Drug use among American high school seniors, 1975–1990. Vol. 1: High school seniors.* (DHHS Pub. No. (ADM)91–1813). Washington, DC: U.S. Government Printing Office.

Kishline, A. (1996). *Moderate drinking: The moderation management guide for those who want to reduce their drinking.* New York: Crown.

Krestan, J. A. (1991). The baby and the bathwater. In T. J. Goodrich (Ed.), *Women and power: Perspectives for family therapy* (pp. 229–233). New York: W. W. Norton.

Krestan, J. A., and Bepko, C. (1991). Codependency: The social construction of female experience. In C. Bepko (Ed.), *Feminism and addiction* (pp. 49–65). New York: Hayworth Press.

Lerner, S. (1997). Chemical reaction. *Ms., 5*(1), 59–76.

Maletta, G. (1982) Alcoholism and the aged. In E. Pattison & E. Kaufman (Eds.), *Encyclopedic handbook of alcoholism.* New York: Gardner Press.

Merikangas, K. R. (1990). The genetic epidemiology of alcoholism. *Psychol Med, 20,* 11–22.

National Council on Alcoholism. (1976). Definition of alcoholism. *Annals of Internal Medicine, 85,* 764.

National Institute for Drug Abuse. (1990). *Substance abuse among Blacks in the U.S.* (Capsule 34).

National Institute for Drug Abuse. (1991). *Substance Abuse Among Hispanics.* (Capsule 30).

Permanen, K. (1991). *Alcohol in human violence.* New York: The Guilford Press.

Pihl, R. O., & Peterson, J. B. (1991). Attention deficit disorders, childhood conduct disorders, and alcoholism: Is there an association? *Alcohol Health & Research World, 15*(1), 25–31.

Steinglass, P. (1987). *The alcoholic family,* New York: Basic Books.

Tafoya, N., & Del Vecchio, A. (1996). Back to the future: An examination of the Native American holocaust experience. In M. McGoldrick, J. Giordano, & J. I. Pearce (Eds.), *Ethnicity and family therapy* (2nd Edition) (pp. 45–65). New York: The Guilford Press.

Tarter, R. E., Alterman, A. I., & Edwards, K. I. (1985). Vulnerability to alcoholism in men: A behavioral-genetic perspective. *Journal of Alcohol Studies, 35*(4), 329–336.

Tartar, R. E., Babene, M., Escallier, E. A., Larid, S. B., & Jacob, T. (1990). Temperament deviation and risk for alcoholism. *Alcoholism: Clinical Experimental Research, 14*(3), 380–382.

Trimpey, J. (1996). *Rational recovery: The new cure for substance abuse addiction.* New York: Pocket Books.

U.S. Department of Health and Human Services. (1990). *Seventh special report to the U.S. Congress on alcohol and health.* (DHHS Pub. No. (ADM)90–1656). Washington, DC: U.S. Government Printing Office.

Vaillant, G. E. (1983). *The natural history of alcoholism.* Cambridge, MA: Harvard University Press.

Vaillant, G. E. (1995). *The natural history of alcoholism revisited.* Cambridge, MA: Harvard University Press.

Wechsler, H. (1996, July/August). Alcohol and the American college campus: A report from the Harvard School of Public Health. *Change.*

Zinberg, N. E., Bean, M. (1981). Alcohol addiction: Toward a more comprehensive definition. In *Dynamic Approaches to the Understanding and Treatment of Alcoholism* (pp. 97–127). M. H. Bean & N. E. Zinberg (Eds.), New York: The Free Press.

CHAPTER 28

VIOLENCE AND THE
FAMILY LIFE CYCLE

MONICA McGOLDRICK
MARY ANNE BROKEN NOSE
MILDRED POTENZA

Today the fear of danger on the streets at the hands of strangers is as strong as ever.... And there is very real danger in the streets...But the cruel irony...is that the real danger of personal attack is in the home...You are more likely to be physically assaulted, beaten, and killed in your own home at the hands of a loved one than anyplace else, or by anyone else in our society.

—R. J. Gelles & M. A. Straus

Unfortunately, violence is a widespread occurrence in families throughout the life cycle in our society as it is in all other patriarchal cultures. It is primarily directed toward women, children, and the elderly, which will be the focus of this chapter. While men experience violence throughout the life cycle, most of it occurs outside the home. The effect of this on the way men relate in intimate and familial relationships is an important and complex topic, unfortunately beyond the scope of this chapter (Barnett, Miller-Perrin, & Perrin, 1997). We do know, for example, that men who are violent with nonfamily members are not necessarily abusive of their wives and children. We can also see that as a culture we encourage male aggression and in some ways have made it a central part of male identity. Male violence is glorified in the media and intertwined with sports, such as football and boxing. Indeed, it has been reported that wife abuse within the home is highest on the night of the Superbowl. Women are also violent at times, often abusing those most dependent on them. They have a high rate of lashing out physically against male and lesbian partners, although less often in ways

that harm them. Sibling violence is also very prevalent and serious with some studies indicating rates as high as 40 percent (Barnett et al., 1997). One of the most widespread forms of violence in the family is corporal punishment. The irony of corporal punishment is that it almost invisible; it is seen as unremarkable, because almost everyone has been spanked or spanks (Straus, 1994). Loving parents regularly and deliberately assault their children, when their children do not do what the parents want. For half of American children, being hit and spanked will be a regular part of their lives from the time they are infants until they are well into their teens (Straus, 1994). It is in the home, at the hands of those who love us the most, that we learn the moral rightness of violence.

To assess issues of abuse in any particular family at any life cycle stage or transition, it is essential to address the societal arrangements that foster oppression and violence by those with power against those with less power: men against women, dominant groups against gays and lesbians, and so forth. We must also assess the various forms of violence: from racial violence to date rape to emotional neglect, from the rages of an alcoholic father of three young children to the intimidating refusal of a 67-year-old man to give his 65-year-old wife any information about or control over their finances. Clinicians must be on guard to assess all couples for the ways in which power, intimidation, and threats of abuse as well as violence itself may organize a couple's relationship and, indeed, all the relationships in a family.

Violence in the family is not just aggression; it is abuse of power. The statistics show clearly that within families, it operates on the basis of the strongest victimizing the weakest. Thus, the greatest volume of abuse is directed against the weakest children, children under the age of 6 (Finkelhor, 1983). The most likely abuser is the more powerful parent: the father. The same is true of spouse abuse; the stronger tends to victimize the weaker. In families in which the woman has less power by virtue of not being in the labor force or having less education, she is at higher risk of abuse. All forms of family abuse occur in the context of psychological abuse and exploitation, a process that victims sometimes describe as "brainwashing" (Finkelhor, 1983). Abuse is clearly associated with family isolation—lack of community ties, friendships, and organizational affiliations (Gelles & Cornell, 1990; Straus & Steinmetz, 1980). It has also been institutionally supported. For example, the dominant churches in the United States have encouraged the use of corporal punishment as an appropriate way of teaching children to "respect authority" (Greven, 1990), and corporal punishment of children is allowed by law in every state in the United States, although some states, such as Texas, qualify this by saying that it must not be "deadly" (Straus, 1994).

In assessing families throughout the life cycle, we must be careful to examine the hidden ways in which abuse, overt and dramatic, as well as subtle forms of intimidation and control, may be organizing family behavior. We must also be attuned to the patterns of violence in different contexts, depending on class, culture, gender, and life cycle phase. Families of color experience double jeopardy, being at once oppressed by both institutional racism and patriarchal oppression. Similarly, gay and lesbian relationships occur within a homophobic society in which their relationships are stigmatized, gay bashing is common, and no legal recognition or protection is offered. Traditional cultures and religions often condone a degree of marital violence. Over 80 percent of women on welfare have experienced domestic violence (Raphael & Tolman, 1997). Having her own money and her own connections is highly protective for a woman against patriarchal abuse. Those without skills, status, money or social connections generally have nowhere to go to avoid abuse (see Figure 28.1 on page 472).

WHY INTERVENTION MUST ADDRESS SOCIAL ACCOUNTABILITY

Abuse and the tolerance of abuse tend to be taught in families from generation to generation. But, like all gender and cultural inequalities, though transmitted through the family, they are generally social issues, not evolving at the interior of the family. Thus, as Almeida and Bograd (1991) have put it,

> *Treatment strategies aimed at shifting the power imbalance within the family alone, without accompanying social sanctions, run the grave risk of entering into a covert alliance with the abuser.... When clinicians only investigate and reconstruct past psychological traumas of abusive men, they beg questions of the men's social responsibility for their violence. (p. 244)*

Therefore, our primary interventions with an abusive father must not relate to questions about his father. That would particularize issues of a social nature. Once the transgenerational patterns of violence are articulated in therapy with a couple in which the husband has abused his wife, treatment has tended to neutralize the husband's accountability, focusing on the couple's joint victimization. Although violence plays out in the interior of the family, it is not an intrafamilial issue (Cleage, 1990; Almeida, Wood, Messineo, & Font, 1998). A man is not violent primarily because his father was violent toward him, but rather because we live in a society that condones violence. While our interventions are obviously directed at changing intrafamilial behaviors, the primary understandings

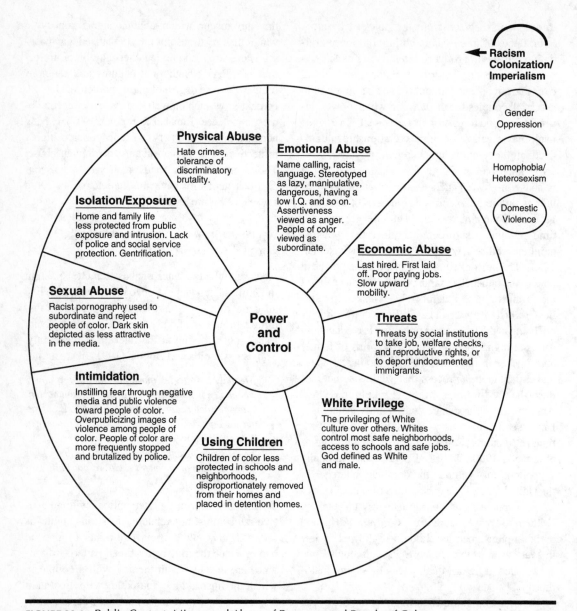

FIGURE 28.1   Public Context: Misuse and Abuse of Power toward People of Color.

Adapted from Almeida, R., Woods, R., Messineo, T., & Font, R. (1992). *Power wheels: The cultural context model.* Somerset, N.J.: Institute for Family Services.

of these problems that we need to convey are social rather than familial. This is an important distinction. Many therapists have failed to relate their therapies sufficiently to the social dynamics of patriarchy, orienting themselves instead to intrapsy-chic issues or the family of origin as the source of primary understanding of a man's violent behavior and a woman's tolerance of it.

The primary context for helping men at all phases of the life cycle to understand and change their patterns of abuse requires placing them in the larger social context and offering them the opportunity to change their behavior in spite of all the societal forces that may support their abuse or pressure them not be accountable for their violence (Almeida et al., 1998; Kivel, 1992). For example, when others label them as "sissies," "wimps," or "fags" for being nonassertive, men are being covertly pressured to undervalue their mothers, sisters, wives, and children and to treat them with disrespect.

There are often wide discrepancies in estimates of family violence, which, until recently, was a well-hidden problem in the U.S. Official estimates of family violence throughout the life cycle are shockingly high, but as we know, many incidents of abuse are never reported, and it is very difficult to get the full picture of its prevalence.

Throughout the life cycle, intimate relationships are much more dangerous for women than for men. Men are more often victimized by strangers, whereas most violence against women is perpetrated by family members, boyfriends, and acquaintances, and these acts usually occur in or near a women's home (Bachman & Saltzman, 1995; Craven, 1997). Violence in the form of corporal punishment against children has been the norm and sexual abuse of children tragically widespread, while abuse of elders appears to be on the increase.

YOUNG ADULTHOOD

- As many as 50 percent of college students are estimated to have been the victims of physical aggression by a dating partner (Pedersen & Thomas, 1992; Stacy, Schandel, Flannery, & Conlon 1994).
- A survivor of acquaintance rape said, "Every day, I sat next to him in class. Every day I passed him in the hallway—the man who raped me. There was nothing I could do. He was a football hero. No one would ever believe me."

Sexual harassment, courtship violence, and acquaintance rape are painful experiences that scar the psyches of their victims. They are experienced on a personal level but in a social environment that tolerates and even encourages their occurrence and denies the enormity of their impact. This promotes self-blame and erodes self-confidence, making it difficult for young people to accomplish the tasks intrinsic to young adulthood, that is, becoming independent and developing careers and intimate relationships. The term "sexual harassment" covers a wide range of behavior, from lewd remarks and dirty jokes to unwanted physical contact and rape. It takes place in the workplace, in schools, and in everyday social situations. Statistics indicate that one out of two women will be harassed during her academic or working life (Fitzgerald, 1993). Women in traditionally male occupations suffer the most (Mansfield, Koch, Henderson, & Vicary, 1991). Sexual harassment creates insecurity and a hostile, threatening work environment for women (Charney & Russell, 1994). Many are not sure how to respond and few file formal complaints. Clinical fallout includes self-blame, the loss of self-esteem, depression, and disempowerment (Hoyer, 1994; Spratlen, 1988). In practical terms, the therapist can act as a coach, rehearsing coping strategies and encouraging clients to get legal advice, learn about their companies' sexual harassment policies, and network with other women to empower themselves against the invalidation of such experiences.

One of the most insidious forms of sexual harassment that women encounter is acquaintance rape. We live in a rape-supportive culture (Koss, 1989; Schwartz & De Keseredy, 1997). Many people think that in certain circumstances, it is okay for a man to force a women to have sex, for example, if they have been dating a long time, if they have had sex before, or if she has "led him on" (Cassidy & Hurrell, 1995; Schwartz & De Keseredy, 1997; Shortland & Goodstein, 1992). Rape myths, such as that a woman "asked to be raped," liked it, or could have stopped it, are widely accepted and are reinforced in popular pornography. Formal and informal male social groups, such as fraternities, sports team, or even the men at the local bar can reinforce the importance of sexual conquest and promote the objectification of women, creating an environment in which rape is acceptable for their members (Schwartz & De Keseredy, 1997). In response to the recent awareness of the epidemic proportions of acquaintance rape, many colleges have initiated rape prevention programs, but these changes are not enough, since the broader social attitudes that allow such behaviors have not changed (Frazier, Valtinson, & Candell, 1994). Young women often do not identify dating violence as abuse and rarely report it to the police, though they frequently confide in friends. Indeed, while it seems counterintuitive, violence seems to increase with the length of the relationship and the depth of commitment (Pedersen & Thomas, 1992). Women often feel that they are as much to blame as their male partners, and men seem more than willing to have them take the blame (LeJeune & Follette, 1994). Women who have more traditional sex-role attitudes are more likely to stay in an abusive relationship (Flynn, 1990). Therefore, it is important in working with young women to focus on how romantic ideals and acceptance of traditional gender roles may be influencing their tolerance of dating violence. This helps to make them conscious of the power dynamics in their relationships and the ways in which they may be controlled by their partner. Conflicts that frequently trigger violence such as jealousy, the use of alcohol, disagreements about sexual intimacy, and verbal abuse also reflect power inequities in couple relationships (Lanner, 1990).

The term "date rape" is truly a misnomer because it implies a romantic relationship between the assailant and the perpetrator. A more appropriate term might be "acquaintance rape." The most common assailants are male friends (Wiehe & Richards, 1995), boyfriends, neighbors, bosses, and fellow employees. Many rapes nationwide occur in the workplace (Bachman, 1994). Women often blame themselves and feel too ashamed to tell anyone. Because acquaintance rape is a betrayal by someone a woman trusts, it can be more psychologically damaging than stranger rape. Survivors frequently experience the symptoms associated with other severe traumas (Petrectic-Jackson & Tobin, 1996). Understandably, rape survivors frequently have difficulty trusting men and have problems with sexual intimacy, expressed by a lack of interest in sex or compulsive sexual activity.

It is important to establish an emotionally safe environment in the wake of a rape. Medical issues and legal options should be explored. It is vital that those around the survivor believe her and not reinforce societal blaming of the victim (Davis, Brickman, & Baker, 1991; Ullman, 1996). Parents, devastated by what has happened, often close down the issue of the rape trauma. Male relatives, intimates, and friends frequently respond in a stereotypical fashion, becoming outraged and preoccupied with thoughts of revenge. Family therapy provides an opportunity for those closest to the survivor to express their feelings and provide genuine support for the victim. Family therapy with the abuser, when possible, similarly expands the potential for social accountability.

> A young man who had been arrested, but not convicted, for participating in a fraternity group rape of a woman at a college fraternity party was coached to have an accountability session with his parents, his siblings, and his wife regarding his participation in this behavior. His parents had initially minimized his actions and stopped discussing the assault as soon as the police backed off. He spoke to his family about his responsibility as a man to be different and to urge other men to be different so that his daughters, and other women would grow up in a different world.

Gay relationships are also plagued by courtship violence and acquaintance rape. This can be especially stressful because they occur within a homophobic environment that offers few resources and supports. Gay men and lesbians also suffer the added insult of being victimized by hate crime. In one survey 75 percent of gay college students said they had been the victims of verbal abuse and 25 percent had been threatened with violence (D'Augelli, 1989). The Anti-Violence Project (1997), a group that monitors such attacks, reports that there is an increase in hate crimes whenever the media or political groups focus on the gay community and that most of the victims of these crimes are young adults (see Figure 28.2).

Interventions with young adults can have a profound influence on the types of relationships

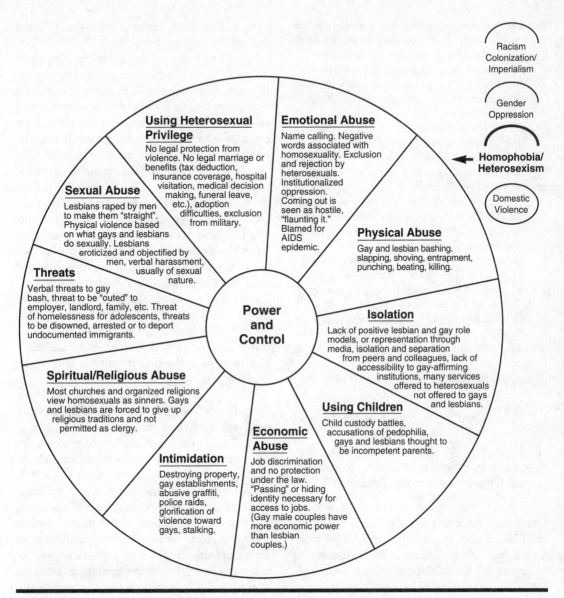

FIGURE 28.2   Public Context: The Misuse and Abuse of Power toward Lesbians and Gays

Adapted from Almeida, R., Woods, R., Messineo, T., & Font, R. (1992). *Power wheels: The cultural context model.* Somerset, N.J.: Institute for Family Services.

they will form at this stage and other stages of their lives.

Marie O'Hara, who sought help for problems with her parents, gradually acknowledged that her father had been violent to her mother, herself, and

her siblings throughout her childhood. Marie was now dating a man who was very jealous and had begun to shove her around. We made many interventions to increase her consciousness about the societal dimensions of abuse. Within a few months, she developed the courage to call for help when her boyfriend became belligerent in a public place, a courageous action that went very much against the grain of her Irish family background. The police came to the scene, and she left the boyfriend in their custody, finding her own way home.

Later, she became engaged to a very different sort of man. By this point, she had the courage to request of her father and her brother that they not participate in her fiancé's bachelor party if the activities became dehumanizing to women. Such a party did occur. Her fiancé left in protest, but her brother and father remained. Marie brought her father and brother into family therapy to confront them. Using the support of her sister and mother, she was able to hold them accountable and express how their actions had hurt and angered her. Her brother refused to accept responsibility and walked out of the session, but her father, with some coaching, was able to apologize to her for breaking his promise and to support her in her wish to have a very different type of relationship with men in the future. He also agreed to try to help his son understand the implications of his behavior.

NEWLY FORMED COUPLE RELATIONSHIPS

- Every nine seconds a woman in the United States is physically abused by her husband (Commonwealth Fund, 1993).
- Researchers have found that even one incident of abuse can organize a couple's relationship for the rest of the marriage (Straus, 1978).

The statistics are alarming. An estimated 3.9 million American women are abused by their husband or intimate partner every year (Commonwealth Fund, 1993). Aggression occurs in one third to one half of all marriages (Straus & Steinmetz, 1980). Women are at times highly aggressive as well, but the type of aggression they use (a slap, push, verbal put-down, or threat) is less emotionally and physically damaging than the acts of violence men use toward women. Women are twice as likely as men to be killed by a spouse or partner (Craven, 1996). And women who do kill their spouses have generally been battered themselves for years, although, ironically, women who murder their spouses are often given longer sentences than men who murder their wives. Domestic violence affects

women of all races, most all of those who are young and poor (Bachman & Saltzman, 1995). The incidence of violence in gay and lesbian relationships is believed to be similar to that among heterosexuals (Barnett, Miller-Perrin, & Perrin, 1997), but for them as for couples of color, the prejudice that they are likely to encounter from legal and social agencies means that they are at greater risk with fewer resources than other families (see Figure 28.2).

Domestic violence takes many forms. Until recently, the general consensus was that sex between a husband and wife could not be rape, since the wife had consented to sex when she took her marriage vows. Until 1976, no man could be charged with raping his wife. In fact, marital rape is often repeated throughout the marriage and tends to be more brutal than stranger rape and frequently involves forced anal sex and the use of objects in the vagina (Bergen, 1996; Campbell & Alford, 1989; Russell, 1990). Research indicates that at least one out of seven married women report that they have experienced marital rape or attempted marital rape (Russell, 1990).

Young women often feel that "love will conquer all," not realizing that violence at the beginning of a marriage is an indication of what is to come. Batterers are notorious for their sincere displays of contrition and can be very charming, attentive, and seductive. Warning signs such as possessiveness and irrational jealousy are commonly misinterpreted as indications of love. Sudden outbursts of rage can easily be attributed to stress. Given the pressure on newlyweds to make the relationship work, it is easy to view abusive incidents as aberrations rather than as the beginning of a pattern. In assessing newly formed couples, the therapist should be alert to a past history of abuse. Violence that begins in courtship is likely to continue into the marriage (Arias, Samois, & O'Leary, 1987). Assessment of power arrangements and especially psychological abuse is particularly important in newly formed couples, because these may be setting a dangerous pattern, which will intensify over time.

Couple relationships have many dimensions, including economics; sexuality; the continuum of

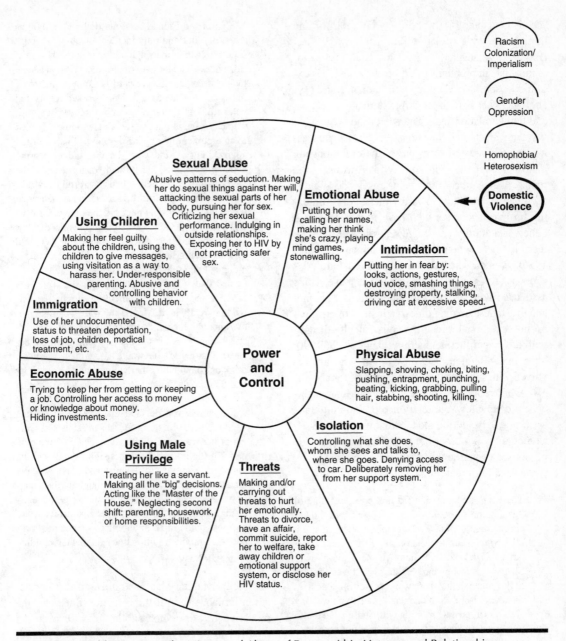

FIGURE 28.3 Public Context: The Misuse and Abuse of Power within Heterosexual Relationships

Adapted from Almeida, R., Woods, R., Messineo, T., & Font, R. (1992). *Power wheels: The cultural context model.* Somerset, N.J.: Institute for Family Services.

power sharing, from partnership to male dominance; boundaries around the couple in relation to extended family, work, friends, and religion; child-

rearing; arrangements regarding chores and leisure activities; emotional connectedness; dependence; control; and physical power (Almeida et al., 1998;

see also Chapter 14). Abuse may be a part of any these in a couple's relationship. The power wheel (Figure 28.3) adapted by Almeida et al. (1998) for clinical use in problems of domestic violence is extremely useful for assessing both violence and psychological abuse in the multiple domains of couple and family relationships. The wheel can be given to partners (in separate meetings) to get their assessment of the power dimensions of their relationship. Who is making the decisions? Who is managing the money? How are conflicts being resolved? What is each partner's attitude toward violence or intimidation in marriage. Men who have more patriarchal beliefs and attitudes and rigid sex role identities are more likely to become violent (Coleman & Straus, 1986). Women who have more traditional attitudes about sex roles are more apt to tolerate abuse. Traits associated with batterers include jealousy, alcohol and drug abuse, mental illness, a history of criminal assault, emotional insecurity, and difficulty dealing with anger, conflict, and stress (Davidovich, 1990; Tolman & Bennett, 1990). Women who are involved with such men are at greater risk for abuse.

Even relatively incidental threats can influence a couple's whole relationship, and clinicians are urged to be alert to the fact that women, as well as men, may not describe their relationship as one of abuse, even though it may be organized by power and intimidation:

> The case of Sharon and Ed is a good example of this. Sharon was being seen in therapy for mild but chronic depression. The therapist noticed that Ed seemed to speak for Sharon more than she did for herself. He also had many theories about why Sharon was feeling the way she was. It was obvious to the clinician that there was a power imbalance in the relationship. Both partners denied there was any abuse. In a separate meeting with Sharon, the therapist first normalized the possibility of violence, stating that in many marriages one partner may lash out at another. She asked specific questions:
> Did Ed ever hit you? No.
> Punch You? No.
> Kick you? No.
> Shove you? Hmm. Well, one time, but it was a long time ago, just after we got married. Sharon then described what had happened.

> Sharon and Ed had been married for six months when the first and only incident of physical abuse occurred in their marriage. It was the Fourth of July. Ed, who worked long hours as a supervisor at a local factory, was looking forward to going to the town fireworks display. Sharon, who worked nights and weekends as a nurse at a community hospital, wanted to spend the day relaxing at home. This led to an argument in which Ed accused Sharon of not appreciating all the work he did and not caring about his feelings. He pushed Sharon against the wall and threatened her with his fist. Frightened, she agreed to go to the fireworks. Sharon said later that it was not the physical hurt, but the rage in his eyes that scared her. They went to the fireworks display. Ed apologized for getting rough with her, and Sharon, seeing his mood improve, became a little indignant and told him that she never wanted to be treated that way again. But inside, she wondered whether she had done something wrong. Ed was working really hard. Maybe she wasn't being sensitive enough. She talked to her mother, who said that every man loses his temper now and then and advised Sharon that he was a good man, he didn't drink or go out with other women, and he didn't hit her. Sharon also talked to her sister, who said that she should have fought back and shouldn't put up with that. Sharon decided that she loved Ed and would forgive him this one transgression. She went out of her way to show her appreciation, taking on more of the household responsibility and cooking his favorite meals. Ed never pushed or physically threatened Sharon again. But throughout their marriage, whenever Ed seemed on the verge of really losing his temper, Sharon would rush to fix whatever was bothering him. Going to see the fireworks became a family tradition that Ed and their children looked forward to every summer.

Neither Ed nor Sharon would consider their relationship abusive. Yet this situation illustrates the pervasive way in which subtle abuse or even the threat of abuse can organize a whole relationship. It also reminds us of the detailed questioning often necessary to clarify the history of abuse. Clarifying the history allows the clinician to formulate an appropriate treatment plan that takes into account the way abuse has organized the internal life of the family.

Conjoint therapy with abusive couples at this or any stage in the life cycle can actually be dangerous.

It may escalate violence, leading to retaliation for events disclosed by the victim in therapy. We strongly recommend that violence be dealt with only in a comprehensive program that emphasizes the safety of the victim, offers separate groups for victim and abuser, and has a strong socioeducational component to educate family members about the social aspects of violence (Almeida et al., 1998).

One of the best programs developed to address violent behavior has been developed by Rhea Almeida and her colleagues (Almeida, 1993; Almedia & Bograd, 1991; Almeida et al, 1998; Almeida, Woods, Messineo, Font, & Heer, 1994) in Somerset, New Jersey. This program is organized around men's groups and women's groups (called "culture circles"), which emphasize social accountability, equitable family relationships, and the development of a community to counter the dominant culture's proviolence attitudes. To break through the denial that is typical of those entering the program, each partner separately attends a socioeducational group for eight weeks, focusing on the way in which social forces of power and oppression cultivate and condone abuse. This approach contextualizes the couple's relationship before they begin to address their personal problems and offers them the possibility of seeing how their ways of relating have been shaped by influences outside their individual personalities and situations.

Young couples need to learn to look at their relationship in a social context. In a group, batterers, who tend to minimize and deny their actions, are confronted by other men who are becoming accountable for their own violent behavior. The supportive environment of the group encourages the batterer to take responsibility for his actions and change his way of relating to his own and other children. The women's group uses a holistic approach to cope with the multiple needs of battered women. Legal information on how to get a restraining order, find a lawyer, or get child support is provided. Therapeutic issues—grief over losing the dream of a happy marriage, self-contempt for tolerating the abuse, anger at the abuser—are addressed. Ordinary practical concerns—how to monitor children's homework, budget a diminished income, or deal with the auto mechanic—are also discussed. For the most part, the people providing this information and support are not the professionals who facilitate the group but other women who have also been victimized by domestic violence. Family members and significant others are invited to provide support or help the therapeutic process. New members learn not only how abuse has permeated their entire relationship, but also how to deal with it. The strength and success of members, who act as sponsors, serve as proof that the women's lives can improve, whether or not the abuser changes or the relationship survives. This process is especially helpful in debunking many of the romantic beliefs that encourage young women to stay in abusive relationships.

Family therapy with newly formed couples needs to focus also on their relationships with their families of origin. Family members who can provide support should become part of the healing process. Violence in the family can be seen within the background of the past generation's ethnicity, beliefs about sex roles, financial, and social circumstances. This understanding should not be used to excuse abusive behavior or minimize its effect on the client, but rather as a starting point in facing what has happened, helping clients to confront abusive relationships in their families of origin as well. The process of confrontation requires careful coaching and depends on the particular history and relationships in each family.

FAMILIES WITH YOUNG CHILDREN

- Almost all American children have been hit by their parents, often for many years. For at least one in five and perhaps almost half, hitting begins in infancy and continues until they leave home. The laws in every state allow parents to hit their children with hairbrush or belt as long as no serious injury results and 28 percent of parents of children age 8 to 10 still hit their children with such instruments (Straus, 1994).
- 50 percent of homeless women and children are fleeing abuse (Zorza, 1991).

- 16 percent of females raped in 1992 were under the age of 12 (Langan & Harlow, 1992).
- Child protective services receive an estimated 2 million reports of child abuse each year (U.S. Department of Health and Human Services (USDHH), 1997).
- It is estimated that five children in the United States die every day because of abuse and neglect (USDHH, 1995).
- Estimates are that over 200,000 children were sexually abused in 1993 (Sedlak & Broadhurst, 1996).

The enormous responsibility of raising children changes a couple's relationship forever. If violence has already been a dynamic, it is likely to increase at this point. Indeed, it is quite common for men to begin abusing their wives during pregnancy. This may be because of the anticipated burdens of the child, because of the wife's new focus away from exclusive devotion to the husband, or perhaps because she is more dependent (Bohn, 1990). Pregnancy also offers no protection from marital rape (Bergen, 1996; Russell, 1990). As their families grow, mothers may leave work because of the expense or lack of daycare, a situation that leaves them especially vulnerable. Women who do not work outside the home, who earn less than 25 percent of the family income, and who have young children at home are at highest risk of abuse (Kalmus & Straus, 1990).

Men who batter their wives may begin abusing their children. Sometimes, this serves as a turning point in the relationship; danger to the children is the most frequently cited reason battered women give for leaving their abuser (Hilton, 1992). Unfortunately, not being able to support those children independently is the most frequent reason they return (Gondolf & Fisher, 1988; Okun, 1986). Even if they are not the target, children who live in violent homes are at high risk of physical and psychological injury. They often feel impelled to try to make peace between their parents or to protect whomever they perceive to be the victim. This puts them in the direct line of fire. The lives of children who witness marital violence are filled with fear. In a sense, they lose both parents. Their fathers are emotionally distant (Holden & Ritchie, 1991). Their mothers are often depressed, anxious, ill, and focused on the behavior of the abuser, with little emotional energy left for their children. It is estimated that up to 10 million children between the ages of 3 and 17 have witnessed parental violence (Straus, 1991).

The relationship between parent and child is socially determined. Historically and culturally, there has been wide variety in what is considered an appropriate parent-child relationship. Children have been seen as a blessing, an obligation, or a burden. What is considered abuse in one setting is seen as good parenting in another. In ancient Greece and Rome, child prostitution was acceptable and legal (Kahr, 1991). Male babies are more highly valued in many societies. Female infanticide has been a common practice in both European and Asian cultures. Little girls everywhere are raised differently from little boys, the most patriarchal cultures being the most oppressive of young girls' development (DeYoung & Ziegler, 1994). Child-rearing practices in the United States have always strongly endorsed corporal punishment. The most vocal advocates of corporal punishment at home and in school today are fundamentalist Christians (Greven, 1990). Corporal punishment is still legal and practiced in school systems in many states, mostly in the South. The states that have the strongest commitment to the use of force for morally legitimate purposes have the highest rates of rape and child abuse. Thus it is a serious issue that so much of the violence conducted against children is carried out by morally righteous people (Straus, 1994). If we lower the amount of corporal punishment of those parents who routinely practice it, we could lower the level of child abuse dramatically. The more people were hit by their parents in their early teens, the more likely they were to be depressed and think of suicide. Corporal punishment contributes to a sense of powerlessness and a lack of internalized moral standards. It also interferes with the likelihood of graduating from college or earning a good income and leads to more troubled child behavior in many dimensions (Straus, 1994). Straus in his extensive study demonstrates that not spanking is in many ways much more conducive to the goals parents hope to attain by spanking. Nonspanking parents are less likely to ignore misbehavior and better able to maintain strong bonds with their children (1994).

Child abuse occurs among all cultures, races, and economic groups. Sadly, the highest rates are among the youngest and poorest children and those who are disabled (Sedlak & Broadhurst, 1996; US-DHH, 1993). Perpetrators of child abuse are usually parents or stepparents who are struggling with addictions, emotional problems, poverty, or other stresses (Dore, Doris, & Wright, 1995; Murphy, Jellinek, Quinn, & Smith 1991; Sedlak & Broadhurst, 1996; Whipple & Webster-Stratton, 1991).

Sexual abuse is defined as interactions between a child and adult or an older child with the goal of the sexual gratification or stimulation of the perpetrator. This covers a wide range of behaviors such as intercourse, fondling, viewing pornography, or posing for pornographic pictures. Because of the secretive nature of sexual abuse, it is believed that most incidents go unreported. Children are vulnerable to sexual abuse from earliest childhood. The most common abusers are family members and others known to the family. The highest number of reports are for children between the ages of 9 and 11 (Sedlak & Broadhurst, 1996). But infants and toddlers are also abused. The rate for girls is at least three times higher than that for boys (Sedlak & Broadhurst, 1996). Boys are even more reluctant to admit to sexual abuse than girls and are often perceived as being less damaged by the experience. They are less likely to receive counseling or be removed from their abusive homes (Black & De Blassie, 1993). This lack of support for boys is particularly disturbing in light of the fact that most perpetrators have a history of having been sexually abused themselves. Male perpetrators of sexual abuse tend to abuse a much higher number of boys over their life course than do men who abuse girls. Children are often threatened by their abuser or made to feel that they have caused the abuse themselves. The long-term effects of sexual abuse include depression, posttraumatic stress disorder (PTSD), anxiety, and problems with sexual relations (Elliot & Brierre, 1992). These problems may be exacerbated by the frequency of the abuse, the kind of sexual activity, the age at onset, the child-abuser relationship, the number of perpetrators, their gender, and whether or not the sexual abuse occurred within the context of other forms of abuse (Heath, Bean, & Freinauer 1996).

The role of the family at this stage in the life cycle is to provide a safe, supportive environment for the growth and nurturance of children. Violence and abuse are incongruent with these tasks. The primary goal of therapy is to help the family to create a safe environment for children by realigning and restructuring the power dynamics within the system. Roles are often reversed in violent homes, with children trying to protect their mother or siblings. Changes in these roles are often met with great resistance. Mothers need to be supported and empowered. Children in abusive homes are often impaired in their emotional and psychosocial development.

Assessment of children's safety is not always easy and requires a different set of skills and knowledge than those needed for work with adults. The therapist must be aware of the norms of development for young children. For example, certain behaviors, such as sexual play or victimization of other children, excessive masturbation, seductive behavior, and genital exposure, are associated with sexual abuse in both preschool and school-age children. Most mothers of incest victims take immediate steps to protect their children, often at great emotional cost to themselves. When there is sexual abuse, which is more often committed by fathers and even more by stepfathers, who play a central role in the emotional, financial, and psychological life of the family, children may feel that by seeking help, they are betraying someone they love and endangering the well-being of the entire family. Other family members may blame the child for talking. It is essential in treating incest that the positive aspects of the victim's and other family members' relationship with the abuser be acknowledged while holding the perpetrator responsible for the abuse and its impact on the child and family. For this reason, treatment programs require that the perpetrator admit to his behavior before relationships can continue. Since protection of the child is paramount, they also require that the offending parent not have unsupervised access to the children.

Children who are being physically abused may have intellectual impairments, learning problems, difficulty concentrating in school, or developmental delays (Barnett et al., 1997). Children who experience or witness abuse at home often exhibit aggressive behavior, which interferes with both their school and social life. Attention needs to be paid to emotional issues underlying these problem behaviors. Very young children may not be able to express themselves verbally; older children often do not respond well to direct questions. Story telling, family puppets, and the use of art and dolls can be effective in gathering information (Gil, 1994). Play therapy and group therapy help children to develop their social skills and deal with their fears, anxiety, depression, and shame.

Ideally, all family members, including the abuser, should be involved in treatment. This does not always happen, and participation in a program does not mean that the abuse will stop. Sometimes, it is necessary for a woman to end the relationship to keep the children safe. The maintenance of a safe home, acknowledging the importance of the abuser's relationships with all family members, and the separation of the abuser from the victim until it is certain that contact will not result in the revictimization of the child are guidelines that apply to work with physically and sexually abused children and those who witness domestic violence.

Therapists should have an understanding of ethnicity, parenting beliefs, and stress levels. They should explore support systems, including extended family and friends, who might be incorporated into treatment plans. While legal definitions of child abuse vary from state to state, all have mandatory reporting laws requiring clinicians to notify the authorities if they suspect abuse. It is important for a clinician to understand these laws and to know what kind of services child protective agencies can offer in their area. Couples with young children need to know that disclosure of psychological, physical, or sexual abuse requires action on the part of the therapist.

Many parents feel that the use of physical punishment is an appropriate way of disciplining a child but are not aware of how dangerous this can be, especially with young children. Most of the children who die from child abuse are under the age of 5; of those, the largest percentage are under the age of 1 (USDHH, 1995). Sometimes, parents have unrealistic expectations about how a child should behave. The clinician can coach parents on management of problem behaviors and help parents to develop a sense of competency in dealing with their children. Battered women often underestimate the amount of violence their children see. When helped to realize how it affects the children, they usually take steps to reduce their exposure.

Women with young children who try to leave their abuser may face seemingly insurmountable obstacles. Cultural norms pressure women not to break up the family; the extended family, especially that of the abusive husband, may not be supportive of her decision to leave. Mothers do not always receive child support, and many are impoverished by divorce. Courts frequently refuse to consider spousal abuse an issue when considering custody. Fathers may try to manipulate the legal system to their advantage in custody, alimony, child support and visitation negotiations. Finally, the woman's safety may be in great jeopardy when she separates. These times are, in fact, the most dangerous for women and are the periods when they are most at risk for increased violence and fatal assault. Harassment, threats, and abuse may continue in spite of divorce, separation, or restraining orders (Craven, 1996).

FAMILIES WITH ADOLESCENTS

- As a group, children between the ages of 12 and 15 have the greatest risk of any age group of being the victim of a violent crime (Bastian, 1995).
- Young Black men between the ages of 12 and 24 are fourteen times more likely to be murdered than the rest of the population (Bastian & Taylor, 1994).
- A recent study of teenage girls revealed that one in four had been physically or sexually abused (Lewin, 1997).
- Physical punishment remains more a part of teenage life than has been realized. Straus

(1994) reports that one third of daughters and 43 percent of sons recall being hit more than six times a year during their adolescence.

As adolescents strive for independence, explore their sexuality, and begin to develop new identities, parents can no longer protect their children or themselves from the world outside their family and often have a difficult time as children rebel and question their authority. In family systems in which power and control are central dynamics, these conflicts easily escalate into violence. While fewer child abuse cases involve adolescents, reports of abuse for this age group are believed to be greatly underestimated. Perhaps this is because adolescents are perceived to be better able to defend themselves or to deserve the punishments they receive (Barth & Derezotes, 1990; Gil, 1996). The truth is that they and infants suffer the most severe injuries (Sedlak & Broadhurst, 1996). Young people from violent homes often leave early, getting themselves into trouble because they left home to escape, rather than because they were ready to move on.

Eliana Gil (1994) distinguishes two different types of parental abuse experienced by adolescents: current abuse and cumulative abuse. Current abuse is rooted in conflicts connected to this particular stage of development, family crises, or inconsistent parenting. Young people who have grown up in a supportive environment up to this point but are now experiencing abuse have a chance to master the developmental tasks of this stage through treatment focused on communication, limit setting, parenting skills, and boundaries. Adolescents who have experienced a lifelong history of cumulative abuse have different needs. They tend to suffer from depression, poor self-esteem, and anxiety and may have trouble developing social skills. In school, they are more likely to have attention and behavioral problems. Their frustration and pain are often expressed through acting-out behaviors. These youngsters are at greater risk for drug and alcohol abuse and have a higher rate of delinquency (Barnett et al., 1997). Gang membership is an appealing option for many. Gangs serve as a pseudo-family, providing protection, power, status, and in some cases profit. Mem-

bers usually share the same racial and ethnic background. This can reinforce cultural identity, especially in areas where the group is a minority. Though usually thought of as an inner-city problem, gangs are expanding in suburban and rural areas (Moore, 1997).

Many young people experience violence in their educational and social environment as well as at home. The greatest health risk for teenage boys is violence from peers, while teenage girls are often abused by siblings and victimized by sexual harassment in school, leading them to experience high levels of depression, eating disorders, and suicide attempts (Lewin, 1997). One study exploring the phenomenon of teen pregnancy found that 70 percent of fathers of children born to adolescent girls were adult males, not teenage boys (Males, 1992). Many of these young mothers had an early history of sexual abuse. Teenagers who live in high-crime areas are not only more frequently victimized; they also witness a great deal of violence, which can have severe psychological consequences (Fitzpatrick & Boldizar, 1993). Very few inner-city families go through the adolescent phase without experiencing a violent death or injury up close.

Gay and lesbian adolescents have an especially difficult time during adolescence as they struggle with sexual identity. In a homophobic society, the first inkling of a homosexual orientation is cause for intense anxiety and denial. Those who do come out are ostracized and risk abandonment by their families and verbal and physical assault by their peers. Those that don't come out suffer in silence.

Many adolescents can be defiant and resistant to therapy. Avoiding power plays with teens, giving them space to discuss their many thoughts and feelings without immediate challenge, and setting clear boundaries are approaches that can help them to develop trusting relationships. Nonverbal forms of therapy, such as art, music, drama, and group therapy can be especially helpful. Gil (1996) recommends establishing an alliance through individual work with the adolescent before beginning conjoint family therapy, which should be undertaken cautiously and only as the adolescent can handle the work and the family is ready to be accountable. Therapists who work with adolescent clients must not make assumptions about their sexual orientation. Instead, they should provide information about human sexuality in a supportive way. There is a large network of organizations and community programs that are designed to meet the special needs of young adults. Clinicians can utilize these and incorporate them into treatment plans.

FAMILIES AT MIDLIFE

- Each year, 1.4 million women between the ages of 45 and 64 are physically abused by their spouses (Wisconsin Coalition Against Domestic Violence, 1995).
- Domestic violence frequently results in severe injury. In one study of women reporting to an emergency room because of domestic violence, 28 percent needed hospitalization and 13 percent needed major medical treatment (Berrios & Grady, 1991).

Midlife is a time of major change. As children leave home, husbands and wives need to renegotiate their relationships with each other, their adult children, and their grandchildren. Men's careers are often at their peak. At the same time, women freed from child care responsibilities may begin to seriously develop their professional skills and interests. This is also a time of losses. Our culture's pairing of youth with beauty leaves little room for middle-aged women. This perceived loss of attractiveness is troublesome for those to whom it has been a prime source of self-esteem and power. The loss of children can be painful, especially for women whose sole focus was on the home and child-rearing and who fear being left alone in an abusive relationship. The incidence of physical assault often declines with age. Overt acts of violence may no longer be needed, as the husband's control is so well established. This does not mean that the relationship is no longer abusive. Often unrecognized is the spouse's ongoing verbal and psychological abuse. Threats, continuous criticism, outbursts of rage, and jealousy can all be used to keep a wife alert and focused on the needs of her husband. Such behavior is especially effective if it is combined with occasional expressions of love

and if the victim is isolated from friends, family, and other sources of support (Andersen, Boulette, & Schwartz, 1991). Psychological abuse is always present in physically abusive relationships, though physical assault may or may not be a part of psychological abuse. One particularly pathological form of psychological abuse has sometimes been referred to as "gaslighting," a reference to the classic movie *Gaslight,* in which the husband tries to drive his wife insane by telling her she is crazy any time she notices the things he is doing in their relationship to mystify her. This is often done by husbands who deny their affairs and call their wives "paranoid" for their suspicions. Years of psychological abuse take their toll. Women in abusive relationships often suffer from low self-esteem, feelings of powerlessness, major depression, anxiety, and PTSD (Gleason, 1993).

An important part of work with women at this stage is identifying the abuse. The most widely held image of a battered woman is that of a young mother with small children (Brandl, 1995). Professionals usually don't consider domestic violence and psychological abuse when assessing a woman at this stage. Doctors don't question pat explanations of bruises and injuries. Clients themselves may have become so used to the way they are treated that they don't consider the relationship abusive. Those with traditional attitudes may consider it normal for a man to "lose his temper now and then." The power wheel is again useful in detecting more subtle types of abuse. Not all women at this stage are in long-term relationships. Some abuse may start in a second marriage. For many though, their marriage represents an investment of twenty or thirty years. Divorce and separation can seem like a negation of everything they value. Groups are especially helpful for women struggling with these issues and for raising consciousness about the nature of psychological and physical dominance, while providing them the support and resources to confront it. Groups also combat isolation and build self-esteem.

A major concern for women at this stage is finances. They fear losing their home and health insurance (Brandl & Raymond, 1997). Abusive men often sabotage their wives' efforts at employment and insist on maintaining total control of the family finances (Raphael & Tolman, 1997). It is not unusual for wives not to know what the couple's financial assets are or even how to manage a checkbook. The therapist should assess what skills a wife will need to develop to have confidence in her ability to function independently from a husband who has fostered dependence.

Relationships with adult children may be strained when midlife women decide to leave their marriage. Even children who have spent a lifetime watching their mother be victimized often become emotionally distant, in part fearing that she will now become dependent on them. They may feel that she deserves the abuse ("she's always nagging Dad"), or they may become abusive to their mother themselves. Although they may have urged their mother to leave for years, they can also have great difficulty letting her go or changing their perception of their parents' marriage. All of these issues need to be addressed if adult children are going to be able to support their mothers' efforts. Adult children will need to renegotiate their relationships with their fathers as well. Unfortunately, abusive men at this stage, as at other phases in the life cycle, often use their children to control and manipulate their wives, sometimes threatening them with emotional or financial abandonment (Brandl, 1995).

OLDER FAMILIES

- The Older Women's League (OWL) estimates that more than 1 million women age 65 and older are victims of abuse each year (Wisconsin Coalition Against Domestic Violence, 1995).
- "After all she survived all these years, things have got to be slowing down now that they are older." (Adult son, having trouble acknowledging that his 78-year-old mother, was still being battered by her 82-year-old husband).
- Abuse that is the result of caregiver stress is not based in a belief system that it is acceptable to use coercion, threats, and physical assault to control someone else's behavior (Brandl, 1995).

As people live longer, more suffer from health problems that interfere with their ability to function independently. Older adults are also systematically oppressed by ageism. Ageism is more than deni-grating images portraying old people as feeble and helpless or as sweet little old ladies and men. It involves a lack of power—less opportunity for employment and lower income. It also involves the lack of resources and services to meet their changing medical and life-style needs (Fullin, 1995). The natural support system for older adults begins to deteriorate as people retire from their jobs and spouses and friends move or pass away. The cost of obtaining the support necessary to maintain independent living is often prohibitive. Women make up the greatest portion of this population, tend to have relatively low retirement incomes and thus find themselves suddenly dependent on their adult children and other family members for support. This is a difficult transition for both the elder adult and the entire family system. Earlier unresolved conflicts often erupt between parents and children or between siblings. As the parent's role changes from one of power and authority to one of dependence, there is a realignment of relationships among family members. The so-called role reversal involves a shift in roles for everyone in the family. Daughters or daughters-in-law usually become the primary caregivers and frequently find themselves torn between their jobs, their own families, and aging relatives. Many are seniors themselves and are beginning to have health problems of their own. A 63-year-old diabetic may be caring for her 85-year-old mother as well as her 65-year-old husband, who has a history of cardiac problems. For this reason, more than at any other stage of the life cycle, it is essential to work with the extended family. A well-made care plan worked out with the oldest daughter may be unworkable if the real power in the family lies with the son who lives fifty miles away. To assess family dynamics and understand the support network that is already in place, genograms should include all family members and those not connected by blood who are important in the everyday life of the older adult. This may include the pastor, the doctor, the next-door neighbor, and/or the home health aide who comes in three days a week. This is especially important in working with older adults of different ethnic groups or sexual orientation. For example, gay and lesbian elders often have an extensive network of friends who act as family. Because their sexual orientation has been considered a crime, a sin, or a psychiatric illness, many same-sex partners may refuse to identify themselves as a couple. Clinicians can respect this need for privacy and focus on the level of support partners can provide (Cook-Daniels, 1998).

Definitions of elder abuse vary from state to state and may include psychological and verbal abuse as well as neglect, financial and physical abuse. While technically this term would encompass wives who are being hit by their husbands or adult children, the emphasis in the field has been on abuse that results from caregiver stress. The experience of domestic violence for older women has been virtually ignored, and until recently, battered women shelters and services have also overlooked older women (Vinton, Altholz, & Lobell-Boesch, 1997). In practice, the distinction between the two can be difficult to discern. But making that distinction is vital, since treatment plans designed to reduce caregiver stress can actually end up blaming the victim ("She's so difficult to care for that I just lost my patience") and supporting the abuser (Brandl & Raymond, 1997).

Ironically, older women are at greatest risk from people who are dependent on them—such as adult children or spouses with a history of drug or alcohol abuse, mental illness, intellectual impairment, and economic problems (Anetzberger, 1987; Bendik, 1992; Kosberg, 1988; Stone, Cafferata, & Sangl, 1987).

Mrs. Foley was an 83-year-old widow with diabetes who lived alone in her small suburban home. Her grandson Tom relocated from another state and asked to live with her while he looked for a job. Tom was 44 and recently divorced. The last time Mrs. Foley had seen Tom was eight years earlier at the funeral of his mother, Mrs. Foley's daughter. Initially, she welcomed Tom, but after a time, his behavior raised suspicion that he was using drugs and alcohol. He was sloppy and offered no help around the house. He resented any criticism from his grandmother and would respond with a litany of complaints that he said his deceased mother had had about her for years. By the time Mrs. Foley became aware that her grandson was stealing from her, she was too afraid and depressed to confront him. She spent more and more

time alone in her room. She began to lose weight and would sometimes forget to take her medication. Her plight was discovered only after she fell and was hospitalized for a broken hip. At the time, she was also suffering from dehydration, and her blood sugar level was dangerously high. Her nurse observed how anxious she became before Tom's visits. When he showed up at the hospital drunk and was verbally abusive to his grandmother, the nurse called adult protective services. The worker interviewed Mrs. Foley, who denied any problems with Tom. The worker also met with Tom, who became quite defensive. He claimed that his grandmother was senile and that none of her statements could be believed. This made the social worker more suspicious. She interviewed Mrs. Foley's neighbors, who painted a clearer picture. They described Tom's comings and goings and expressed their concern about Mrs. Foley. The adult protective worker established rapport with Mrs. Foley during her recovery, and the older woman gradually confided her problems with Tom. She was given information about drug and alcohol addiction and made aware of her legal rights. Since she had no other children or grandchildren, a niece and nephew were contacted and brought into counseling. With their support, Mrs. Foley was able to confront her grandson and threatened to use legal measures unless he left her home. She continued to have a warm and supportive relationship with her sister's children and become more involved with their families.

Spousal mistreatment at earlier life cycle stages often foreshadows elder abuse, but the lack of such a history offers no assurance. Events at this phase can increase tensions between a couple. Retirement, health problems, and decline in sexual functioning can make men whose identity is rooted in power and control feel threatened. Unfortunately, one of the easiest ways for men to feel empowered is by abusing family members, particularly their wives (American Association of Retired Persons, 1993). Frequently, sudden behavioral changes are indicative of health problems. Therefore, all cases of late-onset abuse require a careful medical assessment to detect cognitive changes and the side effects of medication. The clinician should study the dynamics between the couple. Warning signs are similar to those at other stages of the life cycle: verbal abuse, possessiveness, control of finances, unexplained bruises and injuries, and reluctance to allow the partner to speak for herself or himself or be interviewed separately. Adult children and other family members may not be good informants. Many adult children seem embarrassed and ashamed of their parents' behavior and may not be aware of the abuse nor really believe that their parent is in danger. Abused elders themselves may be reluctant to tell a professional the problems they are having if they think it may be reported to a protective agency. The fear of nursing home placement haunts those with chronic illnesses; some feel that it is better to endure the abuse than to risk being taken from their homes. For many older women, leaving a relationship is not a viable option because of the economic realities they face and the traditional values they embrace. Therapy can empower women who stay by helping them to recognize what they are experiencing as abuse and addressing its lifelong consequences. Clinicians can provide information about abuse in later life, help older women to identify their strengths, and validate the importance of their work as wives and mothers. They can also encourage them to make safety plans and provide referrals to local resources (Brandl & Raymond, 1997). Gays and lesbians may have difficulty using many of the services that are usually prescribed for older adults. Fearing the frequent prejudice in traditional social support systems, they may require special legal counseling, since their relationships are often not legally recognized (Cooke-Daniels, 1998).

Older adults suffering from dementia are at greater risk for abuse, especially those who are aggressive toward their caregivers (Cooney & Mortimer 1995: Coyne, Reichman, & Berbig, 1993). Dementia raises particularly thorny problems in assessment because patients may not be able to remember incidents of abuse, or they may suffer from paranoid delusions that focus on mistreatment at the hands of a family member. They may refuse to eat or bathe, putting the caregiver in the position of forcing them to cooperate or risk being charged with neglect. Episodes of sudden belligerence may require physical intervention and restraints that can result in bruises, which may give the appearance of physical abuse. Behavioral or

personality changes, suspiciousness, withdrawal from previous activities, difficulty managing finances, getting lost, minor automobile accidents, neglect of personal hygiene, and other changes in daily activities may be the early signs of dementia. Often, family members do not recognize the significance of such changes and will make excuses or deny the extent of the deterioration. Sometimes, they will interpret the older person's inability to function as willful and become angry and accuse him or her of being stubborn and spiteful. This is particularly difficult if the caregiver has previously had a conflicted relationship with the older person. The professional can sometimes fall into the same trap and may label an elder as uncooperative and unwilling to be helped, when, in fact, the person's judgment may be too impaired to understand the need for help. An assessment and planning session with as many family present as possible can be important, not only for clarifying the situation but for supporting all family members in their shared responsibility and concern for the aging person.

The experience of caring for someone with dementia can be overwhelming and incredibly sad for family members. Husbands may not recognize their wives; mothers may not recognize their children. Basic skills such as bathing, reading, or writing are lost. Communication becomes more difficult as language skills become impaired. Piece by piece, the personality of the person with dementia seems to disappear; yet they are still there and require an ever-increasing level of care. The continued decline of a family member despite the best efforts of those caring for the person, causes feelings of inadequacy, helplessness, and anger. Validating the sadness, anger, frustration, and fear that caregivers often feel helps to counter their burnout and frustration. It is important to normalize and reframe the patient's behavior. For example, a patient with Alzheimer's repeatedly accused his 83-year-old spouse of having an affair. His wife was greatly relieved to learn that delusions of infidelity are common in people with dementia and that her husband hadn't secretly harbored doubts about her throughout their 50-year marriage. In family counseling, caregiving tasks can be redistributed among family members. Options for the immediate situation and long-term care can be presented to everyone at the same time, and conflicts and concerns can be discussed openly. This helps the family to move forward as a whole and to keep the needs of an aging parent from becoming the point of contention among feuding relatives. Such approaches can actually help to prevent abuse by relieving family and caregiver stress before it escalates.

Interventions and treatment goals with abused elders may be different from those at other stages of the life cycle. Home visits and extensive telephone work are important tools in providing care. Clinicians must work with their clients' natural support system. This may mean contacting the family doctor to understand health problems and the side effects of medication or asking a neighbor to provide respite. It may also mean advocating with community agencies especially those that provide concrete services such as transportation or meals on wheels. Family work will focus on realigning relationships with adult children and the abuser, dealing with concerns about health and death, and providing concrete services. Older woman have tended not to use battered women's services, which are often not accessible to them nor designed to meet their needs (Vinton et al., 1997). But they do use programs tailored especially for them, such as the Older Battered Women's Project at the Wisconsin Coalition Against Domestic Violence (Brandl, 1995; Vinton et al., 1997). Elder abuse is a crime. Many states have mandatory reporting laws and agencies to which incidents must be reported. The clinician must be aware of these and work within those guidelines.

CONCLUSION

The study of family violence is relatively new, as is the very concept that it is a social problem. When we address the societal arrangements that foster violence and oppression, we are confronting norms and beliefs that are deeply rooted in the dominant culture. These inequities have been formalized in law, and by religious institutions as if they were sanctioned by God. They have become so widely accepted that they have rarely been noticed, much less questioned.

Victims of violence have more often been stigmatized than supported. They have little legal recourse, and they often receive little support or understanding even from their families and social circle. When we understand that violence is the abuse of power, we are able to recognize it in all its forms—physical abuse, psychological abuse, sexual abuse, economic, political, and social oppression. We call on family therapists not to focus solely on the particular emotional and psychological dynamics of individual relationships and family systems, because this denies the impact of broader social forces on our clients throughout their life cycles that may encourage violence. We must enlarge our focus so that we can work together to support families to stop violence, develop nonviolent ways of resolving conflicts, and challenge the values that have promoted and allowed violence to continue in our society.

REFERENCES

Almeida, R. (1993). Unexamined assumptions and service delivery systems: Feminist theory and racial exclusions. *Journal of Feminist Family Therapy, 5*(1), 3–23.

Almeida, R., & Bograd, M. (1991). Sponsorship: Men holding men accountable for domestic violence. *Journal of Feminist Family Therapy, 2*(3/4), 243–256.

Almeida, R., Woods, R., Messineo, T., & Font, R. (1998). The contextual model. In M. McGoldrick (Ed.), *Revisioning family therapy: Race, gender, and culture in clinical practice.* New York: The Guilford Press.

Almeida, R., Woods, R., Messineo, T., Font, R. J., & Heer, C. (1994). Violence in the lives of the racially and sexually different: A public and private dilemma. *Journal of Feminist Family Therapy, 5*(3/4), 99–126.

American Association of Retired Persons. (1993). *Abused elders or older battered woman? Report on the AARP Forum October 29–30, 1993.* Washington DC: AARP Women's Initiative.

Anderson, S., Boulette, T., & Schwartz, A. (1991). Psychological maltreatment of spouses. In R. Ammerman & M. Hersen (Eds.), *Case studies in family violence* (pp. 293–327). New York: Plenum Press.

Anetzberger, G. J. (1987). *The etiology of elder abuse by adult offspring.* Springfield, IL: Charles C. Thomas.

Anti-Violence Project. (1997). *Anti-lesbian, gay, bisexual, and trangendered violence in 1996.* New York: The New York City Gay and Lesbian Anti-Violence Project.

Arias, I., Samios, M., & O'Leary, K. D. (1987). Prevalence and correlates of physical aggression during courtship. *Journal of Interpersonal Violence, 2,* 82–90.

Bachman, R. (1994). *Violence and theft in the workplace.* (Bureau of Justice Statistics crime data brief, NCJ No. 148199). Rockville, MD: U.S. Department of Justice.

Bachman, R., & Saltzman, L. (1995). *Violence against women: Estimates from the redesigned survey* (Bureau of Justice Statistics special report, NCJ No. 154348). Rockville, MD: U.S. Department of Justice.

Barnett, O. W., Miller-Perrin, C. L., & Perrin, R. D. (1997). *Family violence across the life span.* Thousand Oaks, CA: Sage.

Barth, R. P., & Derezotes, D. S. (1990). *Preventing adolescent abuse: Effective intervention strategies and techniques.* New York: Lexington Books.

Bastian, L. (1995). *Criminal victimization 1993* (NCJ No. 151658). Annapolis Junction, MD: U.S. Department of Justice.

Bastian, L., & Taylor, B. (1994). *Young Black male victims: National crime victimization survey* NCJ-147004). Annapolis Junction, MD: U.S. Department of Justice.

Bendik, M. F. (1992). Reaching the breaking point: Dangers of mistreatment in elder care giving situations. *Journal of Elder Abuse & Neglect, 4*(3), 39–59.

Bergen, R. K. (1996). *Wife rape: Understanding the response of survivors and service providers.* Thousand Oaks, CA: Sage.

Berrios, D. C., and Grady, D. (1991). Domestic violence: Risk factors and outcomes. *The Western Journal of Medicine, 155,* 2.

Black, C. A., & De Blassie, R. (1993). Sexual abuse in male children and adolescents: Indicators, effects and treatments. *Adolescence, 28*(109), 123–133.

Bohn, D. (1990). Domestic violence and pregnancy: Implications for practice. *Journal of Nurse Mid-wifery, 35*(2), 86–98.

Brandl, B. (1995) Older abused/battered women: An invisible population. *Wisconsin Coalition Against Domestic Violence Newsletter, 14*(3), 6–9.

Brandl, B., & Raymond, J. (1997). Unrecognized elder abuse victims: Older abused women. *Journal of Case Management, 6*(2), 62–67.

Campbell, J. C., & Alford, P. (1989). The dark consequences of marital rape. *American Journal of Nursing, 89,* 946–949.

Cassidy, L., & Hurrell, R. M. (1995). The influence of victim's attire on adolescents' judgment of date rape. *Adolescence, 30*(118), 319–323.

Charney, D., & Russell, R. (1994). An overview of sexual harassment. *American Journal of Psychiatry, 151*(1), 10–17.

Cleage, P. (1990). *Mad at Miles: A Blackwoman's guide to truth.* Southfield, MI: The Cleage Group.

Coleman, D. H., & Straus, M. A. (1986). Marital power, conflict, and violence in a nationally representative sample of American couples. *Violence and Victims, 1,* 141–157.

Commonwealth Fund (1993, July 14). *First comprehensive national health survey of American women finds them at significant risk* [News release]. New York: The Commonwealth Fund.

Cook-Daniels, L. (1998). Lesbian, gay male, bisexual and transgendered elders: Elder abuse and neglect issues. *Journal of Elder Abuse and Neglect, 9*(2), 35–50.

Cooney, C., & Mortimer, A. (1995). Elder abuse and dementia: A pilot study. *International Journal of Social Psychiatry, 41*(4), 276–283.

Coyne, A., Reichman, W., & Berbig, L. (1993). The relationship between elder abuse and dementia. *American Journal of Psychiatry, 1*(50), 643–646.

Craven, D. (1996). *Female victims of violent crimes* (Bureau of Justice Statistics selected findings, NCJ No. 162602). Rockville, MD: U.S. Department of Justice.

Craven, D. (1997). *Sex difference in violent victimization, 1994* (Bureau of Justice Statistics special report, NCJ No. 164508). Rockville, MD: U.S. Department of Justice.

D'Augelli, A. (1989). Lesbians' and gay men's experience of discrimination and harassment in a university community. *American Journal of Community Psychology, 7*(3), 317–321.

Davidovich, J. (1990). Men who abuse their spouses: Social psychological supports. *Journal of Offender Counseling, Services & Rehabilitation, 15*(1), 27–44.

Davis, R., Brickman, E., & Baker, T. (1991). Supportive and unsupportive response of others to rape victim: effect on concurrent victim adjustment. *American Journal of Community Psychology, 19*(3), 443–451.

DeYoung, Y., & Zigler, E. (1994). Machismo in two cultures: Relation to punitive child rearing practices. *American Journal of Orthopsychiatry, 64*(3), 386–395.

Dore, M. M., Doris, J., & Wright, P. (1995). Identifying substance abuse in maltreating families: A child welfare challenge. *Child Abuse & Neglect, 19,* 531–543.

Elliot, M., & Brierre, J. (1992). Sexual abuse trauma among professional women: Validating the trauma symptom checklist-40 (TSC-40). *Child Abuse & Neglect, 16,* 391–398.

Finkelhor, D. (1983). Common features of family abuse. In D. Finkelhor, R. J. Gelles, G. T. Hotaling, & M. A. Straus (Eds.), *The dark side of families: Current family violence research* (pp. 17–30). Beverly Hills, CA: Sage.

Fitzgerald, L. (1993). Sexual harassment: Violence against women in the workplace. *American Psychologist, 48*(10), 1070–1076.

Fitzpatrick, K., & Boldizar, J. (1993). The prevalence and consequences of exposure to violence among African American youth. *Journal of American Child & Adolescence Psychiatry, 2*(2), 424–435.

Flynn, C. (1990). Sex roles and women's response to courtship violence. *Journal of Family Violence, 5*(1), 83–94.

Frazier, P., Valtinson, G., & Candell, S. (1994). Evaluation of a coeducational interactive rape prevention program. *Journal of Counseling and Development, 73*(2), 153–158.

Fullin, K. (1995). Men's violence against women: Screening issues for elderly women. *Wisconsin Coalition Against Domestic Violence Newsletter, 14*(3), 12–14.

Gelles, R. J., & Cornell, C. P. (1990). *Intimate violence in families.* Newbury Park, CA: Sage.

Gil, E. (1994). *Play in family therapy.* New York: The Guilford Press.

Gil, E. (1996). *Treating abused adolescents.* New York: The Guilford Press.

Gleason, W. J. (1993). Mental disorders in battered women: An empirical study. *Violence and Victims, 8,* 53–68.

Gondolf E. W., & Fisher, E. R. (1988). *Battered women as survivors: An alternative to treating learned helplessness.* Lexington, MA: Lexington.

Greven, P. (1990). *Spare the child: The religious roots of punishment and the psychological impact of physical abuse.* New York: Alfred A. Knopf.

Heath, V., Bean, R., & Freinauer, L. (1996) Severity of childhood sexual abuse: Symptom difference between men and women. *American Journal of Family Therapy, 24*(4), 305–314.

Hilton, Z. (1992). Battered women's concerns about their children witnessing wife assault. *Journal of Interpersonal Violence, 7*(1), 77–86.

Holden, G. W., & Ritchie, K. L. (1991). Linking extreme marital discord, child rearing, and child behavior problems: Evidence from battered women. *Child Development, 62,* 311–327.

Hoyer, A. (1994). Sexual harassment: Four women describe their experiences: Background and implications for the clinical nurse specialist. *Archives of Psychiatric Nurses, 8*(3), 177–183.

Kalmus, D., & Straus, M. A. (1990). Wife's marital dependency and wife abuse. In M. A. Straus & R. J. Gelles (Eds.), *Physical violence in American families: Risk factors and adaptations to violence in 8,145 families* (pp. 369–382). New Brunswick, NJ: Transaction Books.

Kahr, B. (1991). The sexual molestation of children: Historical perspectives. *The Journal of Psychohistory, 19*(2), 191—219.

Kivel, P. (1992). *Men's work: How to stop the violence that tears our lives apart.* New York: Ballantine.

Kosberg, J. (1988). Preventing elder abuse: Identification of high risk factor prior to placement decisions. *Gerontologist, 28*(1), 43–40.

Koss, M. P. (1989). Hidden rape: Sexual aggression and victimization in a national sample of students in higher education. In M. A. Pirog-Good & J. E. Stets (Eds.), *Violence in dating relationships: Emerging social issues* (pp. 145–168). New York: Praeger.

Langan, P., & Harlow, C. (1992). *Child rape victims, 1992.* (Bureau of Justice Statistics crime data brief NCJ No. 147001), Annapolis Junction, MD: U.S. Department of Justice.

Lanner, M. (1990). Violence or its precipitators: Which is more likely to be identified as a dating problem? *Deviant Behavior, 11*(4), 319–329.

LeJeune, C., & Follette, V. (1994). Taking responsibility: Sex differences in reporting dating violence. *Journal of Interpersonal Violence, 9*(1), 133–140.

Lewin, T. (1997, October 1). Sexual abuse tied to 1 in 4 teen-age girls. *New York Times,* p. A24.

Males, M. (1992). Adult liaison in the "epidemic" of "teenage" birth, pregnancy, and venereal disease. *Journal of Sex Research, 29*(4), 525–545.

Mansfield, P., Koch, P., Henderson J., & Vicary, J. (1991). The job climate for women in traditionally male blue-collar occupation. *Sex Roles, 25*(1–2), 63–79.

Moore, J. (1997). *Highlights of the 1995 national youth gangs survey* (Fact Sheet No. 63). Washington, DC: U.S. Department of Justice.

Murphy, J., Jellinek, M., Quinn, D., & Smith, G. (1991). Substance abuse and serious child mistreatment: Prevalence, risk, and outcome in a court sample. *Child Abuse & Neglect, 15*(3), 197–211.

Okun, L. (1986). *Woman abuse: Facts replacing myths.* Albany: State University of New York Press.

Pedersen, P., & Thomas, C. (1992). Prevalence and correlates of dating violence in a Canadian university. *Canadian Journal of Behavioral Science, 24*(4), 490–501.

Petrectic-Jackson, P., & Tobin, S. (1996). The rape trauma syndrome: symptoms, stages, and hidden victims. In T. L. Jackson (Ed.), *Acquaintance rape: Assessment, treatment and prevention* (pp. 93–144). Sarasota, FL: Professional Resource Press/Professional Resource Exchange.

Raphael, J., & Tolman, R. (1997). *Trapped by poverty, trapped by abuse.* Chicago, IL: The Taylor Institute.

Russell, D. E. H. (1990). *Rape in marriage.* Indianapolis, IN: Indiana University Press.

Schwartz, M., & De Keseredy, W. (1997). *Sexual assault on the college campus: The role of male peer support.* Thousand Oaks, CA: Sage.

Sedlak & Broadhurst (1996). *Executive summary of the third national incidence study of child abuse and neglect.* Washington, DC: U.S. Department of Health and Human Services, Administration for Children and Families.

Shortland, R., & Goodstein, L. (1992). Sexual precedence reduces the perceived legitimacy of sexual refusal: An examination of attributions concerning date rape and consensual sex. *Personality and Social Psychology Bulletin, 18*(6), 756–764.

Spratlen, L. (1988). Sexual harassment counseling. *Journal of Psychosocial Nursing and Mental Health Services, 26*(2), 28–33.

Stacy, C., Schandel, L., Flannery, W., & Conlon, M. (1994). It's not all moonlight and roses: Dating violence at the University of Maine, 1982–1992. *College Student Journal, 28*(1), 2–9.

Stone, R. G., Cafferata, G. L., & Sangl, J. (1987). Caregivers of the frail and elderly: A national profile. *Gerontologist, 27,* 616–626.

Straus, M. A. (1978). Wife beating: How common and why? *Victimology, 2,* 443–348.

Straus, M. A. (1991, September). *Children as witness to marital violence: A risk factor for life-long problems among a nationally representative sample of American men and women.* Paper presented at the Ross Roundtable titled "Children and Violence," Washington, DC.

Straus, M. A. (1994). *Beating the devil out of them: Corporal punishment in American families.* San Francisco: Lexington.

Straus, M. (1998). Corporal punishment in childhood and abusive behavior in adulthood. Keynote Presentation: Ninth Annual Child Abuse Conference: Child Abuse: Can We Prevent It? St. Peters Medical Center, New Brunswick, N. J. April, 18.

Straus, M. A., & Steinmetz, S. (1980). *Behind closed doors: Violence in the American family.* New York: Anchor Press.

Tolman, R., & Bennett, L. (1990). A review of quantitative research on men who batter. *Journal of Interpersonal Violence, 5*(1), 87–118.

Ullman, S. (1996). Social reactions, coping strategies, and self-blame attribution in adjustment to sexual assault. *Psychology of Women Quarterly, 20*(4), 505–526.

U.S. Department of Health and Human Services. (1995). *A nation's shame: Fatal child abuse and neglect in the United States* (Report of the U.S. Advisory Board on Child Abuse and Neglect). Washington, DC: U.S. Government Printing Office.

U.S. Department of Health and Human Services. (1997). *Child maltreatment 1995: Reports from the states to the National Child Abuse and Neglect Data System.* Washington, DC: U.S. Government Printing Office.

Vinton, L., Altholz, J., & Lobell-Boesch, T. (1997). A five-year follow up of domestic violence programming for older battered women. *Journal of Women and Aging, 9*(1/2), 3–14.

Whipple, E., & Webster-Stratton, C. (1991). The role of parental stress in physically abusive families. *Child Abuse & Neglect, 15*(3), 279–291.

Wiehe, V., & Richards, A. (1995). *Intimate betrayal: Understanding and responding to the trauma of an acquaintance rape.* Thousand Oaks, CA: Sage.

Wisconsin Coalition Against Domestic Violence. (1995). Family abuse in later life. *Wisconsin Coalition Against Domestic Violence Newsletter, 14*(3), 1.

Zorza, J. (1991) Women battering: a major cause of homelessness. *Clearinghouse Review, 25*(4), 421–429.

CHAPTER 29

CHRONIC ILLNESS AND THE FAMILY LIFE CYCLE

JOHN S. ROLLAND

When serious illness strikes, the dimension of time becomes a central reference point for families to successfully navigate the experience. The family and each of its members face the formidable challenge of focusing simultaneously on the present and future, mastering the practical and emotional tasks of the immediate situation while charting a course for dealing with the complexities and uncertainties of their problem in an unknown future. Also, families draw on prior multigenerational experiences with illness and loss and core family beliefs to guide them.

Families and clinicians need an effective way to tap into the dimension of time both to comprehend issues of initial timing of an illness and to look toward the future in a more proactive manner. Placing the unfolding of chronic illness or disability into a multigenerational developmental framework facilitates this task. This requires understanding the intertwining of three evolutionary threads: the illness, the individual, and the family life cycles. To think systemically about the interface of these three developmental lines, we need a common language and set of concepts that can be applied to each yet permits consideration of all three simultaneously.

Two steps lay the foundation for such a model. First, we need a bridge between the biomedical and psychosocial worlds—a language that enables chronic disorders to be characterized in psychosocial and longitudinal terms, each condition having a particular personality and expected developmental life course. Second, we need to think simultaneously about the interaction of individual and family development. This is vividly demonstrated

when we consider the impact of an illness on both a couple's relationship and each partner's individual development. The inherent skews that emerge between partners highlight the necessity to consider the interweaving of individual and family life cycle challenges (Rolland, 1994a, 1994b).

This chapter describes the Family Systems-Illness Model, a normative, preventive framework for assessment and intervention with families that are facing chronic and life-threatening conditions (Rolland, 1984, 1987a, 1990, 1994a). This model is based on the systemic interaction between an illness and family that evolves over time. The goodness of fit between the psychosocial demands of the disorder and the family style of functioning and resources are prime determinants of successful versus dysfunctional coping and adaptation. The model distiguishes three dimensions: (1) psychosocial types of disorders, (2) major phases in their natural history, and (3) key family system variables (Figure 29.1). A scheme of the systemic interaction between illness and family might look like the diagram in Figure 29.2. Family variables that are given particular emphasis include the family and individual life cycles, particularly in relation to the time phases of the disorder; multigenerational legacies related to illness and loss; and belief systems.

The first section of this chapter reviews a psychosocial typology and time phases of illness framework. Chronic illnesses are grouped according to key biological similarities and differences that pose distinct psychosocial demands for the ill individual and his or her family, and the prime de-

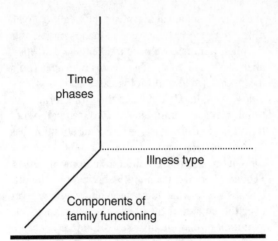

FIGURE 29.1 Three Dimensional Model: Illness Type, Time Phase, Family Functioning

Excerpted from: Rolland, J. S., "Chronic Illness and the Life Cycle: A Conceptual Framework," *Family Process, 26,* no 2, 203–221, 1987. Reprinted with permission from Family Process.

velopmental time phases in the natural evolution of chronic disease are identified. In the following section, integrating key concepts from family and individual developmental theory, the interface of

disease with the individual and family life cycles will be described. Finally, multigenerational aspects of illness, loss, and crisis are considered.

THE SOCIAL CONTEXT OF ILLNESS AND DISABILITIES

It is important to state at the outset that families' experiences of illness and disability are enormously influenced by the dominant culture and the larger health systems embedded in this prevailing culture. Families from diverse minority and ethnic backgrounds and lower socioeconomic strata are disproportionately represented among the current 42 million uninsured and the additional 60 million underinsured people in the United States (U.S. Census Bureau, 1997). For those with health coverage who are underinsured, a major illness often means financial ruin. For millions with disabilities, the assistance that would enable independent living is unobtainable. For these groups, a lack of access to adequate basic health care has major ramifications in terms of the incidence of illness, disease course, survival, quality of life, and a variety of forms of suffering caused by discrimination.

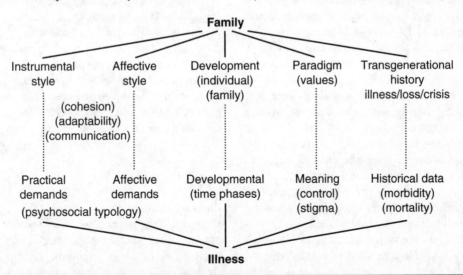

FIGURE 29.2 Interface of Chronic Illness and the Family

Excerpted from: Rolland, J. S. Family Systems and Chronic Illness: A Typological Model, *Journal of Psychotherapy and the Family,* vol 2, no 3, 143–168, 1987. Reprinted with permission from Family Systems Medicine.

In a trend that has been worsening, over 33 percent of Hispanics and 20 percent of African Americans were uninsured in 1997. For these minority groups, chronic diseases are more prevalent, will occur earlier in the life cycle, and, when they occur, will have a worse course and prognosis because of inadequate medical care and limited access to resources. Recent data showing that African Americans' life expectancy is seven years less than that of Whites give a glaring example of these larger societal issues.

Dedicated mental health professionals work under severe constraints in helping affected families. In recent years, most forms of health coverage have severely limited mental health benefits. For the majority of families facing illness, this means that the longstanding difficulties of integrating psychosocial services with traditional biomedical care increase.

As the population of the United States ages, the current 99 million people with chronic conditions will balloon to nearly 150 million by the year 2030 (see Chapter 18). With advances in technology, people will be living longer with chronic illnesses, and the strain on families to provide adequate caregiving will become unprecedented. For example, in 1970, there were twenty-one potential caregivers for each elderly person; by 2030, there will be only six such potential caregivers for each senior citizen (U.S. Census Bureau, 1992). Many factors are involved, including decreasing birth rates; family networks that are getting smaller and more top-heavy, with more older than younger family members; and women entering the workforce in increasing numbers and no longer being available for the traditional female role as unpaid family caregiver. These facts suggest that even the best family-centered systemic clinical model will be inadequate unless the United States develops a humane system of health care in which universal equitable care is a basic human right.

PSYCHOSOCIAL TYPOLOGY OF ILLNESS

The standard disease classification is based on purely biological criteria that are clustered in ways to establish a medical diagnosis and treatment plan rather than the psychosocial demands on patients and their families. We need a schema to conceptualize chronic diseases that remains relevant to both the psychosocial and biological worlds and provides a common language that transforms our usual medical terminology. Two critical issues have hindered us. First, insufficient attention has been given to the areas of diversity and commonality that are inherent in different chronic illnesses. Second, there has been a glossing over of the different ways in which diseases manifest themselves over the course of an illness. Understanding the evolution of chronic diseases is hindered because clinicians often become involved in the care of an individual or family coping with a chronic illness at different points in the illness life cycle. Clinicians rarely follow families through the complete life history of a disease. Chronic illnesses need to be conceptualized in a manner that organizes these similarities and differences over the disease course so that the type and degree of demands relevant to clinical practice are highlighted in a more useful way.

The goal of this typology is to create clinically meaningful and pragmatic categories with similar psychosocial demands for a wide array of chronic conditions affecting individuals across the life span. It conceptualizes broad distinctions of the pattern of onset, course, outcome, type and degree of disability, and level of uncertainty. Although each variable is in actuality a continuum, it will be described here in a categorical manner by the selection of key anchor points.

Onset

Illnesses can be divided into those that either an acute onset, such as strokes, and those that have a gradual onset, such as Alzheimer's disease. For acute-onset illnesses, emotional and practical changes are compressed into a short time, requiring of the family more rapid mobilization of crisis management skills. Families that can tolerate highly charged affective states, exchange roles flexibly, problem solve efficiently, and utilize outside resources will have an advantage in managing acute-onset illnesses. Gradual-onset diseases, such as Parkinson's disease, entail a more protracted period of adjustment.

Course

The course of chronic diseases can take three general forms: progressive, constant, or relapsing/ episodic. With a progressive disease such as Alzheimer's disease, the family is faced with a perpetually symptomatic member in whom disability worsens in a stepwise or gradual way. Periods of relief from the demands of the illness tend to be minimal. The family must live with the prospect of continual role change and adaptation as the disease progresses. Increasing strain on family caretakers is caused by exhaustion, with few periods of relief from the demands of the illness, and by new caretaking tasks over time. Family flexibility, in terms of both internal role reorganization and willingness to use outside resources, is at a premium.

With a constant-course illness, the occurrence of an initial event is followed by a stable biological course. A single heart attack and spinal cord injury are examples. Typically, after an initial period of recovery, the chronic phase is characterized by some clear-cut deficit or limitation. Recurrences can occur, but the individual or family faces a semipermanent change that is stable and predictable over a considerable time span. The potential for family exhaustion exists without the strain of new role demands over time.

Relapsing or episodic course illnesses, such as disk problems and asthma, are distinguished by the alternation of stable low-symptom periods with periods of flare-up or exacerbation. Often, the family can carry on a normal routine. However, the specter of a recurrence hangs over their heads. Relapsing illnesses demand a somewhat different sort of family adaptability. Relative to progressive or constant-course illnesses, they may require the least ongoing caretaking or role reallocation. But the episodic nature of an illness may require a flexibility that permits movement back and forth between two forms of family organization. In a

sense, the family is on call to enact a crisis structure to handle exacerbations of the illness. Strain on the family system is caused by both the frequency of transitions between crisis and noncrisis and the ongoing uncertainty about when a crisis will next occur. The wide psychological discrepancy between periods of normalcy and flare-up is a particularly taxing feature that is unique to relapsing diseases.

Outcome

The likelihood that an illness can be fatal or shorten one's life span has profound psychosocial impact. The most crucial factor is the initial expectation of whether a disease is a likely cause of death. On one end of the continuum are illnesses that do not typically affect the life span, such as arthritis. At the other extreme are illnesses that are clearly progressive and usually fatal, such as metastatic cancer. An intermediate, more unpredictable category includes illnesses that shorten the life span, such as cystic fibrosis and heart disease, and those with the possibility of sudden death, such as hemophilia. A major difference between these kinds of outcome is the degree to which the family experiences anticipatory loss and its pervasive effects on family life (Rolland, 1990, 1994a). The future expectation of loss can make it extremely difficult for a family to maintain a balanced perspective. Families are often caught between a desire for intimacy and a push to let go emotionally of the ill member. A torrent of emotions can distract a family from the myriad of practical tasks and problem solving that maintain family integrity. Also, the tendency to see the ill family member as practically in the coffin can set in motion maladaptive responses that divest the ill member of important responsibilities. The result can be the structural and emotional isolation of the ill person from family life. This kind of psychological alienation has been associated with poor medical outcome in life-threatening illness (Campbell & Patterson, 1995; Derogatis, Abeloff, & Melisartos, 1979; Schmale & Iker, 1971).

When loss is less imminent or certain, illnesses that may shorten life or cause sudden death provide a fertile ground for idiosyncratic family interpretations. The "it could happen" nature of these illnesses creates a nidus for both overprotection by the family and powerful secondary gains for the ill member. This is particularly relevant to childhood illnesses such as hemophilia, juvenile-onset diabetes, and asthma (Minuchin et al. 1975; Minuchin, Rosman, & Baker, 1978).

Incapacitation

Disability can involve impairment of cognition (e.g., Alzheimer's disease), sensation (e.g., blindness), movement (e.g., stroke with paralysis), or stamina (e.g., heart disease); disfigurement (e.g., mastectomy); and conditions associated with social stigma (e.g., AIDS). The extent, kind, and timing of incapacitation imply sharp differences in the degree of family stress. For instance, the combined cognitive and motor deficits caused by a stroke necessitate greater family role reallocation than does a spinal cord injury that leaves cognitive abilities unaffected. In some illnesses, such as stroke, disability is often worst at the beginning. In progressive diseases, such as Alzheimer's disease, disability looms as an increasing problem in later phases of the illness, allowing the family more time to discuss and prepare for anticipated changes and an opportunity for the ill member to participate in disease-related family planning.

By combining the kinds of onset, course, outcome, and incapacitation into a grid format, we generate a typology that clusters illnesses according to similarities and differences in patterns that pose differing psychosocial demands (Table 29.1).

Uncertainty

The predictability of an illness and the degree of uncertainty about the specific way or rate at which it unfolds overlay all the other variables. For illnesses with highly unpredictable courses, such as mulitple sclerosis, family coping and adaptation, especially future planning, are hindered by anticipatory anxiety and ambiguity about what will happen. Families that can put long-term uncertainty

into perspective and sustain hope are best prepared to avoid the risks of exhaustion and dysfunction.

Other important attributes that differentiate illnesses should be considered in a thorough, systemically oriented evaluation. These include the complexity, frequency, and efficacy of a treatment regimen; the amount of home versus hospital-based care required; and the frequency and intensity of symptoms, particularly those that involve pain and suffering.

TIME PHASES OF ILLNESS

Too often, discussions of coping with cancer, managing disability, or dealing with life-threatening illness approach illness as a static state and fail to appreciate the dynamic unfolding of illness as a process over time. The concept of time phases provides a way for clinicians and families to think longitudinally and to understand chronic illness as an ongoing process with expectable landmarks, transitions, and changing demands. Each phase of an illness poses its own psychosocial demands and developmental tasks that require significantly different strengths, attitudes, or changes from a family. The core psychosocial themes in the natural history of chronic disease can be described in three major phases: crisis, chronic, and terminal (Figure 29.3 on page 498).

The *crisis phase* includes any symptomatic period before diagnosis and the the initial period of readjustment after a diagnosis and initial treatment plan. This period holds a number of key tasks for the ill member and family. Moos (1984) describes certain universal, practical, illness-related tasks, including learning to cope with any symptoms or disability, adapting to health care settings and treatments, and establishing and maintaining workable relationships with the health care team. There are also critical tasks of a more general, existential nature. The family needs to create a meaning for the illness that maximizes a sense of mastery and competency. Members must grieve for the loss of the life they knew before illness. They need to gradually accept the illness as permanent while maintaining a sense of continuity between their past and their

TABLE 29.1   Categorization of Chronic Illnesses by Psychosocial Type

		INCAPACITATING		NONINCAPACITATING	
		ACUTE	**GRADUAL**	**ACUTE**	**GRADUAL**
PROGRESSIVE	F A T A L		Lung cancer with CNS metastases AIDS Bone marrow failure Amyotrophic lateral sclerosis	Acute leukemia Pancreatic cancer Metastatic breast cancer Malignant melanoma Lung cancer Liver cancer	Cystic fibrosis*
RELAPSING				Incurable cancers in remission	
PROGRESSIVE	P O S S I B L Y F A T A L · S H O R T E N E D L I F E · S P A N		Emphysema Alzheimer's disease Multi-infarct dementia Multiple sclerosis (late) Chronic alcoholism Huntington's chorea Scleroderma		Juvenile diabetes* Malignant hypertension Insulin-dependent adult-onset diabetes
RELAPSING		Angina	Early multiple sclerosis Episodic alcoholism	Sickle cell disease* Hemophilia*	Systemic lupus erythematosis*
CONSTANT		Stroke Moderate/severe myocardial infarction	P.K.U. and other congenital errors of metabolism	Mild myocardial infarction Cardiac arrhythmia	Hemodialysis treated renal failure Hodgkin's disease
PROGRESSIVE	N O N F A T A L		Parkinson's disease Rheumatoid arthritis Osteoarthritis		Noninsulin-dependent adult-onset diabetes
RELAPSING		Lumbosacral disc disorder		Kidney stones Gout Migraine Seasonal allergy Asthma Epilepsy	Peptic ulcer Ulcerative colitis Chronic bronchitis Irritable bowel syndrome Psoriasis
CONSTANT		Congenital malformations Spinal cord injury Acute blindness Acute deafness Survived severe trauma & burns Posthypoxic syndrome	Nonprogressive mental retardation Cerebral palsy	Benign arrhythmia Congenital heart disease	Malabsorption syndromes Hyper/hypothyroidism Pernicious anemia Controlled hypertension Controlled glaucoma

* = Early
Source: Reprinted from Rolland, J. S. (1984). Toward a psychosocial typology of chronic and life-threatening illness. *Family Systems Medicine, 2,* 245–62. Reprinted with permission of Family Systems Medicine.

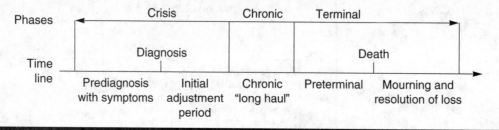

FIGURE 29.3   Time Line and Phases of Illness

From: Rolland, J. S. *Families, Illness and Disability: An Integrative Treatment Model.* New York: Basic Books, 1994.

future. They must pull together to cope with the immediate crisis. In the face of uncertainty, they need to develop flexibility toward future goals, reorienting their hopes and dreams.

The *chronic phase,* whether long or short, is the time span between the initial diagnosis/readjustment and the potential third phase when issues of death and terminal illness predominate. This era can be marked by constancy, progression, or episodic change. It has been referred to as "the long haul" and "day-to-day living with chronic illness" phase. Often, the patient and family have come to grips psychologically and organizationally with permanent changes and have devised an ongoing modus operandi. The family's ability to maintain the semblance of a normal life with a chronic illness and heightened uncertainty is a key task of this period. If the illness is fatal, this is a time of living in limbo. For certain highly debilitating but not clearly fatal illnesses, such as a massive stroke or dementia, the family can feel saddled with an exhausting problem without end. Paradoxically, a family may feel that its only hope to resume a normal life can be realized after the death of their ill member. The maintenance of maximum autonomy for all family members in the face of protracted adversity is a key developmental task that helps to offset these trapped, helpless feelings.

In the *terminal phase,* the inevitability of death becomes apparent and dominates family life. The family must cope with issues of separation, death, mourning, and resumption of family life beyond the loss (Walsh & McGoldrick, 1991).

Families that adapt best to this phase are able to shift their view of mastery from controlling the illness to a successful process of letting go. Optimal coping involves emotional openness as well as dealing with the myriad of practical tasks at hand. This includes seeing this phase as an opportunity to share precious time together, to acknowledge the impending loss, to deal with unfinished business, and to say goodbyes. If they have not decided beforehand, the patient and key family members need to decide about such things as a living will; the extent of medical intervention desired; preferences about dying at home, in the hospital, or at hospice; and wishes about a funeral and memorial service. For illnesses such as heart disease, in which death can occur at any time, or with progressive conditions that can increasingly impair mental functioning (e.g., Alzheimer's disease), it is vital that these conversations are encouraged much earlier in the illness.

Critical *transition* periods link the three time phases. Transitions in the illness life cycle are times when families reevaluate the appropriateness of their previous life structure in the face of new illness-related demands. Unfinished business from the previous phase can complicate or block movement through the transitions. Families or individuals can become permanently frozen in an adaptive structure that has outlived its usefulness (Penn, 1983). For example, the usefulness of pulling together in the crisis phase can become maladaptive and stifling for all family members over a long chronic phase. Enmeshed families, because of their rigid and fused style, would have difficulty negotiating this delicate transition. Because high cohesion may be typical and not dysfunction in some cultures, clinicians need to be cautious not to pathologize a normative cultural pattern. A family that is adept at handling the day-to-day practicalities of a long-term stable illness but limited in its emotional coping skills may encounter difficulty if their family member's disease becomes terminal. The relatively greater demand for affective coping skills in the terminal phase compared to the chronic phase may create a crisis for a family navigating this transition.

The interaction of the time phases and typology of illness provides a framework for a normative psychosocial developmental model for chronic disease that resembles models for human development. The time phases (crisis, chronic, and terminal) can be considered broad developmental periods in the natural history of chronic disease. Each period has certain basic tasks independent of the type of illness. Each type of illness has specific supplementary tasks.

Clinical Implications

This model provides a framework for assessment and clinical intervention with a family facing a serious health problem. It facilitates a grasp of chronic illness and disability in psychosocial terms. Attention to features of onset, course, outcome, and incapacitation provide markers that focus clinical assessment and intervention with a family. For instance, acute-onset illnesses demand high levels of adaptability, problem solving, role reallocation, and balanced cohesion. In such circumstances, helping families to maximize flexibility enables them to adapt more successfully.

An illness timeline delineates psychosocial developmental stages of an illness, each phase with its own unique developmental tasks. It is important for families to address phase-related tasks in sequence to optimize succcessful adaptation over the long haul of a chronic disorder. Therefore, attention to time allows the clinician to assess family strengths and vulnerabilities in relation to the present and future phases of the illness.

The model clarifies treatment planning. First, goal setting is guided by awareness of the components of family functioning that are most relevant to particular types or phases of an illness. Sharing this information with the family and deciding upon specific goals provide a better sense of control and realistic hope to the family. This process empowers families in their journey of living with a chronic disorder. Also, this knowledge educates the family about warning signs that should alert them to call at appropriate times for brief, goal-oriented treatment.

The framework is useful for timing family psychosocial checkups to coincide with key transition points in the illness life cycle. Preventively oriented psychoeducational or support groups for patients and their families (Gonzales, Steinglass, & Reiss, 1989) can be designed to deal with different types of conditions (e.g., progressive, life-threatening, relapsing). Also, brief psychoeducational modules, timed for critical phases of particular types of diseases, enable families to digest manageable portions of a long-term coping process. Modules can be tailored to particular phases of the illness life cycle and family coping skills that are necessary to confront disease-related demands. This provides a cost-effective preventive service that also can identify high-risk families.

The model provides a context into which to integrate other aspects of a comprehensive assessment. This would involve evaluation of a range of common and illness-specific family dynamics in relation to the psychosocial type and time phases of illness. Other important components of an illness-oriented family assessment that are beyond the scope of this chapter include the family's belief system (Rolland, 1998; Wright, Watson, & Bell, 1996); the meaning of the illness to the family; the family's medical crisis planning; the family's capacity to perform home-based medical care; and the family's illness-oriented communication, problem solving, role reallocation, emotional involvement, social support, and availability and use of community resources (see Rolland, 1994a).

Using this typological and developmental model of illness, we can now address the interface of illness, individual, and family development.

INTERFACE OF THE ILLNESS, INDIVIDUAL, AND FAMILY LIFE CYCLES

To place the unfolding of chronic disease into a developmental context, it is crucial to understand the intertwining of three evolutionary threads: the illness, the individual, and the family life cycles. To facilitate dialogue, a language is needed that bridges these developmental threads. Two overarching concepts are that of a life cycle and that of life structure.

Early life cycle frameworks assumed that there was a basic sequence and unfolding of the life course within which individual, family, or illness uniqueness occurs. More recent thinking has modified the notion of an invariant epigenetic process in light of the major influences of cultural, socioeconomic, gender, ethnic, and racial diversity (see Chapter 1). Illness, individual, and family development have in common the notion of phases, each with its own developmental tasks. Carter and McGoldrick have divided the family life cycle into eight phases, in which marker events (e.g., marriage, birth of first child, last child leaving home) herald the transition from one phase to the next. Illness is a significant marker event that can both color the nature of a developmental period and be colored by its timing in the individual and family life cycle.

Life structure refers to the underlying pattern or design of a person or family's life at any given point in the life cycle, composed of various commitments (e.g., job, child-rearing, religious affiliation, leisure) and their relative importance. Levinson (1978, 1986), in his description of individual adult development, describes how individuals' and families' life structures can move between periods of life structure transition and building/ maintaining. Transition periods are sometimes the most vulnerable because previous individual, family, and illness life structures are reappraised in light of new developmental tasks that may require major discontinuous change rather than minor alterations (Hoffman, 1989). The primary goal of a life structure-building/maintaining period is to form a life structure and enrich life within it on the basis of the key choices an individual/family made during the preceding transition period.

Different stages of the family life cycle coincide with shifts between family developmental tasks that require intense bonding or an inside-the-family focus, as in the "families with young children" child-rearing stage, versus stages such as "launching children and moving on" during which the external family boundary is loosened, often emphasizing personal identity and autonomy (Combrinck-Graham, 1985). In life cycle terms, this suggests a fit between family developmental tasks and the relative need for family members to direct their energies inside the family and work together to accomplish those tasks.

These unifying concepts provide a base to discuss the fit among illness, individual, and family development. Each phase in these three kinds of life cycle poses tasks and challenges that move through periods of being more or less in sync with each other. It can be useful to distinguish (1) between child-rearing and non-child-rearing phases in the family life cycle, (2) the alternation of transition and life structure–building/maintaining periods in all the life cycles, and (3) periods of higher and lower psychosocial demands over the course of a chronic illness or disability.

Generally, illness and disability tend to push individual and family developmental processes toward transition and increased cohesion. Analogous to the addition of an infant member at the beginning of the child-rearing phase, the occurrence of chronic illness sets in motion an inside-the-family-focused process of socialization to illness. Symptoms, loss of function, the demands of shifting or new illness-related roles, and the fear of loss through death all require a family to pull together. This inward pull of the disorder risks different normative strains depending on timing with the family's and individual members' phases of development. In clinical assessment, a basic question is "What is the fit between the psychosocial demands of a condition and family and individual life structures and developmental tasks at a particular point in the life cycle?" Also, how will this fit change as the course of the illness unfolds in relation to the family life cycle and the development of each member?

Periods of Child-Rearing and Postlaunching

If illness onset coincides with the launching or postlaunching phases of the family life cycle, it can derail a family's natural momentum. Illness or disability in a young adult may require a heightened dependency and return to the family of origin for caretaking. Each family member's autonomy and individuation are jeopardized. The young adult's ability to establish a life away from home is threatened. Both parents may have to relinquish budding interests outside the family. Family dynamics as well as severity of the condition will influence whether the family's reversion to a child-rearing-like structure is a temporary detour or a permanent reversal. Since enmeshed families frequently face the transition to a more autonomous launching/postlaunching phase with trepidation, a serious illness provides a sanctioned reason to return to the "safety" of the child-rearing period.

Disease onset that coincides with the child-rearing phases in the family life cycle, such as the "families with young children" stage, can foster a prolongation of this period. At worst, the family can become permanently stuck at that phase and enmeshed. When the inward pull of the illness and the phase of the life cycle coincide, there is a risk that they will amplify one another. In families that function marginally before an illness begins, this kind of mutual reinforcement can trigger a runaway process leading to overt family dysfunction. Minuchin et al.'s (1975, 1978) research of psychosomatic families has documented this process in several common childhood illnesses.

When a parent develops a chronic disease during the child-rearing phases of the life cycle, the family's ability to stay on course is most severely taxed. For more serious conditions, the impact of the illness is like the addition of a new infant member, one with special needs that will compete with those of the real children for potentially scarce family resources. In psychosocially milder health problems, efficient reallocation of roles may suf-

fice. A recent case of a family at the "Family with young children" phase illustrates this point.

Scott and his wife Molly presented for treatment six months after Scott had sustained a severe burn injury to both hands that required skin grafting. A year of recuperation was necessary before Scott would be able to return to his job, which required physical labor and full use of his hands. Before this injury, Molly had been at home full time raising their two children, ages 3 and 5. In this case, although Scott was temporarily handicapped in terms of his career, he was physically fit to assume the role of househusband. Initially, both Scott and Molly remained at home, using his disability income to get by. When Molly expressed an interest in finding a job to lessen financial pressures, Scott resisted, and manageable marital strain caused by his injury flared into dysfunctional conflict.

Sufficient resources were available in the system to accommodate the illness and ongoing child-rearing tasks. Their definition of marriage lacked the necessary role flexibility to master the problem. Treatment focused on rethinking his masculine and monolithic definition of "family provider," a definition that had, in fact, emerged in full force during this phase of the family life cycle.

If the disease affecting a parent is severely debilitating (e.g., traumatic brain injury, cervical spinal cord injury), its impact on the child-rearing family is twofold. A "new" family member is added, one parent is essentially lost to the illness, and the other's presence may be diminished by caregiving demands, thereby creating the semblance of a single-parent family with an added child. In acute-onset illnesses, both events can occur simultaneously, in which case family resources may be inadequate to meet the combined child-rearing and caregiving demands. In this situation, families commonly turn to other children and extended-family members to share responsibilities. This can become dysfunctional for children to the extent to which they sacrifice their own developmental needs or a developmental detour for grandparents who must relinquish newly achieved freedom from parenting to resume child care. Yet, we need to be cautious not to pathologize these structural changes, which may be necessary, for instance, in a single-parent household or may be culturally normative expressions of loyalty in some ethnic groups.

If we look at chronic diseases in a more refined way through the lens of the illness typology and time phases, it is readily apparent that the degree of inward pull varies enormously, with important effects on the family life cycle independent of family dynamics. The tendency for a condition to pull a family inward increases with the level of disability or risk of death. Progressive diseases over time inherently require greater cohesion than disorders with a stable, constant course. The continuous addition of new demands as an illness progresses keeps a family's energy focused inward on the illness. In contrast, after a modus operandi has been forged, a constant-course disease (excluding those with severe disability) permits a family greater flexibility to enter or resume life cycle planning. As the following case in the post-launching phase illustrates, the added inward pull exerted by a progressive disease increases the risk of reversing normal family disengagement or freezing a family into a permanently fused state:

> Mr. L., a 54-year-old African American, had become increasingly depressed as a result of severe and progressive complications of his adult-onset diabetes over the past five years, including a leg amputation and renal failure that had recently required instituting home dialysis. For twenty years, Mr. L. had had an uncomplicated constant course, allowing him to lead a full, active life. He was an excellent athlete and engaged in a number of recreational group sports. Short- and long-term family planning had never focused on his illness. This optimistic attitude was reinforced by the fact that two people in Mrs. L.'s family of origin had had diabetes without complications. Their only child, a son (age 26), had uneventfully left home after high school and had recently married. Mr. and Mrs. L. had a stable marriage, in which both maintained many outside independent interests. In short, the family had moved smoothly into the postlaunching phase of the life cycle.
>
> Mr. L.'s disease transformation to a progressive phase, coupled with the incapacitating and life-shortening nature of his complications, had re-versed the normal postlaunching process for all family members. His advancing illness required his wife to take a second job, which necessitated giving up her many involvements with their church. Their son and his wife moved back home to help his mother take care of his father and the house. Mr. L., unable to work and deprived of his athletic social network, was isolated at home and spent his days watching television. He felt that he was a burden to everyone, was blocked in his own midlife development and future plans with his wife, and foresaw a future filled only with suffering.
>
> The goal of family treatment in developmental terms centered on reversing some of the system's overreaction back to a more realistic balance. For Mr. L., this meant both coming to terms with his losses and fears of suffering and death and identifying the abilities and possibilities that were still available to him. This involved reworking his life structure to accommodate his real limitations while maximizing his chances of remaining independent. For instance, although Mr. L could no longer participate on the playing field, he could remain involved in sports through coaching. For Mrs. L. and her son, this meant developing realistic expectations for Mr. L. that reestablished him as an active family member with a share of family responsibilities. This helped the mother and son to resume key aspects of their autonomy within an illness-family system.

Relapsing illnesses alternate between periods of drawing a family inward and periods of release from the immediate demands of disease. However, the on-call state of preparedness that many such illnesses require keeps some part of the family in a higher cohesion mode despite medically asymptomatic periods. Again, this may impede the natural flow of phases in the family life cycle.

One way to think about the time phases of illness is in terms of their involving a progression from a crisis phase requiring intensified cohesion to a chronic phase often demanding less cohesion. A terminal phase forces most families back into being more inwardly focused and cohesive. In other words, the "illness life structure," that a family develops to accommodate each phase in the illness life cycle is influenced by the differing needs for cohesion dictated by each time phase. For example, in a family in which the onset of the illness has coincided with a postlaunching phase of development, the transition to the chronic phase permits a family to resume more of its momentum.

Life Cycle Transition Periods

Clinicians need to be mindful of the timing of the onset of a chronic illness in terms of family and individual transitions. Chronic conditions may precipitate the loss of the family's preillness identity. They force the family into a transition in which one of the family's main tasks is to accommodate the anticipation of further loss and possibly untimely death. When onset of a condition coincides with a transition in the family or individual life cycle, one may expect that issues related to previous, current, and anticipated loss will be magnified. Transition periods are often characterized by upheaval, rethinking of previous and future commitments, and openness to change. This poses a greater risk that the illness may become unnecessarily embedded or inappropriately ignored in plans for the next developmental phase. This can be a major precursor of family dysfunction in chronic disease. By adopting a longitudinal perspective, a clinician can stay attuned to future transitions, particularly overlaps in those of the illness, individual, and family life cycles.

The following example highlights the importance of the illness in relation to future developmental transitions:

In one Hispanic family, the father, a carpenter and primary financial provider, had a mild heart attack. He also suffered from emphysema. At first, his level of impairment was mild and stabilized. This allowed him to continue part-time work. Because their children were all teenagers, his wife was able to undertake part-time work to help maintain financial stability. The oldest son, age 15, seemed relatively unaffected. Two years later, the father experienced a second, more life-threatening heart attack and became totally disabled. His son, now 17, had dreams of going away to college. The specter of financial hardship and the perceived need for a "man in the family" created a serious di-

lemma of choice for the son and the family. This was additionally complicated for this family, which had worked hard to move out of the housing projects and ensure that the children could get a good education for a better future.

In this case, there was a fundamental clash between developmental issues of individuation and family dreams for the next generation at the launching phase of the family life cycle and the ongoing demands of progressive chronic disability on the family. This vignette demonstrates the potential collision between simultaneous transition periods: the illness transition to a more incapacitating and progressive course, the adolescent son's transition to early adulthood, and the family's transition from the "living with teenagers" to "launching young adults" stage. This example also illustrates the significance of the type of illness. An illness that was relapsing or less life-threatening and incapacitating (in contrast to one with a progressive or constant course) might have interfered less with this young man's separation from his family of origin. If his father had an intermittently incapacitating illness, such as disk disease, the son might have moved out but tailored his choices to remain nearby and thus available during acute flare-ups.

Life Structure-Maintaining Periods

Illness onset that coincides with a life structure–building/stable period in family or individual development presents a different challenge. These periods are characterized by the living out of choices that were made during the preceding transition period. Relative to transition periods, the cohesive bonds of the family and individual members are oriented to protect the family unit's and their own current life structures. Milder conditions (nonfatal, only mildly disabling) may require some revision of individual or family life structure but not a radical restructuring that would necessitate a shift to a transitional phase of development. A severe chronic illness will force families into a more complete transition at a time when individual and family inertia is to preserve the momentum of a stable period. To successfully navigate this kind of crisis, family adaptability requires the ability to transform their entire life structure to a prolonged transitional state.

For instance, in the previous example, the father's heart disease rapidly progressed while the oldest son was in a transition period in his own development. The nature of the strain in developmental terms would be quite different if his father's disease progression had occurred when this young man was 26, had already left home, had finished college and secured a first job, and had married and had his first child. In the latter scenario, the oldest son's life structure would be in an inwardly focused, highly cohesive, "Families with young children" stage of the life cycle. Fully accommodating the needs of his family of origin could require a monumental shift of his developmental priorities, creating a potential crisis regarding his loyalty to his family of origin and his new nuclear family. When this illness crisis coincided with a developmental transition period (age 17), having made no permanent commitments, he might have felt very threatened about losing his status as a "single young adult" to a caregiving role that could become his permanent life structure. Later, in his mid-twenties, he would have made developmental choices and would have been in the process of living them out. Not only would he have made commitments, but also they would also be more highly cohesive in nature, focused on his newly formed family. To serve the demands of an illness transition, the son might have needed to shift his previously stable life structure back to a transitional state. And the shift would have happened out of phase with the flow of his individual and nuclear family's development. One precarious way to resolve this dilemma of divided loyalties might be the merging of the two households.

This discussion raises several key clinical points. From a systems viewpoint, at the time of diagnosis, it is important to know the phase of the family life cycle and the stage of individual development of all family members, not just the ill member. First, illness and disability in one family member can profoundly affect the developmental goals of another member. For instance, disability in an infant can be a serious roadblock to a mother's mastery of child-rearing, and a life-threatening illness in a young adult can interfere with the well spouse's readiness to become a parent. Also, family members frequently do not adapt equally well to chronic illness. Each family member's ability to adapt and the rate at which he or she does so are directly related to the individual's own developmental stage and role in the family (Ireys & Burr, 1984).

The timing of chronic illness in the life cycle can be normative or nonnormative ("off-time"). Coping with chronic illness and death are considered normally anticipated tasks in late adulthood, whereas their occurrence earlier is out of phase and tends to be developmentally more disruptive (Neugarten, 1976). As untimely events, chronic diseases can severely disrupt the usual sense of continuity and rhythm of the life cycle. Chronic diseases that occur in the child-rearing period can be most devastating because of their potential impact on family financial and child-rearing responsibilities (Patterson, 1988). The actual impact will depend on the type of illness and the preillness roles of each family member.

The notion of "out-of-phase" illnesses can be conceptualized in a more refined way that highlights patterns of strain related to time. First, since diseases exert an inward pull on most families, they can be more developmentally disruptive to families in the "Families with adolescents," or "launching children" stages of development. Second, the period of transition generated by the onset of a serious illness is particularly "out of phase" if it coincides with a stable, life structure–maintaining period in the individual or family's life cycle. Third, if the particular illness is progressive, relapsing, increasingly incapacitating, and/or life-threatening, then the unfolding phases of the disease will be punctuated by numerous transitions. Under these conditions, a family will need to more frequently alter their illness life structure to accommodate shifting and increasing demands of the disease. This level of demand and uncertainty keeps the illness in the forefront of a family's consciousness, constantly impinging upon their attempts to get back in phase developmentally. Finally, the transition from the crisis to the chronic phase of the illness life cycle is often the key juncture at which the intensity of the family's socialization to living with chronic disease can be relaxed. In this sense, it offers a window of opportunity for the family to recover its developmental course.

Confronted by illness and disability, a family should aim, above all, to deal with the developmental demands of the illness without forcing family members to sacrifice their own or the family's development as a system. It is important to determine whose life plans were canceled, postponed, or altered and when plans put on hold and future developmental issues will be addressed. In this way, clinicians can anticipate life cycle nodal points related to autonomy within the condition versus subjugation to it. Families can be helped to strike a healthier balance with life plans as a way to minimize overall family strain and relationship skews between caregivers and the ill member. It is most useful to assist families to resolve feelings of guilt, overresponsibility, and hopelessness and find family and external resources to enhance freedom both to pursue their own goals and to provide needed care for the ill member.

Early in the experience of illness, families have particular difficulty appraising the need for temporary detours or permanent changes in life cycle plans. Once developmental plans are derailed, the inherent inertia of chronic conditions makes it more difficult to find one's original path. This underscores the importance of timely psychoeducation for families. Also, the process by which life cycle decisions are reached is particularly important. Significant factors include gender-based or culturally defined beliefs about who should assume primary responsibility for caregiving. Cultures and families are quite diverse in their expectations about the relative priority of sacrifice for the family in time of need versus protecting personal goals and plans. A forward-thinking clinical philosophy that uses a life cycle perspective as a way of gaining a positive sense of control and op-

portunity is vital for families dealing with chronic disorders.

MULTIGENERATIONAL EXPERIENCES WITH ILLNESS, LOSS, AND CRISIS

A family's current behavior cannot be adequately comprehended apart from its history (Boszormenyi-Nagy & Sparks, 1973; Bowen, 1978; Byng-Hall, 1988; Framo, 1992; Paul & Grosser, 1965; Walsh & McGoldrick, 1991). This is particularly germane to families that face a chronic condition. A historical inquiry may help to explain and predict the family's current style of coping and adaptation and the creation of meaning about an illness. A multigenerational assessment helps to clarify areas of strength and vulnerability and identifies high risk-families who, burdened by unresolved issues and dysfunctional patterns transmitted across time, cannot absorb the challenges presented by a serious condition.

A chronic illness–oriented genogram focuses on how a family organized itself and adapted as an evolving system around previous illnesses and unexpected crises in the current and previous generations. Patterns of coping, replications, discontinuities, shifts in relationships (i.e., alliances, triangles, cut-offs), and sense of competence are noted (McGoldrick & Gerson, 1985). These patterns are transmitted across generations as family myths, taboos, catastrophic expectations, and belief systems (Seaborn, Lorenz, & Kaplan, 1992; Walsh & McGoldrick, 1991). A central goal is to bring to light areas of consensus and learned differences (Penn, 1983) that are sources of cohesion and conflict. Also, it is useful to inquire about other forms of loss (e.g., divorce, migration), crisis (e.g., lengthy unempolyment, rape, a natural disaster), and protracted adversity (e.g., poverty, racism, war, political oppression). These experiences can provide sources of resilience and effective coping skills in the face of a serious health problem.

Since ethnicity, race, and religion strongly influence how families approach health and illness, any multigenerational assessment should include inquiry into these areas (McGoldrick, Pearce, &

Giordano, 1996). As professionals, we need to be mindful of the cultural differences between ourselves, the patient, and the family. The different ethnic backgrounds of the adults in a family or between a family, professionals, and systems of health care may be a primary reason for discrepancies in beliefs that emerge at the time of a major illness. This is especially common for minority groups (e.g., African American, Asian, and Hispanic) that experience discrimination or marginalization from our prevailing White Anglo culture. Significant ethnic differences, particularly health beliefs, typically emerge in such areas as:

1. beliefs about control,
2. the definition of the appropriate "sick role,"
3. the kind and degree of open communication about the disease,
4. who should be included in the illness caretaking system (e.g., extended family, friends, professionals),
5. who the primary caretaker is (almost always women), and
6. the kind of rituals that are viewed as normative at different stages of an illness (e.g., hospital bedside vigils, healing and funeral rituals) (Imber-Black, 1991).

Health and mental health professionals should become familiar with the belief systems of various ethnic, racial, and religious groups in their community, particularly as these translate into different behavior patterns during illness. For example, traditional Navajo culture holds that thought and language have the power to shape reality and control events (Carrese & Rhodes, 1995). In other words, language can determine reality. From the Navajo world view, discussing the potential complications of a serious illness with a newly diagnosed Navajo patient is harmful and strongly increases the likelihood that such complications will occur. This belief system clashes dramatically with those of health professionals (backed by powerful legal imperatives) that mandate explaining possible complications or promoting advance directives regarding the limits of medical care desired by the ill family member. Carrese and Rhodes, in their study

of Navajo, give one example of a Navajo daughter describing how the risks of bypass surgery were explained to her father: "The surgeon told him that he may not wake up, that this is the risk of every surgery. For the surgeon it was very routine, but the way that my Dad received it, it was almost like a death sentence, and he never consented to the surgery" (p. 828).

Illness Type and Time Phase Issues

The typology of illness and time phases framework helps focus the clinician's multigenerational evaluation. Whereas a family may have certain standard ways of coping with any illness, there may be critical differences in their style and success in adaptation to different types of disorders. It is important to track prior family illnesses for areas of perceived competence, failures, or inexperience. A family may disregard the differences in demands related to different kinds of illnesses and thus may show a disparity in their level of coping with one disease versus another. Inquiry about similar and different types of illnesses (e.g., life-threatening versus non-life-threatening) may find, for instance, that a family dealt successfully with non-life-threatening illnesses but reeled under the weight of the mother's metastatic breast cancer. Such a family might be well equipped to deal with less severe conditions, but it might be particularly vulnerable if another life-threatening illness were to occur. Another family may have experienced only non-life-threatening illnesses and need psychoeducation to successfully cope with the uncertainties particular to life-threatening conditions. Such inquiry clarifies areas of family strength and vulnerability in facing a particular type of disorder. A recent family consultation highlights the importance of family history in uncovering areas of inexperience:

Joe, his wife Ann, and their three teenage children presented for a family evaluation ten months after Joe's diagnosis with moderate-severe asthma. Joe (age 44) had been successfully employed for many years as a spray painter. Apparently, exposure to a new chemical in the paint triggered the onset of asthmatic attacks that necessitated hospitalization and job disability. Initially, his physician told him that improvement would occur but remained non-committal as to the level of chronicity. Although somewhat improved, Joe continued to have persistent and moderate respiratory symptoms. His continued breathing difficulties contributed to a depression, uncharacteristic tempermental outbursts, alcohol abuse, and family discord.

During the initial assessment, I inquired about the family's prior experience coping with chronic disease. This was the nuclear family's first encounter with chronic illness. In their families of origin, they had limited experience. Ann's father had died seven years earlier of a sudden and unexpected heart attack. Joe's brother had died in an accidental drowning. Neither had had experience with disease as an ongoing process. Joe had assumed that improvement meant cure. Illness for both had meant either death or recovery. The physician and family system were not attuned to the hidden risks for this family going through the transition from the crisis to chronic phase of his asthma—the juncture at which the permanency of the disease needed to be addressed.

Another crucial issue was the onset of the father's disability during their children's adolescence and the looming launching phase of the family life cycle. In these situations, adolescents may become symptomatic (e.g., acting-out behavior, school problems, or drug use) as a way of coping with their fears of loss of their father or conflicts about moving ahead with personal goals if family loyalty expectations requires them to assume caregiving roles.

Tracking a family's coping capabilities in the crisis, chronic, and terminal phases of previous chronic illnesses can highlight legacies of strength, and a history of difficulties at a specific time phase can alert a clinician to potentially vulnerable periods for a family over the course of the current chronic illness. A family that was seen in treatment illustrates the interplay of problems coping with a current illness that are fueled by unresolved issues related to disease experiences in one's family of origin. The type of illness and unresolved complications in the terminal phase are critical features of this case.

Angela, her husband Bill, and their 8-year-old son Mark, an Italian Catholic, working-class family, presented for treatment four months after Angela had been injured in a life-threatening head-on auto collision. The driver of the other vehicle was at fault. Angela had sustained a serious concussion. Initially, the medical team was concerned that she might have suffered a cerebral hemorrhage. Ultimately, it was determined that this had not occurred. Over this time, Angela became increasingly depressed and, despite strong reassurance, continued to believe that she had a life-threatening condition and would die from a brain hemorrhage.

During the initial evaluation, she revealed that she was experiencing vivid dreams of meeting her deceased father. Her father, with whom she had been extremely close, had died from a cerebral hemorrhage after a four-year history of a progressive debilitating brain tumor. His illness had been marked by progressive and uncontrolled epileptic seizures. Angela was 14 at the time and was the "baby" in the family, her two siblings being more than ten years her senior. The family had shielded her from his illness. This culminated in her mother deciding to not have Angela attend either the wake or the funeral of her father. This event galvanized her position as the child in need of protection—a dynamic that carried over into her marriage. Despite her hurt, anger, and lack of acceptance of her father's death, she had avoided dealing with her feelings with her mother for over twenty years.

Other family history revealed that Angela's mother's brother had died from a sudden stroke, and her maternal grandfather had died of a stroke when her mother was seven years old. Her mother had experienced an open casket wake for three days at home.

In this situation, Angela's own life-threatening head injury triggered a catastrophic reaction and dramatic resurfacing of previous unresolved traumatic losses involving similar types of illness and injury. In particular, her father's, uncle's, and grandfather's deaths by central nervous system disorders had sensitized her to this type of problem. The fact that she had witnessed the slow, agonizing, and terrifying downhill course of her father only heightened her catastrophic fears.

Therapy focused on a series of tasks that included Angela initiating a series of conversations with her mother about her feelings of having been excluded from her father's funeral and about the pattern of mutual protection between mother and daughter over the years. Angela, then wrote a good-bye letter to her father, experiencing the grief that she had bypassed for so many years. It was particularly important to include her husband throughout this phase of treatment because her grief directly stimulated his own anxiety about the threatened loss of his own aging parents. The final stage of treatment involved a graveside ritual in which Angela, with her family of origin and nuclear family present, read her goodbye letter to her father.

Replication of System Patterns

For any significant chronic illness in either adult's family of origin, a clinician should try to get a picture of how those families organized themselves to handle the range of disease-related emotional and practical tasks. It is important for a clinician to find out what role each played in handling these tasks. Whether the parents (as children) were given too much responsiblity (parentified) or shielded from involvement is of particular importance. What did they learn from those experiences that influences how they think about the current illness? Whether they emerge with a strong sense of competence or failure is essential information. By collecting the above information about each adult's family of origin, one can anticipate areas of conflict and consensus.

Evaluation of the system that existed and evolved around a prior illness includes assessment of the pattern of relationships within that system. In many families, relationship patterns are adaptive, flexible, and cohesively balanced. In other families, these relationships can be dysfunctionally skewed, rigid, enmeshed, disengaged, and/or triangulated. As Penn (1983) and Walker (1983) have described, unresolved issues related to illness and loss frequently remain dormant and suddenly reemerge triggered by a chronic illness in the current nuclear family. Penn describes how particular coalitions that emerge in the context of a chronic illness are isomorphs of those that existed in each adult's family of origin. The following case is an example:

Mr. and Mrs. S. had been married for nine years when their 6-year-old son Jeff developed childhood-onset diabetes. Mrs. S. became very protective of her son and made frequent calls to their pediatrician expressing persistent concerns about Jeff's condition. This occurred despite Jeff's doing well medically and emotionally and frequent reassurances from the physician. At the same time, the previously close marital relationship became more distant, characterized by Mrs. S. arguing with her husband and Mr. S. actively distancing himself from his wife and son.

In Mrs. S.'s family of origin, she had grown up with a tyrannical, alcoholic father. She had witnessed intense conflict between her parents. During her childhood and adolescence, Mrs. S. had tried to "rescue" her mother. To counterbalance her victimized mother, she tried to tend to her mother's needs and cheer her up. She talked frequently to her family physician about the situation at home. However, she felt that she had failed at this, since her mother continued over the years to be stuck and depressed.

Mr. S. grew up in a family in which his father had disabling heart disease. His mother devoted a great deal of time to taking care of his father. Not to further burden his parents, he raised himself, maintaining distance from the primary caretaking relationship between his parents. He stoically viewed this strategy as having been successful. He supported his mother's caregiving efforts by mostly taking care of his own needs.

With their son's illness, Mrs. S., burdened by feelings of guilt at being a failed rescuer, had a second chance to "do it right" and assuage her guilt. The diabetes gave her this opportunity, and it is a culturally sanctioned normative role for a parent, particularly a mother, to protect an ill child. These factors, her unresolved family of origin issues, and the culturally sanctioned roles promoted the enmeshment that developed with her son.

In this situation, Mr. S., though outwardly objecting to the coalition between his wife and son, honors that relationship, as if it would make up for the one he forfeited with his own mother. Further, despite his unmet needs as a child, he believes that the structure, and his role in it, had worked. Both Mr. and Mrs. S. have replicated their particular positions in triangles from their families of origin. In a complementary way, Mrs. S. is a rescuer in a coalition and Mr. S. is in the distant position in the triangle they create with their son.

The roles of each person in this triangle fit traditional cultural norms. The mother is appropriately concerned and tending to her ill child. The father is in the more distant instrumental provider position. For this reason, it can be more difficult for a clinician to ferret out a traditional pattern from the beginnings of a dysfunctional reenactment of family of origin patterns developed around prior experiences with illness, crisis, or loss. Early assessment of multigenerational patterns such as these helps to distinguish normative from problematic responses. Further, it helps to identify the source and degree of commitment to gender-defined caregiving roles. Particularly in crisis situations such as illness onset, couples may fall back on traditional divisions of labor. The climate of fear and uncertainty itself is a powerful stimulus to seek the familiar, time-tested methods of coping. This is reinforced if traditional gender-defined roles worked well in prior situations of illness or crisis. Or, as this case highlights, a sense of failure around a gender-based role can act as a powerful push toward reenactment in the current situation. In this case, Mrs. S. is driven to reenact the role of emotional rescuer, a typically female role that she felt she had failed at with her mother in relation to her father's chronic alcoholism. Psychoeducational guidelines can help her to distinguish what forms and degree of responsiveness are appropriate from those that are excessive and unhelpful. Also, tasks for the husband and couple jointly would be useful to increase a more balanced, shared involvement in the burdens of a chronically ill child. This would counteract the peripheral position of the father.

In this case, early referral by the pediatrician was essential to prevent entrenchment of a long-term dysfunctional relationship pattern. At this early stage, the parents were able to reflect upon the situation, recognize the connection to family of origin issues, and disengage from a destructive path. If these kinds of cases are not detected early, they typically progress over a period of years to highly enmeshed intractable systems. Morbidity is high and may be expressed in a poor medical course and compliance issues, divorce, or child and adolescent behavioral problems.

Reenactment of previous system configurations around an illness can occur largely as an unconscious, automatic process (Byng-Hall, 1988). Further, the dysfunctional complementarity that one sees in these families can emerge specifically within the context of a chronic disease. On detailed inquiry, couples will frequently reveal a tacit unspoken understanding that if an illness occurs, they will reorganize to reenact unfinished business from their families of origin. Typically, the roles that are chosen represent a repetition or reactive opposite of roles that they or the same-sex parent in their family of origin played. This process resembles the unfolding of a genetic template that is activated only under particular biological conditions. It highlights the need for a clinician to distinguish between what constitutes functional family process with and without illness or disability. For families that present in this manner, placing a primary therapeutic emphasis on the resolution of family of origin issues might be the best approach to prevent or rectify an unhealthy triangle.

Distinct from families with dormant, encapsulated illness "time bombs" are those in which illnesses become imbedded within a web of pervasive and longstanding dysfunctional transactions. In this situation, clinicians may collude with a family's resistance to addressing preexisting problems by focusing excessively on the disease itself. If this occurs, a clinician becomes involved in a detouring triangle with the family and the patient, analogous to the dysfunctional triangles formed by parents with an ill child as a way to avert unresolved marital issues (Minuchin et al., 1975, 1978). When a chronic condition reinforces preexisting family dysfunction, the differences between the family's illness and nonillness patterns are less distinct. In the traditional sense of the term "psychosomatic," this kind of family displays a greater level of baseline reactivity; when an illness enters its system, this reactivity gets expressed somatically through a poor medical course and/or treatment noncompliance (Griffith & Griffith, 1994). Such families lack the foundation of a functional nonillness system that can serve as the metaphorical equivalent of a healthy ego in tackling family of origin patterns around disease. The initial focus of therapeutic intervention may need to be targeted more at current nuclear family processes than at multigenerational patterns.

Many families facing chronic conditions have not had dysfunctional multigenerational patterns of adaptation. Yet any family may falter in the face of multiple disease and nondisease stressors that affect it in a relatively short time. With progressive, incapacitating diseases or the concurrence of illnesses in several family members (e.g., families with aging parents), a pragmatic approach that expands the use of resources outside the family is most productive.

Life Cycle Coincidences across Generations

A coincidence of dates across generations is often significant. We often hear statements such as "All the men in my family died of heart attacks by the age of 55." This is a multigenerational statement of biological vulnerability and a legacy and expectation of untimely death. In one case, a man who was vulnerable to stomach ulcers began to eat indiscriminately and drink alcohol excessively, despite medical warnings, when he reached the age of 43, precipitating a crisis requiring surgery. His failure to comply with treatment created a life-threatening situation. It was only after his recovery and upon his forty-fourth birthday that he remarked that his own father had died tragically at age 43 and he had felt an overpowering conflict about surviving past that age.

Knowledge of such age-related multigenerational patterns can alert a clinician to risks of undiagnosable pain syndromes and somatization, compliance issues, blatantly self-destructive behaviors, and realistic fears that may emerge at the time of a diagnosis of an illness or a particular stage of the patient's life cycle. A brief intervention timed with an approaching intergenerational anniversary date is very useful preventively in this type of situation.

CONCLUSION

This chapter offers a conceptual base for thinking about the system created at the interface of chronic illness with the family and individual life cycles. A psychosocial typology and time phases of illness framework facilitate a common language for bridging the worlds of illness, individual, and family development. This developmental landscape is marked by periods of transition, periods of living out decisions and committments, and periods of child-rearing and non-child-rearing. What emerges is the notion of three intertwined lines of development in which there is continual interplay of life structures to carry out individual, family, and illness phase-specific developmental tasks. Families' multigenerational paradigms related to chronic disease, crisis, and loss play upon these three interwoven developmental threads, adding their own texture and pattern.

REFERENCES

Boszormenyi-Nagy, I., & Spark, G. (1973). *Invisible loyalties: Reciprocity in intergenerational family therapy.* New York: Harper & Row.

Bowen, M. (1978). *Family therapy in clinical practice.* New York: Jason Aronson.

Byng-Hall, J. (1988). Scripts and legends in families and family therapy. *Family Process, 27*(2), 167–181.

Campbell, T. L., & Patterson, J. M. (1995). The effectiveness of family interventions in the treatment of physical illness. *Journal of Marital and Family Therapy, 21*(4), 545–583.

Carrese, J., & Rhodes, L. (1995). Western bioethics on the Navajo reservation: Benefit or harm. *Journal of the American Medical Association, 274,* 826–829.

Combrinck-Graham, L. (1985). A developmental model for family systems. *Family Process, 24,* 139–150.

Derogatis, L. R., Abeloff, M. D., & Melisartos, N. (1979). Psychological coping mechanisms and survival time in metastatic breast cancer. *Journal of the American Medical Association, 242,* 1504–1508.

Framo, J. L. (1992). *Family-of-origin therapy: An intergenerational approach.* New York: Brunner/Mazel.

Gonzalez, S., Steinglass, P., & Reiss, D. (1989). Putting the illness in its place: Discussion groups for families with chronic medical illnesses. *Family Process, 28,* 69–87.

Griffith, J., & Griffith, M. (1994). *The body speaks.* New York: Basic Books.

Hoffman, L. (1989). The family life cycle and discontinuous change. In E. Carter & McGoldrick, M. (Eds.), *The changing family life cycle: A framework for family therapy* (2nd ed.). Boston: Allyn and Bacon.

Imber-Black, E. (1991). Rituals and the healing process. In F. Walsh & M. McGoldrick (Eds.), *Living beyond loss: Death in the family.* New York: W. W. Norton.

Ireys, H. T., & Burr, C. K. (1984). Apart and a part: Family issues for young adults with chronic illness and disability. In M. G. Eisenberg, L. C. Sutkin, & M. A. Jansen (Eds.), *Chronic illlness and disability through the life span: Effects on self and family.* New York: Springer.

Levinson, D. J. (1978). *The seasons of a man's life.* New York: Alfred A. Knopf.

Levinson, D. J. (1986). A conception of adult development. *American Psychologist, 41,* 3–13.

McGoldrick, M., & Gerson, R. (1985). *Genograms in family assessment.* New York: W. W. Norton.

McGoldrick, M., Pearce, J. K, & Giordano, J. (1996). *Ethnicity and family therapy* (2nd ed.). New York: The Guilford Press.

Minuchin, S., Baker, L., Rosman, B. L., Liebman, R., Milman, L., & Todd, T. (1975). A conceptual model of psychosomatic illness in children: Family organization and family therapy. *Archives of General Psychiatry, 32,* 1031–1038.

Minuchin, S., Rosman, B. L., & Baker, L. (1978). *Psychosomatic families: Anorexia nervosa in context.* Cambridge, MA: Harvard University Press.

Moos, R. (Ed.). (1984). *Coping with physical illness: Vol. 2. New Perspectives.* New York: Plenum Press.

Neugarten, B. (1976). Adaptation and the life cycle. *The Counselling Psychologist, 6,* 16–20.

Patterson, J. M. (1988). Chronic illness in children and the impact on families. In C. S. Chilman, E. W. Nunnally, & F. M. Cox (Eds.), *Chronic illness and disability,* (pp. 69–107) (Families in Trouble Series, Vol. 2). Newbury Park, CA: Sage.

Paul, N. L., & Grosser, G. (1965). Operational mourning and its role in conjoint family therapy. *Community Mental Health Journal, 1,* 339–345.

Penn, P. (1983). Coalitions and binding interactions in families with chronic illness. *Family Systems Medicine, 1*(2), 16–25.

Rolland, J. S. (1984). Toward a psychosocial typology of chronic and life-threatening illness. *Family Systems Medicine, 2,* 245–263.

Rolland, J. S. (1987a). Chronic illness and the life cycle: A conceptual framework. *Family Process, 26*(2), 203–221.

Rolland, J. S. (1987b). Family illness paradigms: Evolution and significance. *Family Systems Medicine, 5*(4), 467–486.

Rolland, J. S. (1990). Anticipatory loss: A family systems developmental framework. *Family Process, 29*(3), 229–244.

Rolland, J. S. (1994a). *Families, Illness, & Disability: An Integrative Treatment Model.* New York: Basic Books.

Rolland, J. S. (1994b). In sickness and in health: The impact of illness on couples' relationships. *Journal of Marital and Family Therapy, 20*(4), 327–349.

Rolland, J. S. (1998). Beliefs and collaboration in illness: Evolution over time. *Families, Systems & Health* (formerly *Family Systems Medicine) 16,* 7–25.

Schmale, A. H., & Iker, H. (1971). Hopelessness as a predictor of cervical cancer. *Social Science and Medicine, 5,* 95–100.

Seaburn, D., Lorenz, A., & Kaplan, D. (1992). The transgenerational development of chronic illness meanings. *Family Systems Medicine, 10*(4), 385–395.

U.S. Bureau of the Census (1992). *Statistical abstract of the United States.* Washington, DC: U.S. Government Printing Office.

U.S. Bureau of the Census (1997). *Statistical abstract of the United States.* Washington, DC: U.S. Government Printing Office.

Walker, G. (1983). The pact: The caretaker-parent/ill-child coalition in families with chronic illness. *Family Systems Medicine 1*(4), 6–29.

Walsh, F., & McGoldrick, M. (1991) *Living beyond loss: Death in the family.* New York: Norton.

Wright, L., Watson, W., & Bell, J. (1996). *Beliefs: The heart of healing in families and illness.* New York: Basic Books.

CHAPTER 30

INTERACTIONS BETWEEN THE THERAPIST'S AND CLIENT'S LIFE CYCLE STAGES

STEVE LERNER

The family life cycle model developed by Carter and McGoldrick (1980, 1988; see also Chapter 1) provides a richly contextualized, multidimensional framework for understanding the movement of the family through time. This framework helps us to locate the points at which the chronic background anxiety in a family is likely to coincide with the acute stress of navigating a current life cycle transition. These are the times in family life when symptoms and dysfunction are most likely to emerge, in both our own and our clients' families.

These crucial transitions in family life are viewed as being inextricably linked to the sociocultural context in which family life is embedded. Factors such as gender, race, class, ethnicity, and sexual orientation shape the nature of the playing field on which life cycle transitions are negotiated.

In this chapter, I focus on the intersection between the therapist's life cycle stage and that of the family in treatment—a key dimension of the fit between therapist and family as the clinical process unfolds (Simon, 1988). More specifically, I propose that when the therapist brings unresolved issues from a past or current life cycle stage into the clinical work with a family that is struggling to navigate that same life cycle stage, predictable problems may emerge.

Some therapists zoom in zealously to remake the client in the image of their own wished-for but unachieved resolution of a particular life cycle issue, overfunctioning for the client's family as they continue to underfunction in their own. Others will become ineffective, fuzzy thinkers, underfunctioning for both themselves and the family. A therapist

may become overly aloof and distant or, alternatively, may end up in a power struggle with the family. Whatever the error tendency of a particular therapist, it is useful to examine one's functioning through the wide-angle lens of the family life cycle model.

For example, what unresolved life cycle struggle of the therapist's may now be interacting with that of the family, fueling a therapeutic impasse? How might anxiety from other similarities and differences add to the problem in the therapy? Can the therapeutic problem serve as a signal that, when heeded, may result in renewed growth for both the therapist and the clinical family?

Many therapists have studied their own families of origin as part of their professional training. They have worked to identify and modify their part in multigenerational patterns, with an eye toward navigating family relationships and life cycle transitions with greater clarity, objectivity, and calm. Those of us who have worked diligently on our own families may mistakenly believe that we have "done that" and can now focus single-mindedly on the family life cycle of the families we work with. Often, we will be reminded that we cannot leave ourselves out of the picture when we encounter pronounced similarities or differences between our own lives and those of our clients.

DIMENSIONS OF SIMILARITY BETWEEN THERAPIST AND CLIENT

Figure 30.1 lists the family life cycle stage as one of many important dimensions on which the thera-

Multigenerational history

Unresolved emotional issues with significant
others

Typical ways of managing stress

Other family patterns and legacies

Sibling position

Family life cycle

Age

Current life events

Health

Culture

Gender

Race

Class

Ethnicity

Sexual Orientation

Religion

Politics

Community, work system, friendship circle

FIGURE 30.1   Interfacing Dimensions between
Therapist and Family

pist and client will be more or less similar—or out
of sync. When life cycle stages intersect for the
therapist and the clinical family, the therapist can
be at the same stage, an earlier stage, or a later
stage than the family. The details of a particular
stage in the therapist's life and that of the family
(say, the birth or the launching of children) may be
very similar or very different. The match between
the therapist and the clinical family on variables
such as race, ethnicity, gender, class, sibling position, and sexual orientation will also influence the
degree to which the life cycle issues become emotionally loaded in therapy. For example, a young
White therapist, herself the youngest in her own
family, finds herself dealing with an older Mexican American couple, both first-borns, who are
caring for their aging parents. The therapist might
suffer from an overwhelming sense of "juniority"
in the therapy process as her age, ethnicity, birth
order, and lack of life experience combine to
foster feelings of incompetence, both real and
imagined.

BRIEF SCENARIOS: COMPLEX THERAPIST-
FAMILY LIFE CYCLE INTERACTIONS

The potential complexity of therapist-family life
cycle interactions is further illustrated by the following vignettes.

Ann, a middle-aged White therapist, recently came
out to her family after entering her first serious
live-in relationship with a woman. Her father has
not yet accepted her sexual orientation and has refused to meet her partner. This situation is very
painful for Ann, who worries that she could lose
her relationship with her father, who is in failing
health. She also feels responsible for the escalating
tensions in her parents' marriage as they become
increasingly polarized around the issue of accepting her lesbianism.

Ann is now working with a White client who is
seriously dating an African American man. Her client wants to tell her parents about this relationship
but fears that her father, in particular, will not get
past his racist response. The client's family is replete with cut-offs as a patterned way of managing
conflict and differences. How might Ann's own issues and anxieties about the coming out process influence her work with this client?

Don, a White therapist in his twenties, is the
youngest child in his upper-middle-class family.
His father initiated a divorce when Don was 15, following the discovery of his wife's affair. Don began
living with his father after the separation and has
never truly modified his angry, distant relationship
with his mother. He is now seeing a working-class
African American couple who are contemplating
separation after the wife's affair came out into the
open. Their youngest son has just turned 15. What
obstacles might Don face as he not only deals with
the gulf posed by racial, class, and life cycle differences, but also is confronted head-on with all that is
evoked from his own past?

Kathy, an Irish American therapist in her fifties,
lost her mother in a car wreck when she was 12 and
is now the same age that her mother was when she
died. Kathy and her older brother were "protected"
from the facts about the accident, which was
shrouded in layers of secrecy. Her mother had been
intoxicated and caused the crash, which also killed a
young child in another car. Almost from the moment

Kathy's mother's funeral ended, her memory was gradually erased because of the family's shame about her alcoholism and its terrible cost. Their father remarried within the year, and the children were instructed to call their new stepmother "Mom."

Now Kathy is beginning work with an Italian American family in which the mother is dying of complications of diabetes. The parents are grief-stricken and worried about their depressed children but very reluctant to permit an outsider to help them with the enormous tragedy they face. How can Kathy find a way to connect with this family and help them open up their reactions to this upcoming loss of a mother, and how might Kathy's regrets and anxiety about her own past influence her work? How might Kathy's ethnicity and that of the clinical family interact to make this therapy process more difficult (McGoldrick, Giordano, & Pearce, 1996)?

FAMILIES WITH YOUNG CHILDREN: A COMPLEX INTERSECTION

A life cycle stage that is particularly challenging is that of the family with young children (see Chapter 15). With the birth of the first child, a profound realignment of family relationships occur. The whole family diagram shifts one notch upward, and every family member gets a new name: husband and wife become father and mother; siblings become uncles or aunts; parents become grandparents; grandparents become great-grandparents.

The marital couple faces the largest challenge as they adjust to their new roles. Many equal partnerships succumb to the powerful tidal pull of the previous generation's far less equitable gender roles and expectations (Lerner, 1998). Even the most pioneering of couples will struggle with the enormous challenges of this stage and are often left with unresolved dissatisfaction stemming from the compromises and accommodations that began after the first child was born. The marital relationship becomes the crucible in which the seeds of inequality and disillusionment grow, resulting in early divorce or the later dissolution of the marriage when the children are adolescents or have been launched.

Therapists who are not actively examining the pervasive impact of gender on their own and their parents' marriages—or who deny the enormous impact of gender on every aspect of personal and work life—will be limited in helping families to navigate the complexities of life with young children and the marital renegotiations that are required to make things work.

SHE NURTURES/HE EARNS: THE THERAPIST'S TRANSITION GETS IN THE WAY

The following case was presented by a therapist in a small supervision group that met twice monthly. The contract was that supervisees presented clinical cases and their families of origin. My theoretical framework as the supervisor was Bowen family systems theory, informed by feminist theory, and the family life cycle model of Carter and McGoldrick (1980, 1988).

Alan, the therapist, was seeing a married woman who had two young children who had sought help after a period of increasing depression. She was distressed about an upcoming move to another city precipitated by her husband's transfer to the headquarters of his company, which was to take place in six months. She was upset about the prospect of leaving her circle of close women friends and her parents and sisters, who lived nearby. Before having children, she had worked full time, and she remembered those years with nostalgia as a time when she felt free to pursue her dreams. Currently, she had a part-time job that she enjoyed and had found an excellent child care situation that would be impossible to duplicate, since it included her mother caring for her children two afternoons a week. She had tentative plans to pursue more education but had put her career goals on hold since the children arrived.

Alan empathized with her sadness and asked some good questions: What did she know about the new city? Had she visited there with her husband and researched the work and educational opportunities and child care options? But in the therapist's mind, the move was a given, which was precisely how his depressed client saw it. So there were certain questions Alan did not ask.

He did *not* ask: How was the decision to move negotiated between the couple? What impact did her husband's income and earning power (he earned 90 percent of the family's income) have on the decision process? How did she understand the fact that she has acted as though she had no option but to reflexively go along with the move, which she called a "fait accompli"?

Supervision

In supervision, I asked Alan to consider the similarities and differences between the clinical couple's way of navigating their current life cycle transition, and the way in which he and his wife handled their own.

Alan and his wife, both first-borns, had one 2-year-old child. His wife had cut back from a full-time position at a magazine to do freelance work when their baby was born. At the current time, she had decided to go back to work, as her old job has been offered to her. The couple had been arguing over how to divide household and child care responsibilities if she took the position, and Alan just didn't see how it could work. Before having a child, Alan believed in shared parenting but now he did not want his child "raised by a stranger." Also, he made $90 an hour, while his wife would make only $16 an hour in her new position. He said, "Given the high cost of child care, and the reality of how little her job pays, I really wish she'd stay with the freelance work for a few more years." Alan admitted that he felt anxious and defensive when his wife talked about resuming full-time work.

Alan's own parents followed the traditional path: His mother nurtured and his father earned. Their family moved four times because of his father's career, and to his knowledge, his mother never objected. Alan had no idea whether either of them had ever considered another arrangement or how the traditional path suited them.

Supervisory Feedback

In response to Alan's presentation of his clinical case, a female supervisee commented that he had quickly conveyed the underlying message that the move could not, and should not, be questioned. It was as if he were saying, "Cheer up, its not that bad, and besides, with a little elbow grease, you'll have almost as good a situation in the new city." I added that he also did not locate the client's depression, or the move itself, in any larger context: her marriage, her family of origin, or her life cycle stage.

I suggested that Alan's current life cycle issues (i.e., the marital tension surrounding his wife's decision to resume full-time work) were interfacing with his client's in a way that was impeding his objectivity. To move toward a clearer frame of reference on his own life cycle transition and that of the client, I encouraged Alan to open up a discussion with each of his parents about the way in which decisions were made in their own relationship, with particular reference to the four career moves.

Family of Origin Data

Alan's father told him that there had never been any question but that the family would move when his job changed. Like his father before him, he had seen himself as the provider for the family. "That's just the way life was back then," his father said. "Your mother and I never questioned it."

When Alan talked to his mother, he learned that she *had* questioned the moves—but only to herself. The moves had been extremely difficult for her. "I started to feel like a refugee, like my grandmother from Poland, but I didn't see any alternative." She revealed that she had become quite depressed when the fourth move took the family sufficiently far from her home town that she could no longer easily visit her own parents. Her mother had also been upset to lose her close connection to her grandchildren. At that point, Alan's mother had thought of staying behind, but for a number of reasons, it had seemed like an impossible choice. By the time retirement came along, she had become more assertive in the marriage. She had been working outside of the home for several years, which she continued to do after her husband retired. Over time, largely as a result of her growing independence and her husband's mellowing in later life, the decision-making process had shifted to much more of a partnership than it had been before. In a later conversation, she said to Alan, "I might have considered divorce at the time of the fourth move if it had been as common as it is today. But on the other hand, I never really protested or fought it out with your father. Maybe he would have put me before his career—I guess I'll never really know for sure."

Alan reported that the discussions with his parents had got him thinking about his own marriage and whether he was putting it in jeopardy by "following in my father's footsteps where work is concerned—I never wanted to do that!" I commented, "So, Alan, I guess the challenge for you is whether you want to wait until retirement to figure out how to become an equal partner with your wife, or whether you want to try to do that now?" Alan smiled and wryly observed, "If I don't do it now, we won't be together at retirement—my wife is much more outspoken than my mother!" He later reported that he had started to initiate talks with his wife about how they could work together to make room for both of their careers, including the option of his cutting back some on his practice, despite the financial sacrifice, and his spending more time parenting.

In the client's therapy, he began to ask questions about the decision-making process about the planned move. He suggested that his client invite her husband to join her in the sessions, and through further questioning, he helped the couple to explore the pluses and minuses of the move for each of them, their children, and their extended-family relationships. The work that Alan did in his own family paid off. He was now a clearer and more effective questioner who helped the couple to explore a wider range of options because Alan could now see these options himself. Alan was also better able to help the couple examine their own families of origin and life cycle issues as a result of his work on his own.

THE LONG-TERM VIEW: WORKING WITH ONE FAMILY OVER SUCCESSIVE LIFE CYCLE STAGES

As successive life cycle stages bring new challenges, a family may return to the same therapist over decades. Seeing the same family navigate successive life cycle stages offers a unique learning experience for both the therapist and the clinical family. For the therapist, long-term contact can provide direct longitudinal experience with a family other than one's own. For the clinical family, there is the knowledge that they have a coach they can return to—a known quantity who has the background information to help them meet another life challenge. In such a long-term process, it becomes far more likely that particular issues in the therapist's life will coincide with the clinical family's, as was the case in my work with the Vintons, which spanned a period of twenty-five years.

The Vintons initially came to see me with their three children because of the parents' concern about Jane, their oldest child. A one-year therapy ended with decreased symptoms and Jane's successful departure for college. Five years later, with their second child now also out of the home, the couple came back to work on marital issues that had emerged as Sheila went back to work. She was starting something new, while Jack felt stuck in a demanding and ungratifying job. Work on their respective families of origin, in which men were the sole breadwinners and women stayed at home, helped each of them to achieve a more tolerant, less reactive position with each other, as they saw their own struggles as part of a larger family and cultural legacy.

Four years later, the couple returned for additional marital work. They had now launched their youngest son, and the older two children were married. Sheila complained that Jack was unavailable for intimacy, while Jack felt increasingly worn out by his management job, which required frequent travel. This phase of therapy lasted for six months, and when it concluded, Sheila was less focused on Jack. When he was unavailable to do things with her, she made her own plans. For his part, Jack was gradually able to see his irritability and frustration as being related to the pattern of men and work in his family; typically, men worked incredibly hard in thankless jobs that they saw as tickets to a comfortable retirement in their "golden years." Then many of them died before or just after retiring, never having enjoyed what they had worked so hard to achieve.

During this phase of therapy, I was diagnosed with a malignant melanoma at the age of 41. In the face of this personal crisis, I had to cancel and reschedule several sessions. I chose to tell Jack and Sheila about my diagnosis because in our small community, they were likely to hear about it from others. They asked me a number of questions, including my prognosis, which by that time was guardedly positive and later was upgraded to excellent. They appreciated hearing directly from me about my illness, and my disclosure seemed to facilitate their work on their own issues in therapy (Gerson, 1996).

Several years later, Jack, now 57, came in again for individual consultations. He was now eager for retirement and dreamed of opening a small specialty bookstore in a nearby university town. In the midst of this phase of therapy, however, he was diagnosed with lung cancer. His wife joined our sessions at that time.

Jack asked me what had helped me to deal with my cancer diagnosis, and I told him that I had found self-regulation training helpful. During the period after my diagnosis, I had learned biofeedback techniques for anxiety management and immune system mobilization. Later, under supervision, I worked with several clients who were struggling with physical illness. Jack asked whether I could teach him biofeedback, and I agreed. I also arranged for him to meet with my supervisor, Pat Norris, an international expert in the use of biofeedback with cancer patients. Jack became proficient with thermal and muscle biofeedback and found it very helpful. He asked me more about my own experience with cancer, and although he knew that my prognosis had been much better than his, he nevertheless saw my survival as a hopeful sign. "You've been there—you know what I'm up against," he said.

During the next two years, I continued to see Jack as he learned to be his own advocate in the medical system and struggled to regain his strength. He was determined to live long enough to dance at the wedding of his youngest son, which he succeeded in doing. A few days later, I received a call from Jane, the original identified patient, telling me that Jack was dying and the family would like me to come to the hospital. I arrived at his room, where his entire family was assembled, just as he died.

Some weeks after his funeral, which I attended, Sheila resumed therapy to focus on her grief and to help the children cope with their loss. Then, several years later, now a grandmother four times over, she returned to treatment, this time to focus on her new live-in relationship with Elliot, who was divorced with four grown children of his own. Her choice to live with her new partner had elicited strong reactions from her children, who had thought nothing of living with their own lovers before marriage but did not see this as permissible for their mother. In particular, she wanted to work on paving the way for her upcoming marriage to Elliot, which was planned for the following year. We worked together on finding a role for her three children in the wedding, which she carried out beautifully. She mentioned Jack during the ceremony, saying that she felt he would support her moving ahead with her life. She terminated therapy after her remarriage, saying, "You know me. I'll probably be back someday."

My thinking as a family therapist evolved during the many years I worked with the Vinton family. Sharing some aspects of my experience with cancer had deepened my relationship with them and contributed to my ability to work closely with them throughout Jack's illness and dying process. Later, when Sheila contemplated remarriage, both she and I were aware that I brought a very different perspective into the therapy regarding her new relationship with Elliot than I had had in the earlier marital work with Sheila and Jack. This was particularly evident as I helped her to think through the loaded issues of money, power, decision making, and who was responsible for dealing with their respective children as they formed a remarried family. Sheila knew that she and her family had helped to "train" me and "bring me up" as a therapist. As a result, she (and Jack earlier) felt a certain well-earned pride, which I reciprocated, about our ability to work well together.

WORKING WITH LOSS: A LINK BETWEEN LIFE CYCLE STAGES

When I was 20, my mother, age 49, died of breast cancer ten years after her initial diagnosis. For a variety of reasons, her illness and subsequent death were underprocessed in my family; indeed, for some years after her death, my mother was rarely discussed. Over the years, I worked on the impact of her death and tried to modify my part in the silence surrounding it. Some of the payoff from this earlier work was reflected in the way my siblings and I recently rallied to my father's side when he became critically ill and nearly died. Also, during the same time frame, I became a partner with my wife in caring for her elderly parents, who had moved to Topeka to be near us. Going through these experiences brought home the fact that I would not be caring for my mother in her old age. This was a life cycle transition that I would miss, and I felt the loss especially acutely during the crisis with my father and my ongoing involvement in caring for my elderly in-laws.

Not coincidentally, it was during this time that I began to work one day a week in a nursing home in a small Kansas town. The work began when I saw an elderly stroke victim in a rural hospital where I consult. Later, she was transferred to the nursing home, where I continued to see her weekly, first with her daughter and then also with her son. The administrator of the nursing home, impressed with her response to therapy, asked me to start a group for those residents—women mostly in their eighties—who were capable of conversing. Group work seemed especially fitting because these residents, most of whom had known each other throughout their lives in the small town, tended to avoid socializing, retreating to their rooms as soon as meals were over.

I run the group using a multiple family model and do a genogram for each member. Visiting relatives are also invited to attend. Molly, a stroke victim who also suffered from severe gastrointestinal problems, was admitted when her husband Morris could no longer care for her in the home. Her siblings were dead, and Morris was all she had. Molly was quite agitated and periodically during the group sessions would shout, "I want to go home, I want to go home!" Morris, who attended several sessions with her, would become frustrated, guilty, and depressed and try to exhort her to settle down. Then, two months after her admission, he suddenly died of a heart attack.

In a session following Morris's death, Molly dozed off for the first part of the group and then suddenly woke up and shouted, "I have no one! I'm all alone! I have to go home!" I asked Georgia, Maxine, Violet, and Elizabeth, the other group members, what their reactions were to Molly's situation and what they wanted to say to her when she shouted out that she had no one. Georgia, a woman with severe physical problems of her own, said in a clear, strong voice, "Molly, I know you miss Morris. He was a fine man. Would you like me to be your sister? I'd like to be your sister, why, we all would. You're not alone, Molly. Would you like me to be your sister?" Molly nodded. One by one, each other group member voiced her willingness to be a sister to Molly. Then there was a silence, and the women all looked at me. I turned to Molly and said, "Molly, I'm only here on Thursday afternoons, and I can't be your sister. But I'd be glad to be your younger brother." Molly smiled, and the other members laughed.

I think that my investment in these women and my interest in working in a context in which past, current, and impending loss is a constant feature of their lives relate to my current life cycle position, in which I have begun to help the previous generation in their old age. This work enriches my life because the untimely death of my mother precluded the possibility of my being available to her as she aged. I mentioned to the group recently that they were teaching me a great deal about life. Georgia turned to me and said, "If you ever need to go into a nursing home, you'll know just what to expect."

CONCLUSION

The interaction between therapist and family life cycle stages offers both pitfalls and opportunities during the conduct of family therapy. When we get off track by confusing our unresolved issues at a particular stage with those of the clinical family, revisiting how we have been navigating the transitions confronting us and identifying where we are stuck will usually help us to find a more creative direction to take in the therapy. This shift in focus typically requires a review of our own family history and the patterns in which we participate, and a renewed effort to modify our part in them. This may involve the opening up of topics that have not been spoken about before or a return to issues that we dealt with in the past but then too quickly dropped.

The experience that we gain from negotiating life cycle transitions also facilitates our work with families, enabling us to point out options that anxious family members may have overlooked and to ask questions and understand our clients in ways that we might not have been able to do had we not been through similar struggles in our own lives.

Our work with families, perhaps especially when they are most like us or most different from us, requires us to examine our own attitudes, beliefs, stereotypes, relationships, and life choices through many lenses, including our own position in the family life cycle vis-à-vis that of our clients. As one therapist that I talked to recently observed, "You mean I have to keep *that* in mind, too?" I am afraid that we do if we plan to continue growing as people and therapists. In the end, this is the beauty of this rather impossible profession we have chosen.

REFERENCES

Carter, E. A., & Lerner, S. (1997a). *Clinical dilemmas in marriage: The search for equal partnership* [Video]. New York: Guilford Publications.

Carter, E. A., & Lerner, S. (1997b). *Addressing economic inequality in marriage: A new therapeutic approach* [Video]. New York: Guilford Publications.

Carter, E. A., & Lerner, S. (1997c). Who's in the kitchen: Helping men move toward the center of family life [Video]. New York: Guilford Publications.

Carter, E. A., & McGoldrick, M. (Eds.) (1980). *The family life cycle.* New York: Gardner Press.

Carter, E. A., & McGoldrick, M. (Eds.) (1988). *The changing family life cycle: A framework for family therapy* (2nd ed.). New York: Gardner Press.

Carter, E. A., and Peters, J. (1996). *Love, honor and negotiate: Making your marriage work.* New York: Pocket Books.

Gerson, B. (Ed.). (1996). *The therapist as a person: Life crises, life choices, life experiences, and their effects on treatment.* Hillsdale, NJ: The Analytic Press.

Lerner, H. (1998) *The mother dance: What children do to your life.* New York: HarperCollins.

McGoldrick, M., Giordano, J., & Pearce, J. K. (1996). *Ethnicity and family therapy* (2nd ed.). New York: The Guilford Press.

Simon, R. M. (1988). Family life cycle issues in the therapy system. In McGoldrick, M. & Carter, E. A. (Eds.), *The changing family life cycle: A framework for family therapy* (2nd ed.). New York: Gardner Press.

SUBJECT INDEX